Die Unternehmung in der demokratischen Gesellschaft

The Business Corporation in the Democratic Society

Die Unternehmung in der demokratischen Gesellschaft

The Business Corporation in the Democratic Society

Günter Dlugos
zum 65. Geburtstag gewidmet

Herausgegeben von Wolfgang Dorow

Walter de Gruyter · Berlin · New York 1987

Herausgeber

Dr. Wolfgang Dorow, E.A.P. Europäische Wirtschaftshochschule
Paris – Oxford – Berlin

CIP-Kurztitelaufnahme der Deutschen Bibliothek

Die Unternehmung in der demokratischen Gesellschaft : Günter Dlugos zum 65. Geburtstag gewidmet = The business corporation in the democratic society / hrsg. von Wolfgang Dorow. – Berlin ; New York : de Gruyter, 1987.
ISBN 3-11-010293-5
NE: Dorow, Wolfgang [Hrsg.]; Dlugos, Günter: Festschrift; PT

Library of Congress Cataloging-in-Publication Data

Die Unternehmung in der demokratischen Gesellschaft
= The business corporation in the democratic society

English and German.
"Herausgegeben von Wolfgang Dorow."
Includes bibliographies.
1. Management—Employee participation.
2. Democracy. 3. Representative government and representation. 4. Efficiency, Industrial. 5. Dlugos, Günter. I. Dlugos, Günter. II. Dorow, Wolfgang. III. Title. IV. Title: The business corporation in the democratic society.
HD5650.U67 1986 658.3'152 86-32864
ISBN 0-89925-295-8 (U.S.)

Satz und Druck: Buch- und Offsetdruckerei Wagner GmbH, Nördlingen – Bindearbeiten: Lüderitz & Bauer Buchgewerbe GmbH, Berlin – Einbandgestaltung: Lothar Hildebrand, Berlin – Foto: Caroline Dlugos, Berlin – Printed in Germany

Vorwort

Wenn 15 Jahre Institutsarbeit an der Fachrichtung Unternehmungspolitik des Fachbereichs Wirtschaftswissenschaft der Freien Universität Berlin und die Feier des 65. Geburtstages ihres Leiters zusammenfallen, ist dies ein doppelter Anlaß, dessen Persönlichkeit und wissenschaftliches Wirken zu würdigen. Dabei ist es für den Herausgeber nicht nur die Befolgung einer alten akademischen Tradition, sondern vor allem ein persönliches Anliegen, die Würdigung seines akademischen Lehrers im Rahmen einer Festschrift auszudrücken.

Die vorliegende Schrift, die Günter Dlugos zu seinem 65. Geburtstag am 26. November 1985 gewidmet ist, repräsentiert in thematischer Hinsicht zentrale Aspekte seiner Forschungs- und Lehrtätigkeit und ist zugleich ein Spiegelbild der Beziehungen, die zwischen der Fachrichtung Unternehmungspolitik und Wissenschaftlern an in- und ausländischen Universitäten.entstanden sind.

Kristallisationspunkt der breit gefächerten betriebswirtschaftlichen Forschungsinteressen von Günter Dlugos ist die Unternehmungspolitik, in der er mehr als eine auf die strategische Planung konzentrierte „Business Policy" sieht. Er entwikkelte eine interdisziplinär angelegte Konzeption der Analyse und rationalen Bewältigung unternehmungsinterner und unternehmungsexterner Konflikte, die er im Sinne einer „Business Politics" zu einer betriebswirtschaftlich-politologischen Teildisziplin ausbaute. Im Rahmen dieser Konzeption werden die Ziele der Unternehmungsmitglieder sowie die markt- und gesellschaftsbezogenen Ziele der Unternehmungen analysiert und die aus wirtschaftlichen und nicht-wirtschaftlichen Interessen resultierenden Konsens- und Konfliktbereiche herausgearbeitet. Das Aufdecken der hier möglichen Kompatibilitätsspielräume, der Gefahren ihrer Überbeanspruchung und der Möglichkeiten, Konsens durch adäquate Formen der Konflikthandhabung innerhalb eines liberal-demokratisch verfaßten Gesellschaftssystems zurückzugewinnen, wurde zum Leitgedanken seiner unternehmungspolitischen Beiträge. So untersuchte er die Beziehungen zwischen Wertwandel, Konflikt und Konflikthandhabung im Unternehmungssektor, analysierte die gesellschaftspolitischen Implikationen unternehmungsinterner Konflikthandhabung, setzte sich mit dem Problem der Unternehmungseffizienz angesichts konfligierender Interessen auseinander und befaßte sich mit Aspekten der Unternehmungsverfassung, der Mitarbeiterführung sowie mit Grundfragen der Konstituierung einer unternehmungsbezogenen Konfliktforschung. Forschung und Lehre folgen dabei der Methodologie rationaler Diskussion und kritischer Prüfung und wenden sich gegen die Dogmatisierung von Lösungskonzepten.

Für die Festschrift wurde das Thema „Die Unternehmung in der demokratischen Gesellschaft" gewählt, um an die von Günter Dlugos verfolgte Grundfrage nach den Gestaltungsmöglichkeiten und Gestaltungsgrenzen wirtschaftlicher Austauschbeziehungen in einer liberal-demokratischen Gesellschaftsordnung anzuknüpfen. An dieser Schrift haben sich Autoren aus Japan, Kanada, den Vereinigten Staaten, Griechenland, Österreich, Polen und Deutschland beteiligt. Ihre Beiträge behandeln vier Themenschwerpunkte: Die im Kapitel I zusammengefaßten Beiträge behandeln aus der Perspektive verschiedener sozialwissenschaftlicher Disziplinen die theoretischen Grundlagen, die gesellschaftspolitischen Voraussetzungen und Konsequenzen der Demokratisierung des Unternehmungssektors. Dem folgen Analysen ökonomischer Aspekte der Partizipation, die schwergewichtig aus betriebswirtschaftlicher Sicht untersucht werden. Das III. Kapitel umfaßt Beiträge, die das gestellte Thema länderspezifisch im Hinblick auf Probleme im Bereich liberal-demokratisch verfaßter Gesellschaftssysteme aufgreifen. Im abschließenden IV. Kapitel wird zur Erweiterung der kritischen Aufbereitung des Rahmenthemas auch ein Blick auf Partizipationsansätze in Gesellschaftssystemen geworfen, die nicht den liberal-demokratischen Vorstellungen folgen. Wegen der zahlreich vertretenen englischsprachigen Beiträge und um Kommunikationsbrükken zu festigen, erhielt die Festschrift einen zweisprachigen Titel und für englischsprachige Leser eine „Introduction".

Den Autoren danke ich herzlich für die beeindruckende Bereitschaft, sich der Idee einer Festschrift für Günter Dlugos anzuschließen. Auch bin ich ihnen für wertvolle Anregungen und Unterstützungen während der Entstehungsphase der Festschrift zu Dank verpflichtet. Weiterhin gilt mein Dank Frau Hilde Karge, die die Korrespondenz und das Schreiben von Manuskripten erledigte, ohne daß der „Betroffene" auf die Entstehung dieser Festschrift aufmerksam werden konnte, sowie Herrn Frank C. Danesy, M. S. B. A., der großen Anteil an der Vorbereitung und Durchführung dieser Veröffentlichung hat. Schließlich danke ich dem Walter de Gruyter Verlag herzlich für die spontane Zusage, die Festschrift zu veröffentlichen und die finanziellen Lasten großzügig zu übernehmen.

Alle an der Festschrift Beteiligten sprechen Herrn Günter Dlugos die herzlichsten Glückwünsche zu seinem 65. Geburtstag aus, verbunden mit dem Wunsch, daß seine Aktivität noch lange erhalten bleiben möge und die für die nahe und fernere Zukunft bereits geplanten wissenschaftlichen Ziele erfolgreich realisiert werden können.

Wolfgang Dorow
Berlin, im November 1985

Introduction

The following introduction should acquaint the English-speaking reader with the concept behind this book. The contributions to the book deal with a key problem of modern industrial nations which results from an altered understanding of the management and leadership of large corporations in a democratically constituted social environment.

In all modern, industrial nations demand is increasing for extended industrial democracy, particularly in relation to large corporations. This demand has given rise to considerable potential for societal conflict. The aim of this book is to highlight, from an international point of view, the political, psychological and economic implications of industrial democracy in order to obtain a critical view of the specific problems and solutions of the individual nations.

The contributions to this book deal with a wide range of differing approaches to participation: the voluntary representation of employees in the North-American "Quality-of-Work-Life" programme; the legally ensured "Co-Determination Rights" of employees and unions in Germany; the reversal of power distribution in the Yugoslavian model of "Workers'-Self-Management". The contributions elucidate the fact that the internationally differing participation models in the business sector of industrial nations will give rise to widely varying economic potentials.

The contributions also show that the demand for increased participation in the business sector is, at least in Western Europe, part of a wider movement, the aim of which is participative democracy in every area of societal life. The roots of this movement can be traced to interpretations of democracy as expressed by John Stuart Mill – namely that it furthers the intelligence, virtue, practical activity and efficiency of the citizen. The movement also finds its roots in doubts as to the ability of a representative democracy, based solely on governmental bodies, to ensure the best interest of the citizen. Strong apprehension has been voiced, however, as to the possibility of negative economic consequences arising from the movement towards democracy. This apprehension is based on the assumption that the democratization of enterprises would restrict the discretion of the capital investor and of the employer. Simultaneously, authority would be delegated to those who do not have at their disposal the expert knowledge necessary for the making of economically efficient decisions.

Doubts as to the economic efficiency of participation will be more strongly voiced when it is not voluntarily agreed between both partners, but is based on the octroi of the state, and when decision sharing involves not only the employees of an enterprise, but also extends to external interested parties. In this case, management is no longer primarily obliged to fulfill demands made by the investor for economically efficient capital-investment. An additional obligation exists to fulfill the demands of the other participants – although the latter do not bear comparable risks. Due to the increased necessity of dealing with conflicting interests, changes occur in the conditions of the production and profit-distribution processes. These changes, in turn, raise new issues of distributive justice and conflict-resolution.

Modern economic theory (e. g. the property rights theory) holds that economic inefficiency of the enterprise is caused by the attenuation of the property rights of the capital investor. On the other hand, the results of sociological and socio-psychological enquiries testify to the positive effects of participation in decision-making. International comparative analyses of the value of and attitudes towards working-life show that in all industrial nations working conditions are demanded which ensure not only the satisfaction of material needs such as remuneration and job-security, but which also permit the development of personal initiative, opportunities for self-realization and improvement of social interaction in the work-place. The increasing demands of the employee with regard to the social efficiency of his/her working life implies that the traditional system of sanctions as incitement to productivity is, in fact, counterproductive. This system must, at the very least, be complemented by other incitement systems which ensure efficient performance through the fulfillment of broader individual interests.

The problems outlined, are discussed from an international perspective. The contributions included in the *first chapter* deal with the socio-scientific bases and the socio-political implications of the democratization issue. The *second chapter* deals with the economic aspects of the changing conditions of the employer-employee relationship resulting from participation. The *third chapter* gives an overview of the approaches to participation in liberal democratic nations. Finally, the *fourth chapter* deals with models of participation in societies which do not conform to the western concept of liberal democracy.

The editor would like to take this opportunity to thank the authors for their consent to contribute to this "Festschrift", on the occasion of the sixty-fifth birthday of *Günter Dlugos*, who has devoted his academic work to the subject of this book.

Inhaltsverzeichnis

I. Sozialwissenschaftliche und gesellschaftspolitische Aspekte

II. Ökonomische Aspekte

IV. Länderspezifische Probleme – sozialistische Gesellschaftssysteme

Teil I
Sozialwissenschaftliche und gesellschaftspolitische Aspekte

Zum Problem der Unternehmensverfassung – Sozialtechnologische Aspekte des Verfassungsproblems

Hans Albert

Abstract
On the Problem of the Constitution of the Business Corporation – Sociotechnological Aspects of the Constitutional Problem

This paper deals with socio-technological aspects of the problem of companies' constitutions. First the possibility of a social technology according to Max Weber is considered; next two different forms of social regulations, dominant in modern societies, will be characterized. Finally the problem of democracy in organizations will be analyzed under socio-technological aspects.

Mit der Problematik der Unternehmensverfassung hat sich Günter Dlugos in seiner wissenschaftlichen Arbeit immer wieder beschäftigt. Er hat sich außerdem intensiv mit Methodenfragen der Sozialwissenschaften auseinandergesetzt und dabei stets die Frage der praktischen Verwendbarkeit sozialwissenschaftlicher Erkenntnisse im Auge behalten.[1] Es ist daher sicherlich angemessen, ihn mit einem Beitrag zu ehren, der sozialtechnologische Aspekte des Problems der Unternehmensverfassung behandelt. Ich werde dazu zunächst kurz auf die Möglichkeit einer im Sinne Max Webers konzipierten Sozialtechnologie eingehen, dann die beiden in der modernen Gesellschaft dominanten Formen sozialer Regelung charakterisieren, um schließlich auf das Problem der Unternehmensdemokratie unter sozialtechnologischen Gesichtspunkten einzugehen.

1. Sozialtechnologie als praktische Sozialwissenschaft

Die Werturteilsdebatte in den Sozialwissenschaften steht bekanntlich in engem Zusammenhang mit der Frage, wie die Ergebnisse dieser Wissenschaften für die Praxis fruchtbar gemacht werden können. Die Vertreter der Auffassung, man sei dazu auf eine normative Sozialwissenschaft angewiesen – bzw. auf eine Normativierung deskriptiver oder erklärender sozialwissenschaftlicher Disziplinen durch die Einführung expliziter Wertprämissen –, pflegen die Max Webersche Forderung der Wertfreiheit meist mit der Begründung zurückzuweisen, eine Wissenschaft, die dieser Forderung entspreche, müsse für die Praxis des sozialen Lebens ohne Nutzen sein. Nun hat aber Max Weber selbst schon gezeigt, inwiefern sich diese Auffassung nicht halten läßt. Er hat nämlich die Idee einer wertungsfreien Lehre von der Wirtschaftspolitik als Wissenschaft vertreten[2], die man als *sozialtechnologische* Disziplin etwa im Sinne der später von Karl Popper entwickelten Auffassung[3] charakterisieren kann. Daß die Verwertung sozialtechnologischer Aussagen in der Praxis – ihre Anwendung auf konkrete Situationen zur Entscheidung zwischen Handlungsmöglichkeiten – Werturteile voraussetzt, haben die Verfechter einer solchen Auffassung nie bestritten.[4] Dasselbe gilt für die Tatsache, daß Wertgesichtspunkte verschiedenster Art den Hintergrund für die Entwicklung sozialtechnologischer Fragestellungen zu bilden pflegen.

Sozialtechnologische Aussagen sind mit denen der theoretischen Sozialwissenschaften auf ähnliche Weise verknüpft, wie das im naturwissenschaftlichen Bereich der Fall ist. Wenn es für das betreffende Sachgebiet Theorien gibt, die zu entsprechenden Erklärungsleistungen geeignet sind, dann lassen sich daraus unter gewissen Bedingungen technologische Systeme gewinnen, aus denen die für die Lösung praktischer Probleme relevanten Handlungsmöglichkeiten hervorgehen, ohne daß man ihnen einen normativen Gehalt zusprechen könnte. Wir können auch im sozialen Leben das vorhandene technologische Wissen dazu benutzen, unsere Ziele dadurch zu erreichen, daß wir die in ihm als wirksam aufgewiesenen Mittel verwenden. Dabei muß die Sozialwissenschaft – und daher auch die Sozialtechnologie – natürlich der Tatsache Rechnung tragen, daß Normen aller Art Elemente des sozialen Lebens sind, und das bedeutet unter anderem, daß sie als Kausalfaktoren in Betracht kommen. Aber solche Normen und die mit ihnen verbundenen institutionellen Vorkehrungen sind natürlich selbst historisch variable Tatbestände des sozialen Lebens. Wenn wir also in diesem Bereich nach Gesetzmäßigkeiten suchen, dann sind sie nicht in diesen normativen Komponenten des sozialen Lebens zu finden, obwohl solche Komponenten in nomologischen Aussagen eine Rolle spielen können.

Um den tatsächlich vorhandenen normativen Elementen sozialer Tatbestände in der sozialwissenschaftlichen Analyse Rechnung zu tragen, müssen wir sie also nicht als „Gesetze", sondern als faktische Komponenten kausaler Verknüpfungen betrachten, das heißt: als Ursachen oder Wirkungen anderer Elemente des sozialen Lebens. Und in der Sozialtechnologie haben wir sie dementsprechend als Mittel oder als Ziele sozialer Aktionen zu behandeln. Das praktisch relevante Problem, das hier jeweils zur Diskussion steht, ist die Frage, wie man die sozialen Verhältnisse durch die Etablierung von Normen oder durch die Modifikation ihrer normativen Komponenten so beeinflussen kann, daß bestimmte mögliche Ziele erreicht werden können.

Damit haben wir die sozialtechnologischen Grundlagen einer wirksamen Gesetzgebung charakterisiert. Wer die Auffassung akzeptiert, daß eine solche Grundlage erforderlich ist, wird die Idee einer rationalen Jurisprudenz im Sinne einer sozialtechnologischen Disziplin der erwähnten Art nicht zurückweisen können, obwohl die Vorstellung, man könne die Rechtswissenschaft oder einen Teil dieser Wissenschaft technologisch – statt wie gewohnt: normativ – interpretieren, ungewöhnlich zu sein scheint.[5] Übrigens scheint diese Interpretation bei genauer Betrachtung der herkömmlichen Rechtswissenschaft gar nicht so fremd zu sein, denn ihre Vertreter sind es gewohnt, in bestimmten Zusammenhängen teleologische Gesichtspunkte geltend zu machen. Wenn man aber die vielfach impliziten Zielsetzungen des Rechtsdenkens explizit macht und in Rechnung stellt, daß die in Frage kommenden Normen als Mittel für die Erreichung solcher Ziele zu betrachten sind, kommt man ohne Schwierigkeiten zu einer technologischen Auffassung der Jurisprudenz. Eine solche Auffassung hat den Vorteil, daß dabei die Einbettung von Normen in soziale Wirkungszusammenhänge deutlich ist und damit die Notwendigkeit, sich über solche Zusammenhänge Klarheit zu verschaffen. Das bedeutet aber, daß man den Beitrag der theoretischen Sozialwissenschaften zur Aufhellung dieser Zusammenhänge berücksichtigen müßte. Vor allem in der Tradition der politischen Ökonomie gibt es seit langem eine Beziehung dieser Art zur Jurisprudenz, eine Beziehung, die seit einiger Zeit – mit der Entstehung der neuen politischen Ökonomie – wieder stärker ins Blickfeld kommt.[6] Die Problematik der Staatsverfassung hat offenbar sozialtechnologische Aspekte, die nur auf der Grundlage von Resultaten theoretischer Sozialwissenschaften – wie etwa der politischen Ökonomie – adäquat behandelt werden können. Ähnliches gilt aber offenbar für analoge Probleme, wie zum Beispiel das Problem einer bestimmten Bedingungen genügenden Unternehmensverfassung. Ich komme darauf zurück.

2. Markt und Organisation: Steuerungsmechanismen und Anreizmuster

Eine Sozialtechnologie, die als Basis für eine rationale Praxis in Betracht kommen soll, muß eine Analyse der in Frage kommenden Steuerungsmechanimen und der in ihnen wirksamen Anreizmuster involvieren. Das sozialtechnologische Problem, das dabei zu lösen ist, kann in die Form der Frage gebracht werden, wie sich bestimmte Funktionen durch die Kanalisierung individueller Interessen institutionell verankern lassen. Es müssen also institutionelle Vorkehrungen erdacht und verwirklicht werden, die so geartet sind, daß mit ihrer Hilfe die betreffenden Individuen auf Grund ihrer Motivationslage dazu angereizt werden, so zu handeln, daß bestimmte Aufgaben erfüllt werden.

In der heutigen Gesellschaft gibt es vor allem zwei Arten von Regelungsformen, solche, die den Charakter einer *Organisation,* und solche, die den eines *Marktes* haben. Im Gegensatz zu den Gebilden der zweiten Art unterliegen die der ersten Art der Kontrolle durch eine gemeinsame Führung. Unter sozialtechnologischem

Gesichtspunkt handelt es sich um alternative Formen der Steuerung sozialer Prozesse, zwischen denen nach den in Betracht kommenden Leistungsmerkmalen – und den hinter ihnen stehenden Wertgesichtspunkten – eine Wahl getroffen werden kann.[7] Während in Märkten die Koordination der Aktivitäten durch freie Vereinbarungen auf Grund von Angebot und Nachfrage erfolgt, spielen in Organisationen Gebote und Verbote, also Direktiven, eine größere Rolle. Auf Grund von Effizienzvorteilen pflegen im freien Marktverkehr auf vertraglichen Vereinbarungen zwischen den Beteiligten beruhende Organisationen zu entstehen, die dennoch soziologisch als Herrschaftsgebilde einzustufen sind.[8] Eine liberale Politik kann an dieser Tatsache nicht desinteressiert sein. Sie kann zum Beispiel allgemeine Schutzbestimmungen für die Mitglieder solcher Organisationen durchsetzen und darüber hinaus eine Gesetzgebung durchzusetzen suchen, die allgemeine Regeln für den Aufbau solcher Organisationen festlegt, um den Zwangscharakter der in ihnen bestehenden Beziehungen einzuschränken. Man sollte sich nur darüber im klaren sein, inwieweit dabei im Interesse der Freiheit unter Umständen auf eine sonst mögliche Erhöhung der Effizienz verzichtet wird. Daß es aber unter Umständen angebracht sein kann, zwischen höherer Effizienz und größerer Freiheit zu wählen, sollte man nicht in Abrede stellen.[9] Allerdings scheint auch die Erhöhung des Konkurrenzdrucks unter Umständen dazu beitragen zu können, daß die willkürliche Handhabung der Macht in den betreffenden Organisationen vermindert wird.

In den letzten Jahren dürfte sich herausgestellt haben, daß viele Fälle des angeblichen Versagens des Marktmechanismus de facto darauf beruhen, daß die Verfügungsrechte an knappen Gütern nicht in einer Weise festgelegt waren, die zu einem funktionierenden Marktmechanismus hätte führen können. Die vergleichende Analyse verschiedener Steuerungsmechanismen kommt zudem meist zu anderen Konsequenzen als der Beurteilung eines dieser Mechanismen auf dem Hintergrund eines ohnehin nicht realisierbaren Idealzustandes. Was das Eigentumsproblem angeht, so hat schon die schottische Moralphilosophie des 18. Jahrhunderts, von der die politische Ökonomie entscheidende Impulse empfangen hat, seinen engen Zusammenhang mit dem Freiheitsproblem herausgearbeitet. Allerdings können die rechtlichen Regelungen, die der Sicherung eines autonomen Entscheidungsbereiches von Individuen dienen, sehr verschiedenartig sein. Es besteht überdies zum Beispiel Anlaß, auch die Mitgliedschaftsrechte in Organisationen in Betracht zu ziehen, wenn man den Umfang und den Charakter des Spielraums legitimer Handlungsmöglichkeiten für die Individuen bestimmen möchte. Auch sie kommen zum Beispiel für einen Vergleich verschiedener sozialer Ordnungen im Hinblick auf die regulative Idee der Freiheit in Betracht.[10]

3. Unternehmensdemokratie als sozialtechnologisches Problem

Unternehmungen sind, wie schon festgestellt wurde, auch, wenn sie im Rahmen einer freien Marktwirtschaft auftreten, soziologisch gesehen Herrschaftsgebilde, und zwar ungeachtet der Tatsache, daß sie im Rahmen einer solchen Ordnung ihr Personal über den Markt rekrutieren und durch freie Vereinbarungen an sich binden. Daß in ihnen Herrschaft ausgeübt wird, ist, wie schon erwähnt, eine Tatsache, die unter dem Gesichtspunkt der Freiheit negativ zu beurteilen ist, auch wenn die Bedürfnisse der davon Betroffenen sich dem tatsächlichen Zustand so angepaßt haben, daß sie sich damit zufrieden geben.

Die tatsächlichen Verfassungen der in einer Marktwirtschaft auftretenden Unternehmungen sind das Resultat von Entscheidungen, die von den Beteiligten unter Berücksichtigung der vorliegenden normativen Regulierungen – also vor allem der geltenden Gesetze – getroffen wurden. Es kann also keinem Zweifel unterliegen, daß die Gesetzgebung in der Lage ist, einen erheblichen Einfluß auf die Unternehmensverfassungen und damit auf den Ablauf der Willensbildungsprozesse in solchen Organisationen auszuüben. Damit ist sie auch in der Lage, den Charakter der in ihnen bestehenden Herrschaft zu beeinflussen. Sie kann also versuchen, Unternehmensformen zu begünstigen, in denen die im Sinne der Freiheitsidee negativen Aspekte der Herrschaft gemildert sind, und zwar durch Einfluß auf das Marktmilieu der Unternehmungen – zum Beispiel in Richtung auf Erhöhung des Konkurrenzdrucks – und durch Regelungen, die unmittelbar für die Verfassungen von Unternehmungen gelten. Allerdings sollte man sich darüber klar sein, daß durch einen solchen Einfluß unter Umständen Leistungsmerkmale von Unternehmungen negativ beeinflußt werden, die unter anderen Wertgesichtspunkten – vor allem dem der Effizienz im Sinne der Wohlstandsmehrung – relevant sind.

In dieser Perspektive kann auch das Mitbestimmunsproblem gesehen werden. Es gibt bekanntlich heute schon die verschiedensten Mitbestimmungsregelungen in Unternehmensverfassungen, zu denen in unterschiedlicher Weise Stellung genommen wird.[11] Diese Mitbestimmungsregelungen sind teilweise auf freiwilliger Basis zustandegekommen, teilweise durch die Gesetzgebung der betreffenden Staaten begünstigt oder erzwungen worden. Hinter der betreffenden Gesetzgebung stehen jeweils verschiedene Interessen, die auch die Beurteilung der betreffenden Regelungen beeinflussen. Das bedeutet aber keineswegs, daß es keine objektive Beurteilung geben kann, etwa, weil die verschiedenen Wertgesichtspunkte der Beteiligten das nicht erlaubten. Soweit entsprechende sozialwissenschaftliche Erkenntnisse vorliegen, lassen sich vielmehr die *Wirkungen* der betreffenden Regelungen auf die *Steuerung* des sozialen Geschehens und auf die *Lebenssituation* der Betroffenen eruieren, und es läßt sich eine *Beurteilung* dieser Resultate unter verschiedenen *hypothetisch* vorausgesetzten *Wertgesichtspunkten* erreichen, die auch für diejenigen Geltung hat, die den einen oder anderen dieser Gesichtspunkte ablehnen. Die betreffende Beurteilung gilt jedenfalls *relativ* auf die erwähnten Gesichtspunkte und damit *objektiv,* gleichgültig, ob man sich diese Gesichtspunkte *persönlich* zu eigen machen möchte. Natürlich können die Sozialwissenschaften selbst die Wertgesichtspunkte, die von ihnen hypothetisch unterstellt werden, nicht als Resultate objektiver Erkenntnis verbindlich machen wollen. Das alles ist, wie man leicht sieht, mit dem von Max Weber postulierten Prinzip der Wertfreiheit der Wissenschaft vereinbar.[12] So kann etwa auch die ökonomische Analyse keineswegs den Gesichtspunkt der Effizienz als verbindlich erklären, den sie durchaus legitimerweise für die Analyse von Wirkungen der betreffenden Regelungen auf das soziale Geschehen heranziehen kann, indem sie etwa feststellt, daß bestimmte institutionelle Arrangements zu einer ineffizienten Anreizstruktur in dem betreffenden Bereich und damit zur Wohlstandminderung in der betreffenden Gesellschaft führen.[13]

Was die Frage der Effizienzminderung angeht, so kann man für die Analyse von der Tatsache abstrahieren, daß die Effizienz als Leistungsmerkmal sozialer Regelungssysteme positiv bewertet zu werden pflegt. In bezug auf das hier vorliegende Sachproblem ist aber zunächst zweierlei festzustellen: erstens sind die relativen Preise und damit auch die Kosten – einschließlich der Transaktionskosten – abhängig von der jeweiligen Verteilung von Eigentumsrechten, so daß ein Effizienzurteil eigentlich zunächst nur relativ auf eine solche Verteilung sinnvoll ist[14], und zweitens ist die Frage der Beeinflussung der Effizienz durch bestimmte Mitbestimmungsregelungen heute noch hinreichend kontrovers.[15] Dasselbe scheint mir aber auch hinsichtlich der Auswirkungen solcher Regelungen auf die Freiheit der Betroffenen zu gelten.

Ganz allgemein ist es aber anscheinend notwendig, aus der bisherigen Diskussion hinsichtlich unserer sozialtechnologischen Fragestellung zwei Folgerungen zu ziehen: erstens ist es unbedingt erforderlich, für jede solche Analyse die *institutionellen Arrangements,* die durch die betreffenden Mitbestimmungsregelungen zustande kommen, genau zu spezifizieren[16]; und zweitens sind die *Verhaltensannahmen,* mit denen die ökonomische Analyse bisher arbeitet – die individuellen Nutzenfunktionen, die für konkrete Analysen jeweils spezifiziert zu werden pflegen – oft nicht ausreichend, um die genaue *Anreizsituation* zu eruieren, die sich aus den institutionellen und den anderen Bedingungen des individuellen Verhaltens ergibt. Man ist also darauf angewiesen, vielfach mit plausiblen ad hoc-Annahmen zu arbeiten und sich dadurch den Vorwurf eines notdürftig verhüllten a priori-Räsonnements zuzuziehen[17], das de facto unter Umständen durch bestimmte Wertungen motiviert ist. Man kann also mit einem gewissen Recht sagen, daß die sozialtechnologisch entscheidende Frage der faktischen Auswirkungen von Mitbestimmungsregelungen bisher unzureichend geklärt ist, was für alle Interessierten ein wenig befriedigender Zustand ist.

Was nun die Frage angeht, inwieweit die Gesetzgebung überhaupt derartige Regelungen zwangsweise einführen und damit den Unternehmungen aufoktroyieren sollte, so wird dagegen mitunter eingewandt, daß Regelungen, die nicht auf freiwilliger Basis zustandekommen, ohnehin nicht effizient sind und daher auch nicht durch Gesetz verbindlich gemacht werden sollten. Ein solcher Einwand geht von der Voraussetzung aus, daß alle akzeptablen institutionellen Vorkehrungen sich ohne Gesetzgebung spontan entwickeln müssen, eine Voraussetzung, die wohl kaum als selbstverständlich unterstellt werden kann, zumal sie nicht einmal den immer wieder auftretenden Situationen gerecht wird, die den Charakter eines Gefangenen-Dilemmas haben.[18] Sie wird außerdem der Tatsache nicht gerecht, daß es außer dem Gesichtspunkt der Effizienz noch andere Wertgesichtspunkte für die Beurteilung institutioneller Vorkehrungen gibt. Überdies ist das Pareto-Kriterium, das dem Effizienzgesichtspunkt zugrunde liegt, selbst gewissen Einwänden ausgesetzt, die seine Verwendbarkeit in Frage stellen.[19] Der Anschein, man könne mit diesem Kriterium der Tatsache gerecht werden, daß die ökonomische Analyse das Problem der interpersonellen Vergleichbarkeit des Nutzens nicht befriedigend gelöst hat, und dennoch zu ökonomisch begründeten minimalen Werturteilen kommen, die für politische Empfehlungen ausreichend sind, ist unberechtigt. Vom methodologischen Individualismus der ökonomischen Analyse gibt es keinen Weg zur Bewertung sozialer Gesamtgrößen. Für die Anwendung sozialwissenschaftlicher Erkenntnisse zur Unterstützung einer rationalen Politik bleibt man daher auf eine Kombination sozialtechnologischer Analyse mit explizit eingeführten Wertgesichtspunkten angewiesen, die sich nicht aus der Erkenntnis ableiten lassen.

Anmerkungen

1 Vgl. dazu Dlugos 1972, S. 21 ff.; s. auch Dlugos 1977, S. 465 ff. und Dlugos 1981, S. 1 ff.

2 Vgl. Weber 1951, S. 523 f.

3 Vgl. Popper 1965, S. 47 und passim.

4 Vgl. dazu Albert 1976.

5 Vgl. dazu Albert 1979, S. 60 ff.

6 Vgl. dazu etwa Hayek 1971, Buchanan 1984, Bernholz/Breyer 1984.

7 Als Alternativen für den ökonomischen Bereich hat sie vor allem Coase 1953, S. 331 ff., analysiert. Dabei hat er die Rolle der Transaktionskosten und des Effizienzgesichtspunktes für die Wahl zwischen beiden Formen herausgearbeitet. Dieser Gesichtspunkt dominiert auch in dem durch den Coase'schen Aufsatz stark beeinflußten eigentumsrechtlichen Ansatz des ökonomischen Denkens.

8 Da sie unvermeidlich die Selbstbestimmung der Individuen einschränken, stehen sie im Widerspruch zur Freiheitsidee; vgl. dazu z. B. Rowley/Peacock 1975, S. 163 ff. Daß es sich um Herrschaftsgebilde handelt, kann keineswegs damit bestritten werden, daß die betreffenden Beziehungen der Unterordnung auf vertraglichen Vereinbarungen zwischen den Beteiligten beruhen. Das gilt schließlich auch für ein Söldnerheer und für das aktive Offizierskorps einer Wehrpflichtarmee. Niemand würde wohl in diesem Falle den Herrschaftscharakter des betreffenden sozialen Gebildes leugnen.

9 Hinsichtlich dieser Wahl bemerkt Dlugos (1977, S. 473), daß unter Beachtung des wirtschaftlichen Primärzweckes der Unternehmung „... eine wichtige gesellschaftspolitische Aufgabe der Unternehmungsführung darin (bestehe), sich um die Schaffung von Freiräumen für die Selbstentfaltung der Mitarbeiter innerhalb der Unternehmungen zu

bemühen und die Voraussetzungen für den Umgang mit diesen Freiräumen zu entwickeln. Wird diese Aufgabe vernachlässigt, so bleibt eine bedeutsame Chance der Sicherung und Weiterentwicklung der freiheitlich-demokratischen Gesellschaftsordnung ungenützt."

[10] Für eine Analyse der Bedeutung derartiger regulativer Ideen für die menschliche Praxis in allen sozialen Bereichen vgl. Albert 1979.

[11] Vgl. dazu etwa Pejovich 1978 sowie Backhaus/Nutzinger 1982.

[12] Vgl. dazu den Aufsatz von Max Weber 1951 und die anderen einschlägigen Aufsätze Webers in diesem Aufsatzband und Albert 1979.

[13] Vgl. dazu den Aufsatz von Furubotn 1978, deutsche Fassung in Backhaus/Nutzinger 1982, S. 127–181 und die Diskussion dazu in diesem Band: Backhaus 1982, S. 183–201; Furubotn 1982, S. 203–237 und Backhaus 1982, S. 239–281,

[14] Vgl. dazu Schmid 1976, deutsche Fassung in Backhaus/Nutzinger 1982, S. 17–32.

[15] Vgl. etwa Backhaus 1982, S. 241 ff. Fragen der Messung und Bewertung von Effizienzänderungen behandelt Dlugos ausführlich in seinem Beitrag 1981.

[16] Darauf hat vor allem Backhaus aufmerksam gemacht; vgl. die oben erwähnten Arbeiten.

[17] Vgl. dazu die Kritik Nutzingers in Backhaus/Nutzinger 1982, S. 33 ff. und S. 39.

[18] Darauf macht im Zusammenhang mit der Mitbestimmungsproblematik Nutzinger in seinem Beitrag in Backhaus/Nutzinger 1982, S. 43 ff. aufmerksam, besonders auf S. 53, wo die Frage der Geschwindigkeitsbegrenzung für Autos in diesem Sinne analysiert wird.

[19] Vgl. dazu Albert 1979, Abschnitt 19: Pareto-Kriterium, Bedürfniskonstellation und soziale Wohlfahrtsfunktionen, S. 127–132, sowie Schmid 1976, S. 24 ff.

Literatur

Albert, H. (1976): Wertfreiheit als methodisches Prinzip: Zur Frage der Notwendigkeit einer normativen Sozialwissenschaft. In: Albert, H., *Aufklärung und Steuerung*. Hamburg.

Albert, H. (1979): *Traktat über rationale Praxis*. Tübingen.

Backhaus, J. / Nutzinger, H. (Hrsg.) (1982): *Eigentumsrechte und Partizipation*. Frankfurt.

Backhaus, J. (1982): Information und Technologie in der mitbestimmten Unternehmung. In: Backhaus, J. / Nutzinger, H. (Hrsg.), S. 183–201.

Backhaus, J. (1982): Die mitbestimmte Großunternehmung: Eine effiziente Unternehmungsform? In: Backhaus, J. / Nutzinger, H. (Hrsg.), S. 239–281.

Bernholz, P. / Breyer, F. (1984): *Grundlagen der politischen Ökonomie*. 2. Aufl., Tübingen.

Buchanan, J. (1984): *Die Grenzen der Freiheit*. Tübingen.

Coase, R. H. (1937)/(1953): The Nature of the Firm. Economica 1937. In: *Readings in Price Theory*. London 1953, S. 331 ff.

Dlugos, G. (1972): Analytische Wissenschaftstheorie als Regulativ betriebswirtschaftlicher Forschung. In: Dlugos, G. / Eberlein, G. / Steinmann, H. (Hrsg.), *Wissenschaftstheorie und Betriebswirtschaftslehre*. Düsseldorf, S. 21 ff.

Dlugos, G. (1977): Gesellschaftspolitische Implikationen unternehmungsinterner Konflikthandhabung. In: *Die Betriebswirtschaft* 37, S. 465 ff.

Dlugos, G. (1981): Die Unternehmungseffizienz im Interessenkonflikt der Unternehmungsmitglieder. In: Säcker, F. / Zander, E. (Hrsg.), *Mitbestimmung und Effizienz*. S. 1 ff.

Furubotn, E. G. (1978): The Economic Consequences of Codetermination in the Rate and Ressources of Private Investment. In: Pejovich, S. (Hrsg.), S. 131–167, deutsche Fassung in: Backhaus, J. / Nutzinger H. (Hrsg.), S. 127–181.

Furubotn, E. G. (1982): Information, organisatorische Struktur und die möglichen Vorteile der Mitbestimmung. In: Backhaus, J. / Nutzinger, H. (Hrsg.), S. 203–237.

Hayek, F. A. von (1971): *Die Verfassung der Freiheit.* Tübingen.

Nutzinger, H. (1982): Die Mitbestimmungsbewegung in den westlichen Demokratien aus der Sicht der ökonomischen Theorie der Eigentumsrechte. In: Backhaus, J. / Nutzinger, H. (Hrsg.), S. 33 ff.

Nutzinger, H. (1982): Die ökonomische Theorie der Eigentumsrechte – Ein neues Paradigma der Sozialwissenschaften? In: Backhaus, J. / Nutzinger, H. (Hrsg.), S. 43 ff.

Pejovich, S. (Hrsg.) (1978): *The Codetermination Movement in the West.* Lexington, Toronto.

Popper, K. (1965): *Das Elend des Historizismus.* Tübingen.

Rowley, C. K. / Peacock, A. T. (1975): *Welfare Economics. A Liberal Restatement.* London.

Säcker, F. J. / Zander, E. (Hrsg.) (1981): *Mitbestimmung und Effizienz.* Stuttgart.

Schmid, A. A. (1976): The Economics of Property Rights: A Review Article. In: *Journal of Economic Issues* 10, deutsche Fassung in: Backhaus / Nutzinger (Hrsg.), S. 17 ff.

Weber, M. (1951): Der Sinn der „Wertfreiheit" der ökonomischen und soziologischen Wissenschaften. In: Weber, M., *Gesammelte Aufsätze zur Wissenschaftslehre.* 2. Aufl., Tübingen, S. 523.

"Industrial Democracy" Reconsidered

H. T. Wilson

Abstract

Industrial democracy has many variations and is taking many different forms in advanced industrial societies which honour representative democracy and the rule of law. In this sense it must be understood to constitute a complement or supplement to political democracy and the exercise of citizenship in particular, not a substitute for such institutions and practices. The historical record across many countries and cultures shows that the solution to the problem of what I have called political regression *in* Political Management: Redefining the Public Sphere *is to resuscitate citizenship both in and through and outside of established mechanisms and processes. Industrial democracy can only work fruitfully and effectively where such citizenly activity and possibility is alive and well in society as a whole.*

1. Initial Statement of the Problem

I very much appreciate this opportunity to contribute to a reader on the issue of industrial democracy, especially when it is being dedicated to Professor Günter Dlugos on the occasion of his sixty–fifth birthday. A reader on a topic of this importance should not only provide a forum for the exchange of ideas on the relation between practice and theory in economic and political contexts. It should also serve to associate Professor Dlugos' name with an ongoing issue of great concern to all democratic countries, one which should be able to benefit from the concepts, frameworks and thinking of political thought and political science as well as economics and the social and cultural sciences.

It is because my disciplinary background and training is similar to that of Professor Dlugos that I am pleased to be able to argue from the perspective of political thought that a careful rethinking of the theory and practice of industrial democracy is called for for a number of reasons. To some extent these reasons have been alluded to, and in some cases discussed in detail, in my recently published book "Political Management: Redefining the Public Sphere"[1]. My main thesis there was that representative democracy in and through political and legal institution is in dire trouble not only in the so-called Third World but in advanced industrial societies themselves. In the first case, it is the cultural nature and historical evolution of these insistutions which addresses the serious difficulties involved in attempting to transpose them to new nations. When the dependence of these political institutions on capitalism and the market system is remembered, the challenge posed by the desire and determination to install them elsewhere is only underscored[2].

In the second case, however, we must be no less concerned about the presence of *political regression* in advanced industrial societies. An increasing number of properly political functions are being carried out by non-elected officials and members of the judiciary. The kind of apathy and passivity which American political science in particular has associated with "politics" and the so-called "civic cultire" is now being formally institutionalized with the active assistance of the rule of law[3]. Though this problem is quite different from the frequent use of the rule of law in Third World countries as a device for legitimizing repression and violence, the fact that these two pillars of our political and legal system are occasionally at loggerheads can hardly be a source of comfort.

Political regression is evident in delegations of authority within the government structure to bureaucrats, technocrats and regulators and within the legal system to judges and magistrates. In the first instance, it means reliance on administrative structure which is necessitated and justified by monetary or fiscal interventions by government, by the welfare or service state, by foreign and military and defense policy, and by the emergence of an international market with its own trade and business cycles. This structure is much more than the standard bureaucratic variant that Weber discussed, because there is no longer any felt need to even maintain the pretense of a separation between politics and administration. However impossible in practice it may be to make all exercises of administrative discretion accountable to politically elected representatives of the people, maintenance of the distinction as a standard of sorts still existed until recently as a benchmark for all administrative personnel[4].

Nowadays the advent of technocracy threatens this sense of limit by the very nature of its new pre-eminence. The claim is that *political* administration is unavoidable because of the technical complexity and need for speed that characterizes decision making in all democratic governments. The new situation is often cited in order to justify what amounts to a corollary breakdown of the distinction between crisis and non-crisis government with the rise of manifestly political administration. Here it is the view that political problems are capable of administrative solutions which informs the breakdown of accountability mechanisms under the new conditions and pressures[5]. In the event, even the rule of law maxim which says that authority can be delegated but not the respsonsibility for its exercise is lost sight of, save for the occasional plebiscites in which citizens more often that not vote negatively *against* the party in power.

Representation must always be considered a *necessary evil* given the inability of citizens to "present" themselves on political issues, for whatever reasons[6]. This being the case, the representative system must be protected and defended in and through those aspects of the rule of law directly addressed to it. None of the functions and activities mentioned above should be cited as justification for the regression and slippage evident in Western Europe and North America today. Apart from anything else, it gives us less to point to when we try to "persuade" Third World countries, not to even mention those in the Soviet and Chinese orbits, that democracy works and that the rule of law ought to be used to protect and defend representation rather than undermine it. The fact that we have *never* succeeded in reconciling the problem that Aristotle first encountered and raised in response to the collapse of the *polis* and its absorption into a larger territorial imperium gives added impetus to the need to hold firm on representative democracy in the face of efforts to either actively undermine it or take it for granted to a point which amounts to the same thing[7].

2. Industrial Democracy in Comparative Perspective

It is the temptation to give up on the effort to achieve and maintain as close an approximation to the above objective as we possibly can that present arguments in favour of regression, given the requirement of speed and the presence of complexity, only serve to underwrite. Particularly in light of both the theory of economic determinism and the practice of trade union socialism, there has been a very legitimate concern for trying to compensate for the problems of representative democracy by democratizing the workplace through a number of schemes, overlapping and interconnected, and different mainly with regard to matters of emphasis. My understanding of industrial democracy would find it only in countries where one or another form of *political* democracy based on representation and the rule of law exists, and where there has been a tradition of one or another form of capitalism and the market system. Thus I do not treat any of the provisions for "front groups" in the Soviet Union or Comicon countries as indicative of the presence of industrial democracy. The recent situation in Poland only underscores the point that these countries cannot afford industrial democracy because they cannot afford *any* form of democracy whatsoever.

My point in locating industrial democracy in this fashion is to underscore its dependence on representative democracy and the rule of law, alongside the right to join trade unions and collectively bargain with management as the representatives of capital. Industrial democracy tries to build upon and extend democracy in advanced industrial societies through the politicization of the labour-management distinction, moderated by arbitration and mediation when collective bargaining fails. At the same time, collective bargaining is seen to constitute the pre-eminent basis for connecting individuals to the state, even by comparison with both the market and the ballot box as mechanisms of public power and control. This conflict model, designed with an eye to the eventual dismantling of the capitalist system in the United Kingdom, was proposed by Mr. Wedgwood Benn over a decade ago, and constitutes an extreme case to be sure. Yet the idea that collective bargaining ought to possess a status equal to the marketplace and the exercise of citizenship through the ballot box has a readily understandable appeal for many.

At the other extreme is the effort to delimit the conflict that this model can generate by providing for joint decision making and profit sharing. Trade unions effectively give up their right to criticize management whenever they are coopted voluntarily (or involuntarily, as in some Comicon countries) into this general form of industrial democracy, for the obvious reason that they have participated in the decision process, for better or for worse. The link between such participation in the form of co-determination, and profit sharing with employees, becomes problematic when external international economic conditions and related internal difficulties produce a situation in which labour shows losses rather than profits with management. This development is precisely what has caused the present strains and tensions in the practice of codetermination in West Germany. The point here is that political-economic models like co-determination really work only when there is a surplus, because it is far more difficult to get agreement on joint decision-making and suppression of a conflict model when the economic situation is poor than when there is economic growth and a surplus.

Sitting somewhere between these two extremes are the Scandinavian countries and, to a lesser extent, the Netherlands, with their strong committment to the social service state and to trade unionism, all within a culture and society which is relatively stable and homogeneous even given the presence of multi-party rather than two-party systems. Some have even suggested that it is only in countries like these that a multi-party system is compatible with political stability. In these instances, there are labour and/or socialist parties which, however, can only participate in political power if they share it with one or more parties in a coalition. It is the tradition of compromise, among other things, that has contributed to a situation in which these multi-party systems generate continuous system stability, while the two-party system so central to British political and governmental institutions manages to produce intense conflict which austerity only exacerbates because of the status and working conditions of British labour. The reason why industrial democracy tends to be associated with multi-party rather than two-party systems is that coalitions all too frequently generate stalemate, or the sort of compromise on policy that cries out for an alternative, albeit one existing *alongside* the political, party and governmental system.

However frustrating the bias in capitalist systems toward management and against labour, even in the presence of a service and welfare apparatus set alongside the economic system, the victory of a party either directly or indirectly representative of the interests of labour usually leads to policies that even the opposition can roll back when in power only at their peril. This has been the trend in almost every case, save for the United Kingdom under Margaret Thatcher. The likelihood of industrial democracy in England is as slight as in the case of the United States, though for totally different reasons. In the first case it is the titanic gap between capital and labour, and an accumulated rage that is continually fuelled by a class system with no parallel anywhere in the western world. In the second, it is the success of an individualist ethic underwritten by intense nationalism and patriotism unknown in any other democratic country that leads trade union members to describe themselves as middle class individuals and Americans first and union members second, if at all.

The point about industrial democracy is that it seeks to improve the decision and policy process by essentially *complementing* a representative system which is believed to be *incomplete* rather than obsolete. Any attempt to dismantle the system of representation, even in and through mechanisms technically subordinate to the rule of law, will provide the conditions which make workplace democracy virtually impossible to sustain. Yugoslavia is an important and intriguing case, and constitutes the closest approximation to an exception to what I have said thus far. However, the model that is far more likely when democratic traditions are not deeply established before they are dismantled is fascism and/or syndicalism, if history and past practice are to be considered any guide. Industrial democracy requires, as I noted earlier, representative political democracy for it to work; it cannot succeed in the latter's absence. At the same time, It is probably incompatible with either excessive individualism or nationalism, for reasons which have already been suggested. Finally, industrial democracy is difficult to establish or extend during periods of economic contraction and austerity, for reasons that Schumpeter understood perfectly when he wrote *Capitalism, Socialism and Democracy* in 1942[8].

What I want to concentrate on in what follows is the need to resusscitate and/or strengthen and extend representative democracy, at the very least as a prerequisite for industrial democracy if not in place of it in the advanced countries. There may be some sense in the view that the present political apathy and passivity can be left where we find it in advanced industrial societies, on grounds it cannot get any worse. The idea here is that this route to change is sterile and useless, but that no danger is presented by its present condition, whereas I believe that the focus on passivity, apathy, even cynicism and a sense of futility constitutes a grave problem for the present and future. In too many countries is it argued that democratic traditions are deeply rooted enough for this development to cause no problem, but this fails to take account of the regression factor that I have been so concerned about in my recent work. What gives my concern added gravity is the fact that political democracy, far from being something which industrial democracy could conceivably replace, is *absolutely essential* if there are to be any prospects whatsoever for industrial democracy of the sort being discussed in Western Europe at the present time.

3. "Political Management" and Industrial Democracy

Let me now turn to some central features of the diagnosis that informs *Political Management* in order to make a case for beginning with the extant political and governmental system in any effort to improve the quality and frequency of democracy. Let me note in passing that political science has been far less concerned than in should be with the fact of political regression, but that this has much to do with its determination to distance itself from "practical" political problems in pursuit of professional and scientific status as a discipline[9]. In this study, I make reference to politics as an activity that can be effected either in and through established governmental and political processes or through a form of display outside these channels in other sectors of Society. Display can occur no matter which alternative is chosen, and it is important not to feel that there is any greater authenticity attaching to the second form of political expression than the first. Individuation takes place in either case, and it is less the mode or manner used than the way in which it is addressed and discussed in whatever form we choose[10].

Another point which I feel is very important relates directly to the question of the viability and necessity of industrial democracy. Here I am concerned that we *not* entertain the idea that acting in and through established process is in a zero-sum relation to some more "authentic" form of display and individuation, because this leads us to support the view that we need do nothing to ressussicitate and utilize these processes but can rely on others to take over their functions and do them better. It must be clear from what I have already said that I believe such an attitude in practice will make industrial democracy of any type *less* possible, if not impossible altogether. Thus my argument in the book that often it is harder to work thrugh established processes precisely *because* the goal is more difficult to realize, so it would seem, than appealing to some form of display outside them. The mass media of public communication, particularly broadcasting, provide the most tempting platform to engage in such activity.

While there is little doubt that the effects in the short-term are often exponentially greater for this type of display, the long-term effects do not provide us with the same sort of assurance at all. Political concerns of pressing moment come in all types and sizes, and the mass media in a (late) capitalist system like ours will pick and choose who and what to present and publicize and when and how long to do so. Often it is difficult to know whether they are *responding* to the apparent fickleness of publics for news, entertainment and stimulation, or whether they are assisting in the creation of such overall attitudes and mind sets. I suspect that this process involves a great deal of both, but have no way of guaging relative importance, which, in any case, would have to be looked at on a case *by case* basis. What I do think is important to keep in mind is the fact that the processes themselves, and those elements of the rule of law that undergird them, are the *sine qua non* without which the rights and liberties so central to display outside these processes can and will eventually be undermined.

Thus there are two types of display and individuation, but activity "outside" established processes must not be seen to have a privileged place *vis à vis* that which occurs (or hopefully will occur) "inside" them. The frustration of working through established processes is more than compensated for by the fact that those who do so are both reaffirming these processes through utilization, and providing the sort of guarantee that will make other modes, including various forms of industrial democracy (at least in their formative phases) possible. There is also the contact, direct or indirect, that citizens have with formal power holders in government, as well as those in political parties and interest groups, as a consequence of acting through established processes. While it is no doubt true that public posturing does occur and is unavoidable in such activities of individuation, the same can be said for political activity outside these channels. Against the likelihood of a more immediate impact in this latter case, one must stand the greater long-term effect of working thrugh established processes, along with the latent function of affirming the system by so doing.

The history of the mass media's attention to serious issues in our society does not make me feel satisfied that broadcasting in particular ought to be seen as a device for supplementing or supplanting, such processes. While the latter instance is not likely to happen, there have been attempts to achieve greater politicization by employing the new automated electronic and audio-visual technology in order to allow citizens to "vote" on a vast number of "issues" that certainly do arise in the effort to manage a polity democratically and with legality. Such proposals simply show how depoliticized, passive and apathetic citizens have become in advanced industrial societies. They reaffirm not politics and citizenship, but audience and consumer roles instead. Further, They treat the "vote" as citizenly display when it should constitute only the *last act* of citizenly display in the formal context of democratic elections. The vote, so understood, is then viewed as a registry of opinion detached from larger contexts and nothing more[11].

Once the vote is understood to be the last step in a *particular type* of citizenly display and individuation – formal elections – rather than something that can be transferred to the nightly news, the point I have been making about process is only underscored in its urgency and significance. Citizens acquire a sense of the issues not from "voting" on an endless series of individual concerns that are detached and taken out of larger contexts of concern, but from considering these problems over time, and in ways which stress their interrelation and interdependence. Process is time-consuming, I readily admit, but isn't the point precisely that present pressures on governments from many sources are trying to achieve speed and efficiency, and that the ideal of "voting" in this fashion would really *disempower* citizens and reinforce an already dangerous tendency to instant policy-making on the part of governments? In a sense, it is not too much to argue that process, seen in this light, is indeed its own justification, as are the political acts which seek to reaffirm process in politics[12].

I have cited the university and higher education, political and social sciences, local, municipal and metro-urban politics, and the mass media of public communication as alternative vehicles for political management in the book. My reasons for not discussing industrial democracy relate to the context from which I write, and the wholesale nature of these proposals. I am certainly not "against" industrial democracy in any sense, but only wish to suggest that such an approach, as in all cases of political display outside established channels, presupposes and is heavily dependent on the good health and functioning of these channels. Indeed, nothing is clearer than the *highly contingent character* of all forms of organizational politics based on conflict and/or cooperation between labour and management in periods when the formal machinery of government and politics has broken down. In these cases, the ability of a tyrant or dictator to take control of the media effectively turns the apparant "silk purse" of display outside established channels into a "sows ear" for groups working against the status quo, the status quo ante, or outright repression.

The history of the Twentieth Century is already replete with major and minor instances, by global standards, of the *inability* of less formal intermediate institutions (churches, unions, cities, parties, bureaucratic organizations, science, higher education, even capital itself) to effectively defend representative democracy, and the rule of law on which representative institutions are based, from the attack of totalitarian and autocratic leaders, parties and ideologies. The fact that occupancy and effective pre-emption of state and governmental organizations and functions has so often led to suppression of politics and the political as I have defined it should not lead us to despair about the hopelessness of such concerns, efforts and approaches and the embrace of apparently more viable alternatives. This illusion is something that those who have survived the wholesale destruction of labour-management collective bargaining and cooperation, along with other instances of institutional collapse in such situations, could readly verify and authenticate. The successful suppression of politics and the political as they are expressed in and through established representative and legal processes, as well as the processes themselves, and their reconstitution as *state* power through the aegis of totalitarian ideologies, parties and leadership groups, virtually guarantees that all intermediate forms dependent on these processes will themselves be coopted or collapse altogether[13].

Industrial democracy could only function in a different capacity from the way I have described it if it were in fact of a type which sought peacefully, but actively, to bring about an alternative to capitalism in any of its variants. This would in turn raise the question of whether the workplace, even aggregated and generalized to Society as a whole, could ever be capable of replacing these forms and processes, or whether democratic principles and practices, and the rule of law undergirding them, would in turn disappear with the creation of this very different form of collective life. While I readily admit that capitalism, broadly understood, and these particular forms and processes still "belong together", today no less than they did a century ago, this does not mean that I am sanguine about capitalism[14]. But neither does it mean that I take these forms and processes for granted. The only sensible way to transform the world capitalist system into something that is qualitatively superior is to *fully and thoroughly utilize* the institutions, mechanisms and processes that I have been at such pains to defend.

While there is a great deal of scope to operate "outside" them in the ways indicated, working in and through them can now be seen to serve not just the two purposes cited above, but a third concerned with system transformation. No other approach, not even industrial democracy, can do this, for the simple reason that it depends upon and takes totally for granted both representation and the rule of law as a prerequisite for its own effective functioning. Industrial democracy, far from constituting an alternative to what I have called political management, has a vested interest in the resusscitation of the very forms and processes that political management is so concerned about and preoccupied with.

Remarks

1 Wilson 1985.
2 Wilson 1987.
3 See for example Crick 1960; Almond/Verba 1965.
4 See Wilson 1985, chapter 6, pp. 93–122.
5 Ibid.; Wilson 1983, pp. 152–238, and Wilson (forthcoming).
6 See Voegelin 1952, pp. 27–106, and Wilson 1985, chapter 4, pp. 45–67.
7 Wilson 1985 especially chapters 2 and 12, pp. 5–22, 253.
8 New York, Harper and Row.
9 See Crick 1959; Storing 1962; Wilson 1985, chapter 7, pp. 123–124.
10 Wilson 1985, chapters 10 and 12, pp. 193–221, but especially at pp. 253–288.
11 Ibid., pp. 89–91; Thomas 1960.
12 At the same time, this should not be detached from the claim that process lends superiority to the outcomes realized in and through its utilization, because such utilization performs latent as well as manifest functions for the system.
13 See Neumann 1944; Arendt 1960, 1951; Buchheim 1968.
14 See generally Wilson 1977 and Wilson 1984.

Literature

Almond, G. / Verba, S. (1965): *The Civic Culture.* Boston.
Arendt, H. (1960, 1951): *The Origins of Totalitarianism.* New York.
Buchheim, H. (1968): *Totalitarian Rule: Its Nature and Characteristics.* Middleton, Conn.
Clegg, S. / Dow, G. / Boreham, P. (Hrsg.) (1983): *The State, Class and Recession.* London.
Crick, B. (1959): *The American Science of Politics.* Berkeley.
Crick, B. (1960): *In Defense of Politics.* Harmondsworth.
Massey, H. (Hrsg.) (forthcoming): *Political Leadership in Canada.* Toronto.

Neumann, F. (1944): *Behemoth: The Structure and Practice of National Socialism, 1933–1944.* New York.

Storing, H. (Hrsg.) (1962): *Essays on the Scientific Study of Politics.* New York.

Thomas, A. (1960): *Audience, Market, Public: An Evaluation of Canadian Broadcasting.* Occasional Paper 7 (April), University of British Columbia, Department of University Extension.

Voegelin, E. (1952): *The New Science of Politics.* Chicago, pp. 27–106.

Wilson, H. T. (1977): *The American Ideology.* London and Boston.

Wilson, H. T. (1983): Technocracy and Late Capitalist Society. In: Clegg, S. / Dow, G. / Boreham, P. (Hrsg.), *The State, Class, and Recession,* pp. 152–238.

Wilson, H. T. (1984): *Tradition and Innovation.* London and Boston.

Wilson, H. T. (1985): *Political Management.* Berlin and New York

Wilson, H. T. (1987): Notes on Achievement of Communicative Behaviour and Related Difficulties. In: *Dialectical Anthropology.*

Wilson, H. T. (forthcoming): Elites, Meritocracy and Technocracy: Some Implications for Political Leadership. In: Massey, H. (Hrsg.), *Political Leadership in Canada.* Toronto.

Einige grundsätzliche Überlegungen zur Verantwortung von Unternehmungen und Gewerkschaften in der demokratischen Gesellschaft

Alexander Schwan

Abstract

Basic Considerations on the Responsibility of Business Corporations and Trade Unions in the Democratic Society

In a democratic society business corporations and trade unions have – according to their legitimate representation of interests – certain responsibility regarding common welfare.

Common welfare is not a given well-defined variable, but always the result of dynamic political decision processes, which are themselves bound to the constitutional structures and thereby to ethical standards. Realization of common welfare means a political transformation of the fundamental rights and the basic values of the constitution. The basic value of social justice is central for economic interest groups. Social justice includes justified performance ratings, and justice in the allocation of opportunities and participation. This results in the economic organizations' obligation to social partnership. Considering the task of reducing the unemployment rate and the "New Social Question" this obligation is questioned. For that reason a revival of the "concerted action" seems to be desirable.

1. Selbstinteresse und Gemeinwohl

In den hochindustrialisierten Gesellschaften mit demokratischer Verfassung, also in den pluralistischen Gesellschaften des Westens, gelten die wirtschaftlichen Unternehmungen und ihre Interessenorganisationen – d. h. genauer die Organisationen zur Vertretung der Interessen der Unternehmer oder Unternehmensführungen, im weiten Sinne der „Arbeitgeber" – einerseits, die Gewerkschaften als die Organisationen der Interessenvertretung der in den Unternehmungen tätigen Arbeiter und Angestellten – der „Arbeitnehmer" – andererseits gleichsam als die klassischen großen Interessengruppen. Wenn früher die „Herrschaft der Verbände" thematisiert wurde und heute von korporativer Versäulung der gesellschaftlichen Interessen die Rede ist, so sind primär die Unternehmens- und Unternehmerverbände sowie die Gewerkschaften gemeint. Die Verbände und Organisationen in anderen gesellschaftlichen Bereichen, denen der Kultur, der Künste, der Wissenschaften, der Religion, des Bildungswesens, des Sports, der Familie, der caritativen und sozialen Arbeit usw., werden zumeist nur teilweise als Interessengruppen angesprochen. Ihnen werden in aller Regel übergreifende Aufgaben zuerkannt, die sie über reine Interessenorganisationen hinausheben. Die ökonomischen Interessen und hier wiederum die organisierten Großinteressen von „Kapital" und „Arbeit" dagegen gelten als blanke, bloße Interessen, Interessen gleichsam in Reinkultur. Diese ihre „Reinheit" enthebt sie gerade nicht des Odiums, oftmals brutal, rücksichtslos, egoistisch verfochten zu werden, in der Weise gänzlich parteiischer Sonderinteressen.

Haben diese Interessengruppen dennoch eine Verantwortung in der pluralistischen Gesellschaft? Nun, ihre erste Verantwortung liegt gewiß eben in der öffentlichen Geltendmachung der Belange der in ihnen zusammengeschlossenen Mitglieder, die zugleich jedoch Glieder, Bürger, Akteure, Institutionen (in) der gesamten Gesellschaft – und zwar in unterschiedlichsten anderen Rollen – sind, als welche sie die ökonomischen Interessengruppen (Unternehmensverband oder Gewerkschaft) auch transzendieren; in und mit ihrer Interessengruppe haben sie dies zu berücksichtigen und sich demgemäß zu verhalten. Dies hat dann auch die Interessenorganisation selbst zu tun. Zwar tragen die ökonomischen Interessenorganisationen anders als die politischen Parteien, die „bei der politischen Willensbildung des Volkes mit"-wirken (GG Art. 21, Abs. 1), keine direkte staatliche, jedoch sehr wohl eine gesamtgesellschaftliche Verantwortung, eine Mitverantwortung für das Wohl der gesamten Gesellschaft, also für das „Gemeinwohl". Die Art und Artikulation dieser Mitverantwortung ist zugleich an ihren Charakter als ökonomische Interessengruppe gebunden, ist mit ihm integral verbunden und von daher bestimmt und auch begrenzt.

Gibt es aber in der pluralistischen Gesellschaft überhaupt so etwas wie ein erkennbares, definierbares, realisierbares „Gemeinwohl"? Wenn ja, in welchem Sinne? Und wie könnten die „klassischen" Interessengruppen dafür mitverantwortlich sein? Was bedeutet dies für die Art und Orientierung der Vertretung ihrer Sonderinteressen, für ihre erste Verantwortung? Diesen Fragen sei in aller Kürze nachgegangen. Wir müssen uns dabei auf die grundsätzlichsten normativen Überlegungen und auf einige der wichtigsten aktuellen Schlußfolgerungen konzentrieren.[1]

2. Gemeinwohl in der pluralistischen Gesellschaft

In der pluralistischen Gesellschaft und im demokratischen Staatswesen ist „Gemeinwohl“ nach der berühmt gewordenen Formulierung Ernst Fraenkels nun gerade keine vorgegebene, jederzeit absolut zweifelsfrei feststellbare Größe, sondern die immer wieder von neuem zu bestimmende „Resultante“, die sich jeweils erst „aus dem Parallelogramm der ökonomischen, sozialen, politischen und ideologischen Kräfte einer Nation dann ergibt, wenn ein Ausgleich angestrebt und erreicht wird, der objektiv den Mindestanforderungen einer gerechten Sozialordnung entspricht und subjektiv von keiner maßgeblichen Gruppe als Vergewaltigung empfunden wird«.[2] Gemeinwohl ist demnach das jeweilige, nie ein für allemal fixierbare, ständigem Wandel überlieferte Ergebnis des dynamischen gesellschaftlichen und staatlichen Willensbildungs- und Entscheidungsprozesses selbst, an dem die Bürger, Gruppen, gesellschaftlichen, kulturellen, ökonomischen Organisationen, politischen Parteien und staatlichen Organe in unterschiedlichen Funktionen teilhaben. Insofern ist seine konkrete inhaltliche Bestimmung aposteriorischen Charakters. An ihr wirken die verschiedenen Kräfte selbst mit, die dem Gemeinwohl verpflichtet und für es (mit)verantwortlich sind. Ein vorgegebenes, absolut richtiges, apriorisches Gemeinwohl festlegen und durchsetzen zu wollen, würde zur Aufhebung der Pluralität und Freiheit in der Gesellschaft, damit der pluralistischen demokratischen Gesellschaft selbst, würde zu einer autoritären oder totalitären Ordnung führen.

Dennoch deutet die zitierte Definition Fraenkels schon an, daß auch in der pluralistischen Demokratie der gesellschaftliche und staatliche Willensbildungs- und Entscheidungsprozeß sowie die Orientierung der in ihm wirkenden und an ihm beteiligten Kräfte nicht schlechthin willkürlich sein können, wenn das Wohl der Allgemeinheit, das gesamtgesellschaftliche Wohl, das Gemeinwohl erstrebt wird. „Gemeinwohl“ bedeutet folglich keine bloße Leerformel ohne jede inhaltliche Voraussetzung. Vielmehr geht in die Erörterung dieses Gemeinwohlbegriffes bereits die normative Prämisse ein, daß ein Ausgleich der gesellschaftlichen – der ökonomischen, sozialen, politischen und ideologischen – Kräfte im Sinne von Mindestanforderungen einer gerechten Sozialordnung und der Gewährleistung eines prinzipiell gleichen Maßes an Freiheit für die Individuen und die Gruppen angestrebt werden muß. Existenz und Entwicklung der pluralistischen Gesellschaft und des demokratischen Staates sind grundlegend an die Achtung der Würde jedes ihnen zugehörigen Individuums, seiner unveräußerlichen Menschenrechte, seiner Freiheit, seines Anspruchs auf Gerechtigkeit im Sinne von Rechtsgleichheit und sozialer Chancengleichheit, auf Solidarität im Sinne der Hilfe zur Selbsthilfe, auf eine freiheitliche Verfassungs- und Rechtsordnung und auf innere wie äußere Sicherheit gebunden. Diese Grundrechte, denen Pflichten der Individuen und Gruppen einander gegenüber und gegenüber der Gemeinschaft korrespondieren, und die so in ihnen enthaltenen anthropologischen Grundwerte möglichst weitgehend praktisch zum Vollzug zu bringen, macht die Gemeinwohlverwirklichung als

Aufgabe aller Individuen, gesellschaftlichen Kräfte und staatlichen Organe in der pluralistischen Demokratie aus.

In der Pluralismustheorie – der Theorie der pluralistischen Gesellschaft und des demokratischen Staates[3] – ist die Erfahrung leitend, daß die praktische Realisierung der grundlegenden Rechte, Pflichten und Werte im endlichen Leben des Menschen immer nur relativ möglich ist und in ihren konkreten Formen und detaillierten inhaltlichen Fixierungen stets umstritten bleibt. Deshalb enthält das normative Gemeinwohlverständnis nur einen minimalen, bessergesagt fundamentalen Rahmen an unverzichtbaren Wertsetzungen. Innerhalb seiner ist die Willensbildung und Entscheidungsfindung der Individuen und Gruppen auch hinsichtlich dessen, was in jeweiligen Konstellationen im einzelnen als Gemeinwohl begriffen und als mögliche Gemeinwohlverwirklichung angesehen wird, offen und legitimen Konflikten ausgesetzt. Aus den normativen Prämissen ergibt sich jedoch als Bedingung für den Prozeß gemeinwohlorientierter Willensbildung und Entscheidungsfindung weiterhin, daß er an gemeinschaftlich festgelegte Verfahren geknüpft ist und die Übung entsprechender Verhaltensweisen, d. h. gesellschaftlich-politischer Tugenden, erfordert. Sie gehören ebenfalls zu den notwendigen Elementen der Gemeinwohlverwirklichung in der pluralistischen Demokratie. Sie sind Bedingung eines befriedeten Austrags der einzelnen Konflikte und ihrer friedlichen Lösung auf Zeit.

Die genannten Elemente sind in der Verfassung des demokratischen Staates einer pluralistischen Gesellschaft teils kodifiziert, teils inkludent enthalten. So bindet das Grundgesetz der Bundesrepublik Deutschland mit seinem für unrevidierbar erklärten Art. 1 alle staatliche Gewalt explizit, alle Glieder der Gesellschaft implizit an die Anerkennung der Unantastbarkeit der Menschenwürde; diese ist zu achten und zu schützen. Es bezeichnet unverletzliche und unveräußerliche Menschenrechte als die Grundlage jeder menschlichen Gemeinschaft, des Friedens und der Gerechtigkeit in der Welt und entwickelt von daher einen Katalog von Grundrechten (von Freiheits- als Abwehr-, Entfaltungs- und Mitwirkungsrechten der Person, aller Gesellschaftsglieder), die die staatlichen Organe als unmittelbar geltendes Recht binden und somit für sie, aber auch für alle Gesellschaftsglieder und alle gesellschaftlichen Kräfte, Gruppen, Organisationen und Institutionen Richtschnur, Maßstab und Schranke, also insgesamt Orientierungsmarken des Handelns und ihm dienlicher Verhaltensweisen darstellen.

Zu den Grundrechten gehören u. a. das Recht auf freie Meinungsäußerung (Art. 5), auf freie, aber friedliche Versammlung (Art. 8), auf die freie Bildung von Vereinen und Gesellschaften, insbesondere auch von Vereinigungen „zur Wahrung und Förderung der Arbeits- und Wirtschaftsbedingungen" in allen Berufen einschließlich des Rechts auf Arbeitskämpfe, die zu solcher Wahrung und Förderung von diesen Vereinigungen, d. h. den Gewerkschaften, geführt werden (Art. 9), auf Freizügigkeit (Art. 11), auf freie Wahl des Berufs, des Arbeitsplatzes und der Ausbildungsstätte (Art. 12), auf Eigentum, das jedoch sozial „verpflichtet" und dessen Gebrauch „zugleich dem Wohle der Allgemeinheit", also dem

Gemeinwohl, dienen soll (Art. 14). Diese und die anderen Grundrechte dürfen nach Art. 19, Abs. 2 des Grundgesetzes in ihrem „Wesensgehalt" durch gesetzliche Regelungen „in keinem Falle" angetastet werden.

Die Verfassung kodifiziert im weiteren zum Zwecke der rechtlichen Ordnung, Beschränkung und Effektuierung politischer und gesellschaftlicher Macht auf der Grundlage der Volkssouveränität die Gewaltenteilung zwischen den staatlichen Organen und die Art ihres Zusammenwirkens, legt die Verfassungsgebundenheit der Gesetzgebung, die Gesetzmäßigkeit der Verwaltung, die parlamentarische Verantwortung der Regierung und die Unabhängigkeit der Rechtsprechung nach Regularien fest, die uns hier nicht im einzelnen zu beschäftigen haben. Es sind die rechtlichen Regularien eines demokratischen und sozialen Bundesstaates (Art. 20), dessen Grundsätze und Grundstruktur nach Art. 79, Abs. 3 ebenfalls nicht revidierbar sind. Der demokratische Rechtsstaat und das sog. Sozialstaatspostulat (vgl. auch Art. 28, Abs. 1) sind also als kodifizierte Grundbedingungen des Lebens und Handelns in der pluralistischen Gesellschaft selbst wesentliche Inhalte der Gemeinwohlverwirklichung. Anders gesagt: Gemeinwohlverwirklichung ergibt sich in dem Maße, wie die pluralistische, rechtsstaatliche und soziale Demokratie in verfassungskonformem gesellschaftlichem und politischem Handeln und Verhalten aller Beteiligten ethisch, rechtlich, sozial, ökonomisch und kulturell entwickelt wird.

3. Der Grundwert der sozialen Gerechtigkeit

Die damit skizzierten grundsätzlichen Hinweise zum Gemeinwohlbegriff der pluralistischen Gesellschaft zeigen, daß diese Gesellschaft durchaus über einen verbindlichen Fudamentalbestand an einheitlichem Ethos für alle ihre Glieder, Gruppen und Organisationen verfügt, der Bedingung ihrer Lebens- und Entwicklungsfähigkeit ist, so sehr die vielen in ihr wirkenden Kräfte in partieller Autonomie auch ihr je eigenes, aus ihrer Interessenperspektive folgendes Ethos ausbilden. Bei allen Unterschieden und Divergenzen zwischen diesen Kräften muß ein genereller Konsens in der Anerkennung und Praktizierung des fundamentalen einheitlichen Ethos bestehen. Solchen Grundkonsens gilt es immer wieder zu erneuern, zu vertiefen und möglichst zu erweitern, wenn die pluralistische Gesellschaft in der Lage sein soll, Konflikte zu regeln und Probleme zu lösen. Sind es zwar in erster Linie die politischen Parteien, denen im demokratischen Mehrparteiensystem durch alle notwendigen Auseinandersetzungen über die jeweils angemessene konkrete Gemeinwohlverwirklichung auf Zeit und die damit gegebene, ja gebotene Konkurrenz um (kontrollierte und begrenzte) staatliche Entscheidungsmacht hindurch der Grundkonsens in der gemeinsamen Bejahung der elementaren Verfassungsgehalte und des fundamentalen öffentlichen Ethos abverlangt werden müssen, was sie für die Lösung aktueller Fragen kompromißfähig macht, so müssen doch auch die gesellschaftlichen Interessengruppen um der Gemeinwohlverwirklichung willen zu verfassungskonformem und diesem Ethos adäquatem Handeln angehalten werden. Dies beeinträchtigt ihre primäre Zwecksetzung der Vertretung ihrer speziellen Interessen nicht. Damit die pluralistische Gesellschaft nicht unregierbar wird und ihre demokratische Ordnung nicht gefährdet, damit sozialer Ausgleich gewährleistet bleibt und die Interessen aller, auch der nicht in den großen Verbänden Organisierten, gewahrt werden können, bedarf es der ausdrücklichen Verpflichtung der ökonomischen, sozialen, kulturellen und weltanschaulichen Organisationen und Institutionen zu partnerschaftlichem und solidarischem Verhalten. Sofern hier nun die ökonomischen Interessenorganisationen der Unternehmer und der Arbeitnehmer im Vorblick stehen, fragt sich auf der Grundlage des bisher Dargelegten, wie sie vornehmlich dem Grundwert des sozialen Ausgleichs (Fraenkel), weiter gefaßt der sozialen Gerechtigkeit verpflichtet sind und darin ihre vornehmliche Verantwortung in der pluralistischen Gesellschaft finden.

Wenn der Grundwert der sozialen Gerechtigkeit zum Kernbestand des fundamentalen Ethos der pluralistischen, demokratischen Gesellschaft gehört, dann muß er mit dem maßsetzenden Grundwert der Freiheit vermittelbar sein. Zentrales Problem einer Anthropologie und politischen Theorie in demokratischer Perspektive, also gerade auch der Pluralismustheorie, ist seit jeher das des Spannungsverhältnisses von Freiheit und Gleichheit. Zur Freiheit der individuellen und politischen Entfaltung der Person gehört das Prinzip der Gleichheit insofern hinzu, als für alle Bürger einer Gesellschaft eine grundsätzlich gleiche Freiheit gefordert werden muß. Gleichheit ist dann nicht als totale Gleichmacherei mißzuverstehen; so wäre sie der entschiedenste Gegensatz zur Freiheit. Gerade um der Freiheit und Würde der Person – unbedingt jeder einzelnen Person – willen kann man einerseits nicht über die individuellen Unterschiede der Veranlagung, der Herkunft, des Geschlechts, der Sprache, des Glaubens, der geistigen Anschauungen, der materiellen und kulturellen Interessen und der mit alledem verbundenen politischen Bestrebungen hinwegsehen und sich hinwegsetzen wollen. Die in der Freiheit und Würde der Person andererseits unverbrüchlich wurzelnde Gleichheit ist jedoch die Gleichheit aller im Recht und darüber hinaus ein Annäherungswert im sozialen Leben der Individuen, der Bürger, der Glieder einer Gesellschaft, der Mitglieder der pluralistischen, freiheitlichen, demokratischen Gesellschaft.

Eben diesen Annäherungswert können wir soziale Gerechtigkeit nennen. Er besagt, daß jedes Mitglied der Gesellschaft Anspruch darauf hat, angemessene materielle und kulturelle Güter zugeteilt zu erhalten, um sein Leben in Freiheit verwirklichen und führen zu können. Die Einlösung dieses Anspruchs bemißt sich primär nach seinen eigenen Leistungen als Beiträgen für die gesellschaftliche Allgemeinheit, die zugleich Erweise seiner Freiheit, der aktiven Entfaltung seiner Person sind. Doch würde eine absolut verstandene, verabsolutierte Leistungsgerechtigkeit die Gleichheit als gleiche Freiheit vernichten. Es gibt stets Bürger und Gruppen, die aus den verschiedensten Gründen von sich her nicht in der Lage sind, die Leistungen aufzubringen, die ihnen ein angemessenes materielles und kulturelles Leben verbürgen. Deshalb ist es Aufgabe der Gesellschaft, des Staates und der Politik, ihnen immer wieder und gegebenenfalls stets von neuem annähernd gleiche, also wenigstens ähnliche Chancen der Wahrnehmung ihrer Freiheit und der Sicherung ihres Lebens zu eröffnen.

Soziale Gerechtigkeit als Annäherung zur Gleichheit ist folglich neben und mit der Leistungsgerechtigkeit immer auch das Bemühen um Chancengleichheit, ist insofern – da es Chancengleichheit absolut ebenfalls nicht geben kann, das wäre eine ungebührliche Abstraktion – zumindest Chancengerechtigkeit: Einräumung ähnlicher Chancen bei vergleichbaren Bedingungen. Nicht zuletzt durch Partizipationsmöglichkeiten in verschiedenen gesellschaftlichen Bereichen des individuellen Lebensvollzuges wird solche Chancengerechtigkeit eröffnet. Aber auch dann bedarf es oftmals wieder der kompensatorischen Hilfen für die materiell und kulturell schwächer gestellten Mitglieder der Gesellschaft, damit sie Gebrauch von diesen Partizipationsmöglichkeiten nach freiem Ermessen machen können. Um der freien Entfaltung der Individuen und Gruppen willen ist das Bemühen um sozialen Ausgleich und um Strukturen der Partizipation – der Mitwirkung und Mitbestimmung – geboten; zugleich ist dieses Bemühen eine Richtung, die die Freiheit als gleiche Freiheit aller selbst einschlagen muß, die sich also aus dem Ethos der freiheitlichen, demokratischen, pluralistischen Gesellschaft zentral ergibt. Dies gilt im Prinzip. Damit ist über die je konkreten angemessenen Formen des sozialen Ausgleichs und der Partizipation noch nicht definitiv entschieden, vielmehr die Auseinandersetzung erst eröffnet. Die konstitutive Schwierigkeit dieser Auseinandersetzung liegt gerade darin, die Spannung zwischen Leistung, sozialem Ausgleich und Partizipation als den wesentlichen Momenten des Grundwertes der sozialen Gerechtigkeit in der freiheitlichen Gesellschaft auszutragen.

4. Die Aktualität sozialer Partnerschaft

Die gesellschaftliche Mitverantwortung der ökonomischen Verbände, Organisationen und Institutionen, namentlich der großen Interessengruppen im Sinne ihrer Gemeinwohlverpflichtung, ihrer Bindung an die Grundwerte der Verfassung, insbesondere an die Forderung nach sozialer Gerechtigkeit bedeutet, daß sie zu sozialer Partnerschaft angehalten sind. Die soziale Partnerschaft zwischen der organisierten Unternehmens- und Unternehmerseite einerseits, der Arbeitnehmerseite andererseits äußert sich vor allem in den Formen autonomer Tarifpartnerschaft wie der betrieblichen und überbetrieblichen Mitbestimmung. In beiden Feldern geht es um die jeweils situationsgebundene Verwirklichung von sozialer Gerechtigkeit in den herausgestellten Momenten der Leistungsgerechtigkeit, des sozialen Ausgleichs und der Partizipation. Die aus diesen Momenten zu gewinnenden Kriterien müssen jeweils zusammengeführt werden, um bei aller legitimen

Verfechtung der je eigenen Interessen soziale Partnerschaft als Aufgabe erkennen zu können und zu praktizieren. Aneinander finden die einzelnen Momente auch ihre Grenze. Sozialer Ausgleich und Mitbestimmung werden z. B. unerfüllbar und sinnlos, wo sie nicht der Differenzierung nach Leistung das nötige Gewicht lassen, das um der Freiheit, aber auch um einer effizienten Wirtschaft und insgesamt um der Gemeinwohlverwirklichung willen unerläßlich ist. Wenn Mitbestimmungsforderungen heute bis zu dem Anspruch ausgedehnt werden, die Einführung neuer Technologien müsse der Kompetenz der Unternehmensführungen entzogen und den Betriebsräten zuerkannt werden, so kann dies zu gravierender Innovations- und Investitionschwäche der Unternehmen, längerfristig zu ihrer Handlungsunfähigkeit und schließlich zu ihrer Insolvenz führen, was gegen den Sinn leistungsfähigen Wirtschaftens und seiner Befähigung, den Erfordernissen sozialer Sicherung und sozialen Ausgleichs im Interesse aller Beteiligten Rechnung zu tragen, gerade verstößt. Hier erscheint es angebracht, zur Stärkung der sozialen Partnerschaft Kompromißformen zu suchen, die die sozialen Folgekosten der Einführung neuer Technologien der Kontrolle der Betriebsräte und Gewerkschaften unterwerfen und zu diesem Zwecke den Partizipationsinstanzen möglicherweise ein suspensives Veto bei diesbezüglichen Unternehmensentscheidungen zuerkennen, nicht aber diese selbst der Unternehmensführung aus der Hand winden.

Die ernsteste aktuelle Bewährungsprobe für die soziale Partnerschaft der großen ökonomischen Interessengruppen, darüber hinaus für die Überlebens- und Entwicklungsfähigkeit der pluralistischen Gesellschaft und des demokratischen Staates überhaupt ist in der Aufgabe der Bewältigung, zumindest der deutlichen Verminderung der gegenwärtig hohen Arbeitslosigkeit zu sehen. Zu den Rechten und Pflichten der Bürger in der Gesellschaft gehört das generelle Recht auf Arbeit (nicht jedoch auf einen bestimmten Arbeitsplatz ihrer Wahl) und die generelle Verpflichtung zur Arbeit, zur Leistung eines angemessenen Beitrages für die Gesellschaft (nicht jedoch in einer von der Gesellschaft zudiktierbaren bestimmten Art und Weise). Wir machen uns zu dieser wichtigsten sozialpolitischen Thematik der nächsten zehn Jahre die grundsätzlichen Ausführungen zu eigen, die Papst Johannes Paul II. in seiner Enzyklika „Laborem exercens“ niedergelegt hat. Der Papst hat darin völlig zu Recht herausgestellt, daß die Arbeit ein besonderes Wesensmerkmal des Menschen ist, vermittels dessen der Einzelne sich verwirklicht, sich und seine Angehörigen am Leben erhält, zum Aufbau der Familie und der Gesellschaft beiträgt, das Werk der Naturbeherrschung, aber auch der Pflege der Natur vollbringt (also ökonomisch wie ökologisch tätig ist), Kultur schafft, insgesamt Gottes Schöpfungstat nachvollzieht – mit all den Möglichkeiten und Mühen, die dem endlichen Ebenbild Gottes zukommen. Die Arbeit – in den verschiedenen Formen körperlicher und geistiger Tätigkeit weit verstanden – gehört also integral zur Würde der Person.[4] Sie besitzt nach den Worten der Enzyklika prinzipiell „positiven und schöpferischen, erzieherischen und verdienstvollen Charakter“ (LE Nr. 11). Sie ist „der wesentliche Schlüssel in der gesamten sozialen Frage“ (Nr. 3). Gerechter Lohn für geleistete Arbeit und Mitbestimmung über die Organisation der Arbeit stehen den Arbeitenden nicht als Almosen zu, d. h. aus Barmherzigkeit, sondern als ihr Recht (Nr. 19, dazu 14). Johannes Paul II. spricht dezidiert von den ,,*Menschenrechten, die der Arbeit entspringen*" (Nr. 16).

Dem Recht auf Arbeit korrespondiert die generelle und sehr detaillierte Pflicht zur Arbeit. „Die Arbeit ist... eine *Pflicht, eine Verpflichtung des Menschen*, und das *im mehrfachen Sinne dieses Wortes*. Der Mensch muß arbeiten, einmal weil es ihm der Schöpfer aufgetragen hat, dann wegen seiner Menschennatur, für deren Erhaltung und Entwicklung die Arbeit erforderlich ist. Der Mensch schuldet die Arbeit auch seinen Mitmenschen, insbesondere seiner Familie, aber auch der Gesellschaft, der er angehört, der Nation, deren Sohn oder Tochter er ist, der ganzen Menschheitsfamilie, deren Glied er ist: Erbe der Arbeit von Generationen und zugleich Mitgestalter der Zukunft derer, die im Ablauf der Geschichte nach ihm kommen werden" (Nr. 16). Mit diesem ihrem „weiten Bezugssystem" (a. a. O.) ist folglich die Arbeit dann gerade auch eine wesentliche Äußerungsform der personalen und gesellschaftlichen Existenz des Menschen, ja selbst der christlichen Existenz, die zur sozialen Verantwortung, zur Caritas, zur Nächstenliebe in der Nachfolge Christi verpflichtet ist (Nr. 24ff.).

Das Recht auf Arbeit gilt für alle Bürger in ihrer gleichen Würde und Freiheit. Wo es in der Gegenwart nicht für alle realisiert zu werden vermag, sind die angelegentlichsten Anstrengungen geboten, diesen Mißstand – wodurch immer er verursacht ist, was hier nicht des näheren erörtert werden kann – so weit irgend möglich zu beseitigen. Wenn einzelnen Mitgliedern der Gesellschaft (von erheblicher Zahl) die durch die Arbeit gegebene Möglichkeit der Selbstverwirklichung, des Unterhalts der Familie, des produktiven Beitrags für die Gesellschaft auf Dauer vorenthalten wird, wenn ihnen geradezu der Eindruck vermittelt wird, sie würden von der Gesellschaft nicht gebraucht, sie seien überflüssig und bedeuteten lediglich eine Last für sie, dann handelt es sich um ein schweres Vergehen der Gesellschaft gegen die Betroffenen und um einen Verstoß gegen das fundamentale Ethos, auf das sie gegründet ist: gegen die Menschenwürde und die mit ihr verbundenen Grundwerte, insbesondere die der Freiheit und der sozialen Gerechtigkeit; dann wird das Gemeinwohl eindeutig verfehlt.

In dieser Situation sind nicht nur die staatlichen Organe und die politischen Parteien, sondern alle Bürger, Gruppen und gesellschaftlichen Organisationen, insbesondere auch die ökonomischen Interessenverbände gefordert, ihren Beitrag zur Milderung der entstandenen Schwierigkeiten zu leisten. Für die Unternehmens- und Arbeitgeberverbände wie für die Gewerkschaften (die in der Bundesrepublik Deutschland die Arbeitnehmer ja nur zu etwa einem Drittel organisatorisch zusammenschließen und vertreten) kommt es dabei vor allem darauf an, soziale Partnerschaft nicht nur als einen Vorgang, der sich zwischen ihnen zur Wahrung ihrer je eigenen Interessen abspielt, zu begreifen, sondern als eine Verbindung, die zum verantwortlichen Handeln für die Außenstehenden, die Arbeitslosen, befähigt und in „konzertierter Aktion" zusammen mit den zuständigen staatlichen

Instanzen alles daransetzt, diesen Personenkreis wieder in den Arbeitsprozeß einzugliedern. Pointiert gesagt, ist es den ökonomischen Großverbänden also abverlangt, daß sie über ihren Schatten springen und soziale Partnerschaft nicht als das neue Kartell der (Arbeit) Besitzenden gegen die Besitzlosen, der großen Habenden gegen Dritte (Habenichtse) mißverstehen.

Es gilt heute für alle Beteiligten, nicht zuletzt eben für die großen Interessengruppen, in der pluralistischen, freiheitlichen, demokratischen Gesellschaft eine Solidargemeinschaft zu verwirklichen, die zu allseitigen Opfern bereit ist. In ihr muß es möglich sein, daß wegen des Rechtes auf Arbeit für alle Bürger den Einzelnen ein teilweiser Verzicht auf die volle und übervolle Ausschöpfung dieses Rechtes zugemutet wird, indem Maßnahmen wie Arbeitszeitverkürzung, Unterbindung von Überstunden, Einführung von Teilzeitstellen und Zeitverträgen, Vorverlegung der Altersgrenzen usw. getroffen werden, um u. a. auf diesem Wege neue Arbeitsplätze zu schaffen. Da sich damit die Sozialkosten erhöhen, schließen solche Maßnahmen grundsätzlich Lohn- und Gehaltsverzichte, Sonderabgaben und/oder Steuermehrbelastungen ein. Diese Solidargemeinschaft wird folglich mehr als bisher zu einer gewissen Askese, einer Selbstbeschränkung in der Verfolgung der einzelnen partikularen Interessen, genötigt sein. Interessen, Interessengruppen, Interessenvertretungen dürfen als solche dabei aber nicht verketzert werden, bleiben sie doch prinzipiell die berechtigten und notwendigen Antriebskräfte für jene Innovationsbereitschaft, ohne die jedem Versuch der Lösung des Arbeitsproblems die geistigen und materiellen Voraussetzungen entzogen wären. Entscheidend bei alledem ist, daß diese schwierigen Aufgaben, die in die Problemstellung „Lösung der Neuen Sozialen Frage“ gehören, aus Einsicht und in Freiheit, d. h. mit den originären Methoden und Mitteln der pluralistischen Gesellschaft und des demokratischen Staates, in Angriff genommen werden.

Mit dem im September 1985 unternommenen, noch schüchternen ersten Versuch einer Wiederbelebung der „Konzertierten Aktion“ – auch wenn man jede Berufung auf deren frühere Form, ja selbst auf den Namen ängstlich vermied – war ein verheißungsvoller, wenngleich prekärer Anfang dazu gemacht worden. Seine Fortsetzung wäre um der allzu ernsten Sache willen dringend geboten. Hier haben die Unternehmens- und Arbeitgeberverbände wie die Gewerkschaften ihre unabweisbare Verantwortung in und gegenüber der Gesellschaft. Hier können sie sie nachweislich erfüllen oder verfehlen. Sie haben sie dagegen nicht auf den jenseits der Wirtschaft und Arbeitswelt liegenden Gebieten der Friedens- und Sicherheitspolitik, auf denen zumindest die Gewerkschaften sich immer wieder so gern umtun, ohne dazu legitimiert zu sein: weder von ihren Mitgliedern, die darüber höchst unterschiedliche Ansichten haben, noch von ihrer gesellschaftlichen Aufgabenstellung her; diese besagt zwar sehr wohl Mitverantwortung für das Gemeinwohl, aber begrenzt auf jene Belange, Aspekte und Probleme, die mit ihrer ersten Verantwortung der ökonomischen Interessenvertretung verknüpft, d. h. die ökonomisch und sozial relevant sind.

Anmerkungen

[1] Vgl. dazu jetzt Rauscher 1985.
[2] Vgl. Fraenkel 1964, S. 21.
[3] Über die Zusammengehörigkeit von pluralistischer Gesellschaft und demokratischem Staat bzw. von Pluralismus und Demokratie näherhin Schwan 1981, S. 143 ff.
[4] Papst Johannes Paul II. 1981, vgl. das Vorwort sowie die Nr. 1, 4, 6, 9, 10, 16, 25 ff. Im folgenden zitiert: LE.

Literatur

Fraenkel, E. (1964): *Deutschland und die westlichen Demokratien.* Stuttgart.

Papst Johannes Paul II. (1981): Enzyklika „Laborem exercens“ über die menschliche Arbeit zum neunzigsten Jahrestag der Enzyklika „Rerum novarum“, 14. September 1981. *Verlautbarungen des Apostolischen Stuhls.* Sekretariat der Deutschen Bischofskonferenz (Hrsg.), Bonn.

Rauscher, A. (Hrsg.) (1985): *Selbstinteresse und Gemeinwohl. Beiträge zur Ordnung der Wirtschaftsgesellschaft.* Berlin, München.

Schwan, A. (1981): Pluralismus und Wahrheit. In: *Christlicher Glaube in moderner Gesellschaft.* Teilband 19, Freiburg, Basel, Wien.

Zur Kritik des Konsensbegriffs

Werner Becker

Abstract
Critique on the Concept of Consensus

The concept of rational consensus is a part of state philosophy in the classical political liberalism, as well as of the historical philosophy of German idealism and of Marxist socialism. It is currently of great significance for political terminology in Western democracies ("common welfare", "basic consensus", etc.), in certain concepts of rationality in economy, in the economic theory of politics and in philosophical ethics. I criticize the great significance of the concept in these fields, and wish to make it quite clear that is has an "ideological" function because it supports incorrect perceptions of social reality in Western democracies.

Unsere Art Demokratie ist mit Macht und Einfluß einer philosophischen Fiktion eng verbunden. Es ist die Fiktion des rationalen Gesellschaftsvertrags. Sie ist die Grundidee des politischen Liberalismus, der mit den philosophischen Entwürfen von Locke und Montesquieu im 18. Jahrhundert das theoretische Fundament für die liberale, parlamentarisch verfaßte Demokratie der Moderne geliefert hat. Die Idee des Gesellschaftsvertrags selber ist von erheblich höherem Alter. Sie entstammt dem abendländischen, im Mittelalter christlich umgeprägten klassischen Naturrecht, das auch von Locke und Montesquieu noch mit religiös-christlichen Begründungen und Inhalten aufrechterhalten wurde. Im Rahmen der philosophischen Rechtfertigung und der faktischen historischen Entwicklung der liberalen Demokratie sind die christlich-religiösen Wurzeln des liberalen Naturrechts im 19. und 20. Jahrhundert in eine – allerdings absichtsvoll erzeugte – Vergessenheit geraten. Der mit der liberalen Demokratie verschwisterte, ihrer staatlichen Garantie der Meinungsfreiheit sich verdankende weltanschauliche Pluralismus vertrug sich nicht mit der Herausstellung eines christlich-religiösen Menschenbilds auf der Legitimationsebene der Verfassungsprinzipien. Das Gesellschaftsvertragsmodell, von dem bereits Hobbes ausging und das durch Locke, Rousseau und Kant eine hervorragende Bedeutung für die politische Philosophie der liberalen Demokratie gewann, reduzierte sich auf die Annahme, daß die Verfassungen der Staaten in einer Art ‚Ursituation', dem menschlichen, vorgesellschaftlichen ‚Naturzustand', gründen. Diese Ursituation kennt nur Individuen, die keine sozialen Bande miteinander verknüpfen und deren Hauptinteresse auf die Erhaltung der Sicherheit von Leib und Leben, mit anderen Worten: auf die Selbsterhaltung im Rahmen einer für alle geltenden Knappheit von Mitteln zur Befriedigung ihrer Selbsterhaltungsinteressen, ausgerichtet ist. Die von allen Philosophen von Hobbes bis Rousseau und Kant geteilte Voraussetzung der ‚Ursituation' liegt in der Eigennutzorientiertheit der Individuen und ihrer Fähigkeit zu einer vernünftigen Beurteilung ihrer Interessen. Aufgrund ihrer Vernunft sollen die Individuen in der Lage sein, nützliche Handlungen stets schädlichen vorzuziehen, und der Maßstab für die Nützlichkeit besteht in der Mehrung der Selbsterhaltungsfähigkeit.

Dieses Modell einer menschlichen ‚Ursituation', die Annahme des rational seinen Nutzen mehrenden Individuums, ließ sich von seinen christlich-naturrechtlichen Inhalten leicht befreien, weil sein Ansatz mit dem grundlegenden Methodenverständnis der neuzeitlichen Wissenschaft, dem methodischen Individualismus, übereinstimmte. Der methodische Individualismus war die Ausgangsbasis fortschrittlicher Wissenschaftsauffassung seit Galilei, Bacon und Descartes und Hobbes hat ihn zur Rechtfertigung seiner Version des Urzustandsmodells auch ausdrücklich herangezogen. Der weitere Aufstieg der Wissenschaften im Zeichen des ‚methodischen Individualismus' – Isaac Newton ist der symbolträchtige Name – hat die von Locke und Montesquieu herausgestellte Fundierung des ‚Ursituations'-Modells im klassisch-religiösen Naturrecht wieder in den Hintergrund gedrängt, und zwar im Zusammenhang mit einem Systemerfordernis des Liberalismus, das ich schon genannt habe: der Vereinbarkeit einer liberalistischen Legitimationstheorie und der zum Liberalismus gehörenden individuellen Meinungsfreiheit in weltanschaulichen Dingen.

Um die Charakteristik des ‚Ursituationsmodells' vollständig zu machen, ist noch als entscheidendes Element die Zwecksetzung des Ganzen anzufügen, nämlich die Verknüpfung der ‚Ursituation' der sozial unverbundenen Individuen mit der Staatsgründung.

Nach der Auffassung der bedeutenden Staatsphilosophie, die ihre Theorien der Staatsrechtfertigung unter ausdrücklicher Verwendung dieses Modells entwickelt haben, geht die Staatsgründung auf einen Gesellschaftsvertrag aller dazu bereiten Individuen zurück. Der Begriff dafür ist ‚Konsens'. Der Konsensbegriff läßt sich zwanglos dazu benutzen, das Konzept des Gesellschaftsvertrags zu verdeutlichen, weil Vertragsabschlüsse die individuell-frei geäußerte Zustimmung der Vertragspartner voraussetzen. Bei Locke etwa besteht der Konsens der Individuen in der ‚Ursituation' darüber, daß jeder einzelne aus rationaler Abwägung es in seinem Eigeninteresse liegend ansieht, einen Zustand der Absicherung der Grundfreiheiten aller – in erster Linie der freien Verfügung über erworbenen Besitz – einem Zustand ohne derartige allgemeine Sicherheit vorzuziehen. Ich übergehe die Feinheiten der Argumentation, zu denen an erster Stelle die modernen spieltheoretischen Diskussionen über das ‚Gefangenendilemma' gehören. Wichtig für meinen Zweck ist allein die Feststellung des Resultats: Das Staatsgründungskonzept der neuzeitlichen politischen Philosophie von Hobbes bis Kant basiert auf einem Konsens sozial unverbundener Individuen in einer gedachten vorgesellschaftlichen

‚Ursituation'; der Konsens kommt unter der Voraussetzung zustande, daß jedes der Individuen seine Entscheidung rational nach Maßgabe seines Eigeninteresses trifft.

In der politischen Philosophie des 19. Jahrhunderts wurde das skizzierte Gesellschaftsvertragsmodell zu einem Bestandteil der geistesgeschichtlichen Vergangenheit, denn kein prominenter Philosoph des Politischen – weder Hegel, Marx noch J. St. Mill – hat es zur ausdrücklichen Grundlage seines Staatskonzepts gemacht. In der politischen Geschichte des 19. Jahrhunderts spielte es vor dem Hintergrund des Kampfes um die Durchsetzung des allgemeinen Wahlrechts – und damit der Demokratie – in den legitimistischen Monarchien des Spätabsolutismus keine Rolle, einmal, weil es als philosophisch-spekulatives Modell mit allen Mängeln der Ferne von politischer Praktizierbarkeit behaftet ist, zum anderen, weil es sich in seiner populärsten Version, derjenigen von John Locke, mit einem Bekenntnis zur christlich-protestantischen Religion in der naturrechtlichen Begründung seiner Grundrechte verband.

Dennoch verschwand es nicht aus dem Bewußtsein der Philosophen, im Gegenteil: Es wurde normativiert. Die einflußreichsten Philosophen haben aus dem Konsensmodell, wie ich das Modell des Gesellschaftsvertrags abgekürzt nennen will, ein normatives Konzept der Staatsphilosophie gemacht, das als Maßstab einer ‚gerechten' Gesellschaft entsprechend der freiheitlichen Grundwerte des politischen Liberalismus benutzt wird. Ich halte es für einen Unglücksfall in der geschichtlichen Entwicklung der neuzeitlichen Sozial- und Geschichtswissenschaften, daß das Modell der ‚Ursituation' nicht ausgearbeitet wurde zu einem empirischen Forschungsprogramm auf der Linie seiner Verwandtschaft mit dem methodischen Individualismus, einer Verwandtschaft, die bekanntlich schon von Hobbes zur Rechtfertigung des Ansatzes des Gesellschaftsvertragsmodells herangezogen wurde. Der einzige bedeutende Staatsphilosoph des 18. Jahrhunderts, der konsequent ernst mit einer historisch-empirischen Deutung der ‚Ursituation' (im Sinne einer vorgeschichtlichen Situation einer Existenzweise menschlicher Individuen ohne feste soziale Bindungen) gemacht hat, nämlich J. J. Rousseau, fand keine Anhänger für diese in die frühgeschichtliche Existenz des Menschen weisende Absicht. Um so berühmter wurde er für seine Normativierung des Modells: für sein Konzept einer ‚volonté générale' im Sinn des Konsensmodells. Er hat auch die wesentlichen Bedingungen des Konsensmodells formuliert, die unter Absehung von ihrer historisch gemeinten Einbettung in die ‚Ursituation' im Gesellschaftsvertragskonzept von Hobbes bis Kant übrig blieben: zuerst die Annahme, daß das ‚wahre' Verhältnis des Individuums zum Staat seine ungezwungene Freiheit voraussetzt, und zum zweiten, daß alle Individuen sich unter dieser Voraussetzung zu einem rational motivierten Konsens im Hinblick auf gemeinsam geteilte Grundwerte zusammenfinden müssen. Beide Annahmen, die ungezwungene Freiheit der Individuen und der rational motivierte Konsens der Individuen, bilden die Minimalbedingungen des nunmehr normativierten Konsensmodells, das die einflußreichste Staatsphilosophie des 19. und 20. Jahrhunderts unter dem Vorzeichen von

Liberalismus, Sozialismus und Demokratie leitet. In Gestalt dieser Minimalfassung ist es auch heute noch von großer Wirksamkeit, in der politischen Philosophie wie in der realen Politik.

Ich habe angedeutet, daß ich in der Normativierung des Modells der gesellschaftsvertraglichen ,Ursituation' den eigentlichen Sündenfall in der geschichtlichen Entwicklung der neuzeitlichen Sozialphilosophie erblicke. Dabei hat es von Anfang an Rufer gegeben, das individualistische Modell in Richtung auf eine sozialphilosophische und – näherhin sozialwissenschaftliche – Version des in den empirisch vorgehenden Naturwissenschaften des 18. Jahrhunderts sich nachdrücklich bewährenden ,methodischen Individualismus' weiterzuentwickeln. Der prominenteste Rufer war David Hume, der auch ein konsequenter Kritiker von Lockes gesellschaftsvertraglichem Konsensmodell gewesen ist. Er hat bereits eine Art evolutionstheoretische Umfunktionierung des Modells auf der Grundlage des darin enthaltenen ,methodologischen Individualismus' im Auge. Ich zitiere Hume auszugsweise: Nach Meinung der Vertragstheoretiker „erwuchsen nicht nur die frühesten Formen der Staatsgewalt aus der Zustimmung oder besser: freiwilligen Einigung des Volkes; ihnen zufolge ruht die Staatsgewalt auch heute noch, nachdem sie sich zu voller Reife entwickelt hat, lediglich auf diesen Fundamenten. Es nutzt (aber) nichts zu sagen, daß jede Staatsgewalt zunächst einmal auf die allgemeine Zustimmung gegründet ist oder doch gegründet sein sollte. Denn ich behaupte ja, daß die realen gesellschaftlichen Bedingungen nicht so sind, daß sie jemals eine allgemeine Zustimmung auch nur dem Schein nach zulassen würden. Vielmehr geht die Etablierung einer neuen Staatsgewalt in aller Regel auf die Auflösung der alten durch Machtergreifung und Eroberung, das heißt aber auch auf Gewalt zurück." (Hume 1976) Selbstverständlich kann man auch aus der bewegten Staatengeschichte mit ihren revolutionären und kriegerischen Umbrüchen seit Humes Zeit bis heute nur eine nachdrückliche Bestätigung von Humes Auffassung herauslesen. Den historischen positiven Sinn des Gesellschaftsvertragsmodells hat er wie folgt charakterisiert: „Zieht man in Betracht, wie sehr sich die Menschen in ihren körperlichen und geistigen Anlagen und Fähigkeiten gleichen, bevor sie durch Erziehung zivilisiert werden, dann muß man notwendig zugestehen, daß nur ihre eigene Zustimmung sie ursprünglich vereinigen und einer Autorität unterstellen konnte. Verfolgt man die Staatsgewalt bis auf ihre ersten Ursprünge in Urwald und Wüste zurück, so erweisen sich die Menschen als Quelle allen Rechts und aller Macht. Im Interesse von Frieden und Ordnung haben sie sich Gesetze gegeben und dadurch freiwillig ihre angeborene Freiheit aufgegeben. Die Bedingungen, unter denen sie dazu bereit waren, waren entweder Inhalt einer ausdrücklichen Vereinbarung, oder aber sie lagen so klar und offen zutage, daß man glauben konnte, auf eine ausdrückliche Vereinbarung verzichten zu dürfen. Wenn nur dieser Tatbestand gemeint sein soll, wenn man vom ,ursprünglichen Gesellschaftsvertrag' redet, so kann nicht bestritten werden, daß alle Staatsgewalt aus einem Vertrag hervorgeht und daß die Bildung der ältesten und primitivsten Formen menschlichen Zusammenlebens vorwiegend auf diesem Prinzip beruht."

(Hume 1976) Es sind diese Bemerkungen natürlich nicht anders denn als Anregungen zu einer evolutionistischen Betrachtungsweise im Ansatz des methodischen Individualismus zu verstehen, Anregungen, die von Humes Freunden und Kollegen aus dem Kreis der Schottischen Moralphilosophie Adam Ferguson und Adam Smith zwar aufgegriffen, aber nie zu einem empirischen Forschungsprogramm weiterentwickelt wurden. Was sich demgegenüber durchsetzte, war das Konsensmodell in seiner normativierten Gestalt, in der es zum Grundmodell der wirksamsten sozialethischen Entwürfe der Neuzeit wurde. Mit diesem – gerade in seinen politischen Folgen nicht zu überschätzenden – Schritt löste sich die führende europäische Sozialphilosophie endgültig von der Entwicklung der modernen empirischen Wissenschaften ab. Sie hat den Anschluß bis heute nicht mehr gefunden.

Das Konsensmodell wurde normativiert, gerade weil es ein extrem kontrafaktisches Modell darstellt. In den empirischen Wissenschaften hätte ein Modell mit dermaßen kontrafaktischen Annahmen keine große Überlebenschance besessen. Doch gerade die Kontrafaktizität des Modells bewirkte in den Augen der bedeutendsten Sozialphilosophen seine Normativierung, und zwar auf der Folie des Grundgedankens, daß staatliche Verbände von Individuen, die in der Realität historischer Epochen noch nie als Ergebnis freier Konsense gedeutet werden konnten, doch wenigstens an der Konsensidee als einem normativen Maßstab zu messen seien, weil die eigentliche ‚Sozialnatur des Menschen‘ den Konsens als Richtschnur ‚gerechter‘ Gesellschaft vorschreibe. Man sieht: Der sich damit einschleichende Rekurs auf eine ‚wesenhafte‘ bzw. ‚eigentliche‘ Sozialnatur der Menschen führt zwangsläufig zu einer ‚essenzialistischen‘ Interpretation des Konsensmodells, die ebenfalls den Bruch dieses Denkens mit dem Geist der empirischen Wissenschaften der Moderne in aller Deutlichkeit bezeugt.

Die Geschichte der Normativierung des Konsensmodells sei nur skizzenhaft wiedergegeben. Im Rahmen der deutschen Philosophie waren es Fichte und Hegel, die das normativierte Konsensmodell in unterschiedlichen Versionen zum Maßstab ihrer geschichtsphilosophischen Konzepte gemacht haben. In den ‚Grundzügen des gegenwärtigen Zeitalters‘ geht Fichte davon aus, daß es der Sinn der geschichtlichen Entwicklung ist, daß die Menschheit dazu gelangt, ihre eigenen Verhältnisse in völliger Freiheit der Vernunft gemäß zu ordnen. In Hegels Geschichtsphilosophie geht es um die Darstellung eines dialektisch sich entfaltenden ‚Wesens der Geschichte‘, welches ‚zu sich selber kommen soll‘ in einem Endzustand der ‚frei sich selbst begreifenden Vernunft‘, ein Zustand, der ‚vernünftig‘ genannt wird, weil dann die Freiheit der einzelnen mit der Freiheit aller völlig kompatibel ist. Den deutlichsten und politisch folgenreichsten Anklang an das normativierte Konsensmodell in der Linie der Fortsetzer der Philosophen des deutschen Idealismus hat das Modell bei Karl Marx gefunden, und zwar in der Ausmalung des Geschichtszieles gemäß der Geschichtstheorie des dialektischen Materialismus. Ich zitiere ihn dafür mit einer Stelle aus dem ‚Kapital‘: aus dem Kapitel über den ‚Fetischcharakter der Ware‘, in der die Fiktion sozialistischer Verhältnisse mit folgenden Sätzen eingeleitet wird: „Stellen wir uns endlich, zur Abwechslung, einen Verein freier Menschen vor, die mit gemeinschaftlichen Produktionsmitteln arbeiten und ihre vielen individuellen Arbeitskräfte selbstbewußt als eine Arbeitskraft verausgaben... Die gesellschaftlichen Beziehungen der Menschen zu ihren Arbeiten und ihren Arbeitsprodukten bleiben hier durchsichtig einfach in der Produktion sowohl als auch in der Distribution." (Karl Marx) Auch hier wird in aller Deutlichkeit der Anspruch auf eine konsensfähige Gesellschaft erhoben, in der die Freiheit aller Bestand haben soll mit Hilfe einer den Konsens ermöglichenden ‚Vernunft', einer Form ökonomischer Wissenschaft, die nach Marxscher Unterstellung die Verteilungsprobleme einer nicht mehr auf den Markt angewiesenen sozialistischen Gesellschaft ‚vernünftig', d. h. für alle zustimmungsfähig, lösen wird. Es bedarf nicht mehr als eines Hinweises auf die enormen politischen und historischen Auswirkungen der marxistischen Sozialismusidee auf die europäische Geschichte und die Weltgeschichte im vorigen und in unserem Jahrhundert. Es ist eine Idee, die in ihrer Massenwirksamkeit nur mit dem geschichtlichen Erfolg der christlichen Heilsbotschaft aus der europäischen Perspektive verglichen werden kann.

Das normativierte Konsensmodell hat jedoch nicht bloß den modernen geschichtswirksam gewordenen politisch-philosophischen Chiliasmus stärkstens beeinflußt. Auch der klassische Liberalismus, der heute die leitenden Begriffe unserer westlichen Verfassungen – und von da ausgehend das politische Bild der führenden Politiker und der Rechtsprechung, speziell der Verfassungsrechtsprechung – prägt, spricht die Sprache des normativierten Konsensmodells. Diese Sprache des klassischen Liberalismus geht davon aus, daß der liberale und demokratische Staat die Herstellung eines ‚Gemeinwohls' zum Zweck hat, eines ‚Wohles aller', von dem unterstellt wird, daß ihm alle Bürger freiwillig zustimmen können. Die Rolle des Parlamentsabgeordneten wird nach klassischer Verfassungssprache im Sinn einer Repräsentation des ‚Volkes in seiner Gesamtheit' bestimmt. Eben deshalb soll er allein seinem individuellen Gewissen in seinen Entscheidungen über das ‚Gemeinwohl' verpflichtet sein und nicht etwa seiner Partei oder gar gesellschaftlichen Partialinteressen. Bekanntlich sperren wir uns heute noch in den westlichen Staaten gegen das Eingeständnis, daß die Dinge faktisch natürlich anders stehen; daß die Bindung der Abgeordneten an das Parteiinteresse alles überwiegt, was an Interessenvertretung im Sinne des ‚Gemeinwohls' ins Feld geführt werden könnte. Wie sehr wir selber im Bann des Konsensmodells stehen, wird deutlich in unserer geläufigen Reaktion auf die realistische Sichtweise: Wir akzeptieren sie bestenfalls als zynisches Zugeständnis an die Realität, hochherzig bedauernd, daß das Ideal, dem wir uns stärkstens verpflichtet fühlen, leider so schwer in die Wirklichkeit zu übertragen sei. Auch die populäre Interpretation unserer demokratischen Verfassungsgrundformel („die Staatsgewalt geht vom Volke aus"), nach der es sich nicht – wie es richtig zu sehen ist – um die Legitimation der ‚Staatsgewaltausübung' in Form der gewählten Regierungen und Parlamente, sondern letztlich doch um die tatsächliche Staatsgewaltsausübung handeln soll, geht auf die Wirksamkeit des Konsensmodells zurück.

Diese Auffassung speist darüber hinaus die verbreiteten basisdemokratischen Illusionen, die ja nicht auf Ideen der Tradition der athenischen unmittelbaren Demokratie des 5. vorchristlichen Jahrhunderts oder der Schweizerischen Landsgemeinde zurückgehen, sondern auf das Konzept der liberalistischen Idee einer durch vernünftige Einsicht gesteuerten konsensfähigen Gesellschaft. Auch die von den führenden Politikern des Westens mit weitgehender Zustimmung erhobenen Ansprüche auf die Vertretung der Menschenrechte zehrt von der illusionären Unterstellung, es gäbe Grundrechte für Menschen, die konsensfähig seien, weil die Vernunft eines jeden für sie spräche.

Ich will meine Gegenposition im Sinn von Humes Appell zu sozialphilosophischem Realismus – und zwar im Geist der Kritik des wirksamen Konsensideals – an den harmloseren innenpolitischen Begriffen wie ‚Gemeinwohl', ‚Volk' und ‚parlamentarische Repräsentation' verdeutlichen. Aus der Ökonomie wissen wir, daß es keine wissenschaftliche Explikation des Gemeinwohlbegriffs im Sinn einer ‚kollektiven Nutzenfunktion' gibt. Wir brauchen jedoch nicht einmal die Wissenschaft zu bemühen, um zu erkennen, daß die Vokabel vom Gemeinwohl im staatlichen System einer parlamentarischen Demokratie immer eine Formel der politischen Rhetorik mit allerdings hoher Werbewirksamkeit bleiben wird. Als politische Zielvorstellung genommen, kann es in einer liberalen Demokratie wegen der mehrheitsdemokratischen Entscheidungsverfahren nie zu einer konsensfähigen Ermittlung des ‚Gemeinwohls' kommen. Parteien und ihre Abgeordneten in den Parlamentsfraktionen vertreten nicht das ‚Gemeinwohl', sie streben es faktisch nicht einmal an, selbst wenn sie in ihren Parteiprogrammen und den normalen öffentlichen und parlamentarischen Auseinandersetzungen mit Überzeugung stets so reden.

Parteien vertreten in erster Linie Interessen gesellschaftlicher Großgruppen und Abgeordnete und Berufspolitiker sind ganz nach Schumpeters ökonomischer Definition des politischen Geschäfts in der Demokratie an ihrer Wiederwahl und der Bestätigung ihrer Positionen, die sie innehaben, interessiert. Daß bis heute ein Tabu über dem Benutzen dieser Sprache realitätsbezogener Nüchternheit liegt, beweist unsere Fixierung auf die moralischeren, wenn auch illusionären, die Wirklichkeit verfehlenden Kategorien des Konsensmodells. Das Tabu beweist aber auch die Angst vor den Konsequenzen der pluralistischen Demokratie. Auch die Rede von der Einheitlichkeit eines demokratischen Staatsvolkes geht an der politischen Realität vorbei. In parlamentarischen Demokratien gibt es in einer für die gesamtstaatlichen Entscheidungen relevanten Weise nur eine Vielzahl partieller Interessen im Rahmen der staatlichen Pluralismusgarantie. Es gibt in der sozialen Realität nicht das Volk als eine Totalität jenseits des Gruppenpluralismus.

Natürlich existieren volksmäßige Kollektiveigenschaften, ohne die demokratische Staaten schwerlich stabil wären, wie den dominanten deutschen Charakter der Bevölkerungen der Bundesrepublik oder Österreichs. Aber diese nationalen Kollektiveigenschaften spielen in den politischen Entscheidungsprozessen der Mehrheitsdemokratie weder eine Rolle, noch denkt man an sie, wenn man von einer Politik im Namen des Volkes als des demokratischen Souveräns spricht.

Auch die von den meisten wirtschaftspolitisch orientierten Ökonomen unterstellte Annahme eines wirtschaftlichen Gesamtinteresses enthält das Konsensmodell. Es wird häufig, wenn die Forderung nach ‚mehr Markt' gemeint ist, von einer wissenschaftlich zu beweisenden ‚richtigen' oder ‚falschen' Wirtschaftspolitik gesprochen. Maßstab für ‚richtig' oder ‚falsch' ist dabei ein angenommenes Gesamtinteresse, das durch Annäherung an den Modellzustand des ‚vollkommenen Marktes' gefördert und durch die Entfernung davon verfehlt wird. Ebenso entstammen die Gleichgewichtsannahmen des Marktmodells einschließlich der ‚Pareto-Optimalität' dem Konsenskonzept. In Wirklichkeit sollte man es so sehen, daß Gruppen in der Gesellschaft aufgrund ihrer Interessenlage mehr für eine marktlich ausgerichtete Wirtschaftspolitik sind, während andere Gruppen ein durchaus im – auch ökonomischen – Eigeninteresse ihrer Mitglieder liegendes Interesse an staatlicher Verteilungspolitik haben. Das Interesse an ‚mehr Staat' bzw. an einer Erhaltung des staatlichen Anteils an der Verfügung über das Volkseinkommen liegt z. B. schon im Interesse der Mitglieder der staatlichen Bürokratien. Dieses Interesse aus vorgeblich wissenschaftlicher Sicht schlichtweg als ‚falsch' zu erklären, ist ebenso falsch wie das Interesse von Wirtschaftskreisen, die den ökonomischen Liberalismus als ihre Philosophie vertreten, an ‚mehr Markt' deswegen schon ‚richtig' genannt werden kann. Die Berufung auf die Begriffe ‚wahr' und ‚falsch' hat in der Ökonomie einen völlig anderen Sinn als in den empirischen Wissenschaften, ein Umstand, der in der ökonomischen Wissenschaft nicht deutlich zum Ausdruck gebracht wird. In der Physik etwa heißt ‚wahr und falsch' ‚Übereinstimmung und Nichtübereinstimmung' mit den Tatsachen. Wenn Ökonomen die Begriffe ‚wahr' und ‚falsch' gebrauchen, meinen sie die Annäherung an ein und die Abweichung von einem künstlich ausgedachten, in der Wirklichkeit gar nicht vorkommenden Modell. Der unterschiedliche Wortgebrauch wird deutlich, wenn man daran denkt, daß es für Ökonomen in der wirtschaftlichen Realität durchaus ein ‚falsches' Handeln von Wirtschaftssubjekten gibt, während es für ‚normale' empirische Wissenschaftler unsinnig ist anzunehmen, es gäbe ‚falsche' Tatsachen in der Welt. (Für sie kann es selbstverständlich nur ‚falsche' Theorien geben.)

Das Festhalten am Konsensmodell hat sowohl den klassischen Liberalismus als auch die auf ihm aufbauende Ökonomie als Wissenschaft daran gehindert, in eine engere Beziehung zur gesellschaftlichen Wirklichkeit der Moderne zu kommen. Der Ansatz beider unterstellt den Individuen ein gleichbleibendes Interesse an autonomen Entscheidungen. Die Realität moderner Massengesellschaften ist jedoch durch das Bewußtsein der meisten Menschen bestimmt, allein im Rahmen ‚großer Zahlen' individuellen Einfluß ausüben zu können. Dieses Bewußtsein kennzeichnet eine ‚Grundbefindlichkeit' des modernen Menschen. Dennoch darf es aus Gründen der ‚Modellreinheit' im ökonomischen Nutzenmodell nicht berücksichtigt werden. Stellt man es jedoch in Rechnung, dann zeigt sich, daß es gegen die ‚reale' Nutzeneinschätzung der meisten Individuen wäre, von einem ‚hohen' Interesse an autonomen Entscheidungen bei ihnen auszugehen. Die meisten Individuen haben unter der Bedingung großer Zahlen nämlich ein ‚hohes' Interesse an einer Delegation ihrer Autonomie an Kollektive. Dementsprechend war das Interesse von Arbeitern als rationalen Gründen ihres individuellen Nutzens stets bei einer Gewerkschaft besser aufgehoben, als wenn jeder Arbeiter individuell als autonomer marktlicher Anbieter seiner ‚Arbeitskraft' aufgetreten wäre. Durch die Organisation der vielen konnte auch der einzelne etwas erreichen – von der Lohnerhöhung bis zur Verbesserung der Arbeitsbedingungen –, etwas, was jeder einzelne für sich nie hätte erreichen können. Die ‚Kartellierung der Arbeitskraft' lag und liegt mit Sicherheit nicht im Interesse der Unternehmer, von denen die meisten nach wie vor besser fahren, wenn sie individuell-autonome Anbieter bleiben.

Durch ihr Festhalten am Konsensmodell, zu dem die Ausgangsbasis der ‚individuell-autonomen' Entscheidung gehört, hat sich die gesamte ökonomische Wissenschaft in den Ruf gebracht, allein im Dienst von Arbeitgeberinteressen zu stehen. Dieser fatale Ruf ist insofern berechtigt, weil in ihrem Grundmodell die ‚Grundbefindlichkeit' der lohnabhängigen Massen nicht Eingang finden darf.

Dieses Grundmodell entstammt dem liberalistisch-individualistischen Konsenskonzept und vermag deshalb nur autonome Individualentscheidungen von der Art zu berücksichtigen, wie sie in der gesellschaftlichen Realität dem Unternehmerinteresse am meisten entsprechen. Man triebe die Realitätsverzerrung jedoch zu weit, wolle man davon ausgehen, daß die Menschen moderner Massengesellschaften alle ‚Unternehmerinteressen' hätten.

Ein letztes markantes Beispiel für die aktuelle Wirksamkeit des Konsensmodells biete die Lage der modernen Sozialphilosophie. Ich nenne dafür drei Namen aus entgegengesetzten Lagern der Gegenwartsphilosophie: John Rawls, Robert Nozick und Karl Otto Apel. Bei allen dreien spielt das Konsensmodell die ausschlaggebende Rolle: bei Rawls und Nozick als ‚fiktive Ursituation', bei Apel als Zielbegriff einer ‚idealen Kommunikationsgemeinschaft'. In der Sozialphilosophie von heute hat sich eine Art masochistische Einstellung breit gemacht. Zwar sind kaum Philosophen zu nennen, die an die konsenserzeugende Rationalität von Rawls, Nozick oder Apel glauben. Im Gegenteil: In den Debatten um die Konzepte dieser Denker überwiegen – wie sollte es anders sein – die kritischen Einwände und Vorbehalte. Trotzdem beschäftigt man sich mit einer Leidenschaft mit diesen Theorien, die auf weltfernen, unrealistischen Fiktionen aufgebaut sind, als ginge es tatsächlich um das Heil der Welt, in der wir leben. Jedenfalls ist unter den modernen Philosophen die einzige realistische Sichtweise selten, derzufolge jene Sozialphilosophen nichts anderes sind als Bastler möglicher Welten, die mit unserer wirklichen Lebenswelt nie in Berührung kommen werden.

Mein grundsätzlicher Einwand gegen das Konsensmodell ist der, daß es eine verbreitete falsche Sicht unserer gesellschaftlichen wie politischen Wirklichkeit entscheidend mitbewirkt. Es läßt die Realität liberaler Demokratien im Licht unerreichbarer, fiktiver Zielvorstellungen sehen. Es unterstützt die ohnehin vorhandene unrealistische Harmoniesucht. Es erzeugt so falsche Ansprüche an demokratische Politik und vermittelt falsche Rationalitätsmaßstäbe zur Bewertung demokratischer Politik. Es verhindert, Gegnerschaft und Konkurrenz so positiv zu sehen, wie diese Kategorien es angesichts ihrer realen Bedeutung in Politik, Wirtschaft und Wissenschaft verdienen. In der ökonomischen Wissenschaft produziert es eine bedauerliche Wirklichkeitsferne.

Literatur

Hume, D. (1976): Of the Original Contract. In: Hoerster, N., Klassische Texte der Staatsphilosophie. München, S. 165 f.

Marx, K. (1959): Das Kapital I. S. 84.

Angleichung politischer Macht durch erweiterte Partizipation?*
Exemplarische Prüfung von drei Grundtypen erweiterter Partizipation

Gesine Schwan

Abstract

Balancing Political Power Through Extension of Participation?
Comparative Discussion of Three Basic Types of Extended Participation

The title of the article puts forward the question, of whether furthering participation in social subsystems contributes to an equalization of the citizen's political power. The author analyzes the empirical results of three types of social participation: 1. the strengthening of voluntary citizen movement in the USA, 2. the Yugoslav model of self-management and 3. the German model of co-determination. The first leads to a power-addition for the members of the middle-class who primarily undertake such activities. The second, contrary to its intentions, furthers the power of those who dispose of the important knowledge and information, i.e. the management instead of the workers. The third, despite some inevitable inner problems, seems to be best suited to a more equal distribution of decision-making power, because it institutes conterpower elites who tend to become equally well informed and to contribute to more transparence in the political processes in social subsystems.

In der Demokratisierungsdebatte der letzten Jahre wurde die Forderung nach erweiterter Partizipation vielfach mit dem Ziel erhoben, dadurch die ungleiche Verteilung politischer Macht einzuebnen. Ist dieses Ziel realistisch?

Ich konzentriere mich zur Prüfung dieser Frage im folgenden auf empirische Ergebnisse und auf theoretische Überlegungen, die Aufschluß darüber geben können, ob und unter welchen Bedingungen die Erweiterung von Partizipation zur Angleichung politischer Machtverteilung auf die Bürger beträgt. Die gegen Ende der sechziger und zu Beginn der siebziger Jahre unter dem Stichwort „Demokrati-

* Dieser Beitrag enspricht weitgehend Ausführungen zu diesem Thema aus meinem Buch „Sozialismus in der Demokratie? Theorie einer konsequent sozialdemokratischen Politik." Stuttgart, Berlin, Köln, Mainz 1982.

sierung“ lebhaft geforderte Erweiterung der Bereiche und der sozialen Basis von Partizipation nämlich wurde vorwiegend damit begründet, daß materielle Lebensbedingungen, Bildungsmöglichkeiten, Information und insgesamt politische Macht weniger ungleich auf die Gesellschaftsglieder verteilt sein sollten. Mehr Machtgleichheit durch mehr Partizipation? Anders gewendet: Werden durch die Erweiterung von Möglichkeiten zur politischen Teilhabe die Chancen aller Bürger, Ihre Ziele in den politischen Entscheidungsvorgang einzubringen, angeglichen? – Ich will zur Beantwortung dieser Frage drei Beispiele erweiterter Partizipation in Industriegesellschaften genauer betrachten.

1. Erweiterte Partizipation in den USA

Die amerikanischen Untersuchungen, die unser Problem im allgemeinen unter dem Stichwort „responsiveness“ („Empfänglichkeit“, d. h. einer den Forderungen und Interessen der Gesellschaft entsprechenden Politik) untersuchen, verstehen unter Partizipation gemeinhin Beeinflussung der Personal- und Sachentscheidungen auf Regierungsebene durch private Bürger.[1] Vielfach wird diese Beeinflussung anhand von vier Tätigkeiten geprüft: Wählen, Wahlkampfbeteiligung, indirekte Kontaktaufnahme mit Vertretern der Legislative oder der Exekutive und Selbsthilfe bzw. Arbeit im Rahmen der Kommune („communal activity“).[2] Für unsere Frage nach einer Machtangleichung durch erweiterte Partizipation ist es wichtig festzuhalten, daß es sich hier um freiwillige Aktivitäten handelt, die überwiegend durch individuelle Motivation zustande kommen (also kaum infolge institutioneller Mobilisierung etwa durch Parteien oder Verbände). Nun nimmt mit dem Schwierigkeitsgrad der intellektuellen, psychischen und materiellen Voraussetzungen, die für eine Partizipationsart erforderlich sind, die Überrepräsentation der Oberschichten zu. Während für Wahlen und auch für die Kontaktaufnahme mit Vertretern der Legislative oder der Exekutive höhere Bildung keine größere Rolle spielt, gewinnt sie in den USA vermehrte Bedeutung für Wahlkampfunterstützung und kommunale Tätigkeit.[3] Dabei ist zu beachten, daß Ober- und Unterschichten typischerweise unterschiedliche Prioritäten setzen etwa in bezug auf Bildung einerseits, wohlfahrtsstaatliche Maßnahmen anderseits, daß sich allerdings z. B. hinsichtlich der Rassenintegration nicht eindeutige schichtenspezifische Aussagen machen lassen. Prüft man nun, welchen Einfluß gesteigerte Partizipation auf Regierungsentscheidungen ausübt, so zeigt sich in Untersuchungen zur Gemeindepolitik, daß bei sehr niedriger Partizipationsrate alle gleich behandelt werden. Steigt die Partizipationsrate etwas, so werden die Inaktiven zugunsten der Aktiven benachteiligt. Steigt sie abermals, so profitieren wieder alle, allerdings bleibt der Unterschied zwischen der Berücksichtigung der Aktiven und der Inaktiven weiter groß.[4]

Bedenkt man darüber hinaus, daß die am Ende der sechziger und zu Beginn der siebziger Jahre verstärkten sogenannten unkonventionellen, d. h. protestierenden Partizipationsarten, von Demonstrationen bis zu verschiedenen Arten von Boykottmaßnahmen, vorwiegend von Mittelschichtenanhängern getragen wurden und z. T. erheblichen Widerhall im Regierungshandeln fanden, so wird man nicht vom Ausgleich, sondern eher von einem Zuwachs an Macht zugunsten der Mittel- und Oberschichten durch gesteigerte Partizipation sprechen müssen. Dies kann allerdings zugleich durch eine Art Mitsaugeeffekt eine Mobilisierung und damit Machtsteigerung der Unterschichten im Vergleich zu ihrem vorherigen Status einschließen.

Ob gesteigerte Partizipation trotz des mit ihr einhergehenden Machtzuwachses der Mittel- und Oberschichten zu einer Angleichung in bezug auf Einkommen, Status und Bildung führt, hängt vor allem von den Zielen der Partizipanten und vom allgemeinen Organisationshintergrund der Partizipation ab.[5] Sofern wir jedoch nicht darauf bauen wollen, daß die neuen partizipierenden Schichten insgesamt oder überwiegend „altruistisch“, d. h. stellvertretend und zugunsten der Unterschichten handeln, müssen wir tendenziell annehmen, daß die in der Erweiterung freiwilliger Partizipation wachsenden Diskrepanzen in der Machtverteilung auch im Ergebnis der Partizipation sozio-ökonomische Ungleichheiten eher fördern. Zum Vergleich mit den Befunden über die rein freiwillige politische Teilnahme sei nun ein zweites Beispiel gesteigerter Partizipation erörtert:

2. Die Arbeiterselbstverwaltung in Jugoslawien

Das Selbstverständnis der jugoslawischen Demokratietheoretiker, die das Ideal der Arbeiterselbstverwaltung proklamieren, und der Politiker, die es in die Tat überführten, schöpft aus der Tradition der direkten, konsensualen bzw. identitären Demokratie. Für sie stehen Namen wie Rousseau, Marx, aber auch Proudhon (in der antistaatlichen Komponente), sowie in der Gegenwart neomarxistische Theoretiker, die starken Wert auf Dezentralisierung legen, wie André Gorz und die Theoretiker der französischen sozialistischen Strategie der „autogestion“. Es geht nicht nur um (nachträgliche) Arbeiterkontrolle, sondern um dauernde -Selbstverwaltung, nicht um *Mit*bestimmung, sondern um *Selbst*bestimmung. Edvard Kardelj, der inzwischen verstorbene ehemalige Cheftheoretiker des „Bundes der jugoslawischen Kommunisten“, bezeichnete die Diktatur des Proletariats, den neuen jugoslawischen Typ der sozialistischen Demokratie, als eine Macht, die nicht etwa die Demokratisierung der Gesellschaft verhindert, sondern im Gegenteil die Pfade weit für sie öffnet und sie damit sichert, „nicht indem sie die bürgerliche politische Demokratie restauriert, sondern indem sie die sozialistische Selbstverwaltung aufbaut.“[6] Hier ist die klassische Gegenüberstellung von liberaler (bürgerlicher) und radikaler (sozialistischer) Demokratie klar benannt.

Von der radikalen Demokratie im Gewand der Arbeiterselbstverwaltung erwartet sich Neca Jovanov, einer der führenden jugoslawischen Gewerkschaftsfunktionäre, daß sie jeglicher Klassenteilung der Gesellschaft den Boden entzieht, daß sie zur Aufhebung von Herrschaft, zur totalen Befreiung und zur solidarischen Verantwortung der Menschen, schließlich zum Absterben des Staates führt, und dies, weil ihre Institutionen besonders geeignet, besonders effizient seien, die verschiedenen gegensätzlichen Interessen zu manifestieren, demokratisch zu orientieren und zu „entknoten".[7] Immerhin, Jovanov spricht von Konflikten, und als erfahrener Gewerkschaftsfunktionär, der sich zudem ausführlich in empirischen Untersuchungen mit Streiks in Jugoslawien beschäftigt hat, weiß er, wovon er redet.

Zu fragen steht nun, in welchem Maße die Institutionen der Arbeiterselbstverwaltung geeignet sind, die Ziele des jugoslawischen Demokratieverständnisses zu erfüllen. Dazu müssen wir erstens diese Ziele etwas genauer entfalten und zweitens die besonderen Merkmale bzw. das entscheidende Spezifikum der Institutionen der Arbeiterselbstverwaltung etwa im Vergleich zu deutschen Mitbestimmungsregelungen verdeutlichen.

Das fundamentale Ziel der Arbeiterselbstverwaltung ist die endgültige Überwindung des „Grundwiderspruchs" zwischen Kapital und Arbeit, des alle weiteren Ungleichheiten, Ungerechtigkeiten, Klassengegensätze hervorrufenden funktionalen und sozialen Konfliktes zwischen denen, die qua Eigentum über die Produktionsmittel verfügen, und denen, die ihre Arbeitskraft gegen Lohn verkaufen. Enthalten sind in diesem Ziel zum einen die Verwirklichung der Gleichheit unter den Menschen in bezug auf ihre Würde, ihre Möglichkeit, sich selbst zu bestimmen und alle ihre Fähigkeiten kreativ zu entfalten, sowie zumindest annähernd in bezug auf ihr Einkommen; zum anderen gehört dazu, von konkurrierenden und feindseligen zu solidarischen Beziehungen untereinander überzugehen und damit schließlich zu freiheitlicher Integration der Gesamtgesellschaft zu gelangen, ohne die Notwendigkeit staatlicher Herrschaft und auf der Basis materiellen Wohlergehens.[8]

Das entscheidende institutionelle Mittel nun, diese Ziele zu erreichen, ist die Abschaffung des Privateigentums an den Produktionsmitteln. Generell wird das Eigentum als Verfügungsrecht ersetzt durch ein Verfassungsrecht auf Selbstverwaltung und auf Nutzung der vorhandenen Produktionsmittel durch die vereinigten Arbeiter. Die Überwindung der grundlegenden gesellschaftlichen Konflikte und die gleichrangige Verwirklichung von Freiheit, Gleichheit und Solidarität erwartet man davon, daß der Gegensatz zwischen der Kapital- bzw. Ressourcenrentabilität und dem Interesse der arbeitenden Menschen an humaner, sicherer und kreativer Arbeit vom Arbeiter als Konflikt inneralb seiner eigenen Interessen betrachtet und in verantwortlicher Selbstbestimmung gelöst wird. Im fundamentalen Unterschied etwa zu deutschen Mitbestimmungsregelungen soll sich der funktionale Gegensatz zwischen Kapitalrentabilität und Arbeitshumanität nicht institutionell und sozial manifestieren im Gegenüber von sozialen Gruppen bzw. Organisationen mit je eigener Legitimations- und Interessenbasis. Nicht die Repräsentation gegensätzlicher Interessen durch gegensätzliche Gruppen mit je besonderen Rollen, sondern die Verinnerlichung und Lösung des Konflikts durch die einzelne Person – dies ist die Devise. So sollen die selbstbestimmte Würde jedes einzelnen gesichert und die Verfestigung sozialer Privilegien verhindert werden.

Aus diesem Grundgedanken lassen sich alle institutionellen Regelungen der jugoslawischen Arbeiterselbstverwaltung – wie immer sie in den über dreißig Jahren ihres Bestehens auch verändert wurden – herleiten. Aus ihm rühren im besonderen die Konstruktion des von allen Mitgliedern der Unternehmung gewählten Arbeiterrates als des legal wichtigsten Entscheidungsgremiums sowie die des Direktors einschließlich des gesamten Managements als des theoretisch nur ausführenden, praktisch jedoch vielfach eigentlich führenden Organs des Arbeiterrates. Aus ihm folgt auch die theoretische Schwierigkeit, bei allem pragmatischen Freimut eine präzise funktionale Rolle für die Gewerkschaft sowie eine Erklärung von Streiks zu finden, die mit der Arbeiterselbstverwaltung systematisch vereinbar wäre.

Im Unterschied zur jugoslawischen Arbeiterselbstverwaltung geht die deutsche Mitbestimmung (selbst in der gesetzlich bisher außer für die Montanindustrie nicht verwirklichten paritätischen Form) vom bleibenden funktionalen und sich sozial, institutionell und legitimatorisch manifestierenden Gegensatz zwischen Kapital und Arbeit aus. Ich komme darauf zurück. Im folgenden will ich meine Untersuchung exemplarisch auf die Funktion des Direktors einschließlich des Managements in der Arbeiterselbstverwaltung und auf die Rolle von Streiks in Jugoslawien beschränken.

Die Tatsache, daß jugoslawische Arbeiter überhaupt streiken, bestätigt Kardeljs Aussage, daß der Konflikt zwischen Kapital und Arbeit zumindest in der Sicht der Arbeiter nicht zur Zufriedenheit gelöst ist. Innerhalb der Theorie der Arbeiterselbstverwaltung erscheint der Streik zwar als „Pathologie“[9]. Die Arbeiter verwalten sich selbst, bestimmen das Wirtschaftsgeschehen selbst und dürften eigentlich nicht gegen das Ergebnis ihrer Selbstbestimmung streiken. Offenbar haben sie jedoch nicht den Eindruck, daß sie sich selbst bestimmen. Als Ursachen für die Arbeitskonflikte nennt Neca Jovanov in seinen Streikanalysen eine ungünstige Bildungs- und Ausbildungsstruktur, schwierige Positionen der Unternehmungen auf dem Markt, heterogene Interessen der Arbeiterklasse sowie eine ungenügende politische Organisation der Arbeiter auf der umfassenden sozialen Ebene,[10] womit er wahrscheinlich für effektivere und arbeiternähere Gewerkschaften plädiert. Ob dies die einzigen oder die vorwiegenden Streikursachen sind, sei dahingestellt. Sicher jedoch ist, daß in die Entscheidungen über Unternehmensfragen neben den Interessen der Arbeiter in den Unternehmungen auch eine Reihe anderer, vielfach entgegengesetzter Interessen eingehen, sei es von den anderen unternehmensinternen Gruppen, den technischen Angestellten, dem Direktor, oder von Unternehmensexternen, die Eingang finden über gesetzliche Vorgaben, über Marktdaten oder über „Informationen“ von seiten des Managements – handele es sich dabei um die politischen Gemeinden, um konkurrierende Unternehmungen, um Banken, Lieferanten oder Kunden.[11]

In seiner Brust zur Übereinstimmung bringen müßte der jugoslawische Arbeiter theoretisch also nicht nur seine eigenen lang- und kurzfristigen Interessen – z. B. kurzfristig am Lohn und langfristig an der Produktivität seiner Unternehmung –, sondern auch diejenigen der anderen internen und externen, mittelbaren und unmittelbaren Marktteilnehmer. So geht in jede Unternehmensentscheidung ein komplexes Bündel von Zielen und Interessen ein, das um so undurchschaubarer wird und potentiell eher Privilegien fördert, je höher die intellektuellen und ausbildungsmäßigen Anforderungen an die Entscheidungsträger sind. Kann man in diesem Geflecht z. T. gegensätzlicher Interessen einen Vorrang des in kapitalistischen Wirtschaften vorherrschenden Gegensatzes von Kapitalrentabilität und Arbeitshumanität oder einen anderen, funktional gleichartigen Grundkonflikt erkennen? Sicher nicht in den Gegensätzen in bezug auf die unternehmensinterne Einkommensverteilung. Und welche Interessen vertreten die im Streik als Kontrahenten der Arbeiter handelnden Direktoren und Manager, wenn sie, wie im Standardfall, höhere Löhne verweigern wollen? Denkbar ist zunächst, daß sie eigene Fehlentscheidungen zu kaschieren oder eigene finanzielle Vorteile zu verfechten trachten; in der Regel jedoch sind sie gezwungen, Grenzen zu setzen, die aus Gesetzen, Verträgen oder aus den Zwängen des Marktes herrühren, d. h. aus der Beachtung der Interessen der politischen Allgemeinheit als des gesetzlichen Rahmengebers, der Kreditgeber, der Lieferanten, der Abnehmer. Unabhängig von der Frage, wie berechtigt diese Interessen sind, läuft ihre Beachtung doch auf den Zwang zum rentablen Umgang mit den Ressourcen, vor allem dem Kapital, heraus. Zwar steht keine sichtbare Gruppe von Kapitaleigentümern, die eine Rendite erhalten wollen, im Hintergrund – mit Ausnahme vielleicht der Banken, die eine vergleichbare Funktion ausüben –, dennoch kann man sagen, daß der Gegensatz von Kapital- bzw. Ressourcenrentabilität und Arbeitshumanität als zentraler Konflikt, wenn auch unter veränderten Bedingungen, wiedererscheint.

Ist die spezifische institutionelle Regelung der Arbeiterselbstverwaltung unter dieser Bedingung eines fortbestehenden Grundkonfliktes zwischen Ressourcenrentabilität und Arbeitshumanität besonders geeignet, Gleichheit, Gerechtigkeit und Solidarität sowohl innerhalb der Unternehmung als auch in seiner Beziehung zum sozialen Umfeld zu befördern? Bei der Suche nach einer Antwort auf diese Frage springt die Übereinstimmung der namhaften jugoslawischen Soziologen über die Diskrepanz ins Auge, die zwischen Norm und Wirklichkeit der Arbeiterselbstverwaltung besteht. Einige ihrer wichtigsten Befunde seien hier zusammengestellt.

Eine besonders markante Kluft trennt den theoretischen Anspruch der gleichen Machtverteilung innerhalb der jugoslawischen Unternehmungen von der Wirklichkeit unübersehbarer Machtkonzentration beim Direktor und beim Management zuungunsten des Arbeiterrates, des theoretisch dem Management übergeordneten wichtigsten Entscheidungsorgans. Vejnovic hat herausgefunden, daß 98% der endgültigen Entscheidungen des Arbeiterrates identisch sind mit den Vorschlägen, die von den Experten und vom Management kommen.[12] Ein durch Information und Qualifikation weit überlegenes Management steht hier einem faktisch schwachen Arbeiterrat gegenüber, dessen einfache Mitglieder allenfalls in der Lage sind, Vorschlägen zuzustimmen oder sie abzulehnen, nicht jedoch konstruktive Alternativlösungen entgegenzusetzen.[13] Infolgedessen begibt sich der Arbeiterrat auch nur selten in Konfrontation zum Management, was die hierarchische Ordnung der Machtstruktur noch verstärkt.[14] Ein zusätzlicher Grund, dem Management faktisch die Entscheidung zu überlassen, liegt in der Überzeugung vieler Arbeiter, den Managern, die im Unterschied zu den Mitgliedern des Arbeiterrates als Einzelpersonen materiell und kriminalrechtlich belangt werden können, auch das letzte Votum überantworten zu sollen,[15] eine ehrenhafte Einstellung, die jedoch zur eigenen Entmächtigung beiträgt. Man fragt sich überdies, ob das Auseinanderklaffen von theoretischer Entscheidungskompetenz des Arbeiterrates und einer allein auf die Direktoren und das obere Management eingeschränkten Verantwortlichkeit bei weniger „ehrenhaften" Arbeitern nicht umgekehrt zu völlig verantwortungslosen Entscheidungen führen könnte.

Dabei trifft das Management nicht nur die wichtigsten finanziellen und technischen Sachentscheidungen, die die Investitions- und Produktionsplanung insgesamt betreffen, sondern bestimmt auch weitgehend die Kriterien und den faktischen Vollzug der unternehmensinternen Einkommensverteilung.[16] Nach der subjektiven Einschätzung der Unternehmensmitglieder haben gemäß einer Untersuchung aus dem Jahre 1974[17] in vierzehn slowenischen Firmen die Mitglieder des Arbeiterrates ein deutliches Übergewicht gegenüber allen anderen Entscheidungsträgern nur in bezug auf Einstellungs- und Entlassungsfragen sowie auf finanzielle Hilfen für Kollegen und – mit Abstand den größten Einfluß – auf die Verteilung von Wohnungen.[18]

Besonders wichtig nun für die Einschätzung der Arbeiterselbstverwaltung ist hinsichtlich der Machtverteilung die übereinstimmende Erkenntnis jugoslawischer Soziologen, nach der die Machtdiskrepanz zugunsten des Managements nicht ab-, sondern zugenommen hat.[19]

Erstes Fazit: innerhalb der jugoslawischen Unternehmungen findet sich seit Einführung der Arbeiterselbstverwaltung nicht mehr Gleichheit, sondern eine zunehmend ungleiche Verteilung der Macht zugunsten des Managements und zuungunsten der Arbeiter.

Wie steht es mit der Machtgleichheit zwischen den Unternehmungen und in ihrem Verhältnis zur Umwelt? Die 1950 eingeleitete Ablösung der Zentralverwaltungswirtschaft durch die sozialistische Marktwirtschaft minderte zweifellos die Machtkonzentration beim Staate und sorgte so im Verhältnis zu den Unternehmungen für eine Angleichung der Macht. Die Unternehmungen wurden stärker. Uns interessiert hier nun die Frage, ob die mit jeder Marktwirtschaft einhergehende Dynamik der Ungleichheit in den spezifischen Einrichtungen der Arbeiterselbstverwaltung wirksamen Gegenkräften begegnet. Auffällig und durchgängig ist hier auch wieder der empirische Befund zunehmender Machtungleichheit. Besonders deutlich und krass wachsend findet sie sich zwischen „normalen" nicht vorrangig für den Handel mit dem westlichen Ausland produzierenden Unternehmungen einerseits und Banken, Handelsorganisationen sowie für den westlichen Außenhandel produzierenden Unternehmungen anderseits.[20]

Die Macht, die der Staat in bezug auf seinen Einfluß auf die Investitionsentscheidungen durch seine Bankreform aus dem Jahre 1965 an die „Gesellschaft", sprich: an die Banken abgegeben hat, verteilte sich keineswegs gleichmäßig auf die selbstverwalteten Unternehmungen, sondern konzentrierte sich bei den großen Banken. Während diese 1955 nur bei 0,1% der Investitionen auf deren Struktur Einfluß nahmen, stieg der Anteil der von den Banken mitbestimmten Investitionen im Jahre 1969 auf 49,4%.[21] Die Bankreform von 1978, die die Macht der Banken an die Produktionsunternehmen zurückgeben wollte, läßt erwarten, daß sie zwar die Banken geschwächt hat, daß die ungleiche Machtverteilung zwischen den Unternehmungen dagegen eher verstärkt worden ist.

Empirisch ist die Frage, ob die Arbeiterselbstverwaltung sich bisher besonders dafür geeignet hat, der Machtkonzentration entgegenzuwirken, vorerst kaum zu beantworten. Die Konzentration hat zugenommen. Hätte sie dies deutlicher getan ohne Selbstverwaltung? Wir können hier nur eine spekulative Überlegung anstellen: Die Minderung der Bankenmacht setzt wirksame Gegengewichte voraus. Da der Staat seinen Einfluß auf den Wirtschaftsverlauf theoretisch mindern will und dies praktisch auch tut, können sie nur von anderen Selbstverwaltungseinheiten ausgehen. Voraussetzung dafür ist praktisch, daß genügend faktische Gegenmacht gegen ökonomische Giganten vorhanden ist, und theoretisch, daß Konflikte als permanente Bedingung des Verhältnisses zwischen den Selbstverwaltungseinheiten anerkannt werden. Dies hieße weiter, daß von außen auf die Unternehmungen einwirkende, ihnen entgegengesetzte Interessen im unternehmensinternen Entscheidungsablauf deutlich und sichtbar sein müssen, damit ihnen Gegeninteressen ebenso deutlich konfrontiert werden können.

Alles spricht unter den Bedingungen der Arbeiterselbstverwaltung dafür, daß das konsensuale Demokratiekonzept solche deutliche Interessenartikulation und Gegenmachtsstrategie nicht erlaubt oder zumindest nicht fördert, daß die den unternehmensinternen Arbeitern entgegenstehenden Interessen vielmehr eher als unerkennbare „objektive" Daten in die Informationen des Managements an den Arbeiterrat eingehen, um diesen zu „marktkonformem" Verhalten zu bewegen. Hier steht nicht zur Debatte, ob die Manager in ihrer häufigen Manipulation von Informationen[22] pragmatisch richtig handeln, was keineswegs auszuschließen ist. Vielmehr geht es um die demokratietheoretische Überlegung, ob zur Förderung der Gleichheit im Sinne des Machtausgleichs entgegen dem Postulat der konsensualen Demokratietheorie nicht eine Entscheidungsregelung geeignet ist, die den Konflikt als eine unaufhebbare soziale Voraussetzung anerkennt, Interessengegensätze infolgedessen institutionell artikuliert und transparenter macht und so die Voraussetzung für einen Ausgleich schafft. Eine dementsprechende Regelung ersetzt zwar nicht die notwendige faktische ökonomische Gegenmacht. Ein Unternehmen kurz vor dem Bankrott kann mit noch so geeigneten Entscheidungsprozeduren keine Gegenmacht bilden. Aber sind sie nicht die Voraussetzung faktischer ökonomischer Gegenmacht? Wir kommen darauf zurück.

Unser Fazit lautet: Ob die Arbeiterselbstverwaltung den Machtausgleich zwischen den Unternehmungen befördert oder behindert hat, kann bisher empirisch nicht eindeutig entschieden werden. Faktisch hat innerhalb der Unternehmung und in ihrem Verhältnis zueinander die Ungleichheit von Teilhabe und Einfluß und damit von Macht jedenfalls zugenommen. Die konsensuale Prämisse der Theorie der Arbeiterselbstverwaltung bietet keine Grundlage zur klaren Artikulation und Institutionalisierung von gegensätzlichen Interessen und verhindert damit Egalisierung durch Gegenmacht.

3. Die paritätische Mitbestimmung

Als drittes Beispiel gesteigerter Partizipation wollen wir die seit 1951 bestehende paritätische Mitbestimmung in der Montanindustrie der Bundesrepublik Deutschland untersuchen.

Die seit 1951 gesetzlich festgelegte paritätische unternehmerische Mitbestimmung in der deutschen Stahl-, Eisen- und Kohleindustrie ist Gegenstand umfangreicher, kaum noch zu übersehender Forschung geworden. An dieser Stelle sei nur noch einmal an die Grundlinien und -absichten dieser Art industrieller Demokratie erinnert und dann im Überblick geprüft, ob, in welchem Sinne und in welchem Maße sie zur Egalisierung von Macht beigetragen hat.

Der Grundgedanke der paritätischen Mitbestimmung hat sich historisch aus Überlegungen, die während der Weimarer Republik formuliert worden sind, und aus der besonderen Situation der deutschen Nachkriegsindustrie entwickelt, nämlich der politischen und moralischen Kompromittierung vieler Unternehmer im Stahlbereich, der tatkräftigen Fortführung der Produktion durch die Arbeiter nach Absetzung der diskreditierten Unternehmer und des gemeinsamen Interesses von Arbeitern und Unternehmern daran, zusätzliche Demontagen zu verhindern und zu diesem Zweck zusammenzuarbeiten.[23] Aus der Leitidee der Parität folgt, daß die Aufsichtsräte der Unternehmen im Kohle- und Stahlbereich entsprechend den beiden Produktionsfaktoren Kapital und Arbeit paritätisch von der Arbeitgeber- und der Arbeitnehmerseite besetzt sein sollen und daß dieses Gremium durch Mehrheitsbeschluß den Vorstand des Unternehmens wählt, wobei ein Vorstandsmitglied – der Arbeitsdirektor – auf jeden Fall das klare Vertrauen der Arbeitnehmerseite genießen muß. Die Arbeitnehmerseite wird zur Hälfte von den dem Unternehmen angehörigen Arbeitnehmern gewählt, zur Hälfte von den entsprechenden Industriegewerkschaften bestimmt. Die Arbeitgeberseite wird durch die Anteilseigner gewählt. Zusätzlich zur paritätischen unternehmerischen Mitbestimmung gibt es in jedem Unternehmen einen Betriebsrat, der die sozialen Belange der Arbeitnehmer (im Unterschied zu den unternehmerischen) vertreten soll.

Der Grundgedanke der paritätischen Mitbestimmung und die bisherige Praxis werden von zwei Seiten kritisiert und in Frage gestellt: Von den einen wird der Partizipations- und Machtzuwachs der Arbeitnehmerseite als ordnungspolitisch bedenklich und hinderlich für die ökonomische Effizienz angesehen. Durch die in dieser Sicht zu starke Vertretung von Arbeitnehmerinteressen im Unternehmen werde die Arbeitgeberseite in den kollektivvertraglichen Verhandlungen mit den Gewerkschaften über Gebühr geschwächt; Innovationen und Rationalisierung würden gebremst, sofern sie nicht durch Arbeitsplätze schaffende Investitionen ausgeglichen werden könnten; die gemeinsame Interessenlage von Arbeitgeber- und Arbeitnehmerseite, Konflikte bei eventuellen Entlassungen zu vermeiden, würde zu einer konservativen Unternehmenspolitik führen, zum Schaden einer flexiblen Ausweitung von Arbeitsplätzen und damit von unternehmensexternen Arbeitnehmern; gemeinsame Strategien von Arbeit und Kapital in Großunternehmen würden zu einem unwiderstehlichen Druck auf politische Institutionen etwa in bezug auf Subventionen führen; schließlich würden Pionierinvestitionen, die ein besonderes unternehmerisches Risiko bergen, entmutigt, weil die dafür notwendigen Chancen einer dem Risiko entsprechenden Aussicht auf eine hohe Rendite solcher Investitionen wegen der Tendenz in mitbestimmten Unternehmungen, Renditen möglichst niedrig zu halten, kaum noch gegeben seien.[24]

Diese Kritik oder zumindest Problematisierung der paritätischen Mitbestimmung geht fraglos von einem Machtausgleich zwischen Arbeitgebern und Arbeitnehmern aus, der aus der Erweiterung der Partizipation für die Arbeitnehmer herrührt. Dies ist vor allem ein Ausgleich zwischen zwei Gruppen, Organisationen bzw. Kollektiven, den Arbeitnehmern und den Arbeitgebern, nicht zwischen deren individuellen Vertretern oder Anhängern.

Auf der anderen Seite der Kritik an der paritätischen Mitbestimmung wird der Partizipations- und Machtgewinn der Arbeitnehmerseite zwar nicht rundweg bestritten, aber er wird als unzureichend angesehen, um einen gesamtgesellschaftlichen Ausgleich zugunsten der Arbeiter herbeizuführen; das geringe Maß an Machtzuwachs lenke darüber hinaus die Arbeiter von ihren eigentlichen Interessen und Aufgaben ab, es verändere oder durchbreche nicht das Rentabilitätsprinzip als das Erfolgskriterium kapitalistischen Wirtschaftens, sondern integriere die Arbeiter in den Kapitalismus und bringe schließlich nur eine illusionäre Gleichheit für die einzelnen Arbeiter mit sich, weil die einzig Profitierenden die Eliten der Gewerkschaften bzw. die Arbeitnehmervertreter seien, die sich auf diese Weise zusätzlich von ihrer Basis entfernten.[25]

Bedeutsam für unsere weiteren Überlegungen ist der Vorwurf, daß der Zuwachs an Gleichheit für die Arbeitnehmerseite als Kollektiv, der grundsätzlich von niemandem bestritten, sondern nur in der Kritik von „links" wegen seiner vermeintlichen Geringfügigkeit oder wegen seiner Gegenläufigkeit gegen eine kommunistische Ordnung oder gegen eine Strategie mit dem Ziel der Selbstverwaltung kritisiert wird, durch ein Anwachsen der Ungleichheit zwischen den Arbeitnehmereliten und den „einfachen" Arbeitern erkauft werde. Findet die in Jugoslawien beobachtete Tendenz einer Machtkonzentration bei denen, die besser gebildet, informiert und höher in der Hierarchie des Unternehmens angesiedelt sind, eine Parallele in einer Machtkonzentration bei den Arbeitnehmervertretern bzw. bei gewerkschaftlichen Eliten?

Zunächst liegt ein wichtiger Unterschied darin, daß die Gewerkschaftselite im Unternehmensbereich nicht ausschließlich herrscht, sondern lediglich als Gegenelite gegen die Anteilseignerseite fungiert. Da beide ihre Legitimation in Gruppen mit z. T. gegensätzlichen Interessen finden müssen, können sie ihre Macht nicht einfach zu einem Monopol vereinen. Eine solche Vereinigung bei gegensätzlichen Ausgangsinteressen würde die Möglichkeit einer totalen Verschleierung der Gegensätze gegenüber der jeweiligen Wählerbasis voraussetzen, die im Unterschied zur jugoslawischen Arbeiterselbstverwaltung bei der paritätischen Mitbestimmung weder institutionell gefördert, noch faktisch gegeben ist. In der gegenwärtigen empirischen Forschung zur Mitbestimmung, die kritisch nach der Oligarchie- und Elitenbildung fragt, wird das Problem infolgedessen auch nicht in einem zunehmenden Auseinanderklaffen zwischen der Macht der Arbeitnehmervertreter als der Eliten einerseits und derjenigen der Belegschaft andererseits gesehen, auch nicht in einer einseitigen Interessenwahrnehmung oder materiellen Begünstigung der Arbeitnehmereliten. Vielmehr geht es um noch unzureichende Teilnahme der einfachen individuellen Arbeiter am vielfältigen Entscheidungsprozeß innerhalb ihres Unternehmens und um ihre ungenügend oder gar nicht vorhandene Möglichkeit, über die Gestaltung ihrer individuellen Arbeitssituation mitzubestimmen. Der in bezug auf den letzten Punkt entbrannte Streit um die Mitbestimmung am Arbeitsplatz, die durch vom Betriebsrat unabhängige Arbeitsgruppen vorangetrieben und gestaltet werden soll, zeigt, daß Konflikte hier nicht so sehr zwischen den Vertretern der Anteilseigner und den Arbeitnehmern bestehen, sondern zwischen verschiedenen Konzepten und Organisationen der Arbeitnehmervertretung selbst. Ob hier der Vorwurf zutrifft, daß die Gewerkschaften, die eine derartige unabhängig von ihnen organisierte Mitbestimmung ablehnen, nur ihr Vertretungsmonopol und ihre Ungestörtheit gegenüber unbequemen „Basisdemokraten“ verteidigen oder ob mit einer Konkurrenz zwischen gewerkschaftlicher und organisatorisch ungebundener Arbeitnehmervertretung die Schlagkraft der Gewerkschaft unangemessen gefährdet erscheint bzw. mitbestimmungsfeindlichen Agitatoren Machthebel in die Hand gegeben werden, hängt letztlich von der Praxis, die sich in diesen propagierten Partizipationsformen entwickelt, ab. Beide theoretischen Gegenpositionen haben Argumente und Fakten für sich.[26]

In bezug auf das Elitenproblem und die dahinter stehende Machtangleichung ist jedoch nicht so sehr die Frage nach der Mitbestimmung am Arbeitsplatz von Bedeutung, die von ihren Vertretern ausdrücklich als Bestandteil der betrieblichen und unternehmerischen Mitbestimmung propagiert wird, sondern die mangelnde faktische Teilhabe der individuellen Arbeitnehmer an der praktizierten Mitbestimmung auf der Ebene des Betriebes oder der Unternehmung. Hier zeigt sich wie schon bei der Erörterung der Arbeiterselbstverwaltung in Jugoslawien, daß die entscheidende Voraussetzung jeder Partizipation und damit jeder Machtangleichung in der dazu erforderlichen Information der Partizipanten liegt. Information, Kompetenz und Expertenwissen sind für jede effektive Entscheidungsteilhabe unabdingbar.[27] Immerhin wird in der empirischen Forschung deutlich, daß die Informationen sich nicht einseitig in einer Vertretungsspitze sammeln, sondern sich durchaus auf Zwischeneliten, vor allem auf das relativ breite Netz der gewerkschaftlichen Vertrauensleute – in manchen Fällen auch der gewerkschaftlich nicht gebundenen Vertrauensleute im Betrieb – verteilen, wenn der personelle Kreis dieser Eliten auch noch zu begrenzt ist.[28] Auch die Tatsache, daß die verschiedenen Arbeitnehmergruppen im Betrieb und außerhalb sowohl gleich- als auch gegenläufige Interessen haben sowie kurz- und langfristige Ziele verfolgen, eine Tatsache, die sich z. B. anläßlich von Aufsichtsratswahlen in z. T. durchaus heftigen Kämpfen zwischen Betriebsrat und außerbetrieblicher Gewerkschaft zeigt, verhindert die Monopolisierung von Informationen z. B. durch eine in sich geschlossene gewerkschaftliche Elite und sorgt für eine breitere Streuung.

Diejenigen, die die Informationshindernisse gegen eine Verbreiterung und Angleichung der Teilhabe an der Mitbestimmung durch größere Publizität im Unternehmen abbauen wollen, stoßen und verweisen dabei ebenfalls auf den engen Zusammenhang zwischen der Artikulation von Interessenkonflikten und der Verbreitung von Information. Allerdings handelt es sich da nicht um eine einlinige Kausalität, sondern um ein Wechselverhältnis: Je weniger Interesse die Beteiligten zeigen, desto weniger Information gewinnen sie und je weniger Information sie bereits haben, desto weniger Interesse bringen sie auf. Man kann daher zur Erweiterung der Information nicht nur an einem Hebel ansetzen. Immerhin scheint es sich nicht um einen undurchbrechbaren Teufelskreis zu handeln. Die Verbreitung von Information hat in den 30 Jahren nach dem Zweiten Weltkrieg z. B. in der Bundesrepublik deutlich stattgefunden, und eine weitere Steigerung ist durchaus möglich.[29]

Allerdings gibt es für die Egalisierung von Information als Grundlage für die Machtangleichung zwei dem Modell der paritätischen Mitbestimmung immanente Grenzen:

1.) Informationen sind im Arbeitsleben wie überall nicht wert- oder interessenfrei. Die Steigerung ihrer Dichte und ihre Verbreitung bedeutet in der Praxis der Mitbestimmung daher auch nicht einfach eine quantitative Aufstockung. Vielmehr ist gerade mit der Forderung nach breiterer Information für die Arbeitnehmer ausdrücklich oder indirekt zumindest das Postulat verbunden, damit auch die Durchsetzung ihrer Interessen besser zu gewährleisten. Diese Verknüpfung von Information und Interessenvertretung wird am Beispiel des Streits um die Geheimhaltung von Informationen im Aufsichts- oder im Betriebsrat plastisch. Kein Zweifel kann darüber bestehen, daß die den Arbeitnehmervertretern im Betriebs- und mehr noch im Aufsichtsrat auferlegte Verpflichtung, Informationen, vor allem wenn sie die Wettbewerbssituation eines Unternehmens schädigen können, auch vor der Belegschaft geheimzuhalten, eine Barriere gegen die Macht- und Partizipationsgleichheit zwischen Eliten und Basis darstellt. Sie ganz abzuschaffen, kann man aber sinnvollerweise nur fordern, wenn man zugleich die Marktwirtschaft mit der nun einmal zu ihr gehörenden Konkurrenz zwischen den Unternehmen überwinden will, wofür es theoretisch und praktisch bisher als Alternative nur die zentrale Planwirtschaft gibt. In ihr hat Mitbestimmung wiederum keinen Platz, weil hier den einzelnen Unternehmen keine nennenswerten Entscheidungsbefugnisse mehr verbleiben. Zur Mitbestimmung gehören daher untrennbar die Marktwirtschaft und damit verbunden ein Mindestmaß von Geheimhaltungsverpflichtung für die Arbeitnehmervertreter. Wieweit sie ausgedehnt werden muß und wieviel z. B. das Interesse des einzelnen Arbeitnehmers an der Sicherheit seines Arbeitsplatzes bzw. an der Möglichkeit, sich frühzeitig einen anderen zu suchen, einerseits wiegt und das Interesse der Anteilseigner an der Stärkung der Stellung des Unternehmens am Markt, wozu auch manchmal das Verschweigen vorübergehender Schwächen gehören kann, muß in Einzelerörterungen in Kenntnis der konkreten Praxis erwogen werden. Hier gibt es sicher einen beachtlichen Interpretationsspielraum. Eine unüberschreitbare Grenze für das Einreißen der Informationsbarriere zwischen Arbeitnehmervertretern und Belegschaft ist mit dem Modell der Mitbestimmung gleichwohl verbunden.

2.) Eine zweite Grenze zeigt sich darin, daß jeder Mensch nur eine beschränkte Fähigkeit hat, Informationen zu verarbeiten. Praktisch hat sich dies im Rahmen der Mitbestimmung z. B. bei jenen Betriebsratsmitgliedern gezeigt, die auf ihre Freistellung vom Arbeitsprozeß für die Betriebsratsarbeit verzichteten, um mit den Erfahrungen und Informationen des normalen Alltagslebens enger verbunden zu bleiben. Sie mußten diesen Vorteil gegen die damit einhergehende Einbuße an Einfluß auf den Betriebsrat erkaufen.[30] Diese zweite Grenze besteht jedoch in jedem System der Partizipation, nicht nur im Modell der paritätischen Mitbestimmung.

Innerhalb dieser beiden nicht radikal überwindbaren Grenzen gegenüber der Angleichung von Information und damit von Macht – der Geheimhaltungspflicht und der Grenzen der individuellen Fähigkeit, Informationen zu sammeln und zu verarbeiten – bleibt jedoch durchaus Raum für einen Abbau ungerechtfertigter und unbegründeter Ungleichheiten. Die deutschen Gewerkschaften haben seit dem zweiten Weltkrieg dazu schon erheblich beigetragen und ihre Bildungs- und Informationsarbeit geht weiter.

Angesichts der Interessengegensätze nicht nur zwischen den beiden legitimierenden Großgruppen – den Anteilseignern und den Arbeitnehmern –, sondern darüber hinaus auch innerhalb dieser Gruppen, die ihrerseits offen artikuliert und organisatorisch gestützt werden können (genannt wurden z. B. Konflikte zwischen unternehmensinternen und -externen Gewerkschaftsvertretern), ist also die von Robert Michels maßgeblich eingeführte soziologische Zweiteilung zwischen Eliten und Massen für die paritätische Mitbestimmung wie überhaupt für organisierte westliche Demokratien nicht mehr so undifferenziert zutreffend. Es gibt eine Reihe von Zwischeneliten innerhalb der Organisationen, die nicht einfach Transmissionsstationen darstellen, sondern sich wegen unterschiedlicher Unteressen, die sie vertreten, Loyalitäten, an die sie gebunden sind, und Informationen, die sie aus vielfach quer zu den Großorganisationen verlaufenden Kanälen beziehen, gegenseitig auch kontrollieren. Das heißt keineswegs, daß in organisierten westlichen Demokratien das Oligarchie- bzw. Elitenproblem gelöst sei, aber die Aussichtslosigkeit des Michelschen ehernen Gesetzes der Oligarchien muß nicht hingenommen werden.[31]

Für das Modell der paritätischen Mitbestimmung kann man zusammenfassend festhalten, daß es faktisch zum Abbau der Machtungleichheit sowohl zwischen Anteilseignern und Arbeitnehmern als auch innerhalb der zweiten Gruppe beigetragen hat und auch noch weiter beitragen kann, weil es prinzipiell nach dem Konzept der einander kontrollierenden Gegeneliten verfährt und Konsens wie Konflikt miteinander verbindet. Es hat damit unter dem Gesichtspunkt der Machtangleichung einen deutlichen Vorteil gegenüber den beiden Alternativen der rein freiwilligen Partizipation einerseits und dem Modell der Selbstverwaltung andererseits. Denn in bezug auf sie mußten wir feststellen, daß die Tendenz zur Machtanhäufung durch erweiterte Partizipation bei den sozioökonomischen Eliten, die wir in den Erfahrungen mit gesteigerter Partizipation in den USA und in Jugoslawien beobachten konnten und die vorrangig aus der zunehmenden Bedeutung von Ausbildung, Information und Funktion innerhalb von Organisationen herrührt, zunimmt, wenn die Machtkonzentration institutionell gefördert wird (durch die konsensuale Demokratiekonzeption in Jugoslawien) oder wenn ihr nicht durch organisatorische Bildung und Stützung von Gegeneliten entgegengewirkt wird (wie in der vornehmlich freiwilligen, d. h. institutionell nicht mobilisierten Partizipation in den USA). Mithin erscheint erweiterte Partizipation nach dem Modell der Mitbestimmung am ehesten geeignet, zur Angleichung politischer Macht beizutragen.

Anmerkungen

1 Eine der Standardformulierungen lautet: "activities by private citizens... aimed at influencing the selection of governmental personnel and/or the actions they take." Verba/Nie 1972, S. 2.
2 Vgl. Verba/Nie/Jae-on 1971, S. 9.
3 Verba/Nie/Jae-on 1971, S. 58.
4 Verba/Nie 1972, S. 316ff.
5 Vgl. dazu auch Verba/Nie 1972, S. 342.
6 Kardelj 1976 (Zit. übersetzt vom Verf.).
7 Vgl. Jovanov 1972, S. 12.
8 Vgl. Bolcić 1972, S. 97–112; ausführlich den demokratietheoretischen Ursprüngen der Arbeiterselbstverwaltung in Jugoslawien: Horvat/Marković/Supek (Hrsg.) 1975.
9 Vgl. Županov 1978, S. 391.
10 Jovanov 1972, S. 74, 89f.
11 Vgl. Rus 1978, S. 406.

[12] Vgl. Vejnović 1978, S. 271.
[13] Vgl. Bučar 1978, S. 429.
[14] Vgl. Arzensek 1978, S. 379 ff.; vgl. dazu auch Hagemann Klemencić 1974, S. 162 f.
[15] Zvonarević 1978, S. 187.
[16] Vgl. Arzensěk 1978, S. 379; Jovanov 1978, S. 369; Obradović 1978, S. 259.
[17] In den meisten anderen zugänglichen empirischen Untersuchungen der jugoslawischen Soziologie stammen die Daten aus dem Ende der sechziger Jahre, sie sind also leider nicht brandneu; allerdings ergeben sich zu denen aus der ersten Hälfte der siebziger Jahre keine wichtigen Unterschiede.
[18] Vgl. Arzensěk 1978, S. 380.
[19] Vgl. Rus 1978, S. 205; Bučar 1978, S. 420.
[20] Vgl. Gorupić 1978, S. 152; Jovanov 1978, S. 357.
[21] Vgl. Jovanov 1978, S. 357 ff.[22] Vgl. Hagemann/Klemencić 1974, S. 138.
[23] Vgl. Teuteberg 1961.
[24] Vgl. Staehelin 1979, Prosi 1978, Ortlieb 1975, Sachverständigenkommission 1970.
[25] Vgl. Gukelberger 1974, Deppe 1969; so auch die Kritik der Dissertation von Hohmann-Dennhardt 1979, S. 154, 158.
[26] Vgl. dazu Vilmar 1981, S. 271–296.
[27] Vgl. Staehelin 1979, S. 107; Günter/Scholl 1981, S. 141; Kißler/Scholten 1981, S. 185.
[28] Vgl. Inhoffen 1979, S. 127 f.
[29] Vgl. Kißler/Scholten 1981, S. 185, 188, 195, 198 f.; vgl. auch Heinrich 1981, S. 244.
[30] Vgl. Inhoffen 1979, S. 126.
[31] Vgl. dazu auch Lehmbruch 1981, S. 237–264; vgl. auch Willey 1971, S. 49: "In the union political process as in the American, a plurality of power centers and real opposition exists; leadership decisions are often checked; leaders sometimes loose elections; and no ruling elite can be found." Vgl. auch Wilke 1979.

Literatur

Arzenšek, V. (1978): Managerial Legitimacy and Organizational Conflict. In: Obradović, J. / Dunn, W. N (Hrsg.), S. 374–389.

Bolcić, S. (1972): The Value System of a Participatory Economy. In: Pusić, E. (Hrsg.), S. 97–112.

Bučar, F. (1978): Participation of State and Political Organizations in Enterprise Decisions. In: Obradović, N. / Dunn, W. N. (Hrsg.), S. 416–434.

Deppe, F., u. a. (1969): *Kritik der Mitbestimmung. Partnerschaft oder Klassenkampf?* Frankfurt/M.

Diefenbacher, H. / Nutzinger, H. G. (Hrsg.) (1981): *Mitbestimmung. Probleme und Perspektiven der empirischen Forschung.* Frankfurt/M., New York.

Gorupić, D. (1978): The Worker-Managed Enterprise (II). Recent Institutional Changes. In: Obradović, N. / Dunn, W. N. (Hrsg.), S. 137–154.

Gukelberger, W. (1974): Kritik bürgerlicher Mitbestimmungskonzeptionen. In: *Sozialistische Politik* 28, S. 3–58.

Günter, P. / Scholl, W. (1981): Mitbestimmung bei Personal- und Investitionsfragen. In: Diefenbacher, H. / Nutzinger, H. G. (Hrsg.), S. 115–142.

Hagemann, M. / Klemencić, A. (1974): *Die sozialistische Marktwirtschaft Jugoslawiens.* Stuttgart.

Heinrich, M. (1981): Information und Kontrolle bei repräsentativer Mitbestimmung. In: Diefenbacher, H. / Nutzinger, H. G. (Hrsg.), S. 219–248.

Hohmann-Dennhardt, C. (1979): *Entscheidungsstrukturen in Unternehmen und Arbeitnehmerinteressen. Zur Effektivität der Mitbestimmung bei Betriebsänderungen.* Frankfurt/M.

Horvat, B. / Marković, M. / Supek, R. (Hrsg.) (1975): *Self-governing Socialism. A Reader. Bd. 1: Historical Development, Social and Political Philosophy.* New York.

Inhoffen, A. O. (1979): *Die Entlassung von Arbeitnehmern in der mitbestimmten Unternehmung.* Stuttgart.

Jovanov, N. (1972a): Définitions théorique de la notion et de l'essence de l'autogestion en Yougoslavie. In: Pusić, E. (Hrsg.), S. 9–17.

Jovanov, N. (1972b): Le Rapport entre la grève comme conflit social et l'autogestion comme système social. In: Pusić, E. (Hrsg.), S. 52–96.

Jovanov, N. (1978): Strikes and Self-Management. In: Obradović, J. / Dunn, W. N. (Hrsg.), S. 339–373.

Kardelj, E. (1976): *Toward a New Type of Socialist Democracy.* Belgrad.

Kißler, L. / Schulten, U. (1981): Mitbestimmung als Kommunikationsproblem. In: Diefenbacher, H. / Nutzinger, H. G. (Hrsg.), S. 183–218.

Lehmbruch, G. (1981): Die ambivalenten Funktionen politischer Beteiligung in hochindustrialisierten Demokratien. In: Diefenbacher, H. / Nutzinger, H. G. (Hrsg.), S. 237–264.

Obradović, J. (1978): Participation in Enterprise Decision-Making. In: Obradović, N. / Dunn, W. H. (Hrsg.), S. 232–262.

Obradović, J. / Dunn, W. N. (1978): *Workers' Self-Management and Organizational Power in Yugoslavia.* Pittsburgh.

Ortlieb, H.-D. (1975): Mitbestimmung in unserer arbeitsteiligen Leistungsgesellschaft. In: *Hamburger Jahrbuch für Wirtschafts- und Gesellschaftspolitik* 20, S. 27–49.

Prosi, G. (1978): Volkswirtschaftliche Auswirkungen des Mitbestimmungsgesetzes von 1976. Köln.

Pusić, E. (Hrsg.) (1972): *First International Conference on Participation and Self-Management.* Bd. 1, Zagreb.

Rus, V. (1978a): Enterprise Power Structure. In: Obradović, J. / Dunn, W. N. (Hrsg.), S. 199–217.

Rus, V. (1978b): External and Internal Influences on Enterprises. In: Obradović, N. / Dunn, W. N. (Hrsg.), S. 406.

Sachverständigenkommission zur Auswertung der bisherigen Erfahrungen bei der Mitbestimmung. Bochum 1970 (Bundestagsdrucksache VI/334).

Staehelin, R. M. (1979): *Mitbestimmung in Europa.* Zürich.

Teuteberg, H.-J. (1961): *Geschichte der industriellen Mitbestimmung in Deutschland.* Tübingen.

Vejnović, M. (1978): Influence Structure in a Self-Managing Enterprise. In: Obradović, N. / Dunn, W. N. (Hrsg.), S. 263–278.

Verba, S. / Nie, N. H. (1972): *Participation in America.* New York, Evanston, San Francisco, London.

Verba, S. / Nie, N. H. / Jae-on, K. (1971): *The Modes of Democratic Participation.* London.

Vilmar, F. (1981): Mitbestimmung am Arbeitsplatz. Normierungsversuche. In: Diefenbacher, H. / Nutzinger, H. G. (Hrsg.), S. 271–296.

Willey, R. J. (1971): *Democracy in the West German Trade Unions: A Reappraisal of the "Iron Law"*. Sage Professional Papers in Comparative Politics, Series No. 01–023.
Wilke, M. (1979): *Die Funktionäre. Apparat und Demokratie im Deutschen Gewerkschaftsbund*. München.
Zupanov, J. (1978): Two Patterns of Conflict Management in Industry. In: Obradović, J. / Dunn, W. N. (Hrsg.), S. 390–399.
Zvonarević, M. (1978): Social Power, Information and Motivation. In: Obradović, J. / Dunn, W. N. (Hrsg.), S. 175–198.

Zur normativen Ökonomik privater Umverteilung – eine Problemskizze

Werner Steden

Abstract

On the Normative Economics of Private Redistribution – An Outline of Problems

In this paper neoclassical preference theory is taken as the general theoretical basis for an attempt to formulate, in contrast to the Rawlsian theory of justice, a normative economics of (re)distribution.

First, the theory of distributive preferences is presented. In theory, distributive preferences of an individual can be described by a preference function with own income and the incomes of other persons as arguments. That means that distributive preferences involve interpersonal externalities. The shape of the preference function is being discussed on the assumption of various motives (egoism vs. altruism; envy vs. solidarity).

Secondly, the criterion of distributive efficiency in the Paretian sense is formulated and a provisional and loose criterion of distributional justice is added. Using both criteria, individual distributive behaviour is analysed for the two-persons and the general n-persons case. Interpersonal externalities in this context cause distributive inefficiencies, i.e. a failure of private distributive action. Individual norms of distributive justice have a conflicting character which is cleared up by applicating the merit wants argument, and causes further insufficiencies of private distributive action.

Summarizing, the analogous use of both arguments, externalities and merit wants, well-known in allocation theory, allows a clear distinction between individual and collective distributive aims, and indicates the way in which a theory of state distributive action should be developed.

1. Vorbemerkung

Im folgenden geht es um den Entwurf einer normativen Verteilungstheorie. Jedes Mitglied unserer Gesellschaft hegt subjektive Vorstellungen darüber, wie die Früchte des gemeinsamen Produktionsprozesses aufgeteilt werden sollten. Derartige Verteilungsvorstellungen bilden einen wesentlichen Bestandteil individueller

Präferenzsysteme. Sie bestimmen das distributive Individualverhalten der Einzelmenschen untereinander. Sie beeinflussen das Stimmverhalten der Bürger im demokratischen Willensbildungsprozeß, das Verhalten der Politiker bei der Umsetzung des Wählerwillens und das distributive Verhalten der staatlichen Kollektive. Diese Verteilungsvorstellungen lassen sich auch präferenztheoretisch darstellen, und zwar in Form von interpersonellen und sozialen Präferenzabhängigkeiten. Sie sollten daher von der normativen Ökonomik berücksichtigt werden[1].

Das nationalökonomische Denken hat sich dieser Einsicht weitgehend entzogen. Dafür boten sich außerhalb des verteilungstheoretischen Bereichs gute Rechtfertigungsgründe. Die Vernachlässigung interpersoneller und sozialer Präferenzabhängigkeiten brachte der Theorieformulierung nämlich im allgemeinen einen großen Gewinn an formaler Eleganz und Einfachheit und erleichterte die Ableitung einzelner Theoreme ganz entscheidend. Im Bereich der normativen Verteilungstheorie, der es um die Ökonomik des (Um)Verteilungsgeschäfts geht, veränderte die Vernachlässigung aber anders als z. B. im Bereich der Allokationstheorie den Inhalt der zentralen Aussagen oder verhinderte sogar deren Ableitung[2]; sie hätte daher auf keinen Fall hingenommen werden dürfen. Diese Vernachlässigung ist der Hauptgrund dafür, daß es der Wohlfahrtsökonomie bis auf den heutigen Tag nicht gelungen ist, eine normative Verteilungstheorie auszuformulieren.

Im folgenden wird daher von der Annahme interpersoneller und sozialer Präferenzabhängigkeiten als Niederschlag vorgegebener individueller Verteilungsvorstellungen ausgegangen und versucht, die Grundlagen einer normativ ausgerichteten ökonomischen Verteilungstheorie noch einmal neu zu durchdenken. Die Überlegungen erstrecken sich ausschließlich auf den Bereich des privaten (Um)-Verteilungsverhaltens innerhalb der mikroökonomischen Theorie. Sie werden bis zu dem Punkt fortgeführt, wo eine ökonomische Theorie staatlichen Umverteilungshandelns einzusetzen hätte. Die Analyse erfolgt bei fast völligem Absehen von allokativen Effizienzaspekten, jedoch bei Berücksichtigung gewisser ethischer Implikationen, die mit den vorgegebenen subjektiven Verteilungsvorstellungen und dem durch sie gesteuerten Umverteilungshandeln verbunden sein können. Abschnitt 2 enthält die präferenztheoretischen Grundlagen; Abschnitt 3 unterzieht das private Umverteilungshandeln einer normativen Beurteilung.

2. Die präferenztheoretischen Grundlagen

2.1. Allgemeine Formulierung der Präferenzfunktion

Der Einfachheit halber wird im folgenden von einer Welt ausgegangen, in der die einzelnen Wirtschaftssubjekte gezwungen sind, im Erwerbsprozeß den gleichen Freizeitverzicht zu leisten, in der sie über kein Vermögen verfügen, das ihnen ein

Vermögenseinkommen abwerfen könnte[3], und in der volle Transparenz über die Einkommensverhältnisse anderer Personen herrscht. Diese Welt umfasse zur weiteren Vereinfachung nur zwei Personen. Wenn in dieser Welt die beiden Individuen i und j im Prozeß der Einkommensverteilung einander Gerechtigkeit widerfahren lassen wollen, hat das zur Folge, daß die Wohlfahrt des einen von der Wohlfahrt des anderen abhängt. Ihre Präferenzfunktion, mit deren Formulierung die distributive Grundentscheidung der Individuen fixiert ist, läßt sich daher wie folgt spezifizieren:

(1) $U_k = U_k^*(Y_k, U_l)$ $\quad k, l \in \{i, j\}$, $k \neq l$

wobei

U_k = Präferenzniveau des k,
Y_k = Einkommen des k.

Wegen der Unmöglichkeit, das Präferenzniveau eines anderen Menschen in seinem absoluten Niveau kardinal zu messen bzw. mit dem eigenen Präferenzniveau zu vergleichen, sind die beiden Individuen auf subjektive Schätzungen über das Präferenzniveau des jeweils anderen angewiesen. Derartige Schätzungen lassen sich zwar nicht exakt begründen und interpersonell überprüfen, werden aber tatsächlich angestellt. Demnach lautet die Präferenzfunktion statt (1):

(2) $U_k = U_k^*(Y_k, \hat{U}_l)$

mit

$\hat{U}_l$ = Schätzwert des k für das Präferenzniveau des l.

Bei dem Versuch, sich eine Vorstellung von dem Präferenzniveau des anderen zu machen, stellt ein Individuum fest, daß auch das andere Gerechtigkeitsvorstellungen hegt, so daß auch dessen Präferenzniveau von Schätzungen über das Präferenzniveau seines Gegenüber bestimmt ist. Es wird das Präferenzniveau des anderen mit einer Schätzfunktion S abzuschätzen versuchen, in der die vermutete fremde Einschätzung der eigenen Wohlfahrtsposition wiederum als Argument auftritt:

(3) $\hat{U}_l = S_k(Y_l, \hat{\hat{U}}_k)$

mit

S_k = Schätzfunktion des k für das Präferenzniveau des l
$\hat{\hat{U}}_k$ = vermutete Einschätzung des eigenen Präferenzniveaus durch Individuum l

und so fort.

Auf diese Weise ist das Individuum gezwungen, in einem unendlichen Regreß wechselseitig gerichteter Vermutungen die fremden Gerechtigkeitsvorstellungen und die fremde Einschätzung der relativen Wohlfahrtspositionen auszumachen und in sein Gerechtigkeitskalkül einzubeziehen bzw. zu internalisieren. Weisen die dabei in der Art von Funktion (3) unterstellten Schätzfunktionen mit zunehmendem Regreßfortschritt bestimmte Konvergenzeigenschaften auf, kann das gesamte Kalkül in einer mathematisch stark reduzierten Form beschrieben werden. In dieser Form ist das Präferenzniveau der beiden Individuen allein abhängig von der Größe des eigenen und des fremden Einkommens:

$$(4) \qquad U_k = U_k(Y_k, Y_l) \qquad k, l \in \{i, j\} \quad k \neq l$$

Hat ein Individuum keine persönlichen Beziehungen zu dem anderen und damit keine Anhaltspunkte über dessen Gerechtigkeitsvorstellungen oder kann es die über Schätzfunktion (3) ausgemachte Verteilungspräferenz des anderen nicht akzeptieren[4], so kann es sich auf den Grundsatz der Reziprozität oder Gegenseitigkeit als Grundsatz fairen Verhaltens berufen, auf den sich auch der kategorische Imperativ Kants und das christliche Gebot der Nächstenliebe stützen. Es unterstellt dem anderen Individuum auf dem Wege eines zusätzlichen distributiven Werturteils gleiche Gerechtigkeitsnormen und ersetzt die Schätzfunktion (3) durch seine eigene Präferenzfunktion (2), die jetzt aber in reziproker Weise, aus der Perspektive des anderen, also mit vertauschten Personenindices, auf das Verteilungsverhältnis zwischen beiden angewendet wird. Dabei kann das Individuum der Einfachheit halber subjektive Sicherheit hinsichtlich der Wohlfahrt der anderen Person unterstellen. – Auch in diesem Fall gelangt man im Endeffekt zu Präferenzfunktion (4)[5].

Die Präferenzfunktion (4) sei lediglich für positive Einkommen und ordinal gemessene Präferenzniveaus definiert. Sie weise im gesamten Definitionsbereich einen stetigen Verlauf auf und sei, abgesehen von den im folgenden angesprochenen Grenzlinien, zweimal differenzierbar. Innerhalb eines Ausschnitts des Präferenzraumes, der durch eine fest vorgegebene Untergrenze und eine fest vorgegebene Obergrenze der Einkommensaufteilung begrenzt sei, verlaufen ihre Indifferenzkurven strikt konvex zum Koordinatenursprung. Innerhalb des so abgegrenzten Bereichs gelte daher für zwei beliebige gleich bewertete Einkommenssituationen (Y_{i1}, Y_{j1}) und (Y_{i2}, Y_{j2}):

$$(5) \qquad U_k(Y_{ks}, Y_{ls}) < U_k(\varkappa \cdot Y_{k1} + [1 - \varkappa] \cdot Y_{k2}, \; \varkappa \cdot Y_{l1} + [1 - \varkappa] \cdot Y_{l2})$$

für

$$k, l \in \{i, j\} \quad k \neq l$$

$$s \in \{1, 2\}$$
$$O < \varkappa < 1$$
$$O \leqslant G_{ku} < \frac{Y_{ks}}{Y_{ls}} < G_{ko} \leqslant \infty$$

wobei:

G_{ku} = Untergrenze der rel. Einkommensposition des k
G_{ko} = Obergrenze der rel. Einkommensposition des k

Diese Konvexitätsgesellschaft läßt sich im Anschluß an (2) und (3) dadurch begründen, daß die Individuen von ihrem Gerechtigkeitsempfinden her geringfügigen Unterschieden des individuellen Wohlergehens verhältnismäßig gleichgültig gegenüberstehen, während marginale Vergrößerungen der Unterschiede ihrem Gerechtigkeitsempfinden immer stärker widersprechen, daß diese Unterschiede aber generell durch einkommensmäßige Kompensationsleistungen präferenzmäßig ausgeglichen werden können.

Das totale Differential der Funktion bzw. der Niveaugrenznutzen sei nichtnegativ. Für eine beliebige Zahl λ gelte daher:

(6) $$\frac{\vartheta U_k(\lambda \cdot Y_k, \lambda \cdot Y_l)}{\vartheta \lambda} \geqslant O$$

Der Fall eines Niveaugrenznutzens von Null ist hierbei nur von lokaler Bedeutung und das auch nur in einem später noch angesprochenen Spezialfall[6].

Schließlich sei die Funktion homothetisch. Ihre Skalenelastizität sei für Einkommenskombinationen, die präferenzmäßig gleich bewertet werden, gleich, für Einkommenskombinationen, die präferenzmäßig unterschiedlich bewertet werden, dagegen nicht unbedingt gleich. Für eine beliebige positive Zahl λ gelte daher:

(7) $$U_k(\lambda \cdot Y_k, \lambda \cdot Y_l) = U_k(Y_k, Y_l) \cdot V_k(\lambda)$$

wobei die Funktion V_k (λ) wegen der nur ordinalen Bestimmung des Präferenzniveaus bis auf

(8) $$V_k(\lambda) > O$$
$$V_k(1) = 1$$
$$\frac{dV_k(\lambda)}{d\lambda} > o$$

unbestimmt sei.

Aufgrund des homothetischen Charakters (7) ist das Verhältnis der beiden ersten Ableitungen der Funktion, die sog. Grenzrate der Substitution, eine ausschließliche Funktion der relativen Einkommensaufteilung, was alle weiteren Überlegungen vereinfacht:

$$(9) \qquad \frac{U_{kl}}{U_{kk}} = - R_k(Y_k/Y_l)$$

mit

U_{kl} = Grenznutzen des k bezogen auf das Einkommen des l; $k, l \in \{i, j\}$

R = Grenzrate der Substitution

Gleichzeitig wird mit der Annahme dieser Eigenschaft unterstellt, daß die Individuen einen prozentual gleichen Anstieg des eigenen und fremden Einkommens, wie er sich im Laufe des Wachstumsprozesses vollziehen könnte, bei allen u. U. vorhandenen Neidkomplexen positiv bewerten.

2.2. Das individuelle Verteilungsoptimum

Um das private Verteilungshandeln der Individuen vollständig zu beschreiben, sei als nächstes mit Hilfe von (4) bestimmt, wie eines der beiden Individuen i und j die von beiden originär erzielten Einkommen mit Hilfe von Transfers umverteilen würde, wenn es die Macht hätte, seine individuelle Verteilungsvorstellung ungehindert durchzusetzen. Zu diesem Zweck sei angenommen, daß das originär erzielte Einkommen beider zusammengenommen eine fest vorgegebene Größe $\bar{Y}$ sei. Dann gilt für das distributive Entscheidungskalkül des Individuums die Budgetgleichung:

$$(10) \qquad \bar{Y} = \sum_{k=i,j} Y_k$$

Gleichung (10) beschreibt die objektiven Umverteilungsmöglichkeiten zwischen den beiden Individuen, stellt also eine Transformationsfunktion für Umverteilungsaktionen dar, die auch dem späteren gesamtwirtschaftlichen Verteilungskalkül zugrunde gelegt wird.

Wenn das Individuum sich in Hinsicht auf seine distributiven Ziele rational verhält, wird es die Präferenzfunktion (4) unter Wahrung der Budgetbedingungen (10) maximieren und das Gesamteinkommen mit Hilfe von Transfers so auf sich und das andere Individuum aufteilen, daß die Grenzrate der Substitution und die Grenzrate der Transformation einander gleich sind.

$$(11) \qquad \frac{U_{kl}}{U_{kk}} = - \frac{dY_k}{dY_l} = 1$$

Mit der Ableitung des individuellen Verteilungsoptimums in (11) ist das private

Verteilungshandeln, soweit es keinen eigentumsrechtlichen Restriktionen unterliegt, formal eindeutig bestimmt.

2.3. Die Richtung der Verteilungspräferenz

Das individuelle Verteilungsverhalten kann inhaltlich noch stärker präzisiert werden, indem zwei Eigenschaften der Präferenzfunktion (4) unterschieden werden, die als Richtung und Stärke der Verteilungspräferenz bezeichnet seien und im folgenden für eines der beiden Individuen, i, definiert werden. Das Merkmal Richtung der Verteilungspräferenz stellt darauf ab, daß das Individuum i von seiner Wertschätzung her einer bestimmten relativen Aufteilung des Gesamteinkommens vor allen anderen Aufteilungen den Vorzug gibt. Wegen des angenommenen homothetischen Charakters (7) der Präferenzfunktion (4) ist diese durch das individuelle Verteilungsoptimum festgelegte relative Aufteilung unabhängig von der absoluten Größe des Gesamteinkommens. In der Indifferenzkurvenanalyse liegen daher die Tangentialpunkte zwischen je einer Budgetlinie und einer Indifferenzkurve für jedes Gesamteinkommensniveau auf einem Fahrstrahl, der mit einer bestimmten Steigung α ($= dY_i/dY_j$) durch den Ursprung des Koordinatensystems verläuft (Fig. 1). Diese Steigung α des Fahrstrahls dient hier als Maßgröße für die Richtung der Verteilungspräferenz. Verläuft der Fahrstrahl im (Y_i, Y_j)-Diagramm mit einer Steigung von $\alpha = 1$, also auf der 45°-Linie durch den Koordinatenursprung, wird im folgenden von einer Gleichverteilungspräferenz gesprochen.

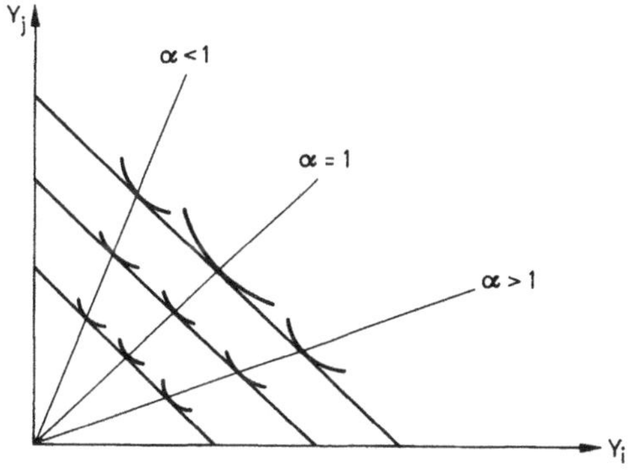

Fig. 1

Könnte man von einer allgemein anerkannten Gleichheit in beruflicher Leistung und persönlicher Bedürftigkeit der Individuen ausgehen und von speziellen Präferenzausprägungen, die sich aus persönlicher Nähe, Sympathie, Antipathie und dergleichen ergeben, absehen, ließen sich die unterschiedlichen Richtungen der Verteilungspräferenz von einem ethischen Standpunkt aus relativ einfach beurteilen. Die oben genannte Gleichverteilungspräferenz entspräche unter diesen Annahmen offensichtlich mehr als jede anders gerichtete Verteilungspräferenz dem allgemeinen Ideal gerechten Verhaltens, wie es im Gebot der christlichen Nächstenliebe und im kategorischen Imperativ von Kant formuliert ist.

Läge das Verteilungsoptimum des i auf dem rechten, unteren Ast der Budgetlinien von Fig. 1 bzw. auf einem Fahrstrahl mit der Steigung $\alpha > 1$, handelte es sich unter den genannten Bedingungen eindeutig um das Phänomen des Egoismus[7]. Egoismus wirkt sich dementsprechend in einer Verzerrung der Präferenzfunktion aus, und zwar in dem Sinne, daß die Indifferenzkurvenschar des i im gesamten Verlauf in Richtung auf die Eigeneinkommens- bzw. Y_i-Achse verzerrt ist. Die marginale Einschätzung des fremden Einkommens, Y_j, im Vergleich zum eigenen Einkommen, Y_i, bzw. die entsprechende Grenzrate der Substitution ist dann auf der Gleichverteilungs- bzw. 45°-Linie für i zwangsläufig kleiner als eins.

Der Fall $\alpha < 1$ kann in ähnlicher Weise gedanklich mit dem Phänomen des Altruismus verknüpft werden. Altruismus ist demnach das volle Gegenstück zum Egoismus und impliziert eine Verzerrung der Präferenzfunktion in die entgegengesetzte Richtung. Am Modellfall einer anonymen Gesellschaft, in der sich jedes Individuum jedem anderen gegenüber unterschiedslos, d. h. ohne Ansehen der Person, verhält, erkennt man, daß eine solche altruistisch bedingte Verzerrung der Präferenzfunktion wahrscheinlich eine verhältnismäßig seltene Erscheinung ist. Im Prinzip müßte der so definierte Altruismus aus der größeren Wertschätzung der Bedürfnisse der fremden Person im Vergleich zu den Bedürfnissen der eigenen Person erklärt werden; d. h. das distributive Verhalten wäre auf den selbstlosen Dienst an den höher bewerteten Bedürfnissen der fremden Person ausgerichtet[8]. Oder dieser Altruismus diente lediglich dazu, sich mit dem Verzicht auf den allgemein zugestandenen materiellen Wohlstand eine subjektiv höher bewertete soziale Anerkennung durch die Gesellschaft zu verschaffen.

Die Annahme einer allgemein anerkannten Gleichheit der Individuen in beruflicher Leistung und persönlicher Bedürftigkeit ist sicher unrealistisch und kann nicht aufrechterhalten werden. Egoismus und Altruismus sind daher nicht die einzigen Ursachen für ein Abweichen individueller Verteilungsvorstellungen von der Gleichverteilungspräferenz. Eine Person kann andere Bedürfnis- und Leistungstatbestände als Zuteilungskriterien im gesellschaftlichen Prozeß der Einkommensbemessung für relevant erachten als die Allgemeinheit. Teilt sie die allgemeine Übereinkunft hinsichtlich der verteilungsrelevanten Bedürfnis- und Leistungstatbestände, kann sie immer noch von anderen Bewertungsgrundsätzen ausgehen als die Allgemeinheit, und das könnte z. B. deswegen legitim sein, weil das bestehende System der Marktpreise seine Bewertungsfunktion infolge der Unvollständigkeit des Wettbewerbs und anderer „imperfections" nur unvollkommen wahrnimmt und weil das verteilungsmäßige Endergebnis des marktlichen Bewertungsprozesses nach allen allokationstheoretischen Überlegungen selbst nicht unabhängig von der zufällig bestehenden Ausgangsverteilung der Ressourcenbestände ist. Hat ein Individuum daher den begründeten Eindruck, daß bei der vorgefundenen Verteilung der Einkommen die gesonderte persönliche Bedürftigkeit oder die spezifische berufliche Leistungsabgabe im Erwerbsprozeß nicht ausreichend erfaßt oder angemessen bewertet wird, so daß daraus für die eigene oder fremde Person ungerechtfertigte Einkommensnachteile entstehen, wird es trotz u. U. gleicher Einkommen für eine Umverteilung zu Gunsten der benachteiligten Personen plädieren. D. h. in Präferenzfunktion (4) wird der Nachteil aus der Schlechterfassung oder Fehlbewertung dieser Tatbestände dadurch ausgeglichen, daß die Verteilungspräferenz von der Gleichverteilung in Richtung auf einen höheren Einkommensanteil der benachteiligten Person abweicht. Neben Egoismus und Altruismus sind also auch Motive der Bedarfs- und Leistungsgerechtigkeit, die bisher nur implizit berücksichtigt wurden, Grund für ein Abweichen der Verteilungspräferenz von der Gleichverteilung[9].

Andererseits läßt sich die Präferenz für eine mehr oder weniger vollständige Gleichverteilung auch nicht zwangsläufig auf Gerechtigkeitsstreben zurückführen und als ethisch wertvoll qualifizieren. Die Literatur führt Unsicherheitsüberlegungen an, die auf Rückversicherungsverhalten und Risikoaversion abstellen. Danach veranlassen die Furcht vor dem Verteilungskampf bzw. vor der Revolution der Einkommensschwachen[10] und der Versuch, sich gegen das Risiko eigener Armut abzusichern[11], die Reichen, einer Umverteilung zu Gunsten der Armen zuzustimmen. Einer solchen (Um)Verteilungspräferenz liegt offensichtlich kein Gerechtigkeitsmotiv zugrunde.

Insgesamt kann daher nur behauptet werden, daß der Präferenzfunktion (4) Verteilungsvorstellungen zugrunde liegen, die sich in den erfaßten Präferenzabhängigkeiten niederschlagen, daß die präferierte Einkommensverteilung infolge des Vorherrschens einer mehr oder weniger egoistischen Grundmotivation wahrscheinlich häufiger von der Gleichverteilungspräferenz in Richtung auf eine höhere eigene Verteilungsposition abweicht als in umgekehrter Richtung und daß die so bestimmte Verteilungspräferenz sowohl durch rein egoistische Bedürfnisse wie durch individuelles, wenn auch egoistisch verzerrtes Gerechtigkeitsstreben motiviert sein kann. Darüber hinaus bleiben die Motive für das durch Präferenzfunktion (4) beschriebene Umverteilungshandeln unbestimmt und können auch nicht ethisch beurteilt werden.

2.4. Die Stärke der Verteilungspräferenz

Das Merkmal Stärke der Verteilungspräferenz stellt darauf ab, mit welcher Intensität ein Individuum in einer bestimmten Verteilungssituation seine spezifischen Verteilungsziele verfolgt. In der üblichen präferenztheoretischen Analyse würde dieses Merkmal durch die oben definierte Grenzrate der Substitution, R, oder die Substitutionselastizität der Präferenzfunktion, bezogen auf die beiden Individualeinkommen Y_i und Y_j erfaßt werden. Es erleichtert jedoch das Verständnis der folgenden, für die normative Verteilungstheorie wichtigen Überlegungen, wenn das Merkmal geometrisch dadurch veranschaulicht wird, wie eng sich in der angesprochenen Verteilungssituation die gerade relevante Indifferenzkurve um den zuvor beschriebenen Fahrstrahl der präferierten Einkommensverteilung schmiegt, d. h. wenn auf die Präferenzeinbußen abgestellt wird, die das Individuum aus der Abweichung vom individuellen Verteilungsoptimum erfährt.

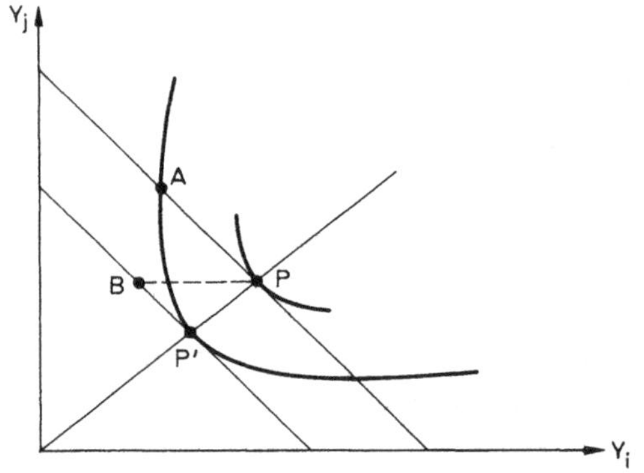

Fig. 2

In Figur 2 wird für Individuum i von zwei Indifferenzkurven und zwei Budgetlinien ausgegangen. Je eine Indifferenzkurve und eine Budgetlinie berühren einander und kennzeichnen damit für unterschiedliche Präferenz- und Einkommensniveaus ein individuelles Verteilungsoptimum, P bzw. P', das auf der Linie der von i präferierten Einkommensverteilung liegt. Die Indifferenzkurve für das niedrigere Präferenzniveau schneidet außerdem die Budgetlinie für das höhere Einkommensniveau in Punkt A. Strecke AP repräsentiert einen reinen Einkommenstransfereffekt bei unverändertem Einkommensniveau. Strecke PP' repräsentiert einen reinen Einkommensniveaueffekt bei unveränderter Einkommensverteilung.

Die Stärke der Verteilungspräferenz kann angesichts der Problematik einer kardinalen Wohlfahrtsmessung durch das Verhältnis von Einkommensniveau- zu Einkommenstransfereffekt gemessen werden. Dieses Maß bringt zum Ausdruck, welche Senkung des allgemeinen Einkommensniveaus i in Kauf zu nehmen bereit wäre, wenn dafür mit Hilfe eines Transfers statt der in A bestehenden Einkommensverteilung die von ihm präferierte Einkommensverteilung durchgesetzt würde, bzw. welche durchschnittlichen subjektiven Opportunitätskosten die Optimumabweichung je Geldeinheit des unterstellten Transfers verursacht. Da der Einkommensniveaueffekt in Figur 2 durch den horizontalen Abstand der beiden Budgetlinien gemessen werden kann, läßt sich das Maß für Punkt A bestimmen als:

$$\pi = \left| \frac{Y_{iB} - Y_{iP}}{Y_{iP} - Y_{iA}} \right| \tag{12}$$

Die Stärke der Verteilungspräferenz läßt sich in ähnlicher Weise auch marginal, d. h. für eine kleine zusätzliche Abweichung vom individuellen Verteilungsoptimum P darstellen, womit die subjektiven Grenzopportunitätskosten der Optimumabweichung ausgedrückt sind. Die algebraische Bestimmung dieser marginalen Stärke der Verteilungspräferenz ergibt im Anschluß an (4):

$$(13) \qquad \pi' = \left| - \frac{U_{ii} - U_{ij}}{\frac{Y_i}{Y_i + Y_j} U_{ii} + \frac{Y_j}{Y_i + Y_j} U_{ij}} \right|$$

und bei Beachtung von (9):

$$(14) \qquad \pi' = \left| - \frac{(Y_i + Y_j) \cdot (1 + R_i)}{Y_i - Y_j \cdot R_i} \right|$$

Mit Maß π und π' können nun die Eigenschaften der Präferenzfunktion (4) weiter veranschaulicht werden. Generell gilt für positive Einkommensniveaus, daß die durchschnittliche Stärke der Verteilungspräferenz und auch ihre Marginalgröße im indiviuellen Verteilungsoptimum des i gleich Null ist ($R_i = -1$). Marginalen Änderungen der Einkommensverteilung steht i im Verteilungsoptimum gleichgültig gegenüber, da die verursachte marginale Präferenzeinbuße nahezu Null ist. Solange die in (5) unterstellte Konvexitätseigenschaft der Präferenzfunktion besteht, führt eine zunehmende Abweichung vom Verteilungsoptimum aber zu zunehmenden marginalen Präferenzeinbußen; mit anderen Worten die beiden Maße π und π' steigen hier kontinuierlich an.

Es müssen zwei Funktionstypen unterschieden werden. Bei dem in der Präferenztheorie üblichen *ersten* Funktionstyp gilt für die in (5) genannten Unter- und Obergrenzen der Einkommensverteilung:

$$(15) \qquad O = G_u < \alpha < G_o = \infty$$

In diesem Fall verlaufen die Indifferenzkurven stets konvex zum Ursprung des Koordinatenraumes (Y_i, Y_j). Sie nähern sich asymptotisch den Koordinantenachsen oder schneiden sie. Die durch Abweichungen vom individuellen Verteilungsoptimum verursachte und in Einkommensniveau-Einheiten gemessene durchschnittliche Präferenzeinbuße nähert sich hier monoton einem kritischen Wert, den sie nicht überschreitet[12]:

$$(16) \qquad \lim_{Y_i/Y_j \to o} \pi \leqslant \frac{1 + \alpha}{\alpha}$$

bzw.

$$(17) \qquad \lim_{Y_i/Y_j \to \infty} \pi \leqslant 1 + \alpha$$

In Hinsicht auf diesen Sachverhalt wird hier von einer Präferenzfunktion mit stets *schwacher* Verteilungspräferenz gesprochen.

Der *zweite* Funktionstyp ist praktisch nur für die Verteilungstheorie von Bedeutung. Hier gilt für die in (5) genannten Unter- und Obergrenzen der Einkommensverteilung, G_u bzw. G_O

(18) $$O < G_u < \alpha < G_o < \infty$$

Innerhalb des durch (18) abgegrenzten Präferenzbereichs nähern sich die Indifferenzkurven, vom individuellen Verteilungsoptimum ausgehend, den Koordinatenachsen; sie schlagen aber, bevor sie diese erreichen, zurück ins Innere des Koordinatenraumes, um sich dort asymptotisch dem Fahrstrahl für die kritische Unter- bzw. Obergrenze der Einkommensverteilung, G_u bzw. G_o, zu nähern oder ihn zu schneiden. Hier steigt die durch Abweichungen vom individuellen Verteilungsoptimum verursachte und in Einkommensniveau-Einheiten gemessene durchschnittliche Präferenzeinbuße über das in (16) bzw. (17) angegebene Niveau hinaus und nähert sich einem kritischen Wert von

(19) $$\frac{1+\alpha}{\alpha} < \lim_{Y_i/Y_j \to G_u} \pi \leqslant \frac{1}{\dfrac{\alpha}{1+\alpha} - \dfrac{G_u}{1+G_u}}$$

bzw.

(20) $$1+\alpha < \lim_{Y_i/Y_j \to G_o} \pi \leqslant \frac{1}{\dfrac{G_o}{1+G_o} - \dfrac{\alpha}{1+\alpha}}$$

Nach Überschreiten der in (18) angegebenen kritischen Unter- bzw. Obergrenze der Einkommensverteilung sinkt die durchschnittliche Präferenzeinbuße wieder auf das in (16) bzw. (17) angegebene Niveau zurück. In Hinsicht darauf, daß die in Einkommensniveau-Einheiten gemessene durchschnittliche Präferenzeinbuße die in (16) bzw. (17) angegebenen Werte übersteigt, wird hier von dem Typ einer Präferenzfunktion mit *starker* Verteilungspräferenz gesprochen.

Dieser zweite Funktionstyp hat eine schwerwiegende präferenztheoretische Implikation. In dem Unterfall, in dem sich die Indifferenzkurven, vom individuellen Verteilungsoptimum ausgehend, der kritischen Unter- bzw. Obergrenze der Einkommensverteilung asymptotisch nähern, verfügt die Präferenzfunktion jenseits des durch G_u und G_o eingegrenzten Bereichs nicht mehr bzw. nur in einem ganz eingeschränkten Sinn über die in (5) genannte Konvexitätseigenschaft[13]. In diesem Außenbereich des Präferenzfeldes setzen sich die Indifferenzkurven aus zwei spitzwinklig im Koordinatenursprung zusammenlaufenden Indifferenzkurvenästen zusammen, die ein *negatives* Präferenzniveau indizieren (Fig. 3). Dies folgt daraus, daß die Linien für die kritischen Verteilungsgrenzen G_u und G_o in dem als stetig angenommenen Präferenzsystem die Funktion einer Indifferenzkurve wahrzunehmen haben, gleichzeitig aber dem homothetischen Charakter (7) der Präferenzfunktion Rechnung tragen müssen, was beides zugleich nur möglich ist, wenn das entsprechende Präferenzniveau den Wert Null hat.

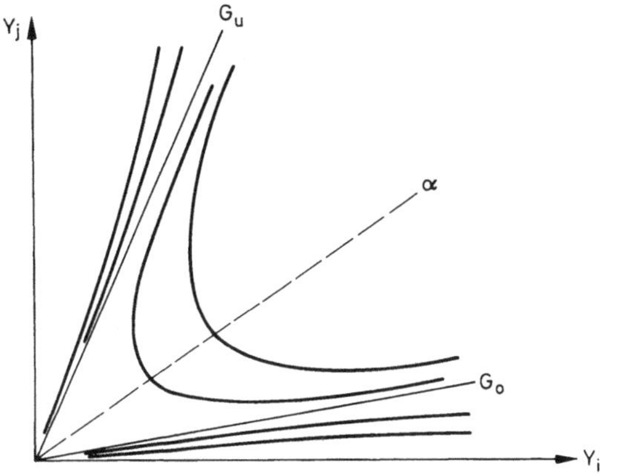

Fig. 3

Diese Implikation ist in dem zweiten Unterfall, in dem die Indifferenzkurven die kritischen Grenzlinien G_u und G_o schneiden und der als ein Mischtyp aus dem vorgenannten Unterfall und dem ersten Funktionstyp angesehen werden kann, nicht enthalten (Fig. 4):

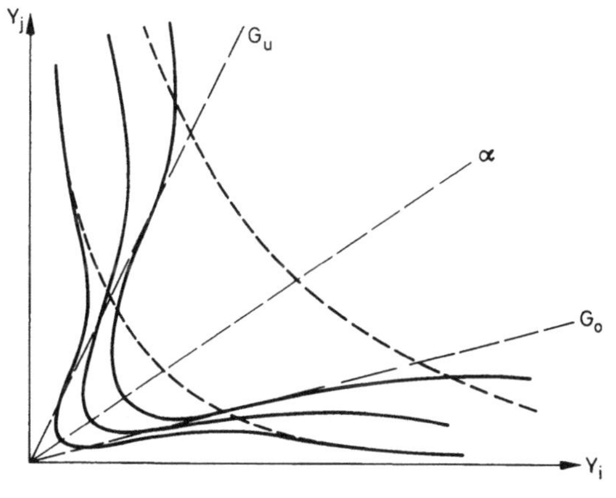

Fig. 4

In Hinsicht auf diese Unterscheidung sei der in Fig. 3 skizzierte Unterfall als der Extremfall einer Präferenzfunktion mit starker Verteilungspräferenz bezeichnet, denn allein in diesem Unterfall erreicht die Stärke der Verteilungspräferenz π den auf der rechten Ungleichungsseite von (19) bzw. (20) angegebenen Maximalwert.

Das Bestehen einer starken Verteilungspräferenz, bei dem es nach Überschreiten eines bestimmten Ausmaßes der Umverteilung[14] zu einem in der Präferenztheorie sonst seltenen und begrenzten Zurückschlagen der Indifferenzkurven von den Koordinatenachsen weg kommt, ist für die Theorie des Umverteilungshandelns von besonderer Bedeutung. Tritt dieses Phänomen an dem der Fremdeinkommensachse zugewandten Indifferenzkurvenast auf, kann dies durch das Vorliegen von Neid erklärt werden. Neidverhalten beruht darauf, daß der – erst positive – Grenznutzen des i, bezogen auf das fremde Einkommen Y_j, nicht nur mit steigendem Y_j sinkt, sondern nach Überschreiten eines bestimmten Y_j-Wertes sogar negativ wird. Neid ist also eine Übersättigungserscheinung[15]. Entsprechend kann das Dual zum Neidverhalten, das ein Zurückschlagen der Indifferenzkurve am anderen Kurvenende bewirkt, durch die Motive Mitleid und Solidarität oder durch Rücksicht auf das beschriebene Neidverhalten des jeweils anderen veranlaßt sein (Fig. 5):

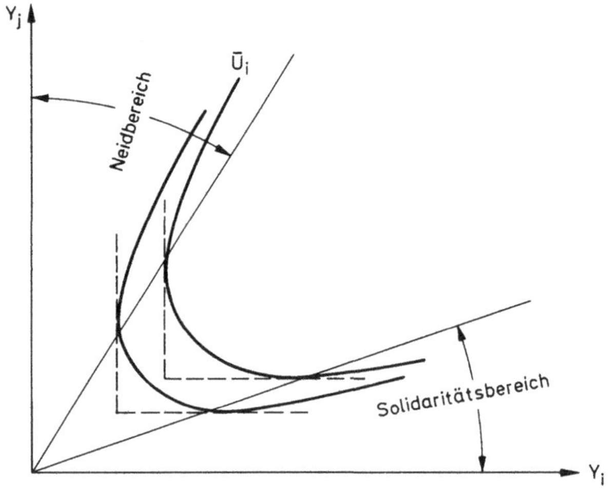

Fig. 5

Es ist jedoch zu beachten, daß die Stärke der Verteilungspräferenz nicht ohne weiteres auf bestimmte Verteilungsmotive wie Neid oder Mitleid zurückgeführt werden kann. Dies wird am ehesten deutlich am Fall einer dritten Person, die die Einkommensverteilung zwischen den Individuen i und j entsprechend beurteilt, ohne einkommensmäßig selbst an dem Verteilungsgeschehen zwischen beiden beteiligt zu sein. Die Behauptung einer starken Verteilungspräferenz besagt nur, daß Abweichungen von den präferierten Verteilungsrelationen zu starken Präferenzeinbußen führen. Das kann auf Neid und Mitleid, einem stark ausgeprägten Gerechtigkeitsempfinden oder irgendeinem anderen Motiv beruhen. Insofern kann allenfalls behauptet werden, daß eine starke Verteilungspräferenz allgemein distributive Strenge oder Intoleranz, eine schwache Verteilungspräferenz distributive Gleichgültigkeit oder Toleranz impliziere. Auch in Hinsicht auf diese Eigenschaft der Präferenzfunktion (4) zeigt sich also, daß die zugrundeliegenden Verteilungsmotive unbestimmt bleiben. Die Präferenztheorie sollte dies zur Kenntnis nehmen und sich darauf beschränken, das individuelle Verteilungshandeln ganz formal durch die beiden Eigenschaften Richtung und Stärke der Verteilungspräferenz zu umschreiben. Zumindest für die normative Argumentation im Rahmen der vorliegenden Analyse dürfte dies ausreichen. Die Motivation und ihre ethische Beurteilung bleiben daher im folgenden auch weitgehend außer Betracht[16].

Die Stärke der Verteilungspräferenz kennzeichnet im übrigen nur eine lokale Eigenschaft der Präferenzfunktion. Die Präferenzfunktion muß diesbezüglich nicht über irgendwelche Symmetrieeigenschaften verfügen. Gleiche transferbedingte Abweichungen vom individuellen Verteilungsoptimum zugunsten des fremden oder des eigenen Einkommens brauchen also nicht zwangsläufig gleiche distributive Präferenzeinbußen zu verursachen. Es könnte sein, daß ein Individuum der unangemessenen fremden Armut gegenüber strenge Solidarität übt, dem unangemessenen fremden Reichtum gegenüber aber hohe Toleranz walten läßt, was für den sozialen Frieden sicher nicht unerheblich wäre. Im Sinne einer strikten definitorischen Trennung der beiden Eigenschaften Richtung und Stärke der Verteilungspräferenz wäre diese asymmetrische Ausgestaltung der Präferenzfunktion theoretisch selbst auf seiten eines Egoisten vorstellbar. Tatsächlich dürfte jedoch die Erfahrung, daß Mitbürger die strenge Solidarität unangemessener fremder Armut gegenüber vermissen lassen, die Individuen veranlassen, sich unangemessenem fremden Reichtum gegenüber nicht mit tolerantem Stillhalten zu begnügen, sondern den subjektiven Anspruch auf Gerechtigkeit aktiv einzufordern. Von daher ist die Bildung der distributiven Präferenzfunktion doch Einflüssen in Richtung auf eine symmetrische Ausgestaltung ausgesetzt.

2.5. Bereitschaft zum Verteilungskampf

Bei Vorliegen einer starken Verteilungspräferenz muß mit einer Bereitschaft des Individuums zum Verteilungskampf gerechnet werden. Die Kampfbereitschaft ist im Neidfall leicht zu erkennen, weil hier das Individuum allein durch den Einkommensschaden des anderen und ohne Erhöhung des eigenen Einkommens präferenzmäßig besser gestellt wird und weil es nur wegen der grundsätzlichen Bejahung der privaten Eigentumsordnung, von dorther drohender Sanktionen, wegen anfallender Konfliktaustragungskosten oder fehlender Mittel von Kampfmaßnahmen Abstand nimmt.

Um das Phänomen der Kampfbereitschaft mit Hilfe von Präferenzfunktion (4) zu präzisieren, wird im folgenden das Präferenzniveau des Individuums i für Verteilungssituationen entlang der vorgegebenen Transformationslinie analysiert. Dabei wird auf den Extremfall einer starken Verteilungspräferenz abgestellt, wie er durch Fig. 3 beschrieben wurde. Ist der strikt konvexe Verlauf der Indifferenzkurven von Fig. 3 innerhalb des durch die Grenzlinien G_u und G_o abgegrenzten Bereichs durch strenge Konkavität der Präferenzfunktion bedingt und die durchgängige Nicht-Konvexität der Indifferenzkurven außerhalb des durch G_u und G_o

abgegrenzten Bereichs durch das vollständige Fehlen jeglicher Konkavitätseigenschaften[17], dann wird das Präferenzniveau entlang der Budgetlinie durch einen Kurvenverlauf zum Ausdruck gebracht, wie er beispielsweise in Fig. 6 skizziert ist.

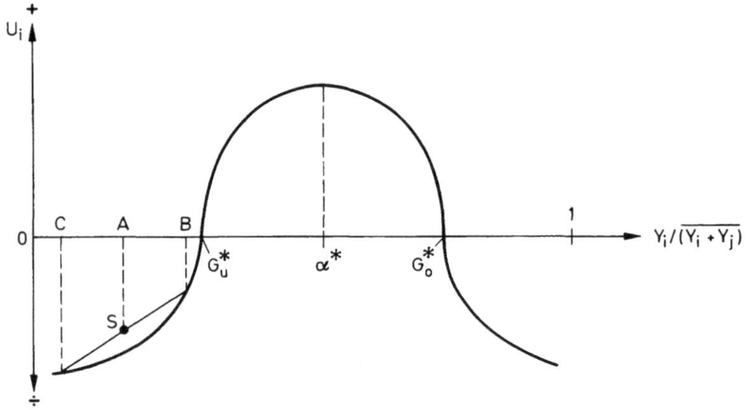

Fig. 6

$\alpha^* = \alpha/(1 + \alpha)$
$G_u^* = G_u/(1 + G_u)$
$G_o^* = G_o/(1 + G_o)$

Es sei angenommen, Individuum i befinde sich verteilungsmäßig zu Beginn in Punkt A von Fig. 6 und damit im Bereich $O < Y_i/Y_j < G_u$; eine Kampfmaßnahme biete ihm mit gleicher Wahrcheinlichkeit eine Verbesserung oder eine entsprechende Verschlechterung seiner relativen Verteilungsposition, und zwar nach Punkt B bzw. C. Dann wird i diese Maßnahme ergreifen, denn der wahrscheinlichkeitsgewogene Durchschnitt der so erreichbaren Präferenzniveaus, der durch den Abstand des Sekantenpunktes S vom Abszissenpunkt A bestimmt ist, liegt über dem Präferenzniveau im Status quo der Ausgangssituation. Es gilt: $O{,}5 \cdot (U_{iB} + U_{iC}) > U_{iA}$.

Befände sich i in der Ausgangssituation innerhalb des Bereichs $G_u < Y_i/Y_j < G_o$, läge der Erwartungsnutzen einer solchen Kampfmaßnahme unter dem sicheren Nutzen des verteilungsmäßigen Status quo. Das Individuum würde daher die Aktion unterlassen, obwohl auch hier schon der Bereich einer starken Verteilungspräferenz erreicht sein könnte.

Die Kampfbereitschaft des i ist also bei Unterschreiten der kritischen Verteilungsuntergrenze G_u durch erhöhte Risikobereitschaft gekennzeichnet. Dies kann als Ausdruck für einen erhöhten Grad der Kampfbereitschaft angesehen werden.

2.6. Verteilungsgruppen im Mehr-Personen-Fall

Verallgemeinert man Präferenzfunktion (4) für den Mehr-Personen-Fall, so läßt sich vorstellen, daß Individuum i die Personen, von denen es präferenzmäßig abhängig ist, nach Art und Umfang seiner Präferenzabhängigkeit zu homogenen Personengruppen ordnet. Diese Gruppen lassen sich ähnlich wie Gütergruppen oder Faktorbündel mit Hilfe der Substitutionselastizität oder auch mit Hilfe der Maße π und π' für die Stärke der Verteilungspräferenz identifizieren.

Sind die distributiven Präferenzfunktionen der Individuen oder verschiedener Gruppen von Individuen in ähnlicher Weise strukturiert, so ist zu erwarten, daß diese sich auch organisatorisch zu distributiven Zweckverbänden zusammenschließen[18]. Dies können Gruppen sein, die über interne Transfers eine Angleichung der relativen Einkommenspositionen unter ihren Mitgliedern vornehmen[19]. Es können Gruppen potentieller Transferempfänger oder Gruppen potentieller Transfergeber sein, die der kollektiven Artikulation und Realisierung distributiver Präferenzen nach außen dienen. Unter Umständen handelt es sich um Angriffs- bzw. Abwehrgruppen im Verteilungskampf[20].

Es gehört wohl zum Charakter einer solchen organisierten Gruppe, gleich ob sie als private Kleingruppe oder als anonyme Großgruppe in Erscheinung tritt, daß der Zusammenschluß einen Prozeß der Abklärung und Rationalisierung der gemeinsamen Verteilungsnormen unter den Mitgliedern nach sich zieht. Aufgrund der Teilnahme an diesem Prozeß kommt es zu einer verstärkten Internalisierung der von der Gruppe vertretenen Verteilungsnormen im Vergleich zu den sonst gehegten Verteilungsnormen. Dies kann dazu führen, daß sich in dem in Abschnitt 2.1 beschriebenen individuellen Gerechtigkeits- bzw. Verteilungskalkül der Mitglieder die gruppenmäßig vertretenen Verteilungsnormen verfestigen oder zu Lasten der anderen Verteilungsnormen ein stärkeres Gewicht erhalten. Mit anderen Worten es ist möglich, daß über die Gruppenmitgliedschaft und ähnlich über die Außenaktivität distributiver Gruppen die Verteilungspräferenzen der Gesellschaftsmitglieder in Richtung und Stärke beeinflußt werden bzw. daß die distributiven Präferenzfunktionen zum Ausdruck spezifischer Gruppen- bzw. Klassenzugehörigkeit werden.

3. Die normative Beurteilung privaten Umverteilungshandelns

3.1. Verteilungsgerechtigkeit versus distributive Effizienz

Im folgenden wird privates Umverteilungshandeln einer normativen Beurteilung unterzogen. Zu diesem Zweck werden als erstes die beiden Begriffe der Verteilungsgerechtigkeit und der distributiven Effizienz abgeklärt, deren Inhalt nicht unabhängig von dem entwickelten präferenztheoretischen Fundament ist.

Die Überlegungen der normativen Ökonomik zur gerechten Verteilung der

Einkommen orientieren sich an der Vorstellung, daß die Aufteilungsmöglichkeiten für ein gegebenes Gesamteinkommen mit Hilfe einer sozialen Wohlfahrtsfunktion bewertet werden könnten und daß unter diesen Aufteilungsmöglichkeiten eine Aufteilung existiere, die jeder anderen Verteilungsalternative wohlfahrtsmäßig überlegen sei. Der nicht ganz eindeutige Inhalt einer solchen Vorstellung läßt sich ein wenig präzisieren, indem man das soziale Wohlfahrtsniveau von der individuellen Wohlfahrt aller Gesellschaftsmitglieder abhängig macht und in der hier vorgezeichneten Weise annimmt, daß die individuelle Wohlfahrt der Gesellschaftsmitglieder nicht nur von der eigenen Einkommensausstattung, sondern auch von der Einkommensausstattung der anderen Personen bestimmt werde[21]. Unter diesen Umständen wird erkennbar, daß die Vorstellungen zur Verteilungsgerechtigkeit inhaltlich nicht ohne Rückgriff auf die subjektiven Verteilungsvorstellungen der einzelnen Gesellschaftsmitglieder zu definieren sind. Zugleich wird erkennbar, daß die Genese der Verteilungsgerechtigkeit innerhalb einer Gesellschaft zwangsläufig einer zirkularen Beziehung zwischen individuellen Verteilungspräferenzen und überindividuellen Gerechtigkeitsnormen unterliegt.

Eine dynamische Betrachtung soll den Sachverhalt veranschaulichen: Auf der ersten Stufe der Genese fällt, hier exogen vorgegeben, die ethische Entscheidung über allgemeine Gerechtigkeitsgrundsätze, relevante Verteilungskriterien und institutionelle Regelungen zu deren effizienter Durchsetzung. Sie läuft z. B. auf eine Verteilung der im gesellschaftlichen Kooperationsprozeß entstandenen Einkommen nach dem Leistungsbeitrag der Individuen und nach ihren Bedürfnissen hinaus und verbietet bestimmte, darüber hinausgehende Diskriminierungen von vornherein als ungerecht. Die Individuen versuchen auf der zweiten Stufe, die Verteilungsgrundsätze in der oben gezeigten Weise zu konkretisieren, wobei sie in dieser Ausgangssituation noch mit gravierender Unsicherheit in der gegenseitigen Einschätzung der individuellen Wohlfahrt zu kämpfen haben. Die Konkretisierung findet ihren Niederschlag in den individuellen Verteilungspräferenzen, die sich in Richtung und Stärke erheblich voneinander unterscheiden können. In einem anschließenden gesellschaftlichen Bewertungsprozeß bildet sich auf der dritten Stufe die soziale Vorstellung, daß in Hinsicht auf die Gesamtheit der so formulierten individuellen Verteilungspräferenzen eine bestimmte Aufteilung des vorhandenen Gesamteinkommens in höchstem Maße gerecht sei. Der hier nicht weiter abzuklärende Inhalt dieser Vorstellung erhält einen den individuellen Verteilungspräferenzen übergeordneten normativen Geltungsanspruch und verlangt auf der vierten und letzten Stufe, anstelle der ursprünglichen, rein subjektiven Konkretisierungen der allgemeinen Gerechtigkeitsgrundsätze internalisiert zu werden. Der Bestand der einheitlich und überindividuell geltenden Norm ist im Einzelfall unabhängig davon, ob sie tatsächlich internalisiert und befolgt wird oder nicht. Wird sie von den Individuen internalisiert, führt dies zu einer Änderung der bestehenden Individualpräferenzen; die beschriebenen Etappen müssen dann noch einmal durchgespielt werden mit dem Ergebnis, daß auch die resultierende Gerechtigkeitsnorm selbst sich gegenüber der ersten Runde ändert.

Man kann sich vorstellen, daß der zirkulare Prozeß in seiner Dynamik ein Endgleichgewicht erreicht, in dem der Inhalt den individuellen Verteilungsvorstellungen und der überindividuellen Gerechtigkeitsnorm keiner Änderung mehr unterliegt. Dieses Endgleichgewicht ist dadurch gekennzeichnet, daß sich die Vorgabe der sozialen Gerechtigkeitsnorm vereinheitlichend auf die Gestalt der individuellen Verteilungspräferenzen ausgewirkt hat[22], daß trotzdem aber keine vollständige oder auch nur überwiegende Übereinstimmung zwischen den sozialen und individuellen Verteilungsnormen erreicht worden ist. Die überindividuelle Gerechtigkeitsnorm des Endgleichgewichts entspricht den üblichen, unpräzisen Gerechtigkeitsvorstellungen der normativen Ökonomik und läßt sich in etwa auch mit den Vorstellungen der Rawls'schen Gerechtigkeitstheorie vergleichen.

Die skizzierte Vorstellung zur Verteilungsgerechtigkeit läßt sich trotz der Problematik des interpersonellen Nutzenvergleichs noch stärker konkretisieren und in ein operationales Beurteilungskriterium fassen. In Anwendung des Grundprinzips der paretianischen Ökonomik kann von der Eigenschaft der distributiven Effizienz gesprochen werden. Ein Verteilungszustand gilt als distributiv effizient, wenn es nicht mehr möglich ist, mit Hilfe der Umverteilung die Verteilungsvorstellungen einer Person stärker durchzusetzen, ohne die Durchsetzung der Verteilungsvorstellungen irgendeiner anderen Person zu beeinträchtigen. Umverteilung fördert demnach die distributive Effizienz, wenn sie einer Person einen distributiven Präferenzgewinn verschafft, ohne irgendeiner anderen Person eine distributive Präferenzeinbuße zuzufügen.

Die Eigenschaft der distributiven Effizienz hat einen plausiblen und klaren Bezug zur überindividuellen Gerechtigkeit. Widerspricht ein Verteilungszustand im Sinne einer totalen distributiven Ineffizienz den subjektiven Verteilungspräferenzen aller Gesellschaftsmitglieder und wird er daher einhellig und nachhaltig abgelehnt, so kann dieser Verteilungszustand plausiblerweise nicht als gerecht bezeichnet werden[23]. Existiert in dem von Nationalökonomen und Ethikern bisher nicht restlos abgeklärten Sinn so etwas wie eine in höchstem Maße gerechte Verteilungslösung, muß diese im Bereich der distributiv effizienten Lösungen gesucht werden. Distributive Effizienz bedeutet also Ausschaltung ungerechter Verteilungsalternativen bzw. Förderung der Gerechtigkeit. Das Pareto-Kriterium erweist sich in diesem Zusammenhang als ein operationales Gerechtigkeitskriterium. Damit ist eine wichtige Beurteilungsbasis gewonnen.

Das Kriterium der distributiven Effizienz unterliegt in seiner ethischen Aussagekraft aber einer gravierenden Beschränkung. Es ist ausschließlich in Hinsicht auf bestehende individuelle Verteilungspräferenzen definiert und geht davon aus, daß diese gesamtgesellschaftlich möglichst effizient realisiert werden sollen. Es orientiert sich nicht an der Gerechtigkeitsnorm, die, obwohl aus den individuellen Verteilungspräferenzen abgeleitet, diesen Individualpräferenzen normativ doch wieder vorgeordnet ist. Inwieweit die Individualpräferenzen im übergeordneten Sinne gerecht sind, bleibt völlig außer acht. Die bestehenden Individualpräferenzen werden also unabhängig von ihrer Übereinstimmung mit der Gerechtigkeitsnorm als letzte Werturteile akzeptiert, die in keinem Einzelfall übergangen werden.

Aus diesem Grund kann sich die normative Beurteilung privaten Umverteilungshandelns, die hier beabsichtigt ist, nicht mit der ausschließlichen Anwendung des paretianischen Kriteriums der distributiven Effizienz begnügen. Sie muß versuchen, die Gerechtigkeitsförderlichkeit dieses Verhaltens darüber hinaus auszumachen. Die Anwendung des Kriteriums der distributiven Effizienz dient dabei aber einer wichtigen Vorabklärung, und es scheint, daß sich auf dieser Basis die Richtung abzeichnet, in der sich das Gerechtigkeitskonzept der normativen Ökonomik in angemessener Weise inhaltlich fixieren läßt.

3.2. Die Pareto-Optimalität freiwilliger Transfers im 2-Personen-Modell

Angenommen in einem geschlossenen 2-Personen-Modell hätten die beiden Individuen i und j eine völlig gleiche, aber in Richtung auf ihr eigenes Einkommen verzerrte Präferenzstruktur. Infolge von Marktunvollkommenheiten auf dem Arbeitsmarkt verdiene i ein hohes und j ein niedriges Einkommen. Hochverdiener i gebe zu, daß seine relative Einkommensposition unter Gerechtigkeitsgesichtspunkten zu hoch sei; Niedrigverdiener j sehe sein Einkommen im Vergleich zu dem des i als ungerecht niedrig an. Bei dieser originären Verteilungssituation, die in Fig. 7 durch Punkt A_i gekennzeichnet ist, wird i, wenn er sich rational verhält, dem j freiwillig einen Einkommenstransfer leisten und diesen Transfer so bemessen, daß er sein durch Marginalbedingung (11) gekennzeichnetes individuelles Verteilungsoptimum erreicht. Dieses individuelle Verteilungsoptimum ist in Fig. 7 durch Punkt P_i gekennzeichnet. Der freiwillige Transfer an j wird entsprechend durch die Strecke A_iP_i gekennzeichnet.

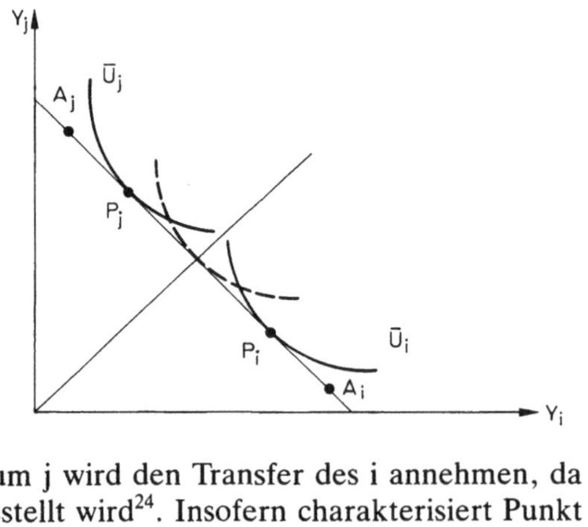

Fig. 7

Individuum j wird den Transfer des i annehmen, da es durch ihn präferenzmäßig besser gestellt wird[24]. Insofern charakterisiert Punkt P_i auch im Sinne des Pareto-Kriteriums ein gesellschaftliches Verteilungsoptimum.

Wäre die Ausgangsverteilung zwischen i und j genau umgekehrt zu Gunsten des j ausgefallen und in Fig. 7 durch Punkt A_j gekennzeichnet gewesen, hätte i von sich aus die Verteilungssituation nicht in Richtung auf sein individuelles Verteilungsoptimum verbessern können, ohne die Eigentumsrechte des anderen zu verletzen. Hier wäre jedoch j bereit gewesen, dem i einen freiwilligen Einkommenstransfer zu leisten, allerdings nur entsprechend der Umverteilungsstrecke A_jP_j, da er in P_j seinerseits sein durch Marginalbedingung (11) gekennzeichnetes individuelles Verteilungsoptimum erreicht hätte.

Abschnitt P_iP_j auf der in Fig. 7 eingezeichneten Transformationsgeraden ist der geometrische Ort aller Pareto-optimalen Einkommensverteilungen, bei denen jede weitere Verteilungsänderung zu Gunsten des einen zu einer präferenzmäßigen Schlechterstellung des anderen führen würde. Allerdings stellen nur die Endpunkte der Strecke individuelle Verteilungsoptima dar, und das auch nur für jeweils einen der beiden. Insofern besteht eine, wenn auch nur unvollständige Analogie zur Kontraktkurve der geometrischen Darstellung allokationstheoretischer Modelle mit Hilfe der Edgeworth-Box[25].

In Hinsicht auf die bestehenden individuellen Verteilungspräferenzen ist privates Umverteilungshandeln also tendenziell effizienzsteigernd. Diese erste allgemeine Feststellung ist völlig analog zu der wirtschaftstheoretischen Aussage über die gesamtwirtschaftliche Vorteilhaftigkeit von ungehinderter Faktormobilität, privater Arbeitsteilung, Freihandel und freier Konsumwahl im allokativen Bereich, die tendenziell selbst in den meisten Fällen eines Vorliegens externer Effekte aufrecht erhalten werden muß.

Zugleich ist privates Umverteilungshandeln tendenziell gerechtigkeitsförderlich. Versuchen die Individuen aufgrund einer Internalisierung von Gerechtigkeitsnormen, einander in ihrem Verhalten gerecht zu werden, oder lassen sie zumindest aufgrund rein egoistischer Vorteilskalküle distributive Rücksicht walten, führt dies zu einer distributiven Annäherung der verfolgten Verhaltenspositionen und reduziert die Menge der Verteilungsalternativen, die grundsätzlich als gerechte Verteilungslösung in Betracht kommen. Praktisch bedeutet das eine graduelle Befriedung der sozialen Beziehungen und eine Zähmung des Verteilungsstreits. Verfolgten die Individuen diese Verhaltensmaxime nicht, käme es in irgendwelchen Verhandlungen zwischen i und j bei der Aufteilung der einkommensmäßigen Verhandlungsvorteile zu einem Streit um Verteilungspositionen, die sich in Fig. 7 auf den gesamten, durch die Koordinatenachsen begrenzten Bereich der Transformationsgeraden erstrecken würden. Infolge der interpersonellen Präferenzabhängigkeiten ist der umstrittene Bereich dagegen auf Abschnitt P_iP_j eingeschränkt.

3.3. Externe Effekte auf seiten Dritter

Interpersonelle Präferenzabhängigkeiten sind ihrer Natur nach externe Effekte. Treten die Präferenzabhängigkeiten auf seiten Dritter in Erscheinung, die weder als Geber noch als Empfänger am Transfergeschehen beteiligt sind, so kann ihr

Externalitätencharakter die Effizienzförderlichkeit privaten Umverteilungshandelns beeinträchtigen. Im geschlossenen 2-Personen-Modell des vorigen Abschnitts sicherte die für das Gelingen des privaten Transfers erforderliche Annahmebereitschaft des Transferempfängers die Effizienzförderlichkeit privaten Umverteilungshandelns. Berücksichtigt man in dem Modell die Existenz von Dritten, ist die Annahme des Transfers durch den Empfänger keine hinreichende Bedingung für eine distributive Effizienzsteigerung mehr. Nach dem Pareto-Kriterium ist erforderlich, daß auch alle Dritten dem Transfer zustimmen. Die beiden Individuen i und j werden die Verteilungspräferenzen dieser Dritten zwar beim Anstellen ihres Verteilungskalküls in dem oben[26] beschriebenen Sinn zu internalisieren versuchen; das sichert jedoch nicht, daß sie eine Verteilungslösung anstreben, die von jedem Dritten tatsächlich gewünscht wird. Da die Eigentumsordnung den Dritten selbst nur die Möglichkeit läßt, das Verhalten von Transfergeber und Transferempfänger über Verhandlungsangebote zu beeinflussen, und da die Wirksamkeit derartiger Verhandlungsangebote begrenzt ist, ist nicht gesichert, daß die externen Präferenzabhängigkeiten der Dritten durch das private Transfersystem angemessen wahrgenommen werden. Insofern kann grundsätzlich nur von einer *Tendenz* zur Steigerung der distributiven Effizienz durch privates Umverteilungshandeln gesprochen werden[27].

Das Problem läßt sich geometrisch veranschaulichen, indem man die distributive Präferenzfunktion (4) für den 3-Personen-Fall verallgemeinert und die Indifferenzkurven eines dritten Individuums, h, bezogen auf die Einkommenspositionen der Individuen i und j, in die graphische Darstellung von Fig. 7 einbezieht[28]. Eine entsprechende Indifferenzkurve des h wurde in Fig. 7 bereits berücksichtigt und durch einen gestrichelten Verlauf kenntlich gemacht. Entscheidend für die Beurteilung des Transfers von Individuum i an Individuum j ist offensichtlich, welche Richtung die Verteilungspräferenz des h gegenüber den Einkommenspositionen von i und j aufweist und wie diese Richtung von der präferierten Verteilung des Transfergebers abweicht. Haben i und j, wie in Fig. 7, eine völlig gleiche Präferenzfunktion und hat Individuum h gegenüber den Einkommenspositionen von i und j eine Gleichverteilungspräferenz, wird es seine Zustimmung zu dem Transfer des i nicht verweigern, da dieser annahmegemäß zu einer Annäherung an die von h präferierte Gleichverteilung führt.

Es muß jedoch damit gerechnet werden, daß die Verteilungspräferenz des h in ihrer Richtung von der Gleichverteilungspräferenz abweicht. Dabei ist besonders der Fall von Bedeutung, daß die Verteilungspräferenz des h weniger stark zugunsten des Transferempfängers gerichtet ist als die des Transfergebers selbst, denn allein in diesem Fall beschränken die distributiven Einwände des Dritten den Bereich, in dem sich das Transferverhalten des i effizienzförderlich auswirkt. Für diesen Fall gibt es die verschiedensten Motive. Das Motiv könnte sein, daß h sich durch i einen unangenehmen Zugzwang ausgesetzt sieht, da er ebenfalls ein Mitglied der reichen Klasse ist und den Altruismus seines Klassengefährten als von der Klassennorm abweichendes Verhalten ablehnt. Es könnte einfach Paternalismus dem Transfergeber i gegenüber oder eine persönliche Aversion oder Neid dem Transferempfänger gegenüber ausschlaggebend sein. Vor allem könnte auch die subjektive Behauptung unterschiedlicher persönlicher Bedürftigkeit oder beruflicher Leistung sowie eine unterschiedliche Ansicht hinsichtlich der Ausgestaltung der Bedarfs- und Leistungskriterien und ihrer Wahrnehmung im originären Verteilungsprozeß eine Rolle spielen. Die Legitimität der von h geäußerten Präferenz und ihre normative Bedeutung für die Beurteilung des von i geleisteten Transfers kann also nicht ohne weiteres bestritten werden.

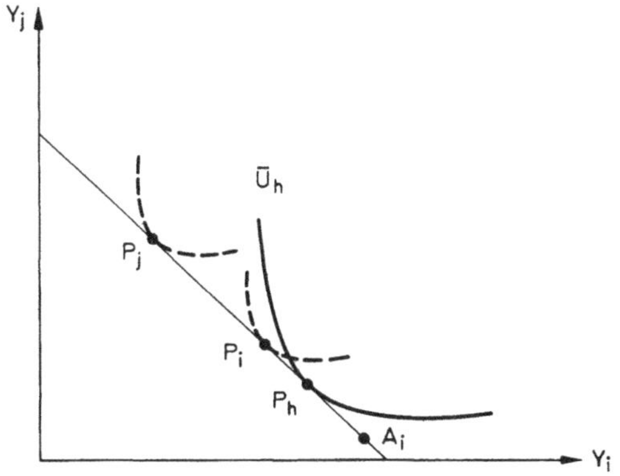

Fig. 8

Liegt aus den genannten Motiven das individuelle Verteilungsoptimum des h, bezogen auf Y_i und Y_j, auf der Transformationslinie rechts unterhalb vom individuellen Verteilungsoptimum des Transfergebers i, P_i, aber links oberhalb der Ausgangsposition A_i, ist nur der Teil des von i geleisteten Transfers effizienzsteigernd, der zu einer Annäherung an die von h präferierte Verteilung, P_h, führt (Fig. 8). Jeder darüber hinausgehende Teil begegnet dem Einwand des h und ist daher umstritten bzw. nicht effizienzsteigernd. Es ist nicht sicher, ob er die Gerechtigkeit zwischen h, i und j fördert oder ihr abträglich ist, denn aufgrund der extremen Ausrichtung der Verteilungspräferenz von h könnte die an sich gerechte Aufteilung der Einkommen zwischen i und j, anders als im geschlossenen 2-Personen-Modell, außerhalb des Abschnitts P_iP_j der Transformationsgeraden liegen.

Die Rolle der externen Präferenzabhängigkeit Dritter wird noch deutlicher, wenn man den nicht ganz untypischen Modellfall einer anonymen Großgesellschaft betrachtet, in der jeder zwar das eigene Einkommen präferenzmäßig höher bewertet als das gleich große Einkommen einer anderen Person, in der Einkommensaufteilung zwei beliebigen fremden Personen gegenüber aber eine Gleichverteilungspräferenz hegt. Hier findet der Transfer des i, der auf eine Angleichung der relativen Einkommenspositionen zwischen i und j abzielt, der sich also vom Reichen zum Armen richtet, bei den vielen Gesellschaftsmitgliedern allgemeine

Zustimmung. Hier ist privates Umverteilungshandeln ohne Einschränkung effizienzsteigernd. Dennoch sind die externen Präferenzabhängigkeiten der vielen Dritten distributiv nicht unerheblich. Das wird verständlich, wenn man einmal annimmt, es gelänge, die distributiven Präferenzen aller Gesellschaftsmitglieder zu bündeln. Wenn das Gerechtigkeitsideal hier nämlich in Hinsicht auf die subjektiven Verteilungspräferenzen *aller* Gesellschaftsmitglieder definiert worden ist und alle am Transfergeschehen zwischen i und j nur mittelbar beteiligten Dritten eine Gleichverteilungspräferenz, bezogen auf Y_i und Y_j, haben und wenn außerdem die Stärke ihrer diesbezüglichen Verteilungspräferenz sehr groß ist, so kann die im überindividuellen Sinne gerechte Verteilungslösung nicht weit von der Gleichverteilung zwischen i und j entfernt sein. Unter diesen Umständen erweist sich das private Umverteilungshandeln des i, das auf Erhalt einer überdurchschnittlich hohen eigenen Einkommensposition bedacht ist, ganz offensichtlich als nur beschränkt gerechtigkeitsförderlich. Mit anderen Worten, wenn die externen Effekte in diesem Fall auch unerheblich für die distributive Effizienz des privaten Umverteilungshandelns im Sinne des Pareto-Prinzips sind, so beeinflussen sie doch im Sinne der eingangs dargelegten Gerechtigkeitskonzeption den Inhalt der über die distributive Effizienznorm hinausgehenden sozialen Gerechtigkeitsnorm und damit den normativen Charakter privaten Umverteilungshandelns. Hierin zeigt sich, daß die externen Präferenzabhängigkeiten Dritter in der ökonomischen Theorie der Gerechtigkeit offensichtlich eine ganz zentrale Stellung einnehmen.

3.4. Große Zahl und Anonymität der Transferempfänger

In mehrfacher Hinsicht wird die Gerechtigkeitsförderlichkeit privaten Verteilungshandelns durch die Existenz einer großen Zahl von Transferempfängern bedroht. Wenn ein einzelner Reicher einer großen Zahl von Armen gegenübersteht, deren relative Einkommensposition er verbessern möchte, so stellt er bald fest, daß er mit seinen privaten Transfers das absolute Einkommensniveau der Empfänger wegen deren großer Zahl nicht wesentlich heben kann. Die Angleichung der relativen Einkommenspositionen vollzieht sich hauptsächlich über die Minderung seines eigenen absoluten Einkommensniveaus, und von daher besteht nach außen hin kein wesentlicher Unterschied zwischen Hergeben und Verstecken des Reichtums. Das Bewußtsein dieses Sachverhalts kann die private Umverteilungsbereitschaft des Reichen lähmen. Dies vollzieht sich aber bereits auf der Stufe der Präferenzbildung, nicht erst auf der Stufe der mehr oder weniger effizienten Präferenzrealisierung.

Zudem verursachen die Information über die Einkommenssituation und Bedürftigkeit der vielen, die als Empfänger freiwilliger Transfers in Betracht gezogen werden müssen, und die Durchführung eines weit verzweigten Transfersystems Kosten, die dem individuellen Verteilungshandeln schnell unüberwindliche Grenzen setzen. Private Organisationen, die die distributiven Individualpräferenzen ansprechen und wahrnehmen, können helfen, diese Kosten gering zu halten, und tragen daher zweifellos in vielfacher Hinsicht dazu bei, die Effizienz privaten Verteilungshandelns zu sichern. Es ist aber fraglich, ob der private Sektor aus sich heraus in der Lage ist, ein effizientes System organisierter Umverteilung zur Verfügung zu stellen, wenn es darum geht, eine allgemein gewünschte, systematische Nivellierung aller interpersoneller Einkommensunterschiede in der Gesamtgesellschaft zu erreichen, denn dies würde einen kollektiven Willensbildungsprozeß und eine freiwillige Offenlegung der individuellen Einkommensverhältnisse voraussetzen.

Die Fähigkeit eines Individuums, sich mit der Verteilungssituation anderer Personen zu identifizieren und deren Verteilungsansprüche wahrzunehmen, ist schließlich rein psychisch gesehen begrenzt und nimmt mit der Zahl der Personen und deren Anonymität ab. U. U. sieht das Individuum die Verteilungssituation anderer Personen mit zunehmender Distanz vom eigenen persönlichen Umfeld sogar als irrelevant an. Wenn auch die Zusammenfassung der potentiellen Transferempfänger in homogenen und sich artikulierenden Verteilungsgruppen die distributive Orientierung und Identifizierung des Transfergebers erleichtert, muß dennoch damit gerechnet werden, daß seine vorrangig auf die überschaubaren Verteilungsverhältnisse ausgerichteten Verteilungspräferenzen infolge der großen Zahl und der Anonymität der potentiellen Transferempfänger in ähnlicher Weise verkürzt sind, wie das häufig für die intertemporalen Individualpräferenzen behauptet wird[29]. Wenn aber einerseits die Gerechtigkeitsnormen sich von der Teilnahme an einem gemeinsamen gesellschaftlichen Kooperationsprozeß herleiten[30], die Teilnehmer an dem Kooperationsprozeß andererseits infolge dieser Präferenzverkürzung keinen über die gesamte Kooperationsgesellschaft reichenden Gemeinsinn aufbringen, so zeigt dies noch einmal, daß die Gerechtigkeitsförderlichkeit eines rein privaten Verteilungshandelns Grenzen unterliegt. Ähnlich wie bei den räumlichen oder zeitlichen Distanzen im allokativen Bereich könnte man hier von „imperfections" der privaten Verteilungsgerechtigkeit sprechen, die durch soziale Distanzen[31] und die subjektiven Kosten ihrer Überwindung verursacht werden. Allerdings müßte eine Verteilungsgerechtigkeit, die ihre Verpflichtung ausschließlich aus der persönlichen Nähe zu anderen Personen ableitet und sich von daher auf einen beschränkten Personenkreis erstreckt, bereits im ethischen Sinne als verkürzt bzw. als meritorisch bezeichnet werden.

3.5. Gegenseitige Präferenzabhängigkeit der potentiellen Transfergeber

Der Einfluß, der von dem Auftreten anderer Reicher auf das Transferverhalten des bisher betrachteten reichen Transfergebers i ausgeht, sei zuerst in der 3-Personen-Version des hier analysierten Modells dargestellt, und zwar unter folgenden vereinfachenden Annahmen: Es existieren zwei Reiche, h und i, als potentielle Transfergeber und ein Armer, j, als potentieller Transferempfänger, die alle drei ein fest vorgegebenes originäres Einkommen beziehen. Jede der drei Personen präferiert eine Ungleichverteilung der Einkommen zu ihren eigenen Gunsten, hegt aber hinsichtlich der Einkommensaufteilung zwischen den beiden anderen Personen eine Gleichverteilungspräferenz. Jeder der beiden Reichen sieht das originäre Einkommen des Armen als unteroptimal an und läßt ihm daher aus dem eigenen originären Einkommen laufend einen Transfer zukommen. Das Einkommen des anderen Reichen sieht er dagegen vor und nach Abwicklung des privaten Transferprozesses als überoptimal an, er muß dies aber aus eigentumsrechtlichen Gründen hinnehmen.

Die Präferenzfunktion des Individuums k laute:

$$U_k = U_k(Y_k, Y_l, Y_m) \qquad k, l, m \in \{h, i, j\} \quad k \neq l \neq m \tag{21}$$

Sie verlaufe im relevanten Bereich konvex zum Koordinatenursprung und verfüge über alle sonstigen Eigenschaften der Präferenzfunktion (4). Zusätzlich sei angenommen, daß sie vollständig streng separabel sei; d. h. es wird unterstellt, daß auf Seiten des Individuums k die Grenzrate der Substitution zwischen je zwei der in (21) eingehenden Einkommen nur von der Größe dieser beiden Einkommen abhängt, dagegen nicht von der Größe des dritten Einkommens[32].

Der Reiche i stellt nun die Einkommensposition und das Transferverhalten des anderen Reichen, h, in Rechnung und bemißt seinen eigenen Transfer an den Armen j so, daß Bedingung (22) bzw. (23) für sein partielles individuelles Verteilungsoptimum dem j gegenüber erreicht ist[33]:

$$U_{ii} = U_{ij} \tag{22}$$

bzw.

$$R_i(Y_i/Y_j) = - \frac{U_{ij}}{U_{ii}} = -1 \tag{23}$$

Solange sich die originäre Einkommensaufteilung und auch das Transferverhalten des anderen Reichen, h, im Zeitablauf nicht ändern, hält i dieses Transfervolumen dem Armen j gegenüber unverändert aufrecht. Sobald jedoch der andere Reiche seinen Transfer an j kürzt, sinkt dessen Einkommen und läßt die Grenzrate der Substitution R_i von (23) c.p. über den Wert von minus eins steigen. Der Reiche i unterliegt dann dem Anreiz, seinerseits den Transfer an j zu erhöhen, bis die Grenzrate der Substitution den Wert von minus eins wieder erreicht. Er kompensiert also den Transferausfall von seiten des h.

Das aufgrund der Transfers erreichte Umverteilungsgleichgewicht der beiden Reichen, h und i, gegenüber dem Armen, j, ist im Sinne des Pareto-Kriteriums effizient. Jeder Reiche stimmt dem Gleichgewichtstransfer des anderen zu, weil er dem fremden Geber und dem fremden Empfänger gegenüber annahmegemäß eine Gleichverteilungspräferenz hat und weil der Transfer zu einer Angleichung der fremden Einkommenspositionen an die präferierte Gleichverteilung beigetragen hat. Freilich ist der Umfang des vom Armen insgesamt empfangenen Transfers von der Richtung der Verteilungspräferenz auf seiten der reichen Transfergeber abhängig bzw. davon, um wieviel diese eigenes Einkommen präferenzmäßig höher bewerten als fremdes Einkommen. Insofern besteht kein Unterschied zum 2-Personen-Modell mit einem Transfergeber und einem Transferempfänger.

Der skizzierte Transferprozeß verläuft nicht wesentlich anders und ist unter Effizienzaspekten auch nicht wesentlich anders zu beurteilen, wenn i die beiden anderen Personen aufgrund eines Klassenbewußtseins präferenzmäßig ungleich behandelt bzw. wenn er dem anderen Reichen, h, aufgrund einer nunmehr klassenmäßig strukturierten Verteilungspräferenz einen höheren prozentualen Einkommensanteil zugesteht als zuvor. Die distributive Problematik dieses Falls liegt nur darin, daß das präferenzmäßige Zugeständnis eines höheren Einkommensanteils an den Klassengefährten zu Lasten des Einkommensanteils gehen könnte, den i präferenzmäßig dem Armen, j, zugesteht. In einem solchen Fall wäre die Herausbildung einer gruppen- bzw. klassenspezifischen Verteilungspräferenz auf seiten des i gerechtigkeitsschädlich.

Der skizzierte Transferprozeß verläuft auch dann nicht wesentlich anders, wenn in dem so konzipierten Modell die Zahl der Reichen und damit der potentiellen Transfergeber unter sonst gleichen Bedingungen als sehr groß angenommen wird. In diesem Fall erhöht sich die Zahl, nicht notwendigerweise der aggregierte Wert der fremden Transfers, die bei dem einzelnen Transfergeber in Rechnung gestellt werden. Der Betrag, der in Form eigener Transfers weggegeben werden muß, um das individuelle Verteilungsoptimum dem Armen, j, gegenüber zu erreichen, wird geringer. Der Transfergeber i verhält sich aber im Prinzip genauso wie im 3-Personen-Modell. Ist das verfügbare Einkommen des Armen trotz der Transferleistung der vielen anderen Reichen im Vergleich zu seinem eigenen Einkommen immer noch unteroptimal, besteht für i ein Anreiz, j seinerseits einen Transfer zu gewähren. Würde i sich angesichts der großen Zahl der fremden Transfergeber aus dem Umverteilungsgeschäft heraushalten, verhielte er sich in Hinsicht auf seine Verteilungspräferenzen irrational, weil er darauf verzichtete, sein partielles Verteilungsoptimum dem Armen gegenüber zu realisieren. Auch hier ist das Endgleichgewicht des Umverteilungsprozesses gegenüber dem Ausgangszustand ohne Umverteilung im Sinne des Pareto-Kriteriums effizient. Es mag sogar sein, daß der arme Transferempfänger, j, im Endgleichgewicht die gleiche Einkommensrelation zum verfügbaren Durchschnittseinkommen der reichen Transfergeber hat wie im 3-Personen-Modell.

Die Verallgemeinerung des Modells für den n-Personen-Fall erlaubt also den normativ wichtigen Schluß, daß das Problem des Free-Rider-Verhaltens als Folge der externen Effekte bei der mikroökonomischen Totalsteuerung interpersoneller Einkommensrelationen durch den dezentralisierten privaten Transferprozeß nicht entsteht, jedenfalls nicht in dem effizienzschädlichen Sinn, der sich auf die Realisierung der Individualpräferenzen bezieht[34]. Der Grund liegt einfach darin, daß die Verteilungspräferenzen auf eine optimale Gestaltung der interpersonellen Einkommens*relationen* abzielen. Wohl kann das Phänomen des Free-Rider-Verhaltens auf der Ebene der Präferenzformulierung, d. h. in einem allgemeineren, ethischen Sinn, auftreten. Es kann sein, daß der einzelne Reiche angesichts der großen Zahl potentieller Transfergeber und der relativen Bedeutungslosigkeit seiner eigenen Beiträge den grundsätzlichen Stellenwert der individuellen Transferleistung innerhalb eines atomistisch strukturierten privaten Transfersystems verkennt und daß er daher glaubt, sein Gerechtigkeitskalkül weniger streng anstellen zu dürfen.

3.6. Private Verteilungsgerechtigkeit als meritorisches Gut

Hinter den distributiven Unzulänglichkeiten privaten Umverteilungshandelns verbirgt sich überwiegend ein fundamentales verteilungstheoretisches Problem: die unterschiedliche Ansicht über die gerechten Verteilungspositionen, die sich im Verteilungsstreit[35] auswirkt und die in dem verbleibenden Konfliktbereich des Transformationsgeradenabschnitts P_iP_j von Fig. 7 zum Ausdruck kommt. Dieses Problem ist aus normativer Sicht in ganz spezifischer Weise zu beurteilen.

Nach den bisherigen Überlegungen sind die individuellen Verteilungsvorstellungen geprägt durch die subjektive Ungewißheit bei der Beurteilung der fremden Wohlfahrtssituation, durch Mühen und Kosten des Gerechtigkeitskalküls (einschließlich der Informationsbeschaffungskosten), durch die mangelnde Konkretisierung der ethischen Gerechtigkeitsnormen für den distributiven Einzelfall und natürlich durch Egoismus. Von diesem Umstand her müssen die individuellen Verteilungsvorstellungen mehr oder weniger stark voneinander abweichen und können dem Anspruch der Gerechtigkeit auf Einheitlichkeit und Allgemeinverbindlichkeit nicht genügen. Da der private Umverteilungsprozeß vor allem durch die subjektive Verteilungsnorm des Transfergebers und nicht durch eine entsprechende überindividuelle Verteilungsnorm gesteuert wird, muß auch das Ergebnis dieses Prozesses als distributiv zufällig und verzerrt angesehen werden. Aus der Sicht der Theorie öffentlicher Güter würde man daher private Verteilungsgerechtigkeit als ein meritorisches Gut bezeichnen.

Aus dieser Sicht des Gerechtigkeitsproblems bietet die Theorie öffentlicher Güter einen Lösungsvorschlag an, der weitgehend kompatibel mit der skizzierten Gerechtigkeitsvorstellung ist: Das Ergebnis des privaten Umverteilungshandelns ist in Hinsicht auf das eigentliche, überindividuelle Verteilungsziel zu korrigieren, und zwar auf eine möglichst wenig autoritäre Weise. Wenn das eigentliche, überindividuelle Verteilungsziel in dem oben skizzierten 2-Personen-Modell noch unbestimmt ist, ist im Fall eines gravierenden Gerechtigkeitsproblems der erforderliche erste Schritt, daß die Individuen, nachdem sie mit Hilfe des rein privaten Verteilungskalküls ihre individuelle Verteilungspräferenz abgeklärt haben, versuchen, im Zuge eines weitergehenden, gemeinsamen Verteilungskalküls eine distributive Übereinkunft zu erzielen. Diese Übereinkunft hätte die Formulierung einer interpersonell abgestimmten und von beiden akzeptierten sozialen Verteilungsnorm zum Gegenstand, der sich das individuelle Umverteilungshandeln anschließend zu unterwerfen hätte. Sie würde den Gedanken einer vertragstheoretischen

Gerechtigkeitslösung auf der Basis der bestehenden Individualpräferenzen praktisch einlösen.

Dieser Lösungsvorschlag ist allerdings mit einer Reihe von Problemen belastet. Die konzipierte Verteilungsnorm leitet sich aus den bestehenden Individualpräferenzen ab. Sie wird nicht, wie in der ethischen Begründung der allgemeinen Gerechtigkeitsnorm bei Rawls, in einem Zustand der Unkenntnis hinsichtlich der Bedürfnis- und Fähigkeitsstruktur sowie der vorgefundenen Ausgangsverteilung formuliert. Vielmehr greift sie auf die bestehenden individuellen Verteilungspräferenzen als normative Instanz zurück. Die individuellen Verteilungspräferenzen sollen bei der Bildung der Übereinkunft so lange vertreten werden, wie sie nicht in offensichtlichem Widerspruch zu übergeordneten Gerechtigkeitsnormen stehen. Dieser Rekurs auf die Individualpräferenzen hat zur Folge, daß die gemeinsame Verteilungsnorm, die sich erst als Ergebnis der angestrebten Übereinkunft herausschält, nicht unbeeinflußt von dem mehr oder weniger zufälligen Charakter der individuellen Verteilungspräferenzen und daher auch nicht distributiv unverzerrt ist. Immerhin kommt es zu einem Kompromiß der mit einander streitenden Verteilungsvorstellungen.

Zugleich zeichnet sich ab, daß die Realisierungschancen des angestrebten Verteilungskompromisses auf der rein privaten Ebene beschränkt sind. Das Zustandekommen einer Übereinkunft in dem oben skizzierten 2-Personen-Modell setzt voraus, daß der Arme, j, seine von den Vorstellungen des Reichen, i, abweichende Verteilungspräferenz äußert. Die bloße Artikulation durch j reicht unter Umständen aber als Anstoß nicht aus, um i zu einem rationalen Diskurs und zu einem Infragestellen seines individuellen Verteilungsoptimums zu bewegen. Möglicherweise muß j einen offenen Verteilungskampf androhen oder inszenieren. Für einen solchen Verteilungskampf ist aber wiederum die ethische Legitimation unsicher, da die hier angesprochene Kompromißlösung werturteilsmäßig auf die mehr oder weniger verzerrten Individualpräferenzen zurückgreift und da es stets schwierig ist, eine offensichtliche Verletzung von Gerechtigkeitsnormen nachzuweisen. Außerdem müssen dem j geeignete Mittel zur Verfügung stehen und die Konfliktaustragungskosten dürfen nicht zu hoch sein. Es besteht daher die Gefahr, daß kein wirksamer Anstoß zu der distributiven Übereinkunft ausgeht und daß im Endgleichgewicht des dezentral gesteuerten privaten Tranferprozesses das System in einem Zustand des nur latenten Verteilungskonflikts verharrt. Droht dem i aufgrund eines Verteilungskampfes jedoch tatsächlich die Gefahr von Einkommensverlusten, zieht er u. U. einen geregelten Kompromiß dem Risiko der Einkommenseinbuße vor und läßt sich die Sicherheit seiner Einkommensposition etwas kosten. Denn das von j angefochtene individuelle Verteilungsoptimum des i befindet sich im Bereich zwischen der oben angesprochenen Ober- und Untergrenze der Einkommensverteilung, G_o bzw. G_u. Ist die Präferenzfunktion, wie in Fig. 6 unterstellt, konkav, verhält i sich risikoscheu.

Wird ein Verteilungskompromiß erzielt, entsteht ein weiteres Problem. Es kann nicht damit gerechnet werden, daß die beteiligten Individuen das Kompromißergebnis so weit akzeptieren, daß sie sich mit seinem Inhalt voll identifizieren und diesen präferenzmäßig internalisieren. Aus der Unsicherheit des interpersonellen Nutzenvergleichs, aus der Einsicht in die Notwendigkeit eines Kompromisses und aus dem ethischen Rückverweis auf die individuellen Verteilungsvorstellungen als Grundlage der Kompromißlösung entsteht eine zwiespältige Motivation, die die vollständige subjektive Unterwerfung unter die ausgehandelte soziale Verteilungsnorm hemmt bzw. verhindert. Aufgrund dessen unterliegen die Konfliktpartner nach Abschluß der Vereinbarung dem Anreiz, das Kompromißergebnis materiell zu unterlaufen. M. a. W. die Kompromißlösung ist instabil. Hier hat man es nach allen bisherigen Überlegungen zum ersten Mal mit einem Free-Rider-Verhalten im üblich definierten Sinn zu tun, da nämlich der aus dem Verteilungskompromiß resultierende Vorteil des sozialen Friedens in Anspruch genommen wird, ohne sich an den subjektiven Kosten des Verteilungskompromisses zu beteiligen. Es bedarf daher der Kontrolle und des Zwanges, um eine angemessene Durchsetzung der Kompromißverteilung zu sichern, und einer übergeordneten Instanz.

Schließlich kann der Verteilungskonflikt und die distributive Übereinkunft zwischen zwei Transferpartnern i und j im Rahmen eines verallgemeinerten n-Personen-Modells nicht stets als ihre rein private Angelegenheit angesehen werden. Ihre Übereinkunft berührt u. U. über interpersonelle Präferenzabhängigkeiten die Verteilungsvorstellungen Dritter, die das Kompromißergebnis billigen oder ablehnen. Bei einer Orientierung der Kompromißlösung an der oben konzipierten sozialen Gerechtigkeitsvorstellung müssen diese Dritten an der Aushandlung des Verteilungskompromisses beteiligt werden. An sich wirkt diese Beteiligung wohltuend objektivierend, da sie die Chancen strategischen Verhaltens auf Seiten der unmittelbaren Konfliktpartner mindert und den davon ausgehenden verzerrenden Präferenzeinfluß mildert. In kritischen Fällen können es auch gerade die am Verteilungskonflikt nur mittelbar beteiligten Dritten sein, die die Initiative zur distributiven Übereinkunft ergreifen. Ist die Zahl dieser Dritten jedoch groß und über die Gesamtgesellschaft verstreut und sind ihre Verteilungspräferenzen aufgrund gemeinsamer Klassenzugehörigkeit überwiegend zugunsten eines der beiden Konfliktpartner ausgerichtet, sind auch von dorther die Chancen einer angemessenen Lösung des Verteilungskonflikts auf privater Ebene gering, und es bedarf u. U. auch insofern einer kollektiven Zwangslösung auf der staatlichen Ebene.

4. Definition privater Verteilungsziele und Schlußfolgerung

Die bisherigen Ausführungen regen den Versuch einer *Definition privater Umverteilungsziele* an. Diese Definition erfolgt in Analogie zur allokationstheoretischen Unterscheidung zwischen privaten und öffentlichen Gütern: Ein rein privates (Um)Verteilungsziel liegt demnach dann vor, wenn ein potentieller Transfergeber i einem potentiellen Transferempfänger j gegenüber eine einkommensbezogene interpersonelle Präferenzabhängigkeit hegt und wenn keine auf die Einkommenspositionen von i und j gerichteten interpersonellen Präferenzabhängigkeiten auf seiten Dritter bestehen.

Die Abgrenzung rein privater Verteilungsziele ist nicht identisch mit der *Abgrenzung rein privater Gerechtigkeitsziele:* Im Anschluß an die Überlegungen von Rawls könnten der potentielle Transfergeber i und der potentielle Transferempfänger j aufgrund ihrer Interaktionen als eine spezifische Kooperationsgesellschaft innerhalb der Gesamtgesellschaft aufgefaßt werden, die aus sich selbst heraus die Legitimationsbasis für spezifische Gerechtigkeitsnormen liefert. Existieren keine ethisch legitimierten externen Präferenzabhängigkeiten Dritter oder müssen bestehende Präferenzabhängigkeiten dieser Art im ethischen Sinn als unerheblich oder illegitim angesehen werden, können die spezifischen Gerechtigkeitsnormen der beiden potentiellen Transferpartner als rein privat bezeichnet werden.

Nach diesem ersten Definitionsversuch privater Verteilungs- und Gerechtigkeitsziele kann zusammenfassend eine allgemeine *Schlußfolgerung* gezogen werden: Zu den normativen Aussagen der Allokationstheorie, die zwischen privaten und öffentlichen Gütern unterscheidet und die eine begrenzte Effizienz des privaten Allokationsmechanismus der Märkte und die Notwendigkeit einer Ergänzung durch einen staatlichen Allokationsmechanismus behauptet, läßt sich auf der Grundlage einer Theorie distributiver Individualpräferenzen ein analoges Aussagesystem für den Bereich der Verteilungstheorie ableiten. In diesem Aussagesystem lassen sich private und öffentliche Umverteilungsziele unterscheiden. Mit seiner Hilfe kann nachgewiesen werden, daß im Bereich der öffentlichen Umverteilungsziele individuelles Umverteilungshandeln nur begrenzt effizient ist und der Ergänzung durch kollektives Umverteilungshandeln bedarf. In analoger Anwendung des Coase-Theorems wird man davon ausgehen müssen, daß die distributive Ineffizienz des individuellen Umverteilungshandelns in bestimmten Fällen über Verhandlungen in privaten Kleingruppen oder über distributive Zweckverbände des privaten Sektors geheilt werden kann. Davon abgesehen liefert das Aussagesystem eine exakte Rechtfertigung für die redistributive staatliche Aktivität und bildet die Grundlage einer bisher nicht ausformulierten Theorie der staatlichen Umverteilungspolitik.

Anmerkungen

[1] Von subjektiven Verteilungsvorstellungen können Ethiker absehen, die außerhalb der ökonomischen Analyse fundamentale Gerechtigkeitsgrundsätze ableiten, um von dorther die grundsätzliche ethische Legitimität konkreter (Um)Verteilungsmaßnahmen zu überprüfen. Für sie sind die subjektiven Verteilungsvorstellungen der vielen einzelnen u. U. kein konstitutives Argument des ethischen Kalküls und der Ableitung der Gerechtigkeitsgrundsätze eher hinderlich. Vgl. die rein formale Ableitung des kategorischen Imperativs bei Kant 1785. Vgl. neuerdings Rawls 1971, Kap. 1, Abschn. 3, der versucht, den

materiellen Gehalt seines Gerechtigkeitsgrundsatzes der Fairneß möglichst voraussetzungsfrei, d.h. ohne Rückgriff auf person- oder situationsbezogene Werturteile der Gesellschaftsmitglieder zu begründen, und in diesem Sinne konsequent von interpersonellen Präferenzabhängigkeiten absieht.

[2] Vgl. das Gerechtigkeitskonzept der klassischen Utilitaristen und die Formulierung der Opfertheorien im Rahmen der finanzwissenschaftlichen Leistungsfähigkeitsdiskussion. Pigou 1951, 3. Aufl., S. 91, hat den modifizierenden Einfluß interpersoneller Nutzenabhängigkeiten in diesem Zusammenhang deutlich gesehen, seine zentrale Bedeutung aber nicht erkannt.

[3] Diese beiden Annahmen, die sich auch auf den Besitz von Humanvermögen erstrecken, erlauben, die methodischen Grundlagen einer Analyse des gesellschaftlichen Verteilungsziels klarer herauszuarbeiten. Bei der vollen inhaltlichen Konkretisierung der dem gesellschaftlichen Verteilungsziel zugrunde liegenden Gerechtigkeitsnorm, die hier nicht angestrebt wird, müssen beide Annahmen selbstverständlich wieder aufgehoben werden.

[4] Der Grund dafür könnte sein, daß die fremden Gerechtigkeitsvorstellungen allzu stark von den eigenen abweichen.

[5] Zweifellos könnte Präferenzfunktion (4) im Anschluß an übliche wohlfahrtstheoretische Überlegungen einfacher hergeleitet werden:
(a) $U_k = P_k(N_k, N_l)$
mit
(b) $N_k = N_k(Y_k)$
(c) $N_l = N_l(Y_l)$
Dabei ist $N_k(\ldots)$ die übliche Nutzenfunktion und $P_k(\ldots)$ eine übergeordnete, von $N_k(\ldots)$ unabhängige distributive Bewertungsfunktion bzw. eine soziale Wohlfahrtsfunktion vom Bergson-Typ.
In dieser Ableitung wird die Wohlfahrt der eigenen Person k durch das Wohlfahrtsniveau der fremden Person l aber nur insoweit beeinflußt, wie dieses vom Einkommen abhängt, dagegen nicht, insoweit es von der Erfüllung bzw. Verletzung der Gerechtigkeitsvorstellung abhängt. Wird jedoch die Wohlfahrt der einen Person, U_k, ausschließlich von der *materiellen* Wohlfahrt der anderen Person, $N_l(Y_l)$, abhängig gemacht, so stellt dies für die Erklärung des individuellen Verteilungshandelns eine analytische Einengung dar, die a priori nicht ohne weiteres gerechtfertigt ist.
Die obigen Zusammenhänge wurden bereits von Becker (1974) explizit angesprochen.

[6] Es handelt sich um den in Fig. 3 beschriebenen Unterfall einer Präferenzfunktion mit starker Verteilungspräferenz sowie um den Bereich dieser Funktion, in dem eine Indifferenzkurve mit den kritischen Grenzlinien G_u und G_o der Einkommensverteilung zusammenfällt.

[7] Der in der ökonomischen Indifferenzkurvenanalyse meist unterstellte Fall, daß keine interpersonellen Präferenzabhängigkeiten vorliegen, kann im oben definierten Sinn mit dem Fall $\alpha = \infty$, also dem Fall des extremen Egoismus, gleichgesetzt werden. Diese, an sich nicht beabsichtigte ethische Implikation wird meist nicht ausreichend gesehen und veranlaßt gelegentlich zu dem Trugschluß, Egoismus sei eine logisch notwendige Implikation des Prinzips der Nutzenmaximierung. Unzweideutig war aber Franziskus von Assisi, wenn er sich zweckrational verhielt, ein „Nutzen"maximierer und dennoch kein Egoist im landläufigen Verständnis.

[8] Man kann vom extremen Egoismus als Normalnull ausgehen und das Verteilungsverhalten allein durch das Vorhandensein einer mehr oder weniger altruistischen Motivation

kennzeichnen. Damit würde dem Aspekt der Sozialisation einer Person Rechnung getragen, die als reiner Egoist geboren wird und erst lernen muß, die legitimen Ansprüche des anderen anzuerkennen. Die Begriffe Altruismus und subjektive Gerechtigkeit wären damit weitgehend deckungsgleich. Dies ist implizit auch die Sicht von Edgeworth (1881), in einer von Collard 1975, S. 355 zitierten Bemerkung. Vgl. auch Manfred Neumann 1980, S. 357. Die obige Definition geht dagegen von der Vorstellung einer ethischen Gerechtigkeitsnorm aus, die unabhängig von der präferenzmäßigen Internalisierung durch die Einzelperson Bestand hat. Gemessen an dieser Normalnull verkörpert Egoismus ein Defizit an subjektiver Gerechtigkeit, Altruismus dagegen einen entsprechenden Überschuß bzw. das, was Rawls als Menschenliebe bezeichnet. Vgl. Rawls 1971, Kap. 3, Abschn. 30 sowie Kap. 7, Abschn. 66.

[9] Zweifellos könnten diese Argumente besser dargestellt werden, wenn die Präferenzfunktion sich nicht nur auf die distributive Beurteilung der individuellen Einkommenspositionen beschränkte, sondern die aus den besonderen Lebensumständen resultierenden Bedürfnistatbestände und die „disutilities" der beruflichen Leistungsabgabe im Erwerbsprozeß explizit als zusätzliche Funktionsargumente berücksichtigte.

[10] Vgl. Brennan 1973, S. 43–67.

[11] Vgl. Buchanan and Tullock 1962, S. 189 ff.

[12] Im Koordinatenraum (Y_i, Y_j) wird die Budgetlinie durch die Koordinatenachsen, den Fahrstrahl der präferierten Einkommensverteilung (α) und die Grenzlinien der kritischen Einkommensverteilung (G_u bzw. G_o) in Teilabschnitte zerlegt. Die Grenzwerte von π in (16) bzw. (17) und ähnlich in (19) bzw. (20) lassen sich durch das Verhältnis dieser Teilstrecken zueinander und daher in der angezeigten Weise durch α, G_u bzw. G_o ausdrücken.

[13] Konvexitätseigenschaft (5) besteht nur insoweit, wie die beiden gleichbewerteten Einkommenssituationen (Y_{i1}, Y_{j1}) und (Y_{i2}, Y_{j2}) sich jeweils auf einem anderen der beiden oben beschriebenen Indifferenzkurvenäste befinden.

[14] Bei Erreichen dieses Ausmaßes gilt

(a) $R_i = 0$

bzw.

(b) $R_i = -\infty$

und daher nach (14)

$$\text{(c)} \qquad \pi' = \frac{Y_i + Y_j}{Y_i}$$

bzw.

$$\text{(d)} \qquad \pi' = \frac{Y_i + Y_j}{Y_j}$$

[15] Die Neiddefinition entspricht völlig der von Rawls angeführten Neiddefinition von Kant. Vgl. Rawls 1971, Kap. 9, Abschn. 80. Vgl. im übrigen auch Bös und Tillmann 1983, S. 637–660. Die dort letztendlich akzeptierte Definition des Neides von Foley 1967 stellt mit dem Kriterium Nutzengewinn des i bei einem gegenseitigen Austausch der Einkommenspositionen von i und j auf eine Asymmetrie oder eine Verzerrung der Präferenzfunktion ab, wie sie hier zur Kennzeichnung von Egoismus und Altruismus herangezogen

wird. Die Foley'sche Definition des Neides erlaubt von daher keine klare begriffliche Trennung von Neid und Egoismus. Neidverhalten setzt z. B. nicht zwangsläufig Egoismus voraus. Der Neid im Falle einer zur Gleichverteilungslinie symmetrischen Präferenzfunktion kann daher mit der Foley'schen Definition nicht erfaßt werden.

[16] Unter Ethikern besteht ein Konsens dahingehend, daß die Gerechtigkeitskonformität des distributiven Handlungsergebnisses für die Lösung des Gerechtigkeitsproblems bedeutsamer ist als die Gerechtigkeitskonformität der distributiven Handlungsmotive. Vgl. Smith 1759, übers. v. Walter Eckstein 1977, S. 127 ff. Zu den diesbezüglichen Vorstellungen der scholastischen Philosophie vgl. Pieper 1953, S. 39 ff. und 68 f.

[17] Zu den Konkavitätseigenschaften und ihren Implikationen vgl. Linde 1981, S. 279–281.

[18] Diese Gruppen sind mehr oder weniger deutlich zu unterscheiden von allokativen Zweckverbänden, wie sie von Tiebout 1956 und Buchanan 1965 konzipiert und untersucht wurden.

[19] Zur Konzeption der Familie als einer so ausgerichteten Kleingruppe vgl. Becker 1974.

[20] Vgl. die umfangreiche Literatur zur ökonomischen Theorie der Gewerkschaften, z. B. das klassische Werk von Ross 1956.

[21] Vgl. Sohmen 1976, S. 20 ff. und S. 363 ff.

[22] Praktisch führt die Vorgabe sozialer Gerechtigkeitsnormen zu einer gewissen, routinemäßigen Entlastung des individuellen Gerechtigkeitskalküls von den Schwierigkeiten des interpersonellen Nutzenvergleichs.

[23] Die stillschweigende Voraussetzung der Aussage ist, daß die Gesamtheit der Gesellschaftsmitglieder identisch ist mit der Gesamtheit der gerecht zu behandelnden Individuen.

[24] Es sei davon abgesehen, daß j den Transfer als entwürdigendes Almosen ansehen und daher die Annahme verweigern könnte.

[25] Die Überlegungen dieses Abschnitts bilden den Inhalt der erstmals von Hochman und Rodgers 1969 formulierten Theorie der Pareto-optimalen Einkommens(um)verteilung.

[26] Vgl. Abschnitt 2.1.

[27] Privates Umverteilungshandeln ist nie distributiv *ineffizient* in dem Sinn, daß eine oder mehrere Personen einen distributiven Präferenzverlust erleiden, ohne daß irgendwelche anderen Personen einen distributiven Präferenzgewinn erfahren. Zumindest zwei Personen erfahren stets einen distributiven Präferenzgewinn, der Transfergeber und der Transferempfänger.

[28] Diese Indifferenzkurven gelten für eine unveränderte Einkommensposition des h.

[29] Es geht dort um die eigene Zukunftsvorsorge. Die Generationenvorsorge fällt bereits unter das distributive Problem.

[30] Vgl. Rawls 1971, Kap. 1 Abschn. 3.

[31] Das Argument der sozialen Distanz findet sich in diesem Zusammenhang bereits bei Edgeworth. Vgl. die Zitate bei Collard 1975, S. 335.

[32] Legt man für einen gegebenen Wert von Y_m einen Schnitt in der (Y_k, Y_l)-Ebene des Präferenzraumes, so ist der Verlauf der Indifferenzkurvenschar in dieser Ebene infolge der Separabilitätseigenschaft völlig unabhängig von dem Wert von Y_m. Lediglich das durch eine jede Indifferenzkurve zum Ausdruck gebrachte Präferenzniveau wird durch den Wert von Y_m beeinflußt. Zur Separabilitätseigenschaft vgl. im übrigen Linde 1981, S. 284 ff.

[33] Im Anschluß an die Definition der Grenzopportunitätskosten der Umverteilung von Abschn. 2.4. könnte nach einer Erweiterung statt (22) geschrieben werden:

(22a) $$\frac{U_{ii} - U_{ih}}{\sum\limits_{k = h,i,j} \gamma_k \cdot U_{ik}} = \frac{U_{ij} - U_{ih}}{\sum\limits_{k = h,i,j} \gamma_k \cdot U_{ik}}$$

D. h. in seinem partiellen Verteilungsoptimum dem j gegenüber bringt i die subjektiven Grenzopportunitätskosten der Umverteilung zwischen i und h einerseits und j und h andererseits zum Ausgleich. Diese Grenzopportunitätskosten sind, da i dem anderen Reichen gegenüber seine Verteilungsvorstellungen nicht durchsetzen kann, größer als Null, während sie im totalen Verteilungsoptimum des i gleich Null wären.

[34] Zur Skepsis gegenüber der Behauptung distributiven Free-Rider-Verhaltens in der Literatur vgl. Sudgen 1982.

[35] Shoup 1969, S. 23 ff., unterscheidet aus diesem Grund zwischen konsensfähigen und konfliktträchtigen Verteilungszielen.

Literatur

Becker, G. S. (1974): A Theory of Social Interactions. In: *Journal of Political Economy* 82, S. 1063–1093.

Bös, D. / Tillmann, G. (1983): Neid und Progressive Besteuerung. In: *Staatsfinanzierung im Wandel.* Schriften des Vereins für Sozialpolitik. N. F., Bd. 134, Berlin, S. 637–660.

Brennan, G. (1973): Pareto Desirable Redistribution: A Non-Altruistic Dimension. In: *Public Choice* XIV, S. 43–67.

Buchanan, J. M. (1965): An Economic Theory of Clubs. In: *Economica* 32, S. 1–14.

Buchanan, J. M. / Tullock, G. (1962): *The Calculus of Consent.* Ann Arbor 1962.

Collard, D. (1975): Edgeworth's Propositions on Altruism. In: *Economic Journal* 85, S. 355.

Eckstein, W. (1977): *Theorie der ethischen Gefühle.* Hamburg.

Edgeworth, F. Y. (1881): *Mathematical Psychics.* London.

Foley, D. (1967): Ressource Allocation and the Public Sector. In: *Yale Economic Essays* 7, S. 45–98.

Hochman, H. M. / Rodgers, J. D. (1969): Pareto Optimal Redistribution. In: *American Economic Review* 59, S. 542–557.

Kant, I. (1785): *Grundlegung zur Metaphysik der Sitten.*

Linde, R. (1981): Produktion II: Produktionsfunktionen. In: Albers, W. (Hrsg.), *Handwörterbuch der Wirtschaftswissenschaft,* Bd. 6. Göttingen u. a., S. 279–281.

Neumann, M. (1980): Nutzen. In: *Handwörterbuch der Wirtschaftswissenschaft,* Bd. 5, S. 349-361.

Pieper, J. (1953): *Über die Gerechtigkeit.* München.

Pigou, A. (1951): *A Study in Public Finance.* 3. Aufl. London.

Rawls, J. (1971): *A Theory of Justice.* Cambridge, Mass.

Ross, A. M. (1956): *Trade Union Wage Policy.* Berkeley and Los Angeles.

Shoup, C. S. (1969): *Public Finance.* Chicago.

Smith, A. (1759): *The Theory of Moral Sentiments.* London. Übers. v. W. Eckstein u. d. T. Theorie der ethischen Gefühle. 2. Aufl., Hamburg 1977.

Sohmen, E. (1976): *Allokationstheorie und Wirtschaftspolitik.* Tübingen.

Sudgen, R. (1982): On the Economics of Philanthropy. In: *Economic Journal* 92, S. 341–350.

Tiebout, C. M. (1956): A Pure Theory of Local Government Expenditure. In: *Journal of Political Economy* 64, S. 416–424.

The Contribution of Social Psychology to Industrial Democracy

Daniel Ondrack

Abstract

The relationship between industrial democracy and social psychology was explored for such variables as individual growth, intrinsic motivation, meaningfulness of work, group cohesion, workforce morale, quality of decisions, and commitment to work. It was generally found that industrial democracy had a positive relationship to most of the social psychological variables and that there was strong social psychological support for the expected outcomes from industrial democracy. However, these relationships were stronger under conditions of direct representation by workers than under conditions of indirect representation. Other important situational moderating variables in the relationship were workers sense of experienced participation, sense of identification with representatives, perceived scope of participation topics, and perceived results of participation activities. Individual differences such as "locus of control" and "inner-other directedness" also act as moderating variables in the relationship. It was concluded that there are strong social psychological foundations for the concept of industrial democracy, but it must also be recognized that the effects of industrial democracy will vary considerably between individuals and situations.

1. Introduction

It is not necessary in this paper to review the purposes of industrial democracy as these are well reviewed elsewhere in the volume. Instead, some of the assumptions about social psychological behavior which underly the concept of industrial democracy will be reviewed. These social psychological assumptions can be thought of as a behavioral model which should explain or predict the dynamics of what is observed (or hoped for) in conditions of industrial democracy. After the development of the theoretical model, some research evidence will be reviewed from the social psychological literature to see if the behavioral model is supported by empirical results.

Roger Brown's classic textbook on social psychology (Brown 1965) tried to define social psychology by listing a series of topics which seem to fall within the field, but Brown admitted that the list was not necessarily comprehensive, nor did the list actually define the field of social psychology. Instead, the list suggested a general domain of subject areas with several overlapping boundaries into psychology and sociology. However, the field does seem to focus on behavior of individuals as influenced by interaction with others and also is concerned with the behavior of groups as a field of study.

Jones and Gerard (1967) have more confidence in their definition as they state that social psychology is a subdiscipline of psychology which involves "the scientific study of the behavior of individuals as a function of social stimuli" (p. 1). However, Jones and Gerard admit that ambiguity exists in the meaning of social stimuli and they in turn list a series of cases of behavioral episodes to illustrate a variety of behaviors which are thought to be within the domain of social psychology. Thus once again, the field is defined by a series of topics which seem to have an underlying, though elusive common thread.

In a more specific approach to social psychology, Tannenbaum (1966) concentrated on social psychology of work organizations. He defined this as the relationship of man to the organization in which he works, the various factors which affect these relationships and the various outcomes for both the person and the organization. Beyond this definition, the field of social psychology in work organizations is illustrated by the subjects in the book: adjustment, conflict, groups, decision-making and outcomes. Some underlying theme or concept of social psychology justifies the choice of these particular topics as being relevant in the social psychology of work, but the theme itself remains elusive.

However, these difficulties in defining social psychology also present an advantage. If the field can be suggested by a range of topics, then one can do a review of social psychology in some context by choosing whichever list of topics one feels is relevant to that context. If the list of topics is a subset of those commonly found in the domain of social psychology, then one can be confident that at least some part of the field of social psychology has been represented in the discussion. In the discussion which follows, no attempt will be made to try to cover all the major topics within the field of social psychology. Instead, the contribution of social psychology to industrial democracy will be reviewed by examining a list of relevant topics in social psychology which form a subset of the possible list and which seem to be relevant to industrial democracy.

2. Some Basic Elements of Industrial Democracy

Industrial democracy has been described by Nightingale (1976) as a form of participation in organizations where there is the right of full joint decision-making; direct participation on shop floor decisions as well as indirect participation in decisions at the very highest levels of the organizations; on issues of company policy as well as on day-to-day issues. The philosophy underlying such participation is power sharing for the purposes (in Nightingale's concept) of alleviating alienation in the workplace, improving labor-management relations and enhancing the productivity of organizations. This concept goes beyond traditional labor-management relationships such as collective bargaining (which essentially focuses on conditions of work), or human relations programs (which focus on the climate of relationships). Instead, the concept involves a redefinition of the fundamental relationship between workers and management away from traditional adversarial relationships to joint partnerships or co-determination of the enterprise. As a variant on the concept, Derber (1969), Jenkins (1974), Trist (1981) have added that authoritarian conditions of work are inconsistent with the philosophy and operations of a society based on democratic ideals. For a society to be striving towards democracy, it is necessary that as many social institutions as possible also operate as democratically as possible. Therefore, industrial democracy is a logical extension of social democracy and just as a social democracy is believed to be a better type of society, then industrial democracy is believed to be a better type of organization or work life. Derber has listed a ten point framework for the necessary conditions for industrial democracy such as equal rights, minority rights, due process, and participation being seen as practiced by individuals and their representatives. Details of industrial democracy theories and practices would of course vary from one country to another or from one socio-economic cultural situation to another, but the basic concepts should remain the same.

In terms of whether industrial democracy achieves some of the avowed purposes, the evidence is mixed. It is not possible in this paper to attempt any comprehensive survey of this question and instead a few representative studies will be cited to illustrate the controversy. On the positive side, Webergen (1985) has concluded that while industrial democracy takes more time and appears to be administratively costly, the results avoid later confrontations which may be even more costly or time consuming. The essential factor for success is a will for cooperation ("in a spirit of confrontation, co-determination cannot succeed" (p. 3)), and on the whole, Webergen is convinced that industrial democracy has contributed a great deal to the „Wirtschaftswunder" of West Germany (p. 3).

A study by Nightingale (1982) concluded that organizations with workplace democracy had greater productivity than similar organizations with conventional management-worker relationships, but that these kinds of results were insufficient to create a momentum for greater adoption of workplace democracy by other organizations. Nightingale also found that the most progress in terms of acceptance by unions and management with the various forms of workplace democracy was with self-directing or semi autonomous work groups. However, work councils were found to be opposed by trade unions as potential alternatives to union representation and board level representation was opposed by management as an intrusion on managerial rights and perogatives, i.e., sharing of power is felt to be a loss of control (Jenkins 1974; Windmuller 1977).

Another issue about industrial democracy is whether it fits with, or is consistent with the socio-cultural situation in a society. Some such as Trist (1981), Walker (1977), feel that social forces common to the Western world will force the adoption of more industrial democracy. Others have argued that social forces in Europe have enouraged industrial democracy, but not in North America (Jenkins 1974; Sturmthal 1977). For example, there is substantial opinion in North America that *both* unions and management are uninterested in industrial democracy (Jenkins 1974) and a strong feeling that collective bargaining is sufficient to satisfy workers needs (Crispo 1978; Goldfinder 1974) and therefore there is no need for industrial democracy (Windmuller 1977). Sturmthal (1977) has also warned about the possibility of unions and management becoming too close together in a system of industrial democracy with the result of alienation of workers from both the union and the employer. Sturmthal also questions whether a union or a federation of unions can meaningfully represent interests of labour when the interests of competitive unions are diverse or when there is diversity of interests among the union membership. Representation at very high levels may come to seem very remote to the interests of rank and file workers while representation through collective bargaining may be of more immediate relevance.

However, King and Van de Vall (1978) have also observed that the collective bargaining model is very traditional in its orienation toward conflict over wages and work conditions. The ideology of conflict may be so ingrained in both parties, that a major barrier to successful cooperation is "the fear of cooperation itself" (p. 187). Those imagined dangers of cooperation would lead both parties to exaggerate the benefits of collective bargaining as a rationalization for avoiding any movement toward industrial democracy.

In summary, there seem to be four models or levels of industrial democracy which could be complementary to each other but could also operate independently from each other. The first is the notion that industrial democracy must occur as a way of life in order to fit in with societal values or the directions of evolving social trends. The second level is that industrial democracy occurs by representation of workers at the highest levels of decision making of the organization. The third level is essentially the same as collective bargaining where workers are represented in decisions about conditions and payments of work. The fourth level is at the shop floor where workers themselves participate in decisions which directly affect their own workplace.

In terms of the impacts of industrial democracy on worker alienation, feelings of job and life satisfaction, intrinsic motivation and sense of personal identity, recent reviews (Nightingale 1982; Trist 1981; King and Van de Vall 1978; and Bartolke et al. 1982), have found the greatest benefits to come from shop floor or direct participation in decision making. Direct participation is perceived by workers as being meaningful control over their workplace while "they are not so likely to see such implications in representative participation" (Bartolke et al. 1982, p. 394).

From a social-psychological perspective, some feeling of participation in decisions and control over one's life may occur from representation, but the evidence does not suggest much impact occurs on perceptions of meaningful power or any reductions in alienation or improvements in satisfaction. For example, in Yugoslavia where representative participation has been in effect for three decades, supervisory relations are reported to be still predominantly authoritarian (King and Van de Vall 1978). In another survey of results of representative participation, Ramsay (1977) concluded that a phenomenon of "phantom participation" existed in most of the case study sites. Participtation was something that was talked about and was supposed to exist, but like a phantom, few had actually seen it or experienced it.

Instead, it appears that the greatest potential impact for industrial democracy on worker alienation, etc., probably lies with shop floor, direct participation rather than forms of indirect participation. The various forms of indirct representation may exist at a level of abstract awareness among workers, but have little psychological reality. Therefore, there is probably very little social-psychological foundation for indirect representation and instead we must look to direct participation for the social-psychology of industrial democracy.

3. Social Psychology of Direct Participation

At the outset, it is necessary to recognize Dachler and Wilpert's (1979) criticisms of research on participation in their excellent review of the topic before proceeding to discuss results of social psychological research. They defined four perspectives or ways of conceptualizing participation, only two of which (human growth and development models, and productivity and efficiency models) have much relationship to social psychology. Dachler and Wilpert state that research on participation has accumulated a considerable amount of empirical data, but:

> ... our analyses have repeatedly shown knowledge about participation to be fragmentary, contradictory, and limited to a relatively few psychological and sociological preconditions and consequences of participation, ... This knowledge hardly begins to reflect the complex questions that participatory social systems pose in their real work settings. (p. 29)

Moreover, the design of research on participatory systems reflects the biases and values of researchers so that only certain kinds of questions are asked and others are not even thought of or considered for asking. For example, if researchers are primarily interested in social psychological issues, they will ask social psychological questions and only report social psychological results. They cannot report results on issues which they had not considered in their research design. While one outcome of this research bias is that more information will be available on social psychological issues, the other outcome is that available information will not be comprehensive, even within a social psychological domain.

Keeping the above caveat in mind about research on industrial democracy, it is

now possible to discuss the following social psychological components of industrial democracy:
3.1. Individual growth
3.2. Intrinsic motivation
3.3. Meaning in work
3.4. Group cohesion
3.5. Workforce morale
3.6. Quality of decisions
3.7. Commitment

These topics are not completely separate conceptually or operationally, but they provide useful approximations of social psychological issues which are assumed to underly some of the dynamics and outcomes of industrial democracy. In other words, this list of topics provides a possible domain for social psychology in industrial democracy.

3.1. Individual Growth

A common element in growth theories or assumptions about worker behavior (McGreger 1960; Argyris 1964; Alderfer 1972), is that people have an inborn need to develop or mature to a state of independence and self-management. This underlying need would manifest itself in the work situation by a desire among workers for what Herzberg (1959) for example, called the motivation factors in work (achievement, recognition, responsibility, advancement, growth and challenge in work). To the extent that workers perceive their work situation to be deficient in these motivation factors, workers would feel a lack of fulfillment in their work and consequently have lower levels of work satisfaction. In turn, low satisfaction with work would have the impacts of less motivation to work, lack of commitment to work or employer, or what one might call alienation from work.

If growth needs were common amongst workers in general, then work which is unfulfilling or even incongruent with these needs (Argyris 1964) would eventually have serious consequences for either productivity and/or general feelings of malaise among the work force. Industrial democracy has been seen as one solution to this sort of problem by offering workers some opportunities for satisfaction of growth needs parallel to the work situation. For example, if the content of work does not provide much opportunity for growth needs satisfaction, the opportunity to participate in decision making about the work place could offer some substitute avenues for satisfaction. By participation in semi autonomous work groups and works councils, workers would have some opportunities for responsibility, growth, achievement, challenge and even recognition. For those who managed to take on roles as representatives in higher level decision councils, there is even the possibility of advancement away from the shop floor which is parallel to advancement within the hierarchical ranks in the organization. There is also the possibility that the outcomes of the participative decision making in industrial democracy might eventually modify the content of work itself so that it becomes more satisfying to growth needs.

In terms of social psychological research, the first question is about the basic premise: is there a basic growth need in people which would drive them to seek fulfillment in work? The research results on this question are unfortunately not very supportive of the basic premise. A review of growth need research by Pfeffer and Salancik (1977) concluded that there was little empirical verification for the concept, but that the growth needs concept was popular due to an intuitive appeal, i.e., it is a way that people like to think or believe that people are, or that social science researchers themselves have high growth needs and believe that everyone else does too. A more appropriate assumption is probably that growth needs are a matter of individual differences and that some people are higher in growth need strength than others (Hackman and Oldham 1980).

If individuals or groups differ in growth need strength, then the opportunities for growth need satisfaction in industrial democracy will appeal to some and not to others. Those low in growth need strength will not perceive industrial democracy as making much difference to their work life and will remain relatively indifferent to the opportunity. For those who are higher in growth need strength, industrial democracy *may* provide an opportunity for some needs satisfaction. The question of whether this happens depends upon whether or not there is sufficient challenging content in the decisions to be made. For example, in a study by Ondrack and Evans (1982), worker participation in decisions was limited to rather low level content and after the novelty of participation had passed, workers did not perceive participation in works councils as being any particular source of satisfaction. Thus participation alone would not be sufficient as an outlet for satsifaction of growth needs. Instead there must be participation in decisions which are perceived to be meaningful in order for industrial democracy to have an impact.

3.2. Intrinsic Motivation

The assumptions about intrinsic motivation are very similar to the assumptions about growth needs in that desire for satisfaction of intrinsic motivation is considered to be something of a basic underlying need common to everyone. Intrinsic motivation refers to the need to have personal challenge in a task or a task that is intriguing to the individual in requiring skills and knowledge that an individual enjoys using. Under this assumption, the opportunity to do the task itself is rewarding to the person independent of other secondary or extrinsic rewards (such as compensation). The simplest examples of intrinsic motivation are the activities that people do in play or recreation. Play and recreation are voluntary and people do them because the activity is rewarding in itself. Thus, the more that the content of a job offers opportunities for intrinsic motivation, the more that people will find great satisfaction in their work. What exactly is intrisically satisfying will differ from individual to individual just as choice of play or recreation differs between individuals.

Intrinsic rewards or satisfactions are an important component of the expectancy theory of work motivation (Vroom 1964) where persons are predicted to be motivated in their work if they have a high expectancy that doing a particular job will result in satisfaction of their particular set of intrinsic work needs. The level of motivation will be even higher if there is also an expectancy that satisfaction from intrinsic rewards will be accompanied by extrinsic rewards (such as career success). Thus a person who likes to do academic research will be motivated primarily by the intrinsic rewards of the task itself, but will also be motivated further if academic research is seen to lead toward career success. Conversely, persons who have little intrinsic interest in academic research may still do the task in order to pursue career success (if they have a high value on career success), but will not obtain much satisfaction from doing the task of academic research.

In the everyday work situation, some workers will find some degree of intrinsic satisfaction in their work and others will not because the work requirements will be a poor match for the worker's individual interests. If sufficient degrees of freedom or opportunities exist, people will gravitate over time to work situations which are more intrinsically interesting, but in conditions of low degrees of freedom, people may be trapped in a poor-match situation. In these circumstances, there will be no intrinsic satisfaction in work and perhaps higher demands for extrinsic rewards to compensate for the lack of intrinsic rewards.

Industrial democracy could be very appealing to those individuals who obtain intrinsic satisfaction from participation in groups, meetings, and decisions in those bodies. Certainly some individuals always seek out such opportunities on or off the job and one must assume that their seeking is driven by their personal intrinsic satisfactions. Others are very much the opposite and shy away from group participation, presumably because their intrinsic satisfactions lie elsewhere. Such individuals may benefit from the results of an industrial democracy system, but will not feel any particular sense of satisfaction from being in such a system. The rewards will be perceived as extrinsic and not associated with their personal intrinsic satisfactions.

For those individuals who are trapped in a poor-match job and whose intrinsic needs can be greatly satisfied by participation in an industrial democracy system, the result will be the same as for growth needs. Participation in the various activities in an industrial democracy system may provide sufficient substitute rewards so that the lack of satisfaction in the job itself can be tolerated.

There is actually very little research to test the concept or the dynamics of intrinsic rewards. It is another concept that has powerful intuitive appeal because it makes such common sense to say that people will be motivated best by what they enjoy doing the most. However, there is some research about tradeoffs between intrinsic and extrinsic rewards. Some research indicates that people feel less intrinsic satisfaction when they receive extrinsic rewards for doing work that they enjoyed doing by itself (Deci 1971; Staw 1975), but others found no such effect (Fisher 1978; Phillips and Lord 1980). Reviews of research on intrinsic and extrinsic rewards have generally concluded that the two types of rewards are additive (Feldman and Arnold 1983) and the anomalous results of Deci have not been extensively supported (Gibson et al. 1985).

In summary, the content of intrinsic motivations is idiosyncratic to individuals and there may or may not be a good match in an industrial democracy situation. Certainly some proportion of workers will obtain satisfaction from participation in meetings and working in semi-autonomous teams and for those people, industrial democracy should enhance their feelings of intrinsic rewards.

3.3. Morale

Morale is an elusive quality in organization life which is easy to sense or recognize when it is high or low, but difficult to define. Essentially it seems to be a collective sense of satisfaction in the workplace which in turn is associated with a collective sense of motivation in work. When morale is "good", energy and productivity are high and people feel good about themselves and their collective effort. Obviously, management in organizations would prefer to have "good" morale rather than poor morale which is characterized by low energy, low interest and low productivity.

An important factor in morale which has been well established in social-psychological research is participation in semi-autonomous work teams. The classic studies by Coch and French (1948), Rice (1958), Trist and Bamforth (1951), the Tavistock Institute (Trist 1981) all provided strong evidence to show that workers organized into semi-autonomous groups had unusual productivity, satisfaction and adaptation to change *provided* that the groups had the right to participate in decisions that affected them and their work. Trist (1981) has described this research tradition as being the foundation for the surge of interest in industrial democracy in Europe in the 1960's and in quality of work life in North America in the 1970's. Trist has gone so far as to describe the industrial democracy/quality of work life movement (combined with new ways of thinking about technology in the work place) as a new paradigm of assumptions and values about the world of work (Trist 1981).

> ... the new paradigm is based on optimum task grouping which encourages multiple broad skills. Workers ... become capable of a much higher degree of internal control, having flexible group resources to meet a greater degree of environmental variance ... which allows commitment to grow and alienation to decrease (p. 43).

With such an impressive research tradition as a foundation, one would expect that group morale should be noticeably improved in industrial democracy with attendent benefits in alienation and productivity. Unfortunately, the evidence is mixed on this question in several ways. For example, morale is often found to be very high in the start-up of a new QWL or participatory work system, but considerable evidence exists to show that the initial high level of morale is difficult to sustain (Goodman 1979). Some question exists about whether high morale is due to the actual opportunity to participate, or the conditions of industrial democracy, or due to some "Hawthorne effect" reaction to the newness of the situation (Ondrack and Evans 1981). Once the newness of the situation wears off, it is possible that morale may drop back to normal or pre-existing levels. In one long term follow-up study of a chemical plant with a reputation for very high morale at the start up of an industrial democracy system, Blackler and Brown (1981) found that six years later, the system hardly existed in memory among employees or managers. The long term outcome was a certain amount of cynicism toward participation on both sides and a definite regression in morale back to preprogram levels.

Secondly, Dachler and Wilpert (1978) have noted that most of reported research on morale and participation is about participation at the level of work place arrangements. Participation at higher levels is seen as relatively unimportant for an impact on morale. Once again, the most potential for a meaningful impact on employee morale from industrial democracy comes more from direct participation at the shop floor level and less so from representative participation at higher levels. The commonly observed initial improvement in group morale in industrial democracy should be viewed with caution as a possibly temporary phenomenon. There is very little evidence to show that such levels of morale are self-sustaining merely because the opportunity for participation exists.

3.4. Group Cohesion

Group cohesion is an important property for the motivation of groups or the satisfaction associated with membership in a group. Cohesiveness is a function of the degree of shared norms, values, goals and behavior styles between the members of a group: the greater the degree of similiarity in shared values, etc., the greater the degree of cohesion. There are a number of effects of cohesion on group and individual behavior. A principal effect is conformity by members to group norms so that behavior by individuals is fairly predictable and behavior by a group is fairly distinctive. Secondly, a sense of group identity can develop so that individuals can feel some degree of pride of association or confidence in identity by belonging to a cohesive group. Finally, morale is generally higher in cohesive groups so that the collective energy or motivation of a group can be at a high level toward tasks perceived to be important to group purposes (Maier 1973; Gibson et al. 1985).

It is this last point which makes group cohesiveness so important in organization performance. If the energy of group cohesiveness is devoted toward organization purposes (or the group goals are consistent with organization goals), then there will be a high level of performance toward goals which benefit the organization (and the group). However, a group could be just as cohesive and have goals which are quite different from management and the energy of the group could be directed toward other purposes (Brown 1984). This means that an important aspect of group cohesiveness is the mutuality or sharing of goals between worker groups and management.

Industrial democracy can contribute to group cohesiveness in two principal ways. First, the opportunity to participate in semi-autonomous groups or workers' councils can increase cohesiveness by providing workers with the opportunity for greater interaction (Trist 1981). If the technological structure of workplace arrangements does not normally encourage worker interaction (Trist and Bamforth 1951), there will be little opportunity for cohesiveness to develop. Various forms of industrial democracy can provide substitute opportunities for interaction to compensate for the lack of opportunities in the routine workplace. Second, participation in decision-making about work arrangements can help to clarify goals and values among workers so that a consensus on goals, values, etc. gradually emerges. Once a consensus is established, then the previously fragmented energy of a collection of individuals can be concentrated into a collective group energy toward the consensus. A third effect of industrial democracy on group cohesiveness is that participation also provides the group with an opportunity to help shape the content or direction of the goals, but this effect will be discussed in the next section on commitment to goals.

In summary, when group cohesiveness is high and group agreement with organization goals is high, then a high level of group performance will be oriented toward achievement of organization goals. Conversely, the same level of energy could be directed away from organization goals if the group does not share organization goals (Gibson et al. 1985, Chapter 8).

Another important aspect of group cohesiveness is the needs of individuals for inclusion in group membership (Cartwright and Zander 1968). Some individuals have a much higher internal locus of control than others (Rotter 1971). Those with high needs for inclusion or high degrees of external control will have higher levels of need satisfaction from group membership. Consequently, their behavior will be more strongly affected by group cohesiveness than will be individuals with high internal control who tend to act more independently of groups. The impact of industrial democracy on forming group cohesion will probably be lesser for inner-directed individuals and the sharing of group and organization goals will have less of an effect as well. However, if the inner directed individuals also share the organization goals, then the level of individual performance will be equally as high as the level of group performance.

For some employers, this issue of individual differences and group cohesion could be quite serious if group cohesion was essential in some way to organization performance, i.e., a crew of a space ship where a high degree of interdependence exists and very high cohesiveness is crucial to survival and task completion. In such circumstances, careful selection of personnel for compatibility with organization goals and extensive development for group cohesiveness would be necessary to enhance the probability of good performance.

3.5. Commitment

Commitment is closely allied to the concept of group cohesiveness because commitment refers to the sense of direction of a group's motivation. If there is high cohesiveness, then there will also be high commitment to a particular direction, goal or group decision, once the decision process has been completed. However, a highly cohesive group can have low commitment if the group does not agree with the content of a decision or possibly the process by which a decision was made. The effect of commitment is that workers will feel a sense of obligation to the decision or course of action which allows them to keep working on a course of action without a need for close supervision. Normally, close supervision is required if a work group does not understand a task or if the group has low commitment to the task (Evans 1970; House 1971). When a group has commitment to a task, they can operate more autonomously or be self-managed in their attention to the task.

Obviously, there are several advantages to an organization if work groups have commitment to decisions or tasks. Overhead expenses can be reduced with group commitment because fewer supervisors are required for the same number of workers (increased span of control), or supervisors can concentrate their attention on other duties (such as planning, resource seeking) rather than on direct supervision. In addition, with commitment workers will feel a personal sense of responsibility for their work and could voluntarily increase cooperation, energy, suggestions and problem solving. These behaviors have the impact of increasing the efficiency of the work place from a bottom-up process rather than from a top-down managerial perspective.

The importance of commitment on group performance was demonstrated in some of the early research studies by Coch and French (1948), Walker and Guest (1952), Miller and Rice (1967) and the Tavistock group (Trist 1981). The results of studies such as these showed quite clearly two important behavior patterns: worker productivity and acceptance of change was greatly affected by worker commitment, and worker commitment was greatly increased by work-group participation in decisions about their work place. Commitment and performance were not nearly so high if workers in groups did not have the opportunity to participate in relevant decison-making. Thus a key factor in building commitment among worker groups was participation in decision-making or some degree of power equalization between workers and management. In some way, the act of participation by groups increases group commitment to the decision.

One answer to how the increased commitment occurs comes from research on dissonance theory (see Brown 1965; Jones and Gerard 1967; and Rokeach 1968 for reviews of dissonance and cognitive consistency theory). In terms of dissonance theory, if people participate or share in decision-making which affects them directly, they must feel commitment to the decision in order to minimize the possibility of dissonance between the decision requirements and personal preferences. If a person does not participate in a decision and the decision requirements are in conflict with personal preferences, there is no dissonance to be avoided because someone else made the decision. Therefore, the worker does not have to feel any sense of commitment (to avoid dissonance) to a decision made by others. When people influence or make the decisions themselves, they must feel commitment toward the decision so that there is no dissonance between personal preferences of behavior and behavior requirements from the decision.

Dissonance theory is a powerful concept in social psychology and is strongly supported by empirical research studies. Thus dissonance theory provides strong support in social psychology theory for increased commitment from shop-floor, direct participation by workers. However, the principles of dissonance theory can also be used to explain why participation by representation may not add much sense of commitment by workers to decision outcomes. If workers feel detached from decisions made indirectly by representatives, then workers would have little sense of dissonance if their personal behavior preferences were different from the decision outcomes. The amount of dissonance felt may not be meaningful because the decisions were made by remote others. However, if the workers strongly identified with the representatives in the higher level decision making bodies in industrial democracy, then the workers might feel a greater sense of commitment to the decisions. An important variable in commitment for any form of decisions by representatives then, is the amount of identification with or psychological distance between workers and their representatives. When workers feel too detached or alienated from their representatives, the power of industrial democracy to obtain worker commitment is greatly diminished.

3.6. Decision Quality

Decision quality refers to the possibility that a decision can be improved or that a decision can be found so that payoffs from the decision are greater than they might have been from some decision of lower quality. Payoffs might be a function of technical elegance of a problem solution, greater acceptance of a solution or greater mutual benefits from a solution. In decision theory (Simon 1960), an optimum decision has the best possible level of satisfaction or payoffs for all parties involved. Since no decision can satisfy the optimum requirements, all decisions must be sub-optimum to some degree. Improving the quality of a decision has the effect of making a decision less sub optimum than some alternative decision (Janis and Mann 1977).

In general, decision quality has the possibility of being improved if more relevant information about the problem is made available to the decision-makers (Maier 1973; Vroom and Yetton 1973). The logic here is that a better informed decision maker has a greater probability of success by virtue of being able to consider more aspects of a problem. A less well informed decision-maker may fail to weigh important considerations because the decision-maker is unaware of their existance. Secondly, decision quality has the possibility of improving if a greater number of alternative solutions are considered before a decision is made or an alternative is selected. If a decision maker can only select alternatives from within a limited range, there is always the possibility that better quality alternatives may exist outside of the limited range. If the decision-maker is unaware of these other alternatives, it is not possible to select them and the decision chosen must be of lower quality. If the range of possible alternatives is expanded, the probability of finding a higher quality alternative is greatly enhanced (Holloman and Henrick 1972). Of course some point of diminishing returns can occur where the addition of more and more alternatives does not contribute any more to quality and may even impede quality by causing information overload on the decision maker. Issues concerning the optimum number of alternatives and information overload are considered in decision and information theory and cannot be pursued here (see Weiss et al. 1982).

Industrial democracy is felt to contribute to decision-quality in both the ways that quality can be improved. First, worker participation in the decision-making process can greatly expand the available, relevant information about the problem (Maier 1973; Vroom and Yetton 1973). Workers can contribute different perspectives on a problem from that of management so that the problem itself may be seen in a different light or that unforeseen consequences of a decision can be more fully explored. Also, workers may have better technical information or different information about a problem than management due to workers' direct experience with operations. Thus even in a situation where management ultimately retains the right to make the decision (Vroom and Yetton's A_2 decision style), they are able to make a much better-informed decision as a result of worker participation.

Secondly, industrial democracy can contribute to decision quality by the generation of more alternatives about a problem. Workers need not be limited to only contributing information, they can also contribute ideas about how a problem may be solved, or contribute alternatives for how a decision may be made. From their perspectives on a problem, they may not only create a wider range of alternatives to enhance the probability of quality, they may exercise some creativity in generating alternatives which may never have occurred to management (Emery 1983). This additional role of workers in industrial democracy requires the management style in the organization to shift from "consultative" (workers contribute information or reactions) to "participative" (workers contribute ideas) in Tannenbaum and Schmidt's (1973) conceptualization of leadership styles. Maier (1973) has also argued that participation in generating decision alternatives has the added effect of creating greater motivation among workers in two ways: greater commitment from having participated in the decision process and greater intrinsic work satisfaction from the challenge of creativity. If workers suggest alternatives and see them implemented, they can also benefit from the motivation components of task identity, task significance, and task feedback (Hackman and Oldham 1975).

A further aspect of decision-quality from industrial democracy is that participation allows (or requires) a decision to be justified before a consensus is reached or the decision is implemented. Consensus-building and decision-justification require that decision-makers convince others of the rationality or logic of their decisions. In doing so, the decision makers' own thinking about the problem and the decision may be clarified in the process, that improving quality (Gibson et al. 1985).

The research on group decision-making has generally shown that decisions from groups have higher quality, more creativity and a greater propensity for riskier alternatives (Arnold and Feldman 1983). However, the decision process is also slower, can be frustrating due to inefficient procedures and can suffer from the phenomenon described by Janis (1973) as "group-think". In group-think, a greater priority exists among a group on maintaining harmony and seeking quick consensus than on seeking better quality alternatives. Such groups may actually suppress creativity and critical examination of alternatives in their unconscious desire to avoid internal conflict. When group-think or other sub-optimizing social processes occur, the benefits of participation on decision quality are greatly reduced.

Another aspect to consider about industrial democracy and decision quality is that the potential for improved quality can exist just as strongly with representative participation. Representatives of workers in higher level decision bodies can create the benefits of more information, more alternatives and more justification just as effectively as in direct participation. This is one of the few areas of social psychology theory discussed in this paper where the benefits of industrial democracy apply equally well at all levels of decision-making. Of course, some might argue that the negative side of participation on decision-making (slowness inefficiency, group-think) can also apply at all levels equally as well.

3.7. Meaningful Work

The concept of meaningful work is a fundamental belief of the proponents of quality of work life (QWL) such as Trist (1981), Hackman and Oldham (1975), Kolodny and Van Beinum (1983). Meaningful work is considered to be an antidote to psychological alienation from work, to some extent possible compensation for economic alienation, and to be a major contributor to quality of life (Kabanoff 1980; Near et al. 1980). The relationship between meaningful work and quality of life is similar to the relationship postulated between job enrichment and growth needs, i.e., there is an assumption that people have an inherent need for meaningful work which is thwarted by traditional work situations (Dachler and Wilpert 1978, pp. 7–8). Greater meaningfulness of work is generally associated with greater enrichment of job content (i.e., satisfaction of intrinsic needs), but could also come from increased task feedback and task significance (Hackman 1977). In Hackman's theory, task feedback allows workers to see where the results of their work go to, or how the results are used. This satisfies their need for closure and may contribute to a sense of meaningfulness as people see how their work fits into a larger system.

Task significance has been defined by Hackman as "the degree to which the job has a substantial impact on the lives or work of other people, whether in the immediate organization or in the external environment" (Hackman 1977, p. 130). If task significance is increased (along with increases in skill variety and task identity), the result is a psychological state which Hackman calls "experienced meaningfulness of work". As with other aspects of the Hackman-Oldham theory of job design and work satisfaction, the experienced meaningfulness of work will be greater for those with high growth need strength than for those with lower growth need strength.

The question for industrial democracy is whether participation, direct or indirect, by workers can add to meaningfulness of work. Hinckley (1985) has concluded that participation can enhance meaningfulness by contributing to worker learning about the organization in such areas as:
- other roles in the organization and how they go about doing their work,
- how the organization functions and the priorities of the larger system,
- how individual output is valued and utilized by others,
- how to influence others and to use power and authority, (pp. 65–66).

However, this conclusion of Hinckley's is not based on empirical evidence, but is a postulated outcome based on his beliefs about the values of participation. The question of the impact of participation on meaningfulness of work probably depends a lot upon the subject matter of the participation opportunities. For example, if direct participation is concerned with conditions of work, means of production scheduling, work assignments and so on, the act of participation may not add any new information about where the work outputs go, how they are used or how they fit into a larger system. Such questions may be outside the boundaries of relevant participation at the work group level and so little would be contributed to task significance and meaningfulness of work.

Participation by representation in meetings to coordinate production between work units may add a lot of information about where the outputs go, how they are used, etc., but this information may only increase the task significance for the individual representative. Similarly, participation by representation at plant or board level meetings may also increase the meaningfulness of work for representatives, but add little significance to the worker levels of the organization. Here it may be argued that once representatives learn about or experience meaningfulness of work by participation, they can communicate this back to the worker bodies they represent. The workers will be better informed as a result, but they still may not have a feeling of "experienced meaningfulness of work." It seems that this reaction can only occur if two conditions are satisfied: direct participation, and sufficiently wide range of topics as the subject matter for participation. Otherwise, it is not seen that industrial democracy will have very much impact on meaningfulness of work except at the intellectual level of workers being better informed by the process.

Conclusion

This review of the social psychology of industrial democracy has examined seven aspects of social psychology (growth, intrinsic motivation, morale, group cohesiveness, commitment, decision quality, meaningful work). Each aspect was discussed in terms of the theoretical or philosopical relationship to industrial democracy and then research results were examined to see if the relationship was supported or not supported. This review of research did not attempt to be comprehensive due to space limitations, but instead looked at principal conclusions from research. This means that some material had to be omitted and some may have been overlooked. However, it is hoped that the material available provided a balanced review of the topics.

In general, the following conclusions were obtained from the review:

a) For the purposes of improving work satisfaction, reducing alienation from work and improving organization productivity, there is more potential impact from direct participation forms of industrial democracy than from indirect representation. Indirect representation at higher levels of decision-making may provide workers with better information about the work place, but better information which comes from work representatives is not much different from better information which comes from management representatives. This will be especially true if workers feel no particular sense of identification with their representatives. However, if workers feel a strong sense of identity with representatives (for example, workers in Poland sense of identification with Solidarity leaders), then indirect representation will provide some benefits similar to direct representation.

b) An important variable in whether workers have a sense of real participation in industrial democracy is their sense of experienced participation. Experienced participation creates a psychological reaction which has the possibility of provoking further reactions such as increased satisfaction, reduced alienation and so on. Some form of participation which is below a threshold level of experienced participation will not provide any psychological responses and workers will appear to be indifferent to the benefits of participation. This penomenon of worker indifference to nominal participation was observed in the studies by Blackler and Brown (1981) and Ondrack and Evans (1981). Consequently, in order for industrial democracy to have an impact of improving satisfaction and productivity, the content of participation must be sufficiently significant to go beyond nominal or trivial participation. This does not mean that the content or agenda for participation always has to be concerned with weighty issues, but the possibility of confronting serious issues has to exist.

c) Another important variable which contributes to experienced participation is the results or outcomes of participation. If workers or their representatives participate in good faith, but find over time that decisions never seem to be implemented or that outcomes never seem to occur, then participation will come to be seen as a hollow exercise. When this perception starts to develop, then experienced participation begins to decline and industrial democracy will be seen as only a ritualistic procedure. In order to combat this development, it is necessary to ensure in some way that decisions actually are implemented or at least that resources are seriously committed toward implementation. This requirement suggests that a significant amount of power sharing has to occur so that worker representatives have the right to force allocation of resources toward decision outcomes. Otherwise, the perception of outcomes resulting from decisions will be dependent solely on the commitment of management toward the decision. This condition of dependency is less likely to create feelings of experienced participation than will a condition of equality.

d) An important theme of social psychological theory is that individual differences have an important moderating effect on behavior in social psychological situations. For example, differences in locus of control or inner-other directedness between individuals will result in stronger or weaker impacts of social forces on behavior patterns. Differences in growth needs will result in stronger or weaker responses to the content of work. The moderating effect of individual differences was noted in almost all of the different aspects of social psychology and industrial democracy discussed in this paper. Because of these differences, it is difficult to reach any firm conclusions about social psychology and industrial democracy without knowing something about the distribution of individual differences in a work group or the norms for a group on some relevant dimension of individual differences. Failure to recognize the importance of individual differences or an uncritical assumption of common characteristics among worker populations have long been a weakness of many theories of industrial democracy.

In summary, there is considerable support for social psychological foundations of industrial democracy to justify expectations that industrial democracy will enhance satisfaction, reduce alienation and encourage greater productivity. However, this is not unqualified support. Social psychological dynamics work best for situations of direct participation and diminish with indirect participation. The appearance of participation through formalities of meetings will also not have much of an impact if there is no experience of participation from power sharing and seeing results of decisions. Finally, the desire for industrial democracy is not a universal need and some proportion of the work force will remain indifferent to the opportunity. However, there is considerable opinion in the literature that the majority of the work force population desire industrial democracy and that these desires are consistent with the democratic ideals of our western industrial society.

If this is true, then social psychological benefits of industrial democracy should be significant for the majority of the population.

Literature

Alderfer, C. P. (1972): *Existence, Relatedness and Growth: Human Needs in Organization Settings*. New York.

Argyris, C. (1964): *Integrating the Individual and the Organization*. New York.

Bartölke, K. / Eschweiler, W. / Fleschenberger D. / Tannenbaum, A. S. (1982): Workers' Participation and the Distribution of Control as Perceived by Members of Ten German Companies. In: *Administrative Science Quarterly* 27 (3), pp. 380–397.

Blackler. F. M. / Brown, C. A. (1981): A New Philosophy of Management: Shell Revisited. In: *Personel Review* 10 (1), pp. 15–21.

Brown, K. (1984): Explaining Group Poor Performance: An Attributional Analysis. In: *Academy of Management Review,* January, pp. 54–63.

Brown, R. (1965): *Social Psychology*. New York.

Cartwright, D. / Zander, A. (1968): *Group Dynamics: Research and Theory*. New York.

Coch, L. / French, J. (1948): Overcoming Resistance to Change. In: *Human Relations*. 1, pp. 512–533.

Crispo, J. (1978): *Industrial Democracy in Western Europe*. Toronto.

Dachler, H. P. / Wilpert, B. (1978): Conceptual Dimensions and Boundaries of Participation in Organizations: A Critical Evaluation. In: *Administrative Science Quarterly* 23, pp. 1–39.

Deci, E. L. (1971): The Effects of Externally Mediated Rewards on Intrinsic Motivation. In: *Journal of Personality and Social Psychology,* pp. 105–15.

Derber, M. (1969): Industrial Democracy as an Organizing Concept for a Theory of Industrial Relations. In: Somers, G. S. (Ed.), *Eassys in Industrial Relations Theory*. Ames, Iowa.

Emery, F. (1983): Sociotechnical Foundations for a New Social Order. In: Kolodny, H. / Van Beinum, H. (Eds.), *The Quality of Working Life and the 1980s*. New York.

Evans, M. (1970): The Effects of Supervisory Behavior on the Path Goal Relationship. In: *Organizational Behavior and Human Performance,* pp. 277–98.

Feldman, D. / Arnold, H. (1983): *Managing Individual and Group Behavior*. New York.

Fisher, C. D. (1978): The Effects of Personal Control, Competence and Extrinsic Reward Systems on Intrinsic Motivation. In: *Organizational Behavior and Human Performance,* June, pp. 273–87.

Gibson, J. / Ivancevich, J. / Donnelly, J. (1985): *Organizations: Behavior, Structure, Processes*. Plano, Texas.

Goldfinger, N., as quoted in Jenkins, D. (1974): *Job Power*. London, p. 315.

Goodman, P. (1979): *Assessing Organizational Change: The Rushton Quality of Work Life Experiment*. New York.

Hackman, R. (1977): Work Design. In: Hackman, J. R. / Suttle, J. L. (Eds.), *Improving Life at Work*. Santa Monica, Calif.

Hackman, J. R. / Oldham, G. R. (1975): Development of the Job Diagnostic Survey. In: *Journal of Applied Psychology,* April, pp. 159–70.

Hackman, J. R. / Oldham, G. R. (1980): *Work Redesign.* Reading, Massachusetts.
Herzberg, F. / Mauser, B. / Snyderman, B. (1959): *The Motivation to Work.* New York.
Hinckley, St. (1985): A Closer Look at Participation. In: *Organizational Dynamics,* Winter, pp. 57–67.
Holloman, Ch. / Henrick, H. (1972): Adequacy of Group Decisions as a Function of the Decision-Making Process. In: *Academy of Management Journal,* June, pp. 175–84.
House, R. (1971): A Path-Goal Theory of Leadership Effectiveness. In: *Administrative Science Quarterly,* September, pp. 321–39.
Janis, I. (1973): *Victims of Groupthink: A Psychological Study of Foreign Policy Decisions and Fiascos.* Boston.
Janis, I. / Mann, L. (1977): *Decision-Making: A Psychological Analysis of Conflict, Choice and Commitment.* New York.
Jenkins, D. (1974): *Job Power.* London.
Jones, E. E. / Gerard, H. B. (1967): *Foundations of Social Psychology.* New York.
Kabanoff, B. (1980): Work and Non-Work: A Review of Models, Methods and Findings. In: *Psychological Bulletin* 88, pp. 60–77.
King, Ch. D. / Van de Vall, M. (1978): *Models of Industrial Democracy.* The Hague.
Kolodny, H. / Van Beinum, H. (Eds). (1983): *The Quality of Working Life and the 1980's.* New York.
Maier, N. (1973): *Psychology in Organizations,* Boston, Houston.
McGregor, D. M. (1960): *The Human Side of Enterprise.* New York.
Miller, E. T. / Rice, A. K. (1967): *Systems of Organization.* London.
Near, J. / Rice, R. / Hunt, R. G. (1980): The Relationship Between Work and Non-Work Domains: A Review of the Empirical Research. In: *Academy of Management Review* 5, pp. 415–429.
Nightingale, D. (1976): Industrial Democracy: A Strategy for Improving Productivity and Labor-Management Relations. In: *The Business Quarterly,* Autumn, pp. 36–42.
Nightingale, D. (1982): *Workplace Democracy: An Enquiry Into Employee Participation in Canadian Work Organizations.* Toronto.
Ondrack, D. / Evans, M. (1981): *Quality of Working Life. Evaluation and Measurement.* Ottawa.
Ondrack, D. / Evans, M. (1982): *The QWL Program at the Lambton Plant of the XYZ Company.* Ottawa, p. 45.
Phillips, J. / Lord, R. (1980): Determinants of Intrinsic Motivation: Locus of Control and Competence Information as Components of Deci's Cognitive Evaluation Theory. In: *Journal of Applied Psychology,* April, pp. 211–18.
Ramsay, H. (1978): Phantom Participation: Patterns of Power and Conflict. Seminar on Power and Influence in Industrial Relations, Brussels, European Institute for Advanced Studies in Management, May, p. 34.
Rice, A. K. (1958): *Productivity and Social Organization: The Ahmedabad Experiment.* London.
Rokeach, M. (1968): *Beliefs, Attitudes and Values.* San Francisco.
Rotter, J. R. (1971): External Control and Internal Control. In: *Psychology Today,* June, pp. 35–40.
Salancik, G. R. / Pfeffer, J. (1977): An Examination of Need Satisfaction Models of Job Attitudes. In: *Administrative Science Quarterly,* September, pp. 427–56.
Simon, H. (1960): *The New Science of Management Decisions.* New York.

Staw, B. (1975): *Intrinsic and Extrinsic Motivation.* Morristown, New Jersey.
Sturmthal, A. F. (1977): Unions and Industrial Democracy. In: *Annals AAPSS* 431, May, pp. 14–21.
Tannenbaum, A. S. (1966): *Social Psychology of Work Organization.* London.
Tannenbaum, A. / Schmidt, W. H. (1968): How to Choose a Leadership Pattern. In: *Harvard Business Review* 36, pp. 95–101.
Trist, E. L. (1981): *The Evolution of Socio-Technical Systems.* Toronto.
Trist, E. L. / Bamforth, K. W. (1951): Some Social and Psychological Consequences of the Long-Wall Method of Coal Getting. In: *Human Relations* 4, pp. 3–38.
Vroom, V. H. (1964): *Work and Motivation.* New York.
Vroom, V. H. / Yetton, P. (1973): *Leadership and Decision Making.* Pittsburgh.
Walker, K. F. (1977): Toward the Participatory Enterprise: A European Trend. In: *Annals AAPSS* 431, May, pp. 1–11.
Walker, C. R. / Guest, H. (1952): *The Man on the Assembly Line.* Cambridge, Mass.
Webergen, J. C. (1985): Co-Determination in Europe. In: *International Management Newsletter* 8 (2), pp. 2–3.
Weiss, H. / Ugen, D. / Sharbaugh, M. (1982): Effect of Life and Job Stress on Information Search Behavior of Organizational Members. In: *Journal of Applied Psychology,* February, pp. 60–66.
Windmuller, J. P. (1977): Industrial Democracy and Industrial Relations. In: *Annals AAPSS* 431, May, pp. 22–31.

Perspektivität als Heuristik
Zum Verhältnis von Politikwissenschaft und Unternehmungspolitik

Jochen Wondracek

Abstract

Perspectivity as a Heuristic Approach
On the Relationship Between Political Science and Business Politics

One of the most interesting elements in the history of science is the attempt to utilize resources of one scientific discipline to develop the range and knowledge base of another discipline. From an epistomological point of view there are a series of problems involved in this process. Besides these epistomological problems, the use of knowledge of one discipline in the area of another discipline involves a number of heuristic and "strategic" issues. These issues will be exemplified and discussed with the help of problems in the area of business administration and its relation to political sciences. This discussion is also a first and very short attempt at a reconstruction of a heuristic process which ended in a new, fruitful interdisciplinary approach to explain human actions in and between companies.

In der langen Geschichte der wissenschaftlichen Thematisierung von menschlichen Lebenszusammenhängen können immer wieder Versuche registriert werden, bestimmte Teilaspekte eines Wissenschaftsbereichs aus der Perspektive einer anderen Wissenschaft zu analysieren.

Diese spezielle Form einer Erkenntnisheuristik kann dabei in verschiedenen Varianten verwendet werden:

Eine dieser Varianten ist die *analoge* Verwendung von Erkenntnissen aus einem anderen Wissenschaftsbereich in dem ausgewählten Bereich. Dabei kann eine direkte oder eine systematisierende Analogie zum Einsatz kommen. Ein Beispiel für eine direkte Analogie ist in letzter Zeit die Bionik, bei der von der Grundthese ausgegangen wird, daß bestimmte Funktionslösungen in der Natur die effizienteste Form für eine Lösung bei der Gestaltung technischer Systeme mit ähnlicher Aufgabenstellung darstellen (z. B. bei der Analogie Gehirn – Computer). Eine systematisierende Analogie geht von der Annahme aus, daß eine ganze Reihe auf den ersten Blick disjunkter Vorgänge mit Hilfe eines generellen Ansatzes systematisiert und synergetisch befruchtend bearbeitet werden kann. Beispiele für eine solche Form der Analogie sind etwa die allgemeine Systemtheorie oder die Kybernetik.

Eine weitere Form von Perspektivität ist die *reduktionistische* Verwendung von Erkenntnissen aus einem anderen Wissenschaftsbereich. Grundannahme ist dabei die These, daß zum einen die zu reduzierende Wissenschaft inferior bezüglich Erkenntnisqualität und/oder Erkenntnisfortschritt ist und daß zum anderen allgemeine Gesetzesmäßigkeiten der überlegenen Wissenschaft grundsätzlich auch im Bereich der zu reduzierenden Wissenschaft ihre Gültigkeit besitzen. Beispiele für eine solche Vorgehensweise sind etwa das Verhältnis von Biologie und Soziologie bzw. Nationalökonomie (Soziobiologie).

Eine dritte Variante der Verwendung von wissenschaftlichen Erkenntnissen in einem anderen Fachgebiet ist die *komplementäre* Nutzung von Ergebnissen in diesem Bereich. Ausgangspunkt dieser Verwendung von Erkenntnissen aus einem anderen Wissenschaftsbereich ist die Diagnose, daß spezielle Teilaspekte des Gegenstandsbereichs der aufnehmenden Wissenschaft überhaupt oder lediglich nur besser aus der Sicht des anderen Wissenschaftsbereichs bearbeitet werden können. Je nach der vorherrschenden Grundannahme über die Regeln wissenschaftlicher Arbeitsteilung führt ein solches Vorgehen zur Bildung einer völlig neuen Disziplin, bei der die Fachvertreter beide, ursprünglich disjunkte Gegenstandsbereiche theoretisch bearbeiten oder zur Herausbildung einer Interdisziplin, in der Fachvertreter aus beiden Bereichen gemeinsam arbeiten. Beispiel für die erste Vorgehensweise ist etwa die Biochemie, für die zweite die Sozialpsychologie.

In allen drei Vorgehensweisen der Verwendung von wissenschaftlichen Erkenntnissen in einem anderen als dem originären Gegenstandsbereich steht der Transferierende vor einer Reihe von Problemen:

Das bedeutendste und in seinen epistomologischen Konsequenzen am weitesten reichende Problem ist die Frage nach der *Isomorphie* zwischen beiden Gegenstandsbereichen. Die Isomorphievermutung ist der Ansatzpunkt für den Versuch, Erklärungen mit Hilfe der gleichrangigen Anwendung von Gesetzen in zwei unterschiedlichen Gegenstandsbereichen zu gewinnen.[1] Formal bedeutet Isomorphie daher, daß das Gesetz G1 im System S1 „dieselbe syntaktische Struktur oder dieselbe logische Form" besitzt wie das Gesetz G2 im System S2[2]. Dies bedeutet, daß alle logischen und damit auch alle mathematischen Konstanten im Falle eines Systemwechsels beibehalten werden können, so daß lediglich alle oder ausgewählte empirische Konstanten geändert werden müssen. Stegmüller schlägt vor, für diese Form der Isomorphie das Attribut „syntaktisch" zu verwenden. In der Regel werden nicht alle Gesetze in beiden Systemen S1 und S2 diesem formalen Anspruch genügen. In diesem Fall wird von Hempel und Stegmüller der Begriff der partiellen Isomorphie eingeführt, mit dem verdeutlicht werden soll, daß eine Isomorphie häufig nur relativ in bezug auf bestimmte Gesetze besteht.

Auch bei einer Relativierung der strengen Isomorphieanforderungen auf nur einige Gesetze wird ein grundsätzliches Dilemma der sowohl der analogen als auch der reduktionistischen sowie komplementären Transferierung von Erkenntnissen von einem Erkenntnisbereich in den anderen deutlich:

Die Überprüfung des Vorhandenseins einer Isomorphie zwischen zwei Erkenntnisbereichen, welche die Voraussetzung für alle drei Vorgehensweisen bildet, kann empirisch erst bestätigt werden, wenn die für den zu untersuchenden Gegenstandsbereich geltenden Gesetze bekannt und in eine isomorphe Struktur gebracht worden sind. Ist diese empirische Bestätigung erbracht, so gründen sich Erklärungen auf die in diesem Bereich tatsächlich geltenden Gesetze und nicht auf die in einem anderen Bereich geltenden Gesetze[3].

Damit wird deutlich, daß bei konsequenter Anwendung der erkenntnislogischen Anforderungen an die Übertragung von Erkenntnissen aus einem Wissenschaftsbereich in einen anderen kein erkenntnisproduktiver Vorteil im strengen Sinne erzielbar ist. Der wesentliche Vorteil dieser Vorgehensweise liegt vielmehr in dem *heuristischen* Wert für die Entdeckung gesetzmäßiger Zusammenhänge[4]: Die sorgfältige Analyse des Erkenntnisbestandes in einem Wissenschaftsbereich und die Feststellung von einigen Isomorphien zwischen beiden Bereichen kann den Forscher z. B. dazu anregen, Hypothesen über das Vorhandensein weiterer Isomorphien aufzustellen und zu überprüfen.

Gerade in den Naturwissenschaften gibt es eine Fülle von Beispielen, die belegen, welche fruchtbare Heuristik eine vergleichende Betrachtung der Erkenntniszustände zweier Wissenschaftsbereiche besitzen kann. Hervorzuheben sind dabei insbesondere Beispiele, bei denen es gelungen ist, Ockhams Prinzip folgend, gegebene Theorien durch basalere, auf einfachere Erkenntniszusammenhänge zurückgreifende Theorien zu ersetzen. Ein Beispiel unter vielen ist etwa die Substitution der Wärmelehre durch eine Theorie der Kinetik von Elementarteilchen oder die Substitution der Vererbungslehre durch eine biochemische Theorie von genetischen Molekularstrukturen.

Stellt man die Frage nach einer ähnlich erfolgreichen Heuristik in den Sozialwissenschaften, so muß die Antwort um einiges differenzierter ausfallen, um die Besonderheiten sozialwissenschaftlicher Erkenntnisgewinnung entsprechend zu berücksichtigen:

Das Gesamtspektrum unterschiedlicher Spezialdisziplinen in den Sozialwissenschaften kann als der Versuch angesehen werden, arbeitsteilig das Agieren und Reagieren von Menschen als Individuum oder im Zusammenhang mit anderen Menschen zu untersuchen. Dabei konzentrieren sich die jeweiligen Spezialdisziplinen auf spezielle Aspekte des Agierens und Reagierens, wobei das Spezifikum der Fragestellung durch die Merkmale des Handelns oder durch das soziale Subsystem, in dem dieses Handeln zu beobachten ist, determiniert wird.

Betrachtet man die einzelnen sozialwissenschaftlichen Spezialdisziplinen, so fällt auf, daß in der Regel beide Varianten der Gegenstandsbestimmung des wissenschaftlichen Erkenntnisbereichs in den grundsätzlichen Erörterungen über diese Fragestellung auffindbar sind. Einige Fachvertreter der jeweiligen Spezialdisziplinen haben daher versucht, die Fragestellung als erkenntnistheoretisch irrelevant auszusondern oder als pragmatisch einfach lösbar darzustellen (Wissenschaft X ist was Wissenschaftler X tun).

In beiden Scheinlösungen wird verkannt, daß eine Klärung des Gegenstandsbereich einer sozialwissenschaftlichen Spezialdisziplin wesentliche Voraussetzung für eine sinnvolle Arbeitsteilung und für eine fruchtbare Nutzung der Erkenntnisse anderer Disziplinen im Sinne einer allgemeinen Erkenntnisheuristik ist.

Erst die präzise Herausarbeitung des spezifischen Gegenstandsbereichs einer Disziplin ermöglicht es daher, jene drei eingangs diskutierten Strategien der Übertragung von Wissensbeständen aus anderen Disziplinen heuristisch fruchtbar für das eigene Erkenntnisbemühen zu nutzen: Bearbeiten Wissenschaftler in der Spezialdisziplin X etwa Fragestellungen, bei denen eine hochgradige Isomorphievermutung zu meinem eigenen Bemühen besteht; sind die Theorieansätze in der Wissenschaft Y für mich Ansatzpunkt, elementare Konzepte auch in meine Fragestellung zu integrieren; gibt es Problemanalysen in der Wissenschaft Z, die notwendig komplementär zu meiner Fragestellung sind, um die Qualität der erzielbaren Aussagen in meiner Disziplin zu verbessern: Alle diese fruchtbaren Anstöße werden wesentlich dadurch erleichtert, daß eine funktionierende Arbeitsteilung unter Beachtung des jeweiligen Spezialwissens sowie gegenseitige Transparenz über das Forschungsbemühen von Wissenschaftlern in verschiedenen Spezialdisziplinen vorhanden ist.

Es kennzeichnet die Schriften von Dlugos von Beginn an[5], daß die Frage nach dem Gegenstandsbereich der Betriebswirtschaftslehre immer im Vordergrund seiner Bemühungen gestanden hat. In der Tradition Kosiols stehend, ist in diesen Erörterungen zum Gegenstandsbereich immer eine Entscheidung für eine *problemorientierte* im Gegensatz zu einer *realfallorientierten* Gegenstandsbestimmung der Betriebswirtschaftslehre getroffen worden.

Als Selektionsmerkmal der Form der Problemorientierung wird in seinen Schriften der Aspekt des *wirtschaftlichen Handelns* ausgewählt, der mit einer Orientierung des Handelns an den Problemen der Güterknappheit näher gekennzeichnet wird. Wirtschaftliches Handeln ist somit eine Handlungsform, die sich an den Konsequenzen des Handelns eines Aktors für den eigenen Geldbestand oder für den anderer orientiert.

In dieser Sichtweise müßte sich betriebswirtschaftliche Forschung in erster Linie an der Erstellung von Aussagen über die Bedingungen rein geldbestandsorientierten Handelns orientieren. Da die Entscheidungsqualität Handelnder in Hinblick auf die Auswahl von Alternativen wesentlich von Informationen abhängt, die der Handelnde über die Geldbestandskonsequenzen der Alternativen hat, werden diese Aussagen um so nützlicher für den Handelnden sein, je genauer der Handelnde über diese Konsequenzen informiert wird. Eine wesentliche Aufgabe der Betriebswirtschaftslehre ist damit die Verbesserung des Wissensstandes Handelnder über die Beziehungszusammenhänge zwischen vorhandenen Alternativen und ihren Geldbeständen.

Bei einer Orientierung an einem so definierten Metaziel betriebswirtschaftlichen Forschungsbemühens wird bei der Analyse tatsächlicher Entscheidungsverläufe in Unternehmungen schnell deutlich, daß einzelne Zielkriterien, die notwendigerweise Bestandteil des Entscheidungsprozesses sind, mit Hilfe der Wissensbestände anderer Wissenschaften unterlegt werden müssen.

Sofort einsichtig ist diese Anforderung bei Sachmittelentscheidungen wie der Anschaffung einer Drehbank. Der Entscheider wird eine Fülle von technischen Details in seine Entscheidung integrieren, die die Qualität der Drehbank wie die Qualität der mit ihrer Hilfe produzierten Güter in seiner Entscheidungsmatrix abbilden. In der Regel handelt es sich dabei um eine allseitig akzeptierte Abgrenzung, daß die Betriebswirtschaftslehre Informationen technischer Art aus dem Bereich der Ingenieurwissenschaften übernimmt. In den meisten Fällen verbleibt es Aufgabe der Betriebswirtschaftslehre, diese Informationen unter Verwendung eines einheitlichen Wertmaßstabes in Hinblick auf die Auswirkungen auf den Geldmittelbestand zu transformieren.

Neben technischen Details sind in den Entscheidungsprozeß häufig weitere Zielkriterien zu integrieren, die die personalen und sozialen Auswirkungen der Entscheidung wie Arbeitszufriedenheit, Konfliktauslösungswahrscheinlichkeit etc. widerspiegeln. Auch dabei ist es Aufgabe der Betriebswirtschaftslehre, Konsequenzen aus den personalen und sozialen Auswirkungen der Entscheidung auf den Geldmittelbestand zu verdeutlichen.

Im Gegensatz zu den zuvor diskutierten technisch unterlegten Zielkriterien ist bei den sozio-personalen Zielkriterien zu beachten, daß die Entscheidung nicht nur von den Konsequenzen auf den Geldmittelbestand abhängig ist, sondern daß soziopersonale Zielkriterien gleichrangig oder sogar dominant werden können. Ein solches *multipel orientiertes Handeln* erhöht aus Sicht der integrierenden Wissenschaft die Notwendigkeit, originäre Erkenntnisse anderer Wissenschaften in einem hohen Ausmaß in die Aussagen der eigenen Wissenschaft aufzunehmen. Dabei können bestimmte Varianten multipel orientierten Handelns auf Grund der Häufigkeit ihres empirisch beobachtbaren Auftretens Anstoß sein, eine spezielle Interdisziplin für diese Form des Handelns zu etablieren.

Zu den besonderen Formen multipel orientierten Handelns zählt in vielen betriebswirtschaftlichen Schriften das Führungshandeln. So führt Heinen aus, daß Willensbildung und Willensdurchsetzung den Gegenstand der Führungslehre auf die Durchsetzungsproblematik konzentriert, mit der Führende gegenüber den Geführten konfrontiert sind.[6] Diese Sichtweise impliziert zugleich, daß selbstverständlich auch die Geführten gegenüber den Führenden eine Durchsetzungsproblematik verspüren, die sich in speziellen, auf die Willensdurchsetzung hin orientierte Handlungen konkretisiert.

Eine Generalisierung dieser sich gegenseitig bedingenden Willensdurchsetzungen kann durch die Sichtweise vorgenommen werden, daß Handelnde in einem gedanklich zweistufigen Zielsetzungsprozeß die Durchsetzung ihrer Primär- oder Grundziele durch ein sekundäres Handeln absichern. Dabei kann dieses Sicherungshandeln nicht nur Innen sondern auch nach Außen wirksam werden, z. B. gegenüber anderen Unternehmungen oder gegenüber anderen gesellschaftlichen Institutionen. Eine so ausgerichtete Spezialdisziplin muß daher in genereller Form sowohl Aussagen über Sicherungskonsequenzen (Nachhaltigkeit der Sicherung, erwünschte und unerwünschte personale Nebenwirkungen) als auch Aussagen über Geldbestandskonsequenzen der Sicherungsalternativen . . ., desweiteren Aussagen über sicherungsorientierte, geldbestandsorientierte und multipel orientierte Entscheidungsergebnisse“[7] erstellen. Die multiple Orientierung an Sicherungs- und Geldbestandsauswirkungen bildet somit für Dlugos die Grundlage zur Errichtung einer eigenen Spezialdisziplin, der betriebswirtschaftlichen Unternehmungspolitik.

Die Begriffswahl „Unternehmungs*politik*“ verdeutlicht die spezifische Perspektivität, die hier zur Anwendung gekommen ist. Ausgangspunkt für die Wahl dieser Heuristik ist eine Isomorphievermutung zwischen bestimmten beobachtbaren Strukturen und Handlungselementen in den Bereichen, die von der politischen Wissenschaft thematisiert werden, und vergleichbaren Strukturen wie Handlungselementen im Unternehmungsbereich. Die heuristische Qualität der Sichtweise von Abläufen im Unternehmungsbereich hängt dabei von dem Ausmaß der Fundierung der Isomorphievermutung sowie von der erkenntnisproduktiven Kraft ab, die von dieser spezifischen Perspektivität ausgeht.

Auf eine besondere Schwierigkeit im sozialwissenschaftlichen Bereich bei der Fundierung der Isomorphievermutung ist bereits weiter oben hingewiesen worden. In der Regel existieren im Wissenschaftsbereich einer Wissenschaft eine Fülle von konkurrierenden Ansätzen zur Thematisierung von Problembereichen der jeweiligen Wissenschaft. Im Gegensatz zu den Naturwissenschaften verbleiben in den Sozialwissenschaften kaum Mögichkeiten, durch empirisch-experimentelle Verfahren die Überlegenheit oder größere heuristische Fruchtbarkeit einer Variante der Problematisierung nachzuweisen. In der Regel verbleiben nur sehr schwache Selektionskriterien, etwa im Bereich der vernünftigen Rede über Sachverhalte oder in der Bereitstellung präziserer Begriffssysteme zur Thematisierung von Problembereichen.

Verwendet man nun Aussagenkomponenten einer Wissenschaft in Verbindung mit einer anderen Disziplin, so ist eine Auswahl unter jenen Varianten zu treffen, die der jeweilig gebenden Wissenschaft immanent sind.

Eine grobe Analyse von verschiedenen Argumentationsmustern im Bereich der Politischen Wissenschaft erlauben eine Reihe von Klassifizierungen:

Eine Reihe von Fachvertretern versuchen, in etwa parallel zu der oben geschilderten Situation in der Betriebswirtschaftslehre, den Aussagenbereich der Politologie auf wenige Realgebilde wie Staat oder staatsnahe Institutionen zu begrenzen. Eine andere Gruppe wiederum versucht, Entscheidungen zu klassifizieren, die entweder hinsichtlich ihrer Art (z. B. bedeutsam) oder hinsichtlich der Personengruppe, die diese Entscheidungen treffen (z. B. Eliten) unterschieden werden können. Im Ergebnis bedeutet dies eine Differenzierung in politische und nichtpolitische Entscheidungen. Wieder andere orientieren sich in dieser Grundfrage an Merkmalen des Handelns, die eine Unterscheidung in politisches und nicht politisches Handeln erlauben. Als „politisch“ wird dabei, generell formuliert, ein Handeln hervorgehoben, das an der Sicherung eigener Ziele orientiert ist.[8]

Innerhalb dieser Variante der Grundorientierung polit-wissenschaftlichen Erkenntnisbemühens sind Argumente zu differenzieren, die, ausgehend von einer spezifischen Anthropologie, ein so hervorgehobenes politisches Handeln unterschiedlich finalisieren. Dabei wird eine grundsätzliche Unterscheidung getroffen, ob politisches Handeln eine Notwendigkeit auf Grund des Verlustes eines Naturzustandes vor der Herausbildung von Sozietäten ist oder ob politisches Handeln der conditio humana wie andere Formen triebunterlegten Handelns zuzurechnen und damit in keiner denkbaren Utopie gesellschaftlicher Zustände überwindbar erscheint.[9]

Die Anerkennung einer Gleichrangigkeit der Rationalität von geldmittelorientiertem und sicherungsorientiertem Handeln in der von Dlugos konzipierten Unternehmungspolitik verdeutlicht, daß bei der Übernahme von politologischen Erkenntnisperspektiven in diese Interdisziplin eine Entscheidung einerseits für einen handlungsorientierten Politikbegriff, andererseits für die vollständige Akzeptanz politischen Handelns als nicht überwindbare, dem Menschen in allen sozialen Situationen zurechenbare Handlungsvariante getroffen worden ist.

Es muß dabei hervorgehoben werden, daß eine solche Sichtweise, insbesondere was die zweite Grundsatzentscheidung betrifft, innerhalb der anderen Teildisziplin der Unternehmungspolitik, der Betriebswirtschaftslehre, als nicht unproblematisch erscheint.

Ausgehend z. B. von einer generellen Zielsetzung des Wirtschaftens in Unternehmungen in Form der Maximierung monitärer Zielkriterien erscheinen Formen der Sicherung der Interessen einzelner Aktoren oder Aktorengruppen als Störungen, Friktionen und somit als Abweichungen von der rationalen Zielverfolgung in wirtschaftlichen Einheiten. Eine „Unternehmungspolitik" in dieser Ausrichtung müßte sich an der Herbeiführung größtmöglicher Rationalität der Organisationsstrukturen, an der Schaffung objektiver Verteilungsregeln und/oder an der Entwicklung intersubjektiv nachvollziehbarer Nutzenkalküle für alle am Unternehmungsgeschehen beteiligten Aktoren oder Aktorengruppen orientieren. Diese Form der „Unternehmungspolitik" endet in ihrer finalen Orientierung konsequenterweise in dem Überflüssigwerden jedweden politischen Handelns in Unternehmungen.

Auch bei einer anderen Orientierung der generellen Zielsetzung des Handelns in Unternehmungen im Sinne einer Überwindung der Entfremdung auf Grund arbeitsteiliger Prozesse erscheint politisches Handeln negativ vorbesetzt. Ausgehend von einer weitreichenden Idealisierung gesellschaftlicher Zustände vor dem Beginn der Industrialisierung fragen eine Reihe von Fachwissenschaftlern, mit Hilfe welcher organisational wie sozialpsychologisch unterlegten Maßnahmen die Authentizität menschlicher Beziehungen wiederhergestellt werden kann. Merkmal für das Fehlen dieser Authentizität ist die Notwendigkeit für den einzelnen Aktor, sein interessengeleitetes Handeln gegen die Interessen seiner Kontrahenten abzusichern.

Zu beiden Positionen, für die eine intensive Austauschbeziehung zwischen vergleichbaren Ansätzen in Soziologie, Politologie, Psychologie und Ökonomie existiert[10], steht der von Dlugos vertretene unternehmungspolitische Ansatz im deutlichen Widerspruch.

Eine nähere Analyse der spezifischen politologischen Perspektivität sicherungsorientierten Handelns in diesem unternehmungspolitischen Ansatz macht deutlich, daß der Ansatz im starken Maße der politischen Anthropologie Thomas Hobbes und den darauf aufbauenden Autoren verbunden ist.

Zentrales Element der Hobbes'schen Anthropologie ist die Zurückweisung der Idee einer göttlichen Ordnung, woraus für Hobbes ableitbar ist, daß kein höchstes Gut oder kein letztes Ziel, wie etwa in den Schriften anderer politischer Philosophen postuliert, existiert. Die Verneinung einer göttlichen Ordnung und damit die Zurückweisung letzter, transzendenter Ziele hat für Hobbes weitreichende Konsequenzen. Zum einen impliziert diese Perspektive, daß die gesellschaftliche Ordnung kein Abbild einer göttlichen Ordnung sondern gestaltbares Menschenwerk ist, zum anderen, daß aus dem Fehlen eines einheitlichen, transzendent begründbaren Wertekosmos die Gleichwertigkeit unterschiedlicher menschlicher Interessen und Werte abgeleitet werden kann.

Ergänzt wird diese generelle Sichtweise um zwei eher naturalistisch unterlegte Annahmen, bei denen zum einen konstatiert wird, daß menschliche Eigenschaften und Fähigkeiten im Mittel nur geringe Abweichungen zeigen und daß zum anderen die verfügbaren Ressourcen, die Menschen sich aneignen können, in ihrer Menge begrenzt sind.

Das Fehlen von deutlichen Unterschieden zwischen den Menschen sowie das Fehlen einer ordnungsstiftenden Kosmologie führen bei begrenzten Ressourcen dazu, daß sich Interessen und Begierden auf eine geringe Anzahl von Objekten, häufig sogar auf dasselbe Objekt richten. Die Folge ist ein allgegenwärtiger Konflikt um die Aneignung oder Verteilung von Gegenständen und Positionen bei relativer Ähnlichkeit der eingesetzten Mittel, Hobbes' „bellum omnium in omnes".

Ausgangspunkt der Hobbes'schen Vorstellung von der Natur des Menschen ist somit ein Menschenbild, in dem der Mensch um seines Vorteils willen mit anderen Menschen um knappe Güter und Positionen ständig in einem konfliktären Verhältnis steht. Dabei unternimmt er immer wieder den Versuch, den anderen an der Durchsetzung seiner Ziele zu hindern, oder – um auf die Darstellungsebene der Dlugos'schen Unternehmungspolitik zu verweisen –, seine Ziele gegen die Ziele der anderen zu sichern. Zur Absicherung seiner Ziele in dem immer wieder auftretenden Durchsetzungskonflikt benötigt der Aktor Macht, für Hobbes der Inbegriff aller Mittel, sich ein anscheinend zukünftiges Gut zu eigen zu machen.[11]

Bis zu diesem Punkt der Rekonstruktion der Hobbes'schen Anthropologie bleibt offen, woher jene Dynamik des Krieges aller gegen alle stammt. Alternativ wäre ansonsten eine Entwicklung denkbar, bei der die gesamtgesellschaftliche Situation durch die Einsicht aller in ein Gleichgewicht der Interessen und Realisierungen gebracht werden könnte. Hobbes ergänzt zur Ausgrenzung dieser alternativen gesellschaftlichen Entwicklung seine Anthropologie um Komponenten einer allgemeinen Trieblehre, bei der Trieb nach Macht unmittelbar zur menschlichen conditio humana zugehörig ist, oder wie Borkenau es ausdrückt: „Bei Hobbes ist... der Wille zur Macht der unmittelbarste Trieb, er ist keineswegs einem ursprünglich friedlichen – liberalen Individuum durch die Not aufgezwungen, unmittelbar ist das Streben nach unbegrenzter Macht im Menschen.«[12]

Die radikale Form der Argumentation ist für Hobbes die geeignete Ausgangsbasis, alle Formen der Einsicht von Menschen zurückweisen und die Verhinderung einer selbstzerfleischenden Auseinandersetzung aller gegen alle mit Hilfe einer mit erheblichen Machtmitteln ausgestatteten Zentralgewalt zu übertragen.

Selbst im Falle einer Relativierung dieser Radikalität der Sichtweise des Menschen als triebgeleitet und machtorientiert verbleibt die Grundeinsicht, politisches Handeln untrennbar der conditio humana zuzurechnen und damit alle Formen des Sicherungshandelns – in welchem sozialen Umfeld auch immer – als eine wesentliche Komponente menschlichen Handelns wissenschaftlich zu analysieren und in Form wissenschaftlicher gestützter Technologien dem Handelnden zur *Erhöhung* seiner Handlungsrationalität zu thematisieren.

Die von uns eingangs problematisierte perspektivische Betrachtung einer Disziplin mit Hilfe der Erkenntnisse einer anderen Disziplin als Grundlage einer fruchtbaren Nutzung dieser Erkenntnisse läßt sich für das Verhältnis „Politische Wissenschaft“ – „Unternehmungspolitik“ somit wie folgt konkretisieren:

Der Transfer von Ansätzen und von Erkenntnissen im Bereich der Politischen Wissenschaft in einen anderen Gegenstandsbereich, hier der Unternehmung, öffnet für den Wissenschaftler *und* für den Anwender auf Grund der dabei gewonnenen wissenschaftlichen Erkenntnisse den Blick für eine notwendigerweise komplexere Analyse von Handlungselementen in der Unternehmung. Er macht zudem deutlich, welchen geistesgeschichtlichen – kulturellen Ursprung alternative, auf einer abweichenden Sichtweise menschlicher Grundbedingungen beruhende Ansätze besitzen und welche abgeleitete Entscheidungen mit der Wahl für diese oder jene Betrachtungsweise des Menschen einhergehen.

Jenseits der Entscheidungen über diese weitreichenden Grundorientierungen innerhalb einer neuen Interdisziplin beeinflußt der Transfer die Errichtung einer konzeptionellen Grundlage für das weitere Forschungsbemühen, indem z. B. bereits auf einige, die Begriffssysteme klärende Diskussionen innerhalb der gebenden Disziplin zurückgegriffen werden kann.

Auch bei der Erstellung von ersten Hypothesen können Ansätze aus dem Bereich der gebenden Wissenschaft übernommen werden, mit der erweiterten Möglichkeit, Ergebnisse aus beiden Bereichen zu vergleichen und in neuen Hypothesen zu verwenden.

Der Summe der Vorteile steht eine Reihe von Zusatzproblemen gegenüber:

So muß der Fachwissenschaftler der übernehmenden Wissenschaft auf Grund der Vielzahl alternativer Ansätze fundierte Wahlentscheidungen treffen, welchen speziellen Ansatz er in den Bereich der neuen Interdisziplin integrieren will. Wir haben oben gezeigt, daß diese Wahl erhebliche Konsequenzen für die weitere Arbeit innerhalb der neuen Interdisziplin besitzen kann; sie muß daher mit viel Sachverstand und damit auch mit viel Aufwand getroffen werden.

Bei einem nachhaltigen Wechsel des Erfahrungsbereichs wie etwa von „Gesellschaft" zur „Unternehmung" sind darüber hinaus stützende Argumente notwendig, um die Zulässigkeit und heuristische Fruchtbarkeit des Vorgehens gegenüber anderen Wissenschaftlern in beiden Bereichen bzw. gegenüber potentiellen Anwendern der neu gewonnenen Erkenntnisse zu verteidigen. Je ungewöhnlicher der Wechsel und je stärker die Abweichung von einem Alltagsverständnis der Aufteilung in wissenschaftliche Gegenstandsbereiche ist, um so umfangreicher und aufwendiger müssen diese Explikationsversuche ausfallen.

Bei einer Abwägung der Vor- und Nachteile der hier skizzierten Übertragung von Ansätzen und Erkenntnissen aus einem Wissenschaftsbereich in den anderen am Beispiel der Fundierung des Dlugos'schen Ansatzes zur Unternehmungspolitik zeigt es sich, daß es glückliche Fälle von Forscherbemühen gibt, ein solches Unterfangen zum Beginn einer äußerst fruchtbaren Diskussion und zur Öffnung von neuen Perspektiven in Wissenschaft und Praxis gelingen zu lassen.

Anmerkungen

[1] Vgl. Stegmüller 1969, S. 133 ff.
[2] Stegmüller 1969, S. 133.
[3] Vgl. Stegmüller 1969, S. 134 f.
[4] Vgl. Hempel 1965, S. 441 f., Stegmüller 1969, S. 135 f.
[5] Vgl. inbesondere Dlugos 1972 sowie Dlugos 1974.
[6] Vgl. Heinen 1978, S. 32.
[7] Vgl. Dlugos/Wondracek 1979, S. 12.
[8] Zur Diskussion vgl. Dorow 1982, S. 20 f.
[9] Vgl. dazu Wondracek 1982 passim.
[10] Vgl. dazu ausführlicher Wondracek 1982.
[11] Vgl. Hobbes 1974, S. 79.
[12] Borkenau 1934, S. 463.

Literatur

Borkenau, E. (1934): *Der Übergang vom feudalen zum bürgerlichen Weltbild.* Studien zur Geschichte der Philosophie der Manufakturperiode. Paris. Reprint: Darmstadt 1971.

Dlugos, G. (1972): Analytische Wissenschaftstheorie als Regulativ betriebswirtschaftlicher Forschung. In: Dlugos, G. / Eberlein, G. / Steinmann, H. (Hrsg.), *Wissenschaftstheorie und Betriebswirtschaftslehre. Eine methodologische Kontroverse.* Düsseldorf, S. 21–53.

Dlugos, G. (1974): Unternehmungspolitik als betriebswirtschaftlich-politologische Teildisziplin. In: Wild, J. (Hrsg.), *Unternehmungsführung.* Festschrift für E. Kosiol zu seinem 75. Geburtstag. Berlin, S. 39–73.

Dlugos, G. / J. Wondracek (1979): Grundüberlegungen zur Konstituierung einer unternehmungsbezogenen Konfliktforschung. In: Dlugos, G. (Hrsg.), *Unternehmungsbezogene Konfliktforschung. Methodologische und forschungsprogrammatische Grundfragen.* Stuttgart, S. 3–30.

Dorow, W. (1982): *Unternehmungspolitik.* Stuttgart, Berlin, Köln, Mainz.

Heinen, E. (1978): Führung als Gegenstand der Betriebswirtschaftslehre. In: Heinen, E., *Betriebswirtschaftliche Führungslehre. Ein entscheidungsorientierter Ansatz.* Wiesbaden, S. 19–44.

Hempel, C. G. (1965): *Aspects of Scientific Explanations.* New York.

Hobbes, T. (1974): *Leviathan.* Erster und zweiter Teil. Stuttgart.

Stegmüller, W. (1969): *Wissenschaftliche Erklärung und Begründung.* Band I, Berlin, Heidelberg, New York.

Wondracek, J. (1982): *Die Verkürzung der politischen Fragestellung in unternehmungsbezogenen Forschungsansätzen.* Dissertation Freie Universität Berlin.

Teil II
Ökonomische Aspekte

Industrial Democracy and Labour Market Behaviour

Klaus Weiermair

Abstract

The paper first critically reviews the treatment of industrial democracy in organization theory and economics. Subsequently, it argues for an alternate more integrative approach, where the latter is to include both social and economic, worker- and management related determinants. These determinants are analyzed in a next step within the context of changing labor markets thus revealing the varying demand for and supply of codetermination and other forms of industrial democracy. Consequences of increased levels of worker participation for the behavior of labour markets are analyzed in the last section of the paper. The article concludes with some reflections on convergency and reversibility of labour market developments across industrialized economies.

1. Introduction

Over the past decades, management on both sides of the Atlantic has become acutely aware of new demands for worker participation be it in the form of increased participation in decision making and improvements in the quality of working life as is true for North America or various forms of codetermination as may be the case in Europe[1]. Management theoreticians and practitioners have reacted to these new environmental demands with changes in organization and work design, style of leadership and patterns of organizational rewards and incentive structures (Galbraith 1977). More often than not, both the intellectual and practical adjustment were incremental in nature, such that new work values and/or increased demands for participation were merely seen and taken as new constraints to the same old paradigm of profit maximization/cost minimization (Davis 1966). While pragmatic and expedient to specific constraints and circumstances of time and value system (culture) such an approach fails to generally recognize the wholistic character of industrial relations systems with respect to its constituent parts. For as has been pointed out some time ago by Dunlop, changes in only a small but integral part of an industrial relations systems will in its consequence lead to dynamic and simultaneous adjustments in the other components compromising the system (Dunlop 1958, p. 26). Changes in the behaviour of labour markets with respect to work values e.g. are likely to impact firms in a number of functional areas such as production and personnel, these transformations at the micro level will in turn lead tu subsequent alterations in the make-up and behaviour of the labour market surrounding the firm. If we were to consult mainstream labour economics and notable exceptions notwithstanding (e.g. Freeman 1979), we equally find little concern with the forementioned interdependencies between labour market behaviour on the one hand and organization characteristics such as forms of worker participation on the other hand. Particularly, where changes have been gradual with no appreciable effects on the laws governing the direction and utilization of manpower at the firm level, as might be true for changes in work values, typical labour market analyses have implicitly assumed intertemporal constancy[2]. Where major legislative reforms were undertaken such as has been the case with West-Germany's codetermination laws, economic analyses have gone to the other extreme and employed the assumption of complete attenuation of property rights, typical for the purely labour managed socialist firm (Pejovich et al. 1978). There also exists a massive literature in sociology and social psychology on changing work values and the demand for worker participation directed both at the level of the firm and the market place[3]. But attempts to formalize deterministic relationships between social phenomena at the micro and macro level have again been few and far apart and best insights as to how alternate social (cultural) environments impact on the firm's and workers' decision making process are still to be glanced from intercountry comparisons involving differing industrial relations systems (Dunlop 1958). The above noted incomplete and hence inadequate treatment of worker participation and related issues derives from an old methodological problem in the theory of the firm. For despite various attempts to combine social (behavioural) and pure economic decisions making parameters in firm theoretical treatises (March/Simon 1958, Cyert/March 1963), and the ongoing debate regarding the inclusion of externalities (Schelling 1971), there has been relatively little progress in developing a general theory of work relations and work behaviour invariant to time and jurisdiction (culture). In this regard, it has been Dlugos' merit to have pioneered a new framework for micro e.g. firm analysis which attempts to overcome the forementioned shortcomings of variable exclusion and external effects (Dlugos 1974). The approach ist probably best translated as a "political science theoretical treatment" of (firm) organization behaviour[4]. It puts the differing goals and interests of those making up the organization and possibly ensuing conflicts between and among goals and organization members into the center of the analysis. Dlugos' contributions are particularly insightful for our task at hand in that it permits a multiple determination of economic hence also work behaviour through organization internal and organization external forces. Put differently, it will assist in the analysis of interrelationships between organization internal phenomena of worker-participation and the structure and behaviour of labour markets surrounding the organization.

The paper will proceed as follows: Part 2 enlists factors on boh the demand and supply side of the labour exchange which have had a decisive influence on the rise of industrial democracy in the past. Brief attempts will be undertaken at the same time to contour their contectual (institutional) setting in the course of historical labour market developments in different jurisdictions. Part 3 will spell out consequences and repercussions of increased worker participation upon the structure and behaviour of labour markets. The paper finishes with some thoughts on the convergency/divergency and reversibility/irreversibility of labour market developments.

2. The Influence of Changing Labour Markets Upon the Demand and Supply of Codetermination and Other Forms of Industrial Democracy

Demand for and establishment of different forms of industrial democracy have progressed unevenly both over time and across different jurisdictions. Proper evaluations of the direction, size and speed of participation movements within the context of given labour markets require therefore a careful screening of economic, social and technological determinants at either side of the market exchange. Before listing demand and supply forces related to worker participation, a distinction between two different though related concepts of participation is in order. Workers may demand more participation and firms offer more of it for reasons of maximizing some other though related goal; in the case of capital owners we assume this to be the net present value of assets in the case of workers the net present value of discounted future earnings. Participation is here viewed as an instrument in the pursuit of specific goals of workers and capital owners. Employment of participation schemes on the part of the employer therefore hinge on their effort or productivity enhancing effects while workers or their representatives (unions) would want more participation to better change, enforce and police their labour contract with the employer. In contrast participation may also represent an end in itself; its consumption in the case of worker may yield higher levels of job satisfaction and job fulfillment as ultimate goals, its provision through the employer may constitute a fringe benefit payment analogous to other job conditions offered. The two concepts of participation as and end and as a means should be kept in mind during our subsequent discussion of participation determinants and consequences. Employer's interest in varying size and form of worker participation should conveniently begin with an examination of production requirements and technology. Mainstream writers on industrial organisation in both the behavioural sciences (industrial sociology and social psychology) and economics invariably have shown labor organization to be a derivative of prevailing product market environments and technology (Chandler 1977; Child/Mansfield 1972; Alchian/Demsetz 1974; Williamson 1980). According to this view causalities run from product market conditions via technology and organisation structure to forms and levels of worker participation, e.g. employer preferences merely represent a mirror image of prior product market adjustments. Stable mass consumption markets with low levels of environmental uncertainty or turbulence are seen as requiring mass production technologies with tight organizational structure and control, strong division of labour and resultant low levels of worker participation in decision making. The organizational structure and control of work essentially becomes a problem of proper monitoring work behaviour by reducing opportunistic shirking (Alchian/Demsetz 1974; Williamson 1975). Hierarchical control emerges as the most efficient way to manage in a work environment otherwise depicted by prevalence of extrinsic incentives (motivation) and rewards (Achlian/Demsetz 1974; Williamson 1980). In contrast, where environments are unstable on account of continuous product changes or other uncertainties flexible systems of production using craft as opposed to mass technology emerge. The latter require looser organizational structure and control both calling for and facilitating high levels of worker autonomy and worker co-decision-making. Reasons of different task uncertainty have also been cited to account for variations in production technology and work organization across different functional areas within given organizations[5]. To the extent that firms find themselves in fiercely competitive markets they are forced to compromise a give market imposed technology. The latter therefore can vary greatly according to different production task e.g. artistic production versus provision of services versus manufacture of specialty steel or automobile assembly, but nevertheless is imposed by the market place. Employers and managers can be regarded here as behaving uniformly at least in the long run. Context offers no choice and institutional arrangements with respect to labour are pure byproducts of markets and technologies over which employers have no control (Alchian/Demsetz 1974). A social optimal distribution of worker participation or industrial democracy is therefore shown to exist since the demand for labour (including its utilization for decision making tasks) is set by markets and fixed by technologies and management has no choice but to provide a matching supply of work with differing degrees of autonomy. There is nothing firms could do to improve the quality of the work process, through worker's co-decision making as it were, unless firms or workers were willing to sacrifice profits and/or wages for non-pecuniary rewards (Furubotn 1978; Hamermesh 1976). Market and associated technology developments certainly have shaped employers' preferences for forms and levels of worker participation throughout the sweep of history. There have been however market situations and circumstances both over time and at any particular point in time which have provided management and employers freedom from market forces thus enabling "managerial discretion". This raises the question as to how employers and management decide on issues of worker participation when their choices over key strategies and structural variables become heavily influenced by personal discretion and assessment of environmental trends. The topic has seen frequent empirical investigations which so far have provided the following results:

1. Work design processes appear to be far less rational than assumed in orthodox theories of the firm; instead they are often determined by central belief systems, management values and organization cultures and subcultures (Klein 1976).

2. When dealing with hard and soft criteria of performance and/or evaluation for alternate forms of work organization, firms and decision makers tend to favour hard and easy to measure performance indicators over soft, qualitative measures (Piore 1969).

3. The implementation of work group autonomy and worker participation schemes is carried out easier for newly built plants or newly merged firms as compared to reorganizations within existing older establishments (Klein 1976).

4. Frequently, management appears to be opposed to the introduction of industrial democracy on account of perceived losses of authority and power (Rosenthal 1980).

5. Most evaluations regarding the effectiveness of job enlargement and worker participation schemes indicate large pay-offs (Nicholas 1982; Walton 1977). However, surprisingly little empirical research has been undertaken to account for varying patterns and speed of diffusion of organizational innovations as compared to investigations of technological diffusion.

The forementioned results, while useful in its own right, have provided little guidance to the formulation of theories dealing with variations in organization form and design. Based on Simon's and March's path breaking analysis of decision making (March 1979; Simon 1960, 1978) economics has seen two further developments in what might be termed "fragments of an economic theory of organization" which is capable of shedding further light on the question of managerial discretion and emerging forms of work organization. The first approach is associated with the work of Williamson et al. (1975, 1980, 1983). It views the creation of alternate forms of work organization inherent in the employment contract as being ultimately determined by its cost of transacting. E.g. a simple alternative to hierarchy is the worker peer group. Stressing learning by doing together, peer groups create productivity gains through team work and a collegial atmosphere at the cost of distributional neutrality and the introduction of power into the labour contract. Peer groups are valuable because they promote consummate cooperation and commitment. Put differently, part of the economic problem of organizing is interpreted as "supplying a satisfying exchange relation" (Williamson 1975, p. 38). When people are committed to their jobs they tend to exhibit a greater sense of identification with the organizational mission, a greater feeling of intrinsic satisfaction from one's duties and a greater feeling of loyalty and affection for the organization. With commitment a closer congruence between individual and organizational goals can be achieved. The need for monitoring devices and rules is reduced. Transaction costs are lowered. An employee can use the corporate goals to "give me a way to make the same decision (the president) would make if he were in my position" (quoted in Ouchi/Johnson 1975, p. 302). This approach thus views worker participation as a managerial strategy designed to boost productivity through expanded jobs, commitment and trust along with greater autonomy of workers. All phenomena are seen as attempts to economize on bounded rationality and lower transaction costs through goal congruence and savings on control devices. Williamson's paradigm leaves no space for the existence of power relations and the development of actual or potential goal and distribution conflicts. Workers provide affirmative job attitudes instead of only perfunctory cooperation through incentives of promotion in a well defined sequence of job/promotion ladders, formal arbitration, grievance procedures and through informal mechanisms (e.g. norms of socialization). Unfortunately, the theory remarkably vague over the emergence of social norms, "corporate atmosphere" and thus the efficient organization of internal labour markets. Theoretical assertions that power sharing between management and workers should provide mutual gains through greater cooperation and that codetermination would therefore eventually substitute collective bargaining (McCain 1980) again offers no testable theory of economic behaviour towards alternative forms of worker participation. In contrast to these narrow "managerial" approaches of worker organization and worker participation, Leibenstein has attempted the formulation of a general theory of work behaviour and organization design (Leibenstein 1976). Contrary to assumption in mainstream economics, Leibenstein first of all shows utility no longer as a strict monotonic negative function of effort but instead represents it as a concave function taking into consideration utility enhancing effects on account of varying levels of intrinsic-motivation. Secondly, an individual's choice of work behaviour e.g., his effort equilibrium is portrayed as a psychological compromise between what an individual would do if completely unconstrained and what is dictated by own's own internalized effort standards, which in turn are formed through observation of others' performance of work. And, finally, instead of using perfect rationality in the sense of the neoclassical "complete constraint concerned calculatedness (Leibenstein, Ibid., p. 1972), Leibenstein adopts a more realistic concept of selective rationality, which in addition to constraint concern takes into consideration the context of decision-making (e.g. patterned versus non-patterned context) and the degree to which interpersonal relations can affect the interpretation of jobs, effort levels and selective rationality itself. The latter is of considerable theoretical importance for it allows the establishment of causal relationships between personal characteristics, organizational culture and design parameters and effort response and as such enables us to study individuals' changes in effort position as a function of personal traits, organization specific characteristics and environmental (market) constraints. Concepts of selective rationality and interpersonal relations allows Leibenstein to explain managerial preferences toward varying forms of work organization/industrial democracy both in terms of economic/technical constraints (structure of product markets, technological requirements of production) as well as social constraints (differing work values and other relevant social norms). The theory is thus capable of comparing and explaining a fair amount of differences in economic organization across cultures (Leibensten 1984). In many ways, Leibenstein's approach is comparable to Dlugos' political framework of analysis. Using the concept of multiple goals, multiple causes of conflict and multiple means of conflict resolution the latter approach similarily permits managerial decisions to be jointly determined by economic, technological and social as well as by firm internal and external forces/actors (Dorow 1979). It is probably fair to say that neither school of thought so far has progressed much beyond heuristic models of firm and worker behaviour and hence little is available in terms of empiricial tests[6]. The two theories nevertheless serve to validate earlier cited empirical findings regarding managerial preferences for and/or objections against varying forms and content of industrial democracy. In addition, a number of the theories' logical conclusions can be employed for predictive or explanatory purposes e.g.: recent managerial experiments and reforms with shop floor control and work organization in the U.S. automobile manufacturing on account of increased competition in its product markets (Katz 1985) have resulted from changes in managerial discretion, selective rationality and organizational innovativeness compatible with Leibenstein's theory of slack and/or X-efficiency (Leibenstein, Ibid., p. 56). Similarily, recognition as to how different firm internal and firm external actors can impact with differing strength and at differing points in time upon a firm's goals and decision making processes (Dlugos 1977) greatly enhances our understanding of the variation in cast of shop floor control and forms of corporate organization observable throughout the western industrialized world[7]. In this way, we can more easily separate firm external actors who are seen as impinging on issues of worker participation as e.g. unions, the state, suppliers or education systems from purely firm internal determinants such as employer and employee interests and concerns. We first discuss employee interests in industrial democracy.

As was pointed out previously, employees view participation as a final utility enhancing intangible good or as an intermediate good which provides individual welfare (income and leisure) through increased power over the firm's allocation decisions. Participation as a pure consumption good appears to be largely determined by workers' levels of educational attainment and past socialization experiences. Workers may want to have more say/power in their jobs (irrespective of whether this power will be used) when they possess greater capacities to gather and handle information relevant to decision making (Shepard/Harrick 1972). Also, they are likely to demand for greater participation in a setting (system) which socializes them to treat participation as a basic right analogous to e.g. freedom of speech as opposed to a setting in which workers were socialized to accept hierarchy as the only viable (natural) form of work organization[8]. We conjecture that over the past two decades, the demand for participation as a consumption good has risen throughout the industrialized world on account of both higher levels of educational attainment among workers and greater socialization towards participation rights. The demand for participation as a means to control and police the employment contract on the other hand appears to vary appreciably across different jurisdictions. Different labour market structures may be one reason for non-uniformity. In the limiting case where employers and employees face perfectly competitive labour markets with zero fixed cost of employment neither employers nor employees would need or want participation schemes. If fixed employment costs of job entry and -exit are zero employees would be able to police employment contracts most effectively through permanent threats of exit. As a corollary there would be no power relationships in the employment system, for workers could readily find employment elsewhere at the going social opportunity value of their services. Put differently, the workers' optimal working and income conditions could be secured through perfect labour markets and near perfect zero cost mobility. While this ideal can be found in isolated labour markets and while North American labour markets genereally display more mobility in comparison to their European counterparts there remain an omnibus of objections against such simplifying assumptions (Weiermair 1985, p. 552, 553). If labour markets were imperfect, this by itself would not imply that employees would automatically opt for more labour participation. For prospective, hence still mobile, workers are willing to join firms in long-term employment jobs with non-zero costs of exit if they are compensated for the additional risk of rent appropriation either through contractually secured profit sharing agreements or written and enforceable guarantees with respect to internal advancement. Workers may however also be satisfied with mere informal assurances upon joining if they hold a high degree of trust in the discretionary behaviour of their prospective peers and superiors. The latter is encouraged in an atmosphere of rich reciprocal social exchange facilitated through personal ties and empathy as well as absence of intensive monitoring (Fox 1974). Furthermore, workers' continued acceptance of informal agreements is likely to be preconditioned by companies' long standing records of employee compensation and treatment being perceived as fair. This suggests that employers' changes or violations of traditional industrial relations norms and practices may constitute another plausible reason for the secular rise in workers' demands for participation. E.g. radical changes in shop floor control, new patterns of manpower adjustment to technological changes, departures from past company training practices or wage concessions can spur worker movements towards greater participation, including codetermination. Participatory arrangements, quality of working life experiments, work redesign and codetermination not surprisingly became big issues in the 70s, in an era of general environmental turbulence and declining confidence in traditional manpower management practices. The latter was as much reflected in the overall climate for legislative participation endeavours (e.g. Works Constitution Act and Codetermination Act in West Germany) and associated changes in firm internal labour market structures in Europe[9], as it was observable in trends towards concession bargaining and provisions of job security clauses in North American industrial relations (Dunlop 1982; Katz 1985). A second plausible explanation for the rise in the demand for industrial democracy and one shared by many conservatives of differing coinage, are expected income and employment benefits expected by workers from improved power distributions in participation agreements (Pejovich 1978). Although power sharing and negotiating for improved working conditions can also be an issue in individual bargaining, more frequently it is pursued within the context of unions and collective bargaining. In their capacity as employee representatives either as works councils or shop stewards, unions behave and act as firm internal forces. Unions represent however also a firm external (societal) force which can influence worker and management through a web of political relationships and institutional linkages. Influence and interests of unions in matters of participation therefore derive from their double role as a social and ideological force and as an organization-internal interest group[10]. Our understanding of unions' present goals, structure and power (including those pertaining to issues of participation) would be contingent upon a discussion of the historically changing role and importance of unions across industrialized countries. Such an endeavour was however beyond the scope of this paper[11]. Though it is safe to state that unions can become a dominant force in the economy, e.g. through socialist governments at the national political level, industry wide bargaining on the economic level, a codetermined selection of the board of directors at the top management level and union dominated works councils at the middle management level, as Swedish and West-German developments in the seventies have demonstrated. Whether accidental or planned such developments towards union dominance could undermine free collective bargaining in that unions end up sitting on both sides of the bargaining table demanding and being granted wages higher than what enterprises could afford. The latter would confirm concerns of those who have put forth the hypothesis that industrial democracy in general and codetermination in particular will raise total labour compensation and lower the rate of private investment[12]. A cursory review of comparative union movements particularly as regards their ideology and militancy reveals considerable diversity. This may suggest that there neither is an unequivocal and persistent correspondence between demands for industrial democracy and unionism nor are trends towards union dominance irreversible. E.g. unionization in the United States presently stands at an alltime low and Europe has seen the rebirth of conservativism. Also, it is worth noting that historically North American "business type" unions have for a number of reasons shown great ambivalence towards industrial democracy, especially in the form of codetermination. Work organization and associated problems of job design, training and career planning became only union concerns during periods of rapid technological change and restructuring of the economy. In Europe this process dates back to the sixties when companies had to make manpower adjustments in response to the changed requirements of an expanded common market. In contrast, North American developments came a decade later and were less abrupt[13]; they were the result of the restructuring of the U.S. economy to meet the new competitive challenges from the Pacific Rim (Piore/Sabel 1984). Thus, the European debate over unions' codetermination came earlier and evolved around issues of work humanization and company training (Weiermair 1985, p. 561–62), while North American unions responded to environmental turbulence with demands for increased job security negotiable within traditional forms of collective bargaining. Other contributing factors towards the reluctance of American unions to embrace labour participation were lack of expertise in matters of job design and training on the part of many small and local unions, associated fears of co-option through management and the greater importance of and faith in the regulatory functions of firm external labour markets and training system[14]. As of late, West-German trade unions too have become disquieted over codetermination effects of labour market segmentation and the closing off of codetermined work places (Tegtmeier 1973, p. 205). The biggest controversy regarding union interests in worker participation, however, at least as far as West-Germany is concerned, arises out of the possibly differing interests between firm-external union nominees and firm-internal works council representatives. According to West-German codetermination laws (1951, 1972, 1976) both groups can be elected for representation at the firms' supervisory boards thus opening the possibility for firm-external union members to exert undue influence on management and workers on matters of work organization. Expressed differently where loyalties built up within a trade union that straddle firms differ from loyalties built up between management and workers within a given firm, conflicts of interest among union representatives and premature and harmful disclosure of firm-specific information to affiliated unions are likely to occur. A more salient issue of union influence is therefore one of union structure and organization and of its political power base. Governments of the left are clearly more inclined to use codetermination as a strategic variable by sending "better educated and towards the whole economy oriented" union representatives into the firm's codetermination bodies in order to fight "enterprise egoism and myopia"[15]. Conservative governments have as a rule been opposed to codetermined forms of worker participation and instead argued for a revitalization of competitive forces in labour markets combined with profit sharing schemes as a way to more effectively control employment contracts and worker incentives. Where unions have occupied a central role in the economy as is e.g. true in West Germany conservatives have taken a more intermediate position on codetermination. In any event, the limits of the combined power of state and unions or state and corporations in matters of industrial democracy must ultimately rest with voter resistance. A clear demonstration of the latter has been the defeat of the Swedish socialist government on account of its famous "Meidner Plan" which foresaw the expansion of codetermination to an eventual total worker control of enterprises. Discussions over the influence of state and unions in codetermination can be best summed up by contrasting European and North American developments. In the former labour has traditionally participated through the political process, while in the latter labour used the strategy of "rewarding friends and punishing enemies".

As a consequence, labour in the U.S. achieved an exemption from the Sherman Anti-trust Act and the Industrial Labor Relations Act (1935), which in their consequences yielded bargaining positions with management superior to their European counterparts, European unions on the other hand have opted to pursue political policies to achieve similar results.

Supplier relationships including banks appear to have had little impact on worker participation[16]. However, high levels of concentration and vertical integration as well as the existence of intertrading groups as is e.g. observable in the Japanese economy would all have the effect of reducing worker mobility and worker transferability and thus make "voice" as opposed to "exit" an equally important regulative device. Finally, varying systems of training and education particularly as regards employer sponsored forms of education can both influence codetermination and in turn are affected by variations in participative schemes. Their discussion is pursued in the next section dealing with labour market consequences of industrial democracy.

3. Forms of Industrial Democracy and Labour Market Behaviour

In dealing with the consequences of increased worker participation, we will restrict our observations to employment system and labour market behaviour. Thus, we exclude aspects of corporate control, management strategies/tactics against union influence and changes in power relations and levels of intra organizational conflict following the introduction of labour participation schemes e.g. West-German codetermination. Equally, excluded are discussions regarding the impact of worker participation upon the functioning and behaviour of capital markets. Before evaluating the performance of labour markets under differing levels of worker-participation it is useful to first spell out differences in the structure and conduct of labour markets emanating from the introduction of industrial democracy. As was shown earlier, workers want to participate in the firm's decision making partly on account of their long-term job attachment and commitment and associated costs of employment exit. An increase in participation and its contractual securement of implementation (either through codetermination laws or participatory clauses in collective agreements) therefore, is likely to cause a rise in employment security and job attachment among employed workers in codetermined firms. Structurally, this amounts to a "closing off" or insulation of codetermined work places and employees from the remaining work force available on the open e.g. firm-external labour market. To the extent that the latter can comprise marginal workers or workers with different, e.g. non-firm specific human capital endowment (e.g. re-entering adult females, youth, part-time workers, older workers or the unemployed), this group can be expected to suffer disproportionately from employment shocks or other environmental turbulence in the economy. Codetermination hardly differs from successful collective bargaining towards full job security for workers covered under the agreement. Either system of worker participation creates social costs of internal accommodation which subsequently become transferred to organizational-external labour markets in the form of social security and unemployment, insurance provisions or other public support/subsidy employment programs (Tegtmeier 1973, pp. 204, 205). Quality of labour and associated levels and forms of human investment represents another phenomenon, which is both a cause and effect of increased participation and which is equally related to the formation of labour market segmentation. Codetermination creates organization internal labour markets by sealing off firm internal manpower allocation processes from forces prevailing in external labour markets. Closure thus reduces the firm's human capital risk associated with labour mobility and at the same time increases worker incentives for self sorting and training to secure improved careers within the firm's extended tenure of employment. Firms are therefore willing to invest in their workers on account of the low outside mobility to be expected from their internally trained work force but they are likely to train for firm-specific, non-transferable skills. This in turn reinforces closure and labour market segmentation. Neither the state nor industrial unions can any longer rely on the controlling position of the organization external labour market and training systems to redress quantitative or qualitative imbalances of manpower. Thus, increasingly they will be forced to use codetermination for central control and concertation. On the basis of diverging interests of management, workers and worker representatives on the one hand and firm-external (union) representatives on the other hand, it is easy to see how conflicts can develop and persist, the decade old debate over humanization of work and industrial type training (Betriebsausbildungsdebatte) in West-Germany being a case in point. Here again, it seems that neither collective bargaining arrangements nor codetermination have been able to prevent the development of segmented labour markets on account of training specificity. More visible differences between codetermination and collective bargaining arrangements exist with respect to the structuring of organization-internal labour markets. Codetermination has made labour a relatively fixed factor of production comparable to capital, which in turn has lead to both quantitative and qualitative changes in manpower management. In part because of pressures for better information and communication, revelation of underlying assumptions and rationale in specific manpower decisions from works councils and the labour director, manpower management became upgraded both in terms of status and skills. It replaced paternalistic and at times "capricious' decision making. The more similar the status of labour as a factor of production became to that of capital the greater was the imperative to manage with the full participation and cooperation of organized labour. Tegtmeier describes this situation as "constraints toward cooperation" created through codetermination (Tegtmeier 1973, p. 148). The organizational rigidity and fixity of labour thus forced firms to better integrate manpower and employment policy with production and investment planning and to early identify future manpower needs and constraints. Among other things, this meant that changes in the structure of the work force had to be carried out through internal mobility in the form of a continuous redeployment and retraining of workers in accordance with the requirements of technological change within firm-internal labour markets. Legal obligations forced firms to offer vacant positions first to the existing work force before turning to external labour market. In consequence, internal labour markets were restructed to now contain long and thin job/training/promotion ladders, a flexible work organization, high internal mobility and a greater acceptance of technological change by the work force. Collective bargaining "North American style" in contrast was much less successful in producing such a restructuring of internal labour markets similarly needed on account of competitive pressures in product markets (Piore/Sabel 1984, p. 240 f.). The latter observations raise some general questions as to the performance characteristics of labour markets with differing degrees of labour participation in terms of such performance criteria as industrial conflict, wages and labour cost, mobility and the experience of labour market imbalances. It is worth noting that jurisdictions with well developed forms of industrial democracy such as West-Germany, Sweden and Austria have shown a better strike record than the rest of the industrialized world with the exception of Japan. Strike records unfortunately do not reflect the total level of industrial conflict in a given industry or jurisdiction for there can also be latent and/or repressed conflict, furthermore, care has to be undertaken to properly define and disentangle cause effect relationships between worker participation and industrial conflict. There is considerable controversy over wage effects associated with industrial democracy in general and codetermination in particular (Backhaus 1979, p. 144). In the past, codetermination and its reforms does not appear to have created excessive wage demands, at least as far as can be discerned statistically. Nothing in the process of codetermination or any other worker participation scheme for that matter, suggests however, that workers will or must continue to be moderate in their demands and seek rewards no greater than those offered by the market place. Whether wage demands will remain moderate and/or conform to market forces will largely hinge upon the stability of the cooperation and accomodation between capital and labour. The collaborative "productivity coalition" observed so far in codetermined West-German firms[17] is likely to be strained by attempts to reduce manpower disequilibria and imbalances in organizational-external labour markets through a process of codetermination.Here we return to the formentioned negative performance aspects of codetermination in terms of structural unemployment particularly youth unemployment. The presently proposed general solution of work sharing and/or reduction in the regular hours of work advanced and propagated by industrial unions in West-Germany through pressures within the process of codetermination was neither in the interest of codetermined employees nor was it in the interest of codetermined enterprises. Expectedly, this created a considerable amount of strain and friction within the system of codetermination. The latter experience clearly also demonstrated the limits of industrial democracy in the form of codetermination e.g. its inability to deal with general labour market imbalances and the temptation to use codetermination for purposes of distribution and redistribution. It is therefore also doubtful that codetermination will continue in its present West-German system of industrial relations. In the final section, we offer some speculations about possible future developments of industrial relations.

4. Concluding Remarks

In the previous section, industrial democracy was shown to be secularly rising albeit with great variations in institutional arrangements across industrialized nations. At the same time, questions were raised about the stability properties of existing labour participation processes. Hence, at this point, it becomes tempting to speculate over future developments particularly as regards the extent to which western industrial relations systems will converge and if so towards which particular system. If the question can be answered successfully, we can also provide a satisfactory answer regarding irreversible labour market developments.

If markets were considered the only regulative device and if there were absolutely no restraints to free trade, industrial relations systems would have to converge towards the most efficient/lowest cost jurisdiction within the trading block of western industrialized nations. Since for some time now, Japan has assumed the role of leader in industrial efficiency, "Japanization" of industrial relations systems would appear a distinct possibility. We believe, however, that the future import of Japanese industrial relations elements will remain restricted to translations of texts on Japanese management, quality control circles and the like. Rarely have markets in history been allowed to make dramatic adjustments involving severe adjustment costs in terms of unemployment and social conflict. Therefore we rather foresee interventions by the state both in the area of trade and in industrial relations thus ameliorating competitive pressures from product markets. In turn, this seems to suggest a convergence of industrial relations, whereas elements of "North American" collective bargaining will become blended with Japanese methods of shop-floor control and/or West-German schemes of worker participation. At this stage, it is impossible to predict the exact outcome of this convergence, for it will largely hinge upon the extent and form of future government intervention. As far as West Germany is concerned, the forementioned effects of codetermination have already introduced elements of "corporatism" into her system of industrial relations. In order to keep the industrial relations system balanced, this will call forth a replacement of industrial unions by company unions. The latter would move West Germany in the direction of the Japanese system of industrial relations and away from a pure West-German model. Clearly, there can be no irreversibility of labour market developments as long as there are at least some competitive pressures in a world of multilateral trade.

Remarks

[1] A good overview of codetermination in West-Germany can be found in: Bundesministerium für Arbeit und Sozialordnung 1978. The wider European context is discussed in: Commission of the European Communities 1975; Batstone/Davies 1976; IDE Research Group 1981. North American perspectives can be found in: Crispo 1978; Pejovich 1978; The Trilateral Commission 1979.

[2] For a good reference see productivity and growth analyses e.g.: Kendrick 1980.

[3] A good overview can be found in: Batstone/Davies 1976.

[4] The authors own and free translation from the German expression "betriebswirtschaftlich-politologische Konzeption" (Dlugos 1974).

[5] For a full discussion of this and related issues see: Galbraith 1977, pp. 174.

[6] For a discussion of empirical finding regarding Leibenstein's X-efficiency Theory see: Lofthouse 1974.

[7] A fascinating historical account of the diverging industrial development in the West can be found in Piore and Sabel's thorough comparative analysis of production conditions and associated systems of industrial relations in major industrialized countries see: Piore/Sabel 1984.

[8] The cultivation of work values most frequently occurs through formal and informal education and training and socialization at the work place. It can vary along a continuum spanning massive indoctrination at one extreme to tradition and custom at the other end of the continuum.

[9] These were reported in a number of different journal and reports see, e.g.: Doleschal/Dombois 1982; Glotz 1984; Everschein et al. 1981.

[10] Depending on the industrial relations system in a specific jurisdiction the two functions can at the extreme either completely overlap, completely differ or represent amalgams of the two forementioned roles.

[11] A good discussion can be found in: Barbash 1972; see also: Shalev 1980, pp. 26–43.

[12] An analysis can be found in Furubotn 1978.

[13] Among the reasons why manpower adjustments were less abrupt in the U.S. was the limited involvement of firms in experiments of job design. Training and novel patterns of bargaining, thus reducing the overall impact, see also Piore/Sabel 1984, pp. 240.

[14] Of particular relevance in this context are differences in the form and focus of occupational/vocational training which can either be employer or market centered.

[15] A good description of codetermination as understood by the adherents of democratic soialism can be found in: Kunze/Christmann 1964, p. 19.

[16] These at least were the findings of the West-German commission of experts on codetermination, for reference see: Mitbestimmungskommission 1970, pp. 29–55.

[17] For an elaboration and some empirical tests, see: Witte 1982, pp. 416–434.

Literature

Alchian, A. / Demsetz, H. (1974): Production, Information Costs and Economic Organization. In: *American Economic Review* 62, pp. 777–795.
Backhaus, J. (1979): *Ökonomik der partizipativen Unternehmung*. Tübingen.
Barbash, J. (1972): *Trade Unions and National Economic Policy*. Baltimore.
Batstone, E. / Davies, P. L. (1976): *Industrial Democracy, European Experience*. London.
Berg, I. / Freedman, M. / Freeman, M. (1978): *Managers and Work Reform: A Limited Engagement*. New York.
Blumberg, P. (1968): *Industrial Democracy: The Sociology of Participation*. New York.
Bohr, K. et al. (Eds.) (1981): *Unternehmensverfassung als Problem der Betriebswirtschaftslehre*. Berlin.
Bundesministerium für Arbeit und Sozialordnung (1978): *Codetermination in the Federal Republic of West Germany*. Bonn.
Chandler, A. (1977): *The Visible Hand*. Cambridge.
Child, J. / Mansfield, C. (1972): Technology, Size and Organization Structure. In: *Sociology* 6, pp. 369–393.
Crispo, J. (1978): *Industrial Democracy in Western Europe. A North American Perspective*. Toronto.
Commission of the European Communities (1975): *Employee Participation and Company Structure*. Bulletin of the European Communities. Brussels.
Davis, L. E. (1966): Design of Jobs. In: *Industrial Relations,* October, pp. 21–45.
Dlugos, G. (1974): Unternehmungspolitik als betriebswirtschaftlich-politologische Teildisziplin. In: Wild, J. (Ed.), *Unternehmungsführung*. Festschrift für Erich Kosiol. Berlin.
Dlugos, G. (1976): Unternehmungspolitik. In: Grochla, E. / Wittmann, W. (Eds.), *Handwörterbuch der Betriebswirtschaft*. Stuttgart.
Dlugos, G. (1978): Mitbestimmung. In: Grochla, E. (Ed.), *Handwörterbuch der Organisation*. Stuttgart, Sp. 4093–4103.
Doleschal, R. / Dombois, R. (Eds.) (1982): *Wohin läuft der VW? Die Automobilproduktion in der Wirtschaftskrise*. Reinbek bei Hamburg.
Dorow, E. (1978): *Unternehmungskonflikte als Gegenstand unternehmungspolitischer Forschung*. Berlin.
Dorow, W. (1979): Konfliktforschung aus unternehmungspolitischer Sicht. In: Dlugos, G. (Hrsg.), *Unternehmungsbezogene Konfliktforschung*. Stuttgart, pp. 354–376.
Dunlop, J. T. (1958): *Industrial Relations Systems*. New York.
Dunlop, J. T. (1982): Working Toward Consensus. In: *Challenge,* July/August, pp. 26–34.
Everschein, W. / Wack, M. / Zauner, K. / Herrman, P. (1981): Anforderungen an zeitgemäße Produktionssysteme. *VDI-Nachrichten,* No. 11, pp. 449–457.
Fox, A. (1974): *Beyond Contract Work, Power and Trust Relations*. London.
Freeman, R. (1979): *Labor Economics*. 2nd edition. Englewood Cliffs.
Furubotn, E. (1978): The Economic Consequences of Codetermination on the Rate and Sources of Private Investment. In: Pejovich, S., *The Codetermination Movement in the West*. Lexington.
Furubotn, E. G. / Pejovich, S. (1974): *The Economics of Property Rights*. Cambridge, Mass.
Galbraith, J. R. (1977): *Organization Design*. Reading, Mass.
Glotz, P. (1984): *Die Arbeit der Zuspitzung*. Berlin.

Hammermesh, D. S. (1976): Economic Consideration in Job Satisfaction Trends. In: *Industrial Relations* 15, (1), pp. 112–114.
Hirschman, A. O. (1970): *Exit, Voice and Loyalty.* Cambridge.
IDE Research Group (1981): *Industrial Democracy in Europe. Oxford Clarendon Press*
Katz, H. C. (1985): Shifting Gears: Changing Labour Relations in the U.S. Auto Industry. Cambridge, Mass.
Kendrick, J. W. (1980): Survey of Factors Contributing to the Decline in U.S. Productivity Growth. In: *Federal Reserve Bank of Boston. The Decline in U.S. Productivity Growth,* Conference Series No. 22. Boston.
Klein, L. (1976): *New Forms of Work Organization.* Cambridge.
Kuehne, R. J. (1980): *Co-determination in Business.* New York.
Kunze, O. / Christmann, A. (1964): *Wirtschaftliche Mitbestimmung im Meinungsstreit* 1, Köln, p. 19.
Lawrence, P. R. / Lorsch, J. W. (1967): *Organisation and Environment: Managing Differentiation and Integration.* Boston.
Leibenstein, H. (1976): *Beyond Economic Man: A New Foundation for Microeconomics.* Cambridge, Mass.
Leibenstein, H. (1984): The Japanese Management System: An X-Efficiency-Game Theory Analysis. In: Aoki, M. (Ed.), *The Economic Analysis of the Japanese Firm.* North Holland.
Lofthouse, S. (1974): Recent Literature Relating to the X-Efficiency and Market Structure Relationship. In: *Zeitschrift für Nationalökonomie* 34, p. 409–423.
March, J. G. (1979): Ambiguity and the Engineering of Choice. In: *International Studies of Management and Organization,* Fall IX (3), pp. 9–40.
McCain, R. A. (1980): A Theory of Codetermination. In: *Zeitschrift für Nationalökonomie* 40 (1–2), pp. 65–90.
Mitbestimmungskommission (1970): *Mitbestimmung im Unternehmen.* Bericht der Sachverständigenkommission zur Auswertung der bisherigen Erfahrungen bei der Mitbestimmung. Bonn, Bundesdrucksache, p. 29–55.
Nicholas, J. M. (1982): *The Comparative Impact of Organization Development Interventions on Hard Criteria Measures.* Academy of Management Review 7 (4), pp. 531–542.
Ouchi, W. G. / Johnson, J. B. (1978): Types of Organization Control and their Relationship to Emotional Wellbeing. *Administrative Science Quarterly,* June 28, pp. 293–317.
Pejovich, S. (1978): *The Codetermination Movement in the West.* Lexington.
Piore, M. (1967): The Impact of the Labour Market upon the Design and Selection of Productive Techniques within the Manufacturing Plant. In: *Quarterly Journal of Economics,* pp. 603–623.
Piore, M. / Sabel, Ch. (1984): *The Second Industrial Divide.* New York.
Rosenthal, R. A. (1980): *On the nature of Managerial Opposition to Industrial Democracy:* An Empirical Investigation, paper presented at the 9th International Atlantic Economics Conference, Freeport, Bahamas.
Schelling, T. (1971): On the Ecology of Micromotives. In: *The Public Interest,* Fall, pp. 59–89.
Shalev, M. (1980): Industrial Relations Theory and the Comparative Study of Industrial Relations and Industrial Conflict. In: *British Journal of Industrial Relations* 18 (1), pp. 26–43.
Shepard, H. / Henrick, N. (1972): *Where Have All the Computers Gone?* New York.

Simon, H. A. (1960): *The New Science of Management Decision*. New York.
Simon, H. A. (1978): On How do Decide What to Do. In: *Bell Journal of Economics* 9 (2), pp. 494–507.
Streeck, W. (1983): *Trade Unions – Structure, Influence, Responsibility. The Case of the German Car Industry*. London.
Tegtmaier, W. (1973): *Wirkungen der Mitbestimmung der Arbeitnehmer*. Göttingen.
The Trilateral Commission (1979): *Collective Bargaining and Participation in Western Europe, North America and Japan*. New York.
Thimm, A. L. (1980): *The False Promise of Codetermination*. Lexington, Mass.
Watson, R. (1977): Work Innovations at Topeka: After Six Years. In: *Journal of Applied Behavioral Science* 13, pp. 422–433.
Weiermair, K. (1985): Worker Incentives and Work Participation: On the Changing Nature of the Employment Relationship. In: *Journal of Management Studies* 22 (5), pp. 547–571.
Williamson, O. E. (1975): *Markets and Hierarchies: Analysis and Antitrust Implications*. New York.
Williamson, O. E. / Harris, J. E. (1975): Understanding the Employment Relationship: The Analysis of Ideosyncratic Exchange. In: *Bell Journal of Economics* 6 (2), pp. 256–278.
Williamson, O. E. (1980): The Organisation of Work: A Comparative Institutional Assessment. In: *Journal of Economic Behaviour and Organisation* 1, pp. 39–60.
Williamson, O. E. / Ouchi, W. G. (1983): The Markets and Hierarchies Programme of Research: Origins, Implications and Prospects. In: Francis, A. / Turk, J. / William, P. (Eds.), *Power, Efficiency and Institutions: A Critical Appraisal of the Markets and Hierarchies Paradigm*. London.
Witte, E. (1982): Das Einflußsystem der Unternehmung in den Jahren 1976 und 1981. Empirische Befunde im Vergleich. In: *Zeitschrift für betriebswirtschaftliche Forschung* 34, pp. 416–434.

Interaction With External Actors as a Guide to Business Efficiency

Wolfgang H. Staehle

Abstract

The following is an attempt to resolve the argument about the "correct" measurement of business efficiency through the application of external rather than internal yardsticks. It does so by focusing on the interactions that take place between a company and relevant interest groups – such as customers, suppliers (of labour, funds, materials, information), competitors and the legislative and executive branches of government – capable of influencing the company's decisions and behaviour in their favour.

Each of these interest groups presents the company with claims (with regard to pay, prices, interest, dividends, taxes, etc.) of a precise type and magnitude which are settled with the company's management by negotiation. As long as the claims are being met to the interest groups' satisfaction, the company itself will be considered efficient. Failing a satisfactory settlement, the interest groups will threaten to withdraw their contributions and/or resort to sanctions.

1. Companies and Their Environment

Advanced societies, through the division of labour, give rise to organisations which justify their existence, rightly or wrongly, on the ground that they perform socially important functions.[1] Organisations exist to achieve certain purposes and objectives. Their members and participants are naturally interested, if only for the sake of their own pride and satisfaction, in their organisations' success, while their managers and organisers are intent, moreover, on running them as efficiently as they can. Basically, companies are private sector organisations (unlike state corporations) trading for profit. Their hallmarks are (a) private ownership of the means of production and (b) resource allocation through the market mechanism. Apart from the profit motive, they also share the power of entrepreneurial decision-making exercised by their owners direct or by managers/executives on their behalf.

The following is primarily concerned with the type of company that predominates in the capitalist system where the output function nowadays, in keeping with present-day principles of market-orientated management, takes precedence over all others, and where processing and input requirements (production/procurement planning) are governed by output conditions (sales planning) accordingly.

Corporate planning throughout must therefore take market factors as its starting point. A company's output is defined as the products or services provided with profit-making intent. It excludes, for the purpose of this argument, other outflows (like wages, taxes, interest and dividends), which represent payment for the company's input.

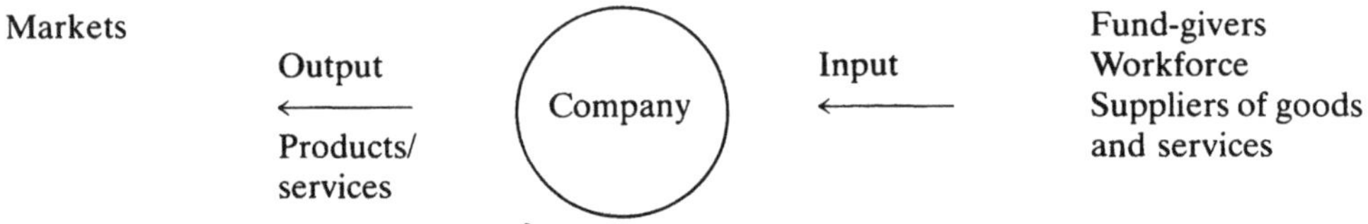

Fig. 1: Output and input functions[2]

A company must procure, husband and perhaps further develop whatever resources it needs for successful operation, and so must offer their owners/purveyors sufficient incentives to make them available to it on agreed terms. They are the input required for processing into the planned output.

The required input must also throughout be of the desired quantity and quality and be available (or at least legally accessible) at the right time and place. If resource owners/ purveyors feel that the contributions they make to keep the company in business are not being adequately matched by the inducemens it offers, they will first protest and then, failing a satisfactory response, opt for a more suitable alternative elsewhere.

Type of resource	Owner/purveyor	Inducements offered by the company
Funds	Shareholders, creditors	Dividend, equity stake interest
Labour	Workforce	Pay, job security, perks
Equipment, materials	Suppliers	Money
Disposable income	Customers	Products, services
Law and order, infrastructure, education, etc.	Government	Taxes

Fig. 2: Resources as company input[3]

Thus companies stay efficient only as long as, somehow or other, acceptable to resource owners/purveyors (input-givers) on account of inducements they offer.

A company can, we are told, be forced out of business simply by disgruntled creditors. But such action will in most cases have been preceded by difficulties with others, notably the company's customers.

It is not only banks and stockholders that must be kept happy. Workers demand a "fair" wage and job security, customers sound goods and quality service at "reasonable" prices, suppliers payment on time, and local authorities the maximum revenue combined with the minimum amount of pollution. Each of these interest groups has different notions of company efficiency, and so has different expectations or aspirations to be satisfied.

Hence, for a company to be efficient, it must first of all keep well in with external interest groups (primarily investors and the like who look for an adequate return on their investment, or are preoccupied with the company's profitability), and only then does it have to satisfy all the internal criteria (productivity, cost efficiency, etc.) by which efficiency is normally measured. This line of thought needs to be discussed in more detail.

2. External Criteria of Company Efficiency

Defining company efficiency in terms of external criteria means, of course, that companies do not conduct a monologue, but are actively and continually engaged in a dialogue with others, whose separate and discernible interests must be taken into account. First and foremost, these are interest groups interacting with companies by way of trade and capable, by hook or by crook, of influencing their future survival.

Approaching the matter in this way gets away from the rather sterile debate about which kind of efficiency matters most, and instead concentrates on how companies and relevant interest groups, capable of influencing companies' actions and behaviour in their favour, interact with each other. It matters little for that purpose whether such groups are identified with the help of the coalition theory[4] or the systems theory[5] approach.

Interest groups agree on the nature and magnitude of the demands, or efficiency criteria, to be met, and declare them to companies in a more or less open manner. They ultimately form the basis of whether companies are to be approved or condemned (cf. Fig. 3).

A show of disapproval will reveal to a company, if nothing else has done, both that it has not been as efficient as it should be and the identity of the interest group(s) of which it has fallen foul. Working out the criteria by which its efficiency is judged is up to the company's management.

An efficient company will, of course, seek to avert disapproval, or worse, that could threaten its survival. It will therefore do whatever it can, through changes in methods of production, technology, organisation, financing, etc., to satisfy the set efficiency criteria, and/or seek to restore its image through an agreed change in those criteria themselves.

Interest groups / Inducements/contributions	Fund-givers	Workforce	Suppliers	Customers	Central government	Local government	Pressure groups
Inducements (approaches to efficiency criteria)	Dividend, interest, collateral	Pay, job satisfaction/security, perks, kudos	Sale proceeds, regular outlet/payment	Use of products and services	Tax revenue, political backing	Tax revenue, quality of life, jobs	Quality of life, "welfare"
Contributions (approaches to possible sanctions)	Funds supplied at risk	Labour, hard work, dedication	Supply of goods, services and goodwill	Payment of bills, word-of-mouth recommendation	Infrastructure, investment incentives, subsidies, legislation	Infrastructure	Publicity, vigilance, active/passive support

Fig. 3: Various interest groups' inducements and contributions[6]

The interaction with external actors that all this involves takes place at several levels (cf. Fig. 4).

This chart can be read horizontally and vertically. Horizontally, the top line shows the trade any organisation (e.g. a company) conducts with resource-givers, or relevant interest groups, under existing, albeit internationally varying, social conditions. Such trade is, at the next level, assessed in terms of efficiency criteria which could entail sanctions or other painful consequences if they are not met. Finally, the three systems involved are shown (within dotted lines) vertically.

2.1. Action System I

Action system I, which stands for all owners/purveyors of resources with whom a company interacts, is concerned with analysis of past and present trading relations, with organisation and analysis of negotiations resulting in the establishment of efficiency criteria[8], with analysis of relative bargaining strengths, and with the application if necessary of suitable sanctions.

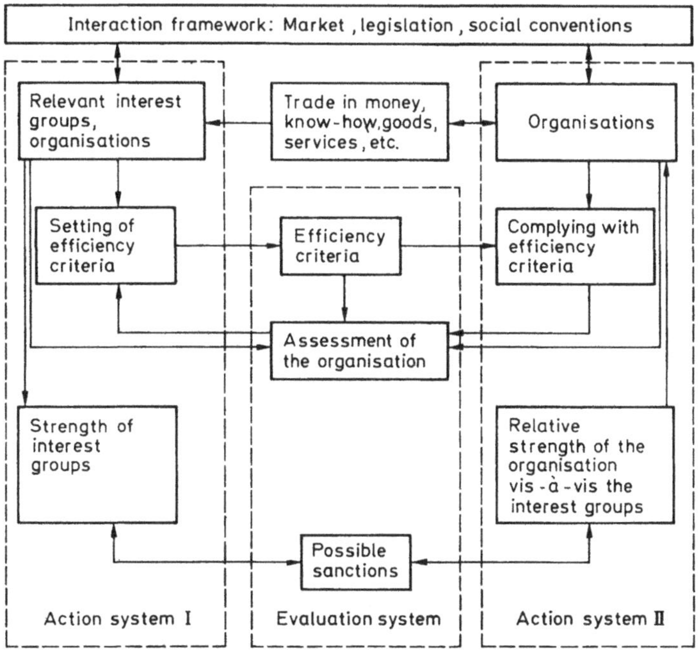

Fig. 4: Efficiency measured through interaction with external actors[7]

2.2. Evaluation System

Principal functions of the evaluation system are to scrutinise whatever efficiency criteria are set, to foresee how one's own organisation will be perceived by others, and to consider sanctions against the company taken, or liable to be taken, by external interest groups.

There are normally negotiations with the company, and within the interest groups themselves, before precise efficiency criteria, in the form of (say) minimum levels of wages, interest rates, product quality, etc., are set and agreed in any given case. In order to evaluate a particular company, generalities comparing, for instance, inducements and contributions, or describing the typical aspirations of different interest groups, are not enough[9]. Each company's efficiency criteria must be related to the specific situation and environment in which it operates.

As for possible sanctions, suffice it here to point out that, just as a company's efficiency is measurable by the inducements that interest groups have to be offered, so the scope for sanctions that can be applied against is indicated by the contributions those same groups, by voting with their feet, can withdraw.

The evaluation system can either be part of action systems I and II – in the guise of a company's Accounting, Audit, Economic or Internal Services department – or exist as an independent entity, whether acting for or appointed by an interest group (TUC, CBI, merchant bank, management consultant) or figuring as an independent arbitrator (OFT, Acas).

2.3. Action System II

In Fig. 4 "organisation" is shorthand for a company's top management, which in this connection has the job of overseeing on-going deals, organising and overseeing negotiations concerning efficiency criteria and performance, assessing the company's and interest groups' relative bargaining strengths, reviewing possible methods of compensation, and taking steps where needs to ensure that the efficiency criteria set are complied with.

It is only when the work of evaluation has been completed that the management can properly proceed (say) to a reformulation of corporate strategies and objectives calculated, through changes (e.g. in products) made after consultation with those concerned, to repair or enhance the company's image.

Possible courses of action/interaction here range from passive, total surrender to external pressures at one extreme – clearly, since some pressures will be more acceptable than others, not a recipe of universal application – to weight-pulling by the sheer exercise of market power at the other.

Perhaps the best way of handling the situation, at least in large companies, might be a two-tier board of directors, with executive directors appointed to undertake the day-to-day management as well as strategic planning and non-executive directors elected, among other things, to look into and reconcile the conflicting claims and aspirations of both inside and outside interests. In this way, efficiency yardsticks of the traditional type could once again come into their own.

Remarks

[1] On what follows, Staehle 1983, pp. 24.
[2] Ibid., p. 36.
[3] Ibid., p. 37.
[4] Cyert/March 1963; Weitzig 1979.
[5] Dill 1958; Gross 1968; Becker/Neuhauser 1975; Meffert 1975; Hill/Fehlbaum/Ulrich 1981.
[6] Staehle 1985, p. 157.
[7] Staehle/Grabatin 1979, p. 97.
[8] Rhenman 1968, 1973; Bircher 1976.
[9] Pickle/Friedlander 1967, pp. 168.

Literature

Becker, S. W. / Neuhauser, D. (1975): *The Efficient Organization*. New York, Oxford, Amsterdam.

Bircher, B. (1976): *Langfristige Unternehmensplanung. Konzepte, Erkenntnisse und Modelle auf systemtheoretischer Grundlage*. Bern, Stuttgart.

Cyert, R. M. / March, J. G. (1963): *A Behavioral Theory of the Firm*. Englewood Cliffs.

Dill, W. R. (1958): Environment as an Influence on Managerial Autonomy. In: *Administrative Science Quarterly* 2, pp. 409–443.

Gross, B. M. (1968): *Organizations and their Managing* (1. Aufl. 1964). New York, London.

Hill, W. / Fehlbaum, R. / Ulrich, P. (1981): *Organisationslehre. Ziele, Instrumente und Bedingungen der Organisation sozialer Systeme*. 1. Band (1. Aufl. 1974), 3. Aufl. Bern, Stuttgart.

Meffert, H. (1975): Marketing und Konsumerismus. In: *Zeitschrift für Betriebswirtschaft* 2, pp. 69–90.

Pickle, H. / Friedlander, F. (1967): Seven Societal Criteria of Organization Success. In: *Personnel Psychology* 20, pp. 165–178.

Rhenman, E. (1980): *Industrial Democracy and Industrial Management*. Assen London.

Rhenman, E. (1973): *Organization Theory for Long-range Planning*. London etc.

Staehle, W. H. (1985): *Management*. 2. Aufl. München.

Staehle, W. H. (1983): *Funktionen des Managements*. Bern, Stuttgart.

Staehle, W. H. / Grabatin, G. (1979): Effizienz von Organisationen. In: *Die Betriebswirtschaft* 1B/1979, pp. 89–102.

Weitzig, J. (1979): *Gesellschaftsorientierte Unternehmenspolitik und Unternehmensverfassung*. Berlin, New York.

Organisationsstrukturen und Partizipationsspielräume

Gerhard Reber

Abstract

Organizational Structures and Discretion for Participation

After a short portrayal of contingency models in the introduction of this paper an extended description of the elements of the participation conception will be given (degree of intensity, contents, participation in different phases of the decision process, direct or indirect participation). The inadequacy of the approach which considers power as a zero-sum-game is shortly dealt with. Main theme of this paper is the discussion of five selected organizational structures which do in reality exist and in which participation is of importance. These are: 1.) statuatory codetermination, 2.) humanization of work (quality of work life), 3.) multi-dimensional, 4.) inexact and 5.) organic structures of organization. Finally some speculative thoughts will be developed about the connection of these structures and their influence on a comprehensive theory of participative organizational structures.

1. Konzeptionen und Definition

(1) Angesichts der gegenwärtig vorherrschenden Kontingenzkonzeptionen[1] nimmt das Thema dieses Beitrags eine Amputation vor: Ohne explizite Betrachtung der „Umwelt" scheinen sich Überlegungen zu Zusammenhängen zwischen Strukturvariablen und Verhaltensweisen in einem Vakuum oder gar im schwerelosen Weltraum abzuspielen, in dem die harten Bedingungen des „Luftdrucks" – insbesondere Aussagen über die Effizienz von Organisationen gemessen als Bewährung in spezifischen Umwelten – übersehen oder künstlich ausgeschaltet werden. Schon aus diesen Gründen des zur Verfügung stehenden Raumes wollen wir uns dieses Versäumnis aufladen. Dies ist vielleicht deshalb nicht so gravierend, weil an vielen anderen Stellen dieses Bandes der hier verlassene Gesamtzusammenhang diskutiert wird. Insofern wollen wir ihn aber im Auge behalten als zweierlei angenommen wird: (a) von der *Umwelt* wird nicht angenommen, daß sie stabil und kalkulierbar ist. Die Organisation steht vor internen Adaptionsnotwendigkeiten, die externe Selektionsmechanismen abfangen sollen. Bei diesen Adaptionsprozessen – gemeint i. w. S. also auch der aktiven Veränderung der Umwelt

durch die Organisation (Dlugos 1981a, S. 66) – gewinnt die Partizipation besondere Bedeutung im Hinblick (b) auf die Beeinflussung der organisationalen Effizienz. Diese Effizienz wird allerdings aufgrund des groben Bezugs zu den Umweltbedingungen nicht differenzierend angesprochen; ebenso unterbleibt eine anspruchsvolle Zusammenfassung von empirischen Forschungsergebnissen zu Bedingungen und Wirkungen von Partizipation, wie sie z. B. von Locke / Schweiger (1978) – allerdings auch ohne kontingenztheoretische Bezugnahme – vorgelegt wurde. Diese Autoren demonstrieren die Komplexität der Zusammenhänge sowie die Uneinheitlichkeit der Forschungsergebnisse. Sie erwähnen, daß „... die Effizienz der Partizipation von einer Vielzahl kontextualer Faktoren abhängt" (S. 325). Lediglich einer dieser Faktorengruppen wenden wir uns zu und spekulieren nur am Rande über die möglichen Effizienzfolgen der strukturell eröffneten Partizipationsspielräume. Hauptziel dieses Beitrags ist es, damit nicht gültige Effizienzurteile abzugeben, sondern in einem Vorstadium hierzu auf ganz unterschiedliche organisatorische Konzeptionen zur Öffnung und Gestaltung dieser Spielräume hinzuweisen.

(2) Partizipation wird sehr unterschiedlich definiert (Locke / Schweiger 1978, S. 266–276). Generelle Übereinstimmung herrscht allerdings darüber, daß zur Partizipation mindestens zwei Personen notwendig sind, die gemeinsam an etwas teilnehmen wollen. Der Gegenstand der Teilnahme soll im folgenden Zusammenhang auf einen *Entscheidungsprozeß* (Tannenbaum / Massarik 1950; Vroom 1973) beschränkt werden, an dem *interne Organisationsmitglieder* beteiligt sind. Die Beteiligung kann a) verschiedene *Intensitätsgrade* haben, b) unterschiedliche *Inhalte* und c) *Phasen* betreffen und d) – eine *direkte* oder *indirekte* Form annehmen (Reber 1970). Des weiteren kann man in bezug auf die Einrichtung der Partizipationsmöglichkeiten zwischen einer *formalen* und einer *informalen* unterscheiden (Locke / Schweiger 1978, S. 275). Die informale Partizipation basiert allein auf persönlichen Beziehungen, Absprachen und Gewohnheiten zwischen Organisationsmitgliedern. Die uns interessierende formal induzierte Partizipation kann kraft Gesetzes, Tarifverträge, Verfassung der Organisation oder einfacher organisatorischer Regelungen installiert sein. Mit diesen Merkmalen ist Partizipation von „Delegation" abgegrenzt. Letztere enthält insbesondere keine Gemeinsamkeit mit anderen Personen, sondern eine hierarchische Arbeitsteilung.

a) In Anlehnung an Tannenbaum / Schmidt (1958) kann die Intensität der Partizipation als ein Kontinuum dargestellt werden, das von keiner Beteiligung (ein Vorgesetzter teilt z. B. seinen Untergebenen eine Entscheidung mit) bis zu einer „vollen" Partizipation (z. B. alle Mitglieder einer Gruppe sind vollständig gleichberechtigt) reicht. Bezogen auf die Partizipation an Führungsentscheidungen haben Vroom / Yetton (1973) diese beiden Extrempunkte mit den Bezeichnungen AI (Führer trifft seine Entscheidungen allein) und GII (Führer ist gleichwertiges und gleichberechtigtes Gruppenmitglied) versehen, Zwischenstufen (AII = Führer holt für seine Entscheidung Informationen bei seinen Untergebenen ein; BI und BII = Führer läßt sich bei seiner Entscheidung von einem (I) oder mehreren (II) seiner Untergebenen beraten) eingefügt und empirisch die jeweiligen Partizipationsintensitäten auf einer Skala von 0–10 bestimmt (AI = 0; AII = 1; BI = 5; BII = 8; GII = 10) (Vroom 1981, S. 185).

b) Inhaltliche Abgrenzungen der Partizipation können vielfältige Formen annehmen. Von wesentlicher Bedeutung für die gesetzliche Mitbestimmung ist z. B. die Abgrenzung zwischen „sozialen, personellen und wirtschaftlichen Angelegenheiten". Locke / Schweiger (1978, S. 276) unterscheiden vier Inhaltskategorien: Routineentscheidungen im Personalbereich (Einstellungen, Entlohnungssysteme, Leistungsbeurteilung usw.), Gestaltung der Arbeitsaufgabe (Zielsetzung, Arbeitsmethoden, Arbeitsverteilung usw.), Arbeitsbedingungen (Pausen, Arbeitszeit usw.) sowie geschäftspolitische Entscheidungen (Gewinnbeteiligung, Kurzarbeit, Sozialleistungen, Investitionen usw.).

Neben diesen eher von der Organisation resp. von der Nachfrage oder den Einsatzmöglichkeiten her differenzierten Inhalten schlagen Kirsch / Scholl eine Gliederung von Partizipationsinhalten auf der Grunlage der Beitragsmöglichkeiten der Partizipienten vor. Sie unterscheiden hiernach „... idealtypisch vier Arten von Partizipation" (Kirsch / Scholl 1977, S. 237 f.): *Pseudo-Partizipation:* Hier geht es letztlich weder um den Einbezug von Werten bzw. Bedürfnissen noch um ein echtes Interesse am Wissen der Beteiligten; lediglich die zwischenmenschlichen Beziehungen sollen verbessert werden und man hofft, daß sich die Partizipienten anschließend mit den Führungsentscheidungen eher identifizieren. Partizipation im Sinne einer *Human-Resources-Strategie* liegt vor, wenn man das Wissenspotential der Partizipienten mobilisieren möchte, während man deren Interessen auszuklammern trachtet. Partizipation im Sinne der *Social-Value-Strategie* ist gegeben, wenn man die Organisationsmitglieder an Entscheidungen beteiligt, weil ihre Werte bzw. Bedürfnisse berücksichtigt werden sollen, andererseits die Notwendigkeit eines ausreichenden Wissens der Partizipienten unterschätzt, so daß die Entscheidungen nicht wirkungsvoll an den Werten ausgerichtet werden können. *Authentische Partizipation* liegt schließlich vor, „... wenn man Partizipationschancen eröffnet, um sowohl eine Artikulation und Berücksichtigung der Bedürfnisse und Werte als auch eine Mobilisierung des Wissens der Geführten zu ermöglichen" (Kirsch / Scholl 1977, S. 238).

Diese Unterscheidung zwischen motivationalen und kognitiven Inhalten der Partizipation spielt auch in einer Abgrenzung Wunderers (1985, S. 246) eine Rolle, obgleich er über die individuellen Bedingungen hinausgeht und Führungs- bzw. Partizipationsbeziehungen auf sozialpsychologischer Ebene anspricht: Er bevorzugt den Begriff „kooperative Führung", bei der er eine „partizipative" („Teilhabe") und eine „prosoziale Dimension" („Teilnahme") unterscheidet. Zu ersterem gehören z. B. Informationsrechte/-pflichten; Begründungsrechte/-pflichten, Vetorecht; zu letzterem Phänomene wie Offenheit, Vertrauen, Verständnis, Akzeptanz, Toleranz usw. Ebenso sprechen Neuberger et al. (1985, S. 86 ff.) die Bedeutung der „sozio-emotionalen Qualität" für die Wirkung von Kooperation und Partizipation an.

Auch die Gliederung der Konfliktarten zur Diagnose des Akzeptanzverhaltens im Führungsmodell Vroom / Yetton enthält eine für die Einschätzung der Wirkung der Partizipation wesentliche Inhaltsdifferenzierung (Vroom 1981, S. 186): Beachtet werden dort Konflikte mit den Organisationszielen, dem Vorgesetzten und zwischen den Untergebenen.

c) Viele Entscheidungen ziehen sich über einen längeren Zeitraum hin und weisen hierbei unterschiedliche Schwerpunkte auf. Es hat sich die Tradition gebildet, die spezifische inhaltliche Abfolge von Entscheidungs- resp. Problemlösungsprozessen in Phasenschemata darzustellen (vgl. z. B. Thomae 1984; Irle 1971; Janis / Mann 1977). Es entstehen dann Sequenzen wie: Problementdeckung, Entwicklung von Alternativen, Bewertung von Alternativen, Auswahl zwischen den Alternativen, Infragestellung und Revision der Bewertung resp. Auswahl. Die Partizipation kann für alle Phasen offen oder auf nur einige beschränkt sein. So kann Gruppenpartizipation für ein „Brain-Storming" zur Problementdeckung zugelassen sein, während die letzte Auswahl zwischen den Lösungsalternativen dem Vorgesetzten vorbehalten bleibt. Formale Festlegungen der Offenheit resp. Geschlossenheit bestimmter Phasen für die Partizipation haben sicherlich Wirkungen, die nicht allein auf die betroffene(n) Phase(n) beschränkt bleiben, sondern den Gesamtprozeß beeinflussen.

d) Ebenfalls im Vroom / Yetton-Modell wird die Bedeutung des Unterschieds zwischen direkter und indirekter Partizipation angesprochen. Dies geht insbesondere auf Arbeiten von Maier (1963, S. 3–19) zurück, der sich besonders mit der Bedeutung der Akzeptanz von Führungsentscheidungen durch die Untergebenen beschäftigt hat. Diese Akzeptanz ist vor allem dann für die Effizienz von Führungsmaßnahmen wichtig, wenn die Durchführung der Maßnahme wesentlich von den Untergebenen bestimmt wird und vom Vorgesetzten schlecht überwacht werden kann. Partizipation wiederum wird als wesentliche Voraussetzung für die Akzeptanz angesehen. Es wird insbesondere eine positive Wirkung auf die Motivation angenommen; daneben ist auch zu erwarten, daß eine gemeinsame Diskussion die kognitiven Aspekte einer Entscheidung und ihre spätere Durchführung – z. B. als Erhöhung des Verständnisses der Arbeitsaufgabe – verbessert.

Diese Überlegungen beziehen sich alle auf die Wirkung direkter Partizipation: der Beteiligte ist in diesen Fällen auch jener, der von Konsequenzen der partizipativ entwickelten Entscheidung betroffen wird. Gerade dieser Aspekt stimuliert motivationale Wirkungen. Indirekte oder repräsentative Partizipation schafft zwei besondere Problemlagen: Der nicht direkt Beteiligte, aber von den Konsequenzen Betroffene bleibt von den oben erwähnten sozio-emotionalen Qualitäten und objektiven Informationen der häufig als Verhandlungen ausgetragenen Partizipationsprozessen ausgeschlossen. Der direkt und repräsentativ Beteiligte steht nicht vor dem Problem der sensiblen Beurteilung der kognitiven und motivationalen Lage der Vertretenen und der Übernahme von Verantwortung für die Reaktion dieser anderen, nicht direkt Beteiligten. Solche Lagen sind besonders offen für Mißtrauen, Halbwahrheiten und Entfremdung und stellen damit besondere Anforderungen an die von Wunderer hervorgehobenen „prosozialen Dimensionen“ der Teilnahme an Entscheidungen.

Die Abgrenzungen zwischen Intensität, Inhalt nach Phasen und Direktheit der Partizipation ist rein analytischer Natur; sie sind im Partizipationserleben der Betroffenen zu einem integrierten Wert verwoben. So ist anzunehmen, daß sich in den von Vroom / Yetton ermittelten Intensitätsgraden von Partizipation in Führungssituationen ein Gesamturteil abgegeben wird, quantitative Aussagen sich damit aus der Integration vielerlei qualitativer Aspekte des Beteiligtseins ergeben.

(3) Partizipation ist ein Prozeß, der unter gleichgestellten Kollegen günstige Voraussetzungen hat, aber auch in dieser Situation zu gravierenden Konflikten führen kann. Die Organisation besteht aber nicht nur aus Gleichgestellten; die mit jeder Organisation verbundene Hierarchie stellt für Partizipationsprozesse i. d. R. eine erschwerende Herausforderung dar: Nicht nur zwischen Kollegen, sondern gegenüber dem Vorgesetzten und den Organisationszielen ergeben sich damit Konfliktmöglichkeiten. Für die Lösung solcher Konflikte ist wesentlich, welche Machtkonzeption Denken, Fühlen und Handeln der Beteiligten bestimmt.

Macht hat, wie jüngst Neuberger et al. (1985, S. 166 ff.) besonders deutlich herausgearbeitet hat, „viele Gesichter“. Deshalb ist es nicht verwunderlich, daß Theoretiker zu vielerlei Interpretationen dieser Gesichter gekommen sind (Reber 1980; Mintzberg 1983; House 1985). Machtphänomene sind so ubiquitär, daß jeder Handelnde mit ihnen laufend zu tun hat und sich Grundvorstellungen über den Einsatz und die Wirkungen von Macht gebildet hat. Nach Neuberger können vier dieser Grundvorstellungen unterschieden werden: Personale und strukturelle Differenzierung, Macht als Kausalität, Macht als Besitz und Macht als Nullsummenspiel. Alle vier Auffassungen haben Konsequenzen für formale und informale Partizipation. Besonders die letztgenannte kann sich als wesentliches Hemmnis für praktizierte Partizipation erweisen.

Wesentlicher Bestandteil der Machtvorstellung als Nullsummenspiel ist die in ihr implizierte Konstanzannahme: Macht gleicht hier einem Kuchen; jeder versucht, sich ein möglichst großes Stück herauszuschneiden und in seinen Besitz zu bringen. Da der Kuchen „konstant“ ist, reduziert jedes individualisierte Stück die Machtchancen für andere. In der Realität ist Macht aber nicht konstant, „. . . sondern ein pulsierendes Phänomen; sie dehnt sich fortwährend aus und schrumpft, konstant ist sie allenfalls in Momentaufnahmen“ (Neuberger et al. 1985, S. 197).

Die Beeinflussung von Macht durch formale Partizipation läßt sich theoretisch z. B. bei Einsatz der strukturellen Machtkonzeption Luhmanns zeigen. Nach seiner Deutung des „Gesichts der Macht“ besteht die Machtausübung in der „Selektion von Verhaltensprämissen für einen anderen“ und ist mithin „strukturabhängige Selektion“ (Luhmann 1969, S. 168). Selektiert in diesem Sinne formale Partizipation neben dem Vorgesetzten zusätzliche Mitwirkende, so kann dies seine Macht erhöhen, wenn die Mitwirkung die Akzeptanz (Motivation) und Qualität (zusätzliche Informationen) seiner Entscheidungen verbessert; sie kann abnehmen, wenn z. B. zu viel Zeit vergeudet wird, gravierende Konflikte im Partizipationsprozeß nicht ausgeräumt werden können usw. Empirisch haben z. B. Bartölke et al. (1982) auf der Grundlage von Vorarbeiten Tannenbaums gezeigt, „. . .daß die von Mitarbeitern jeweils berichtete Machtverteilung in partizipativeren Unternehmen sich von jener in weniger partizipativen unterscheidet. Partizipation scheint nach den Aussagen der von uns Befragten die Macht der Arbeiter zu erhöhen, ohne die Macht der Manager abnehmen zu lassen. Im Gegenteil nehmen sich Manager in den partizipativeren Unternehmen als einflußreicher wahr als dies Manager in den weniger partizipativen Unternehmen tun" (S. 394). Zu gleichen Ergebnissen kommen Kirsch / Scholl auf der Basis eines begrifflich-theoretischen Bezugsrahmens, der ökonomische und politikwissenschaftliche Konzeptionen berücksichtigt (1977) sowie in einer empirischen Überprüfung mitbestimmter Unternehmen, deren Design auf diesem Bezugsrahmen aufbaut (1983). In ihrer Interpretation ihrer empirischen Befunde bewirkt eine „Verringerung innerbetrieblicher Friktionen" die *„Handlungsfähigkeit"* bei stärkerer Mitbestimmung (Kirsch / Scholl 1983, S. 559).

2. Ausgewählte Strukturtypen und ihre Wirkung auf Partizipationsspielräume

Im folgenden werden fünf Strukturtypen angesprochen, die jeweils in der Realität vorkommen und gerade unter dem Aspekt der Eröffnung von Partzipationschancen geschaffen wurden. Der Auswahl liegt keine geschlossene Systematik zugrunde. Dennoch erfolgte sie nicht rein nach Zufälligkeit. Es sollen jeweils ganz unterschiedliche Denktraditionen angesprochen werden, die weniger in einem alternativen Verhältnis zueinander stehen als sich in ihren unterschiedlichen Aspekten ergänzen können. Die fünf Typen sind im einzelnen die *gesetzliche Mitbestimmung, Humanisierung der Arbeit* (resp. „Qualität des Arbeitslebens"), *mehrdimensionale Organiationsstrukturen* (insbesondere die Matrix Organisation), *inexakte* sowie *„organische" Organisationsstrukturen.* Je bekannter der jeweilige Typ ist, desto kürzer müssen und können wir uns relativ zu der zur Verfügung stehenden Literatur fassen; dies auch auf die Gefahr der Verkürzung und Vereinfachung der vorliegenden Materialien und Diskussionsbeiträgen.

2.1. Die gesetzliche Mitbestimmung

Eine von Chmielewicz (1981, S. 296ff.) zusammengestellte Bibliographie zum Themenbereich der Unternehmensverfassung weist über 700 Einzeltitel auf; die überwiegende Mehrzahl dieser Arbeiten beschäftigt sich mit Fragen der gesetzlichen Mitbestimmung. Theisen (1983) macht in einer Sammelrezension zum Thema

„Betriebswirtschaftliche Aspekte und Perspektiven in der Mitbestimmungsdiskussion" – besprochen werden wesentliche Monographien aus den Jahren 1972–1981 – deutlich, daß in dieser Diskussion „institutionelle", auf die Gesamtunternehmung gerichtete Aspekte eine weit untergeordnete Rolle spielen. Der innovative Beitrag der gesetzlichen Mitbestimmung ist im wesentlichen auf die Schaffung zusätzlicher und die Nutzung bestehender, gesellschaftsrechtlich vorgegebener Organe beschränkt (Dlugos 1980; Chmielewicz et al. 1977; Chmielewicz / Inhoffen 1977), ohne daß es zu einer Integration und Verarbeitung zu einer neuen Organisationsstruktur kommt, die für alle Organisationsteile typisch „mitbestimmt" resp. „partizipativ" ist. Dabei steht z. B. der Betriebsrat „neben" Hierarchiestufen während Arbeitnehmervertreter „in" Organen tätig sind. Nur mit wenigen Ausnahmen wird dieses additive, nicht alle Unternehmensebenen umfassende Ergebnis der gesetzlichen Maßnahmen unter betriebswirtschaftlichen (z. B. Budäus 1975; Bartölke / Wächter 1974/1980; Dlugos 1981b; Kappler 1981) und rechtlichen (z. B. Raiser 1973; v. Nell-Breuning 1978) Aspekten als problematisch angesehen. Praktizierte mitbestimmungsstimmige Gesamtorganisationskonzepte liegen auf der Grundlage von freiwilligen Unternehmensverfassungen z. B. für die Glacier Metal Company in England (Brown 1960; Bericht hierüber: Reber 1970) vor; daneben sieht die schwedische Mitbestimmungsgesetzgebung explizite Spielräume zum Aushandeln spezifischer Organisationsstrukturen vor (Goldberg 1983).

Bleibt man bei der gegebenen gesetzlichen Mitbestimmung, so bedeutet dies, daß in der Praxis der Unternehmen fix vorgegebene Mitbestimmungselemente mit sehr unterschiedlichen traditionellen oder modernen Organisationsstrukturen verbunden sind. Dies ergibt sehr unterschiedlich formalisierte Partizipationsspielräume. Dabei kann es dann wenig verwundern, wenn Erfahrungsberichte und empirische Studien die unterschiedlichsten Urteile über die verwirklichten Partizipationsgrade zu Tage fördern. Die vorliegende organisatorische Realität ist damit unvergleichbar; damit liegt eine ideale Situation zum Anheizen ideologischer Gegensätze vor.

Bei all diesen realen und ideologischen Gegensätzen dürfte jedoch unstrittig sein, daß die Mitbestimmungsgesetze für die jeweils Hauptbeteiligten sehr schwierige Rollen geschaffen haben: Die Konzeption der gesetzlichen Mitbestimmung ist nur als indirekte Partizipation operationalisierbar. Der Repräsentierte hat wenig Chancen, die Arbeit seiner Repräsentanten unmittelbar wahrzunehmen, seine Wünsche in den Verhandlungsergebnissen wiederzuerkennen. Sein Detailwissen ist für Entscheidungen an der Unternehmensspitze i. d. R. irrelevant, eine „prosoziale Dimension" (Wunderer) ist für ihn kaum erlebbar; dies schafft häufig Verhältnisse, die einer „Pseudo-Partizipation" (Kirsch / Scholl) gleichkommen sowie – von Vroom / Yetton unbeachtete – Konfliktmöglichkeiten im Verhältnis zwischen Vertretenen und Vertretern. Die Rolle letzterer ist mit Macht ausgestattet, sie verlangt Wissen und Einsatz und ist häufig mit großer Arbeitsbelastung verbunden. Die Machtkomponente deutet auf Entwicklungsmöglichkeiten im Sinne des „eisernen Gesetzes der Oligarchie" (Grunwald 1980) hin; Arbeitsüberlastung macht insensibel gegenüber Differenziertheit der Bedürfnisse und Stimmungen der Vertretenen.

Dies vergröbert die Interessenvertretung auf Hauptkomponenten wie Beschäftigung und Lohnniveau positiven Einfluß der Mitbestimmung auf „Kündigungen" und (Witte 1980. 557). Solche Vertretungsschwerpunkte bleiben selbverständlich wesentliche Interessenschwerpunkte der Vertretenen; hier hat die gesetzliche Mitbestimmung sicherlich ihre Verdienste. Wenig Impulse sind aber in Richtung der Förderung innovativer Entwicklungen gerade von den Vertretern der Belegschaft erkennbar (Säcker 1981). Dies betrifft nicht allein Aspekte wie Produktneuentwicklungen oder frühzeitige Umstrukturierung von Unternehmen, sondern auch Programme zur Humanisierung der Arbeit, neue, partizipative Aspekte fördernde Organisationsformen, Beteiligung der Arbeitnehmer am Ertrag oder Vermögen. All dies scheint zu komplex und riskant für die Interessenvertretung zu sein, deren Alltag – gerade in ökonomisch nicht sehr günstigen Zeiten – mit der Wahrung und Sicherung des Erreichten ausgefüllt ist und die darüber hinaus aktiv sein muß, den Kontakt zu den Vertretenen, deren kritisches Potential auf sie kanalisiert ist, zu pflegen.

Dort, wo die gesetzliche Mitbestimmung überbetriebliche Unterstützung findet – z. B. durch die Paritätische Kommission in Österreich (Nowotny 1978) resp. Verstaatlichung –, verliert die Bedrohung von Unternehmen und Arbeitsplätzen durch externe Selektion (betont insbesondere vom Organizational-Ecology-Ansatz; vgl. z. B. Hannan / Freeman 1977, 1984; Aldrich 1979; McKelvey 1982) zumindest kurzfristig ihre gesamte Schärfe. Dies gibt grundsätzlich der Unternehmensführung die Chance, gefährliche Lagen durch „Adaptionen" zu überwinden. Die Organisationstheorie ist generell optimistisch in dem Sinne, daß die Unternehmensführung „normalerweise" zu solchen Adaptionen fähig ist. Dieser Tendenz stellt der „Ecology"-Ansatz die eher pessimistische These gegenüber, daß Organisationen normalerweise eine hochgradige strukturelle Schwerkraft entwickeln, die organisationale Adaptionen schwierig, wenn nicht ganz unmöglich machen. Welche dieser beiden Theorien macht die gesetzliche Mitbestimmung eher wahr? Einerseits zeigt die repräsentative Partizipation mit zunehmender Stärke eine Dämpfung externaler Selektion und damit auch Festigung der Arbeitsplätze; andererseits kann sie auch die strukturelle Schwerkraft verstärken und damit die Bedürfnisse der Vertretenen auf Beschäftigung und Einkommen mittel- und langfristig nicht sichern. In diesem Sinne müßte es zu den vordringlichen Aufgaben einer machtvollen gesetzlichen Mitbestimmung gehören, Organisationsstrukturen „adaptionsfähig" zu machen. Wie die nachfolgend beschriebenen Konzeptionen zeigen, basiert Adaptionsfähigkeit zu wesentlichen Teilen auf Partizipation auf möglichst allen Organisationsebenen.

2.2. Humanisierung der Arbeit

Ebenso wie bei der gesetzlichen Mitbestimmung liegen zu den Bemühungen um die Humanisierung der Arbeit eine Vielzahl von Literaturbeiträgen vor; so zeigt die Literaturanalyse von Gaugler et al. (1977) bereits 1125 Titel. Neben Gaugler et al. geben Kubicek (1979) und Meadows (1981) einen profilierten Überblick über die Entwicklungslinien und Arbeitsschwerpunkte unter dieser Thematik. Hiernach ist das Gebiet von zwei Konzeptionen geprägt worden. Dieses sind einerseits die Bemühungen um die Neugestaltung der Arbeitsaufgabe im Sinne einer „Bereicherung" (job enrichment) und andererseits der sozio-technische Systemansatz in der Ausprägung von Auffassungen aus dem Tavistock Institute of Human Relations und skandinavischen Anwendungs- und Weiterentwicklungsformen.

Die Beschäftigung mit der Arbeitsbereicherung folgt vor allem den Anregungen Herzbergs (1981). In dem von Hackman / Oldham (1975) entwickelten Fragebogensatz – genannt „Job Diagnostic Survey (JDS)" – liegt ein typisches Ergebnis zur Operationalisierung der Absicht vor, Arbeitsaufgaben so einzurichten, daß die Ausführenden die Chance haben, selbstzweckhafte Leistung, Verantwortung, „Autonomie", „Abwechslung", „psychologisches Wachstum" und Freude an der Arbeit unter Berücksichtigung individueller Unterschiede zu erleben. Stellt man die „psychometrische" und „technokratische" Natur dieser Bemühungen in den Vordergrund, so kann man sie als Fortführung des Taylorismus unter Einbezug weiterentwickelter psychologischer Theorien vor allem aus dem Bereich des Motivationsgeschehens ansehen (Meadows 1981). Delegation und nicht Partizipation wird angestrebt. Ungeachtet dieser Beurteilung ist zu beachten, daß optimalere Arbeitsaufgaben indirekt interpersonale Beziehungen beeinflussen. Bei der Erledigung der Arbeitsaufgabe werden motivationale und kognitive Eigenschaften der betroffenen Personen angesprochen und entwickelt, die von zentraler Bedeutung für Selbstbewußtsein, Fachwissen und Arbeitsfreude sind. Der Aufbau und die Festigung dieser Eigenschaften bilden wesentliche individuale Voraussetzungen für das Streben und die Sinnhaftigkeit von Partizipation.

Der erwähnte sozio-technische Ansatz ist im Gegensatz zu der individualistischen Perspektive der Ansätze zur Arbeitsbereicherung sowohl mikro- als auch makrosozial angelegt (Klein 1959) und erkennt schon bei seinen ersten praktischen Anwendungen, daß die technischen Aspekte der Arbeitssituation ebenso wichtig sind wie die sozialen (Trist / Bamforth 1951). Die mit diesem Ansatz eröffnete Perspektive ist außerordentlich weit. Diese Weite konnte bis heute weder theoretisch noch praktisch konkretisiert werden, die realisierten Anwendungsfelder liegen in der Gestaltung und dem Erforschen der sog. teilautonomen oder selbststeuernden Arbeitsgruppen insbesondere innerhalb skandinavischer Betriebe (Steinmann et al. 1976). Die Partizipation ist hier ein zentrales Thema sowohl in bezug auf die Beziehungen innerhalb der teilautonomen Arbeitsgruppe als auch deren Beziehung zum formalen Vorgesetzten. Obgleich eine Fülle von Erfahrungen über praktizierte Partizipation gewonnen wurde, kam es bisher noch nicht zum

Aufbau entsprechender Partizipationstheorien. Die Ergebnisse bleiben i. d. R. außerordentlich interessante Fälle, die jeweils einmalig sind, dabei aber bei ihrer Darstellung aus dem Streben nach dem Erfassen des Gesamtsystems in historische und gesellschaftliche Zusammenhänge gestellt werden (z. B. Klein 1975). Da das systembezogene Begriffssystem sehr allgemein ist, entstehen subjektive Expertenpotentiale, die als informierte und inspirierte „Change-Agents" praktische Anwendungsfälle schaffen.

Das Fehlen einer einheitlichen geschlossenen Theorie ist allerdings mit einer besonderen Tugend in bezug auf die Partizipationsthematik verbunden. Partizipation im Sprachgebrauch des soziotechnischen Systemansatzes steht vor allem im Zusammenhang mit der *Einführung* von Humanisierungsmaßnahmen. In dieser Perspektive sind die Betroffenen an allen Phasen der Entscheidung der für sie gedachten Maßnahmen unter Zusammenarbeit mit dem „Change-Agent" zu beteiligen. „Aktionsforschung" ist hier das relevante Stichwort (Meadows 1981, S. 526 ff.). In ihrem Rahmen ist „... Humanisierung zweckmäßigerweise als ein aus Einzelschritten bestehender permanenter Lernprozeß zu begreifen, ..." (Kubicek 1979, S. 678).

Mit dem Hinweis auf Lernprozesse wird ein Aspekt angesprochen, der nicht nur für die Einführung von Partizipationschancen wichtig ist, sondern für den gesamten Alltag von Organisationen in instabilen Umwelten. Dies bedeutet auch, daß Lernen auch zum Thema jener Bereiche werden muß, die im Rahmen des sozio-technischen Systemansatzes noch zu wenig Ausformung erfahren haben. Dieses sind Strukturbedingungen der Gesamtorganisation, die Ablöse von dem „Determinismus" der technischen Bedingungen des Arbeitslebens (Friedel-Howe 1982) und deren Flexibilisierung sowie der Einbezug „makrosozialer", d. h. gesamtgesellschaftlicher Bedingungen (Fricke 1971; Strauss-Fehlberg 1978; Kubicek 1979; Meadows 1981; Dlugos 1981).

Die Lernfähigkeit induzierende Aufgaben von Organisationsstrukturen ist das zentrale Anliegen der Konzeption inexakter Organisationsformen, über die später berichtet wird. Die Flexibilisierung der Technik in Werkstätten und Büros greift ein altes Anliegen des sozio-technischen Systemansatzes wiederum auf und scheint insbesondere als Erbe der Aufnahme dieses Ansatzes in Skandinavien aktuelle Beachtung zu finden (vgl. Berichte von Kolodny 1984). Unter gesellschaftlichen Aspekten stellt Meadows den Zusammenhang zwischen sozio-technischem Ansatz und Aktionsforschung mit der Mitbestimmungsdiskussion her. Seinen Überlegungen nach sind gerade jene Kräfte aufgerufen, die die gesetzliche Mitbestimmung durchgesetzt haben, ihre Bestrebungen dahingehend wirksam zu machen, die gesellschaftlichen Voraussetzungen für Forschungen und Anwendungen im Bereich der Humanisierthematik auf allen Systemebenen zu schaffen (Meadows 1981, S. 533 ff.).

2.3. Mehrdimensionale Organisationsstrukturen

Zu den charakteristischen Kennzeichen mehrdimensionaler Organisationstrukturen – häufig auch vereinfachend Matrix-Organisation genannt – gehören die Gliederung der Aufgaben nach mindestens zwei „Dimensionen" sowie die Mehrfachunterstellung von Organisationsmitgliedern (zu vollständigen Definitionen vgl. Davis / Lawrence 1977; Wagner 1978; in Kurzfassung: Reber 1983). Beim praktischen Einsatz dieser Organisationsform ist häufig eine Zweidimensionalität festzustellen: Einer Gliederung nach Verrichtungen resp. Funktionen steht eine nach Objekten (Produkten, Projekten) gegenüber; beide Dimensionen werden in der Mehrfachunterstellung simultan und partizipativ zusammengefügt. Entsprechend dieser Wirkung gilt der Einsatz dieser Organisationsform dann als begründet, wenn für die Zielerreichung der Organisation absolut wesentlich ist, daß eine hohe Anpassungsfähigkeit an Entwicklungen in den betreffenden Dimensionen (z. B. Produkt / Markt einerseits, technisches Wissen/Funktionsbereiche andererseits) erreicht wird, große Unsicherheiten mit entsprechend großen Informationsanforderungen und schwierigen Koordinationsaufgaben zu bewältigen sind und finanzielle sowie personale Ressourcen bestmöglich eingesetzt werden müssen (Davis / Lawrence 1978).

Die angestrebte Anpassungsfähigkeit soll durch die enge Verflechtung der Mitarbeiter in den wichtigsten Dimensionen im Matrixgefüge erreicht werden. Bleibt man bei der häufig gewählten Verknüpfung von Mitarbeitern aus verrichtungs- und objektorientierten Abteilungen, so können die Vorteile beider Dimensionen vereinigt werden: Indem bei der Matrixanordnung das Wissen unterschiedlicher Verrichtungsspezialisten unmittelbar mit dem Informationsstand von am Markt agierenden Objektspezialisten in Verbindung gebracht wird, können folgende Wirkungen erzielt werden (Kolodny 1983, S. 449 f.):

a) Die einer verrichtungsorientierten Organisation inhärente Schwäche der schlechten Reaktion auf spezifische produkt- bzw. projektbezogene Aufgaben kann behoben werden.
b) Der einer objektorientierten Organisation inhärenten Tendenz, die langfristige Kumulation verrichtungsspezialisierten Wissens und Könnens zu hemmen, wird durch das Festhalten an verrichtungsorientierten Abteilungen entgegengewirkt.
c) Die enge Zusammenarbeit beider Dimensionen verbindet Fachexperten mit einem hohen Maß an Offenheit der Organisation gegenüber ihrer Umwelt.

Aus der gegebenen Absicht, weder der einen Dimension noch der anderen einen ungehinderten Vorrang zu geben, ergibt sich die Mehrfachunterstellung von Mitarbeitern aus beiden Bereichen. Dementsprechend ist die Machtstruktur als partizipatives Rollensystem angelegt, das in der Form des „Matrix-Diamanten" (Davis / Lawrence 1977) vier unterschiedliche Schlüsselrollen miteinander verbindet:

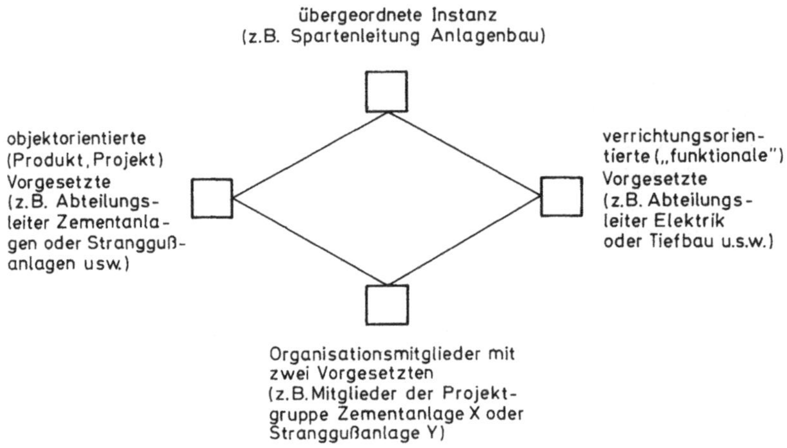

Die Aufgabe der *übergeordneten Instanz* besteht im Kern darin, die Macht im Diamanten so zu verteilen und aufrechtzuerhalten, daß keine einseitige Dominanz die Partizipation überflüssig macht. Außerdem sind die notwendigen informationellen, finanziellen und personalen Ressourcen für die Arbeitsfähigkeit der Matrixmitglieder bereitzustellen.

Die *verrichtungsorientierten Vorgesetzten* und ihre Mitarbeiter verlieren gegenüber einer rein funktionalen Organisation die alleinige formale Bestimmung über den Einsatz des Fachwissens ihrer Abteilung. Auf Anforderung der Objektdimension der Matrix wird die Leistungsfähigkeit ihrer Abteilung für unterschiedliche Objektbedürfnisse nachgefragt und nicht allein von ihnen selbst, sondern auch von den Mitarbeitern und Vorgesetzten der Objektseite beurteilt.

Die *objektorientierten Vorgesetzten* und ihre Mitarbeiter sind für den Erfolg eines „Subganzen" – eben eines Produktes, eines Projektes im Rahmen des gesamten Leistungsangebots ihrer Organisation – verantwortlich. Sie betreuen als „Geschäftsführer" ein komplettes (Sub-)Leistungsangebot unter Einsatz verrichtungsorientierter Spezialisten aus anderen Abteilungen, die ihnen nicht zur Gänze unterstellt sind und deren Spezialwissen sie nicht im gleicen Maße haben.

Bei *Organisationsmitgliedern mit zwei Vorgesetzten* laufen die Gegensätze zwischen den Objekt- und Verrichtungsperspektiven zusammen. Sie haben beide Ansichten in der konkreten Bewältigung ihrer Aufgaben zu integrieren, die auftretenden Konflikte in erster Linie zu bewältigen. Da sie weder der einen noch der anderen Seite zur Gänze unterstellt sind und die übergeordnete Instanz keiner dieser Seiten eine Dominanz ermöglicht, haben sie einen Operationsrahmen, der ihnen Spielraum zum Aufbau von Selbstbewußtsein und relativ freiem Leistungseinsatz gibt.

Das Herzstück der Matrix-Organisation ist bei dem gezeigten Rollenaufbau ein formalisiertes Partizipationssystem, das insbesondere im Middlemanagement seinen Platz hat. Das Modell entstammt dem Kalkül technokratischer Organisatoren, die in erster Linie auf die kognitiven Beiträge der Partizipierenden abzielen. Es ist offensichtlich, daß die Matrix-Struktur hohe Anforderungen an die Kooperations- und Konfliktlösungsfähigkeit der Beteiligten stellt (Lawrence et al. 1977). Vor allem der Umgang mit komplexen Machtkonfigurationen fordert die Rolleninhaber zu schwierigen Abstimmungsprozessen heraus, deren Nichtbewältigung die Nutzung der Vorteile der Matrix-Organisation stark gefährdet (Davis / Lawrence 1978, S. 134ff.).

Die Bewältigung formaler Herausforderungen zur Partizipation wird in Phasen der Einführung, ökonomischer Krisen und der internen Umstrukturierung virulent. Theoretische Auseinandersetzungen mit solchen Entwicklungs- resp. Anpassungsschritten der Matrix haben dem generellen Disput darüber, ob strukturelle Maßnahmen zeitlich vor Maßnahmen zur verhaltensmäßigen Bewältigung stehen sollten oder umgekehrt, auf beiden Seiten Nahrung gegeben. Ein typischer Vertreter des zeitlichen Vorrangs von Lernprozessen in Kleingruppen vor Strukturänderungen ist Argyris (1967). Veränderungen haben in seiner Sicht die Abfolge: Intervention, Reaktion, Feedbackprozesse, Verhaltensänderung, Normen- und Strukturänderungen (Argyris 1982, S. 104ff.). Der gegensätzliche Standpunkt plädiert dafür, zuerst Strukturänderungen einzuleiten; dies allerdings in vorsichtigen kleinen Schritten. Diese Vorgangsweise soll eine Destabilisierung („unfreezing“) des gesamten Systems bewirken, dem einzelnen Mitglied dadurch den „Ernst“ des Veränderungsprozesses sowie die Richtung des Veränderungsprozesses zeigen, ihn aber in seiner individualen und mikrosozialen Lernkapazität nicht überfordern. Kolodny (1979) zeigt in diesem Sinne das schrittweise Entstehen einer „reifen“ Matrix-Organisation aus einer funktionalen Organisation in Zwischenschritten. Dabei läßt er offen, ob die „reife“, voll formalisierte Matrix als letzte optimale Form anzusehen ist oder als Vorstufe zu „freieren“ Partizipationsformen, die unter den Anforderungen formaler Partizipation eingeübt wurden und die diese hohe Formalisierung mit der Reife interpersonaler Kompetenz zumindest im Hinblick auf Detailregelungen überflüssig macht.

2.4. Inexakte Organisationsstrukturen

Das Denken in inexakten Organisationsstrukturen stellt einen relativ jungen Ansatz in der Organisationstheorie dar. Die Anregungen zu dieser Konzeption sind einerseits deskriptiver Art und kommen andererseits aus dem normativen Streben, der oben als Ansatzpunkt der „Ecology-Theorie“ angesprochenen Gefahr zu entgehen, aufgrund einer „strukturellen Schwerkraft“ in Starrheit und Ineffizienz zu verfallen. In beiden Traditionen wird der Partizipation eine wichtige Rolle zugeschrieben.

Die deskriptive Entwicklungslinie überträgt die seit Simon heimisch gewordene Einsicht, daß Personen selten rationale Entscheidungen treffen, auf das organisationale Verhalten. Am extremsten wird diese Position von Cohen, March und Olsen (1972), (March / Olsen 1976) vertreten. Ihr Bezugspunkt sind „organisierte Anarchien“, die gekennzeichnet sind durch unklare Ziele, mangelhaftes Verständnis der eigenen organisationalen Prozesse und Instabilität in der Teilnahme der Organisationsmitglieder. Auf der Grundlage dieser Annahmen „organisationaler Ambiguität“ entwickeln sie ein „Mülleimer“-Entscheidungsmodell, das auch für solche organisationale Zustände testbare Hypothesen über deren Lebensfähigkeit enthält.

In diesem Modell (Cohen et al. 1972, S. 3) wird eine organisationale Entscheidung als Ergebnis des Zusammenwirkens von folgenden vier „Strömen“ angesehen: Probleme, Lösungen, Teilnehmer und Auswahlgelegenheiten (z. B. Fristen, Anfragen, Sitzungstermine). Diese Modellbestandteile werden als relativ unabhängig voneinander angesehen. Dies bedeutet, daß die klassische Reihenfolge von Entscheidungsphasen (Beginn bei der Entwicklung der Problemstellung und Abschluß mit dem Auswahlakt) in rationalen Entscheidungsmodellen in der Realität auf den Kopf gestellt sein kann. Damit ist berücksichtigt, daß in Organisationen für vorgefertigte Lösungen Probleme gesucht werden, auf die sie angewandt werden können; unterbeschäftigte Entscheider Auswahlgelegenheiten suchen, Probleme gelöst werden, die keine sind usw. Probleme, Lösungen und Auswahlgelegenheiten liegen – so das Vorstellungsbild – in einem oder mehreren „Mülleimer“(n), der (die) von den Teilnehmern nicht nur ungeordnet gefüllt, sondern auch ebenso geleert werden. Bei diesen Leerungen kommt es häufig dazu, daß die Teilnehmer von der Problemmenge überflutet werden und dann entweder Entscheidungen ohne Problemaufbereitung („decision by oversight“) oder unter Umgehung der u. U. wichtigsten Probleme getroffen werden („decision by flight“).

Da die Aktivierung der Inhalte des resp. der „Mülleimer“ einer Organisation durch die Teilnehmer erfolgt, kommt dem Mechanismus, der die Beziehungen der Teilnehmer zu den Problemen, Lösungen und Auswahlgelegenheiten ordnet, für den Ausgang des Entscheidungsprozesses wesentliche Bedeutung zu. Dieser Mechanismus wird „Sozialstruktur“ genannt. In ihr wird selektiv die Partizipation von Organisationsmitgliedern an Auswahlgelegenheiten festgelegt. Diese Erkenntnis bestätigt den oben erwähnten Hinweis Luhmanns, nach der in Systemen Macht durch Selektion bestimmter Alternativkonstellationen erzeugt wird (Luhmann 1969, S. 168). Allerdings werden damit lediglich Machtpotentiale zugeteilt; die Reaktion der Teilnehmer entscheidet darüber, wieweit das Partizipationspotential tatsächlich genutzt wird. March / Olson beschäftigen sich unter dem Aspekt der instabilen Teilnahme der Organisationsmitglieder an Auswahlgelegenheiten (z. B. Teilnahme an Fakultätssitzungen) mit den Bedingungen, unter denen Partizipationschancen von den Teilnehmern wahrgenommen werden. Zu den beschriebenen Bedingungen gehören z. B. die Menge und Wichtigkeit der Probleme bei einer Auswahlgelegenheit, Einschätzung der eigenen Einflußchancen, alternative Gelegenheiten, Aufgaben außerhalb der Organisation, zufällige Anwesenheit usw.

Die Feststellung der Bedeutung von Partizipationsstrukturen gerade in schlecht strukturierten organisationalen Entscheidungssituationen resp. „organisierten Anarchien“ fordert den normativen Gedanken heraus, wie Strukturen aussehen müssen, damit die berichteten Unzulänglichkeiten von Entscheidungen nach dem Mülleimermodell vermieden resp. eingedämmt werden können (Moch / Pondy 1977, S. 359). Dieser Weg wird von March / Olsen nicht betreten. Sie bleiben bei der Deskription und verwenden hierzu eine Vielzahl von Fallstudien, Episoden, theoretische Weiterführung aus dem Bereich von Erziehungsorganisationen (March / Olson 1976). Insbesondere von Universitäten nehmen sie als sicher an, daß sie alle Merkmale einer „organisierten Anarchie“ (unklare Ziele, mangelndes Verständnis des eigenen organisationalen Prozesses und instabile Teilnahme) haben und nach dem Mülleimermodell handeln. Liest man diese Beispiele, so kann man sich häufiger als erhofft im Universitätsleben an sie erinnert fühlen. Dabei kann aber auch besonders deutlich werden, wie wenig das Modell zur besseren Gestaltung von Partizipationsprozessen beiträgt.

Der normative Ansatz in inexakten Organisationsstrukturen knüpft an die häufig bestätigte Erfahrung an, daß Organisationen in ihrem Streben „perfekter“, d. h. immer besser organisiert zu werden, Flexibilität verlieren und damit Krisen, insbesondere dynamische Umweltveränderungen nicht bewältigen können. Hieraus ergibt sich die Konsequenz, Organisationen neben einem perfektionierenden Lernen auch mit der Fähigkeit zum „Verlernen“ und „Wiedererlernen“ auszustatten. Pointiert wird dies z. B. von Hedberg (1981, S. 23) vorgetragen:

„Es kommt zu einer zu großen Verschwendung an menschlichen Ressourcen, Kapital, Wissen und Enthusiasmus, wenn man Organisationen sich allein mit ihrer Lernfähigkeit entwickeln läßt. Solche Organisationen umgeben sich mit Mauern, sie wachsen in die Defensive. Sie werden insensitiv für Signale aus der Umwelt und akkumulieren so viele Ressourcen, daß sie es sich nicht leisten können, sich in Bewegung zu setzen, wenn sich die Zeiten ändern. Deshalb müssen die Fähigkeiten zum Lernen, Verlernen und Wiedererlernen gleichermaßen entwickelt werden. Zu lernen, verlernen und wiederlernen ist der organisatorische Lebensweg: Entwicklung endet, wenn eines dieser Beine fehlt.“

Das Gleichgewicht zwischen Lernen – Verlernen – Wiederlernen bedarf der strukturellen Unterstützung. Aphoristisch ausgedrückt sollen Organisationen, die flexibel und anpassungsfähig sein wollen bzw. müssen, „minimale Guthaben“ – d. h. gerade ein wenig mehr als nicht genug – von jenen Eigenschaften (z. B. Konsens, Zufriedenheit, Gutgläubigkeit, Konsistenz und Rationalität) haben, die – nach häufiger Literaturansicht – „gute und ordentliche“ Organisationen charakterisieren (Hedberg et al. 1976, S. 41).

Praktisch bedeutet dies, daß z. B. überlappende, unklare Rollendefinitionen, mehrdeutige, sich widersprechende Ziele und Verantwortungsbereiche, informale Kommunikationskanäle, Konflikte, mangelnde Ressourcen, Krisen, Inkonsistenzen bewußt herbeizuführen sind. Dies geschieht mit dem Ziel, Strukturen vor dem Erstarren zu bewahren und Organisationen in ständige Auseinandersetzung zwischen den Organisationsmitgliedern fit zu erhalten und ihnen Gelegenheit zu geben, ihre Lern- und Verlernprozesse zu kultivieren. Organisationen, die ihre

Anpassungsfähigkeit erhalten wollen, „... bewerten und revidieren ihr Verhalten und erfinden ihre Zukunft ebenso wie sie diese überleben. Zur Förderung solcher 'selfdesigning organizations' sollten die in ihnen Verantwortlichen danach streben, die Wege zu modifizieren, auf denen sie ihre Leistungen bewerten, und inkrementale Experimente in bezug auf die Strategien der Organisation und die Karrieren ihrer Mitglieder stimulieren" (Hedberg et al. 1977, S. 178).

Wesentlich an diesen Ansätzen ist, daß die Entstabilisierung der Strukturen zur Bewahrung der Anpassungsfähigkeit eine hohe Sensibilität in bezug auf das rechte Maß fordert. Herzustellen ist ein „dynamisches Gleichgewicht" (Hedberg 1981, S. 22), ein „... optimaler Kompromiß, um die inkompatiblen Anforderungen von Stabilität und Flexibilität bwältigen zu können" (Weick 1979, S. 229). Ein Zuviel an Stabilität verhindert die Anpassungsfähigkeit, ein Zuwenig bringt die Organisation soweit aus dem Gleichgewicht, daß ihre Existenz auf dem Spiele steht. In diesem Sinne ist die Formulierung eines „minimalen Guthabens" zu verstehen. An anderer Stelle vergleichen Hedberg et al. (1976) die Führung einer solchen Organisation mit der Aufgabe, eine (Kinder-)Wippe ("seesaw") oder Waage im Gleichgewicht zu halten, deren Verlassen auf beiden Seiten (Inflexibilität vs. Desintegration) mit zunehmender Geschwindigkeit zu einem harten Aufprall auf der harten Erde konkurrierender Kräfte in der Umwelt der Organisation führt.

Explizit ist in dieser Konzeption der Suche nach „dynamischen Gleichgewichten" die Partizipation kaum erwähnt. Mit der Entstabilisierung durch inexakte Strukturen entstehen vielfältige Freiräume, die gleichzeitig Partizipationsspielräume sind. Im Gegensatz zu der formalisierten Partizipationsstruktur in der Matrix-Organisation werden diese Spielräume im Informalen belassen. Dies kann aber nicht bedeuten, daß anzunehmen ist, daß diese Akzeptanz und Nutzung dieser Spielräume von den Organisationsmitgliedern umstandslos bewältigt werden kann. Hier ergeben sich Parallelen zu den Erfahrungen mit Prozessen zur Humanisierung der Arbeit. Mit den durch die Inexaktheit eröffneten Spielräume entstehen teilautonome resp. „self-designing" Arbeitsgruppen auf allen Ebenen der Organisation. Die Ergebnisse der Aktionsforschung bzw. der „Organisationsentwicklung" sind nicht allein für die Einführung von Neuerungen, sondern für die Gestaltung permanenter partizipativer Lernprozesse relevant. Inexakte Organisationsstrukturen schaffen die generellen formalen Voraussetzungen; diese sind wichtig, aber im Sinne der Flexibilisierung und Humanisierung nur nutzbar, wenn die Partizipationschancen akzeptiert werden und qualitativ befriedigende Lernleistungen erbracht werden können.

2.5. „Organische" Organisationsstrukturen

Der von Weick (1976) in die Organisationsliteratur eingebrachte Begriff der „losen Verkoppelung" (loose coupling) von Systemteilen weist auf wesentliche Eigenschaften „organischer" Organisationsstrukturen hin. Lose Verkoppelung liegt vor, wenn Systemteile weniger oder für ihre Lebensfähigkeit relativ unbedeutende Variable gemeinsam haben (Weick 1979, S. 111). Organisationen mit in diesem Sinne lose verkoppelten Subsystemen sind potentiell sowohl stabil als auch flexibel. Wenn eine Variable gestört wird, bedeutet dies praktisch, daß die Störung eher begrenzt bleibt als daß das Gesamtsystem wesentlich einbezogen wird. Moch / Pondy (1977, S. 360) nehmen in ihren Anmerkungen, welche normativen Schritte zur besseren Führung von „organisierten Anarchien" grundsätzlich vorstellbar sind, bezug auf diese Eigenschaften loser Verkopplung. Sie empfehlen, daß Organisation mit hoher Ambiguität – sei sie extern (z. B. Marktturbulenz) oder intern (z. B. unterschiedliche Werthaltungen und Normen, unterschiedlich intensiv partizipierende Mitglieder) verursacht – ihre Subsysteme nur lose verkoppeln sollen. „Eine solche Verkopplung besteht in mehr als einfacher Differenzierung. Sie impliziert, daß lose verkoppelte Einheiten Unterschiedlichkeit und Veränderungen eher absorbieren oder internalisieren, als daß sie die Organisation von ihnen abkoppeln. Organisationen sind dann nicht in homogene Abteilungen differenziert. Vielmehr sind sie genau aus dem Grund abgekoppelt, um die Internalisierung von Unterschiedlichkeit zu ermöglichen" (Moch / Pondy 1977, S. 360).

Hedberg fordert bei seinen Überlegungen die Verkürzung und Entlastung von Kommuniktionswegen zu den Kunden und zwischen den Organisationseinheiten (Hedberg 1981, S. 21). Auch dieses Ziel kann durch die lose Verkopplung erreicht werden. Bleiben die so gebildeten Subsysteme klein und überschaubar, schaffen sie gleichzeitig das geeignete „Forum" (Hedberg, ebenda) für partizipative Entscheidungsprozesse. Pusić kommt in seinem Blick auf die Erfahrungen mit der Selbstverwaltung in Jugoslawien zu dem Schluß, daß „tatsächlich selbstverwaltete" Betreibe „Konföderationen von Arbeitsgruppen" zur Voraussetzung haben und Selbstverwaltung am wenigsten zu finden ist in Großbetrieben mit klassischer industrieller Technik (Pusić 1982, S. 424).

Solche theoretischen und praktischen Hinweise machen Organisationsstrukturen gerade unter dem Aspekt der Partizipation attraktiv, die in ihrer Größe überschaubar bleiben und bei loser Verkoppelung dennoch die Vorteile großer Systeme einbeziehen. Die lose Verkoppelung führt zu Strukturformen, die weniger einer Pyramide als etwas komplexen Strukturmodellen aus der Chemie gleichen. Aus diesem Grund verwenden wir den im organisatorischen Sprachgebrauch häufig als Gegensatz zu „pyramidenförmigen", „bürokratischen", „mechanischen" usw. Strukturformen benutzten Begriff „organisch".

Eine konkrete Organisationsstruktur, die von ihrem Gründer und ersten Anwalt „organisch, flexibel, selbst-generierend und dezentralisiert" (Armstrong / Kolodny 1985, S. 9) genannt wird, hat in Kanada und jetzt auch über die Grenzen dieses Landes hinaus besonders auch wegen ihres grandiosen ökonomischen Erfolgs als Zulieferer der Automobilindustrie (Umsatz innrhalb von 27 Jahren von 1000 auf 500 Millionen canad. Dollar, entsprechendem Gewinnwachstum und Zunahme der Beschäftigten auf 5800) Furore gemacht. Sie hat folgende Gestalt (Geschäftsbericht, S. 11):

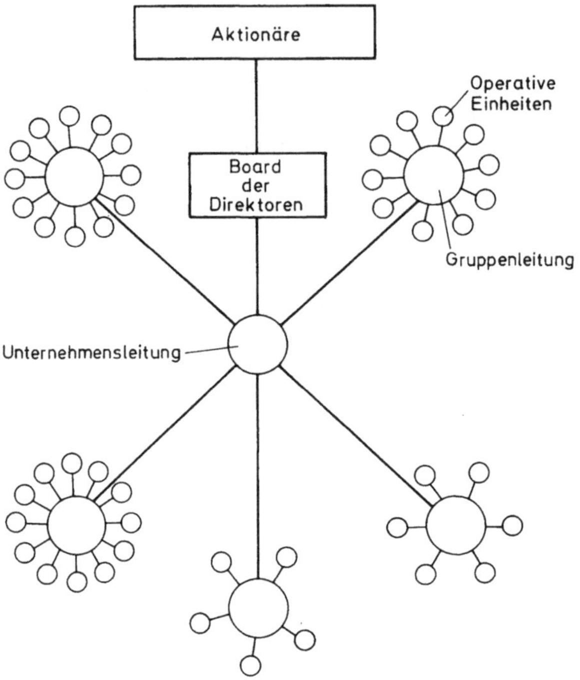

Die Aufgaben der Unternehmens- und der Gruppenleitung sowie der operativen Einheiten werden im Geschäftsbericht 1984 wie folgt zusammengefaßt:

Unternehmensleitung

Die *Unternehmensleitung* ist verantwortlich für die Realisierung der Unternehmenspolitik, die sich ableitet aus der Unternehmensphilosophie, wie sie von dem *Board der Direktoren* artikuliert wird.

Die Priorität der Unternehmensleitung kommt der strategischen Planung zu. Diese umfaßt die Kennzeichnung spezifischer Produkte und Technologien, die von MAGNA zu entwickeln sind, um den Herausforderungen standhalten zu können, die der Markt stellt, dessen Nachfrage wir durch unser Angebot befriedigen wollen. Außerdem gehört hierzu die Gründung von Führungsgruppen, die fähig sind, MAGNAs Qualität, humane Vorstellungen und finanzielle Ziele erfüllen zu können. Als Teilaspekt ihrer Verantwortung sichert und verteilt die *Unternehmensleitung* die finanziellen Ressourcen in Abstimmung mit den *Gruppenleitungen* und überwacht die Leistung der *Operativen Einheiten*.

Die Hauptverwaltung bietet ihre Dienste den *Gruppenleitungen* und *Operativen Leitungen* zur Aufbringung der Mittel für Investitionen, dem Einkauf von Materialien/Vorprodukten und Dienstleistungen an. Dies erlaubt den *Gruppen- und Operativen Einheiten,* Vorteile aus der vereinten Nachfragekraft der MAGNA-Gruppen wahrzunehmen. Dessen ungeachtet liegt die Verantwortung für die Qualität der Produkte und Termintreue bei den Operativen Einheiten; dementsprechend tätigen sie ihren Kauf aus jenen Quellen, die ihren Anforderungen am besten entsprechen.

Gruppenleitung

Die *Operativen Einheiten* sind in Gruppen organisiert – geographisch und nach ihren Märkten – und sind unter einem Team von Gruppenleitern der *Unternehmensleitung* verantwortlich. Ein Gruppenleiter ist für alle Aktivitäten seiner Gruppe verantwortlich und erhält Unterstützung durch einen Marketing-, Finanz- und Personalmanager. Jede Gruppe hat ihr eigenes Verkaufsteam in Detroit, das die normalen, tagtäglichen Kontakte zwischen den Kunden, der *Gruppenleitung* und den *Operativen Einheiten* aufrechterhält. Die für Finanzfragen zuständigen Stäbe überwachen alle finanziellen Aktivitäten einschließlich der Ausgaben und Einnahmen der *Operativen Einheiten.* Jede Gruppe hat ihre eigene Qualitätskontrolle und Personalabteilung, die alle Leistungen der *Operativen Einheiten* beobachtet und ihre Dienste zur Verfügung stellt, wenn sie angefordert werden. Die *Gruppenleitung* achtet außerdem auf die Forschungs- und Technologieentwicklung, die für ihre Gruppe Relevanz besitzt.

Operative Einheiten

Jede *Operative Einheit* stellt eine autonome Geschäftseinheit dar, die von einem Geschäftsführer und einem stellvertretenden Geschäftsführer geleitet wird, die die vollständige Autorität und Verantwortung für ihre Einheit innerhalb weiter und allgemeiner Grundsätze haben, die von der *Unternehmens- und Gruppenleitung* festgelegt wurden. Diese zentralisierten Einheiten beschäftigen im allgemeinen nicht mehr als 100 Mitarbeiter, womit dem Führungsteam enge Kontaktmöglichkeiten mit den Mitarbeitern gegeben werden und sie in der Lage sind, Verantwortung zu übernehmen für alle Einflüsse, die im wesentlichen die Qualität, Effizienz und Profitabilität ihrer Einheit bestimmen.

Neben diesen besonderen Strukturmerkmalen weist die Unternehmensverfassung der MAGNA ein Vermögens- und Gewinnbeteiligungssystem, ein hohes Lohnniveau, intensive Ausbildungsangebote (Lehrlingsausbildung, fachliche Weiterbildung und Führungstrainings), Sozialleistungen an Mitarbeiter (einschließlich Erholungspark, Kinderkrippen) auf. Außerdem sind regelmäßige Spenden für als „beispielgebend" angesehene Aktivitäten in der gesellschaftlichen Umwelt (einschließlich Stipendien für Studenten, Spenden an Universitätsinstitute) vorgesehen.

Die Hierarchie aller Organisationseinheiten ist sehr flach (z. B. die typische Operative Einheit hat neben dem Geschäftsführer einen Stellvertretenden Geschäftsführer, je eine Führungskraft für die Qualitätskontrolle, Instandhaltung, Maschinenwesen, Verwaltung und Produktion sowie Meister oder Vorarbeiter als Schichtführer); die Arbeitsbeziehungen sind wenig formalisiert, die persönlichen Führungsstile zeigen ein sehr uneinheitliches Bild, die Fluktuation ist sehr gering; Organisationsmitglieder äußerten in einer Befragung hohe Zufriedenheit; in einer freien Formulierung kommt es zu der Aussage „MAGNA gibt Menschen bei der Arbeit direkte Partizipation; das Ergebnis ist, daß sie das Gefühl haben, daß die erzielten Resultate direkt aus ihren Anstrengungen enstehen." (Armstrong / Kolodny 1985, S. 25). Der Firmengründer ist zweifellos ein charismatischer Führer, dem es zu gelingen scheint, ein Organisationsklima zu schaffen, in dem

Leistungsbewußtsein und das Gefühl, in einer toleranten Gemeinschaft wichtiges und anerkanntes Mitglied zu sein, integriert sind. Bei der Fülle dieser Eigenheiten ist es schwer, der Organisationsstruktur einen spezifischen Effizienzbeitrag – der Gesamterfolg ist seit der Gründung auch in Zeiten schlechter Konjunktur in der Automobilbranche permanent gewachsen – zuzuweisen; ohne die gewählte Struktur, scheinen allerdings die anderen Elemente ihre Verankerung resp. ihr „Gerüst" zu verlieren.

3. Zusammenfassende Bemerkungen

Die Beschäftigung mit formalen Strukturbedingungen der Partizipation hat gezeigt, daß die Literatur diesem Thema keine besondere Aufmerksamkeit geschenkt hat. Zusammenhängende Theorien, die im Sinne von Kontingenzmodellen die Umwelt der Organisation, die motivationalen und kognitiven Partizipationsbedingungen der beteiligten Personen sowie unterschiedliche Organisationsgrößen, Informations- und Fertigungstechnologien und alle anderen Strukturbedingungen einschließen, scheinen nicht vorzuliegen. Allerdings ließen sich einige Inseln der Theoriebildung sowie praktische Lösungsansätze anprechen. Diese Ansätze lassen sich in zwei sich etwas skurril voneinander abhebende Klassen ordnen: Ansätze, die versuchen Partizipation explizit festzulegen. Hierzu gehören die gesetzliche Mitbestimmung und die Matrix-Organisation. Daneben führen Ansätze zu Partizipation unter Vermeidung der expliziten Zuteilung von Partizipation durch die Beschneidung der Formalisierung – im Falle des Eintretens für inexakte Strukturen – resp. Verkoppelung von kleinen, relativ selbständigen Organisationseinheiten zu offenen Partizipationschancen. Theorie und Praxis der Humanisierung scheinen hier zwischen diesen Klassen zu liegen: bei der Arbeitsgestaltung eher bei der ersten, im Falle der teilautonomen Arbeitsgruppen eher bei der zweiten . . .

Eine andere Klassenbildung könnte unterscheiden zwischen technokratischen Ansätzen (Arbeitsgestaltung, Matrix-Organisation), die Verwendung von Partizipation als Einführungsstrategie (Aktionsforschung im Bereich der Humanisierung) sowie Partizipation als „Alltagsziel" (Matrix-Organisation, inexakte und organische Strukturen) unter mehr oder weniger starker Verwendung von Partizipation bei der Einführung der Partizipationsbedingungen (vgl. die unterschiedlichen Partizipationsstrategien von Argyris einerseits und Kolodny andererseits beim Aufbau von Matrixorganisationen oder der charismatische Aspekt bei MAGNA, der bei der Erstellung der Unternehmenssatzung – zumindest bei der Entwicklung der Leitidee – den Beteiligten keinerlei Partizipation einräumte). Vielleicht ist es gerade die Uneinheitlichkeit der Ansätze, die es ermöglicht, sie mit einiger Phantasie so zusammenzusetzen, daß die Konturen einer Theorie partizipativer Strukturen erkennbar werden. Die gesetzliche Mitbestimmung hat sowohl das gesamtgesellschaftliche Bewußtsein für Partizipation in Betrieben aktiviert als auch Machtstrukturen geschaffen, die Ideen zur „Partizipierung“ von Betrieben genügend Schubkraft geben könnten, falls die Partizipation tatsächlich über die indirekte Form hinaus zum Leitbild der Mitbestimmungsproponenten gehört. Die berichteten Chancen, daß Partizipation den „Machtkuchen“ vergrößern sowie sowohl Stabilität als auch Flexibilität erhöhen kann, sollte auch jene zu Partizipationsexperimenten veranlassen, die nicht „Ideologien“, sondern “Leistung“ resp. nicht gesellschaftliche „Werte“, sondern „wertfreie Mittel“ im Vordergrund des wirtschaftlichen Gestaltens stehend sehen möchten. Bei dieser „ideologischen“ bzw. „instrumentellen“ Schubkraft bliebe zu überlegen, ob eher genaue Partizipationsanleitungen z. B. bei der Arbeitsgestaltung (z. B. im Sinne des erwähnten „Job Diagnostic Survey“) oder der Matrix-Organisation auf der Grundlage der Situationsbedingungen geeignet sind oder ein Vakuum – im Sinne der inexakten Strukturen – geschaffen wird, das Partizipation – gestützt auf entsprechende Maßnahmen der Aktionsforschung – aufsaugen kann. Insgesamt gesehen liefern Modelle organischer Strukturen Anregungen, die für alle anderen Ansätze offen sind: Die Humanisierung der Arbeitsaufgabe als Basis selbstbewußter individualer Partizipation hat dort ebenso ihren Platz wie die Anwendung der Erfahrungen aus teilautonomen Arbeitsgruppen, inexakten Organisationsstrukturen sowie die Anwendung matrixartiger Gebilde bei der Gestaltung des Zusammenwirkens der lose verkoppelten „operativen Einheiten“.

Phantasie trägt häufig etwas weit weg von der Realität; vielleicht lassen sich die ausgewählten Ansätze doch nicht so leicht zusammenfügen wie dies auf den ersten naiven Blick aussieht. Theoretisch und praktisch interessant scheint es aber auf jeden Fall zu sein, die offenen Spekulationen über partizipative Strukturen in mehr Wissen durch vermehrte Anstrengungen im Entwerfen integrierter Konzeptionen und deren Überprüfung zu überführen.

Anmerkung

[1] Es soll nicht in die Diskussion der heute vorliegenden Differenziertheit der „situativen“ resp. „Kontingenzansätze“ eingegriffen werden (vgl. hierzu z. B. Kieser / Kubicek 1983, S. 349–390, House 1984); es wird nur angemerkt, daß eine (vollständige) deterministische Steuerung der Organisation durch ihre Umwelt – etwa im Sinne der reinen „ecologischen“ Konzeption (Singh / House / Tucker 1985) als wenig realistisch angesehen wird.

Literatur

Aldrich, H. E. (1979): *Organizations and Environment,* Englewood Cliffs.

Argyris, C. (1967): Today's Problems with Tomorrow's Organizations. In: *The Journal of Management Studies* 4, S. 31–55.

Argyris, C. (1982): *Reasoning, Learning, and Action.* San Francisco.

Bartölke, K. / Wächter, H. (1974, 1980): Mitbestimmung und betriebswirtschaftliche

Organisationstheorie. In: Koubek, N. / Küller, H.-D. / Scheibe-Lange, I. (1974, 1. Aufl.; 1980, 2. Aufl.), *Betriebswirtschaftliche Probleme der Mitbestimmung*. Frankfurt, S. 66–83.
Bartölke, K. / Eschweiler, W. / Flechsenberger, D. / Tannenbaum, A. S. (1982): Workers' Participation and the Distribution of Control as Perceived by Members of Ten German Companies. In: *Administrative Science Quarterly* 27, S. 380–397.
Brown, J. A. C. (1960): *Exploration in Management*. Harmondsworth.
Budäus, D. (1975): *Entscheidungsprozeß und Mitbestimmung*. Wiesbaden.
Chmielewicz, K. / Großmann, A. / Inhoffen, A. O. / Lutter, M. (1977): Die Mitbestimmung im Aufsichtsrat und Vorstand – Darstellung, Vergleich und Kritik der rechtlichen Regelungen aus juristischer und betriebswirtschaftlicher Sicht. In: *Die Betriebswirtschaft* 37, S. 105–145.
Chmielewicz, K. / Inhoffen, A. O. (1977): Die Mitbestimmung nach dem Betriebsverfassungsgesetz 1972 aus organisatorischer Sicht. In: *Die Betriebswirtschaft* 37, S. 591–613.
Chmielewicz, K. (1981): Bibliographie Unternehmensverfassung. In: Chmielewicz, K. / Coenenberg, A. G. / Köhler, R. / Meffert, H. / Reber, G. / Szyperski, N. (Hrsg.): *Unternehmensverfassung*. Stuttgart, S. 296–317.
Cohen, M. P. / March, J. G. / Olsen, J. P. (1972): A Garbage Can Model of Organizational Choice. In: *Administrative Science Quarterly* 17, S. 1–25.
Davis, S. M. / Lawrence, P. S. (1977): *Matrix*. Reading.
Davis, S. M. / Lawrence, P. S. (1978): Problems of Matrix Organizations. In: *Harvard Business Review* 56, S. 131–142.
Dlugos, G. (1980): Mitbestimmung. In: Grochla, E. (Hrsg.), *Handwörterbuch der Organisation*. 2. Aufl., Stuttgart, Sp. 1343–1356.
Dlugos, G. (1981a): Von der Betriebswirtschaftspolitik zur betriebswirtschaftlich-politologischen Unternehmungspolitik. In: Geist, M. N. / Köhler, R. (Hrsg.), *Die Führung des Betriebes*. Stuttgart, S. 53–70.
Dlugos, G. (1981b): Die Unternehmungseffizienz im Interessenkonflikt der Unternehmungsmitglieder. In: Säcker, F. J. / Zander, E. (Hrsg.), *Mitbestimmung und Effizienz*. Stuttgart, S. 1–18.
Fricke, W. (1975): *Arbeitsorganisation und Qualifikation*. Bonn.
Friedel-Howe, H. (1982): Soziale Technik – Implikationen für die Humanisierung der Arbeit. In: *Die Betriebswirtschaft* 42, S. 13–83.
Gaugler, E. / Kolb, M. / Ling, B. (1977): *Humanisierung der Arbeitswelt und Produktivität*. 2. Aufl., Ludwigshafen.
Goldberg, W. H. (1983): Verhandelte Mitbestimmung. Die Methode der kleinen Schritte oder die Kunst des Möglichen. In: *Die Betriebswirtschaft* 43, S. 381–393.
Grunwald, W. (1980): Das "Eherne Gesetz der Oligarchie". In: Grunwald, W. / Lilge, H.-G. (Hrsg.), *Partizipative Führung*. Bern, S. 245–285.
Hackman, J. R. / Oldham, G. (1975): Development of the Job Diagnostic Survey. In: *Journal of Applied Psychology* 60, S. 159–170.
Hannan, M. T. / Freeman, J. (1977): The Population Ecology of Organizations. In: *American Journal of Sociology* 82, S. 929–964.
Hannan, M. T. / Freeman, J. (1984): Structural Inertia and Organizational Change. In: *American Sociological Review* 49, S. 149–164.
Hedberg, B. L. T. / Nystrom, P. C. / Starbuck, W. H. (1976): Camping on Seesaws: Prescriptions of Self-Designing Organizations. In: *Administrative Science Quarterly* 21, S. 41–65.

Hedberg, B. L. T. (1981): How Organizations Learn and Unlearn. In: Nystrom, P. C. / Starbuck, W. H. (Hrsg.), *Handbook of Organizational Design* 1. Oxford. S. 3–27.
Herzberg, F. (1981): Die Motivations-Hygiene-Theorie. In: Ackermann, K.-F. / Reber, G., *Personalwirtschaft. Motivationale und kognitive Grundlagen.* Stuttgart, S. 109–126.
House, R. J. (1984): *Power in Organizations: A Social Psychological Perspective.* Unveröffentlichtes Manuskript, Toronto.
Irle, M. (1971): *Macht und Entscheidungen in Organisationen.* Frankfurt.
Janis, I. L. / Mann, L. (1977): *Decision Making.* New York.
Kappler, E. (1981): *Ökonomische Beurteilung der Mitbestimmung.* Arbeitspapier Nr. 58 des Fachbereichs Wirtschaftswissenschaften der Gesamthochschule Wuppertal. Wuppertal.
Kieser, A. / Kubicek, H. (1983): *Organisation.* 2. Aufl., Berlin.
Kirsch, W. / Scholl, W. (1977): Demokratisierung – Gefährdung der Handlungsfähigkeit organisatorischer Führungssysteme? In: *Die Betriebswirtschaft* 37, S. 235–246.
Kirsch, W. / Scholl, W. (1983): Was bringt die Mitbestimmung: Eine Gefährdung der Handlungsfähigkeit und/oder Nutzen für die Arbeitnehmer? In: *Die Betriebswirtschaft* 43, S. 541–562.
Klein, L. (1975): *Die Entwicklung neuer Formen der Arbeitsorganisation.* Göttingen.
Klein, M. (1959): Our Adult World and Its Roots in Infancy. In: *Human Relations* 12, S. 291–330.
Kolodny, H. F. (1979): Evolution to a Matrix Organization. In: *Academy of Management Review* 4, S. 543–553.
Kolodny, H. F. (1983): Organisationsformen und erfolgreiche Produktinnovationen: der spezielle Beitrag der Matrix-Organisation. In: *Die Betriebswirtschaft* 43, S. 445–455.
Kolodny, H. F. (1984a): *Product Shops and the Quality of Working Life in Sweden.* Unveröffentlichtes Manuskript, Toronto.
Kolodny, H. F. (1984b): *Work Organizations in Sweden: Some Impressions from 1982–83.* Unveröffentlichtes Manuskript, Toronto.
Kubicek, H. (1979): Dimensionen der Humanisierung des Arbeitslebens. In: *Die Betriebswirtschaft* 39, S. 663–684.
Lawrence, P. R. / Kolodny, H. F. / Davis, S. M. (1977): The Human Side of the Matrix. In: *Organizational Dynamics* 17, S. 43–61.
Locke, F. A. / Schweiger, D. M. (1978): Participation in Decision Making: One More Look. In: Staw, B. M. (Hrsg.), *Research in Organizational Behavior* I. Greenwich, CN, S. 265–339.
Luhmann, N. (1969): Klassische Theorie der Macht. In: *Zeitschrift für Politik* 16, S. 149–170.
Maier, N. R. F. (1963): *ProblemSolving Discussions and Conferences.* New York.
March, J. G. / Olsen, J. P. (et al.) (1976): *Ambiguity and Choice in Organizations.* Bergen.
McKelvey, B. (1982): *Organizational Systematics.* Berkeley.
Meadows, I. S. G. (1981): Qualität des Arbeitslebens: Fortschritte, Probleme und Aussichten. In: *Die Betriebswirtschaft* 41, S. 519–536.
Moch, M. K. / Pondy, L. R. (1977): Ambiguity and Choice in Organizations (Buchbesprechung). In: *Administrative Science Quarterly* 22, S. 351–362.
Nell-Breuning, O. v. (1978): Zielhorizont des Unternehmens und der Mitbestimmung. In: *Die Betriebswirtschaft* 38, S. 265–271.
Neuberger, O. / Conradi, W. / Maier, W. (1985): *Individuelles Handeln und sozialer Einfluß.* Opladen.

Nowotny, E. (1978): Das System der „Sozial- und Wirtschaftspartnerschaft" in Österreich – Gesamtwirtschaftliche und Einzelbetriebliche Formen und Effekte. In: *Die Betriebswirtschaft* 38, S. 273–285.

Raiser, T. (1973): *Marktwirtschaft und paritätische Mitbestimmung*. Heidelberg.

Reber, G. (1970): Mitbestimmung in der unternehmerischen Legislative und Exekutive. In: Marx, A., *Personalführung* 2. Wiesbaden, S. 195–231.

Reber, G. (Hrsg.) (1980): *Macht in Organisationen*. Stuttgart.

Reber, G. (1983): Matrix-Organisation. In: *Die Betriebswirtschaft* 43, S. 666–668.

Säcker, F. J. (1981): The German Model of Codetermination: Programmatic Perspectives, Confrontative Issues and Prospective Developments. In: Dlugos, G. / Weiermair, K. (Hrsg.), *Management Under Differing Value Systems*. Berlin, S. 311–346.

Singh, J. V. / House, R. I. / Tucker, D. J. (1985): *Organizational Change and Organizational Mortality*. University of Toronto. Unveröffentlichtes Manuskript.

Steinmann, H. / Heinrich, M. / Schreyögg, G. (1976): *Theorie und Praxis selbststeuernder Arbeitsgruppen*. Köln.

Strauss-Fehlberg, H. (1978): *Die Forderung nach Humanisierung der Arbeitswelt*. Köln.

Tannenbaum, R. / Massarik F. (1950): Participation by Subordinates in the Managerial Decision-Making Process. In: *The Canadian Journal of Economics and Political Science*; zitiert nach dem Wiederabdruck in: Heckmann, I. L. / Huneryager, S. G. (Hrsg.), *Human Relations in Management*. Cincinnati, S. 378–391.

Tannenbaum, R. / Schmidt, W. H. (1958): How to Choose a Leadership Pattern. In: *Harvard Business Review* 36, S. 95–102.

Theisen, M. R. (1983): Betriebswirtschaftliche Aspekte und Perspektiven in der Mitbestimmungsdiskussion. In: *Die Betriebswirtschaft* 43, S. 123–142.

Thomae, H. (1974): *Konflikt, Entscheidung, Verantwortung*. Stuttgart.

Trist, E. L. / Bamforth, K. W. (1951): Some Social and Psychological Consequences of the Long-Wall Method of Goal-Getting. In: *Human Relations* 4, S. 3–38.

Vroom, V. H. (1973): A new Look at Managerial Decision Making. In: *Organizational Dynamics* 1, S. 66–80.

Vroom, V. H. / Yetton, P. M. (1973): *Leadership and Decision-Making*. Pittsburgh.

Vroom, V. H. (1981): Führungsentscheidungen in Organisationen. In: *Die Betriebswirtschaft* 41, S. 183–193.

Wagner, H. (1978): Mehrdimensionale Organisationsstrukturen. In: *Die Betriebswirtschaft* 38, S. 103–115.

Weick, K. E. (1979): *The Social Psychology of Organizing*. 2. Aufl. Reading.

Witte, E. (1980): Der Einfluß der Arbeitnehmer auf die Unternehmenspolitik. In: *Die Betriebswirtschaft* 40, S. 541–559.

Führung und Partizipation unter dem Einfluß moderner Informationstechniken

Norbert Szyperski

Abstract
Management and Participation Under the Influence of Modern Information Technology

Assessments of the effects of information technologies in organizations are subject to great controversies, since even scientific explorations of this phenomenon can not clarify dissending opinions, an attempt will now be made to consider the different aspects and basic assumptions of the problem. It is intended to describe information technology as an object of human planning and designing and to portray it in terms of a participative basic comprehension of management potentials for improving the presupposition of participation.

1. Darlegung der Perspektive

Die Einführung von Informationstechniken in Unternehmungen und Verwaltungen führt zu teilweise heftigen Kontroversen. Befürworter und Gegner der neuen Systeme bilden weitgehend geschlossene Fronten; abweichende Interessen, Perspektiven und Kontexte bestimmen die jeweiligen Stellungnahmen und erschweren eine rationale Auseinandersetzung erheblich. De facto schreitet die „informationelle Technisierung" jedoch mit steigender Geschwindigkeit fort; neue Anwendungsbereiche werden erschlossen.

Die wissenschaftlichen Bemühungen um die Erforschung gesellschaftlicher und insbesondere innerorganisatorischer Wirkungen der Informationstechniken, die von der Hoffnung geleitet sind, zur Vermeidung negativer Wirkungen beitragen zu können, befinden sich jedoch erst am Anfang.[1] Ungelöste methodische und konzeptionelle Probleme kennzeichnen die Forschungslandschaft:

- Merkmale der Informationstechniken wie Entwicklungsdynamik, Komplexität und Flexibilität der Anwendungsmöglichkeiten und der Einfluß der individuellen Systemgestaltung auf die Systemwirkungen stellen sehr hohe Anforderungen an die wissenschaftliche Erforschung, die in der Regel mit erheblichem time-lag hinter der technischen Entwicklung her hinkt.

- Die Gefahr eines Zirkelschlusses besteht da, wo System-Experten die Wirkungen informationstechnischer Systeme zu erforschen suchen und die Methodik mehr auf systemspezifische Merkmale als auf den Anwendungskontext abgestimmt ist.[2] „... ‚objective' system evaluations conducted by experts reflect their own *Weltanschauung* and not that of the end-users or of persons affected by the problems."[3]
- Unerläßlich ist die Thematisierung und Reflexion auf den zugrunde gelegten Problembezugsrahmen und das Organisationsverständnis, die die Forschungsergebnisse in erheblichem Umfang vorprägen.

Im folgenden wird auf dem Hintergrund eines zu explizierenden Rationalitätsverständnisses der Unternehmensführung und der Partizipation wie auch der Rolle der Informationstechniken versucht, zu der kontroversen Diskussion um die Wirkungen informationstechnischer Systeme auf die Partizipationsinteressen einen Beitrag zu liefern. Hierbei wird kein empirisches, sondern ein technologisches Argument vorgetragen. Es wird dafür plädiert, die vielfältig bestehenden Gestaltungsspielräume im Sinne einer partizipativen Führung zu nutzen.

Die weitreichenden Implikationen der Fragestellung, Konflikt- und Machtaspekte weisen diese deutlich als *unternehmungspolitische* Problemstellung[4] aus.

2. Kontroversen

Die Diskussion um Partizipation und die Einführung von Informationstechniken in Unternehmungen ist durch zwei gegenläufige Argumente markiert: Die Unternehmensführung als Motor der Einführung von Informationstechniken gefährde Partizipationsinteressen der Mitarbeiter, andererseits gefährde Partizipation die Effizienz und Handlungsfähigkeit der Führung.

Im folgenden sollen beide Argumente näher expliziert und erwidert werden, indem Grundannahmen aufgedeckt und mögliche Chancen des Einsatzes von neuen Informationstechniken zur Verbesserung von Partizipation und Führung aufgezeigt werden.

2.1. Zum Verhältnis von Partizipation und Führung

Die traditionelle Vorstellung von der Unternehmensführung[5] als Entscheidungsprozeß des (Top-)Managements aufgrund zum Teil weitgehend gewisser und zum Teil ungewisser Informationen, mit je nach Unternehmung abgestufter Beteiligung weiterer Mitarbeitergruppen an diesen Prozessen, wird zunehmend abgelöst. An seine Stelle tritt die, den praktischen Problemen eher gerecht werdende Betrachtung der Unternehmung als soziales System, in der Führung verstanden wird als sozialer Interaktionsprozeß mit rationaler Argumentation im Rahmen institutioneller Regeln, bezogen auf Wissen und Normen als Orientierungsgrundlagen.

Damit wird die Initiierung und Institutionalisierung von Argumentationsprozessen, um dezentral verteiltes Wissen und vorhandene Kenntnisse zur Entwicklung und kritischen Prüfung von Vorschlägen zu nutzen, zu einer expliziten Aufgabe der Unternehmensführung.

"So reasoning involves dealing with claims with an eye to their context, to competing claims, and to the people who hold them. It calls for a critical evaluation of these ideas by shared standards: a readiness to modify claims in response to criticism (...) A 'reasoned' judgement is thus a judgement in defense of which adequate and appropriate reasons can be produced."[6]

Basis- wie auch Leitungs-Partizipation[7], verstanden als routinemäßige Teilnahme an (Fach-)Diskursen über Entscheidungen von erheblicher Bedeutung, wird zu einem konstitutiven Element der Unternehmungsführung. Diskurse als Möglichkeit und Form der Partizipation dienen zwar auch im politischen Bereich als Garanten von Vernunft und Fortschritt[8], die Forderung nach einer mustergleichen „Demokratisierung der Unternehmung" wird hier jedoch aus grundsätzlichen Erwägungen[9] nicht verfolgt.

2.1.1. Gefährdung der Führung durch Partizipation

Der Haupteinwand gegen die Ausweitung der Partizipation ist die befürchtete Gefährdung der Handlungsfähigkeit der Unternehmensführung, verbunden mit Effizienzverlusten oder gar der Existenzgefährdung der Unternehmung.[10] Wird Führung wie etwa bei Kirsch[11] als kollektiver Problemhandhabungsprozeß verstanden, so sind potentielle Gefährdungen der Handlungsfähigkeit sowohl in den verschiedenen Phasen der Lösungsgenerierung (erschwerte Prozeß-Promotion) wie auch bei der Implementierung der Ergebnisse (Ergebnis-Promotion) zu sehen. Art und Häufigkeit der auftretenden Konflikte bestimmen dabei das Ausmaß der Gefährdung der Führung. Dieses Argument läßt sich, zumindest teilweise, empirisch belegen, es kann jedoch vor dem Hintergrund eines geänderten Führungsverständnisses behandelt werden.

2.1.2. Rationalitätsverständnis der Unternehmensführung

Die Fokussierung auf die Gefährdung der Handlungsfähigkeit läßt die weiteren Funktionen der Führung, Bedürfnisberücksichtigung und Erkenntnisfortschritt, außer acht, Handlungsfähigkeit allein ist jedoch noch keine hinreichende Bedingung rationaler Unternehmensführung. In Abkehr von einer entscheidungstheoretischen, individuell-ökonomischen Betrachtungsweise der Führung, in der Zielerreichung und reines Begründungsdenken dominieren, treten zunehmend Anpassung, Innovation und flexible Reaktionsfähigkeit als praktische Aufgaben der Führung in den Vordergrund. Die Behandlung dieser Aufgaben folgt weniger dem Muster wohlstrukturierter Phasenschemata, sondern eher Modellen von (politischen) Verhandlungsprozessen.[12] In (partizipativen) Prozessen sozialer Interaktion, durch Regeln geleiteter kritischer Diskurse werden Lösungen erarbeitet und abgestimmt. Dabei sind feldspezifische und feldinvariante Diskursregeln zu unterscheiden.[13] Praktische Rationalität begründet die Geltungsansprüche, Regeln dezisionistischer Diskursbegrenzung sichern die Einhaltung zeitlicher Restriktionen.[14]

Möglicherweise wird Partizipation dort weniger als Problem oder Belastung empfunden, wo sie, als Ausdruck eines partizipativen Grundverständnisses der Führung, in routinehaften Verhaltensformen verankert ist und nicht als kodifiziertes System mit starren Ritualen erlebt wird.[15] Fragen der Mitbestimmung in diesem zweiten Sinn (als kodifizierte Mitwirkungssysteme) und damit in Verbindung stehende Fragen der Unternehmungsverfassung werden hier nicht einbezogen, wiewohl viele Bestrebungen bestehen, auch die Einführung und den Einsatz der Informationstechniken zum Gegenstand gesetzlicher Mitbestimmung zu machen.

2.2. Zur Wirkung von Informationstechniken auf Partizipation

Trotz der erwähnten Probleme wissenschaftlicher Wirkungsforschung sollen Risiken und Chancen des Einsatzes der Informationstechniken diskutiert werden, indem auf die zugrunde liegenden Annahmen über Rolle und Funktion der Informationstechniken eingegangen wird.

2.2.1. Gefährdung von Partizipationsinteressen

Ansatzpunkte der Kritik an der Einführung neuer Informationstechniken in Unternehmungen aus der Perspektive der Mitarbeiterbeteiligung sind:
- die drohende Ausweitung des Kompetenzvorsprungs der Unternehmungsführung,
- die Ausdehnung zentraler Kontroll- und Überwachungsmöglichkeiten trotz zunehmender Dezentralisierung der Funktionen sowie
- die Schwächung der Position mancher Mitarbeiter durch drohende Dequalifizierung oder gar durch den Verlust des Arbeitsplatzes.

Weitere Einwände, die sich gegen die Ausweitung der Informationstechniken richten, beziehen sich auf die Änderung von Arbeitsinhalten und Arbeitsqualität, zunehmende Formalisierung und Standardisierung von Arbeitsabläufen, ohne daß damit jedoch unmittelbar Partizipationsinteressen betroffen wären.

Die genannten Einwände und Kritikpunkte haben ihre Berechtigung und sind grundsätzlich ernst zu nehmen, eine differenzierte Abwägung von Chancen und Gefahren, setzt jedoch eine nähere Bestimmung der Rolle der Informationstechniken voraus.

2.2.2. Zur Rolle der Informationstechniken

Die Informationstechniken sind von Menschen erdachte und entwickelte Techniken und Instrumente zur Verfolgung bestimmter Zwecke. In den Grenzen des jeweils Machbaren bestimmt menschlicher Gestaltungswille Funktionsumfang und Einsatzbereiche der Informationstechniken. Damit hängt die Wirkung informationstechnischer Systeme in sozialen und organisationalen Kontexten primär davon ab, wie die vorhandenen Gestaltungsspielräume genutzt werden. Diese bestehen im wesentlichen in drei Bereichen:
- bei der Systemkonzeption in der Auswahl und Ausgestaltung der zu realisierenden Funktionen;
- bei der Implementierung des Systems in der Unternehmung in der Informationspolitik, Beteiligung und Vorbereitung der Betroffenen wie auch schließlich
- bei der laufenden routinemäßigen Nutzung.

Das Ausfüllen der Spielräume ist Aufgabe der Mitarbeiter wie der Führenden, deren jeweilige Interessen und Perspektiven den gesamten Prozeß der Vorbereitung und Durchführung der systemtechnischen Änderungen prägen und sich darin dokumentieren.

Dabei stellt sich zunächst die grundlegende Frage, wie die Rolle der Informationstechniken bestimmt wird, da insbesondere die Vorstellung vom „vermenschlichten Computer“, der, mit künstlicher Intelligenz begabt, den Menschen ersetzt, Ursache mancher Vorbehalte gegen die Informationstechniken ist. Vor dem Hintergrund der oben entwickelten Perspektive von der Unternehmung als System sozialer Interaktionen könnten Informationstechniken dagegen die Funktion von Kommunikations- und eventuell Verhandlungsmedien[16], als Mittler zwischen Menschen und für den Menschen, erfüllen und das hieße in diesem Sinne systemkonform eingesetzt werden. „Das jeweilige Kritierum für diese Intelligenz muß also das pragmatisch passende Verhalten des Mediums sein. Der Kern des Mediums muß nachweislich interessenneutral sein, (...).“[17]

Wird der Informationstechnologie diese Rolle zugewiesen und werden die Gestaltungsspielräume im Sinne der Partizipationsinteressen der Mitarbeiter wie der Führenden genutzt, so könnten Partizipations- und Führungsprozesse sinnvoll unterstützt werden.

3. Potentiale der Informationstechniken zur Verbesserung von Partizipationsvoraussetzungen

Ausgehend von neuen Entwicklungen im Bereich der Informationstechniken soll anhand einiger ausgewählter Aspekte von Partizipation und Führung aufgezeigt werden, wie durch gezielten Einsatz informationstechnischer Instrumente, Führung partizipativer und Partizipation kompetenter werden kann.

3.1. Funktion von Informationstechniken

In Anlehnung an die Entwicklung von Expertensystemen in technischen, naturwissenschaftlichen und juristischen Bereichen wird auch an der Entwicklung derartiger Systeme für betriebswirtschaftliche Anwendungen gearbeitet. Dabei stehen bislang Anwendungen in relativ gut strukturierten, aber komplexen Arbeitsgebieten wie z. B. der Konzernrechnungslegung im Vordergrund. Ein weiteres Anwendungsgebiet ist die Konstruktion intelligenter Retrieval-Systeme, in denen Expertenwissen für das Auffinden gesuchter Informationen in Datenbanken genutzt wird.

Der Einsatz informationstechnischer Systeme als Kommunikationsmedium enthält Potentiale zur Verbesserung der Kommunikation insbesondere dort, wo der persönliche Kontakt gescheut wird oder zu zeitaufwendig ist. Aber nicht nur die reine Informationsübermittlung ist Aufgabe der Informationstechnik, das „Verbundmedium muß (...) die von ihm vermittelten und verknüpften Informationsströme nicht nur technisch präzise behandeln, sondern vor allem ‚verständig' vor dem Hintergrund des jeweiligen Gefüges von Rechten und Pflichten."[18]

Die nächsten Entwicklungsziele informationstechnischer Systeme liegen in der Reduktion des für den Benutzer erforderlichen Wissens zur Handhabung des Systems. Standardisierungs- und Formalisierungsanforderungen an den Benutzer werden durch die Gestaltung der Benutzeroberfläche reduziert, Benutzungswissen wird teilweise in das System selbst verlagert werden können.

3.2. Chancen partizipativer Unternehmensführung

Das geänderte Rationalitätsverständnis der Unternehmensführung rückt als eine zentrale Aufgabe der Führung die Nutzung des Wissens, der Erfahrung, der Kreativität und des Kritikpotentials der Mitarbeiter – und nicht nur der Stabsmitarbeiter – in den Blick. Es lassen sich hierbei Parallelen zu Entwicklungen in den Bereichen Fertigung und Qualitätssicherung ziehen: Die Institutionalisierung von „Lern-Stätten" oder „quality circles" ist unter anderem Ausdruck des Bemühens, die bei den Mitarbeitern vorhandenen Potentiale fruchtbar zu machen und zu nutzen sowie kollektives Problemlösungsverhalten einzuüben. Im folgenden gilt zu zeigen, inwiefern der Einsatz von Informationstechniken dazu beitragen kann, vorhandenes Wissen systematischer zu nutzen und auf diese Weise die Grenzen der handhabbaren Komplexität auszuweiten.

Der Einsatz von Kommunikationsmedien ermöglicht die Beteiligung von mehr Mitarbeitern und die Berücksichtigung ihres umfangreichen Expertenwissens und Kritikpotentials in Verhandlungs- und Abstimmungsprozessen bei gleichzeitig geringerem zeitlichen Aufwand. Dabei sind die Potentiale prozeduraler Verbesserungen durch informationstechnische Instrumente zusätzlich durch organisatorische Regelungen zu erschließen und zu sichern. So könnten Bedürfnisberücksichtigung und Erkenntnisfortschritt ausgedehnt werden, ohne daß die Handlungsfähigkeit gefährdet wäre. Die unten näher auszuführenden Möglichkeiten, qualifikationsbedingte Grenzen der Partizipation auszuweiten, sowie der Zugriff auf formalisierte Informations- und Wissensbasen lassen eine Unterstützung der Unternehmensführung erwarten. Die Entlastung von Routineaufgaben erweitert daneben die Spielräume für direkte und persönliche Interaktion.

3.3. Chancen kompetenter Partizipation

Die wichtigste, von der Einführung neuer Informationstechniken direkt betroffene Voraussetzung für die Partizipation ist die Partizipationskompetenz.[19] Statt einer einseitigen Erhöhung nur der Führungskompetenz durch Informationstechniken besteht durch entsprechende, die Interessen der Betroffenen berücksichtigende Systemkonzeption die Möglichkeit, die Aktivitäts- und Kompetenzpotentiale der Mitarbeiter zu erhöhen. Durch die Nutzung z. B. von Experten- oder Datenbanksystemen können Informationsstand sowie Wissen und Kenntnisse der Mitarbeiter verbessert werden. Damit sind in erster Linie kognitive Elemente der Partizipationskompetenz betroffen, auf deren zentrale Bedeutung für die Handlungsfähigkeit jedoch bereits Lübbe[20] hinweist. In dem Maße wie die Mitarbeiter auf fachspezifische Wissensbestände problemlos zugreifen können und die Informationsflüsse verbessert werden, werden auch sie zunehmend zu kompetenten Gesprächspartnern. Durch Einblick in die Struktur von Entscheidungsregeln wird auch die Argumentationsfähigkeit der Mitarbeiter gesteigert („kommunikative Kompetenz"[21]). Vielseitige Kommunikationsmedien und Netzwerksysteme eröffnen neue Formen indirekter und teilweise informeller Kommunikation wie auch gemeinsamer Problemhandhabung. „Je dichter die Kommunikation in einer Organisation, desto größer die Tendenz zur Informalität, und desto geringer wird die Bürokratisierung der Unternehmung sein."[22]

Zunehmende Professionalisierung sowie das Erfahren von Beteiligungsspielräumen und des Erwünschtseins von Beteiligung tragen sicher ebenfalls zu einer Verbesserung des Partizipationsklimas bei („affektive Dispositionen"[23]).

Diskurse und Argumentationsprozesse, die, gerade auch wenn sie kontrovers geführt werden, zu einer gründlicheren Evaluation eines Problems beitragen können, sollen durch den Einsatz informationstechnischer Systeme keineswegs ersetzt, sondern ganz im Gegenteil in ihrem Gehalt aufgewertet werden. Dies korrespondiert zu dem Bemühen, zunehmend Routinetätigkeiten auch im Verwaltungs- und Planungsbereich auf informationstechnische Systeme zu verlagern und die dadurch entstehenden Spielräume kommunikativ und diskursiv zu nutzen.

4. Fazit: Gestaltungsspielräume nutzen!

Die modernen Informationstechniken eröffnen neue Gestaltungsspielräume auch für die Beziehungen und die Zusammenarbeit in Unternehmungen. Bei allem notwendigen Nachdenken über mögliche Auswirkungen sowie auch über die zu erwartenden Entwicklungslinien dieser Systeme, die letztlich alle instrumentellen Charakter besitzen, bleiben die Fragen nach dem Selbstverständnis der Führung und der praktischen Rationalität im Vordergrund. Angesichts der Möglichkeiten, die hier nur kurz aufgezeigt werden konnten, aber auch wegen der immanenten Gefahren, soll im Rahmen der teilweise sehr kontrovers geführten Diskussion für eine Integration dieser Techniken in die Unternehmensführung und Partizipation plädiert werden. Informationstechniken sind neue Kulturtechniken. Ihre Nutzung sollte sich auch in einer positiv veränderten Unternehmungskultur niederschlagen.

Anmerkungen

[1] „Hope to escape the negative effects of an Information Society by Research", Untertitel zu Szyperski et. al. 1983.
[2] Vgl. Hoos 1983, S. 84.
[3] Bjoern-Andersen 1983, S. 161.
[4] Vgl. zum Problemkreis der Unternehmungspolitik: Dlugos 1976, Sp. 4099–4102.
[5] Vgl. etwa die Kritik am entscheidungstheoretischen Rationalitätskonzept bei Schaffitzel 1982, S. 83–175.
[6] Toulmin et. al. 1979, S. 9.
[7] Vgl. zur Begriffsbestimmung: Backhaus et. al. 1978, S. 76.
[8] Vgl. Kriele 1979, S. 30.
[9] Vgl. etwa Hennis 1973, S. 23, der sich gegen die Übertragung staatlicher Begriffe auf außerstaatliche Sphären mit dem Verweis auf die aristotelische Trennung von polis und oikos wendet.
[10] Vgl. Darstellung und Kritik bei Kirsch, Scholl 1977.
[11] Vgl. Kirsch, Scholl 1977, S. 235 f. in Abkehr von einem begrenzten entscheidungstheoretischen Verständnis.
[12] Vgl. etwa March, Olsen 1977.
[13] Vgl. Toulmin et. al 1979.
[14] Vgl. Sikora 1984.
[15] Vgl. zu dieser Unterscheidung: Wolff 1984, S. 276.
[16] Vgl. Petri 1983.
[17] Petri 1983, S. 44.
[18] Petri 1983, S. 44.
[19] Eine differenzierte Operationalisierung des Begriffs Partizipationskompetenz gibt Friedel-Howe 1985, S. 235 f.
[20] Lübbe 1972, S. 140.
[21] Friedel-Howe 1985, S. 236.
[22] Wolff 1984, S. 277.
[23] Friedel-Howe 1985, S. 236.

Literatur

Backhaus J. / Eger, T. / Nutzinger H. G. (Hrsg.) (1978): *Partizipation in Betrieb und Gesellschaft.* Frankfurt/M., New York.
Bjoern-Andersen, N. (1983): Public Participation in Technology Assessment. In: Szyperski, N. / Grochla, E. / Richter, U. M. / Weitz, W. (Hrsg.), S. 153–167.
Dlugos, G. (1976): Unternehmungspolitik. In: Grochla, E. / Wittmann, W. (Hrsg.). Sp. 4093–4103.
Friedel-Howe, H. (1985): Partizipationskompetenz – Problematik des Konzeptes und seiner Vermittlung im Weiterbildungsansatz. In: *Die Unternehmung* 39, S. 231–245.
Grochla, E. / Wittmann, W. (Hrsg.) (1976): *Handwörterbuch der Betriebswirtschaftslehre.* 4. Aufl., Stuttgart.
Hennis, W. (1973): *Die mißverstandene Demokratie.* Freiburg.
Hinterhuber, H. H. / Laske, S. (Hrsg.) (1984): *Zukunftsorientierte Unternehmungspolitik.* Freiburg.
Hollihn, F. (1978): *Partizipation und Demokratie – Bürgerbeteiligung am kommunalen Planungsprozeß.* Baden-Baden.
Hoos, I. R. (1983): Pitfalls of Current Methodologies of Technology Assessment. In: Szyperski, N. / Grochla, E. / Richter, U. M. / Weitz, W. (Hrsg.), S. 83–89.
Kirsch, W. / Scholl, W. (1977): Demokratisierung – Gefährdung der Handlungsfähigkeit organisatorischer Führungssysteme. In: *Die Betriebswirtschaft* 37 (2), S. 235–266.
Kriele, M. (1979): *Recht und praktische Vernunft.* Göttingen.
Lübbe, H. (1972): *Bewußtsein in der Geschichtswissenschaft.* Freiburg.
March, J. G. / Olsen, J. P. (Hrsg.) (1977): *Ambiguity and Choice in Organizations.* Bergen, Oslo, Tromsö.
Petri, C. A. (1983): Zur „Vermenschlichung“ des Computers. In: *GMD-Spiegel*, Nr. 3/4, S. 42–45.
Schaffitzel, W. (1982): *Das entscheidungstheoretische Rationalitätskonzept in der Betriebswirtschaftslehre – Anspruch und Wirklichkeit.* München.
Sikora, K. (1984): *Theorie des Handelns, Argumentationstheorie und Unternehmungsplanung.* Unveröffentlichtes Manuskript. Köln.
Szyperski, N. / Grochla, E. / Richter, U. M. / Weitz, W. P. (Hrsg.) (1983): *Assessing the Impact of Information Technology.* Braunschweig, Wiesbaden.
Toulmin, S. / Rieke, R. / Janik, A. (1979): *An Introduction to Reasoning.* New York.
Wolff, R. (1984): Kultur und geplanter Wandel von Organisationen – Anmerkungen zu einem ungeklärten Verhältnis. In: Hinterhuber, H. H. / Laske, S. (Hrsg.), S. 261–282.

A Business Political Analysis of Democratic Leadership in the Enterprise

Frank C. Danesy

Abstract

An Enterprise is established in order to fulfill both internal and external purposes. In pursuit of these purposes, goals must be formulated and implemented. The extent to which these activities are considered to be the management's exclusive domain, is dependent upon the political interactions within the enterprise. While the issue of democratic decision making has long been taken into account in the context of leadership studies, the implications of goal diversity and goal conflict have not. In order to gain a better understanding thereof, it is possible to apply the Business Political Approach to the leadership function. In the following the goal securing alternatives will be emphasized, and an attempt will be made to ascertain which of these alternatives are in fact compatible with democratic leadership systems. The author postulates that certain alternatives must be precluded, thereby reducing the leader's alternative set.

1. The Enterprise as a Political System

Enterprises are institutions which are established in order to fulfill the dual purpose of providing external actors with goods or services and internal actors (owners and staff) with an income.[1] When an enterprise fails to fulfill its purpose it is eventually abandoned. Thus attempts are made to insure that the purpose of the enterprise is continuously fulfilled. The activities which are aimed at the successful accomplishment of these attempts are preceeded by a vast variety of decisions. It is postulated that the extent to which these decisions are made and implemented by management is contingent upon the business political system in which management operates.

A system is a collection of elements which in some way interact with one another. Social systems (societies) may be characterized as having two or more individuals who interact, who take each others likely actions into account while acting, and who, at times, act together in pursuit of a common goal. Thus all enterprises may be considered social systems.[2] A political system is a part (subsystem) of a social system in which conflict related aspects of individual behaviour are emphasized. Political phenomena are assumed to be ubiquitous in all social systems.[3] If this is in fact the case, then political phenomena exist in every enterprise, and that every enterprise contains a political system.

Political systems are frequently referred to as being either democratic or authoritarian. Democracies are defined as political systems in which the opportunity to participate in decisions is widely shared among the members of that system. By contrast authoritarian systems restrict the opportunity to participate in the decision process to only a few.[4]

2. Leadership in the Political Context

In the field of management science, various studies related to the styles of leadership may be regarded in the context of political phenomena. While some studies differentiate between leadership orientations (e. g. person oriented or task oriented leadership styles) which are only vaguely connected to the political aspect of organizational behavior, others explicitly address the extent to which organizational members are legitimated to participate in decision processes, thereby referring to the political behavior of organizational members. Dichotomies frequently used in the latter sense include democratic or participative leadership to denote the choice of many and autocratic or directive leaderhsip to denote the choice of few.[5]

The first major research which differentiated leadership styles, as presently signified, and undertook to study the reciprocal process of interaction between the leader and his followers was published by Lewin and Lippitt.[6] Their experiments were designed to determine the effects of democratic and authoritarian leadership styles on the behavior of group members. Those designated as democratic leaders encouraged their followers to decide their own policies, gave them perspective by indicating the steps toward the achievement of their goals, and awarded them the liberty to initiate their own tasks and interactions. Conversely, the authoritarian leaders decided all policies for the group members, dictated the methods and stages of goal attainment individually and in succession, and directed the actions and interactions of each group member.

Lewin and Lippitt treated each leadership style as an ideal type thus isolating one from the other. While this approach undoubtedly has its merits when determining effects on given dependent variables, it is also associated with shortcomings. Dichotomies are often unsatisfactory, since they do not reflect the majority of events which can not be entirely captured by one category or the other. Referring to democratic and authoritarian systems, Dahl points out that "... political systems are neither wholly democratic nor wholly dictatorial".[7] The leadership styles associated with these two political systems may therefore be viewed as opposite points which define the limits of a continuum of leadership styles.

In an attempt to portray the range of leadership styles Tannenbaum and his associates delineate seven modes of decision making.[8] These are determined by the amount of authority which the leader employs and the area of freedom which he grants his subordinates (see fig. 1). The leader's tendency towards a democratic style of leadership increases with the extent to which his subordinates are involved in the decision process, and the extent to which they are permitted to act autonomously. While participation in decisions and autonomy are positively related to eachother, they are both negatively related to the amount of control exercised by the leaders.

At the aggregate societal level "the rights to participate in and to oppose the government, the hallmark of polyarchy, require the State to tolerate and even protect autonomy both for individuals and for organizations. ... By contrast, the development of autonomy threatens the nature of a hegemonic regime and the power of its leaders... Hence in hegemonic regimes, organizations must be kept under the control of the government".[9] It is conceivable that this holds equally true in enterprises.

It appears, however, that while autocratic leadership is severely criticized at the state level, there are leadership situations at the organizational level in which autocratic leadership is accepted. These include situations in which the members are indifferent to the consequences of a decision and the time required to reach a group decision is not justified due to the insignificance of the problem at hand, as

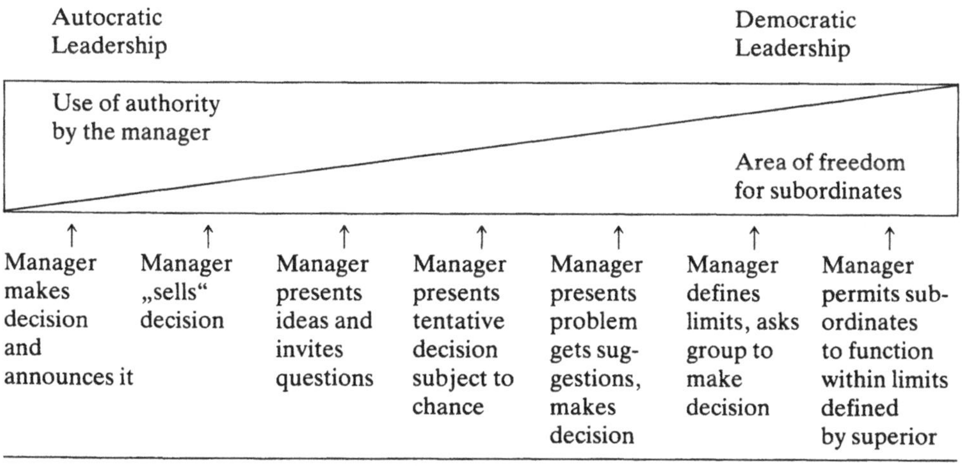

Fig. 1: Continuum of Leadership Behaviour

Adapted from Robert Tannenbaum et al... (1961): Leadership and Organization: A Behavioral Science Approach. New York, p. 69.

well as situations of crises in which immedeate action is necessary, and not sufficient time to reach a group decision is available.

In a normative approach to leadership styles Vroom and Yetton outline five methods of decision making[10]:

Autocratic method # 1 (A 1)
The leader solves the problem or makes the decision himself, using the information available to him at that time.

Autocratic method # 2 (A 2)
The leader obtains the necessary information from his subordinates. He may or may not tell them what the problem is. The role of the subordinates is to supply the leader with the necessary information rather than generating or evaluating solutions.

Consultative method # 1 (C 1)
The leader shares the problem with the relevant subordinates individually without bringing them together as a group. The subordinates are to give ideas and suggestions which may or may not be reflected in the leader's decision.

Consultative method # 2 (C 2)
The leader shares the problem with his subordinates as a group, collectively obtaining their ideas and suggestions. The decision which may or may not reflect the subordinates' influence is made by the leader.

Group method (G)
The leader shares the problem with his subordinates as a group. Together they generate, and evaluate alternatives, and attempt to reach agreement (consensus) on a solution. The role of the leader is essentially that of a chairman. He tries not to influence the group to adopt his solution and is willing to accept and implement any solution that has popular support.

Depending on the situation with which the leader finds himself confronted a certain decision method is recommended (see figure 2).

Regardless of the leadership style, however, it is apparent that conflict can arise. As relationships may be characterized in terms of the frequency and intensity with which conflicts occur, there seems to be sufficient evidence to support the notion that these attributes vary with the type of political system in which the relationship exists. Democratic systems tend to promote frequent manifest conflict which typically occurs at a comparatively low level of intensity. In nondemocratic political systems conflict may be less frequent, but it is also likely to be of greater intensity.[11]

Dahrendorf identifies three attitudes which individuals, groups and societies may have toward conflict. The first attitude is that conflict can be suppressed. This

Is there a quality requirement such that one solution is likely to be more rational than another?	Does the leader have enough information to make a high quality decision?	Is the problem structured?	Is acceptance of decision by subordinates critical to implementation?	Is it reasonably certain that subordinates would accept the decision if it is made by the leader?	Do the subordinates share the organizational goals to be obtained in solving the present problem?	Is conflict among subordinates likely in preferred solution?

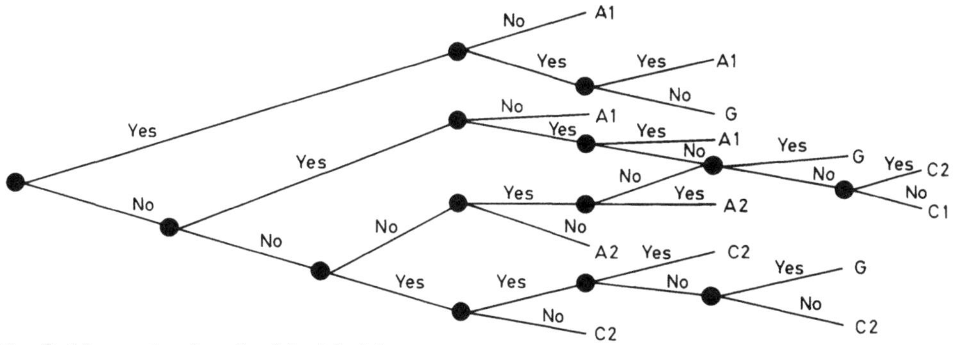

Fig. 2: Normative Leadership Model

Adapted from Victor H. Vroom (1973):
A New Look at Managerial Decision Making. In: *Organizational Dynamics*, p. 70.

approach proves to be ineffective in dealing with conflict, however, since the pressure exerted by those who wish to suppress the conflict is eventually opposed by an impetuous counteracting force of those seeking to express their interests. The second attitude is that conflicts can be solved. Given that conflicts are specific to the functions held by the individuals in conflict, it stands to reason, that their conflicts are structurally fixed, and can, in effect, not be solved. Any attempts to solve conflicts would therefore be illusive. The third approach is to regulate conflict. Arguing from the standpoint that conflicts can not be solved Dahrendorf stipulates that the intensity of conflicts can be reduced if the parties involved succeed in agreeing on rules to which they adhere when in conflict. Such an agreement, however, requires that the parties recognize (a) the inevitability of their conflicts, (b) that conflict intervention must be limited to the structure and not the cause of the conflict, (c) that the conflicts must in some way be chaneled, and finally (d) that they must agree on rules which are mutually accepted and binding.[12] Thus, the management of conflicts becomes a decision problem which, in structure, is comparable with all other decision problems.

3. Conflict Handling as a Decision Problem

It may be assumed that every decision process is triggered by a motivating situation which leads the thought processes of an individual in a certain direction. Given a situation of relative certainty, the process of rational decision making is associated with four problem areas. The first problem area involves the designation of a general goal which has yet to be specified through the decision process. It remains undecided whether the general goal shall be pursued until the decision process has been completed. The second problem area includes the definition of alternatives and of criteria with which the alternatives may be evaluated. On the basis of the criteria defined, the consequences of each alternative must be determined. The evaluation of the consequences and alternatives is subject to the third problem area. These processes are concluded with a set preference structure which enables the individual to make a choice based on a predetermined formal goal (i.e. value maximization or minimization). The implementation of a sufficiently specified goal represents the final problem area.[13]

Given that the general goal in a conflict relationship has been determined, thus eliminating the first problem area, and that the parties involved, have explicitly or implicitly agreed to regulate their conflicts within a democratic framework, the problem next to be solved pertains to the designation of alternatives suited to handle conflicts, and of politico-economic criteria for the evaluation of these alternatives.

The many alternatives discussed in conflict related literature may be devided into two broad categories of political actions. The first category includes those actions with which the actors attempt to influence their adversaries' decision processes. These necessitate direct communication between the opponents, and initiate change only to the extent to which the adversaries voluntarily abandon their preconcieved goals. By comparison, the actions related to the second category exclude direct communication between the opponents, and initiate change by altering the adversaries' environment.[14]

In the business political approach, actions associated with the first category are termed goal delimitations and include the acts of persuasion, manipulation, and the announcement of conditional rewards and penalties. While persuasion and manipulation may be directed at any element of the adversaries' decision process (i.e. general goal actualization, definition of alternatives etc.) and serve to alter preference structures under given circumstances, reward and penalty announcements are conditional statements with which an actor indicates his intention of rewarding compliant behavior and penalizing divergent behavior, thus changing the circumstances under which the adversaries make a decision. Persuasion and manipulation may be differientiated on the basis of the information which the actor imparts. In attempting to influence an adversary by means of persuasion, the actor argues to the best of his knowledge disclosing all information relevant to the present decision. Conversely, manipulation involves the deliberate adulteration, distortion, dilution or overloading of information by the actor.[15]

Actions related to the second category are termed environmental delimitations since they are aimed at structuring the adversaries' immedeate surroundings in such a way to insure compliant behavior. Environmental delimitation may be subdivided into interactions with which the actor attempts to influence a third party (i.e. indirect environmental delimitation) and actions with which he directly structures the adversaries' scope of action (i.e. direct environmental delimitation). The actions utilized to influence a third party are identical with those used to influence the opponent. Thus the persuasion and manipulation of a third party and the announcement of rewards and penalties to the third party are actions of indirect environmental delimitation, which are linked to the purpose of directing the third party's actions against the conflicting activities of the adversary. These actions stand in contrast to the employment of contractual rights, the withdrawal of cooperation, and the implementation of organizational and physical constraints which are actions of direct environmental delimitation, and reduce the discretion of the adversary regardless of whether or not a third party is prepared to comply with the expectations of the actor.[16]

Assuming that both the behavioral and economic effects would be relevant for a choice of political actions, the criteria with which these actions are to be evaluated should reflect both aspects. Thus, the following criteria may be employed are[17]:

1. Extent of behavioral change
2. Duration of behavioral change
3. Costs associated with the action
4. Complimentary effects
5. Adverse effects.

Having established the alternatives and criteria, it is now possible to structure a goal system, which portrays the consequences (k_{ij}), consequence values (w_{ij}), and alternative values (W_i) to be determined (see figure 3). While the evaluation of the consequences and alternatives is likely to the dependent on the frame of reference of the individual making the decision, there are empirical accounts which review the effects (i.e. consequences) of the aforementioned actions, thereby setting the groundwork for the individual's business political choice.[18]

4. Implications of the Democratic System and Consequences of Business Political Actions

As pointed out above, the right to participate in decision processes and to oppose the leadership of a political system is attributed to the democratic system. Because of these rights individuals have greater autonomy vis-a-vis the leadership, and the

Criteria / Alternative	Extent	Duration	Cost	Complemantary effects	Adverse effects	Value of the alternative
Persuasion	$k_{1,1}$ / $w_{1,1}$	$k_{1,2}$ / $w_{1,2}$	$k_{1,3}$ / $w_{1,3}$	$k_{1,4}$ / $w_{1,4}$	$k_{1,5}$ / $w_{1,5}$	W_1
Manipulation	$k_{2,1}$ / $w_{2,1}$	$k_{2,2}$ / $w_{2,2}$	$k_{2,3}$ / $w_{2,3}$	$k_{2,4}$ / $w_{2,4}$	$k_{2,5}$ / $w_{2,5}$	W_2
Announcement of rewards	$k_{3,1}$ / $w_{3,1}$	$k_{3,2}$ / $w_{3,2}$	$k_{3,3}$ / $w_{3,3}$	$k_{3,4}$ / $w_{3,4}$	$k_{3,5}$ / $w_{3,5}$	W_3
Announcement of penalties	$k_{4,1}$ / $w_{4,1}$	$k_{4,2}$ / $w_{4,2}$	$k_{4,3}$ / $w_{4,3}$	$k_{4,4}$ / $w_{4,4}$	$k_{4,5}$ / $w_{4,5}$	W_4
Third party persuasion	$k_{5,1}$ / $w_{5,1}$	$k_{5,2}$ / $w_{5,2}$	$k_{5,3}$ / $w_{5,3}$	$k_{5,4}$ / $w_{5,4}$	$k_{5,5}$ / $w_{5,5}$	W_5
Third party manipulation	$k_{6,1}$ / $w_{6,1}$	$k_{6,2}$ / $w_{6,2}$	$k_{6,3}$ / $w_{6,3}$	$k_{6,4}$ / $w_{6,4}$	$k_{6,5}$ / $w_{6,5}$	W_6
Announcement of rewards to third party	$k_{7,1}$ / $w_{7,1}$	$k_{7,2}$ / $w_{7,2}$	$k_{7,3}$ / $w_{7,3}$	$k_{7,4}$ / $w_{7,4}$	$k_{7,5}$ / $w_{7,5}$	W_7
Announcement of penalties to third party	$k_{8,1}$ / $w_{8,1}$	$k_{8,2}$ / $w_{8,2}$	$k_{8,3}$ / $w_{8,3}$	$k_{8,4}$ / $w_{8,4}$	$k_{8,5}$ / $w_{8,5}$	W_8
Employment of contractual rights	$k_{9,1}$ / $w_{9,1}$	$k_{9,2}$ / $w_{9,2}$	$k_{9,3}$ / $w_{9,3}$	$k_{9,4}$ / $w_{9,4}$	$k_{9,5}$ / $w_{9,5}$	W_9
Withdrawal of cooperation	$k_{10,1}$ / $w_{10,1}$	$k_{10,2}$ / $w_{10,2}$	$k_{10,3}$ / $w_{10,3}$	$k_{10,4}$ / $w_{10,4}$	$k_{10,5}$ / $w_{10,5}$	W_{10}
Organizational constraint	$k_{11,1}$ / $w_{11,1}$	$k_{11,2}$ / $w_{11,2}$	$k_{11,3}$ / $w_{11,3}$	$k_{11,4}$ / $w_{11,4}$	$k_{11,5}$ / $w_{11,5}$	W_{11}
Physical constraint	$k_{12,1}$ / $w_{12,1}$	$k_{12,2}$ / $w_{12,2}$	$k_{12,3}$ / $w_{12,3}$	$k_{12,4}$ / $w_{12,4}$	$k_{12,5}$ / $w_{12,5}$	W_{12}

Fig. 3: Business political goal system

leadership has less opportunity to employ coercion against its opponents. Leaders in a democratic system are more likely to find themselves in networks of reciprocal influence in which disputes are settled by negotiation and bargaining. In autocratic systems, by contrast, the influence of leaders is more unilateral, the means of influence tend to be coercive, and goals are likelier to be attained by hierarchy and command.[19]

Given that punitive measures are precluded in democratic decision situations the political actions available to a leader are significantly reduced. Direct environmental delimitations, which by nature are restrictive, must be excluded from the alternative set. Similarly, the announcements of penalties against an opponent or a third party also seem incompatible with democratic decision making. It is debatable whether the announcement of rewards violates the principles associated with a democratic system, since such an announcement could compel an individual to abandon his opinion against his better judgement. Should this be the case, then the actions left in the alternative set are persuasion and manipulation of opponents or third parties.

Manipulation may be effective in a short term exchange relationship. However, in a leader-member relationship, which is assumed to be long term, the adverse effects may be considerable. If the member recognizes that the leader is employing manipulative forms of influence, he is not likely to accept the leader's opinion. Contingent upon the extent to which the member is dependent on the exchange relationship he may react either with resistant complaining (voice) or counterdependent flight (exit).[20] Even if the leader at a later time attempts to influence the members by means of persuasion instead of manipulation, he may find himself unable to gain acceptance due to the mistrust initiated through his earlier actions.

While it may not be certain that employment of persuasive actions will in effect charge the adversaries' opinion, there appears to be sufficient evidence that the extent to which the arguments are accepted is largely dependent on the credibility of the source, and that if, in deed, an opinion change is brought about, it then tends to be persistent.[21] The complimentary effects of persuasive forms of influence enhance an atmosphere of mutual trust between the conflicting parties, thereby reducing the intensity of conflicts.[22] Although persuasion may require more time than the other forms of communicative delimitation, thus producing greater costs, it may be assumed that the costs incurred are offset by the duration of the opinion change and the reduction of conflict intensity.

Remarks

1 For a detailed analysis of the exchange relationships in the business sector, see Dlugos 1981, pp. 651–676.
2 Parsons/Shils 1951, p. 55; Dahl 1976, pp. 5–8.
3 Dahl 1976, pp. 3–5.

4 Ibid.
5 Stogdill 1974, pp. 365–370, and pp. 386–392.
6 Lewin/Lippitt 1938, pp. 292–300; Lippitt 1930, pp. 43–95.
7 Dahl 1976.
8 Tannenbaum/Weschler/Massarik 1961, pp. 67–79.
9 Dahl 1976, p. 83.
10 Vroom 1973, pp. 66–80; Vroom/Yetton 1973.
11 Dahl 1976, pp. 35–87.
12 Dahrendorf 1962, pp. 225–228.
13 Dlugos 1974, pp. 39–73.
14 Dlugos 1982, pp. 307–311; Dorow 1982, pp. 173–179.
15 Dlugos 1982; Dorow 1982.
16 Ibid.
17 Dlugos 1982, p. 311.
18 See e.g. Klis 1970; Simons 1976; Kiesler/C. Kiesler, S. 1970; Karlins/Abelson 1970; Tedeschi 1972.
19 Dahl 1976.
20 Mann 1967, pp. 89–90.
21 See e.g. Cook/Insko 1968, pp. 322–328; Newcomb 1963, pp. 3–14.
22 Simons 1976, pp. 98–102; Dorow 1982, p. 183.

Literature

Cook, T. / Insko, C. (1968): Persistence of Attitude Change as a Function of Conclusions Reexposure: A Laboratory-Field Experiment. In: *Journal of Personality and Social Psychology 9,* pp. 322–328.
Dahl, R. A. (1976): *Modern Political Analysis.* Englewood Cliffs.
Dahrendorf, R. (1962): *Gesellschaft und Freiheit.* München.
Dlugos, G. (1974): Unternehmungspolitik als betriebswirtschaftlich-politologische Teildisziplin. In: Wild, J. (Ed.) S. 39–73.
Dlugos, G. (1981): The Relationship between Changing Value Systems, Conflicts, and Conflict-Handling in the Enterprise Sector. In: Dlugos, G. / Weiermair, K. (Eds.) pp. 651–676.
Dlugos, G. (1982): Beziehungen zwischen Wertwandel, Konflikt und Konflikthandhabung im Unternehmungssektor. In: Stachowiak, H. (Ed.).
Dlugos, G. / Weiermair, K. (Eds.) (1981): *Management under Differing Value Systems – Political, Social, and Economical Perspectives in a Changing World.* Berlin, New York.
Dorow, W. (1982): *Unternehmungspolitik.* Stuttgart.
Karlins, M. / Abelson, H. J. (1970): *Persuasion: How Opinions and Attitudes are Changed.* New York.
Kiesler, C. A. / Kiesler, S. B. (1970): *Conformity,* Menlo Park, Cal. et. al.
Klis, M. (1970): *Überzeugung und Manipulation.* Wiesbaden.
Lewin, K. / Lippitt, R. (1938): An Experimental Approach to the Study of Autocracy and Democracy – a Preliminary Note. In: *Sociometry* I, pp. 292–300.
Lippitt, R. (1940): An Experimental Study of the Effect of Democratic and Authoritarian Group Atmospheres. In: *University of Iowa Stud.* Child Welf, 16 (3), pp. 43–95.

Mann, R. D. (1967): *Interpersonal Styles and Group Development. An Anaylsis of the Member-Leader-Relationship.* New York.
Newcomb, T. (1963): Persistance and Regression of Changed Attitudes: Long Rang Studies. In: *Journal of Social Issues* 19, pp. 3–14.
Parsons, T. / Shils, E. A. (Eds.) (1951): *Toward a General Theory of Action.* Cambridge, Mass.
Simons, H. W. (1976): *Persuasion: Understanding, Practice, and Analysis.* Menlo Park, Cal. et al.
Stachowiak, H. (Hrsg.) (1982): *Bedürfnisse, Werte und Normen im Wandel.* Bd. II. München et al.
Stogdill, R. M. (1974): *Handbook of Leadership. A Survey of Theory and Research.* New York, London.
Tannenbaum, R. / Waschler, I. R. / Massarik, F. (1961): *Leadership and Organization. A Behavioral Science Approach.* New York et al.
Tedeschi, J. T. (Ed.) (1972): *The Social Influence Processee.* Aldine et al.
Vroom, V. H. (1973): A new Look at Managerial Decision Making. In: *Organizational Dynamics* I, pp. 66–80.
Vroom, V. H. / Yetton, R. (1973): *Leadership and Decision Making.* Pittsburgh, Penn.
Wild, J. (Hrsg.) (1974): *Unternehmungsführung. Festschrift für Erich Kosiol zu seinem 75. Geburtstag.* Berlin.

Handlungsspielräume und Partizipation in der Arbeitsbeziehung – Kritische Anmerkungen zur transaktionskostentheoretischen Interpretation

Wolfgang Dorow

Abstract
Discretion and Participation in the Employment Relationship – Critical Remarks on the Transactions Cost Theoretical Interpretation

The substitution of "hierarchies" for "markets" raises, in a democratic society, questions regarding the qualitative change of economic exchange processes. The alteration of conditions for the safeguarding of the discretionary choice of the exchange partners is a critical element of an economic system which is far from the model of neoclassic theory. The discussion of this question includes a criticism of some of the misleading assumptions of "New Institutional Economics" on distinctive characteristics of "markets" and "hierarchies". Then the question of safeguarding interests in markets and hierarchies against opportunistic behavior is dealt with. Finally, the consequences of participation for the firm's efficiency are evaluated.

1. Einführung

In den liberalen Gesellschaftssystemen des Westens ist in den letzten Jahrzehnten eine beunruhigende Tendenz der Zentralisierung ökonomischer Entscheidungsmacht auf meist weltweit operierende Großunternehmungen zu beobachten. Die Sogkraft dieser Unternehmungen hat eine Stärke erreicht, die ein längerfristiges Überleben gerade auch erfolgreicher Newcomer am Markt in Frage stellt. Newcomer, die ein innovatives, konkurrenzfähiges Produkt entwickelt haben, laufen schnell Gefahr, attraktive Kandidaten einer Einverleibungspolitik der Großunternehmungen zu werden. So ermittelte eine Untersuchung der Harvard Business Review, daß von 314 kleineren innovativen Unternehmungen, die ein Joint Venture mit einer Großunternehmung eingingen, um ihre Schwächen im Bereich der Finanzierung und des Marketing auszugleichen, nach fünf Jahren nur noch 46 weiterbestanden, die übrigen wurden entweder übernommen oder mußten liquidieren.[1] Mit den vertikal und horizontal verlaufenden Konzentrationsprozessen wird der Marktmechanismus als klassisches Konflikthandhabungsinstrument liberaler Wirtschaftspolitik ausgedünnt. Dies hat weitreichende Folgen für die Möglichkeiten der Interessensicherung, nicht nur von Konsumenten und Lieferanten, sondern auch von Arbeitnehmern als Mitglieder von Großunternehmungen.

Betrachtet man die Wahlmöglichkeit zwischen Parteien und die Möglichkeit, Individual- und Gruppeninteressen in dafür geschaffenen Institutionen (Parlamenten) zu artikulieren und durchsetzen zu können, als zentrale Grundlagen eines demokratischen Staates[2], so können die Grundelemente eines liberalen Wirtschaftssystems in analoger Weise bestimmt werden: Die Wirtschaftssubjekte müssen die Möglichkeit haben, zwischen Marktpartnern wählen zu können, oder, wenn diese Wahlfreiheit etwa aufgrund von Monopolsituationen eingeschränkt ist, über Möglichkeiten des Widerspruchs gegen die ihre Interessen verletzenden Entscheidungen des Austauschpartners verfügen. Sollen demokratische Prinzipien auch im Bereich des Wirtschaftssystems gelten, können begründete Forderungen nach Widerspruchsmöglichkeiten für von ökonomischen Entscheidungen Betroffene erhoben werden, sofern sich durch Konzentrationsprozesse die Wahlfreiheit der Betroffenen einschränkt. Die Forderung der Öffentlichkeit nach Publizitätspflicht von Großunternehmungen, die Forderung der Konsumenten und Lieferanten nach Beteiligung an Entscheidungen marktbeherrschender Unternehmungen und die Forderung von Gewerkschaften nach Mitbestimmung in den Unternehmungsorganen werden mit eingeschränkten Wahlmöglichkeiten in einem Wirtschaftssystem, das sich vom Ideal des vollkommenen Marktes weit entfernt hat, begründbar.[3] Die Ersetzung des Marktes durch immer größer werdene Unternehmungen wirft in einer demokratischen Gesellschaft die Frage nach den qualitativen Veränderungen der wirtschaftlichen Austauschbeziehungen und den damit verbundenen Problemen der Entstehung und Handhabung von Interessenkonflikten zwischen den Unternehmungsmitgliedern sowie zwischen Unternehmung und den verbleibenden Marktpartnern auf.

Um diese Frage zu behandeln, werde ich zunächst auf die in der „New Institutional Economics“[4] geführte Diskussion um die Unterschiede von Märkten und Unternehmungen als alternative Institutionen ökonomischer Aktivitäten eingehen, dann die Frage der Sicherung von Interessen in Märkten und Unternehmungen diskutieren, wobei der Akzent auf die interne und externe Arbeitsbeziehung gelegt wird, und schließlich zur These der Property-Rights Theorie[5] Stellung nehmen, daß die Sicherung von Arbeitnehmerinteressen durch Partizipation zu Effizienzverlusten der Unternehmung führe.

Die Fragen des Interessenkonflikts und seiner Handhabungsmöglichkeit im Unternehmungssektor sowie deren Auswirkungen auf die Funktionsfähigkeit von Unternehmungen innerhalb eines liberal-demokratischen Gesellschaftssystems stehen im Mittelpunkt des Forschungsinteresses von Dlugos.[6] Dabei kann die von Dlugos entwickelte Konzeption ökonomisch-politischen Handelns im Unternehmungssektor als äußerst tragfähige Basis einer kritischen Diskussion der im Rahmen der „New Institutional Economics" entwickelten Thesen herangezogen werden.

2. Märkte und Unternehmungen: Einige Bemerkungen zu den Schwierigkeiten ihrer institutionellen Abgrenzung

Die „New Institutional Economics", deren Entstehung mit den Namen Coase[7] und Commons[8] verbunden ist, wirft der neoklassischen Mikroökonomie vor, daß sie eine reine Theorie des Marktverhaltens von Unternehmungen sei und dabei übersehe, daß wirtschaftliche Aktivitäten nicht nur im Markt ablaufen, sondern auch innerhalb von Unternehmungen vollzogen werden. Betrachtet man Märkte und Unternehmungen als unterschiedliche Regelungsformen wirtschaftlichen Handelns, stellt sich das von der Neoklassik nicht beachtete Entscheidungsproblem, in welcher dieser Institutionen Aktoren ihre wirtschaftlichen Handlungen entfalten wollen. Für den individuellen Aktor stellt sich die Frage, ob er seine Forderungen und Leistungszusagen als Marktpartner oder als Unternehmungsmitglied realisieren soll.

Den zentralen Unterschied zwischen den Institutionen Markt und Unternehmung sehen die meisten Vertreter der „New Institutional Economics" unter Berufung auf Coase in der Art und Weise, wie die Zielsetzungen der jeweils beteiligten Aktoren koordiniert werden. Coase definiert den Unterschied zwischen Markt und Unternehmung in seinem bekannten Essay „The Nature of the Firm" wie folgt: „If a workman moves from department Y to department X, he does not go because of a change in relative prices, but because he is ordered to do so ... It can, I think, be assumed that the distinguishing mark of the firm is the supersession of the price mechanism."[9] Der wesentliche Unterschied der Zielkoordination in Unternehmungen und Märkten liegt für Coase also darin, „... daß sie in einer Unternehmung nicht als Reaktion auf Preisrelationen und ihre Änderungen erfolgen, sondern aufgrund von Anweisungen der dafür zuständigen Instanzen der Unternehmensorganisation."[10] In einer Marktwirtschaft gibt es demnach zwei Institutionen wirtschaftlichen Handelns, die sich durch ihre unterschiedlichen Koordinationsmechanismen unterscheiden: „Märkte und Preise einerseits, Unternehmungen und Anweisungen andererseits."[11] Betrachtet man diese idealtypische Abgrenzung von Märkten und Unternehmungen unter dem oben skizzierten Merkmal demokratischer Interessensicherung, bedeutet dies, daß nur Märkte aufgrund ihrer dem Marktmechanismus impliziten Wahlmöglichkeit zwischen alternativen Austauschbeziehungen ein demokratisches Potential enthalten: Jedem Nachfrager oder Anbieter steht es frei, eine Austauschbeziehung zu verlassen, wenn er seine Interessen in einer preisgünstigeren Austauschbeziehung realisieren zu können glaubt. Das eine der beiden zentralen Elemente demokratischer Institutionen, nämlich die Wahlfreiheit, würde somit in einem funktionierenden Markt vorhanden sein: Die Freiheit zwischen Marktpartnern zu wählen, wobei sich aus ökonomischer Sicht diese Wahl am Kriterium „Preis“ orientiert. Demgegenüber sind aus der Sicht der „New Institutional Economics“ Unternehmungen „Hierarchien“[12], in denen die Ziele der Institutionsmitglieder durch Anweisungen des zentralen Koordinators, des „Unternehmers“, aufeinander abgestimmt werden, in denen also keine Freiheitsgrade existieren bzw. diese so reduziert sind, daß die Koordinationskosten im Vergleich zu den Kosten der Marktkoordination geringer sind. Die idealtypische Unternehmung der „New Institutional Economics“ kennt somit weder Handlungsspielräume ihrer Mitglieder, noch das zweite konstitutive Element demokratischer Zielbildung, nämlich, „Widerspruch“ gegen die Anweisungen des zentralen Koordinators zu artikulieren.

Mit diesen aus dem Fehlen beider demokratischen Elemente resultierenden „Transaktionskostenvorteilen“ der Unternehmung gegenüber dem Markt begründet Coase die Existenz von Unternehmungen. Es liegt daher nahe, jede institutionelle Bedingung, die die Ursachen dieser Transaktionskostenvorteile aufhebt, als Quelle von Ineffizienz zu bekämpfen.[13]

Akzeptiert man die hier getroffene Unterscheidung von Märkten und Unternehmungen, muß man Unternehmungen als besonders problematische Institutionen innerhalb eines demokratischen Wirtschafts- und Gesellschaftssystems betrachten. Während im Markt die Zielkoordination in der Vorstellung des Transaktionskostenansatzes *freiwillig* zwischen autonom handelnden Austauschpartnern erfolgt, wird sie in Unternehmungen durch die mit Sanktionen verbundenen Anweisungen des zentralen Koordinators *erzwungen.* Werden die hierarchischen, mit Zwangsmitteln verbundenen Anweisungen als typisches Koordinationsmittel der Unternehmung betrachtet, stellt sie folglich eine die demokratischen Grundwerte verletzende Institution dar.[14] Gegen diese Argumentation wenden die Vertreter der „New Institutional Economics“ jedoch ein, daß die Mitglieder der Unternehmung sich freiwillig zum Beitritt entschließen und die Unternehmung auch wieder freiwillig verlassen können.[15] Nun entkräftet dieser Einwand aber weder die These, daß die internen Bedingungen der Unternehmung als „Hierarchie“ Chancen zur Interessensicherung der dem zentralen Koordinator untergeordneten Unternehmungsmitglieder ausschließen, noch kann dieser Einwand akzeptiert werden, wenn die „exit“-Option[16] aufgrund immer unvollkommener werdender Märkte, bedingt durch zunehmende Unternehmungszusammenschlüsse, in ihrer realen Bedeutung abnimmt.

Gegen die Abgrenzung von Märkten und Unternehmungen durch die Merkmale der freiwilligen und erzwungenen Koordination haben sich vor allem Alchian und Demsetz[17] in einem im Rahmen der „New Institutional Economics“ sehr umstrittenen Aufsatz gewendet. Sie verneinen, daß sich eine Marktaustauschbeziehung von einer Arbeitsbeziehung mit dem von Coase behaupteten Koordinationsaspekt unterscheiden lassen. Ihr paradigmatisches Beispiel lautet: „Telling an employee to type this letter rather than to file that document is like my telling a grocer to sell me this tuna rather than that brand of bread."[18] Nach der Ansicht von Alchian und Demsetz hat die Unternehmung „... no power of fiat, no disciplinary action any different in the slightest degree from ordinary market contracting between any two people."[19] Sie wenden sich damit gegen die weithin in der „New Institutional Economics" geteilte Auffassung, daß die Besonderheit der Unternehmung die Akzeptanz eines Direktionsrechtes sei, mit dem die Unternehmung als Herrschaftssystem vom Markt als System freiwilliger Austauschvereinbarungen abzugrenzen sei.[20] Diese Argumentation, gegen die sich Alchian und Demsetz wenden, geht sogar so weit, daß behauptet wird, die unternehmungsinternen Arbeitsbeziehungen stellten eine Transformation von „eigentlichen Marktbeziehungen" in bürokratisch-administrativ verwaltete Beschäftigungsbeziehungen dar, bei deren Verwaltung ökonomischen Effizienzaspekten eine nur nachgeordnete Bedeutung zukäme. Nutzinger behauptet, daß der Markt durch freie Koordination, die Unternehmung dagegen durch die Subordination der Mitarbeiter charakterisiert sei.[21] Für ihn stellt daher ebenfalls die Autoritätsbeziehung zwischen Arbeitgeber und Arbeitnehmer das Unterscheidungsmerkmal des „Arbeitskontraktes" vom gewöhnlichen „Marktkontrakt" dar: „This contract comprises a *general* agreement ‚to obey the directions' of the entrepreneur or his delegate within the contractual legal limits."[22] Nach Nutzingers Vorstellung ist der Marktkontrakt hingegen durch eine mehr oder weniger (!) detaillierte Bestimmung des ausgehandelten Austauschobjektes definiert. Zu diesen Versuchen, unternehmungsinterne und -externe Beziehungen voneinander abzugrenzen, stellen Alchian und Demsetz schließlich fest: „To speak of managing, directing or assigning workers to various tasks is a deceptive way of noting that the employer is continually involved in renegotiating of contracts on terms that must be acceptable to both parties."[23] Auch das Merkmal, daß Arbeitsverträge im Gegensatz zu beispielsweise Kauf- oder Werkverträgen als Dauerschuldverhältnisse angelegt seien, lassen Alchian und Demsetz nicht gelten. Für sie ist das typologische Merkmal der Unternehmung vielmehr die *Team-Produktion* als kooperative Leistungserstellung verschiedener Input-Eigentümer, die durch einen zentralen Vertragspartner koordiniert wird: „It is the centralised contractual agent in a team productive process – not some superior authoritarian directive or disciplinning power".[24] Die spezifische Funktion dieses central agent sehen sie in der Überwachungs- und Anreizfunktion gegenüber den Input-Gebern. Sie begründen damit die Transaktionskostenvorteile der Unternehmung gegenüber dem Markt etwas anders als Coase und Williamson. Während letztere die Transaktionskostenvorteile aus der „Anweisung" als schneller und präziser Koordinationsform der Unternehmung, mit der langwierige und kostenintensive Vertragsabschlüsse zwischen Marktpartnern ersetzt werden, ableiten, begründen Alchian und Demsetz die Überlegenheit der Unternehmung mit der Spezialistenfunktion des „central agent", der die Handlungsspielräume überwacht und begrenzt, wobei er alle möglichen Determinierungsprozesse[25], also nicht nur die „Anweisung", anwendet. Aber auch das von Alchian und Demsetz präferierte Team-Modell der Unternehmung bleibt letztlich unbefriedigend, weil es nicht die Frage beantwortet, welche Input-Geber denn nun als Mitglieder der Unternehmung zu betrachten sind.

Dlugos[26] bemerkt dazu, daß diese Frage letztlich eine definitorische sei, die sich zweckmäßigerweise am Kriterium des rechtlichen Rahmens der Unternehmungsverfassung orientiert: Danach sind Mitglieder der Unternehmung die Träger der Mitarbeiterfunktion und der Eigenkapitalgeberfunktion sowie die Träger von Funktionen der gesetzlichen und statuarischen Unternehmungsorgane. Auf dieser Grundlage unterscheidet Dlugos als unternehmungsinterne Grundfunktionen die Mitarbeiter- und die Eigenkapitalgeberfunktion, als unternehmungsexterne Grundfunktionen die Lieferanten/Dienstleisterfunktion, die Fremdkapitalgeberfunktion, die Abnehmerfunktion und die Mitgliedsfunktion der Unternehmung in einem Gemeinwesen.

Folglich wird die Unternehmung von Dlugos als ein Zentrum interner und externer Austauschbeziehungen charakterisiert, die aus wechselseitigen Verknüpfungen von Forderungen und Leistungszusagen der Austauschpartner bestehen. Legt man die Dlugos'sche Konzeption der Unternehmung als Austauschzentrum zugrunde, die wiederum nur den Rahmen für die Analyse der einseitigen und wechselseitigen mikropolitischen Aktivitäten der Austauschpartner, mit denen sie ihre Forderungen und Leistungszusagen durch Einsatz von Machtgrundlagen abzusichern suchen, abgibt, wird die Untauglichkeit der Abgrenzungsversuche von Märkten und Unternehmungen durch die „New Institutional Economics“ überdeutlich. Trotz dieser Unklarheiten bleibt die vom Transaktionskostenansatz aufgeworfene Frage, warum unternehmungsexterne (marktliche) Austauschbeziehungen in unternehmungsinterne Beziehungen transformiert werden, von höchster Relevanz. Die Effizienzvorteile der Unternehmung gegenüber dem Markt, die Coase und mit ihm Williamson auf die spezifische Determinierungsform der Anweisung, Alchian und Demsetz dagegen auf die Spezialistenfunktion des central agent als Verhandlungs- und Überwachungszentrale gegenüber den Kontaktpartnern zurückführen, bestehen jedoch nur innerhalb enger Grenzen. Im folgenden wollen wir uns mit diesen Grenzen befassen.

3. Die Gefährdung der Unternehmungseffizienz durch Opportunismus

Im Rahmen des Transaktionskostenansatzes stellt opportunistisches Verhalten von Austauschpartnern den Angelpunkt der Erklärung ökonomischer Ineffizienz dar. Unter opportunistischem Verhalten versteht Williamson[27] die Verfolgung egoistischer Interessen unter Einschluß arglistiger Täuschungen des Austauschpartners. Opportunistisches Verhalten in diesem Sinne setzt die Existenz schwer überwachbarer und kontrollierbarer Handlungsspielräume der Aktoren voraus. Da opportunistisch nutzbare Handlungsspielräume mit dem neoklassischen Modell des vollkommenen Marktes unvereinbar sind, erhebt sich die Frage, wie es zu derartigen

Abweichungen vom Idealmodell der Neoklassik kommen kann. Im Modell des vollkommenen Marktes würden nämlich opportunistisch genutzte Handlungsspielräume sofort durch die exit-Entscheidung des getäuschten Austauschpartners eleminiert werden. Die Wettbewerbssituation würde verhindern, daß Aktoren sich gegenüber ihren Austauschpartnern Vorteile durch opportunistisches Handeln verschaffen könnten.

Die Entstehung opportunistisch nutzbarer Handlungsspielräume in realen Austauschbeziehungen führt Williamson auf drei Variablen zurück[28]: Erstens auf die begrenzte Rationalität der Aktoren, zweitens die Unsicherheit und Komplexität der Entscheidungsbedingungen und drittens die begrenzte Anzahl von Austauschalternativen, die dem Aktor zur Verfügung stehen. Das gleichzeitige Auftreten dieser Variablen verhindert, daß die Austauschpartner künftige Situationen sicher prognostizieren und sämtliche damit verbundenen Rechte und Pflichten vertraglich festlegen können. Insofern verbleiben immer Handlungsspielräume, die die Austauschpartner zu opportunistischen Aktivitäten nutzen können. Um sich gegen das opportunistische Verhalten des Austauschpartners absichern zu können, sind zusätzlich zu den transaktionskostenintensiven Verhandlungen über die wechselseitigen Forderungen und Leistungszusagen Überwachungs- und schließlich Durchsetzungsmaßnahmen bei Abweichungen von den Vereinbarungen notwendig.

Das dem neoklassischen Marktmodell implizite Mittel der Sicherung gegen opportunistisches Handeln wird durch die den Aktoren in der Realität nur begrenzt zur Verfügung stehenden Austauschalternativen weitgehend unwirksam: Da ein „small numbers exchange" die Abwanderungsmöglichkeit der Aktoren einschränkt, vermindert sich die Einsetzbarkeit der Abwanderungsdrohung als Mittel der Determinierung opportunistischen Handelns des Austauschpartners. Die Einschränkung der Abwanderungsmöglichkeit setzt die Austauschpartner letztlich der Gefahr des transaktionskostenverursachenden Opportunismus aus. Die transaktionskostengünstige Lösung des Determinierungsproblems sieht Williamson nun im Aufbau einer „Hierarchie", d.h. einer Unternehmung. Die Substitution marktlicher Austauschbeziehungen durch unternehmungsinterne Austauschbeziehungen auf der Basis eines Arbeitsvertrages bringt dabei nicht nur den Vorteil, durch ein spezifisches Kontroll- und Anreizsystem die Nutzung von Handlungsspielräumen der Mitarbeiter zu überwachen und zu steuern, sondern sie ermöglicht auch, durch adaptive, sequentielle Zielsetzungsprozesse die Probleme der begrenzten Rationalität und der Umweltunsicherheit und -komplexität besser zu beherrschen.[29]

Allerdings bestehen diese Transaktionskostenvorteile der Unternehmung gegenüber dem Markt nur innerhalb enger Grenzen, die von der Unternehmungsgröße abhängig gemacht werden.

Mit der Ausdehnung der „Hierarchie", häufig bedingt durch ein spezifisches Anreizsystem des Managements, das Status und Einkommen der Leistungskräfte von der Mitarbeiterzahl abhängig macht und insofern eine opportunistische Vergrößerung von Leitungsspannen und Leitungstiefen auslöst, kommt es zu Störungen des mehrstufigen Informationsflusses, die teilweise zur Abschirmung der eigenen Handlungsspielräume manipulativ herbeigeführt werden. Dadurch erhält die Unternehmungsspitze Informationen, die ein falsches Image von der Problemsituation der Unternehmung vermitteln und die vor allem zu Steuerungs- und Kontrollverlusten gegenüber den Handlungsspielräumen der Mitarbeiter führen. Mit zunehmender Unternehmungsgröße entwickelt sich außerdem eine Verantwortungsverflechtung im Rahmen des multipersonalen Zielsetzungsprozesses, die die Determinierung opportunistischen Handelns einzelner Entscheidungsbeteiligter ebenfalls erschwert. Williamson stellt daher die These auf, daß die übliche Stab-Linien-Organisation (U-form) infolge dieser größenbedingten Determinierungsprobleme schnell auf Effizienzgrenzen stößt. Um bei zunehmender Unternehmungsgröße opportunistisches Verhalten vermindern zu können, sind strukturelle Eingriffe in Form der Divisionalisierung notwendig. Williamson behauptet daher, daß die multidivisionale Organisationsstruktur (M-form) die Lösung des Transaktionskostenproblems großer Unternehmungen darstellt, da sie eindeutig abgrenzbare Verantwortungsbereiche (profit center) mit verbesserten Möglichkeiten der Determinierung von Handlungsspielräumen bietet. Die divisionale Organisation stellt also eine Wiederannäherung an das Ideal der eindeutigen Verantwortungs- und Anordnungsbeziehungen der „Hierarchie" dar, deren Vorteile durch eine zunehmende Unternehmungsgröße aufgehoben wurden. Die Umstrukturierung soll für den „central agent" die Möglichkeit, kollidierende Handlungsspielräume der Unternehmungsmitglieder durch die transaktionskostenminimale „Anweisung" zu determinieren, zurückgewinnen. Indem jegliche Begrenzung des Handlungsspielraumes des „central agent" als Quelle von Transaktionskosten betrachtet wird, wird konsequenterweise auch die Partizipation an seinen Rechten (property rights) als Quelle von Effezienzverminderungen betrachtet.[30] Es ist daher nicht verwunderlich, daß die Vertreter des Transaktionskostenansatzes die Effizienzsicherung der Unternehmung stets als Problem der Erhaltung der Durchsetzungsfähigkeit des „central agent", nicht aber als Problem der Beteiligung von Unternehmungsmitgliedern an seinen Entscheidungen betrachten. Mit diesem Problem wollen wir uns abschließend beschäftigen.

4. Arbeitnehmerpartizipation aus transaktionskostentheoretischer Sicht

Wendet man das neoklassische Idealmodell des vollkommenen Marktes auf die Arbeitsbeziehung an, ist das Problem der Partizipationsforderung der Arbeitnehmer nicht relevant: Jeder Arbeitnehmer kann – sofern noch keine Gleichgewichtssituation entstanden ist – bei Unzufriedenheit mit den Forderungen und Leistungszusagen des Arbeitgebers in eine ihn besserstellende konkurrierende Arbeitsbeziehung überwechseln. Die Williamsonsche Analyse der Ursachen des Abweichens vom Idealmodell zeigt jedoch, daß dieses „Abwanderungskonstrukt" wenig Realitätsgehalt besitzt.

Reale Arbeitsmärkte sind durch eingeschränkte Abwanderungsmöglichkeiten charakterisiert und im allgemeinen werden Arbeitnehmer nicht Beschäftigungen finden, die genau ihren Nutzenvorstellungen entsprechen. In dieser Situation nicht-übereinstimmender Forderungen und Leistungszusagen von Arbeitgebern und Arbeitnehmern sind folgende Reaktionsmöglichkeiten denkbar: 1. Die Arbeitnehmer verzichten auf eine Absicherung ihrer Interessen und akzeptieren die konfligierenden Forderungen und Leistungszusagen des Arbeitgebers, d. h. sie passen sich ohne jeglichen Determinierungsversuch an.

2. Die Arbeitnehmer verhalten sich opportunistisch, um in den Grenzen schwer kontrollierbarer Handlungsspielräume ihre Eigeninteressen zumindest teilweise zu realisieren. 3. Die Arbeitnehmer bauen gewerkschaftliche Gegenmacht bzw. Rahmenbedingungen für „collective voice" im Sinne Hirschmanns auf, um ihre nicht erfüllten Forderungen und überbeanspruchten Leistungszusagen gegen die konfligierenden Forderungen und Leistungszusagen des Arbeitgebers abzusichern. Die erste Alternative ist aus transaktionstheoretischer Sicht die günstigste, da hier keine Transaktionskosten der Anpassung der Arbeitnehmerinteressen an das Arbeitgeberinteresse entstehen. Die zweite Alternative stellt den Schwerpunkt der Analysen von Williamson und Alchian und Demsetz dar und wirft die Frage nach der transaktionskostenminimalen Determinierung von Arbeitnehmeropportunismus auf. Gemäß den Grundannahmen des Transaktionskostenansatzes überrascht es nicht, daß jede Form von Gegenmacht oder „voice" als Mittel der Determinierung konfligierender Interessen des Arbeitgebers als eine Gefährdung der von diesem formulierten „Unternehmungseffizienz" betrachtet wird. Hinsichtlich der Wirkung von Arbeitnehmerpartizipation gilt dann auch konsequenterweise: „Grundsätzlich gilt, daß Partizipation eine ineffiziente Anreizstruktur zur Folge hat."[31] Denn die Besitzer des Eigenkapitals bzw. ihre Vertreter erleiden einen beträchtlichen Machtverlust, der ihren Handlungsspielraum in Hinblick auf die Bestimmung der Unternehmungsziele, die Gestaltung des Produktionsprozesses oder die Zusammensetzung der „Produktionsteams" einengt. Da sich die Partizipation nicht nur auf eine Umgestaltung des Prozesses der Wertschöpfungserzielung, sondern auch auf eine Wertschöpfungsumverteilung richtet, sinken die Erträge der Eigentümer. „Dauerhaft gesenkte Kapitalerträge werden wahrscheinlich die Investitions- und Innovationsaktivitäten hemmen, so daß die partizipative Unternehmung im besten Fall weniger dynamisch und weniger produktiv als die traditionelle kapitalistische Unternehmungskooperation sein wird."[32] Es ist nicht verwunderlich, daß die Transaktionskostentheorie und hier im engeren Sinne der Property Rights-Ansatz die vorzuziehende Lösung des Problems der Sicherung von Arbeitnehmerinteressen im Ausbau differenzierter Arbeitsmärkte sieht, die durch konkurrierende Systeme von Arbeitsbeziehungen mit unterschiedlichen trade-off Angeboten von monetären und nicht-monetären Leistungszusagen des Arbeitge-

bers charakterisiert sind. In geradezu extremer Weise bringt dies Gallaway[33] zum Ausdruck, der in der Abwanderung von Arbeitnehmern aus sie nicht zufriedenstellende Arbeitsbeziehungen in konkurrierende Arbeitsbeziehungen die optimale Form der demokratischen Beteiligung an Arbeitgeberzielsetzungsprozessen sieht: „This is certainly worker participation in decisions that affect their lives; worker participation, incidentally that does not carry with it all the disruptive economic consequences that attend the more obvious forms of worker control over enterprise decision making that we have been discussing."[34] Gallaway übersieht den von Hirschman in ähnlichem Zusammenhang geäußerten Einwand, daß „voting with one's feet" aufgrund unzutreffender, sich nicht erfüllender Erwartungen lediglich eine ziellose Wanderungsbewegung zwischen den Arbeitsmärkten auslöst und darüber hinaus die Arbeitgeber nicht über die Ursachen der Unzufriedenheit informiert. Des weiteren ist darauf hinzuweisen, daß die Transaktionskostentheorie die produktiven Wirkungen einer kanalisierten partizipativen Konfliktaustragung unter den realen Bedingungen begrenzter Abwanderungsmöglichkeiten weitgehend unberücksichtigt läßt. Gerade die angloamerikanische Industrial Relations-Forschung zeigt aber, daß in den Ländern, in denen keine bzw. nur rudimentäre gesetzliche Mindestregelungen der Arbeitnehmerpartizipation bestehen, Streikhäufigkeit und Streikdauer besonders hoch sind. Dem weiteren Argument, daß Mitbestimmung in den westlichen Ländern nicht auf freiwilligen Vereinbarungen zwischen den Austauschpartnern des Arbeitsmarktes beruht, sondern durch staatliche Gesetze erzwungen ist, kann erstens entgegnet werden, daß eine Fülle von Modellen freiwilliger Partizipation in westlichen Ländern realisiert worden ist, die über die gesetzlichen Rahmenregelungen hinausgehen, und zweitens, daß zumindest die Frage zu untersuchen wäre, ob der Staat bei der Realisation von Mitbestimmungsmodellen unter dem Einfluß der Arbeitsmarktparteien und unter Abwägung ihrer kollidierenden Interessen die Funktion eines transaktionskostenminimierenden „conflict agent" übernommen hat.

Der transaktionskostentheoretischen These, daß die Partizipation die Möglichkeit opportunistischen Handelns der Arbeitnehmer verstärkt, transaktionskostenintensive Auseinandersetzungen in der Arbeitsbeziehung fördert und aufgrund veränderter Anreizstrukturen für Anteilseigner letztlich zum Effizienzverlust der Unternehmung führt, steht die These gegenüber, daß Partizipation zu kooperativem, kompromißorientierten Handeln führt und durch eine kanalisierte Konfliktaustragung transaktionskostenintensive Auseinandersetzungen in der Arbeitsbeziehung reduziert, wodurch die Aussagen über die negativen Wirkungen für die Anteilseigner-Anreize relativiert werden.

Kehren wir zu unserer Ausgangsüberlegung der permanten Inkorporation von Marktaustauschbeziehungen zu internen Beziehungen durch Großunternehmungen zurück, stellt sich die Frage, ob nicht innerhalb eines liberal-demokratischen Staatswesens die dadurch eingeschränkte exit-Option durch eine entsprechende Vermehrung der voice-Option auszugleichen wäre, um auf diese Weise Chancen der Gleichgewichtserzielung von Forderungen und Leistungszusagen wiederzugewinnen. Während der Transaktionskostenansatz in der voice-Alternative lediglich ein Instrument der Absicherung von opportunistischer Interessenverfolgung der Mitarbeiter sieht und in ihr eine Ursache des „Leistungsversagens" von Unternehmungen vermutet, zeigt die Equity-Theorie, daß fehlende Möglichkeiten der Absicherung von Interessen der Austauschpartner eine Reduktion der Leistungszusagen auslösen, also ebenfalls zum „Leistungsversagen" der Unternehmung führen können.

Die Verbesserung der voice-Option ist dabei nicht nur unter dem Gesichtspunkt der Wirkungen auf die ökonomische Effizienz der Austauschbeziehungen, sondern auch unter dem Gesichtspunkt der Erfüllung demokratischer Grundwerte im Unternehmungssektor zu beurteilen. Auf diese Fragen gibt Dlugos, der sich zu diesem Problemkreis mehrfach geäußert hat, folgende Antwort: „Mitbestimmung ist einerseits ein Instrument zur Verbesserung der wirtschaftlichen und sozialen Unternehmungseffizienz aus der Sicht der Arbeitnehmer..., andererseits ein Instrument zur Sicherung wechselseitiger konstruktiver Zusammenarbeit und pressionsbegrenzender Konflikthandhabung. Wenn wahrscheinlich auch hieraus Effizienzvorteile sowohl für die Kontrakteinnahmen-Empfänger als auch für die Residualeinnahmen-Empfänger resultieren, so wäre Mitbestimmung unvollständig beurteilt, solange neben den Auswirkungen auf die Unternehmungseffizienz nicht auch der Beitrag der Mitbestimmung zur Sicherung des sozialen Friedens in den Unternehmungen und in der Gesellschaft berücksichtigt werden würde."[35] Diese Aussage soll als Beleg unserer abschließenden These dienen, daß bei zunehmender Einschränkung der exit-Option die Übertragung von Mitbestimmungs-Property Rights auf die Mitarbeiter notwendig wird, wenn die soziale und ökonomische Unternehmungseffizienz gesichert werden soll.

Anmerkungen

1 Vgl. Hlavacek/Dovey/Biondo 1983.
2 Zu Kriterien des demokratischen Staates vgl. Cohen 1973.
3 Zu Begründungsproblemen einer interessenpluralistischen Unternehmungsverfassung vgl. Steinmann 1969.
4 Zum Konzept der New Institutional Economics: McGuiness 1983, S. 180ff.; Williamson 1975, S. 1ff.
5 Als Gründungsväter dieser Forschungsrichtung gelten A. Alchian und H. Demsetz sowie E. G. Furubotn und S. Pejovich. Forschungsziel der Property Rights Theorie ist die Einbeziehung „sozialer Institutionen" wie Verfügungs-, Handlungs- oder Eigentumsrechte in die neoklassische Theorie. Die „Property Rights" an Wirtschaftsgütern werden als bestimmende Faktoren wirtschaftlichen Handelns betrachtet. Vgl. hierzu auch Schüller 1983.
6 Vgl. hierzu Dlugos 1977, 1982, 1984.
7 Coase 1937, 1956.
8 Commons 1924.

[9] Coase 1956, S. 333 f.
[10] Bössmann 1983, S. 106.
[11] Bössmann 1983, S. 106.
[12] So bezeichnet Williamson (1975) die alternativen bzw. substitutiven Regelungsformen wirtschaftlichen Handelns als „Markets und Hierarchies".
[13] Vgl. hierzu auch Leibensteins „Theorie der X-Effizienz", die Ineffizienzen der Unternehmung auf die Verfolgung von Eigeninteressen im Rahmen von Handlungsspielräumen der Unternehmungsmitglieder zurückführt.
[14] Zu den Grundwerten liberal-demokratischer Systeme vgl. Schwan 1981.
[15] Vgl. Gallaway 1978.
[16] Vgl. Hirschman 1974.
[17] Alchian/Demsetz 1972. – Zur Kritik vgl. Nutzinger 1978.
[18] Alchian/Demsetz 1972, S. 777.
[19] Alchian/Demsetz 1972, S. 777.
[20] Vgl. Becker 1985, S. 29.
[21] Vgl. Nutzinger 1978, S. 47.
[22] Nutzinger 1978, S. 53.
[23] Alchian/Demsetz 1977, S. 777.
[24] Alchian/Demsetz 1977, S. 778.
[25] Zur Interpretation der Konflikthandhabung als Determinierungsprozeß vgl. Dlugos 1974, 1977.
[26] Vgl. Dlugos 1981.
[27] Williamson 1975, S. 26.
[28] Diese Variablen faßt Williamson (1975) im sogenannten Organizational Failures Framework zusammen, mit dem er das Leistungsversagen von Märkten und Hierarchien erklärt. Vgl. auch Willmann 1983.
[29] Vgl. Williamson 1975, S. 40.
[30] Gallaway 1978 und Furubotn 1982.
[31] Furubotn 1982, S. 206.
[32] Furubotn 1982, S. 205 f.
[33] Vgl. Gallaway 1978.
[34] Gallaway 1978, S. 188.
[35] Dlugos 1981, S. 18.

Literatur

Alchian, A. A. / Demsetz, H. (1972): Production, Information Costs and Economic Organizations. In: *American Economic Review* 62, S. 177 ff.

Backhaus, J. / Eger, T. / Nutzinger, H. G. (Hrsg.) (1978): *Partizipation in Betrieb und Gesellschaft.* Frankfurt/M., New York.

Backhaus, J. / Nutzinger, H. G. (Hrsg.) (1982): *Eigentumsrechte und Partizipation.* Frankfurt/M.

Becker, H. (1985): *Transaktionskostentheoretische Interpretation interner Arbeitsmärkte.* Berlin.

Bössmann, E. (1983): Unternehmungen, Märkte, Transaktionskosten: Die Koordination ökonomischer Aktivitäten. In: *Wirtschaftswissenschaftliches Studium* 12, S. 105 ff.

Coase, R. (1937): The Nature of the Firm: In: *Economica* 4, S. 386–405. Wiederabdruck 1956. In: Stigler, G. J. / Boulding, K. E. (Hrsg.), *Reading in Price Theory*. London, S. 331 ff.
Cohen, C. (1973): *Democracy*. Toronto.
Commons, J. R. (1924): *Legal Foundations of Capitalism*. New York.
De Alessi, L. (1983): Property Rights, Transaction Costs, and X-Efficiency. An Essay in Economic Theory. In: *American Economic Review* 73, S. 69 ff.
Demsetz, H. (1967): Toward a Theory of Property Rights. In: *American Economic Review*, 57, S. 347 ff.
Dlugos, G. (1974): Unternehmungspolitik als betriebswirtschaftlich-politische Teildisziplin. In: Wild, J. (Hrsg.), Berlin, S. 39 ff.
Dlugos, G. (1977): Gesellschaftspolitische Implikationen unternehmungsinterner Konflikthandhabung. In: *Die Betriebswirtschaft* 37, S. 465 ff.
Dlugos, G. (1981): Die Unternehmungseffizienz im Interessenkonflikt der Unternehmungsmitglieder. In: Säcker, F. J. / Zander, E. (Hrsg.), S. 1–18.
Dlugos, G. (1982): Beziehungen zwischen Wertwandel, Konflikt und Konflikthandhabung im Unternehmungssektor. In: Stachowiak, H. (Hrsg.), S. 293 ff.
Dlugos, G. (1984): Die Lehre von der Unternehmungspolitik – eine vergleichende Analyse der Konzeptionen. In: *Die Betriebswirtschaft* 44, S. 287 ff.
Dlugos, G. / Weiermair, K. (Hrsg.) (1981): *Management under Differing Value Systems*. Berlin, New York.
Francis A. / Turk, J. / Willman, P. (Hrsg.) (1983): *Power, Efficiency and Institutions*. A Critical Appraisal of the „Markets and Hierarchies" Paradigm. London.
Furubotn, E. G. (1982): Information, organisatorische Struktur und die möglichen Vorteile der Mitbestimmung. In: Backhaus, J. / Nutzinger, H. G. (Hrsg.), S. 203 ff.
Furubotn, E. G. / Pejovich, S. (1974): *The Economics of Property Rights*. Cambridge, Mass.
Gallaway, L. (1978): The Economic Consequences of Codetermination on Employment and Income Distribution. In: Pejovich, S. (Hrsg.), S. 169 ff.
Hirschman, A. O. (1974): *Abwanderung und Widerspruch*. Tübingen.
Hlavacek, J. D. / Dovey, B. M. / Biondo, J. M. (1983): Erfolge mit Joint Ventures. In: *Harvard Manager*, S. 83 ff.
Jensen, M. C. / Meckling, W. H. (1976): Theory of the Firm: Managerial Behavior, Agency Costs and Ownership Structure. In: *Journal of Financial Economics*, S. 305 ff.
Leibenstein, H. (1966). X-Efficiency Versus Allocative Efficiency. In. *American Economic Review* 56, S. 392 ff.
Linsenbühler, G. (1984): Theorie der X-Effizienz. In: *Wirtschaftswissenschaftliches Studium* 8, S. 424 ff.
McGuiness, T. (1983): Markets and Hierarchies: A Suitable Framework for an Evaluation of Organizational Change? In: Francis, A. / Turk, J. / Willman, P. (Hrsg.), S. 180 ff.
Nutzinger, H. G. (1978): The Firm as a Social Institution: The Failure of the Contractarian Viewpoint. In: Backhaus, J. / Eger, T. / Nutzinger, H. G. (Hrsg.), S. 45 ff.
Nutzinger, H. G. (1982): Die ökonomische Theorie der Eigentumsrechte – ein neues Problem in den Sozialwissenschaften? In: Backhaus, J. / Nutzinger, H. G. (Hrsg.), S. 43 ff.
Pejovich, S. (Hrsg.) (1978): *The Codetermination Movement in the West*. Lexington, Ma., Toronto.
Perrow, C. (1981): Markets, Hierarchies and Hegemony. In: Van de Ven, A. H. / Joyce, W. F. (Hrsg.), S. 371 ff.

Säcker, F. J. / Zander, E. (Hrsg.) (1981): *Mitbestimmung und Effizienz*. Stuttgart.
Schüller, A. (1983): Property Rights, Theorie der Firma und wettbewerbliches Marktsystem. In: Schüller, A. (Hrsg.), S. 145 ff.
Schüller, A. (Hrsg.) (1983): *Property Rights und ökonomische Theorie*. München.
Schwan, A. (1981): Fundamental Values of Western Democracies. In: Dlugos, G./Weiermair, K. (Hrsg.), S. 3 ff.
Stachowiak, H. (Hrsg.) (1982): *Bedürfnisse, Werte und Normen im Wandel. Bd. II, Methoden und Analysen*. München.
Steinmann, H. (1969): *Das Großunternehmen im Interessenkonflikt*. Stuttgart.
Van de Ven, A. H. / Joyce, W. F. (Hrsg.) (1981): *Perspectives on Organization Design and Behavior*. New York etc.
Wild, J. (Hrsg.) (1974): *Unternehmungsführung. Festschrift für Erich Kosiol zu seinem 75. Geburtstag*. Berlin.
Williamson, O. E. (1975): *Markets and Hierarchies: Analysis and Antitrust Implications*. London.
Williamson, O. E. (1979): Transactions-Cost-Economics: The Governance of Contractual Relations. In: *The Journal of Law and Economics* 22, S. 233 ff.
Williamson, O. E. / Wachter, M. L. / Harris, J. E. (1975): Understanding the Employment Relation: The Analysis of Idiosyncratic Exchange. In: *The Bell Journal of Economics* 6, S. 250 ff.
Willman, P. (1983): The Organizational Failures Framework and Industrial Sociology. In: Francis, A. / Turk, J. / Willman, R. (Hrsg.), S. 117 ff.

Control of Industrial Democracy Through Social Reporting

Bikki Jaggi

Abstract

This paper examines the role of social reports within the framework of industrial democracy. After explaining the concept of industrial democracy as understood in this paper, part 1 reviews the objectives and forms of industrial democracy and identifies the information needs of participation bodies concerned with operationalization of this concept. In the second part, corporate social responsibility and the underlying principles on which it is based, are critically reviewed. The third part presents the framework for social reporting and discusses problems and issues involved in measuring and processing social information.

1. Framework of Industrial Democracy for Social Reporting

1.1. Concept and Objectives of Industrial Democracy

The nature of industrial democracy is understood differently in different countries. In democratic countries this concept is generally understood in terms of workers' participation in the management process. The interpretation of workers' participation, however, will be influenced by several factors, the most important being the participation objectives.

In the early stages of the development of industrial democracy, labor unions played an important role in the participation process and the participation objectives to a great extent were molded by the union goals. Later on, unions' support for workers' participation started declining. However, despite this decline, employers continued encouraging workers' participation. Employers' motivation for the participative process was derived from the notion of increased productivity by gaining workers' confidence and enhancing their morale. As a consequence, a change in the objectives for workers' participation became evident.

The major objective for the participative process has been described as industrial peace through harmonious relations between management and workers[1]. In pursuit of this goal, the participative process serves as a means of pacifying the conflict between managers' desire for efficiency and workers' desires to enhance their security and welfare.

1.2. Forms of Industrial Democracy

The development of workers' participation at various levels progressed at different rates among democratic countries. At the plant level, a steady progress has been witnessed by almost all countries. At the board level, the progress has not been uniform among various countries. Consequently, there are variations in the arrangement and degree of participation, and the configuration of participative bodies differs from country to country. We will briefly review the important approaches to identify the social information needs of participative bodies.

1.2.1. Scandinavian Approach

The form of workers' participation in Scandinavian countries is greatly influenced by the cooperative efforts of employers and workers in determining the agreements. The works councils were first established in Sweden, Denmark and Norway in the mid and late forties. These councils have management as well as workers' representatives, and they are entitled to commercial information. In 1971, the works councils in Denmark received substantial powers of co-determination in personnel matters and of coinfluence. For a variety of reasons, industrial calm existed in these countries for a long time and there was no substantial change in the works councils' functions. However, in 1971 workers' representation on Swedish Company board was demanded[2]. In 1973, a law was enacted which provided workers' representation on the company boards; one representative from each class of workers – manual and white collar – were added on the boards. New legislation in Norway also provided for two-tier boards. As a result of these developments, information needs of the participative bodies changed.

1.2.2. The West German Approach

In West Germany, the concept of industrial democracy can be traced back as far as 1848, when works councils were proposed by the constitutional assembly at Frankfurt. However, the most important developments took place in 1951 and 1952, which were signified by the Co-determination Act for Coal and Steel 1951, and the Works Councils Act 1952. The latter was amended in 1972 to give greater powers to works councils.

In West Germany, the concept of two-tier board system is well accepted. The supervisory board, which includes workers' representatives, appoints the members of the management board, and supervises their policy formulations and implementations. The supervisory boards of the companies in the coal and steel producing industry have an equal number of shareholder and employee representatives.

In addition to employee representation at the board level, the works council act stipulates that companies with twenty or more employees should establish a company works council. All employees have a vote in the election of works councils. The 1952/72 Act prohibits the deviation of employers and employees from all laws, regulations, and collective agreements. The councils do, however, take part in setting rules on work hours, hearing of dismissal appeals, work allocation, etc. The important aspect of works councils with regard to this presentation relates to their right to information and co-determination in certain matters affecting the business so that they can play an important role in the decision making process.

1.2.3. Approaches in Other European Countries

In Netherlands, works councils are well accepted by the firms, but they are primarily consultative bodies. They, however, have a greater say on social and personnel matters which are not covered by collective bargaining. In 1970, a two-tier management structure has also been introduced in Netherlands. The supervisory boards members may be nominated by the shareholders, the works councils or by the board itself. However, they must be accepted by the board subject to a right of veto by either the shareholders or the works councils.

The works councils are also required by French firms with more than 50 employees. The nature of works councils in France is largely consulative. These councils are, however, entitled to reports on the company's commercial plans and performance. The two-tier board system is not practiced by French companies. But the works councils may nominate two members to attend board meetings of the Joint Stocks companies as observers. They are not the legal members and have no vote.

In Italy works councils have been in existence since 1966. These works councils are required in all firms with more than 40 employees. The main function of Italian Works Councils is to maintain normal relations between workers and managers. The councils may, however, make representations on the correct observance of safety, health and welfare laws and collective agreements. The Italian councils have a limited access to information, they are entitled to information on personnel and social matters only.

1.3. Information Needs for Industrial Democracy

The success and effectiveness of industrial democracy to a great extent will depend upon the availability of information to works councils and other participative bodies. Since the nature of participative bodies differs with countries, there is no consistency in the rights of these bodies to different types of information. Consequently, depending upon the quality and quantity of information provided to them their success differs. An analysis of the success of participative bodies in different countries has provided evidence to the difference in their success rate.

In the case of France, co-determination has not been able to create wide enough interest in the broad masses of workers that a noticeable effect can be discovered[3]. The Scandinavian and German experiences are considered to be successful to some extent. However, questions have been raised whether the participative system accomplishes the objective of efficiency and promotes the development of workers' positive attitudes.

In view of the differences in objectives, organizational structure, and powers of the participative bodies, there can be no universal agreement on their organizational efficiency. The IDE study has examined this issue with regard to several European countries[4]. The results indicate that in the case of Northern countries, power-sharing, cooperation, and positive relations with supervisors were highly valued. The study, however, did not find conclusive evidence with regard to democratic countries.

Whatever the nature, objectives or forms of participatory bodies, industrial democracy requires that relevant and adequate information is provided to these bodies. An important component of this information will relate to the firm's social performance. It is important that participative bodies are provided with detailed information on social inputs and outputs, which will provide the basis for judgment on the firm's social performance. Before we discuss the format of social reports, we will examine the rationale and basis for corporate social responsibility.

2. Rationale for Corporate Social Performance

Though corporate social responsibility has been receiving wide recognition in European countries, its utility is still being debated in the United States. Whether corporate social responsibility is well grounded will depend upon the support provided by the theoretical principles. We will examine the rationale for corporate social responsibility on the basis of four principles – economic, social contract, quality of life and ethical[5].

2.1. Corporate Social Performance Based on Economic Principle

The liberatarian economists who advocate a total laissez faire policy, perceive the market rather than any regulatory body as the ultimate judge and guarantor of social freedom. On the other extreme, the radical economists, who believe in a decentralized and participative system in which workers become partners in running corporations are highly critical of contemporary capitalism and the role of market in determining social values. In between these extrems, are the social and institutional economists.

The social economists see a strong relationship between social and economic systems. John Maurice Clark[6], who was among the earliest economists recognized the existence of social costs and viewed economics as a theory of efficiency. He divided efficiency into social and private efficiency, whereby social efficiency was referred to as the production of social values and private efficiency as the production of marketable values. Clark urged businesses to assume social responsibility for overhead costs which were within the framework of social efficiency[7]. His analysis supported the thesis that these aspects of corporations which contribute to a betterment of standard of living, are likely to generate admiration and respect, and the negative aspects will lead to society's distrust resulting in dissatisfaction, hostility, and ultimately to the questioning of the corporate role in society.

The institutional economists, who have been concerned about the interaction between corporations and society, consider conventional economics largely limited to the study of maximizing behavior, which makes it irrelevant for solving the prevailing issues. In the pre-1939 period, Thorstein Veblen[8] and other institutional economists basically rejected the orthodox Marshallian economics. Now, the institutionalists view economics as the study of complex institutions concerned with meeting the material needs of human race and they study the impact of various social disciplines on the economic behavior of individuals and corporations.

The views of social and institutional economists provide stront support to the concept that corporate social responsibility is well grounded in economic principles. These principles determine the role of corporations in the society and define the scope and nature of corporate activities.

2.2. Corporate Social Performance Based on Social Contract Principle

The social contract argument for corporate social responsibility surfaced in several discussions, but it was formalized by Ramanathan in 1976[9]. This argument is based on the notion that business firms do not exist in a vacuum, instead they are a part of society, which creates and supports them. Furthermore, corporations owe their existence to laws which have been developed by society. Thus, society's support for the existence of business may be dependent upon their performance which is considered socially desirable. An implicit assumption in these arguments is that there is a contract between businesses and society which requires socially desirable behavior from firms in return for rewards. If businesses engage in socially undesirable behavior, society may be forced to take steps to penalize such businesses. The steps may include boycott of their products and services, modification of existing laws or development of new laws to restrict activities of such businesses.

The contract argument requires development of certain criteria which can be used for evaluating corporate social performance to judge whether businesses' social behavior meets society's expectations. Social scientists have attempted to develop social goals, which can be considered analogous to economic indicators. On the basis of the macro level criteria, micro level criteria applicable to a specific firm can be developed and adopted for social reporting. Unfortunately, despite sustained efforts, there has been no consensus of opinion with regard to social goals. In the absence of macro level social goals, the alternative is to develop social goals at the micro level directly. Firms should establish their own social goals depending upon the nature of their business and prepare social reports to show the degree of accomplishment of these goals. This approach will, however, need certain guidelines so that a comparative analysis can be made across different firms with regard to their social performance. Therefore, a general framework for social goals and social reporting would be desirable.

2.3. Social Reporting Based on the Quality of Life Argument

The corporate social responsibility is also supported on the basis of the quality of life argument. The social costs of economic development which have been increasing at staggering proportions, started affecting different aspects of the quality of life. The increase in social costs and realization of quality of life issues resulted in a shift of society's attitude toward industrializiation. This shift has especially been caused by the power of labor unions, protection of physical environments in the form of air and water pollution and impetus to the movement of social justice.

As a result of this shift, society started perceiving businesses being responsible for social ills, and attempting to maximize profit by exploiting environmental and social systems. These perceptions and attitudes forced society to re-evaluate their expectations from businesses. It was realized that increased economic development at all costs would not be desirable. Only industrial development which does not reduce the quality of life should be encouraged.

2.4. Corporate Social Performance Based on Ethical Principles

The ethical principles also provide support to the expectation of good social performance from corporations. It is believed that corporations should be considered as corporate citizens and they should be expected to be good corporate citizens. The social responsibility advocates argue that businesses ought to engage in social responsibilities that go beyond compliance with law and include measures which provide evidence for corporations to be good citizens. To prove their good intentions and behavior, corporations should especially be involved in correcting some of the social ills of the society. The social responsibility school maintains that the unethical behavior of corporations should not be tolerated.

The constructionism school, however, criticizes the notion of corporate social responsibility and advocates that profit maximization is the only acceptable objective of business corporations. Milton Friedman, a strong opponent of corporate social responsibility, maintains that businesses serve society best when they restrict their activities to profit maximization and participate in social activities only to the extent that they are necessary to their own well being[10]. Despite this criticism, the general feeling is that corporations' unethical behavior will be detrimental to them. Thus, the concept of good citizenship has received wide recognition.

3. Social Reporting as a Tool for Control of Industrial Democracy

A proper functioning of industrial democracy and evaluation of corporate social responsibility performance requires that corporate performance, especially social performance, is continuously monitored and evaluated. In addition to financial reports, accruate and timely social reports are prepared to provide relevant social information to users. There is, however, no consensus of opinion as to how corporate activities with regard to the performance of social responsibility can be measured and what reporting format should be used. Several attempts have been made to develop suitable formats. Important approaches to social reporting will be briefly reviewed and measurement problems relating to the corporate social performance will be presented.

3.1. Nature of Social Reporting

The nature of social reporting, which is also known as social accounting, has been understood differently in the literature. David Linowes defined it as an application of accounting in the field of social sciences[11]. According to Mobley, socio-economic accounting refers to the "ordering, measuring and analysis of the social and economic consequences of governmental and enterpreneurial behavior"[12]. Whatever the definition, the objective of social reporting is to measure the impact of corporate activities on the quality of life, and disclose information relating to these activities. Thus, the social reports in general are expected to identify, measure and evaluate those aspects of corporate activities which are essential to maintain adequate quality of life for all associated with the firm.

3.2. Social Reporting Formats

An important reason for the absence of a generally accepted social reporting format probably lies in the fact that a theoretical framework has not been developed so far. A general framework is desirable to identify users of social reports and crystalize the objectives and principles needed for the preparation of these reports.

The business and accounting literature in German as well as the English language suggests several formats. The suggested formats can be grouped into four categories – descriptive-narrative approach, operating statement format approach, comprehensive approach, and goal-oriented approach. Each of these approaches has positive aspects as well as weaknesses. We will briefly evaluate these approaches and also examine whether suggested formats are capable of providing relevant social information to interested individuals and/or institutions.

3.2.1. Descriptive-Narrative Approach

The most common form of social reporting has so far been in the nature of narrative description of social activities undertaken by the firms. The firms have attempted to highlight in a descriptive form the positive aspects of these activities, and no special format is followed in this approach. A review of annual reports, however, indicates that some firms use the President's letter to highlight their social responsibility-related activities and others provide this information in the general discussion of business. Some firms also use special reports showing the impact of their social performance-related activities. An example of such a format is provided by the Scovill Manufacturing Company in the United States.

The narrative description of social reporting cannot be considered a useful format for social reporting. The major deficiency of this format lies in its inability to provide the basis for evaluation of social performance by the firm. As mentioned above, this type of social reporting presents the positive aspects only and the negative aspects of corporate activities on the social and physical environments are ignored. Therefore, such a report will not serve any useful purpose for evaluating a firm's social performance. A realistic appraisal of corporate social performance should include positive as well as negative impacts of its activities.

Despite deficiencies and weaknesses inherent in the narrative description of the firms' activities, this format cannot be ignored. The reporting in this format at least exhibits a degree of management's concern for cosial responsibility. Furthermore, this approach does not need any special accounting systems to keep track of the activities and thus, social reporting becomes simple and easy. Because of the non-availability of a generally accepted social reporting format, several difficulties are encountered in measuring the social impact of corporate activities. Until better measurement techniques become available, the descriptive narrative approach can be used.

3.2.2. Operating Statement Format

Another important approach which attracted several researchers' attention can be described as the operation statement format approach. According to this approach, the firm is required to present positive as well as negative aspects of its activities. The positive aspects are broadly termed as "social benefits" and negative aspects as "social costs". Similar to an operating statement, net "social contribution" can be determined by taking the difference between social benefits and social costs. The main problem associated with this approach relates to the measurement of social costs and social benefits. In view of the measurement problems, this format for social reporting has not found favor with many firms.

3.2.3. A Comprehensive Approach

Another important approach which was developed and used by Abt Associates[13], is based on the concept of annual statements consisting of an income statement and a balance sheet. The objective of this approach is to determine the full impact of corporate activities on different constitutents. Because of the measurement problems, this approach has not been adopted by other companies.

3.2.4. Goal-Oriented Approach

This approach was discussed by US firms in early 1970s, but it was not fully accepted in the United States. Lately, this approach has found favor with German and other European firms. According to this approach, annual reports first describe the goals chosen by the firm depending upton the nature of its business and social demands of the society. Then, activities which are undertaken in pursuit of these goals, are enumerated and analyzed. Where possible, description of these activities is supported by data and graphs.

Deutsche Shell's annual report provides the best illustration of this approach[14]. Realizing that changes in the social environment require an analogous change in the goals of the firm, the management of Deutsche Shell recognized the need for different goals. In addition to achieving a reasonable return on investment, the following goals received their attention: 1. Meeting consumer's needs as determined by the market conditions. 2. Development of new processes and products. 3. Consideration of employee interest, and 4. Regard for public concern. The major goals are divided into subgoals. The first part of the report contains discussion of these subgoals as well as description of the activities in pursuit of these goals.

A critical review of this approach would however indicate that its major emphasis is to highlight the fact that the major portion of the firm's resources are being devoted to its employees in the form of salaries and other benefits. Thus, the report is basically employee oriented, and its major objective is to provide information to participatory bodies showing the firm's concern for its employees. Additionally, the report points toward safety of its products. The firm's concern for environment is exhibited only on a minimal base.

3.3. Measurement of Social Performance

The progress for social reporting to a great extent will depend upon our capability to measure social performance of firms in terms of social costs and social benefits. Despite several attempts, no well accepted measurement principles and techniques have been developed so far. Efforts are underway to come to a general consensus for the solution of social performance measurement problems. The following areas of social performance measurement are identified to which efforts can be directed[15]:

- Identification of the set of activities that have social relevance,
- Extent of the efforts being expended in each of the identified socially relevant activities,
- Measurement of immediate outputs of social actions and processes, and
- Evaluation of the worth of the output in spite of the lack and difficulty of measurement values in most cases.

One way to identify the origins of social cost and social benefits is to determine how detriments and contributions occur. Once the activities that give rise to social costs and benefits are determined and particular detriments or contributions are identified, the effects on people can be calculated.

4. Conclusion

The above presentation demonstrates that proper social reporting is critical for control of industrial democracy. Extensive research work is needed to find solutions to the measurement and reporting problems.

5. Summary

The paper examines the role of social reports within the framework of industrial democracy. The major objective of industrial democracy, which is understood as a participative process in the democratic countries, is to achieve industrial peace through harmonious relations between management and workers. Depending upon the form, arrangement and degree of participation, the social information needs of the participative bodies will differ. In some countries, such as Germany, the participative process is evident from the plant through the board level, and the social information needs of the participative bodies are extensive. In other countries, such as France and the USA, the participative process has not yet received the wide acceptance, and therefore, the need for social information is not greatly felt. It can, however, be argued that the process and control of industrial democracy will to a great extent depend upon the availability of relevant, adequate, and timely social information.

The generation of social information by firms is justified on the ground that this information is needed to evaluate the social performance of these firms. The corporate social responsibility has been supported by the theoretical principles of economics, social contract, quality of life and ethics. Despite some criticism of corporate social responsibility, there is a general feeling that corporations should behave as good corporate citizens, and that their unethical behavior will prove to be detrimental to them.

Despite a general agreement that the success and control of industrial democracy require social information, the issue arises whether corporate social performance can be adequately and accurately measured and which form would be most suitable for social reporting. Unfortunately, the development of measurement techniques for corporate social performance are lagging behind. In view of the absence of generally accepted measurement techniques, there is no consensus with regard to the reporting format, The suggested reporting formats generally suffer from the weakness of proper measurement. Some of the suggested formats are: descriptive-narration of corporate social activities, operating statement, a comprehensive statement, and the goal-oriented statement. The goal-oriented approach has been used by several European firms, especially German firms. The Deutsche Shell's annual report is a good illustration of this approach. Despite its popularity with European firms, this approach does not fully solve the social reporting problems. The main emphasis of this approach is on employees, and the firm's for environment is exhibited on a minimal basis.

Additional research is needed to find solutions to the measurement problem and to develop the reporting format which will cover every aspect of corporate social responsibility.

Remarks

1 For objectives of industrial democracy, refer to International Research Group IDE 1981; Blumberg 1968; Macbeath 1973.
2 Macbeath 1973, p. 13.
3 Macbeath 1973, p. 10.
4 IDE 1981.
5 For detailed discussion of these principles refer to Belkaoui 1984.
6 Clark 1936.
7 Clark 1923.
8 For example, see Veblen 1912.
9 Ramanathan 1976, pp. 516–983.
10 Friedman 1970.
11 Linowes 1972.
12 Mobley 1970, pp. 762–768.

[13] Abt Associates, Inc. 1973.
[14] Deutsche Shell Company 1977. Also see Jaggi 1980, pp. 35–45.
[15] Freedman/Stagliano 1985, pp. 3–30.

Literature

Abt Associates, Inc. (1973): *Annual Report and Social Audit.* Belkaoui, A. (1984): Socio-Economic Accounting. Westport, Connecticut.

Blumberg, P. (1968): *Industrial Democracy.* London.

Clark, J. M. (1923): *Studies in the Economics of Overhead Costs.* Chicago.

Clark, J. M. (1936): *Preface to Social Economics.* New York.

Deutsche Shall Company (1977): *Annual Report.*

Freedman, M. / Stagliano, A. S. (1985): A Taxonomic Approach to Defining Industrial Social Costs. In: *Advances in Accounting* 2, pp. 3–30.

Friedman, M. (1970): Social Responsibility is to Increase Profit. In: *New York Times Magazine,* September 13.

International Research Group (1981): *Industrial Democracy in Europe: IDE.* Oxford.

Jaggi, B. (1980): An Analysis of Corporate Social Reporting in Germany. In: *International Journal of Accounting Education and Research*, pp. 35–45.

Linowes, D. F. (1972): *An Approach to Socio-Economic Accounting.* New York.

Macbeath, I. (1973): *The European Approach to Worker-Management Relationships.* New York, London.

Mobley, S. C. (1970): The Challenges of Socio-Economic Accounting. In: *The Accounting Review,* October, pp. 762–768.

Ramanathan, K. V. (1976): Toward a Theory of Corporate Social Accounting. In: *The Accounting Review,* July, pp. 516–983.

Veblen, Th. (1912): *The Theory of the Leisure Class.* New York.

Teil III
Länderspezifische Probleme – liberal-demokratische Gesellschaftssysteme

Partizipation in Unternehmungen – international vergleichende Analysen

Bernhard Wilpert

Abstract
Participation in Business Corporations –
International Comparative Analyses

The paper discusses the findings of seven large scale international comparative research studies on participation. Starting with a discussion of participation as an organization-theoretical concept, it reviews methodological approaches and findings of the research conducted by Hofstede (1980), Tannenbaum et al. (1974), Heller and Wilpert (1981), King and van de Vall (1978), IDE (1981), Maurice et al (1980), Crouch and Pizzorno (1978) and discusses them in terms of their differential scope in treating individual, organizational and societal factors.

1. Einleitung

Die Begrifflichkeit zur Beteiligung von Beschäftigten an Unternehmensentscheidungen gleicht weithin einem schwer durchdringbaren Dschungel. Dem haben auch diverse, um Präzision bemühte Versuche zur Begriffsklärung wenig Abbruch getan (vgl. hierzu Dachler/Wilpert 1978, 1980; Greenberg 1975; Lammers 1967; Walker 1975). Der Vielfalt verwendeter Terme – ebenso wie die vielfältige Verwendung einzelner Begriffe – entsprechen einer schier unübersehbaren Anzahl unterschiedlichster Forschungen der letzten zwei–drei Dekaden zum Thema Partizipation. Mag man mit Mulder (1971, S. 31) diese Veröffentlichungswelle auch als Indiz dafür werten, daß es sich bei der Partizipation um das „lebenswichtigste Organisationsproblem unserer Zeit" handle, so darf dennoch nicht übersehen werden, daß den Löwenanteil dieser Arbeiten ein durchaus begrenzter, lokaler Charakter auszeichnet. Die meisten Studien bleiben auf wenige Organisationen oder Unternehmungen nur eines nationalen Kontextes begrenzt. Systematische internationale Vergleiche sind rar, was wohl mit der Fülle und Komplexität sowohl theoretischer und methodologischer als auch organisatorischer Probleme solcher Vergleiche zusammenhängen dürfte (Jacob/Jacob 1984).

Immerhin sind in den letzten Jahren einige Arbeiten erschienen, die sich direkt oder indirekt der Partizipation in Unternehmungen international vergleichend widmen. Es verlockt daher, die wichtigsten dieser Bemühungen synoptisch im Hinblick auf ihren je unterschiedlichen Ansatz und ihre Erträge zu betrachten. Dies soll im folgenden nach einer grundsätzlicheren theoretischen Reflektion versucht werden.

2. Partizipation als organisationswissenschaftliches Konzept

Partizipation wird für die Zwecke dieses Beitrags verstanden als Beteiligung von Organisationsmitgliedern an Entscheidungen zum Zwecke der Rückbindung dieser Entscheidungen an die Interessen der Organisationsmitglieder. Der Finalitätsaspekt der Definition – Rückbindung an Interessen – grenzt dieses Begriffsverständnis ab von einer Beteiligung i. S. bloßer Präsenz der Organisationsmitglieder. Die im Unternehmensalltag realiter auffindbare Partizipation ist offensichtlich variabel und beeinflußt durch vielerlei Faktoren. Wenigstens vier grundlegende analytische Dimensionen lassen sich zu einem besseren Verständnis des Realphänomens Partizipation benennen (Dachler/Wilpert 1978):

- Sozial-/gesellschaftstheoretische Prämissen, welche die beteiligten Akteure leiten und ihre Ziele bzw. Interessen mit definieren. Mit Greenberg (1975) lassen sich wenigstens vier grundlegende Richtungen unterscheiden: Demokratietheorien, Sozialismustheorien, persönliche Wachstumstheorien und Produktivitäts- bzw. Effizienzorientierungen.
- Merkmale der Partizipationsformen. Hier kommen durchaus unterschiedliche Aspekte ins Spiel, etwa die Frage nach dem Grad der formalen, statutorischen Ausgestaltung von Partizipationsregeln und -strukturen im Gegensatz zur informellen, schriftlich nicht fixierten Partizipation; desgleichen die wichtige Unterscheidung indirekter, über Mandatsträger vermittelter und direkter, persönlicher Partizipation eines Organisationsmitglieds oder von Mitgliedergruppen (Lammers 1967). Hierher gehören auch der Zugang der Mitglieder zu Entscheidungsprozessen i. S. unterschiedlicher Informations- und Beeinflussungschancen des Entscheidungsprozesses (Heller 1971; IDE 1981; Wilpert 1977), die Merkmale der Entscheidung selbst (Inhalt, Relevanz, Komplexität) und nicht zuletzt deren soziale Reichweite i. S. der Einbeziehung unterschiedlicher Mitgliedergruppen in den Entscheidungsprozeß.
- Organisationale Kontextbedingungen sowohl des kulturellen, historischen und sozio-ökonomischen Umfeldes (etwa Rechts- und Wirtschaftsverfassung, Wirtschaftszyklen, technischer und wirtschaftlicher Entwicklungsstand) und des institutionellen Umfeldes (System der Arbeitsbeziehungen, Grundorientierungen der Sozialisationsinstanzen Familie, Schule, Gewerkschaften etc.). Hierzu wären auch Merkmale der Organisation selbst zu zählen (Größe, Technologie, Struktur, Kompetenzverteilung und Einstellungen der Belegschaft).

– Konsequenzen der Partizipation in mehrebenenanalytischer Perspektive: der individuellen Ebene (Sozialisationsergebnisse, Partizipationskompetenz), der organisationalen Ebene (betriebswirtschaftliche, soziale Folgen) und der gesellschaftlichen Ebene (Demokratisierung, nationalökonomische Folgen).

Es soll nicht beansprucht werden, mit den vier genannten analytischen Dimensionen sämtliche denkbaren Analyseperspektiven zu erfassen. Immerhin dürften damit die für organisationswissenschaftliche Fragestellungen wichtigsten Dimensionen zum Verständnis der Partizipation benannt sein. Sie sollen daher auch für die Analyse der wichtigsten international vergleichenden Partizipationsforschungen jüngeren Datums herangezogen werden.

3. Kultur und Partizipation

Die Frage, ob Organisationsmerkmale kulturabhängig oder kultur-,frei' sind, d. h. ob und inwieweit unterschiedliche kulturelle Umwelten bei sonst gleichen Voraussetzungen (etwa der Technologie, Größe und Ziele einer Organisation) Organisationsstrukturen und -prozesse maßgeblich prägen, hat seit langem die Vertreter interkultureller Organisationsvergleiche beschäftigt (England 1975; England et al. 1979; Farmer/Richman 1964; Haire et al. 1966; Hofstede 1978; Kerr et al. 1960/1966; Lammers/Hickson 1979; Negandhi/Prasad 1971). Mithin mußte diese Frage früher und später auch auf Aspekte der Partizipation bezogen werden. Hofstedes Studie (1980) von Einstellungen und Wertpräferenzen bei ca. 60 000 Belegschaftsmitgliedern (zwei Erhebungszeitpunkte: 1967–69, 1971–73) einer großen U.S.-amerikanischen multinationalen Unternehmung, befaßt sich zwar nur indirekt mit Partizipationsproblemen, ist aber allein aufgrund der gigantischen Datenbasis als einmalig anzusehen. Sie ist nur insofern etwas eng begrenzt, als sie sich in der Erfassung der Wertpräferenzen ausschließlich auf Berichte der Beschäftigten verläßt. Diese für unseren Zusammenhang wichtige Wertdimension (wir berücksichtigen hier nicht die vielen anderen Befunde der Studie) ist die „Machtdistanz" des Untergebenen zum Vorgesetzten, die durch drei relativ breit angelegte Fragen erhoben wird: eine Frage zur Häufigkeit, mit welcher der Untergebene Angst hat, seinen Widerspruch gegenüber dem Vorgesetzten zu artikulieren und je eine Frage über den jetzigen und den gewünschten Vorgesetzten. Die vorgegebenen Antwortkategorien liegen auf einem Kontinuum der Entscheidungsfindung: autokratisch, ex post Erläuterung, Konsultation mit Untergebenen, Gruppenentscheidung. Der Machtdistanzindex besteht aus dem Aggregat der Antworten auf diese drei Fragen. Er mag auch als Index der Partizipationspräferenz gewertet werden.

Die signifikanten nationalen Unterschiede, die Hofstede im über alle Befragten eines Landes gemittelten Machtdistanzindex findet, interpretiert er als Folge kultureller Unterschiede. Der Index korreliert hoch mit national aggregierten Produktivitätsindices und mit seiner Hilfe gelingt es Hofstede, die beteiligten

Länder verschiedenen Gruppierungen (Cluster) zuzuordnen, die teilweise mit den von Haire et al. (1966) gefundenen Ländergruppierungen übereinstimmen. In Studien, die weniger als Hofstede und Haire et al. mit Einstellungsskalen, sondern eher mit Messungen des Partizipations*verhaltens* arbeiten (Heller/Wilpert 1981; IDE 1981), konnten diese Cluster jedoch nicht entsprechend repliziert werden. Kulturelle Kontextbedingungen, so ließe sich also vermuten, scheinen in sehr viel engerem Zusammenhang mit den in Organisationen sich herausbildenden Partizipationseinstellungen als mit Partizipationsverhalten zu stehen. Inwieweit es sich bei den von Hofstede gefundenen Zusammenhängen zwischen Partizipationseinstellung und ökonomischen Resultaten um Kausalzusammenhänge handelt, muß angesichts seiner korrelativ gewonnenen Belege offen bleiben.

4. Hierarchie und Partizipation

Tannenbaum und Mitarbeiter (1974) bemühen sich, die Zusammenhänge zwischen hierarchischen Ebenen innerhalb einer Unternehmung und der wahrgenommenen inner-organisatorischen Einflußverteilung in fünf Ländern (Italien, Israel, Jugoslawien, Österreich, USA) zu erhellen. Die Länderauswahl erfolgte z. T. mit der Absicht, nationale Unterschiede formaler Strukturiertheit der Partizipation (i. S. rechtlich fixierter Entscheidungsstrukturen) und informaler Partizipationsformen (i. S. des Managementstils und der Teilung der Autorität der Vorgesetzten mit Untergebenen) in die Untersuchung einzubeziehen. In jedem beteiligten Land wurde versucht, zehn Unternehmungen nach Größe und Industriesektor vergleichbar auszuwählen (insges. 70). Befragt wurden „Hierarchieketten" miteinander verbundener Vorgesetzter und Untergebener (N 3500) durch sämtliche Hierarchieebenen der Unternehmung nach dem Ausmaß des „Sagens im Unternehmen" (Skala von viel – wenig), das die verschiedenen Ebenen in der Organisation haben. Die Mittelwerte des wahrgenommenen Einflusses pro Ebene bildet den sog. „Kontrollgraph", dessen Neigung als Maß der Einflußverteilung interpretiert wird: Je steiler desto ungleicher, je flacher desto gleicher ist die Einflußverteilung.

Am egalitärsten finden Tannenbaum und Mitarbeiter israelische Kibbutzim und jugoslawische Unternehmungen; italienische und amerikanische Organisationen haben eine weit ungleichere Einflußverteilung über die Hierarchieebenen. Signifikante Zusammenhänge bestehen zwischen hohen Einflußausprägungen einerseits und Arbeitszufriedenheit, hoher Arbeitsmotivation und geringerer Magengeschwürsymptomatik. Partizipatives Verhalten von Vorgesetzten steht in engem Zusammenhang mit Untergebenenzufriedenheit. Ohne im einzelnen den Formalisierungsgrad der nationalen Partizipationssysteme gemessen zu haben, meinen die Autoren, einen Zusammenhang hoher Formalisierung (Israel, Jugoslawien) mit dem wahrgenommenen Einfluß identifizieren zu können. Andererseits fungiere informelle Partizipation (USA) als funktionales Äquivalent, um Hierarchieeffekte abzuschwächen.

Der Kontrollgraph als Maß der hierarchischen Einflußverteilung ist aufgrund seines globalen Meßverfahrens insofern in die Kritik gekommen, als er eher als allgemeines Maß des Organisationsklimas verstanden werden kann (Gundelach/ Tetzschner 1976), was auch seine engen Beziehungen zu Zufriedenheits- und Motivationsmaßen erklären mag. Auch sind die Zusammenhänge zwischen Formalisierung und Einflußverteilung eher intuitiv erfaßt als von Tannenbaum und Mitarbeitern systematisch messend nachgewiesen worden. Dennoch stellt die Studie einen wichtigen Fortschritt internationaler Organisationskomparatistik und des Partizipatationsvergleichs dar.

5. Kompetenz und Partizipation

In einer Studie des oberen Managements von 129 großen, erfolgreichen und nach Industriesektor vergleichbaren Unternehmungen in acht Ländern (Bundesrepublik, England, Frankreich, Israel, Niederlande, Spanien, Schweden, USA) untersuchten Heller und Wilpert (1981) die Kooperations- und Partizipationsweisen von 625 Vorgesetzten: Untergebenen Dyaden in Entscheidungsfindungsprozessen. Die Vorgesetztenebene stellte die Ebene unmittelbar unterhalb des Vorstands dar. Zur Ebene 2 gehörten die unmittelbar untergebenen, engsten Mitarbeiter des jeweiligen Vorgesetzten aus Ebene 1. Als Datengewinnungsverfahren diente die Gruppen-Feedback-Analyse (GFA; Heller 1969): In einem ersten Schritt werden pro Hierarchieebene und Unternehmung Daten mit Hilfe eines standardisierten Fragebogens erhoben, die in einem zweiten Schritt umgehend an die Teilnehmer anonym rückgekoppelt und in einem dritten Schritt mit den Teilnehmern diskutiert und im Hinblick auf die je spezifische Situation der Unternehmung und Managementfunktion interpretiert wurden. Zentrale Forschungsfrage war auf die Bedingungen (Aufgabe, Organisationsstruktur, Umweltturbulenz, Technologie, individuelle Kompetenz) gerichtet, unter denen partizipatives Verhalten beobachtet wird. Vorgegeben wurden 12 spezifische Entscheidungen, in denen u. a. das Verhalten des Vorgesetzten in der Selbstbeurteilung und durch den Untergebenen anhand eines „Einfluß-Macht-Kontinuums (EMK)“ beurteilt wurde (EMK: „eigene Entscheidung ohne Erläuterung – eigene Entscheidung mit Erläuterung – vorherige Konsultation – gemeinsame Entscheidung – Delegation der Entscheidung auf Untergebenen“).

Neben dem allgemeinen Befund, daß sich der Entscheidungsstil in den Dyaden flexibel nach bestimmten situativen Bedingungen richtet (Umweltturbulenz, Dispositionsspielraum), unterstreichen die Ergebnisse der Studie die besondere Bedeutung, die der objektiven und wahrgenommenen fachlichen und interpersonellen Kompetenz der Dyadenmitglieder zukommt: je stärker derartige Kompetenzen verfügbar sind, desto intensiver erfolgt eine Beteiligung der Vertreter der Ebene 2. In der Verbesserung der Entscheidungsqualität und besseren Nutzung der Mitarbeiterkompetenz sehen die befragten 1600 Manager mehrheitlich die Hauptfunktion der Partizipation. Darüber hinaus zeigen sich signifikante nationale Unterschiede im Entscheidungsverhalten der Manager aus verschiedenen Ländern: Israelische Manager (nicht aus Kibbutzim!) liegen im autoritären, schwedische Manager im partizipativen Spektrum des EMK. Amerikanische Manager unterscheiden sich nicht von ihren europäischen Kollegen, was als Gegenbeleg für das von Servan-Schreiber (1967) postulierte transatlantische Managementgap gewertet werden kann.

Aspekte des Partizipationsverhaltens unter unterschiedlichen organisationalen und Umweltkontexten stehen in dieser Studie im Vordergrund. Am Rande werden sozialtheoretisch relevante Grundhaltungen der Manager zur Partizipation und Folgewirkungen der Partizipation (z. B. Ressourcennutzung) thematisiert.

6. Modelle der Industriedemokratie

Einen ganz anderen Interessenschwerpunkt setzen King und van de Vall (1978) in ihrer vergleichenden Studie der Formalsysteme, d. h. der schriftlich fixierten Partizipationsnormen der, nach ihren Aussagen, „drei führenden Modelle": des britischen „joint Consultation", der jugoslawischen Arbeiterselbstverwaltung und der deutschen Montanmitbestimmung. Der Systemvergleich erfolgt anhand von acht Dimensionen: 1. Intensität vorgeschriebener Partizipation, 2. horizontale Reichweite (Partizipationsthemen), 3. Zugang der Beschäftigten zu unterschiedlichen Entscheidungsphasen, 4. soziale Reichweite hinsichtlich der Beteiligung verschiedener Organisationsebenen, 5. Repräsentativität (Verhältnis Beschäftigter: Mandatsträger und die Art der Verbindung unter Mandatsträgern), 6. Ausbildungsstand (formale oder informell durch Partizipationslernen), 7. gewerkschaftliche Grundhaltung gegenüber Partizipation, 8. Konfliktregulierungseffizienz der Partizipation.

Das britische System der „joint Consultation" erhält auf diesen Dimensionen im Vergleich zur jugoslawischen Arbeiterselbstverwaltung und der deutschen Montanmitbestimmung die niedrigsten Werte. Die Autoren erheben keine Daten über das tatsächliche Partizipationsverhalten in diesen drei Systemen, sondern bleiben fast ausschließlich im Rahmen eines Rechtssystemvergleichs, der allerdings erstmals systematisch messend überzeugende Ergebnisse liefert; bis zu ihrer Veröffentlichung dominierte bei international vergleichenden Darstellungen eine allein die rechtlichen/normativen Bestimmungen qualitativ beschreibende Vorgehensweise.

7. Industrielle Demokratie in Europa

Unabhängig von King und van de Vall, aber parallel zu ihren Arbeiten, entwikkelte das internationale Industrial Democracy in Europe Team ein Vorhaben, das in einem Zwölf-Länder-Vergleich systematisch messend sowohl die rechtlich vorgeschriebene Partizipation (de jure) als auch die tatsächliche Partizipation (de facto) und ihre Folgen für die Bewertung des jeweiligen Partizipationsmodells durch die Beschäftigten untersuchte (IDE 1976, 1981). Insgesamt wurden 134 nach Größe und Industriesektoren vergleichbare Unternehmungen aus Belgien, der Bundesrepublik, Dänemark, England, Finnland, Frankreich, Italien, Israel, Jugoslawien, den Niederlanden, Norwegen und Schweden untersucht (1975–77) und ca. 1000 Schlüsselpersonen sowie ca. 8000 zufällig aus den Unternehmen ausgewählte Beschäftigte befragt. Die Größenklassen der Unternehmungen waren so gewählt (< 100, 100–500, 500–1500 Beschäftigte), daß für sie in der Bundesrepublik vor allem die Betriebsverfassung den gültigen Rechtsrahmen abgab.

Die normativen, formalen Vorgaben für die innerbetriebliche Partizipation (Gesetze, Kollektivverträge, Führungsrichtlinien etc.) wurden auf dem Wege einer Dokumentenanalyse hinsichtlich der vorgeschriebenen Partizipationsintensität einzelner Gruppen (z. B. Arbeiter, Mandatsträger, Management) bei 16 spezifischen Entscheidungen (darunter Routine- und strategische Entscheidungen) untersucht. Die Erhebung der de facto Partizipation erfolgte durch Befragung der tatsächlichen Beteiligungsintensität der Beschäftigten in den gleichen 16 Entscheidungen.

Jugoslawische Unternehmungen zeigen den höchsten Grad der Formalisierung der Partizipation, englische den geringsten. Bei den meisten der beteiligten Länder spielen gesetzliche Verankerungen der Partizipationsnormen die relativ wichtigste Rolle (im Vergleich zu Kollektivverträgen oder Führungsrichtlinien). In der de facto-Partizipation wurde allgemein (Ausnahme: Jugoslawien) ein niedriges Partizipationsniveau festgestellt, das zudem überall durch starke Hierarchieeffekte beeinflußt ist. Andererseits zeigte sich, daß die normativ vorgeschriebene Partizipationsintensität zugleich der beste Prädikator tatsächlicher Partizipationsintensität ist, gefolgt vom „Mobilisationsgrad" der Beschäftigten (gewerkschaftlicher Organisationsgrad und „Repräsentativität" sensu King und van de Vall). In der Bewertung des jeweiligen Partizipationssystems waren die Befragten der Länder am positivsten, deren Mandatsträgerinstitutionen (z. B. Betriebsräte) das höchste Niveau sowohl von de jure als auch de facto Partizipation hatten.

Der IDE-Studie scheint damit erstmals gelungen zu sein, das in der internationalen Komparatistik durchgängig schwierige Problem zu lösen, Merkmale des umfassenden Partizipationssystems (etwa Betriebsverfassung), organisatorische Kontextbedingungen (Größe, gewerkschaftlicher Organisationsgrad usw.) und tatsächliches Partizipationsniveau und individuelle Bewertungen der Betroffenen systematisch messend miteinander in Beziehung zu setzen. Bei weitgehender Übernahme des theoretischen Ansatzes aus den IDE-Forschungen wurden von einem Teil des IDE-Teams aus drei Ländern (England, Jugoslawien, Niederlande; sieben

Unternehmungen; 88 Befragte) die methodischen Vorgehensweisen durch Längsschnittanalysen und Beobachtungsverfahren ergänzt, welche die wesentlichsten Befunde der IDE-Studie bestätigen (Heller et al. 1977; DIO 1979).

8. Gesellschaftliche Unterschiede, Organisationsstrukturen und Partizipation

Das zentrale Forschungsinteresse der Arbeiten von Maurice et al. (1980) gilt weniger der Partizipation als vielmehr der Frage nach den Ursachen unterschiedlicher hierarchischer Unternehmungsstrukturierung in Deutschland, England und Frankreich. Insofern als Hierarchien auch Ausdruck der organisationsinternen Arbeitsteilung sind, hat diese Fragestellung zumindest auch mittelbare Bedeutung für Probleme der Partizipation in dem von uns definierten Sinne. Je zwölf Unternehmungen pro Land, nach Größe, Technologie und Produkt in etwa vergleichbar, stellen die Untersuchungsobjekte der Studie dar, die sich vorwiegend qualitativer Interviews als Methodik bedient.

Ungeachtet der Ähnlichkeiten aller Firmen in ihrer Suche nach optimalen, rationellen Organisationsstrukturen zeigen die Ergebnisse doch länderspezifische Lösungen und charakteristische Merkmale. So ist etwa der Anteil formal qualifizierter Arbeitnehmer in deutschen Unternehmungen höher als die entsprechenden Anteile französischer und britischer Unternehmungen. Entsprechend der Bildungs- und Qualifikationsstruktur der Beschäftigten ist der Grad der Dezentralisierung von Entscheidungsprozessen auf untere Ebenen der Hierarchie in deutschen Unternehmen am ausgeprägtesten. Die Forschungsgruppe um Maurice geht einen Schritt weiter und bezieht nun diese Unterschiede sowohl auf das jeweilige umgreifende nationale Erziehungssystem und die damit verbundene berufliche Stratifizierung als auch das je existierende System der Arbeitsbeziehungen.

Maurice et al. versuchen ähnlich wie die IDE-Studie Zusammenhänge zwischen gesellschaftlich-institutionellem Umfeld und innerorganisatorischen Strukturen, d. h. auch der Verteilung von Einflußchancen auf Unternehmensentscheidungen aufzuhellen. Der qualitative Forschungsansatz liefert dafür eine Fülle reicher Detailbeschreibungen dieser Wechselwirkungen.

9. Klassenkonflikt und Partizipation

Crouch und Pizzorno (1978) weiten in ihren Arbeiten die Forschungsperspektive im Vergleich zu den bislang erörterten noch einmal aus. Sie beziehen historische Entwicklungen in ihre Untersuchungen über Veränderungen im System der Arbeitsbeziehungen in sechs Ländern ein: Belgien, Bundesrepublik, England, Frankreich, Italien, Niederlande. Im Vordergrund stehen Sekunäranalysen anderweitig verfügbarer Daten über betriebliche Gewerkschaftsarbeit, Streikfrequenzen, nationale Strategien im Zusammenhang mit einem angespannten sozialen Klima der untersuchten Länder.

Obwohl nicht explizit das Thema der Arbeiten von Crouch/Pizzorno und Mitarbeitern, so treten Partizipationsprobleme wenigstens an zwei Stellen in den Mittelpunkt der Betrachtung: einmal in der Diskussion von Gegenmachtstrategien der Gewerkschaften (durchaus verstanden als Sicherung und Determinierung von Handlungsspielräumen unter Konfliktbedingungen, vgl. Dlugos 1974) als einer eigenen Form der Interessendurchsetzung neben statutorisch-formalen und informalen Partizipationsformen; zum anderen bei dem im Zeitraum seit 1968 in den einbezogenen Ländern beobachtbaren Trend zur Dezentralisierung der Arbeitsbeziehungen und zum Entstehen neuer Verhandlungsstrukturen auf betrieblicher Ebene. Die von den Autoren beobachteten korrespondierenden Bemühungen, solchen „lokalen" Strukturen auch eine angemessene Rechtsbasis und Institutionalisierung zu geben, wird dabei als unmittelbarer Ausfluß der Streikwelle zu Anfang der 70er Jahre interpretiert.

Das makro-analytische und historische Vorgehen dieser Arbeiten wirft fundamentale Fragen über den Zusammenhang historischer bzw. ökonomischer Entwicklungen und den Stellenwert und die Entfaltungschancen der Partizipation in Industrieländern auf, auch wenn die Schlußfolgerungen methodenbedingt eher Hinweis- als Beweischarakter tragen. Selbst die möglicherweise Ergebnis-verzerrende Auswahl der untersuchten Länder (Poole 1984) schmälert nicht das Verdienst der Autoren, einen Zugang der historischen und strukturanalytischen Untersuchung von Partizipationsphänomen aufgezeigt zu haben.

10. Schluß

Die Sequenz der dargestellten Arbeiten (s. Synopse) zu einem internationalen Vergleich der Partizipation in Unternehmungen folgt weder dem Erscheinungsdatum ihrer Veröffentlichung noch stellt sie eine wertende Rangreihe dar. Vielmehr sollte sie verdeutlichen, daß es oft sinnvoll, manchmal unerläßlich sein kann, zunehmend umfassendere Systemebene in die Analyse einzubeziehen, will man zu einem adäquaten Verständnis von Partizipation gelangen. Dies heißt nicht, daß eine solche Perspektivenausweitung von jedem Forschungsbemühen zu fordern ist, denn es mögen Forschungsinteresse oder forschungsökonomische Möglichkeiten dem widersprechen. Es kommt jedoch darauf an, für die Komplexität der Faktoren, die das Bild der Partizipation in Unternehmungen prägt, sensibilisiert zu sein. Ein weiterer Gesichtspunkt war für die Reihung wichtig: Die ersten drei Arbeiten handeln vor allem von informeller Partizipation, während die nachfolgenden teils

Tab. 1: Synopse: Forschungsschwerpunkte der referierten international vergleichenden Arbeiten zur Partizipation

Analytische Dimension / Forschung	Gesellsch.-theoretische Orientierung	Merkmale des Partizipations-systems	Organisatorischer Kontext	Folgen der Partizipation
Hofstede	–	–	+	+
Tannenbaum et al.	–	0	+	+
Heller/Wilpert	0	+	+	0
King/van de Vall	–	+	0	–
IDE/DIO	–	+	+	+
Maurice et al.	–	+	+	–
Crouch Pizzorno	+	+	+	0

Legende: – nicht behandelt
0 teilweise behandelt
\+ zentral behandelt

ausschließlich, teils auch von formaler Partizipation i. S. ihrer Institutionalisierung bzw. Verrechtlichung handeln.

Den meisten der referierten Arbeiten eignet jedoch eine Schwäche, die in ihrer methodischen Vorgehensweise begründet ist: Es handelt sich vorwiegend um Querschnittstudien, bei denen dynamische Aspekte der Partizipation und Entscheidungsbeeinflussung ausgeblendet bleiben wie etwa Koalitionsbildung, Machtausübung, Verweigerung, Interessenausgleich und Konflikthandhabung. Nur eine Berücksichtigung der Zeitdimension innerhalb von Längsschnittstudien wäre in der Lage, diese Begrenzungen angemessen zu überwinden. Auf mikroanalytischer Ebene wird dies in der DIO-Studie ebenso versucht wie auf makro-analytischer Ebene die Arbeiten von Crouch/Pizzorno mit Mitarbeitern. Unbeschadet dessen zeigt sich, daß die wenigen international vergleichenden Vorhaben zu Problemen der Partizipation in Unternehmungen wertvolle Aufschlüsse über Funktion und Wirkungswise dieses zentralen organisationswissenschaftlichen Konzepts zu vermitteln in der Lage sind.

Literatur

Crouch, C./Pizzorno, A. (1978): *The Resurgence of Class Conflict in Western Europe since 1968,* Vol. I and II. London.

Dachler, H. P./Wilpert, B. (1978): Conceptual Dimensions and Boundaries of Participation

in Organizations: A Critical Evaluation. In: *Administrative Science Quarterly* 23, März, S. 1–39.
Dachler, H. P./Wilpert, B. (1980): Dimensionen der Partizipation: Zu einem organisationswissenschaftlichen Analyserahmen. In: Grunwald, W./Lilge, H.-G. (Hrsg.), S. 80–98.
DIO (Decisions in Organizations) (1979): Participative Decision-Making: A Comparative Study. In: *Industrial Relations* 18, S. 295–309.
Dlugos, G. (1974): Unternehmungspolitik als betriebswirtschaftlich-politologische Teildisziplin. In: Wild, J. (Hrsg.), S. 39–74.
England, G. W. (1975): *The Manager and his Values: An International Perspective from the United States, Japan, Korea, India and Australia.* Cambridge, Mass.
England, G. W./Negandhi, A. R./Wilpert, B. (Hrsg.) (1979): *Organizational Functioning in Cross-Cultural Perspective.* Kent, Ohio.
Farmer, R./Richman, B. M. (1964): A Model for Research in Comparative Management. In: *California Management Review* VII (2), S. 55–68.
Greenberg, E. S. (1975): The Consequences of Worker Participation: A Clarification ot the Theoretical Literature: In: *Social Science Quarterly,* S. 191–209.
Grunwald, W./Lilge, H.-G. (Hrsg.) (1980): *Partizipative Führung.* Bern.
Gundelach, P./Tetzschner, H. (1976): Measurement of Influence in Organizations – Critique of the Control-Graph Method. In: *Acta Sociologica* 19 (1), S. 49–63.
Haire, M./Ghiselli, E. E./Porter, L. W. (1966): *Managerial Thinking: An International Study.* New York, London, Sidney.
Heller, F. A. (1969): Group Feed-Back Analysis: A Method of Field Research. In: *Psychological Bulletin* 72 (2), S. 108–117.
Heller, F. A. (1971): *Managerial Decision Making.* Assen, London.
Heller, F. A./Wilpert, B. (1981): *Competence and Power in Managerial Decision Making.* New York, London.
Heller, F. A./Drenth, P. J. D./Koopman, P./Rus, V. (1977): A Longitudinal Study in Participative Decision-Making. In: *Human Relations* 30 (7), S. 567–587.
Hofstede, G. (1978): Kultur und Organisation. In: Grochla, E., *Handwörterbuch der Organisation.* 2. Aufl., Stuttgart.
Hofstede, G. (1980): *Culture's Consequences. International Differences in Work-Related Values.* London.
Industrial Democracy in Europe (IDE) – International Research Group (1976): Industrial Democracy in Europe: An International Comparative Study. In: *Social Science Information 15,* S. 177–203.
Industrial Democracy in Europe (IDE) – International Research Group (1981): *Industrial Democracy in Europe.* London.
Jacob, B./Jacob, P. (1974): Values and the Active Community. In: Wilpert, B./Sorge, A. (Hrsg.), S. 317–336.
Kerr, C./Dunlop, J. T./Harbison, F./Myers, C. (1980): *Industrialism and Industrial Man.* Cambridge, Mass.
Kerr, C. u. a. (1966): *Der Mensch in der industriellen Gesellschaft.* Frankfurt/M.
King, C. D./Van de Vall, M. (1978): *Models of Industrial Democracy.* The Hague, Paris, New York.
Lammers, C. J. (1967): Power and Participation in Decision Making in Formal Organizations. In: *American Journal of Sociology* 73 (2), S. 201–217.
Lammers, C. J./Hickson, D. (Hrsg.) (1979): *Organizations Alike and Unlike.* London.

Maurice, M./Sorge, A./Warner, M. (1980): Societal Differences in Organizing Manufacturing Units: A Comparison of France, West Germany and Great Britain. In: *Organization Studies* 1 (1), S. 59–86.

Mulder, M. (1971): Power Equalization through Participation. In: *Administrative Science Quarterly,* S. 31–38.

Negandhi, A. R./Prasad, S. B. (1971): *Comparative Management.* New York.

Pool, M. (1984): Comparative Approaches to Industrial Conflict – An Assessment of „The Resurgence of Class Conflict in Western Europe since 1968". In: Wilpert, B./Sorge, A. (Hrsg.): International Perspectives on Organizational Democracy. In: *International Yearbook of Organizational Democracy.* Chichester, S. 197–213.

Servan-Schreiber, H.-J. (1967): *Le Défi Américain.* Paris.

Tannenbaum, A. S./Kavcič, B./Rosner, M./Vianello, M./Wiesner, G. (1974): *Hierarchy in Organizations.* San Francisco.

Walker, K. F. (1975): Mitbestimmung im internationalen Vergleich. In: *Soziale Welt* 26 (2), S. 150–173.

Wild, J. (Hrsg.) (1974): *Unternehmungsführung. Festschrift für Erich Kosiol zu seinem 75. Geburtstag.* Berlin.

Wilpert, B. (1977): *Führung in deutschen Unternehmen.* Berlin, New York.

Wilpert, B./Sorge, A. (Hrsg.): *International Perspectives on Organizational Democracy* II. Chichester, New York.

Gestaltungsmöglichkeiten der Kooperation zwischen Unternehmung und Betriebsrat

Ernst Zander

Abstract

Possible Designs for the Cooperation between Management and Works' Councils

In the Federal Republic of Germany the possibilities for organizing cooperation between companies and works councils are limited by the Labor-Management Relations Act. A compromise between the interests of both partners is intended. The law does not restrict management's autonomy, but does, however, require that the works council be involved in the codetermination process.

The possibilities for the flexibility of this cooperation dependend on two factors: the consideration of the legally stipulated system of works council's rights of participation and the form of cooperation. The law calls for cooperation in good faith, a willingness to compromise, and attempts to find balanced solutions by equal partners. Yet employers are not bound to any principle that commits them to provide works councils with maximum rights, because companies have to be able to structure cooperations with works' councils in a flexible way in order to develop. Thus it becomes possible for them to serve the interests of the company and its employees.

1. Einführung

Die Unternehmung ist in der demokratischen Gesellschaft nicht mehr nur ein Instrument der Anteilseigner, es ist aber auch keine Beute der Arbeitnehmer. Es ist ein aliud, eine dritte Größe, eine Institution, in der Gesellschafterinteressen mit Arbeitnehmerinteressen zusammentreffen und unter Wahrung der Belange des gemeinen Wohls ausgeglichen werden müssen.

Der Interessenausgleich hat in der Bundesrepublik Deutschland vor allem zwischen dem Unternehmen und seinem Betriebsrat zu erfolgen. § 2 des Betriebsverfassungsgesetzes von 1972[1] liefert dafür die Maxime: Es ist das Kooperationsgebot. Diese vom Gesetz verlangte und von der praktischen Alltagsvernunft gebotene Zusammenarbeit zwischen Unternehmung und Betriebsrat kann in vielfältiger Weise gestaltet werden.

2. Gestaltung der Kooperation – Aufgabe unternehmerischer Personalpolitik

Erfolgreiche Möglichkeiten solcher Gestaltung aufzuspüren, ist vornehmste Aufgabe einer unternehmerischen Personalpolitik. Personal- und Sozialpolitik ist ein wichtiger Bestandteil der gesamtunternehmerischen Politik.[2] Das Personal- und Sozialwesen nimmt die Arbeitgeberfunktion der Unternehmung wahr und verkörpert zugleich die soziale Verantwortung des Unternehmens gegenüber Mitarbeitern und Gesellschaft. Sie wird von der Erkenntnis beherrscht, daß die Sicherung der Existenz des Unternehmens die Voraussetzung für die Sicherung der Arbeitsplätze der Mitarbeiter ist.

Diesem Ziel hat auch die Gestaltung der Kooperation mit dem Betriebsrat zu dienen. Dabei hat die Unternehmung das historische, wirtschaftliche und soziale Umfeld zu beachten; von ihm wird die Unternehmenspolitik entscheidend geprägt. Änderungen dieses Umfelds haben deshalb notwendig auch Einfluß auf die Kooperationsbeziehungen der Betriebspartner.

So waren in den 50er und 60er Jahren in den deutschen Unternehmungen Einstellung, Personalentwicklung, soziale Leistungen Schlüsselbegriffe, die die Binnenkooperation in der Unternehmung charakterisierten. Zwar kam auch seinerzeit die personalwirtschaftliche Rationalität nicht zu kurz: Systeme der Arbeitsbewertung und der Leistungsbeurteilung aus jener Zeit zeugen hiervon.[3] Jedoch gehörten Begriffe wie Strukturanpassung, Einstellungsstop, Aufhebungsvertrag, vorzeitige Pensionierung, Interessenausgleich und Sozialplan damals – anders als heute – nicht zum personal- und sozialpolitischen Alltagsinstrumentarium. Die allgemeine wirtschaftliche und soziale Entwicklung in allen westlichen Industrieländern hat zu dieser Inhaltsänderung der Unternehmenspolitik geführt. Zu den überkommenen personalwirtschaftlichen Aufgaben ist als zentrales Thema die sinnvolle und flexible Anpassung der Personalpolitik an die gewandelte soziale Umwelt getreten.[4]

3. Betriebsverfassung im Wandel

Die Gestaltungsmöglichkeiten einer zeitgemäßen Kooperation von Unternehmung und Betriebsrat hängen entscheidend von der Betriebsverfassung ab. Die Betriebsverfassung 1985 ist nicht mehr die bei Erlaß des Gesetzes im Jahre 1972. Die betriebliche Praxis, vor allem aber die arbeitsgerichtliche Rechtsprechung in der Bundesrepublik Deutschland hat für einen tiefgreifenden Wandel gesorgt; eine Wende keineswegs zum Besseren. Es ist nicht zu verkennen, daß die deutschen Arbeitsgerichte zuweilen mit recht grobschlächtigen Mitteln in den vom Gesetz gewollten Interessenausgleich von Arbeitgebern und Arbeitnehmern eingreifen.

Das gilt vor allem für die Gerichte der 1. Instanz. Hier gibt es bedenkliche Entwicklungen, denn es werden neue bürokratische Hürden errichtet und damit den auf Effizienz angewiesenen Unternehmen zusätzliche Probleme bereitet. Das gilt vor allem für die Neigung der Arbeitsgerichte, mit Hilfe des Instruments der einstweiligen Verfügung eine Art neue Betriebsverfassung zu schaffen. Dadurch wird z. B. der vom Gesetzgeber *bewußt* als nicht erzwingbar ausgestaltete Interessenausgleich des § 112 BetrVG im Wege von einstweiligen Verfügungen gegen Kündigungen praktisch in den Rang eines paritätischen Mitbestimmungsrechts gehoben.[5]

Außerdem erstarken Unterrichtungs- und Beratungsrechte oder bloße Anwendungsregeln, wie der Grundsatz der vertrauensvollen Zusammenarbeit (§ 2 BetrVG), auf dem Umweg über die einstweilige Verfügung zu quasi-paritätischen Mitbestimmungsrechten. Damit entsteht die Gefahr, daß schließlich jede bisher mitbestimmungsfreie unternehmerische Maßnahme der Entscheidung des Betriebsrats unterworfen wird. Es genügte die einfache Behauptung, mit der Maßnahme werde die vertrauensvolle Zusammenarbeit gestört oder ein Informationsanspruch des Betriebsrats sei noch nicht erfüllt.

Sorgen bereitet auch der zuweilen anzutreffende Mißbrauch des Instruments Sozialplan. Er dient mehr und mehr der Umverteilung verbliebenen Vermögens. Damit droht das Arbeitsverhältnis als Austauschverhältnis von Entgelt und Leistung aus dem Blickfeld zu geraten. Der Arbeitsplatz wird zum Eigentumstitel des Arbeitsplatzinhabers, so daß es nahe liegt, für seinen Verlust eine Art Enteignungsentschädigung zu fordern.

Ein klassisches Beispiel für die Einengung von Gestaltungsmöglichkeiten ist der jüngst ergangene Beschluß des Großen Senats des Bundesarbeitsgericht[6] zum Weiterbeschäftigungsanspruch des gekündigten Arbeitnehmers. Mit diesem Beschluß wird eine Art vorläufige Vollstreckbarkeit des erstinstanzlichen arbeitsgerichtlichen Urteils eingeführt. Die Entscheidung geht an der gesetzlichen Ausnahmeregelung des § 102 BetrVG vorbei, die den Weiterbeschäftigungsanspruch vom Widerspruch des Betriebsrats abhängig macht.

Angesichts dieser Tendenzen der arbeitsgerichtlichen Judikatur kommt es entscheidend darauf an, die in der deutschen Betriebsverfassung liegenden Möglichkeiten sachgerechter Gestaltung der Zusammenarbeit mit den Betriebsräten auszuschöpfen. Zwar sind die Betriebsverfassungsgesetze einst als Schutzgesetzte für die Arbeitnehmer ins Leben getreten; sie waren und sind im Kern Normenwerke über die Organisation und die Aufgaben der Betriebsräte. Das Reichsgesetz von 1920 brachte dies noch in seinem Titel zum Ausdruck: „Betriebsrätegesetz".

Aber schon die Neufassung des Jahres 1952 nannte sich „Betriebsverfassungsgesetz". Das Nachkriegsgesetz wollte also *nicht* mehr nur Organisationsregeln für Betriebsräte schaffen und seine Aufgaben beschreiben; es wollte als Grundgesetz für den Betrieb verstanden werden, als Verfassung des Betriebs.

4. Die Leitungsautonomie der Unternehmung

Damit wurd die Unternehmung – insbesondere in ihrer Eigenschaft als Arbeitgeber – stärker ins Blickfeld gerückt. Sie erscheint nunmehr als Träger einer der beiden Hauptrollen im betriebsverfassungsrechtlichen Zusammenspiel mit ihrem Partner, dem Betriebsrat. Das Betriebsverfassungsgesetz ist daher auch Schutzrecht für die Unternehmung.

Die Leitungsautonomie der Unternehmung wird vom Gesetz nämlich nicht eingeschränkt (§ 77 Abs. 1 BetrVG). Das Unternehmen behält das Organisationsrecht und ist allein für alle Planungen und für die Durchführung der Entscheidungen zuständig. Arbeitsvertragsrechtlich gesprochen, behält es allein das Direktionsrecht; es entsteht *kein* Mitdirektionsrecht des Betriebsrats.

Um ein Gleichnis aus dem Immobilienrecht zu verweden: Mit dem Leitungsrecht des Unternehmers ist es wie mit dem Grundeigentum; es war in der Zeit vor dem verfaßten Betrieb sozusagen unbelastet. Das Betriebsverfassungsgesetz hat mit den vielfältigen Beteiligungsrechten des Betriebsrats Hypotheken und Grundschulden bestellt. Zwar liegt die Leitungskompetenz nach wie vor allein beim Unternehmen; aber es darf von ihr erst Gebrauch machen, wenn es zuvor den Betriebsrat in der vom Gesetz jeweils vorgesehenen Form beteiligt hat.

Der Gestaltungsspielraum hängt demnach grundsätzlich von zwei Faktoren ab, nämlich von der Beachtung des gesetzlich austarierenden Systems der Beteiligungsrechte des Betriebsrats und von der Art der Zusammenarbeit der Betriebspartner.

5. Das System der Beteiligungsrechte

Was zunächst die Belastungsskala angeht, so reicht sie von der Null-Beteiligung bis zur paritätischen Mitbestimmung. Es besteht also kein einheitliches gesetzliches Mitbestimmungsrecht des Betriebsrats. Eine Unternehmungspraxis, die das ignoriert, muß sich in ihrer unternehmerischen Leitungsfreiheit ungebührlich eingeengt fühlen. Es kommt zur Sicherung eines hohen Maßes an Entscheidungsautonomie darauf an, das System abgestufter Beteiligungsrechte des Betriebsrats so zu beachten, wie es vom Betriebsverfassungsgesetz geschaffen worden ist.

Dieses System reicht von der bloßen Information über die angekoppelte Beratung, die Anhörung, verschieden ausgestaltete Widerspruchsrechte und die Zustimmung, bis hin zur paritätischen Mitbestimmung bei sozialen Angelegenheiten, die Initiativrechte des Betriebsrats einschließt. Zum Verständnis dieser Abstufung mag der Gedanke förderlich sein, der Gesetzgeber habe den Kernbereich wirtschaftlich-unternehmerischer Betätigungsfreiheit nicht zuletzt aus verfassungsrechtlichen Gründen weitgehend unangetastet lassen wollen, während er im Gebiet personeller Entscheidungen und sog. Sozialangelegenheiten meinte, den Einfluß des Betriebsrats deutlich erhöhen zu sollen.

Zur Respektierung des gesetzlich vorgegebenen Systems von Leitungsautonomie des Arbeitgebers und Beteiligungsrechten des Betriebsrats gehört ferner die Erkenntnis, daß sich die Beteiligungsrechte in personellen und sozialen Angelegenheiten grundsätzlich einer Ausweitung durch Tarifvertrag oder Betriebsvereinbarung entziehen. Nur ausnahmsweise und lediglich bei Vorhandensein gesetzlicher Öffnungsklauseln – wie etwa im Falle des § 102 Abs. 6 BetrVG – ist eine Ausdehnung zulässig; für den sozialen Bereich läßt § 88 BetrVG freiwillige Betriebsvereinbarungen in den dort beschriebenen Grenzen zu.

Die Kooperation der Betriebspartner in deutschen Unternehmungen hängt aber nicht nur von der gesetzlich gewollten Balance ihrer Rechte und Pflichten ab. Zweiter, wesentlicher Faktor ist ihre vertrauensvolle Zusammenarbeit.

6. Vertrauensvolle Zusammenarbeit der Betriebspartner

Das Betriebsverfassungsgesetz 1972 fordert diese Art der Kooperation und verlangt weiter den Verzicht auf Arbeitskämpfe der Betriebsparteien. Es will den Betriebsfrieden, den ungestörten Arbeitsablauf und die Gleichbehandlung aller Betriebsangehörigen sichern.

Das Gesetz gebietet Kooperation, nicht Konfrontation. Es lebt vom Gedanken vertrauensvoller Zusammenarbeit. Vertrauensvolle Zusammenarbeit meint den Willen zum Ausgleich und das Streben nach ausgewogenen Lösungen durch gleichwertige Partner.

Daher hat die Art und Weise des Umgangs des Unternehmens mit dem Betriebsrat maßgebenden Einfluß auf die Gestaltung der Zusammenarbeit. Wer seinen Partner nicht ernst nimmt oder wer ihn im Ungewissen läßt, darf sich über einen ängstlich am Gesetz klebenden Betriebsrat nicht wundern. Eine solche Betriebsvertretung wird keine Rechtsposition aufgeben und sei sie noch so belanglos. Nur ein kenntnisreicher, selbstbewußter und vom Unternehmen geachteter Betriebsrat kann ihm den nötigen Gestaltungsspielraum verschaffen. Dieser Betriebsrat wird seine Entscheidungen selbst treffen, im Bewußtsein, daß er – zusammen mit dem Arbeitgeber – Hauptorgan der Betriebsverfassung ist und nicht die Gewerkschaft.

Das Gesetz hat nämlich den Betriebspartnern – Arbeitgeber und Betriebsrat – die Vorrangstellung eingeräumt. Gewerkschaften und Arbeitgeberverbände spielen in der Bundesrepublik Deutschland – vom Gesetz her betrachtet – in der Betriebsverfassung nur Nebenrollen; sie sind ihre Hilfsorgane. Die betriebliche Interessenvertretung der Arbeitnehmer ist also nicht in erster Linie Sache der Gewerkschaften, sondern von ihnen unabhängiger Betriebsräte. Sie sind als Institution nicht zur Loyalität gegenüber einer Gewerkschaft verpflichtet, sondern zur Loyalität gegenüber dem Betrieb. Sein Wohl zu achten ist ebenso gesetzliche Pflicht wie die Förderung des Wohls der Belegschaft.

7. Gestaltungsspielraum des Betriebsrats

Das Kooperationsgebot verpflichtet den Betriebsrat, seine Beteiligungsrechte sachgerecht und zweckmäßig wahrzunehmen. Dazu gehört eine Rechtsausübung, die der Unternehmung den erforderlichen Gestaltungsspielraum läßt und ihn nicht durch engherzige und kleinliche Ausnutzung bloß formaler Rechtsposition einengt.

Zwar darf der Betriebsrat auf die Ausübung seiner gesetzlichen Rechte nicht von sich aus verzichten und sozusagen auf illegale Weise die Möglichkeiten des Arbeitgebers vergrößern, denn das Betriebsverfassungsgesetz hat dem Betriebsrat die Beteiligungsrechte nicht um seiner selbst willen verliehen, es sind vielmehr sog. „Pflichtrechte", deren Ausübung den Interessen der verfaßten Arbeitnehmerschaft und des Betriebs dienen soll. Jedoch bedeutet nicht schon jede Nichtausübung von Rechten eine pflichtwidrige Unterlassung; dem Betriebsrat steht in vielen Fällen ein Ermessensspielraum zu.

Zum Teil ist dieser Ermessensspielraum im Gesetz selbst angelegt, wie z. B. bei der innerbetrieblichen Stellenausschreibung. Nach § 93 BetrVG kann der Betriebsrat eine Ausschreibung verlangen, er muß es aber nicht. Beispielsweise wird er darauf verzichten, wenn sie ersichtlich sinnlos ist, so etwa, wenn ein Spezialist gesucht wird, den es im Betrieb nicht gibt und den man auch durch Umschulung aus der Belegschaft heraus nicht entwickeln kann. Ein Bestehen auf der Ausschreibung wäre in einem solchen Fall geradezu rechtsmißbräuchlich.

Die Einräumung größerer Gestaltungsmöglichkeiten ist ferner von der Rechtsprechung der Arbeitsgerichte anerkannt. So ergibt sich aus § 87 Abs. 1 Ziff. 3 BetrVG, daß der Betriebsrat bei jeder Anordnung von Überstunden mit kollektivem Bezug mitzubestimmen hat. Jeder Praktiker weiß, daß das oft gar nicht geht. Es kommt häufig genug vor, daß die Notwendigkeit von Mehrarbeit buchstäblich in letzter Minute erkannt wird. Oft ist dann gar kein Betriebsrat mehr greifbar. In einem solchen Falle ist es zulässig, von dem Betriebsrat die pauschale Zustimmung zur Anordnung von Mehrarbeit in gleichliegenden, immer wieder auftretenden Eilfällen einzuholen.[7] In diesen Zusammenhang gehört auch das Problem flexibler Gestaltung der betrieblichen Arbeitszeiten, bei dem sich gerade in jüngster Zeit beiden Betriebspartnern ein großer Gestaltungsspielraum eröffnet hat.[8]

Eine Absprache mit dem Betriebsrat ist ferner bei Versetzungen nützlich, denn der vom Gesetz selbst in § 95 Abs. 3 BetrVG definierte Begriff ist in der betrieblichen Praxis wenig brauchbar. Wollte man ihn buchstabengetreu anwenden, so würde sehr viel Sand ins Getriebe geraten. Daher ist es auch in einem solchen Falle nützlich, mit dem Betriebsrat eine Absprache darüber zu treffen, was als Versetzung im betrieblichen Alltag gelten soll.

In allen diesen Fällen könnte man von pflichtgebundener Nichtausübung von Rechten bzw. von pflichtgemäßer Modifikation gesetzlich vorgeschriebener Verfahrensabläufe sprechen. Das Gebot der vertrauensvollen Zusammenarbeit verpflichtet den Betriebsrat zum Wohle des Betriebs und damit auch der Arbeitnehmer, die personalpolitische Flexibilität nicht ohne Not oder gar willkürlich einzuschränken. Vielmehr ist stets eine Form der Interessenwahrnehmung zu wählen, die einen möglichst geringen Eingriff darstellt.

8. Gestaltungsmöglichkeiten des Arbeitgebers

Gestaltungsmöglichkeiten ergeben sich für den Arbeitgeber sogar aus der richtigen Anwendung der Rechtsprechung des Bundesarbeitsgerichts. So ist z. B. dieses Gericht bei den neuen Technologien nicht der gewerkschaftlich initiierten Auffassung von der Allzuständigkeit der Betriebsräte für neue technische Entwicklungen gefolgt, sondern hat die Mitbestimmung auf wenige – wenn auch inhaltsreiche – Tatbestände beschränkt.[9] Eine sorgfältige Analyse der bisher ergangenen Entscheidungen läßt jedoch auch in diesen Fällen Möglichkeiten erkennen, die der personalpolitischen Gestaltungskraft gegeben sind.

Von ganz besonderer Bedeutung ist in diesem Zusammenhang die Rechtsprechung des Bundesarbeitsgerichts zu so wichtigen personalpolitischen Instrumenten wie Anforderungsprofilen[10], Stellenbeschreibungen[11] und vor allem zu Führungsrichtlinien.[12] Der Anspruch mancher Betriebsräte, bei der Aufstellung von Anforderungsprofilen und Stellenbeschreibungen mitzubestimmen und über ein weitgehendes Beteiligungsrecht an der Entwicklung von Leitlinien für die Führung und Zusammenarbeit Einfluß auf die Führung der Unternehmen zu gewinnen, ist abgewiesen worden. Damit hält sich das Bundesarbeitsgericht an das bundesverfassungsgerichtliche Gebot, wonach jede Mitbestimmung der Arbeitnehmer sich daran messen lassen müsse, ob die Funktionsfähigkeit der Wirtschaft geschmälert wird. Mitbestimmung der Arbeitnehmer ist nicht Selbstzweck, sondern Mittel des sozialen Ausgleichs.

Freiräume der Gestaltung sind schließlich selbst dort gegeben, wo eine exzessive Rechtsinterpretation zunächst auf das Gegenteil hinzudeuten scheint. Als Beispiel kann das Problem der Betriebsänderung durch bloßen Personalabbau dienen. Nach § 112a BetrVG liegt eine interessenausgleichs- und sozialplanpflichtige Betriebsänderung schon dann vor, wenn die Belegschaft auch ohne Reduzierung sächlicher Betriebsmittel in bestimmtem Umfang abgebaut wird. Das Unternehmen handelt nicht rechtsmißbräuchlich, das bei einem notwendigen Personalabbau jeweils unterhalb dieser Quote bleibt. Es kann auch nicht zweifelhaft sein, daß seine Pflicht zur Aufstellung eines Sozialplans in einem Großunternehmen dann nicht besteht, wenn es sich bei der betroffenen Unternehmenseinheit um einen Kleinbetrieb mit in der Regel nicht mehr als 20 wahlberechtigten Arbeitnehmern handelt.

Überhaupt liegen einige Gestaltungsmöglichkeiten in der Beachtung der im Gesetz an vielen Stellen genannten Zahlenschwellen. Das gilt nicht nur für die Bildung und die zahlenmäßige Größe von Betriebsräten, sondern z. B. auch für die

1000-Mitarbeiter-Grenze, deren Überschreiten dem Betriebsrat ein Initiativrecht zur Aufstellung von Auswahlrichtlinien verleiht, einem Instrument, das in vielen Fällen zu nichts anderem als zur Bürokratisierung taugt und überdies die Gefahr fruchtloser Auslegungsstreitigkeiten in sich birgt.

So wie Betriebsräte mit Recht Möglichkeiten wahrnehmen, die ihnen das Gesetz einräumt, ist es genauso legitim, wenn die Unternehmung von ihrem Organisationsrecht mit dem Ziel Gebrauch macht, eine günstige Gestaltungsform zu erreichen. Es gibt das Gebot vertrauensvoller Zusammenarbeit, aber es gibt kein an den Arbeitgeber adressiertes Gebot der Verschaffung oder Erhaltung maximaler Rechtspositionen des Betriebsrats, denn die Unternehmungen bedürfen zu ihrer Entfaltung flexibler Gestaltungsmöglichkeiten der Kooperation mit dem Betriebsrat. Dies ist zur Sicherung der Existenz der Unternehmen und zur Verbesserung der Wettbewerbsfähigkeit der Volkswirtschaft im internationalen Vergleich unerläßlich.

Anmerkungen

[1] Dazu umfassend Glaubrecht / Halberstadt / Zander 1985.
[2] Vgl. zu Gegenstand und Teilgebieten der Unternehmungspolitik Dlugos 1976.
[3] Vgl. dazu Zander 1980 a.
[4] Vgl. Zander 1980 b.
[5] Vgl. LAG Hamburg vom 13. 11. 1981. In: *Der Betrieb* 1982, S. 1522.
[6] *Der Betrieb* 1985, S. 551.
[7] So das Bundesarbeitsgericht im Beschluß vom 2. 3. 1982. In: *Der Betrieb* 1982, S. 1115.
[8] Dazu näher Glaubrecht / Wagner / Zander 1985.
[9] Vgl. die Entscheidungen vom 6. 12. 1983. In: *Der Betrieb* 1984, S. 775.
[10] Beschluß vom 31. 5. 1983. In: *Der Betrieb* 1983, S. 2311.
[11] Beschluß vom 31. 1. 1984. In: *Der Betrieb* 1984, S. 1199.
[12] Beschluß vom 23. 10. 1984. In: *Der Betrieb* 1985, S. 495.

Literatur

Dlugos, G. (1976): Unternehmungspolitik. In: *Handwörterbuch der Betriebswirtschaft,* 4. Aufl., Stuttgart, Sp. 4093 ff.

Glaubrecht, H. / Halberstadt, G. / Zander, E.: *Betriebsverfassung in Recht und Praxis.* Losebl., Freiburg i. Br. 1977 ff.

Glaubrecht, H. / Wagner, D. / Zander, E. (1985): *Arbeitszeit im Wandel.* 2. Aufl., Freiburg.

Zander, E. (1980 a): *Handbuch der Gehaltsfestsetzung.* 4. Aufl., Heidelberg.

Zander, E. (1980 b): *Führung in den 80er Jahren.* Heidelberg.

Erlebte Expertenmacht – Berichte über die faktische Machtverteilung zwischen Unternehmensführung und Kontrollorgan in einem Unternehmen der Arbeiterselbstverwaltung[1]

Horst Steinmann und Helmut Müller

Abstract

Experienced Power of Experts – Reports on the Factual Distribution of Power Between Management and Supervisory Board in a Workers' Self-Managed Company

In the theory and practice of workers' self-government the problem of expert power of the company's management – compared with the laymen in the controlling body (supervisory, advisory board) – has always been of great importance, because this actual superiority of the management means a limitation to the legally intended power allocation at the top-management level. This paper does not deal with the problem in a theoretical way, but, rather focusses on an empirical research project in which the subjective views of members of the supervisory board in the Porst group were investigated. More than half of the members of this controlling body were representatives of the employees. The ways the representatives reacted to the management's expert power are typified. The results show a tension between the control of management on the one hand and the confidence in the members of management on the other. Knowing this should be an incentive to reconsider the features of the interrelation between the management and the representation of interests. In this context three theses will be formulated and briefly discussed.

1. Das Problem

Die Unternehmensverfassung fixiert den institutionellen Rahmen, der die Umsetzung der verfassungskonstituierenden Interessen in die Unternehmenspolitik sicherstellen soll; ihre Funktionsfähigkeit bemißt sich deshalb letztlich daran, wieweit sie diesen Zweck auch wirklich dauerhaft zu erfüllen in der Lage ist. Vor dem

Hintergrund dieser Zwecksetzung wird die in den kapitalistischen Ländern seit Jahrzehnten andauernde Diskussion um die „Trennung von Eigentum und Verfügungsgewalt“ verständlich und das Unbehagen nachvollziehbar, das sich in dieser Diskussion ausdrückt.[2] Dort, wo sich das Management gegenüber den (Klein-) Aktionärsinteressen zu verselbständigen droht (Managerkontrolle), geht ja eine wichtige Funktionsbedingung des kapitalistischen Systems verloren.

Eine der zentralen Ursachen für diese Verselbständigungstendenzen ist bekanntlich die Professionalisierung des Management. Wenn es so ist, daß die Probleme, die mit der Führung eines (Groß-)Unternehmens verbunden sind, im Prinzip nur noch von solchen Personen effizient gelöst werden können, die eine entsprechende berufliche Ausbildung durchgemacht und lange Erfahrungen als Manager gesammelt haben, dann ist damit eine Situation entstanden, die jeden Versuch von vornherein zum Scheitern verurteilt, die verfassungskonstituierenden Interessen mit Hilfe institutioneller Regelungen im unternehmerischen Entscheidungsprozeß ausreichend und dauerhaft zur Geltung zu bringen. Die „Herrschaft der Manager“ wird zur notwendigen Funktionsbedingung erfolgreichen großbetrieblichen Wirtschaftens.

Man mag diese kritische Situation für die kapitalistische Unternehmensverfassung, insbesondere bei der Aktiengesellschaft, noch herunterzuspielen versuchen, wie es etwa die „Theorie der Verfügungsrechte“ anstrebt, indem sie die Aktionäre für ihre Interessenwahrung auf den Kapitalmarkt (Kauf und Verkauf der Aktien) verweist und die Trennung von Eigentum und Verfügungsgewalt dann nicht nur als Scheinproblem abstempelt, sondern sogar positiv umdeutet.[3] Diese Argumentationsstrategie, die von der behaupteten bzw. unterstellten funktionalen Äquivalenz von „Voice“ und „Exit“, von Binnensteuerung durch Argumentation und Außensteuerung durch Markt und Tausch, lebt, ist aber jedenfalls dort nicht mehr möglich, wo die Unternehmensverfassung gerade nicht (allein) auf die Kapitalrationalität, die Kapitalinteressen und die Kapitalbeziehungen, abheben will. Man denke etwa an die Mitbestimmte Unternehmung oder Reformmodelle zur Arbeiterselbstverwaltung. Hier geht es um Binnenstrukturen der Unternehmensverfassung, die für den Interessenausgleich und die interessenbezogene Steuerung der Unternehmenspolitik auf unternehmensinterne argumentative Prozesse der Willensbildung und Entscheidungsfindung angewiesen sind. Bei derartigen Verfassungsstrukturen stellt sich also das Problem der Managerherrschaft, Experte versus Laie, unausweichlich. Wie werden derartige Verfassungen mit diesem Problem fertig und vor allem: Wie erleben die Beteiligten dieses Problem und wie reagieren sie darauf?

Diesen Fragen soll hier im Rahmen des verfügbaren Raumes anhand einer *Fallstudie* nachgegangen werden, die bei der Porst-Gruppe, Nürnberg, durchgeführt wurde. Dieses Unternehmen praktizierte von 1972 bis 1980 ein Selbstverwaltungsmodell, das u. a. einen überparitätisch mit Arbeitnehmervertretern besetzten Beirat vorsah.[4] Die Rechte des Beirates gegenüber der Unternehmensführung waren denen des Aufsichtsrates der Aktiengesellschaft nachgebildet, gingen aber in einem hier besonders wichtigen Punkt darüber hinaus: Dem Beirat war in der Porst-Verfassung ein Zustimmungsvorbehalt zur gesamten Unternehmensplanung eingeräumt worden, so daß im Vergleich zu § 111, Abs. 4 AktG (zustimmungspflichtige Geschäfte) besonders günstige rechtliche Voraussetzungen für die Einflußnahme auf die Unternehmenspolitik gegeben waren. Dies insofern, als nicht nur punktuell einzelne Geschäfte, sondern alle unternehmenspolitischen Handlungsabsichten des Managements in ihrem Gesamtzusammenhang und in ihrer wechselseitigen Bedingtheit einer interessenbezogenen Einwirkung offenstanden. Ist es dem Beirat gelungen, diese seine *juristische* Machtstellung auch *faktisch* gegenüber den Experten der Geschäftsführung zum Tragen zu bringen, oder hat sich die Expertenmacht des Managements durchsetzen können?

Es soll hier nicht der Versuch einer *objektiven* Einschätzung der Einfluß-Strukturen zwischen Geschäftsleitung und dem Beirat unternommen werden. Vielmehr soll die aufgeworfene Frage aus der *subjektiven* Sicht einiger Beiräte beantwortet werden, die in halbstrukturierten Interviews danach befragt wurden, wie sie ihre Rolle im Rahmen der Beratung und Verabschiedung der jährlichen Unternehmensplanung erlebt haben; zum Teil versuchten die Interviewpartner auch selbst, gewisse Konsequenzen aus der Deutung ihrer Rolle zu ziehen. Die Interviewpartner waren teils Arbeiter, teils leitende Angestellte[5], die in mindestens einer der drei Beiratsperioden (1972–1975, 1975–1978; 1978–1980) ihr Mandat auf Grund demokratischer Wahlen erhalten hatten.

Für das Verständnis der Antworten ist es noch wichtig darauf hinzuweisen, daß die allgemeinen Rahmenbedingungen für die Nutzung der dem Beirat eingeräumten Machtbefugnisse – verglichen etwa mit der Praxis der Aufsichtsratsmitbestimmung – relativ günstig waren, auf jeden Fall sich im Zuge von Lernprozessen von Jahr zu Jahr verbesserten. Das gilt insbesondere für die Informationen, die dem Beirat von der Geschäftsführung für seine Beratungen zur Verfügung gestellt wurden; das gilt aber auch für die gesamte Unternehmenskultur, die der Verfassungsabsicht nach auf die Selbstbestimmung der Arbeitnehmer ausgerichtet sein sollte.[6]

2. Erlebte Expertenmacht – drei Reaktionsweisen

2.1. Die Beratung über die Unternehmensplanung: Typisches Verlaufsmuster

Der Entscheidung des Beirates über die vorgelegte Jahresplanung ging regelmäßig eine sehr ausführliche und langwierige Beratung voraus. Beteiligt daran waren nicht nur die Beiratsmitglieder, sondern auch die Geschäftsführung und hin und wieder externe Experten, wenn diese wesentliche Teile der Unternehmensplanung vorbereitet hatten. Die Geschäftsführung erläuterte immer die rechtzeitig vorgelegten Unterlagen und trat dann mit den Beiratsmitgliedern in einen Gedankenaustausch ein, etwa um bestimmte Planannahmen weiter zu hinterfragen oder über konkrete Maßnahmen genauer zu unterrichten, die gewöhnlich nicht in der Jahresplanung ausgewiesen wurden. Diese war vielmehr eine Umsatz- und Kosten- sowie Investitionsplanung; später wurden auch Planbilanzen und Plan-Gewinn- und Verlust-Rechnungen vorgelegt. Im Zuge der Beratungen entwickelte sich dann – mehr oder weniger tiefgehend – eine inhaltliche Auseinandersetzung, in deren Verlauf die Beiratsmitglieder mit dem Sachverstand des Management konfrontiert wurden, wenn es um die Verteidigung konträrer Positionen ging, sei es, daß gewisse Basisannahmen der Planung für die Ausgrenzung des unternehmerischen Handlungsspielraums strittig waren oder die Art der Nutzung des Handlungsspielraums in Form konkreter strategischer Maßnahmen zur Debatte stand. Hier wurde dann häufiger der Punkt erreicht, wo das Problem der Expertenmacht virulent wurde. Die Geschäftsführung war regelmäßig in der Lage, vom Beirat vorgetragene Argumente zu entkräften und jeweils weitere Gründe für ihre eigenen Vorstellungen anzuführen, z. T. unter Rückgriff auf externe Gutachten. Derartige Situationen wurden von den Arbeiter-Beiräten (Basisvertreter) häufiger berichtet als von den höherqualifizierten Beiratsmitgliedern.

Die folgenden Ausschnitte aus Interviews mit Arbeitnehmervertretern zeigen, wie verschiedene Beiratsmitglieder diese Expertenmacht des Managements erlebten und warum trotz mancher Bedenken und kritischen Fragen eine Ablehnung oder Modifikation der Jahresplanung außerordentlich selten war.

Interviewausschnitt 1 (ltd. Angestellter):
„Wir haben natürlich gefragt, was passiert, wenn die Planung verfehlt wird. Dies kam dadurch zum Ausdruck, daß wir eine Planung nicht verabschieden wollten, weil sie nach unserer Meinung zu hoch angesetzt war. Ich glaube, 1978 war die Planung mit 20 oder 22% Umsatzzuwachs angesetzt. Ich sagte: ‚Mehr als 12% sind nicht drin und nicht machbar, weil man abwägen muß, was passiert, wenn die Konkurrenz attackiert, wenn die Konjunktur sich anders entwickelt?‘ Dies alles wurde aus der Überlegung her aufgezeigt, daß eine Umsatzausweitung ja zusätzliche Investitionen erfordert und gewaltig Kapital bindet. Man schiebt dann Kostenblöcke vor sich her und weiß noch nicht, ob der Erfolg auch tatsächlich eintritt. Das Gegenargument der Geschäftsleitung war immer: ‚Geplant ist ein Gewinn von 12 Mio. DM. Wenn die Planungsannahmen nicht eintreten, dann sind es eben 6 Mio. DM, das ist ja auch etwas!‘ Mit solchen Argumenten wurden wir Beiräte matt gesetzt, und wir konnten nichts mehr gegen die Planung einbringen. Das Argument der Geschäftsleitung war: ‚Die Planung ist zwar hoch angesetzt, aber es sind Sicherheitsfaktoren eingebaut, die ausreichen, wenn die Planungsannahmen nicht erfüllt werden.‘ Es wurde auch immer in Betracht gezogen, ob Arbeitsplätze durch evtl. Planabweichungen gefährdet wären oder nicht. Die Geschäftsleitung sagte, daß durch evtl. Planabweichungen keine Arbeitsplätze gefährdet wären. In den Beiratssitzungen spielten somit die Wirkungen von Planabweichungen eine durchaus große Rolle; die entsprechenden Fragen wurden jedoch von der Geschäftsleitung überzeugend beantwortet, und gegen die Antworten konnten wir keine Gegenargumente anführen."

Die Beiräte sahen umso eher die Möglichkeit, kritische Fragen an die Geschäftsleitung zu stellen, je stärker die vorgelegten Zahlen von vergleichbaren Vergangenheitswerten abwichen. Die Ausgangsbasis für die Diskussionen waren deshalb oft die aus einer Differenzbetrachtung zu den Daten früherer Jahre gewonnenen und zunächst nicht plausibel erscheinenden *Abweichungen*. Die vorgetragenen Fragen und Bedenken der Beiratsmitglieder wurden jedoch, wie der folgende Gesprächsausschnitt zeigt, von der Geschäftsführung auch dann so beantwortet, daß sich die Fragesteller zufriedengeben mußten.

Interviewausschnitt 2 (Basisvertreter):
„Wir konnten in den Beiratssitzungen nur dann auf etwas hinweisen, wenn wir gravierende Probleme sahen, beispielsweise, wenn der Werbeetat um 40% erhöht worden wäre. Hier konnten wir nachfragen und konnten erfahren, aus welchen Gründen dies erforderlich war. Weiter konnten wir verschiedene Vorhaben erfahren, die sich aus der Erhöhung des Werbeetats ergaben. Wir konnten fragen, ob dies nötig sei, ob wir das Geld dazu haben. Dann mußten wir doch letztlich der Person und dem Bereich das Vertrauen aussprechen und die Fähigkeit zugestehen, dies alles richtig zu machen. (...) Mehr oder weniger ist die vorgelegte Planung ja ein Zahlenwerk, und bestimmte gravierende Zahlen sind beim Durchsehen, beim Durcharbeiten ins Auge gestochen. Dann hat man sich überlegt, weshalb muß dies so sein, und hat sich die Gründe dann erklären lassen. Nur sah man dann keine Chance, dieser Antwort zu widersprechen. Die Geschäftsleitung trug dann eben ihre Gründe vor, legte auch Fakten dar, und dann hat man letztlich doch der Geschäftsleitung das Vertrauen schenken müssen, daß die Planung und die Kosten auf die richtigen Daten zurückgehen. Wir hatten letztlich bei der Verabschiedung der Planung das Gefühl, man hat eine Planung verabschiedet, die doch nicht so gravierende Fehler aufweist. Kein Beirat konnte ein Argument anführen und der Geschäftsleitung mitteilen, hier läge die Geschäftsleitung mit der Einschätzung ihrer Annahmen völlig daneben. Wir haben unsere Bedenken in verschiedenen Punkten angemeldet, haben uns auch erklären lassen, weshalb dies nur so möglich ist, und haben dann letztlich schon das Vertrauen der Geschäftsleitung gegenüber gehabt, daß dies alles seine Richtigkeit hat."

Zusätzliche Schwierigkeiten entstanden dadurch, daß die Geschäftsleitung auf Bedenken der Beiräte gegen bestimmte Vorhaben hin und wieder mit der Aufforderung reagierte, doch selbst einen „besseren Vorschlag" vorzulegen. Dazu war der Beirat natürlich nicht in der Lage. Bei einigen wenigen Versuchen, zu einzelnen Vorhaben Alternativen zu entwickeln, konnte die Geschäftsleitung plausibel deren Unterlegenheit gegenüber dem eigenen Vorschlag darlegen.

Ähnliche Einschätzungsprobleme, wie sie sich bei der Verabschiedung der Unternehmensplanung ergaben, tauchten auch dann auf, wenn der Beirat im Rahmen der ex post-Kontrolle zu *Entscheidungen im abgelaufenen Geschäftsjahr* Stellung nehmen sollte, die vom Plan abwichen, sich aber nach Auffassung der Geschäftsführung als notwendig erwiesen hatten, um veränderten Gegebenheiten Rechnung zu tragen. Die Geschäftsleitung legte hier die relevanten Gründe dar, und wiederum stand der Beirat vor der schwierigen Aufgabe, sie auf ihre Stichhaltigkeit zu überprüfen. Der folgende Interviewausschnitt charakterisiert die Situation aus der Sicht eines Arbeitnehmervertreters, der leitender Angestellter war.

Interviewausschnitt 3 (ltd. Angestellter):
„Was wollen Sie denn dazu sagen, wenn die Geschäftsleitung darlegt, daß aus Gründen der Konkurrenzfähigkeit die Entwicklung auf dem Spiegelreflexkamera-Markt so war, daß eine 10%ige Preissenkung eingeleitet werden mußte, um halbwegs die Absatzzahlen zu realisieren. Ich kann doch nicht sagen, ihr hättet die gleiche Menge verkauft, wenn ihr die Preise hochgelassen hättet. Man kann eigentlich die Entwicklung nur noch zur Kenntnis nehmen."

Die Stellung der Geschäftsführung während der Beiratssitzungen wurde auch durch die bei vielen wichtigen Maßnahmen, insbesondere aus dem Marketingbereich, übliche Praxis gestärkt, bei der Entscheidungsvorbereitung *externe Berater* hinzuzuziehen. Waren diese externen Spezialisten bei der Diskussion anwesend, so unterstützten sie natürlich die Argumentation des Managements. Aber auch dann, wenn Spezialisten zu den Beiratssitzungen nicht hinzugezogen wurden, genügten Hinweise der Geschäftsführung auf die vorliegenden Gutachten, um kritische Fragen der Beiratsmitglieder zu entkräften. Die folgende Aussage eines leitenden Angestellten zeigt am Beispiel der Begutachtung der Werbemaßnahmen, welchen Schwierigkeiten sich die Beiräte gegenübersahen:

Interviewausschnitt 4 (ltd. Angestellter):
„Der Werbeetat lag bei 10% des Umsatzes von Photo Porst, ich glaube das letzte Mal bei 18 oder 17 Mio. DM. Ich sagte, ein solcher Etat sei doch eigentlich zu hoch für uns. Der Sprecher der Geschäftsleitung antwortete, dies sei ein Spezialgebiet und man müsse sich in die Tiefen der Werbung einarbeiten und sich außerordentlich intensiv damit befassen, um überhaupt ein Urteil abgeben zu können. Zur Begutachtung der Werbekonzeption müssen Sie absoluter Fachmann sein. In abgemilderter Form trifft diese Aussage natürlich auch für andere Bereiche zu. Aber vom Volumen her ist natürlich die Begutachtung der Werbekampagnen ein außerordentlich großer Brocken. Wenn Sie der Geschäftsleitung als Beirat vorwerfen, manche Werbeausgaben seien hinausgeworfenes Geld, so kommen sofort die Gegenargumente, die nachweisen, daß die Maßnahmen erfolgversprechend seien. Meist ist ja irgendeine Unternehmens- und Marketing-Beratungsgesellschaft angehängt, die aus den Tiefen der Werbepsychologie interpretiert, daß genau jetzt der richtige Zeitpunkt für diese Maßnahmen ist. Wie wollen Sie denn die Aussage widerlegen, daß die Kunden, die im Weihnachtsgeschäft nichts gekauft haben, jetzt noch genügend Kaufkraft haben und genau jetzt Kameras kaufen? Es ist ja das Problem, daß man bei vielem emotional entscheiden und urteilen muß und von der Sache inhaltlich nicht den vollen Einblick hat."

Lediglich bei ganz wenigen Vorhaben, die massiv die von den Beiräten vertretenen Interessen berührten, ohne daß von der Geschäftsleitung hierfür während der Diskussion eine klare Notwendigkeit für genau die beabsichtigten Maßnahmen einsichtig gemacht werden konnte, setzte sich der Beirat gegenüber der Geschäftsleitung durch. Ein Beispiel hierfür war die Forderung der Geschäftsführung nach einer tariflichen Nullrunde.[7]

2.2 Reaktion einzelner Beiräte auf die erlebte Expertenmacht

Aus den Interviews haben sich im wesentlichen drei verschiedene Reaktionsweisen der Beiratsmitglieder auf die erlebte Expertenmacht der Geschäftsführung herausgeschält, die man wie folgt typisieren kann:
- Resignative Distanz zur eigenen Rolle als Beirat;
- Aktivierung des gesunden Menschenverstandes und
- Reduzierung von Komplexität durch Vertrauen.

2.2.1. Resignative Distanz zur eigenen Rolle

Hauptsächlich zwei nicht am Unternehmensstandort beschäftigte Arbeitnehmervertreter, aber auch einige Basisvertreter, reagierten auf die erlebte Expertenmacht der Geschäftsführung mit einer – unterschiedlich stark ausgeprägten – resignativen, distanzierten Haltung gegenüber den Anforderungen der Beiratsrolle. Sie gingen relativ unvorbereitet in die Sitzungen, weil sie – wegen der räumlichen oder sozialen Distanz – im Gegensatz zu anderen Beiratsmitgliedern keine Möglichkeit sahen, informelle Kontakte für weitere Informationen zu nutzen oder an Vorbereitungssitzungen teilzunehmen. Diese Beiratsmitglieder spielten dann ihre Rolle gleichsam „achselzuckend" und resigniert; sie spürten deutlich die Grenzen ihrer Leistungsfähigkeit bei der Überwachung des Managements. Ihr Abstimmungsverhalten orientierte sich z. T. an dem Vertreter der Hausbank im Beirat, der von ihnen als noch am sachverständigsten angesehen wurde.

Der folgende Interviewausschnitt ist ein typisches Beispiel für diese resignative Reaktionsweise:

Interviewausschnitt 5 (ltd. Angestellter, nicht am Unternehmensstandort beschäftigt):
„Man war in der Beiratssitzung eigentlich ein klein wenig überfordert. Denn um eine Jahresplanung wirklich beurteilen zu können, müßte man wahnsinnig viel Zeit aufwenden. Vielleicht nicht soviel Zeit wie derjenige, der die Planung erstellt hat, jedoch mindestens die Hälfte davon. Sehen Sie, wenn dort beispielsweise stand, der Agenturbereich plant die Eröffnung von 50 weiteren Agenturen, d. h. es wird folgender Mehrumsatz geplant etc., und um solche Fragen ging es ja regelmäßig. Zu solchen Vorschlägen können Sie eigentlich nicht viel mehr sagen außer: ‚Ich wünsche euch viel Glück! Es wird schon gehen! Wie wollt ihr denn das machen?' (...) Ich war immer sehr pragmatisch und sagte mir, ich habe auch keine besseren Ideen als die Geschäftsleitung, und habe dann im Prinzip auch zugestimmt. (...) Wenn eine Planung nicht so dargestellt wird, daß man von vornherein sagen kann, dies geht so nicht und dies ist ein Unsinn, wird man schon gerne zustimmen und diese Planung probieren. Denn die Hauptfrage war immer, wer wird denn das Ganze bezahlen. Umgekehrt formuliert: Wenn der Bankier und die Bank zustimmten, gab es keinen Grund mehr, dies nicht zu probieren, und solch utopische und unrealistische Planung hat die Geschäftsleitung ja auch nicht vorgelegt. Das kann man ihr wirklich nicht vorwerfen. Man war überall ein bißchen stolz, das Vertrauen ehrte uns, aber, ganz ehrlich, im Nachhinein finde ich die Rolle, die ich abgegeben habe, für nicht gut. Den anderen Beiratskollegen ging es ähnlich."

Die erlebte Expertenmacht der Geschäftsführung veranlaßte diesen Beiratsvertreter dazu, über eine Neudefinition der Beiratsrolle nachzudenken. Er skizzierte im Interview seine entsprechenden Gedanken. Er verglich die Rolle des Beirates mit der eines Richters. Im Gegensatz zur Gerichtsverhandlung träten in der Beiratssitzung aber nur Personen auf, die eine ausschließlich *entlastende* Funktion wahrnähmen. Die *belastende* Funktion des mit dem Streitgegenstand bestens vertrauten Staatsanwaltes fehle dagegen:

Interviewausschnitt 6 (Interviewpartner wie 5):

„Wissen Sie, wie ich meinen Beirat gestalten würde? Die Beiräte wären bei mir wie die Schöffen vor Gericht. Sie bräuchten sich im Prinzip auch nicht vorzubereiten. Die säßen eigentlich nur da, würden von der Geschäftsleitung hören, was die Geschäftsleitung will, und würden dann von einer fachlich qualifizierten Gegenseite, die auch die Planungsunterlagen lange vorher durchgesehen hat und die man nicht erst auf Chancen und Risiken hinweisen muß, sondern diese aufgrund ihrer Qualifikation selbst erkennt, die Gegenargumentation hören. Aus meiner Sicht wäre dies für die internen Beiräte[8] (...) der richtige Weg. Ohne den externen Beiräten wehtun zu wollen, ich glaube auch, für die wäre es der bessere Weg. Ich kann mir noch aus Meinung und Gegenmeinung ein Urteil bilden. Eine eigene Gegenmeinung gegenüber der Geschäftsführung zu entwickeln und zu begründen, halte ich für ein Unding."

Gerade dies, ein mehr ins Detail gehendes eigenes Urteil zu entwickeln, war aber das Anliegen einiger anderer Beiräte und insofern eine zweite eigenständige Reaktionsweise auf die erlebte Expertenmacht.

2.2.2. Aktivierung des gesunden Menschenverstandes

Ihre Urteilsbildung gegenüber den Vorschlägen der Geschäftsführung gründeten vor allem zwei Basisvertreter auf den „gesunden Menschenverstand". Ein Interviewpartner explizierte diese seine Vorstellung am Beispiel eines Problems, das in einer Beiratssitzung im Zusammenhang mit bestimmten fehlgeschlagenen Werbemaßnahmen des abgelaufenen Jahres auftauchte. Da die für das betreffende Jahr genehmigte Jahresplanung nur das Werbebudget fixierte, ohne daß bereits detaillierte Werbemaßnahmen aus den Unterlagen ersichtlich waren, wurde die ganze Problematik erst in der Rückschau für den Beirat aktuell. Die beiden Beiräte leiteten aus dem Fehlschlag der Vergangenheit die Forderung ab, für die Zukunft nicht nur das Werbebudget, sondern auch die Werbekonzeption selbst in ihren groben Zügen zum Gegenstand einer inhaltlichen Diskussion zu machen; sie fühlten sich ausreichend qualifiziert, die von den Fachleuten entwickelten Konzeptionen auf ihre Erfolgswahrscheinlichkeit hin zu beurteilen. Allerdings konnten sie im Beirat keine Mehrheit für ihre Forderung finden. Ganz offenbar befürchteten die übrigen Beiräte, mit einem solchen Schritt die Grenze zwischen Geschäftsführung und Überwachung zu überschreiten.

Die Sichtweise, wie sie für die beiden Basisvertreter charakteristisch war, wird mit folgendem Interviewausschnitt umrissen:

Interviewausschnitt 7 (Basisvertreter):
„Hier ist der gesunde Menschenverstand entscheidend. Es gibt Dinge, in die verbohren sich Werbefachleute. Die Idee mag gut sein, aber die Ideen kommen nicht an. Ich hatte wirklich einige Werbeprojekte zu kritisieren, die ich für vollkommen absurd angesehen habe und die auch in der Praxis fehlgeschlagen sind. Man hätte dies für meine Begriffe vorher sehen müssen. Ich sage, hier hilft uns auch der gesunde Menschenverstand weiter. Ich hätte es gerne gesehen, wenn manche der kostspieligen Werbeprojekte durch den Beirat zustimmungspflichtig gewesen wären. Aber dies ist ja nicht der Fall. Das Werbebudget wird mit der gesamten Planung verabschiedet. Da steht nicht, daß Sie die ‚Minute des Jahres‘[9] verabschiedet haben und daß der VfL Bochum mit ‚PORST‘ herumsausen darf. Darüber entscheidet im Detail der Beirat nicht, da er davon überhaupt nichts erfährt. Sie können dann im Nachhinein gegen einzelne Maßnahmen Sturm laufen und sagen, wie konnte dieses und jenes passieren. Der VfL Bochum erhält jährlich von uns DM 300 000,–. Sehen Sie sich weiter die von der neuen Werbeagentur gemachte Anzeigenkampagne der letzten Zeit an. Der Kunde will nicht hören, es gibt ‚Porst‘, der Kunde will auf Artikel hingewiesen werden; wobei ich von der Imagewerbung sogar etwas halte, wenn etwas dahintersteckt, d. h. die Kunden bisher auch zufrieden waren. Wenn Sie dann hören: ‚Porst, das ist ja alles gut. Was nützt es mir aber als Porst-Kunde, wenn ich mir eine Kamera gekauft habe oder Bilder zurückerhalten habe und enttäuscht bin, weil ich laufend Reparaturen damit habe und die Bilder falsch entwickelt sind?‘ Und wenn dann die Imagewerbung kommt und auf die Porst-Qualität hingewiesen wird, dann kann ich nur lachen. Es tritt höchstens noch der negative Effekt auf, daß ich mit meinen Kollegen über die Anzeige spreche und meine negativen Erfahrungen mit der Reklame vergleiche. Es besteht sogar die Gefahr einer Negativ-Werbung, wenn die schlechten Kundenerfahrungen mit den großen Sprüchen konfrontiert werden. Jedenfalls besteht diese Gefahr eher, als wenn der Kunde mit seinen Erfahrungen allein bliebe und nicht mit der großspurigen Werbung konfrontiert werden würde. Diese Werbung könnte in zwei bis drei Jahren für uns gut sein, wenn wir es schaffen, unsere Qualität zu verbessern. Der Zeitpunkt dieser Werbekonzeption war falsch."

Ein weiterer Interviewausschnitt unterstreicht an einem zweiten Beispiel die Auffassung, mit Hilfe des gesunden Menschenverstandes könne auch der Beirat die Zweckmäßigkeit von Maßnahmen der Unternehmensführung ausreichend beurteilen:

Interviewausschnitt 8 (Basisvertreter):
„Ein bezeichnendes Beispiel war die Einführung des ‚sprechenden Bildes‘.[10] Wir haben auch bei diesem Projekt vom Aufwand und von den Details her nicht erfahren, was geplant ist. Wir haben dann schon nachgehakt und gefragt, was alles geschehen soll, und wir haben schon gefragt, ob dies in dem Umfang sein muß. Ich weiß nicht, ob nicht auch die Geschäftsleitung heute der Auffassung ist, daß dies mit weniger Aufwand auch zu machen gewesen wäre. Ich meine, diese riesigen Einladungen, das riesige Zelt, mit dem dieses Projekt vorgestellt wurde, waren nicht nötig. Ich glaube, die gleiche Präsentationswirkung hätte man auch mit anderen Maßnahmen erreichen können."

Die hier beschriebenen Reaktionen der Basisvertreter resultierten offensichtlich aus einem Verlust an Vertrauen in die fachliche Kompetenz der Spezialisten der Werbeabteilung und der für die gescheiterten Maßnahmen verantwortlichen Geschäftsführer. Ihre Schlußfolgerung daraus war weniger, für die Zukunft personelle Konsequenzen im Management zu ziehen, sondern gleichsam die „Eindringtiefe“ des Beirates in die Planung zu erhöhen. Dazu wäre dann allerdings auch eine detailliertere, nicht nur auf Formal- sondern auch auf Sachziele abstellende Planvorlage an den Beirat erforderlich gewesen.

2.2.3. Reduzierung von Komplexität durch Vertrauen

Eine dritte Gruppe von Beiratsmitgliedern erlebte die Expertenmacht der Geschäftsführung und sah letztlich keine Möglichkeit, dieser ein eigenes ebenso gut fundiertes Argumentationspotential entgegenzusetzen. Diese Beiratsmitglieder akzeptierten dieses Spannungsverhältnis und überbrückten es durch einen Vertrauensvorschuß, der nach Ablauf des Geschäftsjahres bei der Diskussion des Jahresabschlusses und vor allem bei der Entlastung der Geschäftsführer auf seine Berechtigung hin überprüft werden sollte. Man setzte sich damit deutlich in Gegensatz zu der zweiten Position, die man als „Beckmesserei und Fliegenbeinzählerei“ charakterisierte. Es komme darauf an, die Grundrichtung der Unternehmenspolitik im Hinblick auf ihre Wirkungen für die im Beirat vertretenen Interessengruppen zu überprüfen, im übrigen aber die Details den Experten zu überlassen und sich vorzubehalten, die Geschäftsführung dann ex post daraufhin zu bewerten, inwieweit ihre Einschätzung der künftigen Entwicklung richtig war und realisiert werden konnte. Der Unterschied zur ersten Reaktionsweise besteht hier darin, daß die Notwendigkeit und die Grenzen der Kategorie „Vertrauen“ im Kontext der Überwachungsaufgabe des Beirates viel deutlicher gesehen wurden; Vertrauen wurde von diesen Beiräten nicht als ausschließende Alternative zur Kontrolle und im Sinne einer resignativen Laissez-Faire-Einstellung thematisiert, sondern eher als eine *Restkategorie,* die sich in die übrigen Überwachungsaktivitäten des Beirates sinnvoll einordnete. Ihre Devise hieß nicht: „Vertrauen statt Kontrolle“, sondern: „Kontrolle soweit wie möglich – Vertrauen soweit noch nötig.“

Zwei Gesprächsausschnitte sollen diese Deutung der Beiratsrolle veranschaulichen[11]:

Interviewausschnitt 9 (ltd. Angestellter):

„Es ist die alte Qualifikationsfrage der Aufsichtsräte, die ja im Grunde genommen im Detail immer weniger wissen als die Geschäftsleitung, und die Chance, dies alles aufzuarbeiten, ohnehin nur bis zu einem gewissen Grad haben. Sie können also nur global prüfen, ob sorgfältig gearbeitet wurde oder nicht. Zweitens kommt die Risikoabwägung, die irgendwo auch zur Vertrauensfrage gehört. Es ist ja nicht zufällig die Aufgabe des Beirates, dem Vorstand das Vertrauen permanent auszusprechen. Mit diesem etwas globalen Bereich muß man als Beirat leben. Man kann nicht fordern, der Beirat solle den gleichen Informationsstand wie die Geschäftsleitung haben. Es mag auch nicht immer günstig sein, zu sehr im Detail zu stecken. Ich glaube, daß es viel wichtiger ist, generell zu sagen: ‚Hat die Geschäftsleitung hier richtig gearbeitet? Ist die Grundrichtung richtig? Können wir Sorgfalt unterstellen? Gibt es beim Endergebnis der Planung die Notwendigkeit, sagen zu müssen: Jetzt müssen wir die Geschäftsleitung wieder nach Hause schicken?‘ Aber möglichst kein

,Fummel im Detail', weil dies äußerst unergiebig und unfruchtbar ist. Dies muß auch zu Frustrationen bei den Beiräten führen, da die Detailkenntnis bei der Geschäftsleitung doch – hoffentlich – so groß ist."

Interviewausschnitt 10 (Gewerkschaftssekretär; zugleich Mitglied in einem nach dem Mitbestimmungsgesetz 1976 mitbestimmten Aufsichtsrat):
„Als Beirat habe ich in der Phase der Ausarbeitung einer Planung ganz klar wenig Einfluß. Kann ich auch nicht haben, denn ich muß den Fachleuten, die im Tagesgeschäft stecken, vertrauen. Diesen Leuten muß ich das Vertrauen entgegenbringen, sonst klappt die Zusammenarbeit überhaupt nicht. Ich muß mich darauf verlassen können, daß sie vernünftig den Markt kennen. Dies erwarte ich ganz einfach, sonst würde ich die Qualifikation dieser Leute in Frage stellen. Wenn ich kein Vertrauen mehr in diese Geschäftsführung habe, so bleibt mir als Beiratsmitglied nichts anderes übrig, als diese Geschäftsführung abzuberufen, zumindest Teile der Geschäftsführung abzuberufen. Wir haben dies bei Porst ja in den letzten Jahren immer wieder gehabt, daß Geschäftsführer wie bei keinem anderen, klassischen Unternehmen berufen und abberufen wurden. Wenn die Vertrauensbasis nicht mehr vorhanden ist, können Sie alles andere vergessen. Wenn man der Geschäftsführung vorwerfen kann, daß sie mit ihren Planungen seit zwei Jahren völlig daneben liegt, so spreche ich damit der Geschäftsführung die Qualifikation ab. Wir machten dies auch deutlich. Wenn wir an der Nase herumgeführt worden wären, so wäre ganz schnell eine Korrektur geschehen. Wir haben dies in all den Jahren getan. Der Beirat ist doch im Prinzip darauf angewiesen, von der Geschäftsführung die richtigen Informationen zu erhalten. Nur dann, wenn Sie berechtigte Zweifel an der Fähigkeit oder am guten Willen der Geschäftsführung haben, wird die Sache problematisch, und Sie müssen die Geschäftsführung abberufen. In jedem anderen mitbestimmten Unternehmen ist das doch immer das Gleiche. Der Vorstand muß seinem Aufsichtsrat genau sagen, was los ist, denn beide tragen die Verantwortung. Hier darf nicht gemauschelt und manipuliert werden. Wenn festgestellt wird, daß dem Beirat etwas vorgegaukelt wird, dann ist dies sicher einmal machbar. Beim zweiten Mal, und die Ergebnisse des Geschäftsjahres zeigen dies ja, wird die Unfähigkeit dieser Geschäftsführung erkennbar, und man wird mißtrauisch. Und man läßt sich nicht ein zweites Mal aufs Kreuz legen. Ein Beirat wäre auch überfordert, wenn er bei einzelnen Kompetenz- und Sachproblemen in die Geschäftsführung eingreifen würde. Ich meine, dies ist nicht Aufgabe eines Aufsichtsrates oder Beirates."

Auffallend ist, daß diese dritte Reaktionsweise vor allem bei solchen Beiratsmitgliedern zu beobachten war, die auf extern gewonnene Erfahrungen als Aufsichtsräte zurückgreifen konnten oder die als leitende Angestellte relativ zu den Basisvertretern über geringere Qualifikationsdefizite gegenüber der Geschäftsleitung verfügten. Diese Personen erlebten im Gegensatz zu den anderen Beiratsmitgliedern das Spannungsfeld zwischen „Unternehmensführung" und „Kontrolle" eher als normal und beherrschbar, vor allem aber auch als durch weitere Bemühungen um eine noch intensivere Detaillierung der Kontrollaktivitäten nicht aufhebbar.

3. Einige kommentierende Anmerkungen

Es ist unschwer erkennbar, daß in den drei referierten Reaktionsweisen der Beiratsmitglieder auf die von ihnen erlebte Expertenmacht der Unternehmensführung Problemfelder thematisiert wurden, die auch in der theoretischen Diskussion immer schon eine gewichtige Rolle gespielt haben. Diese interessante Parallelität läßt sich in drei Thesen verdichten; ihre kurze Kommentierung soll abschließend wenigstens andeuten, daß das Problem der Expertenmacht insgesamt durchaus differenzierter gesehen werden muß, als es die Pauschal-These von der strukturellen Unterlegenheit des Laien gegenüber dem Fachmann nahelegt. Die drei Thesen lauten:

1. Dort, wo es um die *normativen Grundlagen* der Unternehmenspolitik geht, gibt es keine Experten; jeder ist im Hinblick auf die zu treffenden Wertentscheidungen Fachmann (oder Laie).

2. Dort, wo die Wahl geeigneter *technischer* Mittel ansteht, geht mit dem Spezialistenurteil des Experten häufig zugleich eine Ausblendung von lebenspraktischen Zusammenhängen des Alltags einher; dem „Expertentum des Spezialisten" läßt sich insoweit das „Expertentum des Alltags" (common sense) gegenüberstellen.

3. *Vertrauen* ist die notwendige Kompensation für die nie vollständig aufzuhebende faktische Machtdifferenz zwischen technischen Experten (Unternehmensführung) und Laien (Beiratsmitgliedern); dabei geht es aber nicht um „blindes Vertrauen", sondern um eine Residualkategorie, deren Bedeutung sich nach der Reichweite einer sinnvoll gestalteten *Kontrolle* richten muß.

Die *erste These* ist zumindest implizit in dem angesprochenen „Schöffenmodell" enthalten. Die Vorstellung, durch Argumentation und Gegenargumentation die Grundlagen der Unternehmensplanung zu explizieren, kann sich ja nicht nur auf die technischen Wirkungszusammenhänge beziehen, sondern betrifft notwendigerweise und insbesondere auch die normativen Ausgangsannahmen, mit deren Hilfe überhaupt erst Planungsprobleme im Rahmen einer hochselektiven Modellkonstruktion aus dem (systemischen) Gesamtzusammenhang der Lebenspraxis ausgegrenzt werden können. Damit werden Verbindungslinien zur neueren betriebswirtschaftlichen Planungsdiskussion deutlich, wenn man etwa an die Arbeiten von Churchman und W. Ulrich denkt.[12] Zu erinnern ist in diesem Kontext auch an die Idee der „dialektischen Planung" für schwach strukturierte strategische Probleme.[13] Die dialektische Planung soll ja der Idee nach durch Konfrontation von mindestens zwei unterschiedlichen Positionen verschiedene *Sichtweisen* der Entscheidungssituation aufdecken und explizite und implizite Voraussetzungen der strategischen Planung deutlich machen und problematisieren.

Die *zweite These* nimmt den Gedanken aus den Interviewausschnitten 7 und 8 auf, daß mit dem „gesunden Menschenverstand" bis zu einem gewissen Grade erfolgreich gegen Expertenvorschläge argumentiert werden kann. Hier ist an die Einsicht anzuknüpfen, daß Spezialisierung nur über Selektion möglich ist. In dem

Maße, wie Experten immer sachverständiger in bestimmten Angelegenheiten werden, besteht die Gefahr, daß sie – weil sie von den vielseitigen Problemlagen der Lebenspraxis abstrahieren müssen – schließlich das Teil für das Ganze setzen und dadurch zu für die Praxis ungeeigneten Lösungen kommen. Und in dem Maße, wie dieser Spezialisierungsprozeß sich auch noch arbeitsteilig im Rahmen der Managementhierarchie und unter großer Distanz von der Handlungsebene vollzieht, erhöht sich die Gefahr, daß der Blick für die Totalität des Lebenszusammenhangs verloren geht. Hier liegt die Chance des Laien, soweit er aus der Lebenserfahrung immer wieder die von den Spezialisten ausgeblendeten, aber (möglicherweise) problemrelevanten Aspekte in die Argumentation einbringen kann. In diese Richtung zielt die Kritik des erwähnten Beiratsmitgliedes sowohl an der Werbeidee der „Minute des Jahres“ wie auch an der Idee des „sprechenden Bildes“. Daß Spezialisierung und Arbeitsteilung in der Managementhierarchie zu unpraktischen Problemlösungen führen können, wird auch aus den Erfahrungsberichten von de Loreans bei General Motors deutlich.[14]

Die *dritte These* schließlich zielt auf eine neue Deutung des Verhältnisses von Unternehmensführung und Aufsichtsrat und knüpft damit speziell auch an die entsprechenden Überlegungen in der Mitbestimmungsdiskussion an. Zu erinnern ist hier an die These von Brinkmann-Herz über die strukturelle Ungeeignetheit des Aufsichtsrates zur Kontrolle der Unternehmensführung.[15] Brinkman-Herz kommt zu diesem Urteil, indem sie an die durch das Aktiengesetz vorgegebene strukturelle Arbeitsteilung von Vorstand und Aufsichtsrat anknüpft, sodann *implizit* von beiden Organen die gleiche Qualifikation und die gleiche Involvierung in den Entscheidungsprozeß fordert und – nachdem dies natürlich nicht möglich ist – die zugrunde liegende Entscheidungsstruktur der Ineffizienz bezichtigt. Sie legt einen Maßstab von Kontrolle an, der auf den Nachvollzug eines jeden einzelnen Schrittes des phasenmäßig und personell ausdifferenzierten Entscheidungsprozesses zielt. Mit diesem „utopischen“ Kontrollmaßstab ist dann das Urteil natürlich bereits vorbestimmt. Erst wenn man einen realistischen Maßstab von Kontrolle anlegt, wie er sich in einigen Interviewauszügen angedeutet hat, und zugleich das Verhältnis von Kontrolle und Vertrauen sinnvoll fixiert, bietet sich eine Chance, zu einem vernünftigen Verständnis der gesamten Überwachungsproblematik des Aufsichtsrates zu kommen.

Die Überlegungen, die verschiedene Beiratsmitglieder zur Bedeutung des Vertrauens im Rahmen ihrer Kontrollbeziehung zur Geschäftsführung der Porst-Gruppe angestellt haben, verweisen darauf, daß Vertrauen eben *nicht* als das funktionale Äquivalent zur Kontrolle anzusehen ist; denn Vertrauen in dem von ihnen gebrauchten Sinne beginnt gerade dort, wo die Leistungsfähigkeit der Kontrolle (auf der Basis geeigneter Institutionen und gut ausgebildeter und informierter, vorbereiteter Personen) *endet.* Erst an dieser Grenze wird die von Luhmann erwähnte „Zeitdifferenz der Leistungsbeziehungen“[16] erreicht, die durch Vertrauen als „riskante Vorleistung“[17] überbrückt werden muß. An dem Punkt, an dem die strukturell bedingte Leistungsfähigkeit des Beirates bzw.

Aufsichtsrates bei der Begutachtung der Unternehmensplanung endet, löst sich die Geschäftsführung aus der Kongruenz der Kooperationsbeziehung und gewinnt einen zeitlich begrenzten Vorteil an direkt nicht mehr kontrollierbaren Gestaltungsmöglichkeiten. An dieser Stelle geht Kontrolle *notwendigerweise* in Vertrauen über, dessen Mißbrauch dann nur noch ex post durch prozessuale Vorkehrungen und personelle Sanktionen (die gleichwohl vorsteuernde Wirkungen entfalten können)[18] kompensiert werden kann.

Insgesamt verweisen die in den Interviewausschnitten wiedergegebenen subjektiven Erfahrungen von Interessenvertretern mit der Expertenmacht der Unternehmensführung ebenso wie theoretische Reflektionen also darauf, die Eigenart der Interkationsbeziehungen zwischen Unternehmensführung (Vorstand) und Interessenvertretungsorgan (Aufsichts- oder Beirat) nicht über den Leisten undifferenzierter und unangemessener Maßstäbe von Kontrolle zu schlagen.[19] Worauf es vielmehr ankommt ist, das prekäre Gleichgewicht zwischen dem, was Kontrolle hier sinnvollerweise heißen kann und muß, und dem notwendigen Ausmaß an Vertrauen in seinen Funktionsbedingungen genauer zu durchdenken und zwar in eine Richtung, wie sie durch die drei angesprochenen Thesen nahegelegt wird. Erst dann wird sich auch die eingangs aufgeworfene Frage beantworten lassen, ob und wann man sinnvollerweise davon sprechen kann, daß die faktische Macht der „Experten" der Unternehmensführung die juristische Machtbasis der „Laien" im Beirat überformt hat.

Anmerkungen

1 Günter Dlugos hat in seiner Forschungsarbeit besonders die Konfliktbezüge wirtschaftlichen Handelns bearbeitet und in seinen Publikationen die institutionellen und personellen Konsequenzen für die Unternehmensführung und eine Lehre von der Unternehmenspolitik betont. Das gleichgelagerte Interesse für Fragen der Unternehmensverfassung hat uns in vielen Kommissionssitzungen zusammengeführt. Dort habe ich die faire und abwägende, immer sachbezogene kritisch-rationale Argumentation von Günter Dlugos schätzen gelernt. So konnte über Jahre eine persönliche Beziehung entstehen, die ich nicht missen möchte und die auch durch unterschiedliche wissenschaftstheoretische Positionen keineswegs beeinträchtigt, eher befruchtet wird. In dem vorliegenden Beitrag, einem „Praxisbericht", werden Schwierigkeiten „dialogischer Verständigung" zwischen Experten der Unternehmensführung und Arbeitnehmervertretern thematisiert, auf die der Jubilar in seinen Publikationen immer wieder aufmerksam gemacht hat. (Vgl. insbesondere Dlugos 1977, 1981).

2 Vgl. zur empirischen Relevanz dieses Trennungsphänomens für die Bundesrepublik Deutschland Steinmann / Schreyögg / Dütthorn 1983 (mit weiteren Literaturnachweisen).

3 Vgl. dazu insbesondere Ridder-Aab 1980 und Hessen 1979.

4 Zur Grundstruktur dieses Modells vgl. Steinmann / Heinrich / Müller 1979.

5 Die Termini „Arbeiter" und „leitende Angestellte" wurden hier gewählt, um die unterschiedlichen Qualifikationen der Basisvertreter und der hoch qualifizierten Arbeit-

nehmervertreter im Beirat zu kennzeichnen. Sie sind nicht identisch mit den arbeitsrechtlichen Begriffen, wie sie für Arbeitnehmervertreter im Aufsichtsrat in § 15 Abs. 2 i. V. m. § 3 MitbestG unter Bezugnahme auf § 6 Abs. 1 bzw. § 5 Abs. 3 BetrVG Anwendung finden.

[6] Vgl. dazu näher Müller 1986, S. 83 ff.

[7] Vgl. dazu näher Müller 1986, S. 254.

[8] Als interne Beiräte wurden diejenigen fünf Beiratsmitglieder bezeichnet, die als Arbeitnehmervertreter direkt durch die Belegschaft in den aus neun Personen bestehenden Beirat gewählt wurden. Die vier externen Beiräte dagegen durften nicht der Porst-Gruppe angehören. Je zwei von ihnen wurden von den beiden Gesellschaftern der Porst Verwaltungsgesellschaft bestellt. Vgl. dazu genauer Steinmann / Heinrich 1977.

[9] Die „Minute des Jahres" war eine Marketingaktion, bei der möglichst viele Personen während einer vorher mit viel Aufwand bekanntgegebenen Minute irgendein sie interessierendes Motiv photographieren sollten. Das zur Porst-Gruppe gehörende Photolabor eurocop sollte die Filme entwickeln und Bilder herstellen. Aus allen eingesandten Filmen sollte eine Dokumentation in Form eines Bildbandes und – mit einer Auswahl der Bilder – einer Wanderausstellung durchgeführt werden. Unter den Einsendern wurden Preise, darunter eine Weltreise, verlost.

[10] Beim „Sprechenden Bild" wurde ein Porst-Königsbild im (teureren) „Welt"-Format kostenlos mit einem Magnetbandstreifen versehen, der an der Rückseite angebracht wurde. Mit einem Gerät, das von Porst vertrieben wurde, war es möglich, einen ca. 5 Sekunden langen Text auf das Band zu sprechen bzw. abzuhören. Zur Präsentation des „sprechenden Bildes" wurde in Schwabach ein Zirkus-Zelt aufgebaut, in dem die zahlreichen geladenen Gäste bewirtet wurden. Der Präsentationsaufwand belief sich auf fast eine halbe Million DM.

[11] Anklänge in dieser Richtung auch im Interviewausschnitt 2 oben S. 259 dieses Beitrages.

[12] Ulrich 1983, insbes. S. 225 ff., mit weiteren Literaturnachweisen.

[13] Vgl. z. B. Mason 1969, B 403 ff.; kritisch dazu Schreyögg 1984, S. 283 f.

[14] Vgl. Wright 1979, insbes. S. 229 ff.

[15] Brinkmann-Herz 1972, insbes. S. 150.

[16] Luhmann 1964, S. 72.

[17] Luhmann 1973, S. 23.

[18] Vgl. Teichmann 1973, S. 458.

[19] Zu einer genaueren Explikation der Bedeutung von Vertrauen und Mißtrauen für die Kontrollrolle des Aufsichtsrates vgl. Steinmann / Klaus 1987.

Literatur

Brinkmann-Herz, D. (1972): *Entscheidungsprozesse in den Aufsichtsräten der Montanindustrie.* Berlin.

Dlugos, G. (1977): Gesellschaftspolitische Implikationen unternehmungsinterner Konflikthandhabung. In: *Die Betriebswirtschaft* 37, S. 465–474.

Dlugos, G. (1981): The Relationship Between Changing Value Systems, Conflicts, and Conflict-Handling in the Enterprise-Sector. In: Dlugos, G., Weiermair, K. (Eds.), *Management Under Differing Value Systems.* Berlin, New York, S. 651–676.

Hessen, R. (1979): *In Defense of the Corporation.* Stanford.

Luhmann, N. (1964): *Funktionen und Folgen formaler Organisation.* Berlin.

Luhmann, N. (1973): *Vertrauen – Ein Mechanismus der Reduktion sozialer Komplexität.* 2. erw. Aufl., Stuttgart.

Mason, R. O. (1969): A Dialectical Approach to Strategic Planning. In: *Management Science* 15, S. B 403–B 414.

Müller, H. (1986): *Mitbestimmung im Aufsichtsrat und Kontrolle der Unternehmenspolitik.* Eine empirische Untersuchung zur Handhabung repräsentativer Mitbestimmung in einem Mitarbeiterunternehmen. Frankfurt am Main, Bern, New York.

Ridder-Aab, Ch.-M. (1980): *Die moderne Aktiengesellschaft im Lichte der Theorie der Eigentumsrechte.* Frankfurt am Main–New York.

Schreyögg, G. (1984): *Unternehmensstrategie. Grundfragen einer Theorie strategischer Unternehmensführung.* Berlin, New York.

Steinmann, H. / Heinrich, M. (1977). Porst-Modell und Marktwirtschaft. In: *Die Betriebswirtschaft* 37, S. 577–589.

Steinmann, H. / Heinrich, M. / Müller, H. (1979): Idee und Wirklichkeit des Porst-Modells. Probleme der Demokratisierung von Betriebsstrukturen. In: *Die Betriebswirtschaft* 39, S. 289–302.

Steinmann, H. / Klaus, H. (1987): Zur Rolle des Aufsichtsrates als Kontrollorgan. In: Die Aktiengesellschaft 32.

Steinmann, H. / Schreyögg, G. / Dütthorn, C. (1983): Managerkontrolle in deutschen Großunternehmen – 1972 und 1979 im Vergleich. In: *Zeitschrift für Betriebswirtschaft* 53, S. 4–25.

Teichmann, H. (1973): Zur Eignung des Aufsichtsrates als Organ der Mitbestimmung im Unternehmen. In: *Zeitschrift für Wirtschafts- und Sozialwissenschaften* 39, S. 445–465.

Ulrich, W. (1983): *Critical Heuristics of Social Planning. A new Approach to Practical Philosophy.* Bern, Stuttgart.

Wright, J. P. (1979): *On a Clear Day you can see General Motors. John Z. de Lorean's Look Inside the Automotive Giant.* New York.

Codetermination: Its Relevance for Canada

John Crispo

Abstract

The purpose of this essay is to assess the relevance of West-German-style codetermination for the Canadian industrial relations system. The reason for writing the essay is to ascertain whether any such codetermination scheme is likely to contribute to the resolution of the problems normally associated with the collective bargaining process in Canada.

The essay begins by reviewing the usual criticisms that are made of industrial relations in Canada with a view to explaining the seemingly never-ending Canadian quest for a brave new foreign world of industrial relations that might work in Canada. This provides a backdrop against which to offer a perspective on West Germany's codetermination system from a Canadian point of view. It is then possible to analyze the relevance of this system for Canada's industrial relations.

1. Criticisms of the Canadian Industrial Relations System

Industrial relations in Canada are often the subject of a great deal of misguided and/or misleading criticism. Three major criticisms are usually offered, each of which is endemic to the system because of the nature of the environment within which it is operating.

One criticism is that the Canadian industrial relations system is too decentralized and fragmented. Employers, unions and the collective bargaining process itself are all vulnerable to this criticism. Indeed, in virtually every respect, Canadian industrial relations are among the most decentralized and fragmented in the world. But there is a simple and largely unavoidable explanation for this phenomenon. It reflects Canada's decentralized federal-provincial distribution of powers in the industrial relations sphere and the fragmented approach of each level of government to the recognition of unions. The solution to these problems lies within Canada and not abroad, assuming the need and resolve to tackle them.

A second criticism reflects the fact that Canada normally vies with Italy for leadership in the international strike league. Relatively speaking Canada is very strike prone but again the explanation lies within Canada's borders and not beyond them. Although there are other reasons for Canada's strike-proneness, two leading causes derive from the decentrallized and fragmented nature of the collective bargaining process and the comparatively high proportion of resource industries in Canada, industries that have a high strike propensity the world over.

The third criticism is that Canada's industrial relations system is inflation prone. Compared to other causes of inflation in Canada wage-push is seldom a major factor even though it often appears to be because of the disproportionate media attention attracted by wage increases relative to most other cost and income increases. The fact of the matter is that collective bargaining is normally no more inflation-prone than most other cost-and-income-setting mechanisms in Canada.

2. The Search for a Brave New World

Discontent with the Canadian industrial relations system periodically leads largely ill-informed observers to look wistfully abroad for alternative models that might improve the situation in Canada. This quest for foreign panaceas goes back many years and ranges over a rich variety of foreign industrial relations experiences.

The search for a foreign panacea began fairly soon after World War II even though Canada's many postwar advantages spared the country the need to worry about its industrial relations or any other troublesome phenomena until the late 1950's and early 1960's. The first target of Canada's admiration was the Netherland's industrial relations system. This fascination lasted until Holland had its great wage price explosion in 1965. Canada's attention was then diverted to Sweden with its famous middle way that seemed to promise both peace on the industrial relations front and prosperity on the economic front. Less Canadian attention has been focussed on Sweden's system as that peace and prosperity has proven more elusive.

More recently Canadians-like all North Americans-have devoted considerable attention to Japan Inc. with all its unique industrial relations characteristics. Theory Z became the buzz word of North American managers who became especially fascinated by the relatively cooperative role which enterprise unions seem to play in the Japanese system of industrial relations. The thought of more hard-working and loyal workers appealed to North American managers even if they were somewhat dubious about the concomitant practices of lifetime employment and seniority wages. Canadians-like their American counterparts-still do not seem to be that aware of the double standard in Japan's dual-labour-market and other features of the Japanese industrial relations system that do not make it that attractive an alternative.

3. Codetermination From a Canadian Perspective

West Germany's codetermination system has hardly been ignored during Canada's continuing obsession with foreign industrial relations models. For a time during the 1970's West Germany's economic miracle received much favourable coverage in Canada and much credit for this miracle was given to the codetermination process.

To begin it should be stressed that many Canadians equate West Germany's codetermination system solely with the representation of workers and unions on company boards. Many Canadians know little about the distinction between Canadian boards of directors and West Germany's supervisory boards. They know even less about the three different systems of codetermination at the supervisory board level let alone about the special role of the labour director on the management boards in the coal and steel industries.

Worse still there is precious little comprehension in Canada of the way in which codetermination in the narrow sense of that term fits into West Germany's overall system of industrial democracy. Little or no attention is paid in Canada to the integral part which works councils play in company codetermination systems in West Germany. Rather, there is a superficial tendency to equate West Germany's works councils with North America's local unions which, of course, is a gross oversimplification.

There is also little or no appreciation of how codetermination at the micro level in West Germany interrelates with more tripartite endeavours at the macro or national level. Whether it is in form of the now-defunct Concerted Action Committee or tripartite-decision-making in the labour bureaus or social security systems, there is virtually no awareness of how all these pieces come together to form a comprehensive approach to codetermination or industrial democracy.

Even in terms of the narrow sense of codetermination at the company supervisory board level in West Germany there is little or no understanding of how it works let alone of the pros and cons involved. Before turning to some of these pros and cons it is essential to appreciate the tradeoffs that characterize an effective codetermination process at the company level. In essence, successful tradeoffs at this level would seem to embody something like the following approach. At the supervisory board level worker and union representatives appear to insist on at least an equal voice in all social matters effecting the work force.

In return, and provided the management and shareholder representatives are totally open with them, the worker and union representatives seem to more or less go along with their accounting, financial, marketing and production policies as long as they do not jeopardize the income and job security of the workers. When that happens-as it did during the protracted recession-worker and union representatives on supervisory boards invariably insist on much more say in the company's affairs. The author was among those who felt that this might lead to unmanageable tensions on these boards, especially if more left wing radicals were elected on the worker and union side.

While this did seem to happen in a number of cases, the protracted recession proved so sobering from everyone's point of view that cooperation competed with protagonism as a means to cope with the challenge. As a result those like the author who expressed grave misgivings about the viability of codetermination during extended hard times proved to be unduly pessimistic. Codetermination has proven to have more staying power than even some of its staunchest advocates may have envisaged.

Turning to some of the pros and cons of codetermination in West Germany, space will permit only a few general observations. If one believes in more worker involvement in decision-making at all levels of society codetermination in the narrow sense of that term has a major role to play in an overall system of industrial democracy. Even within such a comprehensive process of industrial democracy, however, the average worker may not feel that involved. After all it is still very much a representative system of democracy rather than one entailing individual worker participation. This is left to the realm of shopfloor democracy under various forms of the quality-of-working-life movement none of which are that advanced in West Germany or anywhere else.

Much of the debate about codetermination has revolved around its impact on management effectiveness, the moreso as efficiency, innovation and productivity improvements have become the hallmarks of success and survival in an increasingly competitive world. Codetermination has clearly had one very healthy effect in this context. Better informed worker and union representatives have come to realize how important increased competitiveness has become and therefore have come to accept the need for change to achieve that objective. Many of them now clearly associate their workers long term income and job security with the attainment of that objective.

But there is another side to the coin. Worker and union representatives cannot afford to ignore the adjustment costs associated with changes required to make their company's more competitive. Accordingly, they are bound to push for costly social plans that cushion the impact of these changes on those adversely effected by them. As a result there are frequent management complaints about the compromises, delays and even politics that are required to work out necessary accommodation among all the interests involved.

It is difficult for an outsider to make an informed judgement on these interrelated pros and cons of codetermination in West Germany. In the first place it has to be acknowledged that the codetermination process has helped many firms with their down-sizing problems. But there have been heavy financial costs in the form of severance and the like not to mention the aforementioned compromise, delays and politics. In the latter context, however, it may well be that what firms lose in the process of arriving at accommodations for changes they more than make up in the actual implementation stage of those changes assuming that by then they are largely resistance-free.

Perhaps the ultimate judgement of codetermination must be based on the overall performance of the West German economy. Codetermination got some of the credit for West Germany's earlier economic miracle. It remains to be seen how much blame or credit codetermination receives for whatever fate now awaits the West Germany economy. Mind you, there are always so many other variables involved that it is difficult to sort out any causes or effects among the relevant interrelationships.

4. The Relevance of Codetermination for Canada

In general caution is required when attempting to transplant or transfer parts of one country's industrial relations systems to that of another. This is because there are often very deep-rooted attitudinal and institutional differences involved. In the case of Canada and West Germany, for example, there is on the attitudinal side an isolated and ostracized labour movement in Canada compared to what is often referred to as a social partner in West Germany. Institutionally, collective bargaining is essentially Canada's only system of industrial democracy whereas collective bargaining is only one part of West Germany's much more comprehensive system of industrial democracy.

While distinctions such as these do not rule out transplants or transfers between the two countries systems of industrial relations they to suggest that adaptations rather than adoptions would be the more appropriate way to proceed. As for codetermination in the narrow sense of that concept it has already had more of an impact on North America than one might have surmised a short time ago. What is even more surprising is that it has had a much greater impact-small as it may be-in the U.S. than in Canada. If anything one would have expected the reverse if only because of the United States almost religious commitment to capitalism or free enterprise.

Even in the U.S. codetermination has made only limited headway and then only really in a token sense. The fact that codetermination made any progress in the U.S. is to be attributed to the strain and trauma associated with the concession bargaining that took place during that country's recent recession-depression. In a few cases, highlighted by the Chrysler Corporation and a couple of the major airlines, the unions involved insisted on some representation on the company board as part of the quid pro quo for the concessions to which they agreed. For the most part, however, neither American labour nor American management have changed their minds on the subject of codetermination. While showing more interest in codetermination-like measures than in the past, organized labour in the U.S. still remains largely committed to a basically adversarial role in its relations with management. At the same time the vast majority of managements in the U.S. remain adamantly opposed to anything like codetermination.

In Canada there is virtually nothing to report of significance on the codetermination front. Despite the urgings of one former federal minister of labour and other simple-minded exponents of codetermination in Canada no major union has pressed for it and no major company has expressed any interest in it. Hopefully this is not because they reject out of hand any concept which is foreign to them. Rather one would like to think that it is because codetermination would not necessarily have that much of an impact on the three criticisms which are usually aimed at Canada's collective bargaining process. Codetermination could do little or nothing to reverse the basic causes of Canada's decentralized and fragmented collective bargaining process. While it might be expected to help reverse the alleged strike and inflation proneness of that process the extent to which it could have any marked effect in these respects is highly debatable.

5. Conclusion

Some variation of codetermination may yet emerge in Canada if, as and when the country faces up to the serious competitive challenge that confronts it. Certainly labour and management in Canada are going to have to reach beyond their traditional adversarial relations to more cooperative relations unless they want to live with an ongoing fight over shares of a national pie that could actually diminish in size. This will be the end result if Canadians do not find a more constructive way to come to grips with the need to become more competitive.

At the very least labour and management in Canada have to find a more mutually acceptable way to share the benefits and the costs of the adjustment required to meet the competitiveness challenge. This suggests the need for varying combinations and permutations of both gains-sharing and labour-adjustment-cost-sharing. How this is going to be accomplished-assuming it is accomplished at all-will obviously vary from case to case. Where it does occur labour and management will find themselves with a complimentary mix of adversarial and cooperative relations. As this happens concepts such as codetermination may not seem as foreign to them. They might even begin to adapt some of them to their own particular needs.

Dispute Resolution and the Quality of Labour-Management Decision Making

Roy J. Adams and Hoyt N. Wheeler

Abstract

The thesis developed in this paper is that the quality of decisions arrived at via labour-management negotiations is critically affected by the nature of the mechanism used to resolve decision-making impasses.

Decisions are considered to be of high quality when they produce high values of productivity, democratic participation and employee security and dignity. The implications of five impasse resolution devices-unilateral decision-making, consensus, strike/lockout, arbitration and choice of procedures – for performance on the noted dimensions are explored.

1. Introduction

Across various national industrial relations systems there exists a wide array of institutions for making decisions having to do with terms and conditions of employment. Among the most important are those in which organizations of employees deal with managerial representatives of capital in regular, formal, negotiations. These institutions must of necessity involve some means of resolving deadlocks which occur when one or both of the sides becomes convinced that further negotiating would be unavailing. When comparing these impasse resolving mechanisms, either within or across national systems, it would be helpful, we believe, to have some way of evaluating them. A fundamental criterion for such an evaluation is the quality of the decisions which the decision-making institutions produce when they employ different impasse resolving mechanisms. To employ this criterion one must, of course, define the concept of decision quality.

We provide such a definition in this paper and then explore the relationship between the quality of decisions reached in institutions where labour and management jointly decide employment-related issues, and the devices utilized in those institutions to resolve impasses. The analysis focuses entirely at the level of the enterprise.

The particular labour-management decision-making institutions that we have in mind are practices such as: 1.) North American collective bargaining; 2.) the nexus of collective bargaining, works council-management negotiations and workers' participation on boards of directors utilized in West Germany; and, 3.) the combination of wage bargaining and consultation for consensus which is practiced in Japan.

Decisions taken by labour and management may be thought of as being of higher or lower quality depending upon the extent to which they add to or detract from several goals. These are goals which we assert to be fundamental in all modern democracies. We would argue that they are goals which must be met by labour-management decision-making institutions in order for them to serve their function within a democratic society. By these standards, we believe that the following goals should be used to measure the quality of decisions:[1]

- Democratic participation: Decisions should be arrived at through meaningful participation in the decision by all those affected by it.
- Employee Security and Dignity: The interests of persons serving in the role of "employee" in income, income security, and individual liberty and dignity should be met to a reasonable degree.
- Productivity: Efficiency and effectiveness in the production of goods and services, which meet goals that are generally considered to be the responsibility of managers and in the interests of capitalists and consumers, should be served to a reasonable degree.

In short, good decisions are those which serve both employee and productivity needs and involve meaningful participation of those affected. In order for a decision to be judged of high quality, it should serve *all* of these objectives to a reasonable degree. That is, a decision which was arrived at democratically, and served employee needs, but was unsatisfactory with respect to productivity, would not be judged to be a good decision. Nor would a decision which resulted in high productivity be considered a good one if taken autocratically or to the serious detriment of employees.

It should be noted that in addition to concerns about the quality of the decisions themselves, there are important questions regarding the costs of the process. That is, it may be possible to arrive at a high quality decision, but pay an unacceptable price for arriving at it. This might be the case if the decision-making mechanisms were associated with a high degree of industrial conflict, financial and other costs associated with the process, a loss of voluntarism, or a low probability of the process resulting in a decision at all in most cases. Although these process costs are not our chief concern in this paper, they will be mentioned at appropriate points.

In all the systems noted above – North American collective bargaining, German bargaining and co-determination and Japanese bargaining and consultation – impasses may, and often do, occur. In these, and other, systems there are a number of alternatives available for resolving these impasses. We will consider the following procedures in this paper:[2]

– Unilateral decision making by either labour or management.

- Consensus: If either side refuses to agree to a course of action proposed by the other side, that course of action must be abandoned.
- Strike/Lockout: If labour disagrees with a course of action proposed by management it may withdraw its services; if management cannot secure agreement from labour relative to a desired course of action it may withhold income and work.
- Arbitration: If the parties are unable to reach an agreement either may require the decision to be made by a neutual third party.
- Choice of Procedures: One side or the other, or both, has the option of choosing either the strike/lockout path to impasse resolution or arbitration.

The above procedures may be invoked where many issues are being simultaneously discussed (multiple-issue decision making) or situations where only a single issue is being addressed (single issue decision making).

The primary focus of the discussion which follows will be on the theoretical relationships between these dispute resolution techniques and the quality of decisions. However, in order to illustrate the points made we will draw upon real world practices, most often with reference to North America, West Germany, and Japan.[3]

2. Unilateral Decision Making

In some real world situations, issues which are nominally subject to joint decision involve impasse resolution procedures which provide for unilateral resolution by management. It might be argued that such schemes should not be classified as joint decision-making institutions at all, since they are ultimately controlled by management. However, they differ from purely unilateral decision making in that they involve some negotiations between organized labour and management prior to a decision being made by management. Such negotiations do provide an avenue for some employee input into decisions. Perhaps more importantly, they put in motion employee efforts to reach desired outcomes which, if frustrated, may give rise to either collective or individual aggressive action by employees.[4]

Examples of unilateral management impasse resolution institutions are provided by German, United States, and Japanese procedures for Federal civil servants as well as by German private sector procedures regarding certain issues which are subject to joint works council-management discussion.

In unilateral management impasse resolution schemes, there appears to be a tendency for management, in times of economic (or political) stress, to emphasize productivity at the cost of employee interests. As a result employees often seek more adequate (from their point of view) procedures. Over time such schemes not uncommonly produce periods of severe conflict as labour protests against what it considers management's failure, to live up to past understandings or, to be reasonable in its determinations. Such a scenario has become very common in several of the developed countries, particularly among public sector employees. The transition of company unions into independent unions in the United States during the 1930s also fits this pattern.[5]

Unilateral impasse resolution by employee organizations is a rare phenomenon in the democratic world. The closest thing to this in the United States may be craft union procedures for the resolution of jurisdictional disputes. Another example exists in Sweden where, if there is an impasse over the interpretation of a labour-management agreement, the worker side may initially decide. However, such issues are finally decided by the courts. This Swedish procedure clearly gives priority to employee interests over productivity, although unions are, as a practical matter, required to behave in a responsible manner in order to avoid government sanctions.

3. Consensus

In the contemporary democratic world consensus is often spoken of as a highly desirable method of economic decision making. As it is closely associated with Japan and the success of the Japanese economic system, "consensus" is currently considered to be an ideal worthy of emulation in the West. In fact, however, decision making by consensus as we have defined it is practically a non-existent entity in labour-management relations.

This form of decision making involves both sides having a veto. Thus, if labour strongly opposes any course of action proposed by management, management must abandon that course of action. This, of course, is a proposition which management in many countries finds highly unpalatable. Because either side may bring decision making to a standstill, successful consensus systems require both sides to work very hard to discover mutually acceptable solutions to problems. It also requires that the two sides use their veto power very sparingly. Where both sides follow these principles consensus decision making tends to produce high quality decisions in terms of our criteria. Both productivity and employee needs are enhanced and the degree of democratic participation is high.

Consensus, however, may be unilaterally abandoned by either side. If it is abandoned, the result is likely to be very poor quality decisions. If, for example, management abandons consensus for unilateral decision making it makes industrial conflict highly probable. This, by definition, destroys democratic participation. Likewise, if labour continually refuses to act favorably on management proposals management is placed in a position where it has little choice but to abandon consensus. An inability to decide also works to the detriment of productivity.

Consensus systems may also have high process costs. Because it may take a considerable period to produce a decision, opportunities which require quick action may be lost, to the detriment of all concerned.

Very few pure consensus systems exist in the real world. Where one side holds great power over the other consensus is largely a sham. Also, the Japanese consensus system works (where it does work) perhaps not because of altruism or cultural heritage, but instead because of fear of the consequences of a lack of consensus. During the first decades after World War II in Japan labour-management decision making deteriorated into highly hostile conflict in a number of industries. The memory of those conflicts and fear of their revival may play a large role in the success of contemporary consensus decision making in Japan. Today, strikes often result when consensus breaks down. The parties also engage in various forms of legal maneuveuring, which in some cases produces a result somewhat similar to arbitration.[6]

In short, consensus is a very good, if fragile, system of decision making. However, several conditions (sincere good will of both sides, fear of the alternatives) must be met if the system is to function effectively.

4. Strike/Lockout

At the root of all labour-management decision making is the possibility of a work stoppage. The strike has traditionally been considered by organized labour to be one of its most cherished possessions. Many countries have imbedded the right to strike in their constitutions, and this right has been upheld by international organizations such as the International Labour Office.

The strike is not only a technique for settling impasses, but also influences the conduct of the parties in negotiations. Ideally, it induces them to engage in meaningful decision making, and to reach agreement.

Apparently the right to strike and the strike-threat system are consistent with high levels of both employee welfare and productivity.[7] The system has been widely used during the past century in precisely those countries which have experienced the greatest economic and social gains (United States, West Germany, Sweden, Japan), although it has not been present in some of the currently most successful segments of the United States system. It is a well established and effective system of representative democratic participation.

The system, however, does have substantial drawbacks. First, the power generated by resort to, or threat of, a strike is unequally distributed among employee groups. Such groups as metal workers, railway workers and miners have used the strike weapon with great success. On the other hand, the strike has not been so useful in the hands of textile workers, retail clerks and employees in small service organizations of various sorts. Thus, the strike threat may produce meaningful participation for metal workers, but not for hotel and restaurant employees. Where a strike threat is not credible there exists, in effect, a system which involves unilateral management impasse resolving.

Another drawback of the strike-threat system is that it may, and sometimes does, produce significant process costs. If a strike occurs, industrial peace is shattered and significant economic burdens are assumed by both workers and management, and perhaps by society at large. This may result in the loss of income and job security to workers, loss of output to enterprise, and a disruption of the lives of others who are not involved in the strike. An auto or mining strike, for example, affects more than the automobile or mining communities.

It is sometimes argued that strikes have a positive aspect in that they release pent-up frustrations. Modern psychological findings, however, refute this "flush toilet" theory of aggression.[8] Indeed, it is fairly clear that aggression, rather than decreasing the likelihood of further aggression, instead increases it.

Another drawback of the strike/lockout system is that in cases where the power of labour is overwhelming, and the relationship between labour and management is cool, the result may be the insistence by labour on the establishment and maintenance of rigid rules which hinder flexibility and competitiveness, and therefore productivity.[9]

Thus, although the right to strike and the strike system has proven to be, on balance, useful and workable, it is certainly not an ideal system. Its advantages are great but its costs and risks are high.

5. Arbitration

Because of the drawbacks of the strike-threat system, policy makers have long sought an alternative to the strike which would have its benefits but not its negative effects. The primary alternative devised for these purposes has been arbitration. We use the term "arbitration" here in a very broad sense to mean any system in which a neutral third party finally decides the issues in dispute. In practice, there are many variations.

Arbitration exists in many of the industrialized democratic countries. In several societies it is considered to be unacceptable for various categories of government employees to strike. Arbitration has, therefore, been offered in its stead. In addition, in Australia and New Zealand arbitration is the principal means of impasse resolution in disputes involving *all* organized employees.

Theoretically, arbitration should produce meaningful participation without the necessity for resort to hostile conflict. In some systems it has apparently had precisely that effect. For example, with respect to several issues under works council-management decision making in West Germany, impasses must be submitted, in the last resort, to arbitration. There is, however, very little use made of arbitration in this system. Instead labour and management work hard to avoid arbitration, mainly because they fear that an arbitrator who is unfamiliar with all of the details of the enterprise will require the implementation of inappropriate and unworkable schemes. Therefore, the threat of arbitration is an effective sanction which prompts the parties to settle issues in a process which is very much like consensus decision making.

Contrarily, arbitration in Australia appears to have had a preverse effect. Instead of jointly deciding common issues via consensus-like procedures, the parties have moved in the opposite direction. Rather than talking to each other they compile briefs for arguments to the arbitrator. Instead of trying to convince each other of the reasonableness of their proposals they try to convince the arbitrator.

In the terminology that has evolved in the United States, arbitration in Australia has had a "chilling effect" on labour-management negotiations. It has also had a "narcotic effect" in that the parties regularly resort to arbitration instead of settling issues on their own. These same effects have been observed in some, but not all, other arbitration systems.

Why does arbitration produce a narcotic or chilling effect in some systems? The classic theoretical explanation for the chilling effect is that the parties will anticipate that the arbitrator will split the difference between whatever are their final positions. Therefore, it is in each party's interest to fail to move toward agreement, as a more moderate final position will produce a worse arbitration result.[10] This suggests that the nature of the issues to be decided in the system is very important. Where the issue can be easily divided, like wages, the parties may be more likely to resort to arbitration. Where the issue is more complex and multifaceted, and resistant to difference-splitting, e.g., training, the parties may be more likely to avoid arbitration and reach agreement.[11]

Arbitration appears to be highly consistent with high levels of employee benefits and productivity. Although it is sometimes accused of producing rigid rules, there appears to be no clear evidence that this is the case. Indeed, arbitration has been rather flexible in many of its usages. To the degree that arbitration provides for both labour and management to consider the full range of issues, along with reasoned arguments for their positions on those issues, it would appear that the requirements of democratic participation would be reasonably well met. However, the final determination is by an outside third party, not by the parties themselves. This is at least somewhat constrained participation.

There are some considerable process advantages and disadvantages in arbitration. First, one might argue that it is a highly civilized process, another step in a long march of humanity from barbarism to law. Decisions are made on the basis of reason, not on the basis of economic power. On the other hand, traditional norms of voluntarism would appear to be violated, at least to some degree, by the final decision being made by a third party. The financial cost of the process may also be rather high, although considerably lower than that of the strike/lockout system.

In short, arbitration often serves our criteria for high quality outcomes quite well. Process costs, however, may be rather high.

6. Choice of Procedures

Choice of procedures is a concept which attempts to combine the best aspects of the strike/lockout and arbitration systems. It has a number of variations. In one, management has the option to invoke arbitration at the point of impasse in order to avoid a strike. In another, the union must choose, before negotiations begin, the dispute resolution technique (arbitration or strike) to be used should an impasse occur. In a third, *either* labour or management may choose arbitration in lieu of the strike, but the parties may, subsequent to impasse, agree jointly to the strike.

Empirical research suggests that such systems tend to score highly on our criteria.[12] Meaningful participation, even by employees who have little capacity to mount a strike threat, is present in those systems where the union is given the option. This allows employee interests to be well served. So long as the interest in productivity is not neglected, this would seem to produce reasonably high quality decisions. On the other hand, giving the employer the option to invoke arbitration may serve the productivity interest very well, but result in little participation and inadequate serving of employee interest. The variation which provides for either side to select arbitration may be the best balanced of the choice of procedures systems. The right to strike could be preserved by a requirement that a majority of the affected employees must agree to any proposal by management or union to arbitrate disputed issues.

Process costs appear to be fairly low in choice of procedures systems. The evidence is that the incidence of strikes is considerably lower than in strike/lockout systems. Some voluntarism is preserved. Financial costs would be the same as a strike/lockout or arbitration system, depending upon the option selected.

7. Multi-Issue vs. Single-Issue Decision Making

Joint labour management decision-making institutions vary on one other structural dimension which has important consequences for the quality of decisions. This dimension is the number of issues involved in the process at the same time. Some institutions are multi-issue. Others are single-issue.

Multi-issue strike systems such as North American collective bargaining have the special feature of producing trade-off dynamics. Because a large number of issues are involved, it is common for a side to "drop" an issue, or trade off one for another. With respect to dropped or traded off issues, the depth and meaningfulness of participation is quite limited. That is, a decision may be made on an issue without a thorough discussion of it, or any clear attempt to reach consensus. This being the case, a resolution of the issue would not be expected to be of high quality under any of our criteria. The probability of settlement is enhanced because it puts in the hands of parties one other instrument for reaching agreement, i.e., a trade off. However, the quality of the result reached may suffer.

In single-issue decision making the trade-off dynamic does not operate. For example, in West Germany and Japan (in contrast to North America) wages are negotiated separately from issues such as safety, training and response to technological change. In West Germany co-decision issues are specified in the law, and on each issue employee and management representatives must come to an agreement or face the possibility of arbitration on that issue.

In Japan there is extensive consultation in search of consensus on each issue. Although there is no definite sanction in the event of impasse at any single consultation round, there is nevertheless in the typical large Japanese corporation a strong propensity to reach consensus on each issue without trading off. Because consensus is reached on an issue-by-issue basis, we consider this system to be single-issue.

By comparison to multi-issue systems, single-issue systems appear more likely to produce high quality decisions. Participation may be more meaningful. The integrative potential of bargaining items is more likely to be fully explored. Both employee interests and productivity seem to be at least as well served. Indeed, Japanologists are in general agreement that Japan's economic success is due in part to the ability of Japanese firms to involve employees in decision-making at the shop floor level in the manner described above. They also generally agree that employee participation in quality improvement would not have been successful in the environment of hostile discord which is often engendered in the multi-issue strike/lockout system.[13]

8. Conclusions

On the basis of the above discussion, we reach several conclusions:

a) The type of impasse resolution procedure utilized has effects upon the quality of decisions in joint-labour management decision-making institutions.
b) Unilateral impasse resolving mechanisms are likely to lead to low quality decisions.
c) Impasse resolution by consensus has excellent potential for high quality decisions. Its main weaknesses lie in its potential for breaking down and leading to increased hostility and its high process costs.
d) The strike/lockout alternative has proven generally to produce high quality decisions. However, because of high process costs and its tendency to sometimes produce very low outcomes with respect to either employee interests or productivity (if power is out of balance), it is less than the ideal system.
e) Arbitration as a device for resolving impasses must be considered as the primary alternative to the strike because of its ability to produce final resolutions while

preserving both the essential interests of employees and productivity. It is also reasonably high with respect to participation. On the other hand, there are high process costs in the loss of voluntarism, particularly where a "chilling effect" leads to overuse of the system.

f) Choice of procedures is an impasse resolving scheme which has considerable potential for creating high quality decisions. Because of its flexibility, it may combine some of the best features of both strike and arbitration systems. Its greatest drawback lies in the potential for one side becoming predominant because it has the power of choice.

g) Single-issue joint labour-management decision making institutions are likely to produce higher quality decisions than multi-issue systems.

Most of the literature evaluating impasse resolving procedures has focused upon process variables. The preservation of industrial peace (strike rates), losses of production due to strikes, financial costs of arbitration, losses of voluntarism under arbitration, the delays inherent in consensus decision-making, and other -process related matters are undoubtedly important. Most appealing from a scholarly perspective, they are relatively easy to measure. They also do not require one to decide what is "good" as to substantive outcomes. Yet, it seems to us that this ignores the fundamental question. After all, these mechanisms exist to perform substantive functions. If they do not perform them well, it is of little use that the costs of their processes are low. The substantive outcomes are those with which employers, employees and the public have to live for extended periods of time. They affect large numbers of citizens on a daily basis. The fact that the question of substantive quality is difficult to answer does not excuse a failure to ask it.

We believe that our brief analysis demonstrates that it is possible to speak to the question of decision quality in the context of impasse resolving mechanisms in a systematic and useful way. It is, of course, possible to pose different criteria and reach different conclusions. It is our hope that this attempt at addressing this question will, at the least, direct attention to the substance of labour-management decision making.

9. Summary

This paper argues that an important criterion for evaluating dispute resolving mechanisms in various industrial relations systems is the quality of the decisions produced by those mechanisms. Decision quality is defined as involving several goals believed to be fundamental in all modern democracies: 1.) democratic participation in decisions; 2.) employee security and dignity; and, 3.) productivity.

The dispute resolution procedures analyzed include: unilateral resolution by either labour or management; consensus; strike/lockout; arbitration; and, choice of procedures. These are viewed as they are operationalized in North American collective bargaining, German bargaining and co-determination and Japanese bargaining and consultation.

Several conclusions are reached. Perhaps the primary finding is that the type of impasse procedure utilized to resolve disputes does affect decision quality. Unilateral resolution is unlikely to produce high quality decisions. Consensus has great potential for effecting high quality decisions, but may produce great hostility when it breaks down. Strike/lockout has served reasonably well, but has the potential for producing very low quality decisions in some situations. Arbitration scores high on the criteria, but involves a loss of voluntarism. Choice of procedures is a new mechanism which may combine the best features of the strike/lockout and arbitration systems, but has the potential for producing a power imbalance. Systems which consider a single issue at a time have some advantage over multiple-issue systems.

Remarks

[1] These are goals which several serious students of the subject have identified as being central to the basic fabric of modern democratic society. See Derber 1970; Summers 1979, pp. 29–49; Weiler 1983, pp. 1769–1827.
[2] See Goldman 1982, pp. 201–225 for a somewhat different typology.
[3] Earlier papers presenting some of the ideas further developed here are: Adams 1986; Adams (1985); Ponak/Wheeler 1980, pp. 292–308.
[4] Wheeler 1985.
[5] Nelson 1982, pp. 335–357.
[6] See Shirai 1983, pp. 369–382; Koshiro 1983, pp. 205–257; Tokunaga 1983, pp. 313–329.
[7] Freeman / Medoff 1984.
[8] Eibl-Eibesfeldt 1974, pp. 243–246; Bandura 1977, p. 161.
[9] Although one would expect that rule rigidity would hinder productivity, the evidence in support of this is mixed. See Freeman / Medoff 1984; Kochan / Piore 1984, pp. 177–189.
[10] Stevens 1966, pp. 38–52.
[11] Some evidence that there is a rational basis for this distinction is found in Wheeler 1974, pp. 176–184.
[12] Ponak / Wheeler 1980.
[13] MacMillan 1984.

Literature

Adams, R. J. (1985): Should works councils be used as industrial relations policy? In: *Monthly Labor Review* 108 (7) (May), pp. 25–29.

Adams, R. J. (1986): Two Policy Approaches to Labour-Management Decision Making at the Level of the Enterprise. In: Riddell, W. Craig (Ed.), pp. 87–109.

Bandura, A. (1977): *Social Learning Theory*. Englewood Cliffs, N. J..

Blainpain, R. / Millard, F. (Hrsg.) (1982): *Comparative Labour Law and Industrial Relations*. Deventer, Netherlands.

Derber, M. (1970): *The American Idea of Industrial Democracy 1865–1965*. Urbana.
Goldman, A. (1982): Settlement of Disputes over Interests. In. Blainpain, R. / Millard, F. (Hrsg.), pp. 201–225.
Eibl-Eibesfeldt, I. (1974): *Love and Hate*. Trans. by Strachan, G.. New York.
Freeman, R. B. / Medoff, J. L. (1984): *What Do Unions Do?* New York.
Kochan, T. / Piore, M. (1984): Will the New Industrial Relations Last? Implications for the American Labor Movement. In: *Annals of the American Academy of Political and Social Science* 273 (May), pp. 177–189.
Koshiro, K. (1983): Development of Collective Bargaining in Postwar Japan. In: Shirai, T. (Hrsg.), pp. 205–257.
Nelson, D. / MacMillan, C. J. (1984): *The Japanese Industrial Relations System*. New York (1982): The Company Union Movement 1900–1937: A Reexamination. In: *Business History Review* 56 (4) (Autumn), pp. 335–357.
Ponak, A. / Wheeler, H. N. (1980): Choice of Procedures in Canada and the United States. In: *Industrial Relations* 19 (3) (Fall), pp. 292–308.
Riddell, W. Craig (Ed.) (1986): *Labour-Management Cooperation in Canada*, Toronto.
Shirai, T. (1983): A Supplement: Characteristics of Japanese Management and Their Personnel Policies. In: Shirai, T. (Hrsg.), pp. 369–382.
Shirai, T. (Hrsg.) (1983): *Contemporary Industrial Relations in Japan*. Madison.
Stevens, C. (1966): Is Compulsory Arbitration Compatible with Bargaining? In: *Industrial Relations* 5 (February), pp. 38–52.
Summers, C. W. (1979): Industrial Democracy: American's Unfulfilled Promises. In: *Cleveland State Law Review* 28, pp. 24–49.
Tokunaga, K. (1983): A Marxist Interpretation of Japanese Industrial Relations with Special Reference to Large Private Enterprises. In: Shirai, T. (Hrsg.), pp. 313–329.
Weiler, P. (1983): Promises to Keep: Securing Workers' Rights to Self-Organization under the NLRA. In: *Harvard Law Review* 96 (June), pp. 1769–1827.
Wheeler, H. N. (1974): Is Compromise the Rule in Fire Fighter Arbitration? In: *Arbitration Journal* 29 (3) (September), pp. 176–184.
Wheeler, H. N. (1985): *Industrial Conflict: An Integrative Theory*. Columbia, S. C.

Die Entwicklung der Unternehmungsdemokratie in Griechenland

Andreas Nikolopoulos

Abstract
The Development of Enterprise Democracy in Greece

This paper describes the development of democracy in Greek companies. In this context two aspects are accentuated:
a) the abolition of the right to lock-out employees and
b) the securing of the existence of collective representation in companies with at least 40 employees.
These changes are differentiated with regard to their legally intended effects and their actual consequences on the discretion of the employees. While considering these trends, two alternative political developments in Greece will be reflected.

1. Einleitung

Die Entwicklung der Unternehmungsdemokratie in Griechenland hat aus mehreren Gründen eine besondere Bedeutung. Die Arbeitnehmer-Arbeitgeber-Beziehungen zeigen noch keinen homogenen Charakter, da die Entwicklungen der letzten drei Jahre auf diesem Gebiet eine Reihe unterschiedlicher neuer Ansätze hervorgebracht haben. Diese Ansätze, die wirtschaftliche und politische Bedeutung im unternehmungsinternen und -externen Bereich erwerben, sind primär auf Veränderungen im politischen Rahmen des Landes zurückzuführen. Die Problematik der Unternehmungsdemokratie setzt die Diskussion über dazu gehörende Begriffe voraus, wie zum Beispiel „Demokratie" bzw. „Demokratisierung" im Unternehmungssektor. Der Begriff „Demokratie" wird eingegrenzt, wenn er in Zusammenhang mit der Gestaltung der Verhältnisse in einem speziellen gesellschaftlichen Subsystem gebracht wird[1]. Diese Eingrenzung findet ihren Ausdruck etwa in folgender Definition: „... die industrielle Demokratie kann als das Gesamtfeld der Arbeitgeber-Arbeitnehmer-Beziehungen bezeichnet werden, in dem gegenseitige und verfahrengemäß geregelte bzw. gesicherte Einwirkungsmöglichkeiten zwischen Aktoren bzw. institutionalisierten Aktorengruppen – mit Interessen ökonomischer und/oder politischer Art – bestehen."[2] Bei der Definition des Begriffs „Demokratisierung" gewinnt die Problematik der Machtmessung der

Beteiligten im System der Arbeitsbeziehungen eine besondere Bedeutung, da als „Demokratisierung" die Minderung der Machtdifferenzen zwischen den Beteiligten in einer Machtbeziehung bezeichnet wird.[3] Obwohl die Problematik der Machtmessung noch Anlaß zu starken Auseinandersetzungen – sowohl im Bereich der Methodik als auch bezüglich der Auswirkungen bestimmter Strukturen bzw. Strategien (wie z. B. Mitbestimmung) – gibt, können hier Bemerkungen globaler Art über die Entwicklungen bzw. die Entwicklungstendenzen der nominalen und der realen Handlungsspielräume der beteiligten Aktoren zum Ausdruck gebracht werden. Für diesen Zweck sind vorerst die charakteristischen Merkmale der Arbeitgeber-Arbeitnehmer-Beziehungen zu diskutieren. Diese Diskussion wird die Beurteilung der Demokratisierung des Unternehmungssektors und folglich die Erfassung der Entwicklungstendenzen dieser Beziehungen erleichtern.

2. Die Merkmale der Arbeitgeber-Arbeitnehmer-Beziehung in Griechenland

Die Arbeitgeber-Arbeitnehmer-Beziehung ist unter zwei Aspekten zu betrachten. Der erste Aspekt betrifft den Charakter, der zweite die Funktionsweise der Arbeitgeber-Arbeitnehmer-Beziehung. Der Charakter der Arbeitsbeziehung hat sich während der letzten vier Jahre stabilisiert, da trotz des Regierungswechsels vom Oktober 1981 (d. h. der Übernahme der Macht durch die Sozialisten) wesentliche Teile dieses Charakters unberührt geblieben sind bzw. sich verstärkt haben. Zu diesem Aspekt gehören folgende Punkte:

- Die parteiliche Orientierung der griechischen Gewerkschaftsbewegung. Jede größere politische Partei nimmt Einfluß auf die Arbeitsbeziehungen durch eine eigene „syndikalistische Partei". Diese Parteien verstehen sich nur mittelbar als Vertretungsorgane der Arbeitnehmer. Diese Orientierung ist im allgemeinen mit den Strukturen der Arbeitsbeziehungen Frankreichs und Italiens vergleichbar.
- Die Intervention der jeweiligen Regierung im Bereich der Arbeitsbeziehungen. Diese Intervention findet ihren Ausdruck zum einen in den gesetzlichen Regelungen der Tarifautonomie. Diese Regelungen erlauben den staatlichen Organen, den Inhalt der Tarifverträge mittelbar oder unmittelbar zu bestimmen.[4] Dazu ist zu berücksichtigen, daß die Regierung seit 1982 eine in die Einzelheiten gehende Politik betreibt, die durch automatische Lohn- und Gehaltserhöhungen eine Anpassung an den Preisindex zu erreichen sucht. Diese automatische Anpassung (die sog. A T A: Automatische Anpassung an den Preisindex) gilt unmittelbar für den öffentlichen und mittelbar für den privaten Sektor. Zum anderen sind die Strukturen des griechischen Gewerkschaftsbundes (d. h. des höchsten Vertretungsorgans der Arbeitnehmer) hervorzuheben. Dieser Bund

wird seit Mitte der 40er Jahre jeweils von denjenigen Funktionären bzw. syndikalistischen Parteien kontrolliert, die ideologisch bzw. politisch mit den entsprechenden Regierungsparteien eng verbunden sind.[5]

Aufgrund dieser Charakteristika ist festzustellen, daß die griechischen Arbeitsbeziehungen durch parteipolitische Auseinandersetzungen geprägt sind. Die politischen Entwicklungen sind für die Gestaltung der Arbeitsbeziehungen von großer Bedeutung, zumal die ideologischen Gräben zwischen den einflußreichsten politischen Parteien als nahezu unüberbrückbar gelten. Will man also die Entwicklungstendenzen der griechischen Arbeitsbeziehungen erfassen, so muß man zunächst die verschiedenen allgemeinpolitischen Entwicklungstendenzen betrachten. Die gegenwärtige Funktionsweise der griechischen Arbeitsbeziehung wird vereinfacht in der Abb. 1 dargestellt.

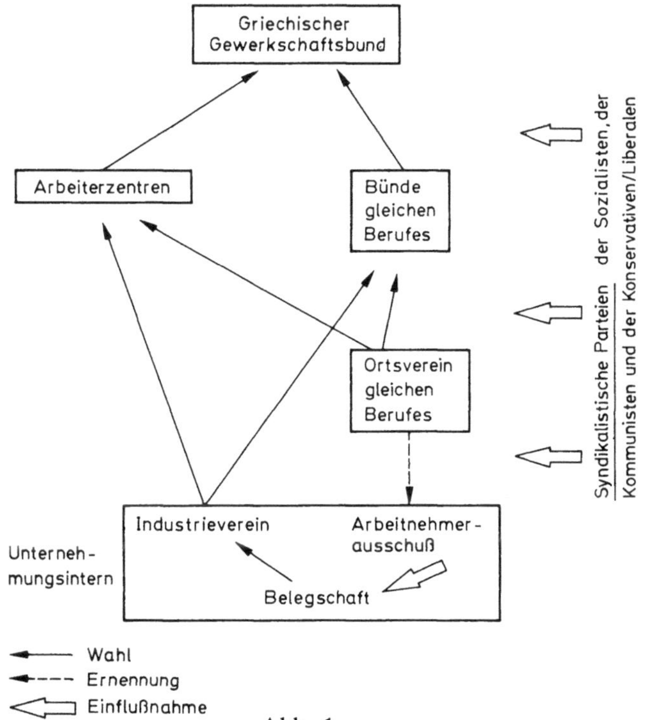

Abb. 1

Die syndikalistischen Parteien üben im ganzen System der Arbeitsbeziehungen ideologischen Einfluß aus. Unternehmungsintern übernehmen der sogenannte Industrieverein (genannt auch: Unternehmungsverein oder Arbeitnehmerverein) und/oder der Arbeitnehmerausschuß die Funktion der kollektiven Repräsentation der Arbeitnehmer. Sowohl der Industrieverein als auch der Arbeitnehmerausschuß vertreten die Arbeitnehmer einer einzigen Unternehmung: Ein Unterschied zeigt sich hauptsächlich bei der Wahl ihrer Vorstände: Der Vorstand des Industrievereins, der eine juristische Person ist, wird von den Arbeitnehmern der Unternehmung gewählt. Dagegen wird der Vorstand des Arbeitnehmerausschusses praktisch von den Ortsvereinen des gleichen Berufes ernannt, die außerhalb der Unternehmung organisiert sind und die Arbeitnehmer desselben Berufes oder desselben Industriezweiges eines Ortes umfassen. Der Industrieverein und die Ortsvereine gleichen Berufes werden als Berufsvereine bezeichnet. Sie gelten als Organisationen ersten Grades. Die Vertreter der Berufsvereine wählen die Vorstände der Bünde gleichen Berufes (sie betragen z. Z. 77) und der Arbeiterzentren (ihre Gesamtzahl: 84). Erstere repräsentieren diejenigen Organisationen ersten Grades, die Arbeitnehmer derselben bzw. ähnlicher Industriezweige organisieren. Die Arbeiterzentren vertreten die Organisationen ersten Grades an demselben Ort. Gewöhnlich werden sie in der Hauptstadt eines Verwaltungsbezirks gegründet. Die Bünde gleichen Berufes und die Arbeiterzentren gelten dementsprechend als Organisationen (oder Vereinigungen) zweiten Grades. Die Vertreter dieser Organisationen wählen den 45köpfigen Vorstand des Griechischen Gewerkschaftsbundes (G S E E, d. h.: Allgemeiner Bund der Arbeiter Griechenlands), der als Organisation dritten Grades gilt.[6]

3. Zur Beurteilung der Demokratisierung des Unternehmungssektors

Die einleitenden Bemerkungen zum Begriff „Demokratisierung" sollen zur Beurteilung der demokratischen Entwicklung des Unternehmungssektors in Griechenland herangezogen werden. Für diese Beurteilung sind zuerst die formalen Entwicklungen der gesetzlichen Bestimmungen zu diskutieren. Danach ist die Bedeutung von Situationsvariablen für die gesetzlichen Bestimmungen zu berücksichtigen, damit die realen Strukturen der Demokratisierung des Unternehmungssektors in Griechenland zutreffend beurteilt werden können.

3.1. Die Entwicklungen auf der Basis der formalen Bestimmungen

Während der letzten drei Jahre ist eine Entwicklung der formalen Bestimmungen in Richtung auf eine Demokratisierung im Unternehmungssektor festzustellen: Die formalen Handlungsspielräume der Arbeitnehmer werden zu Lasten der Handlungsspielräume der Arbeitgeber erweitert. Diese Entwicklung beruht hauptsächlich auf dem Gesetz 1264 vom 1. 7. 1982: „Über die Demokratisierung der syndikalistischen Bewegung und die Konsolidierung der syndikalistischen Freiheiten der Arbeitnehmer". Dieses ersetzte das Gesetz 330 vom 29. 5. 1976: „Über die Berufsvereine und -verbände und über die Wahrung der syndikalistischen

Freiheit".[7] Die wichtigsten Punkte dieser gesetzlichen Entwicklung sind die folgenden:

- Das Recht auf kollektive Vertretung der Arbeitnehmer auf der Unternehmungsebene wird von Unternehmungen mit mindestens 100 Beschäftigen (Gesetz 330/1976) auf Unternehmungen mit mindestens 40 Arbeitnehmer erweitert. Diese kollektive Vertretung wird meistens von den Industrievereinen übernommen. Da diese Vereine juristische Personen sind, hat jeder von ihnen eine eigene Verfassung (Art. 1).
- Die Vorstandsmitglieder (bzw. die Mitglieder des provisorischen Vorstands) dieser Vereine dürfen nicht entlassen werden (Art. 14), mit Ausnahme von „Extremfällen" (Art. 14 § 10). Dieser Kündigungsschutz betrifft mindestens sieben Vorstandsmitglieder – bei Vereinen mit mindestens 200 Mitgliedern – und maximal elf Vorstandsmitglieder – bei Vereinen mit mehr als 1000 Mitgliedern – (Art. 14, § 5, 6, 7). Für diesen Zweck sind Verfahren vorgesehen (Art. 15 § 1), die keine Möglichkeit für eine mittelfristige Entfernung dieser Mitglieder aus dem Betrieb erlauben (Art. 15 § 2)[8].
- Der obengenannte Kündigungsschutz bleibt auch in denjenigen Fällen unberührt, in denen ein Verein illegale Streiks organisiert hat (im Gegensatz zum Gesetz 330/1976, Art. 32 § 2, Art. 33 § 1, 2 und Art. 38 § 1, 2).
- Es besteht ein Zustimmungsrecht des Berufsvereins im Falle einer Versetzung eines seiner Vorstandsmitglieder (Art. 14 § 9).
- Es ist die Einrichtung von Gewerkschaftssektionen vorgesehen, die die Kommunikation zwischen der Belegschaft und dem Berufsverein fördern (Art. 16).
- Die Möglichkeiten für die Ausbildung der Vorstandsmitglieder der Vereine (Art. 17 § 2) wurden erheblich erweitert.
- Die obengenannten Rechte – mit Ausnahme des ersten – werden als Mindestrechte bezeichnet; sie können dementsprechend durch betriebliche Vereinbarungen erweitert werden (Art. 18 § 1, 2).
- Für die Ausrufung eines Streiks wird die entsprechende Entscheidung der Vollversammlung des Berufsvereins vorausgesetzt (Art. 20 § 1). Bei Arbeitsniederlegungen, die nur einige Stunden dauern und die sich nicht innerhalb eines Tages und einer Woche wiederholen, reicht lediglich die Entscheidung seines Vorstandes aus (Art. 20 § 1). Über die Vorhaben des Vereins in bezug auf Streiks bzw. Arbeitsniederlegungen muß der Arbeitgeber 24 Stunden vorher benachrichtigt werden (Art. 19 § 1).
- Die Aussperrung ist illegal (Art. 22 § 1).
- Durch die Übergangsbestimmungen dieses Gesetzes (insb. Art. 24) müssen die Arbeitgeber alle bisher (d. h. seit der Geltung des Gesetzes 330/1976) entlassenen Vorstandsmitglieder der syndikalistischen Organisationen wieder einstellen.

Diese Bestimmungen zeigen auf, daß sowohl die horizontalen als auch die vertikalen Handlungsspielräume von Arbeitgebern und Arbeitnehmern formal mangelhaft determiniert wurden. Es handelt sich eher um „offene" Beziehungen, deren Gestaltung bzw. Entwicklung stark von Situationsvariablen abhängt. Außer den oben genannten Bestimmungen bestehen eine Reihe von Regelungen, die sich noch im Stadium des Gesetzentwurfes befinden. Diese Entwürfe werden im Punkt 4 im Rahmen der Entwicklungstendenzen der Unternehmungsdemokratie in Griechenland behandelt.

3.2. Die Situationsvariablen

Die Situationsvariablen beinhalten eine Reihe von Strukturen, die eine sehr wichtige Rolle bei der realen Entwicklung des Machtpotentials (d. h. Ankündigung von Sanktionen, Überzeugung, Manipulation)[9] und des Machtbereichs (d. h. Entwicklungsfelder)[10] der Arbeitgeber und Arbeitnehmer spielen können. Diese Zusammenhänge stellt die Abb. 2 dar.

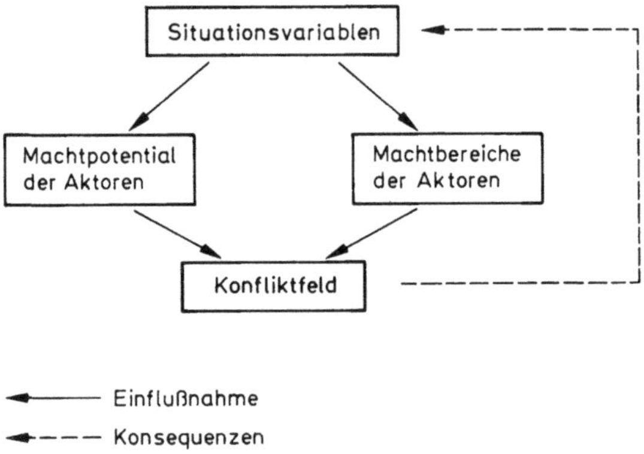

Abb. 2

Die Situationsvariablen werden folgendermaßen gegliedert[11]:

a) Wirtschaftliche Strukturen
  - aa) Arbeitsmarktsituation,
  - ab) wirtschaftliche Notwendigkeiten,
  - ac) wirtschaftliche Engpässe,
  - ad) wirtschaftliche/technologische Möglichkeiten

b) Politische Strukturen
  - ba) Merkmale der unternehmungsinternen und -externen Aktoren
    - baa) Organisationsstruktur und Entscheidungsfindung,
    - bab) ideologische Ausrichtung,
    - bac) besondere Fähigkeiten,
    - bad) spezielle Ziele,
    - bae) Unterstützungen
  - bb) Vorstellungen der Regierungspartei
    - bba) Ideologische Ausrichtung,

bbb) Verhalten im Falle von offenen Konflikten,
bbc) Möglichkeiten der Ausübung von Druck durch Dritte
c) Gesetzliche Strukturen
ca) Institutionalisierungsgrad der Handlungsspielräume der beteiligten Akteren,
cb) Entwicklung der Rechtssprechung

Zu a):

Die Arbeitsmarktsituation zeigt während der letzten Jahre eine negative Entwicklung. Zur Zeit existiert eine offizielle Arbeitslosenquote von insgesamt 8%, im städtischen Bereich von 12%[12]. Das hohe Niveau der Arbeitslosigkeit wirkt sich negativ auf die Intensität von manifesten Konflikten aus. Diese Auswirkung nimmt bei offenen (d. h. schlecht strukturierten) Konfliktbeziehungen zu. Zum Beleg dieser Argumente können folgende Daten über Streiks in Griechenland (s. Abb. 3) angeführt werden.

Kriterien / Jahr	Streikbewegungen	Streikende	ausgefallene Arbeitsstunden
1982	888	348.861	9.218.614
1983	675	224.315	3.881.829
1984	462	155.321	3.350.331

Abb. 3: Daten über Streikbewegungen, Streikende und ausgefallene Arbeitsstunden in Griechenland während der Jahre 1982–1984*

* Unveröffentlichte offizielle Angaben des griechischen Arbeitsministeriums

Die Daten dieser Tabelle betreffen sowohl die öffentlichen als auch die privaten Unternehmungen. Da während der letzten drei Jahre längere Streiks im öffentlichen Bereich stattgefunden haben, ist die wirkliche Zahl der Streiks im Rahmen der Privatwirtschaft als wesentlich geringer einzuschätzen. Eine Spezifizierung der obengenannten Daten kann nicht geleistet werden, da der griechische Arbeitsminister seit 1983 den Mitarbeitern seines Ministeriums verboten hat, irgendwelche Daten über Streiks in Griechenland der Öffentlichkeit bekannt zu geben. Die Existenz von wirtschaftlichen Notwendigkeiten für die Unternehmung (z. B. die Bewältigung eines hohen Auftragsvolumens) kann die Schlagkraft von negativen Sanktionen (z. B. Streiks) der Arbeitnehmerseite erhöhen und die Arbeitgeberseite empfindlicher treffen. Diese Ereignisse sind seltener im Falle einer Rezession, in der sich Griechenland seit mehreren Jahren befindet, wie aus der Abb. 4

hervorgeht. Die wirtschaftlichen Engpässe griechischer Unternehmungen spiegeln sich erstens in den Rentabilitätskennziffern (Abb. 4). Zweitens ist der Fall der sog. problematischen Unternehmungen zu erläutern. Diese Unternehmungen, deren Zahl sich bis 1. 4. 1985 auf 43 belief, gehören überwiegend zu den 200 größten Unternehmungen Griechenlands. Die Führung dieser Unternehmungen wird von der staatlichen Organisation „Anstalt für den Wiederaufbau von Unternehmungen“ eingesetzt[13]. Das Ziel dieser Anstalt besteht in der Wiederherstellung der Konkurrenzfähigkeit dieser Unternehmungen, die wegen ihrer finanziellen Überbelastung in Frage gestellt wurde[14]. Wenn dazu berücksichtigt wird, daß bis jetzt insgesamt 127 größere Unternehmungen die Hilfe dieser Anstalt beantragt haben, dann ergibt dies ein repräsentatives Bild der wirtschaftlichen Engpaßsituation der griechischen Industrie. Diese Entwicklung stimmt weitgehend mit den Prognosen über die Integrationsschwierigkeiten der griechischen Industrie im Hinblick auf den Beitritt Griechenlands zur EG überein.[15] Diese Schwierigkeiten werden außerdem von den statistischen Angaben (Mitte 1982) der griechischen Regierung

Kriterien / Jahr	Index der Produktion in der Industrie* (Basisjahr: 1970)	Bruttoprivatinvestitionen in konstanten Preisen** (in Mill. Drachmen)	Rentabilität in der griechischen Industrie (%)***	
			des eig. Kapitals	des Gesamtkapitals
1979	192,8	76.385	8,0	2,1
1980	194,8	70.465	7,8	1,8
1981	192,3	63.196	5,4	1,2
1982	182,4	60.370	– 4,7	– 1,2
1983	181,5	56.600	n. V.	n. V.
1984	n. V.	n. V.	n. V.	n. V.

* Nationales griechisches statistisches Amt, monatliche statistische Berichte, aus: The Greek Economy in Figures, Athens 1984, S. 209

** dito, S. 114

*** Federation of Greek Industries (Ed.): Greek Industry, annual Series

Abb. 4: Daten über die industrielle Produktion und Rentabilität sowie über die Privatinvestitionen in Griechenland

gegenüber der EG unterstrichen[16]. Aufgrund des oben Dargestellten sind die wirtschaftlichen bzw. technologischen Möglichkeiten der griechischen Unternehmungen noch als gering einzuschätzen.

Zu b):

Die Merkmale der Arbeitgeber-Arbeitnehmer-Beziehung in Griechenland zeigen während der letzten zehn Jahre eine gewisse Stabilität. Für die Arbeitgeber gilt, daß sie eine sehr zentralistische Organisationsstruktur bzw. Entscheidungsfindung bevorzugen und die kollektive Repräsentation der Arbeitnehmer in der Unternehmung ablehnen[17]. Wegen der bestehenden Rezession orientieren sich ihre Ziele am Überleben ihrer Unternehmungen. Die Arbeitnehmerseite strebt eine kollektive Repräsentation an, von der sie glaubt, ihre Interessen besser durchsetzen zu können[18]. Die Vertretungsorgane der Arbeitnehmer haben aus verschiedenen Gründen eine parteiliche Orientierung[19]. Dementsprechend sind zusätzlich zu ihren Zielen auch die Ziele derjenigen politischen Partei in Betracht zu ziehen, deren Funktionäre die Mehrheit der Vorstandssitze in einem Verein besitzen. Deswegen ist mit der Unterstützung aus entsprechenden politischen Richtungen gegenüber den Vertretungsorganen der Arbeitnehmer zu rechnen. Die Regierungspartei kann eine sehr wichtige Rolle in diesem Konfliktfeld spielen, da das Arbeitsministerium praktisch für das gesamte Schlichtungssystem verantwortlich ist.[20]

Die Entscheidungen der Schlichtungstellen sind verpflichtend für die Betroffenen. Diese Beziehungen erlauben im Rahmen der parlamentarischen Demokratie die Ausübung von offenem Druck auf die Entscheidungen der Regierungspartei bzw. des Arbeitsministeriums in konkreten Konfliktfällen. Der Erfolg dieser Einflußnahme hängt hauptsächlich von der Art und der Stärke der sich daraus ergebenden politischen Konsequenzen für die Regierungspartei ab. Dafür spielen sowohl die Mitgliederzahl eines Vereins als auch die Auswirkungen auf die öffentliche Meinung eine besonders wichtige Rolle.

Zu c):

Die formalen Handlungsspielräume der Arbeitgeber und der Arbeitnehmer sind bereits dargestellt worden. Als bedeutendste Entwicklung im Rahmen der entsprechenden Rechtssprechung gilt eine gerichtliche Entscheidung vom März 1985. Nach dieser Entscheidung ist die Aussperrung illegal, selbst wenn sie als Verteidigungsmittel der Arbeitgeber gegen einen illegalen Streik angewendet wird.

3.3. Zur Problematik der realen Demokratisierung des Unternehmungssektors

Die formalen Bestimmungen für die Unternehmungsdemokratisierung in Griechenland betreffen hauptsächlich zwei Bereiche:

- die Absicherung der Einrichtung und des formalen Funktionierens eines Berufsvereins. Diese Absicherung ergibt sich sowohl aus dem strengen Kündigungs-

schutz seiner Vorstandsmitglieder als auch aus der Förderung der Gewerkschaftssektionen;
- die radikale Erweiterung des Streikrechts durch die Aufhebung einer Reihe von diesbezüglichen Bedingungen bzw. Voraussetzungen, die von dem bis Juli 1982 geltenden Gesetz 330/1976 gestellt wurden.

Diese formalen Bereiche der Unternehmungsdemokratisierung werden real von Situationsvariablen negativ oder positiv beeinflußt. Die gegenwärtige Arbeitsmarktsituation und die politischen Strukturen spielen eine besonders negative Rolle für die Unternehmungsdemokratisierung. Die jetzige Arbeitsmarktsituation bewirkt eine Entmutigung der Belegschaft im Hinblick auf ihre Beteiligung an den Aktivitäten der Berufsvereine. Der negative Einfluß der politischen Strukturen auf den Bereich der Unternehmungsdemokratisierung ergibt sich in zweierlei Hinsicht. In erster Linie ist die Kontrolle des überwiegenden Teils der Berufsvereine durch Funktionäre zu nennen, die ideologisch zur Regierungspartei bzw. zu Parteien gehören, die der Regierungspartei nahestehen. Da manifeste Konflikte größerer Intensität[21] (z. B. Streiks) eine gesamtpolitische Bedeutung haben, neigen die Funktionäre der Berufsvereine zur Vermeidung solcher Konfliktentwicklungen. Dabei ist zu berücksichtigen, daß die überwiegende Zahl der Basisorganisationen von der sozialistischen und der kommunistischen Partei, die im Rahmen der Arbeitspolitik zusammenarbeiten, kontrolliert werden. Diese Kontrolle wird allerdings schwierig, wenn die Konflikte zwischen der Belegschaft und der Unternehmungsführung eine erhebliche Intensität annehmen und/oder wenn auf der parteipolitischen Ebene Spannungen zwischen der Regierungspartei und der Kommunistischen Partei Griechenlands auftreten, wie dies z. B. 1982 bzw. in den ersten Monaten des Jahres 1985 der Fall war. Die syndikalistische Partei der Konservativen/Liberalen kann lediglich zur Bewältigung von Konflikten beitragen, die im Rahmen öffentlicher Unternehmungen stattfinden.

In zweiter Linie ist die traditionelle staatliche Schlichtungspolitik anzuführen, die prinzipiell dem Arbeitsministerium obliegt. Das Ausmaß staatlicher Einflußnahme zeigt sich in der Entwicklung der Streikbewegungen der letzten Jahre (s. Abb. 3). Alle anderen Situationsvariablen beeinflussen unter den herrschenden Bedingungen die Arbeitsbeziehungen kaum. Die wirtschaftlichen Notwendigkeiten als Einflußgröße auf die Arbeitgeber-Arbeitnehmer-Konflikte sind im Falle der gegenwärtigen Rezession eher als Ausnahme zu betrachten.

Unter dem Gesichtspunkt der Überwindung bestehender wirtschaftlicher Engpässe wären kooperative Beziehungen zwischen den beteiligten Aktoren erforderlich. Diese Entwicklung konnte jedoch wegen der oben genannten Merkmale der griechischen Arbeitsbeziehungen bzw. der Organisationsstruktur der Unternehmungen sowie der Ablehnung der kollektiven Repräsentation der Arbeitnehmer durch die Arbeitgeber nicht eintreten.

Aus dieser Darstellung ergibt sich, daß die Unternehmungsdemokratie in Griechenland überwiegend aus der Sicherung der Existenz der kollektiven Repräsentation der Arbeitnehmer in der Unternehmung besteht.

4. Die Entwicklungstendenzen der Unternehmungsdemokratie in Griechenland

Im folgenden sollen die Entwicklungstendenzen der griechischen Arbeiterbeziehungen unter dem Gesichtspunkt der Entwicklung der politischen Strukturen diskutiert werden. Dabei kann von zwei Annahmen ausgegangen werden. Die erste besteht darin, daß die sozialistische Partei für weitere vier Jahre an der Macht bleibt, die zweite betrifft den Fall, daß die Konservativen/Liberalen die Macht nach den kommenden Wahlen übernehmen werden.

Wenn die Sozialisten die Regierung für weitere vier Jahre bilden sollten, sind folgende Entwicklungen zu erwarten: im unternehmungsexternen Bereich (d. h. in den Bünden gleichen Berufes und in den Arbeiterzentren, s. Abb. 1), können sich einige Machtverschiebungen zugunsten der Kommunisten und der Konservativen/Liberalen (d. h. zuungunsten der Sozialisten) ergeben. Diese Machtverschiebungen, die wegen der Verfolgung einer strengen Politik der Lohn- bzw. der Gehaltserhöhungen durch die Regierungspartei auftreten können, werden jedoch nicht zu einem Umsturz der bestehenden Machtverhältnisse im griechischen Gewerkschaftsbund führen. Im Prinzip können diese Verschiebungen die Streikaktionen im öffentlichen Bereich positiv beeinflussen. Im Bereich der privaten Wirtschaft dagegen ist mit dieser Entwicklung nicht zu rechnen. Auf der Unternehmungsebene ist die weitere Einrichtung bzw. weitere Existenz der Industrievereine (zuungunsten der konkurrierenden Ortsvereine gleicher Berufe) anzunehmen. Die folgenden Abbildungen sprechen für diese Tendenz.[22] In der Abb. 5 wird die Bedeutung der Industrievereine als Repräsentationsorgane dargestellt. Deutlich ist die weitere Einrichtung von Industrievereinen nach der Veränderung des politischen Rahmens Ende 1981 bzw. der entsprechenden gesetzlichen Regelungen im Juli 1982 zu sehen, die auch in den kleineren Unternehmungen die kollektive Repräsentation der Arbeitnehmer auf Unternehmungsebene ermöglicht haben. Aus der Abb. 6 und dort insbesondere aus der Spalte 3b ergibt sich, daß die kollektive Verhandlung der Arbeitnehmer wesentlich von der Unternehmungsgröße abhängig ist. Die sogenannten „besonderen Fälle" betreffen überwiegend öffentliche Unternehmungen, in denen die Arbeitnehmer durch eine Kombination von Basisorganisationen (d. h. sowohl Industrievereinen als auch Arbeitnehmerausschüssen bzw. Betriebsräten) kollektiv vertreten werden. Die Unterschiede in der Gesamtzahl der Industrievereine bzw. Arbeitnehmerausschüsse der Abb. 5 (Spalte 1a und 2a) und der Abb. 6 (Spalte 4aa und 4ba) sind auf die Tatsache zurückzuführen, daß in einigen Unternehmungen mehrere Industrievereine bzw. Arbeitnehmerausschüsse gegründet wurden, was nur aus der Abb. 5 ersichtlich ist, da in der Abb. 6 lediglich die Unternehmungen mit mindestens einem Repräsentationsorgan der Arbeitnehmer erfaßt wurden. Da die Industrievereine die speziellen Tarifverträge[23] fördern, was von den geltenden formalen Bestimmungen praktisch ausgeschlossen ist (Gesetz 3239/von 1955)[24], ist eine Revision der entspre-

Repräsentationsformen	Industrieverein (1)		Arbeitnehmerausschuss (2)		Betriebsrat (3)		Besondere Fälle (4)	
Jahr	Abs. (1a)	Verh. (1b)	Abs. (2a)	Verh. (2b)	Abs. (3a)	Verh. (3b)	Abs. (4a)	Verh. (4b)
bis 1974	53	16%	7	19%	–	–	8	58%
1975	33	10%	1	3%	–	–	–	–
1976	21	6%	4	11%	–	–	–	–
1977	11	3%	–	–	–	–	1	7%
1978	12	4%	1	3%	–	–	1	7%
1979	9	3%	2	6%	–	–	–	–
1980	15	4%	1	3%	–	–	1	7%
1981	19	6%	4	11%	–	–	1	7%
1982	93	27%	8	22%	–	–	1	7%
1983	49	13%	3	8%	1	100	1	7%
1984	23	7%	5	14%	–	–	–	–
1985 (bis Februar)	2	1%	–	–	–	–	–	–
Summe	340	100	36	100	1	100	14	100

Abb. 5: Die eingerichteten Repräsentationsorgane der Arbeitnehmer in den griechischen Unternehmungen pro Jahr (provisorische Ergebnisse)

chenden gesetzlichen Regelungen zugunsten dieser Tarifverträge sehr wahrscheinlich. Die Tendenz zur weiteren Entwicklung von Industrievereinen kann trotz der erwarteten Verabschiedung der Gesetzentwürfe „Über die Gründung von Arbeitnehmerausschüssen" (auf der Basis des internationalen Arbeitsvertrags 135[25]) und „Über die Hygiene und die Sicherheit der Arbeitnehmer"[26] nicht beeinträchtigt werden. Da die Streitfälle zwischen diesen Organen und der Unternehmungsführung nicht zufriedenstellend institutionalisiert wurden, ist zu erwarten, daß der

Kriterien / Beschäftigung	Gesamtzahl der Unternehmungen (1)		Beteiligungsgrad (2)		Repräsentationsgrad (3)		Art der Repräsentation (4)							
							Ind. verein (4a)		Arbeitn. auss. (4b)		Betr. rat (4c)		Bes. Fälle (4d)	
	Abs. (1a)	Verh. (1b)	Abs. (2a)	Verh. (2b)	Abs. (3a)	Verh. (3b)	Abs. (4aa)	Verh. (4ab)	Abs. (4ba)	Verh. (4bb)	Abs. (4ca)	Verh. (4cb)	Abs. (4da)	Verh. (4db)
40–99 Arb.	1168	56%	278	24%	109	39%	87	31%	19	7%	–	–	3	1%
100–149	283	14%	66	23%	56	85%	49	74%	6	9%	–	–	1	2%
150–199	160	8%	53	33%	40	75%	38	72%	2	4%	–	–	–	–
200–449	310	15%	83	27%	78	94%	72	87%	4	5%	–	–	2	2%
500–999	82	4%	32	39%	32	100%	30	94%	1	3%	1	3%		
über 1000	66	3%	24	36%	24	100%	15	63%	1	4%	–	–	8	33%
Summe	2069 – 36* = 2033	100	536	26%	339	63%	291	86%	33	10%	1	–	14	4%

* Diese Unternehmungen haben ihre Tätigkeit eingestellt.

Abb. 6: Daten über den Grad und die Art der kollektiven Repräsentation der Arbeitnehmer in bezug auf die Beschäftigung in den griechischen Unternehmungen (provisorische Ergebnisse)

Industrieverein, der größere Entscheidungskompetenzen für die Handhabung der Unternehmungskonflikte hat, beide obengenannten Repräsentationsorgane unter seiner Kontrolle hält. Ihre Gründung kann jedoch zur Spezifizierung bzw. Festlegung der Beziehungen der Arbeitnehmer und der Arbeitgeber führen, die durch das Gesetz 1264 von 1982 nicht gegeben ist. Damit wird ersichtlich, daß das größere Gewicht der Verhandlungen zwischen den obengenannten Aktoren auf Unternehmungsebene liegen wird. Die Tendenzen im öffentlichen Sektor, d. h. in den sogenannten „sozialisierten Unternehmungen“, sprechen deutlich für ein Führungssystem, das vergleichbar mit dem entsprechenden in den nationalisierten Unternehmungen Frankreichs (d. h. Prinzip der „Tripatisme“) ist. Insoweit handelt es sich ebenfalls um eine Tendenz zur Demokratisierung in diesen Unternehmungen[27].

Tritt der Fall ein, daß die Konservativen/Liberalen an die Macht kommen, werden quasi gegensätzliche Entwicklungen erwartet: die Machtverhältnisse im griechischen Gewerkschaftsbund werden sich radikal ändern, da keine griechische Regierung – unter der herrschenden Polarisierung – ihren Gegnern die Möglichkeit geben würde, sie durch einen nationalen Streik, den nur der griechische Gewerkschaftsbund organisieren darf, zu erpressen. Mit anderen Worten, die Tradition der staatlichen Politik wird in diesem Bereich fortgesetzt (s. oben). Da die Einflußnahme der Konservativen/Liberalen auf die Basisorganisationen (Berufsverein) gering ist, sind Entwicklungen zu erwarten, die sich auf die Eingrenzung des Handlungsspielraums der Industrievereine beziehen, wie es auch im Gesetz 330 von 1976 der Fall war. Diese Eingrenzung ist primär im Rahmen der Streikrechte und sekundär bei der Absicherung des formalen Funktionierens der Industrievereine anzunehmen. Diese Tendenzen sprechen für eine Rücknahme des bestehenden Verhandlungssystems im unternehmungsinternen Bereich zugunsten des externen Bereichs. Wegen der Bedingungen der wirtschaftlichen Strukturen sind keine diesbezüglichen erfolgreichen Gegenaktionen seitens der Betroffenen (d.h. der politischen Gegner der Konservativen/Liberalen) vorstellbar.

5. Unternehmungspolitische Konsequenzen

Die eben diskutierten Veränderungsmöglichkeiten des politischen Systems würden zu unterschiedlichen formalen Differenzierungen der Handlungsspielräume von Arbeitgebern und Arbeitnehmern führen. Bei der ersten politischen Alternative werden die Arbeitgeber mit den Arbeitnehmervertretern über eine Reihe von Themen verhandeln müssen, über die sie bis jetzt selbst entscheiden konnten. Dementsprechend handelt es sich um eine weitere formale Eingrenzung des Handlungsspielraums der Arbeitgeber. Allerdings ist dabei sowohl das niedrige Ausbildungsniveau der Arbeitnehmervertreter zu berücksichtigen als auch die Tatsache, daß die Führung der meisten Basisorganisationen manifeste Konflikte größerer Intensität zu vermeiden versuchen würde. Dadurch besteht die Chance für die Entwicklung einer kooperativen Beziehung. Die Realisierung einer kooperativen Beziehung setzt aber auch eine entsprechende Initiative der Arbeitgeberseite (z.B. im Bereich der Ausbildung der Arbeitnehmervertreter) voraus.

Im Falle der Verwirklichung der zweiten politischen Alternative werden – im Vergleich zum gegenwärtigen Stand – die formalen Handlungsspielräume der Arbeitgeber erweitert. Diese Erweiterung kann zur Verschlechterung der Arbeitsbeziehungen bzw. mittelfristig zur Intensivierung der manifesten Konflikte führen. Wenn die Vermeidung dieser Entwicklung erwünscht wird, dann ist wieder die oben genannte (d.h. die im Rahmen der ersten Alternative vorgeschlagene) Politik von der Arbeitgeberseite zu verfolgen, obwohl in diesem Fall die Schwierigkeiten für die Realisierung dieser Politik wesentlich größer sind, da die Vertreter der Basisorganisationen aus politischen Gründen weniger kooperationsbereit wären.

Daraus ist ersichtlich, daß in allen Fällen die Rolle der Arbeitgeber für die weitere Entwicklung der Unternehmungsdemokratie in Griechenland entscheidend ist. Die Bedeutung dieser Rolle wird wesentlich durch die Tatsache verstärkt, daß die höheren Organisationen der Arbeitnehmer nicht in der Lage sind, die

Voraussetzungen für die Realisierung von kooperativen Arbeitsbeziehungen zu erfüllen. Für die Erfüllung dieses Vorhabens müssen dementsprechend die Arbeitgeber die Initiative ergreifen, was sich allerdings bis jetzt noch nicht absehen läßt.

Anmerkungen

[1] Biedenkopf 1972, S. 137.
[2] Nikolopoulos 1980, S. 15.
[3] Habermas 1973, S. 170; Krüger 1977, S. 250; Muszynski 1975.
[4] Gesetz 3239 von 1955.
[5] Vgl. Nikolopoulos 1980, S. 118 ff.
Einige Wochen vor den Wahlen von 1981 hat der damalige Vorstand des griechischen Gewerkschaftsbundes, der von den Konservativen/Liberalen kontrolliert wurde, die vorzeitige Einberufung des Kongresses für die Wahl eines neuen Vorstands beschlossen. Die Mitglieder des neugewählten Vorstands zeigten keine andere ideologische Orientierung im Vergleich zum früheren Vorstand. Kurz nach der Übernahme der Regierung durch die Sozialisten wurde der Vorstand des griechischen Gewerkschaftsbundes durch gerichtliche Entscheidung gestürzt, da der vorherige Kongreß als nicht repräsentativ bezeichnet wurde. Der neue Vorstand des griechischen Gewerkschaftsbundes, der vom Gericht ernannt wurde, wurde prinzipiell aus Funktionären der syndikalistischen Partei, die die Sozialisten im Rahmen des Syndikalismus vertritt, gebildet. Nach zwei Jahren hat dieser Vorstand den neuen Kongreß des griechischen Gewerkschaftsbundes organisiert. Auf diesem Kongreß hat die syndikalistische Partei der Sozialisten die absolute Mehrheit erhalten.
[6] Vgl. Nikolopoulos 1980, S. 75 ff.
[7] Ders., S. 75 ff.
[8] Zu den entsprechenden Bestimmungen des vorigen Status vgl. Nikolopoulos 1980, S. 110 ff.
[9] Dlugos 1977, S. 468; Bütow / Dorow 1977, S. 305.
[10] Nikolopoulos 1984, S. 166 ff.
[11] Nikolopoulos 1984, S. 195.
[12] Nationales Statistisches Amt Griechenlands 1984.
Zusätzlich werden Daten berücksichtigt, die eine provisorische Einschätzung ermöglichen.
[13] Gesetz 1386 von 1983.
[14] Ihre Schulden sollen z. Z. über 200 Milliarden Drachmen (d. h. umgerechnet ca. 5 Milliarden DM) betragen. Aus: Interview des griechischen Finanzministers vom 22. 11. 1984 bzw. Angaben vom 11. 2. 1985.
[15] Buck 1978; Hummen 1977.
[16] Griechisches Außenministerium 1982.
[17] Nikolopoulos 1980, S. 203 ff.
[18] Nikolopoulos 1980, S. 144 ff.
[19] Nikolopoulos 1980, S. 79 ff.
[20] Katsanevas 1977, S. 137 ff.
[21] Über die Intensität der Konflikte Nikolopoulos 1984, S. 144.

[22] Nikolopoulos 1987.
In diesen Abbildungen werden die provisorischen Ergebnisse aus einer empirischen Erhebung in allen Unternehmungen Griechenlands dargestellt, in denen ein Repräsentationsorgan der Arbeitnehmer bestehen könnte. Die Gesamtzahl dieser Unternehmungen (d. h. mit Beschäftigung über 40 Arbeitnehmer) beträgt 2069. 36 davon haben ihre Tätigkeit eingestellt. Die Beteiligung an dieser Befragung liegt dementsprechend um 26% (536:(2069–36)).

[23] Die speziellen Tarifverträge betreffen eine einzige Unternehmung, die zwischen der entsprechenden Basisorganisation und der Unternehmungsführung vereinbart wurden.

[24] Nikolopoulos 1980, S. 104 ff.

[25] Die Rechte dieser Ausschüsse erinnern an die Funktion des Betriebsrats nach dem deutschen Betriebsverfassungsgesetz. Sie sind jedoch viel geringer im Vergleich zu den entsprechenden der deutschen Betriebsräte.

[26] Somit wird durch die Bildung von speziellen Ausschüssen bzw. durch die Beschäftigung von Fachleuten (Sicherheitsingenieuren und Arbeitsmedizinern) die Verbesserung der Arbeitsbedingungen und die Minderung der Arbeitsunfälle bezweckt.

[27] Der juristische Status dieser Unternehmungen basiert auf dem Gesetz 1385 von 1983. Dieses Gesetz hat wegen seines Artikels 4 viel Kritik erfahren, da damit das Streikrecht der Arbeitnehmer in diesen Unternehmungen begrenzt wird. Die „Sozialisierung" dieser Unternehmungen wird durch Präsidialdekrete verwirklicht. Bis jetzt wurden drei Unternehmungen sozialisiert (Staatliche Telefongesellschaft, Staatliche Elektrizitätsgesellschaft, Staatliche Eisenbahn).

Literatur

Biedenkopf, K. H. (1972): *Mitbestimmung*. Köln.

Boulding, K. E. (1957): Organization and Conflict. In: *Journal of Conflict Resolution*, 1, S. 122.

Boulding, K. E. (1962): *Conflict and Defence. A general Theory*. New York.

Buck, K. H. (1978): *Griechenland und die Europäische Gemeinschaft*. Bonn.

Bütow, L. / Dorow, W. (1977): Zielsetzung und Zielsicherung als Kernfunktion des Managements. In: *Zeitschrift für Betriebswirtschaftslehre*, 45/5, S. 289 ff.

Clegg, H. A. (1963): *A new Approach of Industrial Democarcy*. Oxford/Blackwell.

Däubler, W. (1971): Fortschritte im italienischen Arbeitsrecht. In: *Arbeit und Recht*, 19. Köln.

Dlugos, G. (1972): Analytische Wissenschaftstheorie als Regulativ betriebswirtschaftlicher Forschung. In: Dlugos / Eberlein / Steinmann (Hrsg.), *Wissenschaftstheorie und Betriebswirtschaftslehre*. Düsseldorf, S. 21 ff.

Dlugos, G. (1974): Die Unternehmungspolitik als betriebswirtschaftlich-politologische Teildisziplin. In: Wild, J. (Hrsg.), *Unternehmungsführung. Festschrift für E. Kosiol zu seinem 75. Geburtstag*. Berlin, S. 39.

Dlugos, G. (1976): Unternehmungspolitik. In: Grochla, E. / Wittmann, W. (Hrsg.): *Handwörterbuch der Betriebswirtschaft*. Stuttgart, S. 4093.

Dlugos, G. (1977): Gesellschaftspolitische Implikationen unternehmungsinterner Konflikthandhabung. In: *Die Betriebswirtschaft* 37, S. 465.

Dlugos, G. (1981): Die Unternehmungseffizienz im Interessenkonflikt der Unternehmungsmitglieder. In: Säcker, F. J. / Zander, E. (Hrsg.), *Mitbestimmung und Effizienz*. Stuttgart, S. 1.

Dlugos, G. (1981): Von der Betriebswirtschaftspolitik zur betriebswirtschaftlich-politologischen Unternehmungspolitik. In: Geist, M. N. / Köhler, R. (Hrsg.), *Die Führung des Betriebes*. Stuttgart, S. 55.

Dlugos, G. / Wondracek, J. (1979): Grundüberlegungen zur Konstituierung einer unternehmungsbezogenen Konfliktforschung. In: Dlugos, G. (Hrsg.), *Unternehmungsbezogene Konfliktforschung*. Stuttgart, S. 3.

Dorow, W. (1977): *Unternehmungskonflikte als Gegenstand unternehmungspolitischer Forschung*. Berlin.

Dorow, W. (1982): *Unternehmungspolitik*. Stuttgart usw.

Dorow, W. / Wondracek, J. (1977): Demokratisierung in Unternehmen: Anspruch, Formen, Grenzen. In: Molden, O. (Hrsg.), *Zu den Grenzen der Freiheit – Europäisches Forum Alpbach 1976*. München, Zürich, Innsbruck, S. 312.

Galtung, J. (1965): Institutionalized Conflict Resolution. A Theoretical Paradigm. In: *Journal of Peace Research* 2, S. 248.

Gesetzesblätter: 3239/von 1955, 330/v. 1976, 1264/v. 1982, 1320/v. 1983, 1365/v. 1983, 1386/v. 1983, 1387/v. 1983, 1483/v. 1984.

Griechisches Außenministerium (Hrsg.) (1982): *Die Thesen der griechischen Regierung für die Beziehungen Griechenlands mit der Europäischen Gemeinschaft*. Athen. (unveröff.)

Habermas, J. (1973): Legitimationsprobleme im Spätkapitalismus. Frankfurt/M.

Hummen, W. (1977): *Griechenland in die Europäische Gemeinschaft*. Berlin.

Katsanevas, Th. (1977): Die Arbeitsverhältnisse in Griechenland. In: *Zentrum für Planung und ökonomische Forschungen* (Hrsg.), Athen. (unveröff.)

Klis, M. (1970): *Überzeugung und Manipulation*. Wiesbaden.

Krüger, W. (1974): *Macht in der Unternehmung*. Stuttgart.

Krüger, W. (1977): Machttheoretische Perspektiven der Partizipation und Demokratisierung. In: Reber, G. (Hrsg.), *Veröffentlichung des Verbandes der Hochschullehrer für Betriebswirtschaft*. Stuttgart, S. 250 ff.

Krüger, W. (1980): Unternehmungsprozeß und Operationalisierung der Macht. In: Reber, G. (Hrsg.), S. 123 ff.

Muszynski, B. (1975): *Wirtschaftliche Mitbestimmung zwischen Konflikt- und Harmoniekonzeptionen*. Meisenheim am Glan.

Nationales Statistisches Amt Griechenlands (1984): *Arbeitsstatistik*. Athen.

Nikolopoulos, A. (1980): *Chancen einer industriellen Demokratie in Griechenland* (Diss.). Berlin.

Nikolopoulos, A. (1984): *Ein Handlungsmodell im Rahmen der industriellen Arbeitsbeziehungen (griechisch)*. Athen.

Nikolopoulos, A. (1987): *Die Struktur der kollektiven Repräsentation der Arbeitnehmer in den griechischen Unternehmungen* (n. n. veröff.). Athen.

Oechsler, W. A. (1979): *Konfliktmanagement*. Wiesbaden.

Pohmer, D./Schweitzer, M. (1974): Macht und Mitbestimmung im ökonomischen Entscheidungsprozeß. In: Wild, J. (Hrsg.), *Unternehmungsführung. Festschrift für E. Kosiol zu seinem 75. Geburtstag*. Berlin, S. 77 ff.

Reber, G. (Hrsg.) (1980): *Macht in Organisationen*. Stuttgart.

Sokianos, N. (1981): *Die Zielanalyse als ein Instrument des Konfliktmanagements*. Berlin.

The Structure of the Enterprise Union and the Present Situation of Labour Participation in Japan

Yoshiaki Takahashi

Abstract

In this article the labour-management joint consultation system and the small group "self-management" are discussed. Both systems are analysed with respect to the structure of the Japanese enterprise union. Japanese labour-management joint consultation has generally operated on the employer's initiative, because it functions not as co-determination machinery but as communication machinery. Following the period of high economic growth in Japan the small group "self-management" system has been changed to the autonomous type from the older voluntary type. The official job relationship at the working level has been brought in the processes of negotiation or joint consultation under influence of the management, because most Japanese labour unions are organized per plant or enterprise.

1. Introduction

Japan and Western countries share two systems for solving problems between employer and employee.

One is the collective bargaining system in Japan, established by the labour act which focuses on the negotiation of wages, holiday allowances and other labour conditions. In Japan, collective bargaining is conducted on a per enterprise basis, because, as is widely known, Japanese labour unions have been organized per enterprise. This situation is different from Western countries where industrial or craft unions prevail. The second is the labour-management joint consultation system which in Japan is not based on law but on a composite of individual agreements reached through collective bargaining in each enterprise. The subjects for discussion in labour-management joint consultation are, therefore, ordinarily different in each company.

It is said in Japan that the labour-management joint consultation system and the so called small "self-management" groups are workers' participation systems. But the procedure of workers' participation in Japan is different from that in Scandinavian countries and West Germany. In Japan neither the joint consultation system, as above mentioned, nor the system of small group activities were realized by legislation or by national agreement between both sides of industry. In most cases these two systems were introduced on the employer's initiative or by agreement between the employer and the labour union of each company. Compared to Western systems with respect to democratization and efficiency in an enterprise, it is possible to point out many different negative and positive points in the Japanese worker participation system.

In the second chapter of this article the structure of Japanese enterprise union is explained. The third and fourth chapter will deal with the present situation of the labour-management joint consultation system and the small "self management" group system at the work place level. The final chapter discusses some problematic points of the labour participation system in Japan.

2. The Structure of Enterprise Unions

2.1. Labour Union Organization

The basic unit of union organization is that which is organized within a company (in-company-union). This differs from national trade union organizations in other countries (see table 1). An union has a strong say within a company but as it is separate from other unions, its social influence is weak. To compensate for this weakness, federations are formed with the individual unions as dominant members.

There are two types of federations: lateral, national federations, called National Centers, and vertical industry federations. Most unions join both types of federations. Nationwide there are nearly 74.500 individual labour unions with approximately 12.5 millions of members. This is approximately 30% of total wage earners. However, there is a big difference between the organization rate of large companies and small companies (see table 1, 2, 3).

Tab. 1: Number of union and membership according to the type of union organization

Type of union organization	no. of unions		no. of union	
Enterprise union	65.337	94.2%	11.361.378	91.4%
Crafts union	720	1.0%	169.569	1.4%
Industry trade union	1.775	2.6%	682.728	5.5%
Others	1.501	2.2%	259.299	2.0%

Source: Ministry of Labor, Basic Survey of Trade Union, 1975

Tab. 2: Development of unions, membership and rate of oganizations

Year	no. of unions	no. of membership (per 1.000 person)	proportion organized (%)
1970	60.954	11.605	35.4
1975	69.333	12.590	34.4
1980	72.693	12.369	30.8
1983	74.486	12.520	29.7

Source: Ministry of Labor, Basic Survey of Trade Union, 1983. In: *Japan Labor Bulletin* 1984

Tab. 3: Proportion of trade unions in private sector according to the size of enterprise

no. of employees	total (in 1.000 persons)	rate of organisation (in %)
over 1.000	5.013	57
300– 999	1.430	16
100– 299	1.039	11
30– 29	459	5
under 29	68	1
average	867	9

Source: Ministry of Labor, Basic Survey of Trade Union, 1983

Vertical industry federations are organized by the companies which belong to the industry concerned. Most of these industrial federations are coalitions of enterprise unions and therefore serve only as advisory bodies. Their functions are restricted to exchanging information and granting mutual assistance. Decisions are not binding on affiliated unions. The lack of authority of the main body over the member unions is caused by the strong independence of the affiliated enterprise unions (Hanami 1979, p. 90). The federations with a large membership are shown in table 4.

There are four national federations (National Centers of Trade Unions) over these industry wide federations (see table 5).

1. SOHYO – General Council of Trade Unions in Japan, under the influence of Japan Socialist Party and Japan Communist Party
2. DOMEI – Japanese Confederation of Labour, under the influence of Japan Democratic Socialist Party
3. CHURITSU-ROREN – Federation of Independent Trade Unions
4. SHINSANBETS – National Federation of Industrial Organization

Overlapping these there are:

Tab. 4: Main large federation (1983)

trade union (affiliation)	official name (occupation or industry)	membership (thousand)
Public sector		
Jichiro (sohyo)	all Japan prefectual and municipal workers' unions	1.275
Nikkyoso (sohyo)	Japan teachers' unions	677
Dentsuroren (sohyo)	joint council of telecommunication industry trade unions	328
Kokuro (sohyo)	national railways workers' union	224
Zentei (sohyo)	Japan postal workers' union	182
Private sector		
Denkiroren (Churitsuroren)	Japanese federation of electric machine workers	586
Jidoshasoren (Churitsuroren)	confederation of Japan automobile workers' union	530
Zensendomei (domei)	the Japanese federation of textile garment, chemical, distributive and allied industry workers' unions	479
Seihororen (Churitsuroren)	Japan life insurance workers' unions	357
Tekkororen (sohyo)	Japanese federation of iron and steel workers' union	222

Source: Ministry of Labor, Basic Survey of Trade Unions, 1983

1. ZEMIN-ROKYO – Japanese Private Sector Trade Union
2. IMF-JC – Japan Council International Metal Workers Federation
3. KO-ROKOY – Council of Public Corporation and National Enterprise Workers' Union

They have been formed to act together based on shared ideals and strategy. SOHYO and DOMEI, the large National Centers in Japan, have different ideals and strategies. The activities of SOHYO, the majority of whose members are government employees, have a strong tint of class struggle. Compared to this, the nucleus of DOMEI is the union of large private enterprises, affiliated on block to the ICFTU (International Confederation of Free Trade Unions), which follows the ideal of social democracy adopted in the Frankfurt Declaration (1951).

Thus the main feature of labour union organizations in Japan is its matrix of national and industrial federations with in-company-unions as the nucleus.

Tab. 5: Membership distribution among the 4 national federations

1 Sohyo	49 "tan-sans" (federations)	452.5 (in 10.000 persons)	33.5% of the total org.labour
private sector	29 "tan-sans"	150.8	33.3% of Sohyo membership
public sector	20 "tan-sans"	301.7	66.7% of Sohyo membership
2 Domei	31 "tan-sans" (federations)	218.2	17.6% of total org. labour
private sector	23 "tan-sans"	201.6	94.2% of Domei membership
public sector	8 "tan-sans"	16.5	7.6% of Domei membership
3 Churitsuroren	10 "tan-sans" 5 unit unions	132.1	10.7% of total org. labour
private sector	10 "tan-sans"	132.0	99.9% of churitsuroren membership
public sector	5 unit unions	6.1	0.1% of churitsuroren membership
4 Shinsanbetsu	4 "tan-sans"	6.1	0.5% of total org. labour
5 others	34 independent	467.9	37.8% of total org. labour

Source: Ministry of Labor, Basic Survey of Trade Unions, 1978

2.2. In-Company-Unions (Enterprise Unions)

The in-company-unions act independently on their own initiative. The labour agreement, directly influencing the interests of the workers, is decided by collective bargaining or by labour-management conference within the company. National centers or industrial federations, as above suggested, do not have the right to negotiate directly on problems between labour and management in individual companies.

Recently, in wage and hours negotiation (which labour consider to be desirable if decided on an overall nation-wide basis), unified negotiations have been realised on industrial and regional levels through the strong request of labour. Yet, the final agreement is generally concluded within the company. It is rare for an agreement to be concluded between the employers' association and the national center or industrial labour organization and applied uniformly to the labour and management in individual companies.

There are differing views on why the enterprise union was organized in Japan; the following is that which this author supports. In the face of repression by the state and the prohibition of three basic workers' rights, the Japanese labour movement developed quickly after the Second World War. Difficult economic conditions caused by inflation strengthened the drive to safeguard the workers' standard of living. Because the managers' side had sabotaged normal production activity, this labour movement was oriented toward having white collar and blue collar (workers) together controlling production for the sake of their own standard of living.

The goals of the workers' side were: to remove the traditional grade system, to reform the management organization, to set up a participation system, to obtain recognition of the labour union, to contract labour agreements, to democratize management and to expand workers' rights. During the early development of union organizations, labour decided to establish a joint effort of white and blue collar workers to organize unions at the enterprise or plant level. This is the reason why Japanese trade unions are organized at the company level (Yoshikawa 1980, pp. 269–281).

But we must not overlook that the managers' side has made an effort to determine the structure of the enterprise union. Hazama writes about this point as follows: "It was a major concern of the managers' side in this period to reverse the predominant position of the workers in Japanese companies just after the Second World War. The managers' side sought to recover its position in relation to the workers' side, so that it could regain its original rights. For this purpose the managers' side took three measures. The first was to make labour relations vertical, thus weakening the horizontal solidarity of workers per district or per industry and strenghthening labour relations per enterprise. The second was to make a cooperation relationship with labour and to recover the order at the work places by removing those union members who propagated radical thoughts and were aggressive toward the managers' side. The third was to establish the 'rights' of management by setting up a new labour management system in every company." (Hazama 1981, p. 256)

Through these measures by the managers' side the Japanese trade union's form has been fixed as an enterprise union. Article 2 of the Labour Union Law stipulates that all regular employees may be organized in unit unions regardless of their job, hierarchical level (below section head) and qualifications, provided that they are not in charge of labour management (see chapter 5).

2.3. Labour Movement at a Turning Point

Japanese enterprise unions have not had a long history. In 1945, just after the Second World War, a trade union law was enacted and three basic rights (to organize to bargain collectively and to strike) were ensured. These were prohibited during the war. With it the Japanese labour movement was able to have a strong influence on Japanese society in those days. Also the Labour Standard Law was established in 1947. In 1946 NIHON RORO SODOMEI (Japan Confederation of Labour) which had existed from 1920 to 1940, was established again and SANBETSU (National Congress of Industry Trades Unions) was organized in August 1946. The SANBETSU was under the strong influence of the communist party, but it was dissolved with the red purge in 1955, and SOHYO, which is anticommunist and still exists, was organized in the same year. In SOHYO there have been socialists and communists on the one hand, and moderate socialists on the other. In 1956 the moderate wing of the socialists separated and organized ZENRO (Japan Trade Union), which developed into the present DOMEI (Japanese Confederation of Labour). Though collective bargaining was done per industry before the dissolution of SANBETSU, this was rejected by management and the bargaining style was changed gradually into bargaining per enterprise.

Now it is said that labour unions are behind the organizing of body which could represent the view of workers throughout the country. That is why the issue of unifying the separate unions into one organization is drawing attention. But because this movement is done under the initiative of DOMEI, and the workers of the left wing in the unions are against this movement. Eventually a new federation, ZENMIN-ROKYO was formed in 1982. It cuts across the four national federations SOHYO, DOMEI, CHURITSU-ROREN and SHINSANBETS and consists of 41 industrial federations and 4.25 million workers in private companies. Against this movement, members of left wing groups in these unions and other unions (about 1.2 million), have organized TOITSU-ROSO-KON (National Unified Congress of Revolutionary Labour Unions) informally.

3. The Present Situation of the Labour-Management Joint Consultation System in Japan

Some major inquiries into the Japanese labour-management joint consultation system have been made by the Social and Economic Congress of Japan (Shakai Keizai Kokumin Kaigi 1975), the Ministry of Labour (1978) and the Japan Productivity Center (1966, 1968, 1972, 1975, 1981). In this article analysis of the present situation of the labour management joint consultation system will be based on two current and exhaustive studies. One is the inquiry conducted in 1981 by the Japan Productivity Center into 1710 companies whose stock were listed at all Japan

Stock Exchanges (available answers 533, percentage of collected answers 32.0%). Another is the inquiry conducted in 1977 by Kimoto, Professor of Meiji University, into 1750 labour unions (available answers 230, percentage of collected answers 12.99%).

3.1. General Character of the Labour-Management Joint Consultation System

According to the Japan Productivity Center 94 per cent of large companies employing more than 1.000 employees, and 90 per cent of the 482 companies recorded have labour-management consultation machineries. This figure for the companies employing less than 1.000 employees is nearly 80 per cent (fig. 1).

At which level in these companies has labour-management joint consultation been established? 66.8 per cent of all 434 companies have this machinery not only at the enterprise level but also at the plant and work place level. In relation to the size of enterprises 92.0 per cent of companies employing more than 5.000 employees have joint consultation machineries at three levels, while 68.9 per cent of companies with 4.900–8.000 employees and only 49.3 per cent of companies with less than 1.000 employees have them at three levels. This difference is in part due to the fact that some small size enterprises have only one plant level (table 6). A time-frame for the development of the labour-management joint consultation system in these companies is shown in fig. 2. This machinery has generally been established more rapidly in larger companies.

Fig. 1: Percentage of companies which have labour-management joint consultation machineries

Source: Japan Productivity Center. The Subjects of the labour-management joint consultation system in a new stage 1981, p. 18

Tab. 6: At which level is labour-management joint consultation machinery established?
434 companies (%)

size of enterprise / item	all companies	more than 10.000 employees	5.000 ~ 9.999	1.000 ~ 4.999	500 ~ 999	300 ~ 499	less than 300
1) only at enterprise level	138(31.8)	0(0.0)	6(11.3)	58(29.6)	38(44.2)	19(51.4)	17(63.0)
2) at enterprise and plant lebel	218(50.2)	23(65.7)	33(62.3)	98(50.0)	42(48.8)	15(40.5)	7(25.9)
3) at enterpr. and work place level	12(2.8)	2(5.7)	1(1.9)	5(2.6)	2(2.3)	2(5.4)	0(0.0)
4) at enterpr., plant + work place level	60(13.8)	10(28.6)	12(22.6)	32(16.3)	3(3.5)	1(2.7)	2(7.4)
5) only at plant level	6(1.4)	0(0.0)	1(1.9)	3(1.5)	1(1.2)	0(0.0)	1(3.7)
total	434(100.0)	35(8.1)	53(12.2)	196(45.2)	86(19.8)	37(8.5)	27(6.2)

Source: Japan Productivity Center, op. cit., p. 30

In the Japanese Company, where labour relations have been established through agreements and from practices recognized over time, for what specific purposes does the labour-management joint consultation system exist? As shown on table 7, the percentage of answers "to explain the situation of the business and the intention of the managers side toward the labour side and to gain their understanding and co-operation" and so that "the communication between labour and management functions smoothly and a dispute between both sides can be avoided" amounts to 60.8 per cent and 56.7 per cent respectiveley. The percentage of answers "to strengthen the worker's right of speach in the decision making at the enterprise level as well as work place level" amounts to only 0.9 per cent. Therefore, it is said that the Japanese labour-management joint consultation system has created an able machinery for the communication and understanding between both sides.

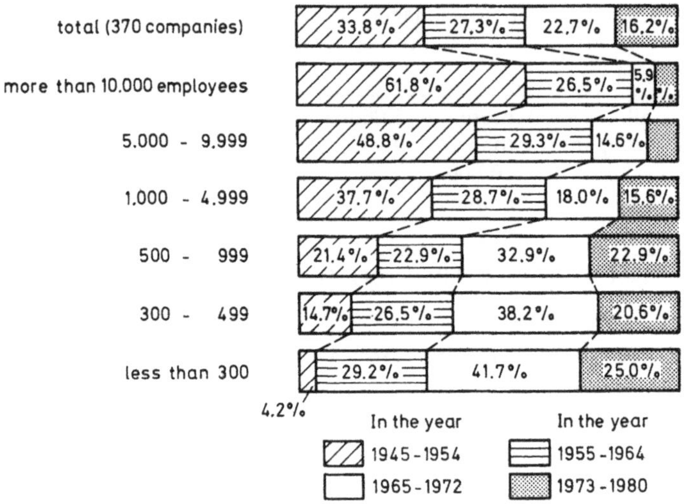

Source: Japan Productivity Center, op. cit., p. 18

Fig. 2: Time-frame of the establishment of labour-management joint consultation

Labour-management joint consultation can be distinguished into three general categories:

1. Joint consultation is held only periodically (8%)
2. Joint consultation is held in the case of need and periodically (70%)
3. Joint consultation is held only in the case of need (21.4%).

Less joint consultation is held at the plant and work place level than at the enterprise level. Furthermore, different situations exist as to the initiation of joint consultation between employer and employee:

1. Either side has the prerogative to initiate consultation (43.1%)
2. Both employer and labour union can suggest consultation but confirmation depends on the decision of a subsequent conference (52.2%), and
3. other (4.7%).

The following statistics have been gathered as to the actual frequency of periodical joint consultation in these companies between September 30., 1979, and August 31., 1980: 12 times per year, 23.2 per cent; less than 6 times, 48.8 per cent; and more than 12 times, 7.6 per cent. On the average, joint consultation based on need occurred 8.6 times during the year.

Tab. 7: On which purposes, according to the labour-agreement or the practice, the labour-management joint consultation system was established

	items (purposes)	number of answers	(%)
(1)	to solve the problems between labour and management before the collective bargaining	85	(19.6)
(2)	for the purpose that the communication between labour and management functions smoothly by which a dispute between both sides can be avoided	246	(56.7)
(3)	for the purpose that both side study and consult co-operatively and concretely about the high productivity	61	(14.1)
(4)	to explain the situation of the business and the intention of the manager side for the labour side and to gain their understanding and co-operation	264	(60.8)
(5)	to consult beforehand with the labour side about the new business development and the introduction of the new technique which exerts a serious influence on the conditions of work and personnel problem	40	(9.2)
(6)	to exchange views on the basic management policy and planning between labour and management for the sake of the promotion of democratization and efficiency	141	(32.5)
(7)	to strengthen the worker's right of speaking on the decision making of the enterprise level as well as work place level	4	(0.9)
(8)	other	9	(2.1)
	total	850	(195.9)

Note: The companies inquiered into could select two item

Source: Japan Productivity Center, op. cit., p. 30

3.2. The Connection Between Labour-Management Joint Consultation and Collective Bargaining, and the Subjects for Discussion in Both Systems

The connection between labour-management joint consultation and collective bargaining, according to the inquiry by Kimoto, is shown on table 8. Three types have been identified to describe this relationship:

1. No-distinction exists (adhesive type)
2. There is a clear distinction (separate type)
3. The discussion by both sides as carried from joint consultation to collective bargaining, when the discussion does not reach a conclusion (pre-bargaining type).

Tab. 8: The connection between labour-management joint consultation system and collective bargaining

	kind of type	number of companies	(%)
1)	The labour-management joint consultation system distinguished with the collective bargaining and has a same function of it	47	22.0
2)	The labour-management joint consultation system does not with the collective bargaining	84	40.1
	i) Joint consultation system is a machinery of consultation, communication and notice	68	31.8
	ii) Joint consultation system is a machinery of co-determination	18	8.4
3)	According to the agreement or the practice labour-management joint consultation system is a machinery of pre-bargaining	51	23.8
4)	other	2	1.0
5)	total	230	100.0

Source: Kimoto, The Present Situation and Problems of "Worker Participation" in Japan, p. 5

Since 1950 the Japanese Productivity Center has consistently offered the recommendation that both systems should be separated and this idea be subsequently adapted in Japanese industries. From this inquiry it can be seen that this separation has not developed as quickly as it might have. The adhesive type applies to 41.0 per cent of labour unions required into which belonging to the SOHYO federation (General Council of Trade Unions in Japan), while characterizing only 21.0 per cent of the labour unions which belong to the DOMEI federation (Japan Confederation of Labour). The difference between federations may depend upon the principles of SOHYO which state: "The connection between the labour-management joint consultation system and collective bargaining is proper when collective bargaining has a more important function than the labour-management joint consultation system. The function of the labour-management joint consultation system is enough to fill the roll of the pre-bargaining." (Kimoto 1979, p. 5)

Which subjects are put up for discussion in the collective bargaining and in the labour-management joint consultation systems? While the subjects for discussion in collective bargaining center around conditions of the labour contract such as wage, work time and holidays, labour-management joint consultation extends discussion to all matters concerned with management and labour. With the exception of some areas such as wages and holiday allowances, each system is distinguishable with respect to subjects for discussion. 147 labour unions (68.7% of all unions inquired into) answered that agreement is not possible without the mutual consent of both parties in labour-management joint consultation (table 9).

Tab. 9: Subjects for discussion in joint consultation and collective bargaining

subjects for consultation or bargaining / system to solve the problems	management policy	financial statement	closing of plant or reduction of business	reform of job organization	job evaluation	production planning	facilities planning	introduction of new machine and technique	time-motion study	basic personnel policy	employee cut	reassignment	personnel change	educating and training	rationalization of production and office work	sanitation	social welfare	wage and semiannual bonus	work time and holiday	interpretation and application of labour agreement	grievance machinery
on the collective bargaining	8.3	6.9	8.6	6.0	3.0	2.2	2.6	4.3	2.6	5.7	12.2	12.6	4.8	4.3	7.4	8.7	17.4	59.1	40.0	16.9	7.4
on the labour-management joint consultation	58.6	50.9	21.3	53.0	24.8	67.4	50.3	33.9	22.4	44.3	13.0	43.5	38.7	38.7	41.3	55.7	46.1	17.8	34.8	23.5	36.1
on the both system	13.4	7.8	9.1	6.0	3.0	7.8	1.8	5.2	3.0	7.4	7.8	9.1	7.4	4.3	6.5	8.7	12.2	14.8	10.0	7.8	8.7
no answer (there was no such case)	19.5	34.3	60.8	34.7	69.1	30.9	39.6	56.5	72.0	42.6	67.0	34.8	44.8	52.6	44.8	27.0	24.3	8.3	15.6	51.7	47.9

Note: The figure in the table refer to percentage of all 230 companies answered

Source: Kimoto, op. cit., p. 5

However, it should be noted that 24% stated that for decisions to be made agreement between both is not necessary. In this instance labour-management joint consultation "is not a determination machinery" (Kimoto 1979, p. 6).

In the table 10 findings of subjects for discussion in labour-management joint consultation and the degree of labour participation are compared between inquiries done by the Japan Productivity Center in 1980 (column C), 1975 (column B) and 1963 (column A). A high degree of "consultation and co-determination" is evident on "labour conditions" and on "reform of job conditions", "reassignment temporal release from work" and "employee cut" in the area of personnel matters. But a high percentage of "consultation" and "giving notices and explanation" is shown on "management matters", "production matters" and other items in the area of "personnel matters" (basic personnel policy, standard of personnel change, education and training plans).

A comparison between the inquiries of 1963 and 1980 reveals that in most cases the percentage of issues subject to "consultation and co-determination" decreases. Furthermore, for matters such as "introduction of new machinery and techniques" employers were generally only required to "give notice and explanations" and "consult" with labour, although such matters exert a big influence on conditions of labour at the work place level.

Generally, therefore, the labour-management joint consultation system in Japan has gradually been operated on the employers initiative.

Tab. 10: Subjects for discussion on the joint consultation system and the degree of labour participation

(%)

	of consultation	consultation and codetermination			consultation			giving notices and explanation			other (there was not such a case)		
	year items	A	B	C	A	B	C	A	B	C	A	B	C
manage-ment matters	- management policy	0.8	0.4	0.2	5.5	5.3	5.4	90.4	84.5	89.0	3.4	9.8	5.4
	- rationalization of production and office work	7.7	3.3	5.9	44.2	34.9	38.2	43.9	52.3	50.5	4.2	9.5	5.4
	- result of business	0.5	0.0	0.0	3.3	1.7	2.0	91.3	87.5	93.2	4.9	10.8	4.9
	- finance statement	0.6	0.0	0.0	6.0	2.3	0.5	85.0	77.8	87.1	8.5	19.9	12.3
	- reorganization and abolishment of enterprise	14.4	7.2	9.1	38.0	26.7	33.2	43.9	58.7	53.6	3.7	7.4	4.2
production matters	- production planning	3.8	3.2	2.3	21.8	14.3	12.5	66.9	66.9	75.2	7.4	18.6	10.0
	- facilities planning	2.5	0.4	1.3	21.8	8.7	11.5	69.5	70.1	73.9	6.2	20.8	13.3
	- introduction of new machine and technique	3.5	0.6	2.5	21.5	9.8	12.6	64.9	61.6	66.0	10.1	28.0	18.9
	- measurement of productivity	7.7	0.2	2.7	29.6	15.6	14.2	46.2	38.4	45.2	17.2	45.8	38.0
personnel matters	- basic personnel policy	16.5	4.4	2.8	29.0	22.5	18.6	47.6	45.6	60.6	7.0	27.5	18.1
	- standard of personnel change	13.7	6.5	5.8	36.3	25.8	25.8	42.0	38.7	43.9	8.0	29.0	24.6
	- education and training plan	4.9	0.8	1.8	24.0	17.0	13.0	59.2	44.3	54.2	11.8	37.9	31.0
	- reform of job conditions	x	27.9	34.2	x	41.0	40.5	x	12.4	13.8	x	18.7	11.6
	- reassignment, temporal release from work and employee cut	x	42.5	47.0	x	37.1	32.3	x	6.2	10.9	x	14.2	9.8
social matters	- sanitation	23.6	10.4	12.1	55.5	64.1	61.9	14.2	18.4	18.6	6.7	7.1	7.4
	- social welfare	26.7	11.2	12.8	54.9	69.5	63.9	14.1	14.1	17.7	4.3	5.2	5.6
labour conditions matters	- wage system	74.0	66.4	69.0	22.7	22.4	20.5	2.9	0.6	4.4	0.2	10.6	6.1
	- worktime, holiday etc.		69.9	70.7		19.9	20.6		0.0	3.1		10.2	5.6
the rest	- interpretation and application of labour agreement	69.6	68.4	62.2	26.8	27.5	28.7	1.1	0.6	2.9	2.4	13.5	6.1
	- grievance machinery	51.8	36.4	36.4	40.1	41.1	45.8	1.9	3.6	4.2	6.1	18.9	13.6
	- change of work rules	40.4	36.0	33.3	43.1	35.8	30.3	12.2	11.8	24.2	4.3	16.4	12.1

Note: 1. A: The report of the Japan Productivity Center "A technological innovation and labour-management joint consultation system" 1964; number of the companies inquired (available answers): 764; the time when the inquiry was done: August 1963

2. B: The report of the Japan Productivity Center "The labour-management joint consultation system in Japan – its present situation and subject" 1976; number of the companies inquired (available answers): 643; the time when the inquiry was done: July – August 1975

3. C: The report of the Japan Productivity Center "The subjects of the labour-management joint consultation system in a new stage" 1981; number of the companies inquired (available answers): 553; the time when the inquiry was done: August–Oktober 1980

4. x: signal means that it did not become the object of the question

5. Reference: Kimoto "Participation of labour union", 1977

4. The Present Situation of Japanese Style Participation at the Work Place Level

4.1. The Popularization of Small Group "Self-Management"

A prevalent form of labour participation at the work place level in Japan is the small "self-management" group, such as the QC (quality control) or ZD (zero defects) circles. Generally speaking the small group "self-management" has been introduced for the following reasons. On one hand "it is to develop design, manufacture and supply products that are the most economical, of the greatest use, and which will satisfy the customer" (Ishikawa 1980, p. 60). On the other hand "the quality of work can be entranced when each employees strives voluntarily to be creative in the course of his daily work assignment" (Katoh 1982, p. 38). These activities were introduced in Japanese companies in order to realize "high efficiency" and "humanization of work".

It was in the middle of 1960 shortly after Japan had entered its stage of high economic growth, that companies in Japan began to adopt the small group "self-management" system. In most cases this system was introduced on the employers initiative to improve workers' motivation. It was a matter of course that Japanese high economic growth was attributable to technological innovation and the rapid introduction of automation and computerization. While this mechnization of production facilities and organization did bring on corporate prosperity, it also has turned the work of workers into automatic routine and repetitive work. The workers who engage in such work, not only blue-collar but also white collar workers, are forced daily to perform fragmented and meaningless tasks.

Despite the rapid modernization of Japan's economy, the wage system remained as it had in the past; with wages increases based on service years or seniority. It was therefore very difficult for highly educated young workers to maintain a high degree of motivation. To overcome this situation, Japanese companies were forced to modify the traditional wage system, and to introduce the modern American management method in which not only service years but also the ability of workers is reflected by the wages. The quality control system was also introduced as a modern management method from America into Japanese companies.

Small group activities have usually been done away from the job and outside regular work time. The issues that these small groups themselves elect to tackle are generally such non-regular problems as quality control, zero-defect or job safety. Each group, independently, outside regular working hours, and somewhere away from the regular place of work such as the lounge or the dining room, gets together from time to time, according to a self-imposed shedule, to study the area of concern. (Odaka 1982, p. 230)

In spite of their introduction on management's initiative, small group activities have spread during the period of high economic growth in both large companies and small-medium sized Japanese firms. In particular, young, skilled workers and highly educated workers have participated in these activities. Odaka elaborates further on this point: "Yet another reason is probably that it could be easily implemented and its introduction did not require a replanning of regular duties, a reshuffing of personnel, a recording of the shop organization, or any other major expenditure of time, effort and expense. Encouraged by its convenience and effectiveness, supporters of the system of voluntary group activities often proudly referred to it as Japanese-style self-management." (Odaka 1982, p. 229)

Popularization of the workers' small group activity has been rapid. According to a recent inquiry by Japan's Labour Ministry, over one-third of all Japanese firms have small QC or ZD groups, with the percentage rising to 69 per cent among large companies. According to the 1975 Annual Report of the Japan Iron and Steel Federation, 169 plants of its 45 member firms has such small groups, totalling over 30.000 groups to which approximately 230.000 workers attended (82.5 per cent of all workers of member firms).

4.2. Transfer from the Voluntary Type to the Autonomous Type

Criticism about voluntary small group activities has emerged since the mid-1970's, from within these same groups. According to Hayashi's article of 1976, surveying the Japan Iron and Steel Federation, the following problems discourage the full realization of QC circle activities:

- poor leadership,
- difficulties in scheduling appropriate times for activities,
- deciding on an appropriate theme or programme for the group,
- inappropriate award systems for the groups achievements,
- overtime pay is not encouraged for the circle activities after hours (Hayashi 1983, p. 8).

Most of these problems depend upon, as mentioned briefly above, the structure of the voluntary small group acitivity. Because of these criticisms and complaints "a number of corporations attempted", according to Odaka, "in the late 1970's, to transform the old system of voluntary study activity by small informal groups into a system of full-fledged autonomous activities to be carried out by small groups in connection with their regular work. Furthermore, a number of corporations promoted a transitional system of intermediate small group activities." (Odaka 1982, p. 232) As a result, there are today three types of small group activities in Japanese companies:

Voluntary type: Small study groups of volunteers allowed to engage in spontaneous study and training activities outside regular work hours.

Transitional type: Intermediate or mixed groups falling between or consisting of older and new type features.

Autonomous type: Small groups which engage in regular productive work and which are allowed autonomously to determine their operational procedures and to be responsible for the results (Odaka 1982, p. 232).

A study of the above three types was conducted by Osaka and his instructor in 1977–1978 surveying 60 companies placed in the Keihin (Tokyo-Yokohami) industrial belt. The findings shown on table 11 indicates that almost 60 per cent of all companies surveyed use the typical old voluntary type, although both transitional and autonomous small group activities account for 26.7 per cent and 16.7 per cent, 90 per cent of the 16 companies with autonomous type groups reported that employee moral was improved as a result of the institution of these new small group activities, as compared to only 5.9 per cent of the companies with voluntary type group. From this survey Odaka arrives at the following conclusion: "It will be

Tab. 11: Types of small group activities and employee morale

	no. of works where small group activities are found	no. of works where employee morale improved	no. of works where employee morale was unchanged	no. of works where employee morale deteriorated
voluntary type	34 (56.7%)	2 of 34 (5.9%)	28 of 34 (82.4%)	4 of 34 (11.8%)
transitional type	16 (26.7%)	8 of 16 (50.0%)	8 of 16 (50.0%)	0 of 16 (0%)
autonomous type	10 (16.7%)	9 of 10 (90.0%)	1 of 10 (10.0%)	0 of 10 (0%)
total	60 (100%)	19 of 60 (31.7%)	37 of 60 (61.7%)	4 of 60 (6.7%)

Source: Odaka, ibid., p. 223

easy to imagine why autonomous group activities in Japanese industry are gradually shifting away from the old voluntary type to the newer autonomous regular-work type." (Odaka 1982, p. 234)

5. The Problems of the Japanese Style Labour Participation System

The preceding chapters have discussed the structure of the enterprise union and Japanese-style labour participation with reference to systems like labour-management joint consultation and small group "self-management" activities. The labour-management joint consultation system was developed in 1965 and the tripartite (government, labour and management) joint consultation system at the national level was established after the oil shock. Communication has been established at every level between employer and employee through such joint consultation systems. However, the relationship between management and labour unions in Japan is not as simple as it may seem, because of different opinions between labour federations. The existence of four National Trade Union Centers (SOHYO, DOMEI, CHURITSURODEN and SHINSANBETSU) and several independent unions, illustrate this point.

According to Kimoto's inquiry (mentioned above) each federation represents a different perspective for its member unions on the subject of worker participation. This difference becomes more apparent in view on issues like small group activities such as QC, ZD and production quotas imposed by management. While most labour unions belonging to DOMEI agree with the small group activity, about 40 per cent of labour unions belonging to SOHYO and SHINSANBETSU are against this system. On the other hand most Japanese labour unions not only SOHYO but also DOMEI are not in favour of the system of worker participation on the board of the directors (see table 12, Kimoto 1977, p. 11).

The structure of enterprise unions limits the effectiveness of labour union activity. Levels of union organization, such as headquarters, chapter and group are parallel to components such as the central, plant, department and sections or supervisors, in the official management organization of the enterprise or plant. Each level of labour is in constant interface with its corresponding management level. This fragmentation of labour and influence of management discourages a healthy level of negotiation in collective bargaining or labour-management joint consultation on specific issues.

Another problem concerns the regulation of membership eligibility. Article 2 of the Labour Union Law in Japan stipulates, as mentioned in chapter two, that all regular employees may be organized in unions regardless of their job, hierarchical level (below section head) and qualifications, provided that they are not on charge

Tab. 12: Labour unions' views on the labour-management joint consultation system, small groups' control and worker participation on the board of directors in Japan

items	federations/ size of enterprise	per federations						per size of enterprise						
		Sohyo	Domei	Churitsuroren	Shinsanbetsu	independent	other (no writing on)	less than 299	300–499	500–999	1.000–4.999	5.000–9.999	more than 10.000	average
labour-management joint consultation system	positive	72.0	93.5	90.2	100	88.8	93.3	79.3	79.2	82.9	90.2	96.7	90.0	87.4
	negative	18.6	2.2	0.0	0.0	6.3	0.0	10.5	12.5	8.6	4.3	3.3	0.0	6.1
	other	9.3	4.3	7.3	0.0	5.0	6.7	6.9	8.3	8.6	5.4	0.0	10.0	6.1
	no writing on	0.0	0.0	2.4	0.0	0.0	0.0	3.4	0.0	0.0	0.0	0.0	0.0	0.4
small groups' control (QC, ZD, control by goal)	positive	39.5	82.6	51.2	40.0	56.3	66.7	44.8	45.8	65.7	60.9	50.0	75.0	57.8
	negative	39.5	0.0	14.6	40.0	18.6	6.7	37.9	29.2	17.1	14.1	10.0	5.0	17.8
	other	18.6	15.2	29.3	20.0	22.5	26.7	13.8	25.0	14.3	21.7	36.7	20.0	21.7
	no writing on	2.3	2.2	4.9	0.0	2.5	0.0	3.4	0.0	2.9	3.3	3.3	0.0	2.6
worker participation on the board of directors	positive	7.0	4.3	7.3	20.0	11.3	20.0	17.2	4.2	8.6	2.0	0.0	5.0	9.1
	negative	62.8	28.3	53.7	60.0	48.8	53.3	51.7	41.7	48.6	44.6	66.7	45.0	48.7
	other	25.6	63.0	34.1	20.0	36.3	26.7	24.1	54.2	40.0	39.1	26.7	50.0	38.3
	no writing on	4.7	4.3	4.9	0.0	3.8	0.0	6.9	0.0	2.9	4.3	6.7	0.0	4.0
	total	100 (43)	100 (46)	100 (41)	100 (5)	100 (80)	100 (15)	100 (29)	100 (24)	100 (35)	100 (92)	100 (30)	100 (20)	100 (230)

Note: The bracketed number means real number of labour unions inquired into

Source: Kimoto, ibid., p. 11

of labour management. This fact means nothing less than that the policy of the opinion of management filters easily into the minds of union members. The ambiguous position of lower management gives credence to the idea that their activity as labour union members is questionable. The lower manager or supervisor at the work place level have double roles as union members and lower management. For example, the subsection head stands opposite his subordinates as a member of the official management organization while acting in co-operation as a member of the union, in the joint consultation and collective bargaining systems. In practice there are, it is said, many cases where supervisors are elected as representatives for the union organization at the work place level.

It is therefore, quite easy to understand the degree of influence on labour unions by the management in the individual enterprise. While the supporter of Japanese style worker participation says that the enterprise union is the strongest point from the view of effectiveness, it is clear that the structure of enterprise unions is a negative influence in the further democratization of the enterprise.

Literature

Hanami, T. (1979): *Labour Relations in Japan Today*. Tokyo, New York.

Hayashi, M. (1983): *The Japanese Style of Small-Group QC-Circle Activity*. Research Papers No. 2 of the Institute of Business Research. Chuo University, Tokyo.

Hazama, H. (1981): *The Employer's Organization and Industrial Relations in Japan* (Japanese). Tokyo.

Ishikawa, K. (1980): *The Japanese Style of Quality Control* (Japanese). Nikka Giren. Tokyo.

Japan Productivity Center (1981): *The Subjects of the Labour-Management Joint Cosultation System in a New Stage* (The Report in Japanese). Tokyo.

Japan Productivity Center (1964): *A Technological Innovation and Labour-Management Joint Cosultation System*. Tokyo.

Japan Productivity Center (1976): *The Labour-Management Joint Consultation System in Japan – Its Present Situation and Subjects*. Tokyo.

Joshikawa, E. (1982): Japanese Personnel and Labour Management. Tokyo.

Katoh, T. (1982): *Productivity and Labour-Management Relations* (Japanese). Tokyo.

Kimoto, Sh. (1979): The Present Situation and Problems of "Worker-Partizipation" in Japan. In: *The Bulletin of the Institute of Social Science Meiji University*. (Japanese).

Kimoto, Sh. (1977): *"The Partizipation" of Labour Union*. (Japanese) Tokyo.

Odaka, K. (1982): The Japanese Style of Workers Self-Management: From the Voluntary to the Autonomous Group. In: Ishikawa, A./Rus, V. and Woodhouse, T. (Eds.): *Employment and Partizipation – Industrial Democracy in Crisis*. Tokyo.

Yoshikawa, E. (1982): *Japanese Personnel and Labour Management*. (Japanese) Tokyo.

Teil IV
Länderspezifische Probleme – sozialistische Gesellschaftssysteme

Die jugoslawische Unternehmung im Spannungsfeld zwischen Demokratisierung und Wirtschaftlichkeit

Gudrun Lemân

Abstract
The Yugoslav Enterprise Between Democracy and Efficiency

In Yugoslav enterprises the decentralization of decisions has extended considerably. The result is a great number of elected committees which are difficult to survey. This development – which started in 1974 – lead to a pseudo-democratization. The employees are overwhelmed by the requirements of this kind of basic democracy. Informal decision oligarchies which are under no democratic control fulfill the necessary tasks. The economic efficiency decreased. The most important reasons for this are the separation of authority and responsibility and the system of social property which leaves no room for a material interest in innovations or in the establishment of new enterprises.

The conclusion might be drawn that the existing kind of basic democracy in Yugoslavian enterprises is incompatible with an efficient management.

1. Einleitung

Die jugoslawische Arbeiterselbstverwaltung hat ihren Ursprung in der Staatsideologie. Dem vom Staat verordneten System der Arbeiterselbstverwaltung liegt die normative Vorstellung zugrunde, daß die jugoslawischen Arbeiter die Macht in den Betrieben gleichberechtigt – fundamental-demokratisch – ausüben sollen. Das Selbstverwaltungsprinzip wurde in allen Bereichen der Wirtschaft und der öffentlichen Dienste eingeführt. Damit sind die gesellschaftspolitischen Grundsätze von der Wahl der Entscheidungsträger und deren Kontrolle durch die Wähler sowie der basisdemokratischen Abstimmung in Betrieb und Gemeinwesen gleichermaßen eingeführt worden. Auf der Ebene des jugoslawischen Staates blieb es jedoch bei der staatstragenden Rolle der kommunistischen Partei.

Wie es bei Dlugos heißt, muß die Erfüllung gesellschaftlicher Aufgaben durch die Unternehmung mit ihren ursprünglichen Zielen – Gewinnerzielung und Bereitstellung von Leistungen – kompatibel sein. Diese Forderung gilt unabhängig vom Wirtschaftssystem. Ebenfalls systemindifferent gilt sein Satz: Gibt es keine Freiräume für die Selbstentfaltung der Mitarbeiter, so bleibt eine bedeutsame Chance für die Weiterentwicklung einer demokratischen Gesellschaftsordnung ungenutzt (Dlugos 1977, S. 473). Demnach müßte das System der jugoslawischen Arbeiterselbstverwaltung die besten Voraussetzungen für die Entwicklung einer demokratischen Gesellschaftsordnung bieten. Schon bei einem oberflächlichen Vergleich Jugoslawiens mit den staatssozialistischen Ländern zeigt sich deutlich, daß in Jugoslawien tatsächlich demokratische Verhaltensweisen bereits heute vielerorts internalisiert wurden.

Es sollen in diesem Beitrag einige Aspekte der jugoslawischen Unternehmung aus dem Blickwinkel des Betriebswirts betrachtet werden. Dabei wird sich die Frage erheben, bis zu welchem Grade die betriebliche Selbstverwaltung in ihrer heutigen Ausprägung und wirtschaftliche Effizienz kompatibel sind.

2. Die Ziele

Nach jugoslawischer Auffassung gehört die Unternehmensdezentralisation zu den wesentlichen Bestandteilen des Selbstverwaltungssozialismus auf betriebswirtschaftlichem Gebiet. Seit 1971 ist die Basisorganisation der Wirtschaft nicht mehr die Unternehmung, sondern die kleinstmögliche ökonomische Einheit, die Grundorganisation der vereinten Arbeit. Die Unternehmung (Arbeitsorganisation) entsteht durch den Abschluß eines Selbstverwaltungsabkommens zwischen den Grundorganisationen über die Vereinigung zu einer Arbeitsorganisation. Die Unternehmerfunktionen wurden mit der neuen Verfassung von 1974 auf die Ebene der Grundorganisationen übertragen. Diese konsequente Dezentralisation verfolgte ehrgeizige Ziele: die Veränderung der Machtstruktur, die Veränderung der Situation des Menschen in der Grundorganisation und die Veränderung des gesellschaftlichen Systems.

Durch die Dezentralisierung soll für den einzelnen Arbeiter auch in einer Großunternehmung der Zusammenhang zwischen Aufwand und Ertrag durchschaubar gemacht werden. Alle Kollektivmitglieder sollen als gewählte Mitglieder der Selbstverwaltungsorgane die Unternehmerfunktionen ausfüllen können. Durch dieses System der Selbstverwaltung in den Grundorganisationen soll allen Mitgliedern des Arbeitskollektivs (der Association) die Möglichkeit eröffnet werden, ihre Interessen in der Basisorganisation wirksam zu vertreten und – durch Delegation von Vertretern – auch in den Organen der Gebietskörperschaften.[1]

Ein weiteres ideologisch motiviertes Ziel ist der Abbau der staatlichen Herrschaftsfunktionen in den Betrieben. Das staatliche Eigentum an den Produktionsmitteln wurde abgeschafft, dadurch ging auch die Entscheidungsbefugnis über die Investitionen an die Betriebe. Das Management wird nicht mehr vom Staat eingesetzt. Die Entlohnung orientiert sich nicht an Tarifverträgen – für die es keine Partner gibt –, sondern wird von den Unternehmungen durch Selbstverwaltungsverträge vereinbart. Steuern und Abgaben wurden durch „Beiträge“ zu den jeweiligen selbstverwalteten Interessengemeinschaften (den ehemaligen öffentlichen Diensten) ersetzt. An die Stelle der zentralen Wirtschaftsplanung ist die „konvergente Planung“, die von den Grundorganisationen ausgeht, getreten (Lemân 1982, S. 42 ff.). In den durch Gesetze und Verordnungen determinierten betrieblichen Organisationsstrukturen ist die Zielvorstellung der Gleichberechtigung und Solidarität, Kooperation und Marktkonkurrenz, sowie einer „kooperativen Konkurrenz“ (Gorupić 1978, S. 340) enthalten. Diese die gesamte Organisationsgestaltung durchziehende harmonistische Auffassung bedeutet die Aufhebung der Polarisierung, die sich bei uns im Verhältnis Arbeitgeber:Arbeitnehmer, Eigentümer:Lohnempfänger usw. zeigt. Sie ist eine wesentliche Ursache spezifischer Instabilitäten, auf die noch einzugehen sein wird.

3. Besonderheiten der Organisation im jugoslawischen selbstverwalteten Betrieb

Die Einführung der Arbeiterselbstverwaltung in den jugoslawischen Unternehmungen hat zur Formulierung spezifischer Organisationsprinzipien geführt. Idealtypisch betrachtet arbeitet das Kollektiv nicht auf eine ex ante, von oben festgesetzte Aufgabe hin, sondern es einigt sich über ein Unternehmensziel und die entsprechenden organisatorischen und technischen Maßnahmen. Die betriebliche Organisation steht vor der Aufgabe, entsprechende Strukturen zu schaffen, die eine gleichberechtigte Teilhabe an der Macht für alle Kollektivmitglieder tendenziell ermöglichen. Denn in der jugoslawischen Unternehmung wird dem demokratischen Entscheidungsprinzip: ein Mann, eine Stimme eindeutig der Vorrang eingeräumt. Je wichtiger die Entscheidungen sind, umso mehr Kollektivmitglieder sind nach dem Willen des Gesetzgebers an ihnen beteiligt. Das Arbeitskollektiv wird als Kollektivunternehmer aufgefaßt, die Unternehmung als Assoziation der Produzenten. Die unternehmerischen Aufgaben werden entweder vom Gesamtkollektiv unmittelbar wahrgenommen oder mittelbar von den Organen der Arbeiterselbstverwaltung. Die organisatorische Grundeinheit ist die Grundorganisation der vereinten Arbeit.

3.1. Die Selbstverwaltung, ihre Organe und die professionelle Leitung

Die formale Organisation beruht auf zwei Hierarchien: der Legislative (Arbeiterselbstverwaltung) und der Exekutive (Leitung). Der Direktor, der vom Arbeiterrat unter Mitwirkung der lokalen politischen Vertreter gewählt wird, steht an der

Spitze der Exekutive und ist gleichzeitig ausführendes Organ der Legislative.
Eine schematische Darstellung könnte wie folgt aussehen:

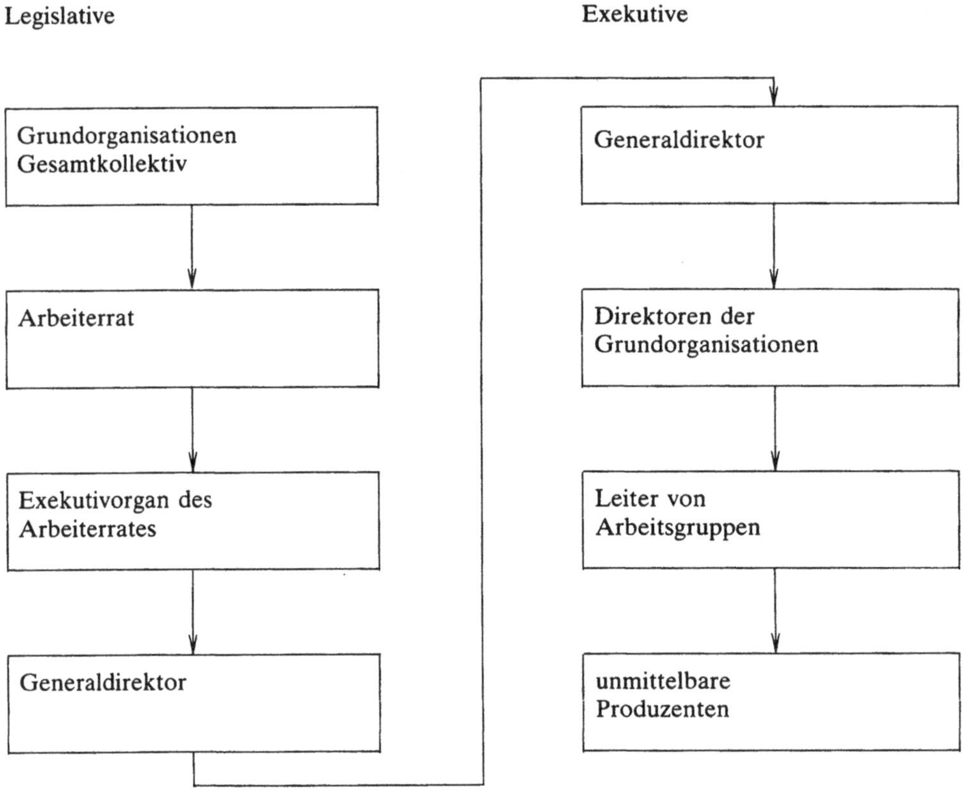

Abb. 1: Die Selbstverwaltung, ihre Organe und die professionelle Leitung

Die Gremien der Arbeiterselbstverwaltung treten nur von Zeit zu Zeit zusammen, um die Grundlinien der Unternehmenspolitik zu bestimmen und die Einkommensverteilung vorzunehmen. Dagegen arbeitet das professionelle Management permanent an der fachlichen Vorbereitung von Entscheidungen und deren operativer Durchführung. Die Mitglieder der Selbstverwaltung werden für eine Mandatsperiode gewählt, die Funktionsträger der Leitung und Verwaltung werden auf Dauer eingestellt. Lediglich die Direktoren müssen sich alle vier Jahre einer Wiederwahl stellen und bei dieser Gelegenheit Rechenschaft über ihr Programm ablegen. Das bedeutet unter anderem, daß sich der Direktor bei allen seinen Handlungen die Unterstützung der Arbeiter sichern muß.

Die Übergänge zwischen leitenden, verwaltenden und ausführenden Funktionen sind fließend. Die Kombination der Organisationsprinzipien der demokratischen

Selbstverwaltung einerseits und des Prinzips der Hierarchie der Leitungsorgane andererseits schafft spezifische Probleme.

3.2. Die Koordination

Da die unternehmerischen Funktionen bei den ökonomischen Teilbereichen der Unternehmungen liegen, ist ein großes Maß an Koordination erforderlich. Formal ist im jugoslawischen Unternehmen die Funktion der Leitung und der professionellen Verwaltung auf die technische Koordination beschränkt. Interessenkoordination und politische Entscheidungen gehören zu den Kompetenzen der Selbstverwaltung.[2] Die Dezentralisierung bestimmter Entscheidungsfunktionen erfordert immer die Zentralisierung anderer Entscheidungsfunktionen, um die wirtschaftliche Tätigkeit in den organisatorischen Teilbereichen auf ein gemeinsames Ziel hin auszurichten. Werden Aufgaben zentralisiert, führt das zur Einschränkung der Entscheidungsfreiheit der Beschäftigten in den Grundorganisationen. Bleiben Entscheidungsbefugnisse, die in allen Grundorganisationen gleichermaßen auftreten – wie z. B. die Einkommensverteilung – dezentralisiert, führt dies zu einer Vervielfältigung des Aufwands. Im Zusammenhang unserer Themenstellung ist die Frage interessant, wie sich die Erfordernisse von Dezentralisation und Koordination auf die Erreichung der Ziele Demokratie und Effizienz auswirken. Nach der jugoslawischen herrschenden betriebswirtschaftlichen Meinung kann die technische Umsetzung von Entscheidungen ohne Demokratieverlust den Experten anvertraut werden, während die gewählten autonomen Selbstverwaltungsorgane diejenige Wertskala suchen, die den vorhandenen Wertvorstellungen der Gemeinschaft am besten entspricht. Die professionelle Verwaltung soll die Gruppenziele verwirklichen, sie aber nicht bestimmen (Horvat 1973, S. 112). Dabei wird der faktische Einfluß außer Acht gelassen, den die Fachspezialisten (Technostruktur) durch ihre Mitwirkung bei der Entscheidungsvorbereitung ausüben.

Die zentralen Führungsentscheidungen, die das Unternehmungsziel und alle damit zusammenhängenden Strategien und Richtlinien umfassen und somit Koordinierungsentscheidungen sind, werden unter Beteiligung aller Grundorganisationen der vereinten Arbeit getroffen. Sie begrenzen den Entscheidungsfreiraum der Grundorganisationen. Es findet somit eine Arbeitsteilung der Entscheidungen statt, der eine hierarchische (Herrschafts-)Organisation entspricht (Hondrich 1970, S. 65).

Zu den wichtigsten formalisierten Koordinationsinstrumenten der jugoslawischen Unternehmungen gehören die Selbstverwaltungsabkommen, die Unternehmensstatute und die übrigen innerbetrieblichen rechtsetzenden Akte. Zu den betriebswirtschaftlich-rechnungstechnischen Instrumenten der Koordination gehören das betriebliche Rechnungswesen mit der Bestimmung der innerbetrieblichen

Verrechnungspreise für den Leistungsaustausch zwischen den Grundorganisationen, die Plankostenrechnung und das Instrumentarium der internen finanzwirtschaftlichen Verflechtung mit internen Banken u. a. Institutionen.

4. Systemimmanente Beeinflussungsfaktoren der Effizienz

Von allen Kollektivmitgliedern gemeinsam werden die grundlegenden Entscheidungen über weitreichende Innovationen, Umstellung des Produktionsprogramms, Statute und Einkommensverteilung getroffen. Aber ist die Beschlußfassung in der Basisversammlung wirklich demokratisch? Die Organisation ist umso komplexer je größer die Zahl der Kollektivmitglieder ist und umso komplizierter werden auch die Entscheidungen, über die abgestimmt werden muß. Die Interessen in den Basisgruppen sind heterogen, und es bilden sich Cliquen und Koalitionen, die die Entscheidungen in ihrem Sinne zu beeinflussen suchen. Um verantwortliche Grundsatzentscheidungen über den Geschäftsgang ihrer Unternehmungen treffen zu können, müßten die Arbeiter ein umfassendes Wissen über Marktchancen, Investitionspolitik, Personalplanung und Kostenrechnung haben. Diese Spezialkenntnisse sind aber nur durch Arbeitsteilung und Spezialisierung zu erlangen. Dies ist nebenberuflich und ehrenamtlich nicht zu leisten. Das erforderliche Wissen steht den Basiseinheiten nicht zur Verfügung. Außerdem ist der Wert von Vollversammlungen zweifelhaft, wenn man an den Konformitätsdruck denkt, der häufig bei solchen Versammlungen herrscht und an die manipulativen Potentiale der Experten und der Vertreter der politischen Organisationen. In der Realität weicht die Verteilung der Macht erheblich von der normativ gleichmäßigen Machtverteilung innerhalb der Kollektive ab. Wie schon früh in verschiedenen empirischen Untersuchungen nachgewiesen wurde (Županov 1969; Obradović 1972, Kavčić 1972; Rus 1974; Vejnović 1974; Soergel 1979 u. a.), verfügen die Angehörigen der Leitungshierarchie und der fachlich spezialisierten Dienststellen über die größten Machtressourcen. Durch die Komplexität der Koordinierung zwischen den einzelnen Grundorganisationen und die Vielzahl der Räte und Ausschüsse der Selbstverwaltung wird das betriebliche Selbstverwaltungssystem unübersichtlich und kompliziert. Gerade die Vielfalt der Organe, Organisationsstrukturen und Beschlüsse ermöglicht es der Technostruktur, aber auch bestimmten informellen Gruppen – wie Vertretern der Partei, lokaler Interessen oder Banken – die Entscheidungen in ihrem Sinne zu beeinflussen. Sie verstoßen damit gegen die normative Konzeption der Selbstverwaltung. Kompetenzabgrenzungen werden schwierig. Die Kongruenz von Entscheidung und Verantwortung geht verloren.

Das Management muß sich nach verschiedenen Seiten hin absichern. So ist der Direktor dem Staat gegenüber für die Wahrung des „gesellschaftlichen Interesses" verantwortlich, dem Arbeitskollektiv gegenüber für erfolgreiches Management und Gewinnerzielung. Staat und kommunistische Partei suchen über die Betriebe ihre programmatischen Zielvorstellungen zu verwirklichen wie z. B. Schaffung neuer Arbeitsplätze, Umweltschutz, die Realisierung bestimmter Investitionen u. a. Staat und Partei haben die Möglichkeit, den Direktor moralischen, sachlichen und auch finanziellen (Kredite)Pressionen auszusetzen. Die Interessen von Staat und Arbeitskollektiv sind nicht deckungsgleich. Verliert der Direktor die Unterstützung des Kollektivs, kann er abgewählt werden. Man kann sich leicht vorstellen, wie schwierig es unter diesen Umständen ist, Entscheidungen durchzusetzen. Adizes hat bei den Inhabern von Führungspositionen in jugoslawischen Unternehmungen folgende dysfunktionale Haltungen beobachtet:

- physischer oder geistiger Rückzug aus Konfliktsituationen,
- aggressives Verhalten und die Tendenz, andere wegen der Mißerfolge zu beschuldigen, ohne die Ursachen der Probleme zu beseitigen,
- Verlust des Selbstvertrauens und Resignation.

Der Direktor spielt als professioneller Manager eine Schlüsselrolle bei der fachlichen Vorbereitung der Entscheidungen. Richtige und damit effiziente Entscheidungen kann er häufig aber nur durchbringen, wenn er bestenfalls durch Argumente und Überredungskunst den Arbeiterrat überzeugt oder – im schlechteren Falle – durch Zugeständnisse und Manipulation auf die Beschlußfassung einwirkt. Bei erfolgreichen Entscheidungen wird sich der Arbeiterrat diese als sein Verdienst anrechnen. Bei Fehlschlägen wird der Direktor als schlechter Ratgeber gerügt oder abgewählt. Es gibt keine entsprechende Motivation für das Leitungspersonal.

Die Situation überforderter Selbstverwaltungsorgane schildert Horvat (1984, S. 217) anschaulich: „... ökonomische Einheiten kämpfen gegeneinander und Sitzungen dauern ad nauseam. Anstatt zu verschwinden kann die Entfremdung sogar zunehmen. Die zwischenmenschlichen Beziehungen werden sich ausdrücklich verschlechtern und die Effizienz sinkt. Der Glaube an die Selbstverwaltung wird erschüttert."

Aus seinen Erfahrungen als Direktor eines wissenschaftlichen Instituts berichtet Horvat (1984, S. 212) folgendes: „In einigen Fällen versuchte der (Arbeiter-)Rat mich als Direktor dazu zu zwingen, bestimmte Handlungen vorzunehmen (oder nicht vorzunehmen), von denen ich genau wußte, daß sie der Institution schaden würden. Nachdem es mir nicht gelungen war, den Rat davon zu überzeugen, meine Vorschläge anzunehmen, bot ich an, den Beschluß der Mehrheit unter der Bedingung durchzuführen, daß der Rat für die Folgen die Verantwortung übernimmt und das Kollektiv darüber vorher unterrichtete. ... Ich war vollkommen überrascht, als mein Vorschlag einen Sturm der Mißbilligung hervorrief. Man sagte mir, daß der Rat welchen Beschluß auch immer fassen könnte und der Direktor ihn auf eigenes Risiko durchzuführen hätte. Dann wurde mein Rücktrittsangebot als Erpressung verurteilt."

Die Unsicherheit der Rollenerwartung der Leitungsorgane – aber auch der Selbstverwaltungsorgane – führt vor allem in Krisensituationen zu Ineffizienz und

Fehlverhalten. So wird sich ein passiver Manager leicht der Verantwortung entziehen, indem er das ganze Risiko auf den Arbeiterrat abwälzt. Der „Manipulator" wird es verstehen, seine eigenen Entscheidungen durchzubringen und die persönliche Verantwortung dennoch zu umgehen.

Die divergierenden Interessen der an den Entscheidungen beteiligten Beschäftigten führen zu langwierigen Aushandlungsprozessen, die hohe Kosten verursachen. Die Mitgliedschaft in Selbstverwaltungsorganen ist auf zwei Jahre begrenzt. Entscheidungen über komplexe Innovationen mit langfristiger Wirkung reichen weit über die Mandatsdauer der Entscheidungsträger hinaus. Die Mitglieder der Selbstverwaltungsorgane haben in erster Linie ein Interesse an kurzfristigen Einkommenserhöhungen. Große Investitionen in neue Technologien verlangen eine hohe Risikobereitschaft der Arbeitskollektive. Für einzelne Kollektivmitglieder können sich mit der Einführung der Neuerungen Schwierigkeiten ergeben, sei es durch die Notwendigkeit, neue Techniken zu erlernen, den Arbeitsplatz zu wechseln oder ganz aus dem Unternehmen auszuscheiden (Rationalisierung). Die Innovation kann sich als finanzielles Fiasko erweisen und die persönlichen Einkommen der Beschäftigten auf lange Zeit mindern. Wie die jugoslawische Erfahrung zeigt, sind die Arbeiter aber nicht bereit, ein über ihren realen Einflußbereich hinausgehendes Risiko zu tragen (Županov 1967). Alle diese Faktoren können zu einer Opposition gegen Innovationsentscheidungen in der Unternehmung führen.[3]

Bei kollektiven Entscheidungsprozessen gibt es viele Möglichkeiten, unerwünschte Entscheidungen zu verhindern: durch Verweigerung der Zustimmung, durch Zusatzanträge, Verweisung an eine Kommission und Wiedervorlage usw. Aber auch wenn es schließlich zu einer Entscheidung kommt, sind wegen der langen Diskussionsprozesse die Konsensfindungskosten hoch. Die Stellung derjenigen Gremien und Personen, die strategische Unternehmensziele definieren und durchsetzen könnten, ist schwach. Die Zersplitterung in selbständige Grundorganisationen und die systemimmanente geringe Arbeitsteilung und Spezialisierung sowie das aus der vorgegebenen Organisationsstruktur und der Eigentumsordnung herrührende geringe Interesse an gemeinsamem Wirtschaften wirken sich zusätzlich hemmend aus (Iversen 1984, S. 43).

Selbstverwaltungsprinzip und Eigentumsordnung führen zu einer weiteren Dysfunktionalität im jugoslawischen System. Es gibt für bestehende Unternehmungen keine Anreize zu Gründung eines neuen Selbstverwaltungsunternehmens. Gründet eine bestehende Unternehmung einen neuen Betrieb, so konstituiert sich dieser, sobald die Gründungsphase abgeschlossen ist, als Grundorganisation der vereinten Arbeit mit eigenen Selbstverwaltungs- und Gewinnverwendungsrechten. Die gesetzlichen Regelungen definieren die Rechte der Arbeitskollektive vergleichsweise stark, die Rechte der Kapitalgeber hingegen schwach. Diese Konstruktion der Eigentumsrechte wirkt sich äußerst ungünstig auf die Effizienz der Entwicklungspolitik innerhalb Jugoslawiens aus. Gründen florierende Unternehmungen aus den entwickelten Gebieten eine Tochterunternehmung in den an Arbeitskräften und Rohstoffen reichen unterentwickelten Regionen, geschieht folgendes: Die Tochterunternehmung richtet sich bei der Lohnbemessung nach dem Lohnniveau der Mutter in der entwickelten Region. Damit entfällt das Lohngefälle als Motiv für die Unternehmensgründung. Bei der Gewinnverteilung treten Mutter und Tochter als gleichberechtigte Partner in Erscheinung. Der akkumulierte Teil des Einkommens kann nicht ohne weiteres aus dem Betrieb herausgezogen werden (Eger 1980, S. 67). Die Tochterunternehmung kann, da sie rechtlich völlig selbständig ist, auch nicht zu einer bevorzugten Belieferung der Mutterunternehmung verpflichtet werden. Somit entfällt auch dieses Motiv für die Unternehmensgründung. Professor Eugen Pusić berichtete Ende der siebziger Jahre über eine gemeinschaftliche Investition mehrerer Zagreber Unternehmungen. Elf Unternehmungen hatten für ein gemeinsames Rechenzentrum 3 IBM-Computer angeschafft und zu deren Bedienung 17 Arbeitskräfte eingestellt. Nachdem die Computer installiert waren, konstituierten die 17 Beschäftigten eine Grundorganisation der vereinten Arbeit und begannen, die Leistungen des Rechenzentrums zu Marktpreisen an die Gründerunternehmen zu verkaufen. Die Angelegenheit wurde vor das kroatische Verfassungsgericht gebracht. Das Rechenzentrum bekam Recht. Sobald der Gründungsvorgang abgeschlossen ist, geht das Anlagevermögen in gesellschaftliches Eigentum über.

Nachdem an verschiedenen Beispielen die negativen wirtschaftlichen Auswirkungen der basisdemokratischen Entscheidungen in den jugoslawischen Betrieben beleuchtet wurden, soll die Aufmerksamkeit auf eine soziale Komponente gelenkt werden. Die Herausnahme der Betriebe aus der staatlichen Einflußsphäre und die Maximierung der Selbstverwaltungsrechte hat zu sozialen Folgen geführt, die gerade jene Gruppen benachteiligen, die ihre Rechte in den Basisgruppen besonders wirksam wahrnehmen sollten: die ungelernten und angelernten Arbeiter.

Zu den wichtigsten Kompetenzen der Selbstverwaltungsorgane gehört die innerbetriebliche Einkommensverteilung. Über die Bewertung der einzelnen Arbeitsplätze entscheidet der zentrale Arbeiterrat. Entscheidungsvorlagen werden von einer Kommission des Arbeiterrates ausgearbeitet. In den Kommissionen des Arbeiterrates haben die qualifizierten Arbeiter und die Führungskräfte eine ausgeprägte Vormachtstellung. Ungelernte Arbeiter sind hier kaum vertreten. Entsprechend der Zusammensetzung der Entscheidungsgremien fällt die Einkommensverteilung in der Regel zuungunsten der Unqualifizierten aus. Die soziale Ungleichheit setzt sich im Erziehungswesen und besonders folgenschwer für die Betroffenen bei der Zuteilung der knappen Wohnungen und von Krediten der Unternehmung fort.

Der Tatbestand, daß die Leitungshierarchie großen Einfluß auf die Beschlüsse der Selbstverwaltungsorgane hat, zeigt, daß die extreme Dezentralisierung und Ausweitung der Selbstverwaltungsrechte (Entprofessionalisierung der Leitung) nicht wirklich zu dem erstrebten Herrschaftsabbau und zur Demokratisierung geführt hat. Die Befreiung von Herrschaftsdruck kann im Organisationsgefüge der Unternehmung nur durch fortwährende Steigerung der Spezialisierung, die tendenziell alle Kollektivmitglieder funktional unabkömmlich und gleichwertig macht, erreicht werden.[4]

5. Einige Schlußfolgerungen

Ökonomische Rationalität ist für die jugoslawische Wirtschaft lebenswichtig. Die Geschichte hat immer wieder gezeigt, daß wirtschaftliche Schwierigkeiten zur Infragestellung des gesamten politischen Systems führen können. Es sei hier nur an die immer wieder aufflammenden Nationalitätenauseinandersetzungen erinnert. Nur wenn die Unternehmungen durch rentable Produktionsweise und marktgerechte Produktion eine stabile wirtschaftliche Entwicklung ermöglichen, können die gesellschaftspolitischen Ziele der Arbeiterselbstverwaltung verwirklicht werden.

Das Dilemma der Arbeiterselbstverwaltung liegt darin, daß dem Zusammenhang zwischen Herrschaft, Demokratie und Leistung zu wenig Aufmerksamkeit gewidmet wird. Werden die formalen basisdemokratischen Strukturen in der Selbstverwaltung über das Maß hinaus ausgedehnt, das durch die Beschäftigten aufgrund ihrer Kenntnisse und Leistungsfähigkeit mit Leben erfüllt werden kann, wird das Gegenteil von Demokratie erreicht. Es kommt zu einer Scheindemokratisierung. „Unterhalb der formal demokratischen Strukturen konstituiert sich eine Oligarchie aus alten oder neuen Herren, die die erwarteten Herrschaftsleistungen, in erster Linie Systemintegration und Effektivitätssteigerung, erfüllen." (Hondrich 1973, S. 101)[5, 6]

Der jugoslawische Ökonom Branko Horvat hat die Erscheinungsformen der Selbstverwaltung in den Unternehmungen analysiert und die Ursachen der Ineffizienz herausgearbeitet. Er vertritt jedoch ganz im Sinne der offiziellen jugoslawischen Politik die Auffassung, daß die erfolgreiche Entwicklung der Arbeiterselbstverwaltung unter bestimmten Voraussetzungen möglich ist:

- industrielle Tradition und gut ausgebildete Arbeitskräfte,
- lange Tradition der politischen Demokratie,
- hohe persönliche Einkommen, die die Erfüllung der essentiellen Bedürfnisse ermöglichen,
- verkürzte Arbeitszeit und Zeit für die Partizipation,
- hoher Bildungsstand, der die Barrieren der Kommunikation abzubauen hilft.[7]

Es liegen nun aber Erfahrungen mit der Selbstverwaltung aus hochindustrialisierten Ländern vor, die die oben zitierten Voraussetzungen relativieren. Obgleich hier die von Horvat genannten Voraussetzungen gewiß als gegeben angenommen werden können, haben sich ähnliche Effizienzeinbußen wie in Jugoslawien gezeigt.[8]

Bei der heutigen Ausgestaltung der Arbeiterselbstverwaltung in Jugoslawien sind Basisdemokratie und Effizienz nicht vereinbar. Zusammenfassend seien noch einmal die Gründe dafür genannt:

- Entscheidung und Verantwortung sind nicht kongruent,
- die Unsicherheit der Rollenerwartung führt zu dysfunktionalen Verhaltensweisen,
- die Eigentumsordnung verhindert ein materielles Interesse der Arbeitskollektive

an Neugründungen von Unternehmungen und an der Einführung von Innovationen,
- die reale Machtverteilung entspricht nicht der normativen Konzeption, die sich in der rechtlich bestimmten Ausgestaltung der Organisation niederschlägt. Eine wirksame Kontrolle der wirklichen Entscheidungsträger ist nicht möglich, was wiederum die Demokratie der Beschlußfassung infrage stellt.

Die angeführten Einwände bedeuten jedoch nicht, daß eine gleichzeitige Erreichung von demokratischen Beziehungen auf Unternehmungsebene und Effektivität des Wirtschaftens generell unmöglich wäre. Der Zusammenhang ist jedoch äußerst komplex. Die beiden Zielvorstellungen werden in der Regel nicht gleichzeitig und jeweils nur mit Einschränkungen auf der einen oder anderen Seite verwirklicht werden können. Es steht außerhalb jeden Zweifels, daß ein Zusammenhang besteht zwischen der Möglichkeit der demokratischen Selbstentfaltung des Betriebsbürgers, wie sie in dem eingangs zitierten Satz von Dlugos postuliert wird, und der Chance für die Entwicklung einer demokratischen Gesellschaftsordnung. Effizienz des Wirtschaftens aber ist nötig, um die Lebensgrundlagen für eine humane Gesellschaftsordnung zu schaffen. Von einem bestimmten Niveau der Bedürfnisbefriedigung an kann zugunsten der Entwicklung einer demokratischeren Entscheidungsstruktur und einer humaneren Atmosphäre in den Betrieben wahrscheinlich auf einen Effizienzanstieg verzichtet werden.[9] Moderne industrielle Produktion, die eine Voraussetzung für die Überwindung der Armut darstellt, und Basisdemokratie sind nicht zu vereinbaren. Dies zeigt das jugoslawische Beispiel deutlich. Der Einfluß des professionellen Managements, der de facto bereits dominiert, müßte rechtlich abgesichert werden. Jedoch ist Demokratie im Popperschen Sinne einer Machtkontrolle und der Möglichkeit der Absetzung der Herrschenden durch die Beherrschten mit einer Leitungsrolle der Technostruktur in der jugoslawischen selbstverwalteten Unternehmung durchaus vereinbar.

Anmerkungen

1 Zum Delegations- und Versammlungssystem ausführlich Furtak 1975, S. 68 ff.
2 Vgl. Lemân 1976, S. 70 ff.
3 Adizes 1971, S. 248 ff.
4 Vgl. dazu Leipold 1978.
5 Siehe auch Hondrich 1970, S. 209.
6 Zum Zusammenhang zwischen Demokratisierung und Leistung s. Lemân 1976, S. 103 ff.
7 Horvat 1984, S. 218.
8 Vgl. Chmielewicz 1975, S. 109 ff. und die dort angegebene Literatur. Chmielewicz zitiert die Analyse des Zeit-Redakteurs Zimmer über gescheiterte Experimente mit selbstverwalteten Verlagen in der Bundesrepublik. „Nichts habe geklappt ... es sei immer nur diskutiert und wenig gearbeitet worden, man habe Kalkulationen über den Daumen gepeilt, fahrlässige Verträge abgeschlossen, unrealisierbare Pläne gemacht, und die Bewirtungsrechnungen seien kilometerlang gewesen."

[9] Narr/Naschold 1971, S. 55: „Allerdings ist keine Gesellschaft ohne jegliche Entfremdung und Unterdrückung möglich. Der Grad und die Verteilung der Entfremdung sind ausschlaggebend."

Literatur

Adizes, I. (1971): *Industrial Democracy: Yugoslav Style.* New York.

Chmielewicz, K. (1975): *Arbeitnehmerinteressen und Kapitalismuskritik in der Betriebswirtschaftslehre.* Reinbeck.

Dlugos, G. (1977): Gesellschaftspolitische Implikationen unternehmungsinterner Konflikthandhabung. In: *Die Betriebswirtschaft* 37, S. 465–474.

Eger, T. (1980): *Das regionale Entwicklungsgefälle in Jugoslawien.* Paderborn.

Furtak, R. K. (1975): *Jugoslawien. Politik, Gesellschaft, Wirtschaft.* Hamburg.

Horvat, B. (1973): *Die Arbeiterselbstverwaltung. Das jugoslawische Wirtschaftsmodell.* München.

Horvat, B. (1984): *Politička ekonomija socijalizma.* Zagreb.

Hondrich, K. O. (1970): *Theorie der Herrschaft.* Frankfurt.

Iversen, H.-C. (1984): *Die jugoslawische Wirtschaftskrise; Merkmale, Ursachen und wirtschaftspolitische Reaktionen.* Berichte des Bundesinstituts für ostwissenschaftliche und internationale Studien. Köln.

Kavčič, B. (1972): Kdo ima vpliv v naših podjetih. 8. Kongres zveze sindikata Slovenija, Ljubljana.

Lemân, G. (1976): *Das jugoslawische Modell. Wege zur Demokratisierung der Wirtschaft.* Frankfurt am Main, Köln.

Lemân, G. (1982): *Wirtschaftsplanung im System der jugoslawischen Arbeiterselbstverwaltung.* Berichte des Bundesinstituts für ostwissenschaftliche und internationale Studien. Köln.

Leipold, H. (1978): Assoziation versus Hierarchie. In: Backhaus u. a. (Hrsg.), *Partizipation in Betrieb und Gesellschaft.* Frankfurt, New York.

Narr, W.-D./F. Naschold (1971): *Theorie der Demokratie.* Stuttgart, Berlin, Köln, Mainz.

Obradović, J. (1972): Distribution of Participation in the Process of Decision-Making on Problems related to the Economic Activity of the Company. In: *Participation and Self-Management.* Zagreb.

Rus, V. (1974): Samoupravljanje i podela rada. In: *Naše teme* 6.

Soergel, W. (1979): *Arbeiterselbstverwaltung oder Managersozialismus.* München.

Vejnović, M. (1974): Struktura Utjecaja u samoupravnoj radnoj organizaciji. In: *Naše teme* 6.

Županov, J. (1969): *Samoupravljanje i društvena moć.* Zagreb.

Županov, J. (1967): Proizvodjać i riziko. In: *Ekonomist.*

Entscheidungsberechtigungen und Mitwirkung der Unternehmungsleitung, Arbeiterselbstverwaltung und Gewerkschaften im Bereich der Entlohnungen in Polen

Mieczyslaw Napierala

Abstract

Decision Rights and Participation of Management, Workers' Self-Administration, and Unions in the Field of Wage Payment in Poland

When discussing the economic reforms in Poland the socialization of the company's management poses one of the most important questions. The newly introduced management model, which grants widespread authority to the autonomous worker organizations, has fundamentally changed the concept of management. In the companies two authorities now exist: a director and a workers' council, each of which have certain decision and control rights. Both are confronted with one of the fundamental problems posed to the Polish economy by the wage demands of the employees: should the profits be reinvested into the development of the company or should they be distributed as wages and premiums among the labour force.

Die komplexe gesellschaftlich-wirtschaftliche Aufgabe eines sozialistischen Staates ist es, eine Befriedigung immer wachsender gesellschaftlicher Bedürfnisse zu erreichen. Jedes einzelne Unternehmen hat zur Realisierung dieses Ziels beizutragen. In den 80er Jahren ist es zu einer Umgestaltung des Leitungssystems der Unternehmungen sowie des zugrunde liegenden ökonomischen Modells gekommen. Folgende Veränderungen sind eingetreten:

1. Eine weitgehende ökonomische Selbständigkeit, die sich sowohl auf die laufende als auch auf die Entwicklungstätigkeit der Unternehmung bezieht,
2. die volle Verantwortlichkeit der Unternehmung für die erzielten produktionsbezogenen und ökonomischen Ergebnisse,
3. die volle Abhängigkeit der materiellen Situation der Mitarbeiter und der Unternehmungsentwicklung von der finanziellen Lage der Unternehmung, d. h. von den erzielten Wirtschaftsergebnissen,
4. die Mitbeteiligung der Mitarbeiter und ihrer Vertretung an Unternehmungsentscheidungen. Die rechtliche Position der Unternehmung wurde völlig neu gere-

gelt, der rechtliche Schutz ihrer Selbständigkeit gesichert und ein gesetzliches Mitbestimmungsrecht gewährleistet.

Das Gesetz von 1981 über staatliche Unternehmungen hat eine neue rechtliche Lage der Unternehmung geschaffen. Man hat sich für die Einführung von bisher in unserer Gesetzgebung nicht üblichen Regelungen entschieden. Besonders auffällig sind Regelungen, welche die selbständige Unternehmungstätigkeit betreffen. Es wird angenommen, daß Selbständigkeit vor allem die Möglichkeit des Entscheidungstreffens im eigenen Namen und auf eigene Rechnung in allen Tätigkeitsbereichen der Unternehmung bedeutet (s. Abb. 1).

Die Ziel- und Aufgabensetzung gehört zum Wirkungsbereich der Planung (Abb. 2). Das Gesetz von 1982 über die gesellschaftswirtschaftliche Planung hat auf neuartige Weise die Funktionen und den Bereich der Zentralplanung geregelt und den Unternehmungen die volle Freiheit hinsichtlich der laufenden und prospektiven Planung ihrer Tätigkeit überlassen. Der Zentralplan hat für die Unternehmung vor allem Informationsfunktionen (Stand und Richtungen der Wirtschaftsaktivität), Abstimmungsfunktionen der Unternehmungsinteressen mit den Interessen der Gesellschaft (Regelwirkungsweisen gegenüber dem ökonomischen System der Unternehmung) und Entscheidungsfunktionen in bezug auf die Nationaleinkommensverteilung und die Grundproportionen der Wirtschaftsentwicklung.

Die Systembedingungen der Unternehmungstätigkeit umfassen vorrangig ökonomische Parameter, die die Innovationsprozesse in den Unternehmungen begünstigen und sogar erzwingen sollen und sie an der Befriedigung von gesellschaftlichen Bedürfnissen orientieren.

Solche ökonomischen Parameter können z. B. sein: Durch den Staat festgelegte und geschützte Preise von Erzeugnissen, Zinssätze der Investitions- und Umsatzkredite, die Devisenkurse, Umsatz-Gewinnsteuersätze sowie Besteuerungsquoten des Individualeinkommens, minimale Lohnsätze, Abschreibungssätze usw.

Auf ganz neue Weise wurde schließlich die Mitarbeiterbeteiligung an der Unternehmungsleitung geregelt. Die Mitarbeiter der Unternehmung bilden eine Gemeinschaft, die über ihre Funktionsfähigkeit, ihre Tätigkeitsergebnisse und über den Rang der Unternehmung in der Gesellschaft mitentscheidet.

Für die gesetzliche Bestimmung des Rangs und der gesellschaftlichen Rolle der Selbstverwaltung sind politische, ökonomische, soziologische, psychologische, praxeologische und rechtliche Gründe wichtig.

Die Gestaltung der gesetzlichen Regelung der Arbeiterselbstverwaltung stellte eine recht schwierige Aufgabe dar. Bei den unterschiedlichen Auffassungen und Forderungen war eine vernünftige und zugleich realistische Lösung problematisch. Häufig konnten nur Ausgleichslösungen gefunden werden.

Die Institution der Arbeiterselbstverwaltung bewirkte wesentliche Veränderungen für die Unternehmungsleitung im Bereich der Entscheidungsberechtigung und Verantwortlichkeit. In der Unternehmung gibt es drei Entscheidungsorgane: Die

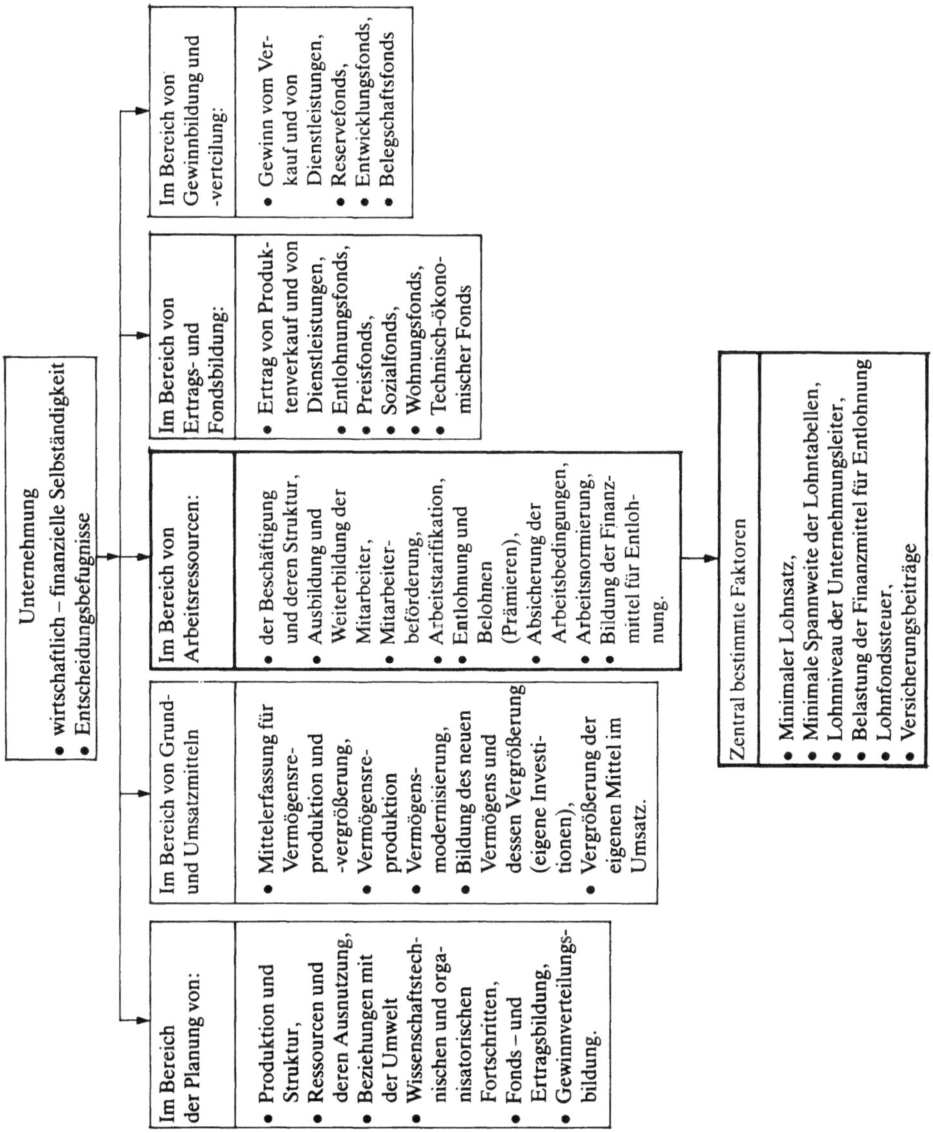

Abb. 1: Entscheidungsbefugnisse der Unternehmung

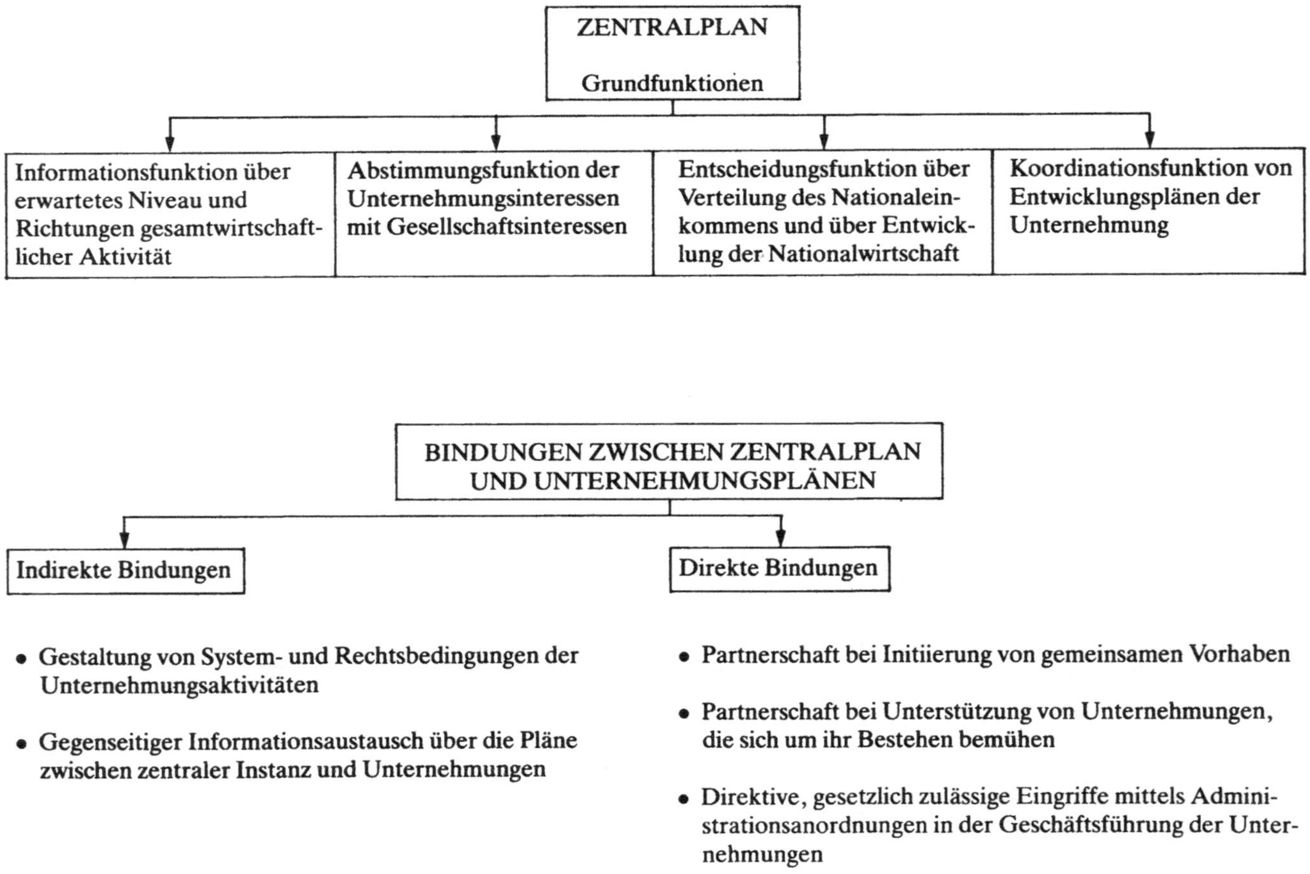

Abb. 2. Zentralplanfunktionen sowie die Bindungen zwischen Zentralplan und Unternehmungsplänen

Generalversammlung der Mitarbeiter ggf. der Delegierten, den Belegschaftsrat als Vertretung der Mitarbeiter und den Unternehmungsleiter. Aufgrund der Mehrzahl von Organen entstehen oft ernste Probleme hinsichtlich der Leitungseffizienz.

Für die Gestaltung der Relationen zwischen diesen Organen in einer Institution gibt es theoretisch drei Alternativen:

Bei der ersten Alternative besteht zwischen den Organen ein hierarchischer Zusammenhang, d. h. das untergeordnete Organ wird verpflichtet, die Direktiven des höherrangigen Organs auszuführen. Bei der zweiten Alternative realisieren die Organe ihre gesetzlichen Befugnisse unabhängig voneinander in dem ihnen zugestandenen Umfang. Bei der letzten Alternative gelten zwischen den Organen Partnerschaftsverhältnisse, die geprägt sind durch das Bestehen einer gewissen gegenseitigen Unabhängigkeit, die gleichzeitig aber einen gewissen Grad der Unterordnung voraussetzt. Diese Unterordnung und Abgrenzung ist vor allem im Hinblick auf eventuelle Streitigkeiten relevant.

Jedes dieser Organe entscheidet in unterschiedlichen Angelegenheiten, keines wird aber berechtigt, die Entscheidung des anderen außer Kraft zu setzen. Sie agieren nebeneinander; die Entscheidungen des einen sind obligatorisch für das zweite, solange sie rechtlich nicht in Frage gestellt werden können. Das Gesetz von 1981 gesteht aber diesen Organen selbständige Entscheidungsfunktionen zu. Auf diese Weise wird die Unternehmung von drei Organen und nicht nur von einem Organ geleitet. Selbstverständlich hat der Unternehmungsdirektor die größten Befugnisse u. a. bezüglich der Steuerung der laufenden Unternehmungsaktivitäten.

Ohne auf Einzelheiten eingehen zu wollen, basiert die Abgrenzung der Kompetenzen von Selbstverwaltungsorganen und dem Unternehmungsleiter auf folgenden Grundsätzen:

- Die Kompetenzen der Selbstverwaltungsorgane wurden durch die gesetzlichen Vorschriften ausführlich festgelegt. Die in diesen Grenzen durch die Selbstverwaltungsorgane getroffenen Beschlüsse sind für den Unternehmungsleiter verbindlich, es sei denn, er ist in der Lage, sie als rechtswidrig hinzustellen. Im Rahmen der Zuständigkeit der entscheidenden Selbstverwaltungsorgane handelt der Unternehmungsleiter also nur als Ausführungsorgan.
- Die Entscheidungskompetenzen des Unternehmungsleiters sind nur negativ definiert, sie sind nicht ausführlich im Gesetz aufgezählt. Alle Angelegenheiten, die nicht in den Kompetenzbereich der Selbstverwaltungsorgane und nicht in die Kompetenz der Staatsorgane fallen, werden durch den Direktor geregelt.
- Die enge Abgrenzung hinsichtlich der Eigenschaften von Unternehmungsorganen betrifft lediglich die Entscheidungskompetenzen. Es betrifft dagegen nicht die Begutachtungskompetenzen von Initial- oder Kontrollorganen. Auf diesem Gebiet können sich die Kompetenzen der einzelnen Organe überschneiden.
- Die Unternehmungsorgane sind nicht berechtigt, sich gegenseitig in ihren Kompetenzen zu vertreten.
- Falls es zweifelhaft ist, welches Unternehmungsorgan für die Entscheidung eines

bestimmten Problems zuständig ist, darf man annehmen, daß es der Unternehmungsdirektor ist, da seine Entscheidungskompetenzen der Selbstverwaltung nicht ausführlich bestimmt sind.

Der Selbständigkeitsbereich der Unternehmung determiniert den Kompetenzenkreis ihrer Organe, obwohl es dabei nicht immer volle Einmütigkeit gibt. Der Kompetenzbereich der Unternehmungsorgane kann nicht den Selbständigkeitsbereich der Unternehmung überschreiten, er kann hingegen enger werden. Letzteres tritt z. B. dann ein, wenn das Gesetz das Recht der Entscheidung über eine Unternehmungsangelegenheit anderen Subjekten außerhalb der Unternehmung (beispielsweise dem Gründungsorgan) zuerkennt.[1] Die Selbständigkeit dieser Organisationseinheit ist infolge des neuen Gesetzes über staatliche Unternehmungen zum konstruktiven Element des Begriffs Staatsunternehmung geworden. Es ist bekannt, daß in der vorigen Periode die Selbständigkeit der Unternehmungen vor allem durch die Tätigkeit sog. übergeordneter Einheiten in der subjektbezogenen Wirtschaftsstruktur beeinflußt wurde; man hat sich darum in der neuen Regelung für die Auflösung der Vereinigungen, für die Begrenzung der Rechte des Gründungsorgans sowie für die Annahme eines Modells der Unternehmungsverbände entschieden, welches die Umgestaltung der Verbände in klassische Zwischenebenen mit den entsprechenden Entscheidungsberechtigungen gegenüber den Unternehmungen unmöglich macht.[2]

Dies bedeutet, daß die Unternehmungsorgane selbständig Beschlüsse fassen und ihre Tätigkeit in allen Angelegenheiten der Unternehmung gemäß den Rechtsvorschriften und im Hinblick auf die Erfüllung der Unternehmungsfunktionen organisieren. Andere Aktoren sind nur dann berechtigt, Entscheidungen, die direkt die Unternehmung betreffen, zu treffen, wenn die diesbezüglichen Kompetenzen eindeutig festgelegt wurden. Das begrenzt die Eingriffsmöglichkeiten der Gründungsorgane auf die Fälle, die in den Rechtsvorschriften vorgesehen sind, und stärkt die Unternehmungsselbständigkeit.

Der Kompetenzbereich der Arbeiterselbstverwaltung in der staatlichen Unternehmung wurde nach langen Überlegungen und Diskussionen gesetzlich festgelegt. Dabei ging es nicht nur darum, durch die gewährten Kompetenzen der Selbstverwaltung die Rolle des faktischen Verwalters zuzuerkennen; das Selbstverwaltungsorgan sollte auch nicht durch Aufgaben, die zu schwer oder nicht realisierbar sind, überlastet werden. Außerdem soll der Unternehmungsleiter nicht entmündigt werden.

Die Arbeiterselbstverwaltungsorgane haben folgende Entscheidungsberechtigungen:

(1) Die allgemeine Versammlung der Mitarbeiter
- verabschiedet die Satzung der Unternehmung,
- verabschiedet die Verteilung des für die Belegschaft bestimmten Gewinns,
- beurteilt jährlich die Tätigkeit des Belegschaftsrats und des Direktors der Unternehmung,
- verabschiedet die mehrjährigen Pläne der Unternehmung,

- verabschiedet die Satzung der Arbeiterselbstverwaltung.

(2) Der Belegschaftsrat der Unternehmung ist berechtigt,
- die Änderungen im Jahresplan zu erbringen und den Plan zu verabschieden,
- die Jahresberichte und die Bilanz der Unternehmung zu bestätigen,
- über die Initiativen der Unternehmung zu entscheiden,
- sich mit der Bildung von gemeinsamen oder gemischten Unternehmungen einverstanden zu erklären (darunter auch die Unternehmungen mit fremdem Kapital),
- über die Bildung von Unternehmungsverbänden zu beschließen,
- Zustimmungsrechte zur Gliederung und Verbindung der Unternehmungen wahrzunehmen,
- zur Beschlußfassung über das Wohnungs- und Sozialbauwesen,
- zu Beschlüssen zu Änderungen der Produktion,
- über die Verteilung der Erträge bzw. des Gewinns zu entscheiden,
- die Arbeitsordnung der Unternehmung zu verabschieden,
- das Referendum in der Unternehmung durchzuführen,
- den Unternehmungsleiter zu berufen und abzuberufen.

Die Analyse der Liste der Entscheidungsberechtigungen der allgemeinen Versammlung und des Belegschaftsrates erlaubt es, vier Kategorien von Beschlüssen der Selbstverwaltungsorgane zu unterscheiden:

Zur ersten Kategorie gehören Beschlüsse, kraft deren die Selbstverwaltungsorgane Grundsätzliches festlegen, wie z. B. Betriebsverfassung, Selbstverwaltungsordnung, Arbeitsordnung. Die erwähnten Beschlüsse besitzen normativen Charakter. Die Befolgung dieser Beschlüsse ist nicht nur für den Unternehmungsleiter, sondern auch für die Mitarbeiter verbindlich. Zur Ausführung dieser Beschlüsse sind zusätzliche Entscheidungen des Unternehmungsleiters erforderlich. Sanktionen für den Fall der Nichtbefolgung dieser Beschlüsse durch die Mitarbeiter kann ausschließlich der Unternehmungsleiter festlegen.

Zur zweiten Kategorie gehören Beschlüsse, deren Adressat und Ausführender allein der Direktor der Unternehmung ist. Sie betreffen folgende Fragen: Ertrags- und Gewinnverteilung, Investitionstätigkeit, betrieblicher Wohnungs- und Sozialbau, Änderungen des Tätigkeitsprofils der Unternehmung, Beitritt der Unternehmung als Kollektivmitglied in gesellschaftliche Organisationen. Diese Beschlüsse bewirken von sich aus keine rechtlichen Folgen in Angelegenheiten der Unternehmung. Diese Kategorie von Selbstverwaltungsbeschlüssen ist zweistufig. Zuerst wird die Entscheidung der jeweiligen Frage durch das betreffende Selbstverwaltungsorgan getroffen; dann wird auf dieser Grundlage der Unternehmungsleiter verpflichtet, die Ausführungsentscheidung zu treffen. Die Entscheidung des Selbstverwaltungsorgans hat normalerweise allgemeinen Richtungscharakter, während die Unternehmungsleiterentscheidung Durchführungscharakter besitzt. Die zweite Entscheidung darf die erste inhaltlich nicht verletzen.

Zur dritten Kategorie gehören Beschlüsse, aufgrund deren ein Selbstverwaltungsorgan sich einverstanden erklärt, bestimmte Entscheidungen oder bestimmte

Aktivitäten durch den Unternehmungsleiter aufzunehmen. Sie betreffen folgende Fragen: Beitritt der Unternehmung zu den Unternehmungsverbänden oder Errichtung einer gemeinsamen bzw. gemischten Unternehmung sowie Berufung und Abberufung von Stellvertretern des Direktors. Die Beschlüsse dieser Gruppe ermächtigen nur den Unternehmungsleiter zur Entscheidungsfindung. Der Unternehmungsdirektor wird aber nicht verpflichtet, eine Entscheidung zu fassen, sondern nur dazu berechtigt. Die Berechtigung ist nicht gleichbedeutend mit einer Verpflichtung. Eine Entscheidung ohne oder entgegen einer Berechtigung würde regelwidrig sein und müßte durch das Selbstverwaltungsorgan aufgehoben werden.

Zur vierten Kategorie gehören Beschlüsse der Selbstverwaltungsorgane, die sich nicht auf den Unternehmungsleiter, sondern auf andere Subjekte beziehen. Sie betreffen: Die Teilung und Zusammenfügung der Unternehmung, Referendum der Belegschaft, Wahl von Vertretern des Belegschaftsrates zum Verbandsrat, Berufung und Abberufung des Direktors. Diese Beschlüsse sind von unterschiedlichem Charakter. Manche von ihnen sind als Entscheidungen zu sehen, andere berechtigen nur andere Subjekte zur Entscheidungsfindung.

Allgemein kann man feststellen, daß der Gestaltungsprozeß der Arbeiterselbstverwaltung noch nicht gänzlich beendet ist. Die Selbstverwaltungsorgane befaßten sich bisher vor allem mit den formalrechtlichen und organisatorischen Problemen. In der Mehrheit der Unternehmungen erfüllen sie eigentlich noch nicht die Funktionen, die ihnen als dem Träger der ökonomischen Macht in der Reformkonzeption des Leitungssystems zugedacht wurde. Hiermit soll aber nicht gesagt werden, daß die Arbeiterselbstverwaltungsorgane gar keinen Einfluß auf die wirtschaftliche Lage der Unternehmungen haben.

Die vom Autor durchgeführten Untersuchungen in 20 Unternehmungen in verschiedenen Industriebranchen beweisen, daß die Selbstverwaltungsorgane sich vornehmlich mit der laufenden ökonomischen Situation der Unternehmung beschäftigen. Möglicherweise ist dies eine Anpassungsreaktion auf die ökonomisch-finanzielle Unstabilität der Unternehmungen. Es kann aber auch eine Folge der wiederholten Versuche der Beschränkung der Unternehmungsselbständigkeit durch die Gründungsorgane sein. Wenn die Selbstverwaltungsorgane aber entscheidenden Einfluß auf die Gestaltung der Unternehmungszukunft nehmen wollen, müssen sie sich verstärkt für strategische Fragestellungen interessieren. Es darf auch nicht übersehen werden, daß die Eingriffe der Selbstverwaltungsorgane in die operative Leitung zum einen einen Kompetenzstreit auslösen und zum anderen die Verantwortlichkeit des Unternehmungsleiters schwächen.

Die Mitarbeiter der staatlichen Unternehmung werden nicht nur durch das Organ der Arbeiterselbstverwaltung, sondern zusätzlich auch durch die Gewerkschaften vertreten. Das neue Gesetz über die Gewerkschaften aus dem Jahr 1982 regelt drei Problembereiche (s. Abb. 3).

Der erste betrifft den Schutz und die Verteidigung von Rechten der Arbeitnehmer, der zweite die Entlohnung der Arbeitnehmer und der dritte die sozialen Rahmenbedingungen der Arbeit.

Zum ersten Problembereich zählen zum Beispiel:
a) Die Neueinstellung von Arbeitnehmern,
b) die Entlassung von Arbeitnehmern,
c) der innerbetriebliche Aufstieg von Arbeitnehmern,
d) die Weiterbildung,
e) die Arbeitsschutzmaßnahmen und
f) der Jugendarbeitsschutz.

Bei a) bis c) ist die Zustimmung der Gewerkschaft obligatorisch. Bei d) bis f) haben die Gewerkschaften Vorschlagsrechte und Kontrollfunktionen (s. Abb. 3).

Zum zweiten Problembereich zählen:
a) Das Tarifvertragsrecht,
b) Entlohnungsformen, insbesondere Prämiensysteme, und
c) Arbeitsnormen.

Bei der Gestaltung von Tarifverträgen sind die Gewerkschaften Verhandlungspartner; bei den Entlohnungsformen ist die Zustimmung der Gewerkschaften zu Vorschlägen des Betriebs notwendig. Bei der Einhaltung von Arbeitsnormen üben die Gewerkschaften Kontrollfunktionen aus. Ich möchte anmerken, daß die Tarifparteien nicht über die Mindestlöhne bestimmen können. Diese werden zur Zeit vom Staat festgelegt. Es ist allerdings beabsichtigt, diese Mindestlöhne zwischen Regierungsvertretern und der Gewerkschaftsspitze auszuhandeln. Die Tarifpartner, d. h. die Betriebsleitungen und die Gewerkschaften, können jedoch die Lohntabellen im einzelnen aushandeln. Darüber hinaus können sie auch die Abhängigkeiten zwischen der durchschnittlichen Lohnsteigerung und der Arbeitsproduktivitätssteigerung mit aushandeln.

Zum dritten Problembereich, d. h. zu den sozialen Rahmenbedingungen der Arbeit, gehören:
a) Die Verteilung des Sozialfonds,
b) die Verteilung des Wohnungsfonds und
c) Impulse hinsichtlich des betrieblichen Gesundheitsdienstes.

Bei der Verteilung des Sozialfonds und des Wohnungsfonds können die Gewerkschaften initiativ und kontrollierend tätig werden. Auf dem Gebiet des betrieblichen Gesundheitsdienstes haben die Gewerkschaften Vorschlagsrecht und können sich auch finanziell beteiligen. Der betriebliche Gesundheitsdienst schließt auch vorbeugende Maßnahmen zur Früherkennung von Krankheiten und zur Abwendung von Gesundheitsbedrohungen ein. Auf diesem Gebiet ist die Zusammenarbeit mit dem Arbeitsschutz notwendig.

Gemäß dem Gesetz über Gewerkschaften und dem Arbeitsgesetzbuch gibt es folgende Mitwirkungsformen des Unternehmungsleiters bei den Gewerkschaften:

- Beratungen mit den Gewerkschaften während der Entscheidungsvorbereitung,
- Entscheidungsfindung gemeinsam mit der Gewerkschaftsorganisation,
- Zustimmung der Gewerkschaften.

Abschließend möchte ich bemerken:

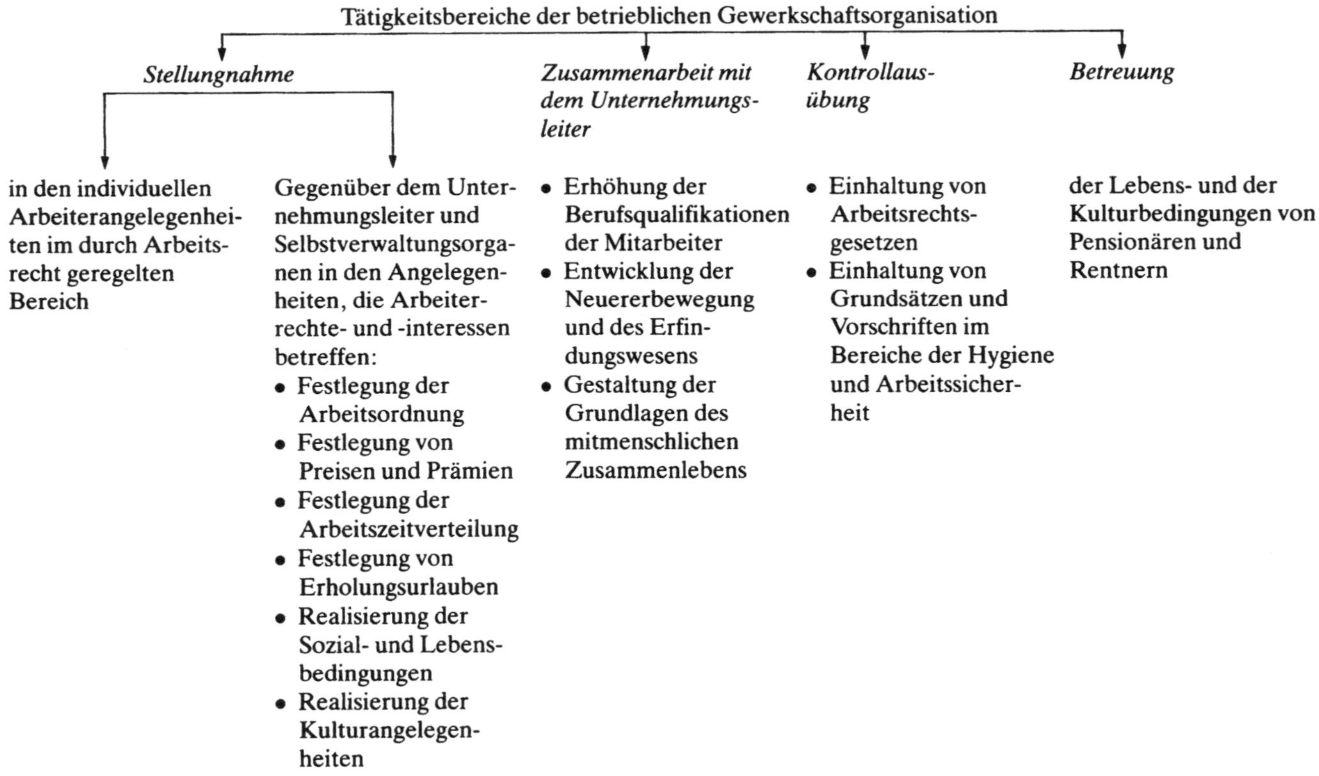

Abb. 3: Tätigkeitsbereiche der Betriebsgewerkschaften.

1. Das neue Gewerkschaftsgesetz garantiert den Gewerkschaften volle Unabhängigkeit.
2. Darüber hinaus definiert dieses Gesetz verschiedene Instrumente für die Gewerkschaften, unter anderem auch das Streikrecht.
3. Das Gesetz umfaßt Regelungen für die Wahl von Gewerkschaftsvertretern sowie Rahmenbedingungen für den Ablauf von Verhandlungen zwischen den Gewerkschaften und den Unternehmungsleitungen.
4. Das Gesetz normiert nur Grundprobleme, nicht aber Angelegenheiten, deren Komplexität erst in der Praxis zum Vorschein kommt.

Die Arbeiterselbstverwaltung und die Gewerkschaften bilden Grundelemente des gesellschaftlichen Systems einer sozialistischen Staatsunternehmung. Sie sind selbständige Arbeitervertretungen, welche die gesetzlichen Berechtigungen sowie die daraus abgeleiteten Aufgaben und Pflichten realisieren. Obwohl der Interessengegenstand dieser Organe in großem Maße gemeinschaftlich ist, realisiert jedes von ihnen seine Befugnisse und seine Aufgaben aufgrund verschiedener Gesetze. Hauptgegenstand des Interesses der Arbeiterselbstverwaltungsorgane sind die betrieblichen Prozesse, während die Gewerkschaften als Hauptziel ihrer Tätigkeit den Schutz der Rechte und Interessen von Mitarbeitern betrachten.

Die Selbstverwaltung hat Anteil an der Unternehmungsleitung; in der reformierten Unternehmung sind als wichtigste Funktionen anzunehmen:

Kurzfristig: Gewinnbildung und -verteilung in der laufenden Periode.

Langfristig: Verteilung der Gewinne zugunsten der Konsumptionszwecke der Mitarbeiter oder für die Entwicklungsziele der Unternehmung.

Die Gewerkschaften haben vorrangig Interesse an der kurzfristigen Gewinnverteilung, während die Arbeiterselbstverwaltung sich auch mit den langfristigen Aspekten auseinandersetzen muß. Hier ist also eine potentielle Konfliktzone vorhanden, die sich sicher nicht allein durch Gesetzesvorschriften regeln läßt. Sie bieten aber zumindest einen gewissen Rahmen für die Handhabung der Konflikte und Kompetenzstreitigkeiten.

Der Charakter der Konflikte zwischen den Organen ist abhängig von ihrer Stellung im Wirtschaftssystem. Grundvoraussetzung der Relation: Selbstverwaltung – Unternehmungsleiter stellt die ökonomische Selbständigkeit der Unternehmung und eine wachsende Stabilität der Bedingungen ihrer Tätigkeit dar. Für die Beziehung: Arbeiterselbstverwaltung – Gewerkschaften aber entscheidet der Rang der Gewerkschaften und ihre Fähigkeit, ein neues Handlungsmodell unter Verzicht auf einen Teil ihrer bisherigen Rechte zugunsten der Selbstverwaltung zu erarbeiten. Selbstverständlich muß ein derart komplexer Prozeß lange dauern; er erfordert außerdem gegenseitigen Respekt und Akzeptanzbereitschaft von allen Beteiligten.

Die Pflicht zur Zusammenarbeit der Arbeiterselbstverwaltung und ihrer Organe mit den Gewerkschaften ergibt sich aus dem Art. 36 des Gesetzes über Arbeiterselbstverwaltung. Dieser besagt, daß bei Beschlüssen der Arbeiterselbstverwaltung, die Angelegenheiten aus dem Wirkungsbereich der Gewerkschaften betreffen, eine Stellungnahme der Gewerkschaft erforderlich ist. Beispiele für solche Angelegenheiten sind:

- Die Betriebssatzung, welche durch die Generalversammlung der Mitarbeiter oder der Delegierten verabschiedet wird.
- Die Arbeitsordnung der Unternehmung.
- Die Jahres- und mehrjährigen Pläne der Unternehmung.
- Die Investitionspläne der Unternehmung.
- Das Funktionieren des Rationalisierungskomitees.
- Die Verteilung des verfügbaren Gewinns der Unternehmung und Nutzung der sich daraus ergebenden Fonds.
- Der Betriebswohnungs- und Sozialbau.

Die Stellungnahme der Gewerkschaften ist jeweils vor der endgültigen Beschlußfassung einzuholen.

Entsprechend dem Gesetz ist der Belegschaftsrat berechtigt, die gesamte Unternehmungstätigkeit zu kontrollieren einschließlich der Sozial- und Wohnungsfondswirtschaft. Das ist aber nicht gleichbedeutend mit einer Entscheidungsberechtigung in individuellen Fällen wie Wohnungszuteilung oder Sozialleistungen. Solche Entscheidungen kommen dem Direktor – nach Einholung der Meinung des Belegschaftsrates und der Gewerkschaften – zu.

Die Verfahrensordnungen bezüglich der Sozialleistungen, die aus Gewinn und zu Lasten der Kosten finanziert werden, legt der Unternehmungsleiter nach der Einholung der Meinung von Belegschaftsrat und Gewerkschaften fest.

Eine wesentliche Frage, die die Mitwirkung aller die Unternehmung und ihre Belegschaft repräsentierenden Partner erfordert, stellen die Lohnfragen dar. Die Kompliziertheit dieses Problems hat mehrere Gründe:

1. Aus der vollen Unternehmungselbständigkeit im Bereich der Entlohnungsgestaltung und -steigerung; dies betrifft:
   a) Arbeitstarife,
   b) Lohnformen,
   c) Prämiensysteme,
   d) Sicherung der Finanzmittel für Entlohnungszwecke, die von der Finanzlage der Unternehmung abhängt.
2. Aus dem erheblichen Druck der Mitarbeiter auf Lohnsteigerung im Hinblick auf den Inflationsprozeß.
3. Aus den verhältnismäßig großen Möglichkeiten der Unternehmung, die Geldmittel für Löhne und Lohnerhöhungen durch Preissteigerung von Erzeugnissen (vor allem von knappen) zu sichern.
4. Aus der langjährigen Vernachlässigung im Bereich der Arbeitsnormierung, da die Normen oft viel mehr die Löhne und weniger den Arbeitsaufwand regulierten.
5. Aus dem außergewöhnlich begrenzten Einfluß der Gewerkschaften auf die Gestaltung von Entlohnungssystemen in den 70er Jahren.
6. Aus den Kompetenzen der Arbeiterselbstverwaltung im Bereich der Gewinnverteilung, darunter des Gewinns, der der Belegschaft zusteht, u.s.w.

Das Gesetz vom Januar 1984 über die betrieblichen Entlohnungssysteme umfaßt das Recht der Unternehmungen, Betriebsvereinbarungen zu schließen und aufgrund dieser die Löhne zu bestimmen. Das Gesetz erlaubt – ohne besondere rechtliche Beschränkungen und bei bestimmten ökonomischen Begrenzungen –, die Löhne entsprechend den Qualifikationen, den Arbeitsbedingungen und den Arbeitsergebnissen selbständig zu gestalten.

Dieses Recht der Unternehmung auf dem Gebiet der Lohngestaltung ist deshalb besonders außergewöhnlich, da die Mitarbeiter bis vor kurzem nicht einmal mittelbaren Einfluß auf die Festlegung der Entlohnungsregeln für die Arbeit hatten. Das vor zehn Jahren veröffentlichte und bis heute geltende Arbeitsgesetzbuch hatte die Bedeutung der Tarifverträge wesentlich beschränkt[3]. Artikel Nr. 79 des Arbeitsgesetzbuches bestimmt, daß der Ministerrat im Einverständnis mit dem Zentralrat der Gewerkschaften die Entlohnungsregeln sowie die Zubilligung anderer mit der Arbeit verbundener Sozialleistungen bestimmt. Die Festlegung dieser Regeln liegt aktuell in der Kompetenz der Unternehmungen. Das angeführte Gesetz ermöglicht, betriebliche Entlohnungssysteme unter Nichtbeachtung einiger Vorschriften der Tarifverträge und des Arbeitsgesetzbuches zu bilden[4]. Sie werden durch die Regelungen, die in der Unternehmung ausgearbeitet und ausgehandelt werden, ersetzt. Es wird quasi eine Art Gesellschaftsvertrag zwischen den Mitarbeitern und der Unternehmungsleitung geschlossen. Der Vertrag wird rechtskräftig nach der Akzeptanz durch das Gründungsorgan und nach der Registrierung durch das Ministerium für Arbeit, Löhne und Sozialwesen. Die beiden Zentralinstitutionen verifizieren die Vereinbarung nach der Gesetzesgerechtigkeit in rechtlicher und ökonomischer Hinsicht.

Das Gesetz vom Januar 1984 hat auf diese Weise einem bedeutungsvollen Vergesellschaftungsprozeß des Lohnsystems den Anstoß gegeben. Das heißt, daß die Arbeiten an dem neuen Entlohnungssystem unter Mitwirkung der Gewerkschaftsorganisation und der Selbstverwaltung geführt werden, wobei die Belegschaft laufend darüber informiert ist. Diese parallel geführten Informations- und Aufklärungsaktivitäten sollen die Billigung der Belegschaft für neue Lohnlösungen gewährleisten.

Diese Vereinbarung schließen also zwei Organe ab, die teilweise verschiedene Interessen, jedenfalls jedoch andersartige Präferenzen repräsentieren, besonders bezüglich

a) der Gestaltung der Relation zwischen dem Lohn- und Arbeitsproduktivitätszuwachs,
b) der Gestaltung der Relation zwischen dem Lohnanstieg und der Inflationsrate,
c) der erforderlichen Arbeitsbedingungen und der Gestaltung von Lohnzuschlägen, die mit beschwerlichen Arbeitsbedingungen verbunden sind,
d) der Gestaltung von Relationen in den Lohntabellen u.s.w.

Es ist offensichtlich unmöglich, alle oben erwähnten Probleme im einzelnen zu besprechen. Es soll darum nur auf manche von ihnen hingewiesen werden.

Von besonderer Bedeutung ist das Tarifsystem. Das in der Industrie geltende

Tarifsystem unterlag lange Zeit keinen Veränderungen. Es kam nur zu kleinen Modifikationen, ohne den Grundaufbau zu ändern. Dieses Tarifsystem entsprach deshalb nicht dem aktuellen Streben nach anforderungsgerechter und qualitätsbezogener Arbeitsentlohnung. Dies betraf insbesondere die Lohntabellen, weil

1. ihre Spannweiten – d. h. das Verhältnis zwischen den Lohnsätzen der höchsten und der niedrigsten Gruppe – nicht ausreichend waren,
2. der Zuwachs von Lohnsätzen der aufeinanderfolgenden Gruppen zu klein war, um einen Anreiz zur Qualifikationserhöhung auszuüben,
3. die Anzahl von Lohngruppen hinsichtlich einer anforderungsbezogenen Arbeitsdifferenzierung als zu klein angesehen wurde, usw. Vor allem aber war das Niveau von Lohnansätzen in den einzelnen Gruppen zu gering, und darüber hinaus entsprach der Zuwachs dieser Lohnsätze der Erhöhung der Unterhaltskosten nicht. Als Folge kam es zu Manipulationen an den Arbeitsnormen und bei der Eingruppierung der Arbeiten und der Arbeiter. Dies führte zu hohen Übererfüllungen der Arbeitsnormen, die infolgedessen ihre Rolle als objektiver Maßstab des Arbeitsaufwandes verloren. Außerdem kam es zur Deformierung der Lohnstruktur. Der Tarifverdienst betrug weniger als 50% des Gesamtverdienstes.

Diese Unvollkommenheit des Tarifsystems zeigt gleichzeitig Probleme, die einer Lösung sowie der gegenseitigen Verständigung der Partner der Betriebsvereinbarung bedürfen.

Von grundlegender Bedeutung ist die Steigerung der Lohnsätze und ihre gerechte Differenzierung. Die Steigerung der Lohnsätze ist mit der Verminderung einer ganzen Reihe von Lohnzuschlägen, die mit der Arbeit und mit der Arbeitsproduktivität unmittelbar in keiner Relation stehen, verbunden. Außerdem wird dabei eine tiefgreifende Prüfung von Arbeitsnormen erforderlich, um die Stimulationsfunktion der Entlohnung wiederherzustellen.

Die Differenzierung der Lohnsätze erfordert die Ausarbeitung von Kriterien, die die Arbeitsanforderungen, die Arbeitskomplexität und Verantwortlichkeit sowie die Arbeitsschwere und Bedingungen ihrer Ausführung charakterisieren können. Dieser Bereich der Arbeitsforschung wurde ohne Zweifel vernachlässigt.

Im Tarifsystembereich bleibt endlich als Grundlage der Einstufung der Arbeiter die Tarifordnung. Die aktuell in der Unternehmung abgeschlossenen Lohnvereinbarungen sind nicht imstande, alle Fragen des Tarifsystems zu lösen. Sie können dennoch geeignete Voraussetzungen für langfristige Absichten bilden, die der Reihe nach unter Beteiligung und unter Kontrolle der Vereinbarungspartner gelöst werden. Es wird vorausgesetzt, daß der minimale Lohnsatz systematisch zur Steigerung der Lebenshaltungskosten proportional korrigiert wird. Die Realisierung dieses gesetzlichen Prinzips durch die staatlichen Organe wird unter der Kontrolle der Gewerkschaften bleiben. Die Korrektur des minimalen Lohnsatzes wird offensichtlich unentbehrliche Veränderungen in den Betriebslohntabellen erzwingen. Auf diese Weise wird der erforderliche Anteil des Tariflohns an der Gesamtentlohnung sichergestellt.

Einer Neuordnung bedarf auch der zweite Bereich der Entlohnungsfragen, der die geeignete Lohnform und das Prämiensystem – anders gesagt: die Entlohnung, die der Arbeitsleistung entspricht – betrifft. Zu diesem Problemkreis gehören ebenfalls Strukturierungsfragen der Arbeit und vornehmlich auch der Arbeitsbereicherung. Die Auswahl von Lohnformen wird eng mit der Möglichkeit der Quantifizierung von Arbeitsaufwand und von Arbeitsergebnissen verbunden. Dies bezieht sich auch auf das Prämiensystem, das zusätzliche Arbeitsleistung belohnen soll.

Die dominierende Lohnform – vor allem in der Industrie – ist aber der Akkordlohn. Der Akkord stimuliert Arbeitsproduktivitätssteigerungen, wenn er auf den richtigen Arbeitsnormen unter Beachtung des rationellen Niveaus der Grundlohnsätze basiert. Das Ordnen der Arbeitsnormen sowie die Steigerung von Grundlohnsätzen sollen als Faktoren, die die richtige Steuerung des Akkordlohns begünstigen, angesehen werden. Das ganze Prämiensystem erfordert eine Rationalisierung. Dies betrifft Kriterien und Prämiengrundlagen, weiterhin die Funktion der Prämie in der Gesamtentlohnung, die Relation Prämie – Grundentlohnung, den Prämienumfang u.s.w. Die aktuell abgeschlossenen Vereinbarungen umfassen auch Grundfragen, die laufend gelöst und in Einklang gebracht werden müssen, wie zum Beispiel

- Beschränkungen des Akkordlohns in begründetem Ausmaß in Anbetracht der Möglichkeit der Messung von Arbeitsaufwand und Arbeitsleistung,
- Verbreiterung des Gruppenakkords zu Lasten des individuellen Akkords, im Hinblick auf die Möglichkeit der Messung von kollektiven Arbeitsergebnissen,
- Begrenzung der Anzahl der Prämiengründe und Bindung der Prämien an quantitativ meßbare Arbeitsergebnisse,
- Beschränkung der Prämierungshöhe in vernünftigen Grenzen in der Gesamtentlohnung des Arbeiters.

Der Mitarbeiter muß an den Effekten der Arbeitsproduktivität und Arbeitseffektivitätssteigerung seinen Anteil in Form der Lohnsteigerung erhalten, den die Unternehmung dagegen in Form der Gewinnsteigerung erhält. An einem Teil dieses Gewinns wird andererseits die Belegschaft – nämlich in Form der Prämien oder aber des Sozial- oder Wohnungsfonds – partizipieren.

Es soll betont werden, daß die betrieblichen Lohnvereinbarungen einen langfristigen Forschungs- und Ordnungsprozeß der Unternehmung initiiert haben. Er umfaßt:

- die Untersuchung der Arbeitsbedingungen an den Arbeitsstellen unter Berücksichtigung der Arbeitsschwere und der Belohnungen seitens der Arbeitsumwelt,
- die technische Arbeitsnormierung unter Einbeziehung von ergonomischen Kriterien der Arbeitsbelastung,
- die Möglichkeiten der Arbeitsbereicherung durch die Auswahl von autonomen Arbeitsformen und Ausführungsweisen,
- die Verbesserung der Tarifordnungsbearbeitung einschließlich ihrer Grundlagen, d. h. der Grundsätze und der Kriterien der Differenzierung von Qualitätsmerkmalen der Arbeit,

– die Anpassung des Prämiensystems unter Berücksichtigung von quantitativen Kriterien der Arbeitseffekte.

Das Recht zur Ausnutzung des Gesetzes haben über 7500 Unternehmungen, zusammen mit den Genossenschaften ungefähr 10000 Organisationseinheiten. Bis Ende 1984 wurden über 1000 Lohnvereinbarungen unterschrieben, die über 2 Millionen Mitarbeiter umfassen. Aus den in 25 Unternehmungen durch den Verfasser durchgeführten Untersuchungen, die schon ausgehandelte Vereinbarungen realisiert haben, ergibt sich, daß die Konsultations-, Abstimmungs- und Akzeptanzstufe der neuen Grundsätze und Lohnregeln bis auf wenige Ausnahmen konfliktlos verlief. Die abgeschlossenen Vereinbarungen umfassen zugleich Grundregelungen im Bereich der Löhne (grundsätzliche Lohntabellen, Entlohnungsformen sowie Prämien- und Arbeitsnormierungssysteme), wobei weitere und kontinuierliche Arbeiten zur Verbesserung der Arbeitstarife sowie über Entlohnungs- und Prämienformen, die der spezifischen Lage der Produktion und Produktionsorganisation am besten entsprechen, vorausgesetzt werden.

Die abgeschlossenen Lohnvereinbarungen brachten in kurzer Zeit in der Mehrheit der Unternehmungen positive Ergebnisse im Bereich der Arbeitsproduktivität. Man kann daher vermuten, daß die betrieblichen Lohnvereinbarungen zum Gestaltungsinstrument der erwünschten Arbeitereinstellungen werden. Man hofft, daß dieses Instrument zu leistungsorientierten Arbeiten motivieren wird.

Anmerkungen

1 Gründungsorgan der Staatsunternehmung ist das Branchenministerium bzw. ein Organ der örtlichen Staatsverwaltung.

2 Unternehmungsverbände werden obligatorisch in den eng bestimmten Wirtschaftszweigen und Branchen, vor allem aber freiwillig gebildet bei der Zustimmung für den Beitritt seitens der Arbeiterselbstverwaltung. Sie erfüllen vornehmlich Organisations-, Anregungs- und Koordinationsfunktionen.

3 Die Geschichte der Arbeitstarifverträge in der VRP beinhaltet sowohl die Entwicklungsphasen als auch ungünstige Regressionen. Wegen Mangels von Modifizierungen des Arbeitsrechtes vor 1975 haben die Verträge eine bedeutsame Rolle in der Ordnung und Gestaltung des Arbeitsrechtes – indem sie den Rechtsregelungen zuvorkommen und gesetzliche Vorschriften konkretisieren – gespielt. In der Evolution von Tarifverträgen unterscheiden sich in dieser Periode die stürmische Entwicklung in den Jahren 1946–1949 – weiterhin die mit der fortgeschrittenen Zentralisation des Leitungssystems in den Jahren 1950–1955 verbundene Regression, der erneute Aufschwung nach 1956 bis 1975, als das neu verabschiedete Arbeitsgesetzbuch die Regulierungsaufgabe von Arbeitsverhältnissen übernommen hat, wobei das Arbeitsgesetzbuch das Bestehen der Tarifverträge beibehält, gleichzeitig aber ihren Inhalt drastisch beschränkt.

4 Bis heute haben 77 Tarifverträge Gültigkeit, die in der zweiten Hälfte der 70er Jahre abgeschlossen wurden und die ungefähr 9 Mio. Mitarbeiter erfassen.

Literatur:

Bar, L. (1984a): Fundamenty prawne reformy. Dwa trudne lata. In: *Zycie Gospodarcze*, nr 4.
Bar, L. (1984b): Losy refory w rękach załóg. In: *Zycie Gospodarcze*, nr 41.
Borkowska, St. (1982): O motywowaniu kadry kierowniczej. In: *Doskonalenie Kadr Kierowniczych*, nr 4.
Borkowska, St. (1985): Sterowanie relacjami płac. In: *Zycie Gospodarcze*, nr 3.
Gliński, B. (1982): Modele motywowania – próba zarysu z punktu widzenia nauk zarządzania. In: *Doskonalenie Kadr Kierowniczych*, nr 4.
Groszek, M. (1984): Samorząd – dyrektor – związek zawodowy. Jałowe spory. In: *Zycie Gospodarcze*, nr 10.
Janowska, Z. (1984): Wzbogacanie treści pracy jako element motywacji pracowniczej. In: *Ekonomika i Organizacja Pracy*, nr 7–8.
Kabaj, M. (1982): Wartościowanie pracy. In: *Zycie Gospodarcze*, cz. 1. nr 27 i cz. 2. nr 46.
Kabaj, M. (1984): Reforma a zatrudnienie. In: *Ekonomika i Organizacja Pracy*, nr 4 (cz. I) i nr 5 (cz. II).
Koraszewska, H. (1984): Metody tworzenia funduszu płac w krajach socjalistycznych. In: *Ekonomika i Organizacja Pracy*, nr 7–8.
Kordaszewski, J. (1960): *Kwalifikowanie pracy robotników przemysłowych.* Warszawa.
Kordaszewski, J. (1967): *Praca i zatrudnienie w przemyśle.* Warszawa.
Kordaszewski, J. (1982): Patologia systemu pracy i kierunki jego poprawy, cz. I i cz II. In: *Przegląd Techniczny*, nr 14 i nr 15.
Krencik, W., (1972): *Podstawy i kierunki polityki płac w PRL.* Warszawa.
Krencik, W. (1977):*Płaca a wzrost gospodarczy.* Warszawa.
Krencik, W. (1982): Zróżnicowanie i rozpiętość płac. In: *Zycie Gospodarcze*, nr 5.
Krencik, W. (1982): System kierowania polityką płac. In: *Zycie Gospodarcze*, nr 8.
Lamparski, M. (1984): Prawne zagadnienia samodzielności przedsiębiorstw państwowych. In: *Organizacja – Metody – Technika*, nr 10.
Masewicz, W. (1983): Związek zawodowy w społecznym systemie przedsiębiorstwa. In: *Ekonomika i Organizacja Pracy*, nr 10–11.
Małkowski, J. (1984): Kryteria oceny przygotowania przedsiębiorstwa do wprowadzenia zakładowego systemu wynagradzania. In: *Ekonomika i Organizacja Pracy*, nr 10–11.
Melich, A. (1977): System płac i zachęt materialnych – drogi usprawnienia. In: *Nowe Drogi*, nr 1.
Melich, A. (1982): Problemy wynagradzania za pracę kierowniczą. In: *Doskonalenie Kadr Kierowniczych*, nr 4.
Sajkiewicz, A. (1984): Struktury procesów pracy jako czynnik stabilizacji załogi. In: *Ekonomika i Organizacja Pracy*, nr 2.
Szul, R. (1982): Warunki sprawnego funkcjonowania samorządności w gospodarce socjalistycznej. In: *Ekonomista*, nr 5–6.
Sokołowski, J. (1978): Tabela płac – stan aktualny i kierunki modernizacji. In: *G. Pl.*, nr 11.
Ziemann, B. Technika współzarządzania: Stosunek między organami (1) (1984): *Życie Gospodarcze*, nr 41, Podział Kompetencji (2) (1984): *Życie Gospodarcze*, nr 52/53, Referendum (3) (1985): *Życie Gospodarcze*, nr 4, Uchwały (4) (1984): *Życie Gospodarcze*, nr 8.

Gesetze und Verordnungen

Kodeks pracy, "Dziennik Ustaw" 1974, nr 24, poz. 141.
Ustawa z dnia 25 września 1981 r. o przedsiębiorstwach państwowych, "Dziennik Ustaw" 1981 r., nr 24, poz. 122.
Ustawa z dnia 25 września 1981 r. o samorządzie załogi przedsiębiorstwa państwowego, "Dziennik Ustaw" 1981 nr 24, poz. 123.
Ustawa z dnia 26 lutego 1982 r. o planowaniu społecznogospodarczym, "Dziennik Ustaw" 1982, nr 32, poz. 216.
Ustawa z dnia 8 października 1982 r. o związkach zawodowych, "Dziennik Ustaw" 1982, nr 43, poz. 216.
Ustawa z dnia 26 stycznia 1984 r. o zasadach tworzenia zakładowych systemów wynagradzania, "Dziennik Ustaw" 1984, nr 5, poz. 25.

Partizipationschancen der sowjetischen Unternehmung

Hans-Erich Gramatzki

Abstract
Participation Opportunities for Soviet Enterprises

Participation in a centrally planned and administered economy must comprise two aspects of division of power, first between state and enterprise and second between top enterprise management and the work force. However, thus far enterprise management has had only limited decision making power and is still extremely restricted by the "board of governors" at the center. The main conclusions of this contribution are that real participation can be far greater than participation by law, secondly that the rebuilding of the economic mechanism giving more scope for enterprise decision making will take a long time, and finally that the "subjective factor" (personal initiative) will become extremely important for the Soviet leadership in the 80s and 90s. This applies not only to top and mid-level management, but also to the shop floor level.

Einleitung

In diesem Beitrag geht es um das Doppelproblem der „Entscheidungsteilung" zwischen staatlicher Administration und Unternehmung einerseits, Unternehmungsleitung und Belegschaft andererseits. Belegschaften können prinzipiell nur dann stärker an Entscheidungen *in* der Unternehmung partizipieren, wenn *die* Unternehmung im Gesamtsystem hinreichend an Entscheidungen beteiligt ist. Dies ist zwar weitgehend eine Trivialität, wird aber dennoch nur selten in dieser offenen Form in der UdSSR so ausgesprochen. Die ,,*Teilnahme*" der „Werktätigen" an Entscheidungen wird auch – dem Prinzip des „demokratischen Zentralismus" entsprechend – anders definiert als in pluralistisch verfaßten Gesellschaftssystemen. Sie ist einerseits sehr hoch angesiedelt: die Werktätigen seien *Miteigentümer der Produktionsmittel* und zum anderen sehr niedrig: die Werktätigen hätten umfassende Möglichkeiten der „Teilnahme" an der *Umsetzung* von Entscheidungen bzw. Plänen. Neben dieser immer noch aktuellen, stark ideologisch fixierten „Teilnahme" gibt es – entsprechend den Partizipationsforderungen in westlichen Ländern – natürlich auch in der UdSSR eine Diskussion über die Notwendigkeit verstärkter unmittelbarer Entscheidungsbeteiligung der Belegschaften und Elemente realisierter Partizipation im westlichen Sinne.

Negative Rahmenbedingungen für Partizipation liegen in der UdSSR einmal in der starken Lokalisierung betrieblich relevanter Entscheidungen außerhalb der Unternehmungen und zum anderen in gesamtgesellschaftlichen Demokratie-Defiziten, für die vor allem die Partei verantwortlich ist: Partei und Wirtschaftsbürokratie sind gemeinsam verantwortlich dafür, wenn der jetzt viel genannte „Unternehmungsgeist" im Vergleich zu westlichen Industrieländern stark unterentwickelt ist. *Positive Rahmenbedingungen* für Partizipation sind gegeben durch Vollbeschäftigung und mehr noch durch Knappheit qualifizierter Arbeitskräfte, durch gesamtwirtschaftliche Entwicklungsaufgaben und durch vielfältige Friktionen im Betriebsablauf. Die Entwicklungsaufgaben und die Friktionen schaffen Entscheidungsspielräume, Möglichkeiten für „Spontaneitäten".

Das aktuelle sowjetische Wirtschafts- und Lenkungssystem stellt eine Mischung aus autoritärer (direkter, direktivischer) und partizipativer Führung dar, bei zweifellos dominierender autoritär-direktivischer Komponente, mit einem kräftigen Schuß „Laisser faire", was z. B. in einem Begriff wie „planlose Wirtschaft" zum Ausdruck kommt. Diese Laisser-faire-Komponente ist in den einzelnen sozialistischen Ländern unterschiedlich ausgeprägt.

Wenn auch die vorhandenen Partizipationsgremien überbetrieblicher wie innerbetrieblicher Art Raum für echte Partizipation geben und auch – unterschiedlich – genutzt werden, so sind diese Gremien bislang dennoch rechtlich wie faktisch „unterentwickelt" und sehr stark Akklamationsorgane. Wie bei uns spielen bei Partizipation häufig informelle Kontakte bzw. Kanäle eine wichtigere Rolle als formal „berechtigte" Institutionen. Sicherlich liegen aber die normative und die faktische Seite der Partizipation in der UdSSR noch weiter auseinander als bei uns. Auch die Rechtsunklarheiten sind zweifellos größer.

In der sowjetischen Literatur, aber auch in der westlichen, wird die *Position* der sowjetischen Unternehmung zum Teil extrem unterschiedlich dargestellt. Dies ist bedingt durch Lücken empirischen Wissens (Überwiegen „punktueller" bzw. „anekdotischer" Informationen), ideologische „Verzerrungen" und selektive Wahrnehmungen, durch unterschiedliche Bewertungen von seiten verschiedener Fachdisziplinen und eine unzureichende interdisziplinäre Forschung, durch den jeweiligen Zweck einer Untersuchung und die durch ihn mitbestimmte Untersuchungsmethode. In einigen Fällen steht die Bestimmtheit des Urteils über die sowjetische Unternehmung im umgekehrten Verhältnis zum empirischen Wissen und kann daher nicht einmal die Kennzeichnung „Idealtypisierung" für sich beanspruchen. Fehlendes Wissen besteht zum Teil hinsichtlich der westlichen Realität – dem „Ostforscher" fehlt dann ein adäquates Referenzmodell für die Analyse der sowjetischen Unternehmung –, zum Teil hinsichtlich der sowjetischen, deren Komplexität nicht hinreichend erfaßt wird. Und dann gibt es noch die durch einen ideologischen bias verursachten Verzerrungen von Realität. Zwei Extrembewertungen seien nachfolgend dargestellt. E. Hamer behauptet, daß es in „den

Zentralverwaltungswirtschaften keine Unternehmer" gäbe, „weil diese in den Betrieben nicht schöpferisch, selbständig und verantwortlich führen können, sondern persönlich wie sachlich weisungsgebunden nur dafür zu sorgen haben, daß der Betrieb das ihm gesetzte Soll erfüllt. Allenfalls die paar Spitzenfunktionäre im Zentralplanungsbüro könnten in diesem Sinne Initiatoren sein. Die Leiter der zentralverwalteten Unternehmen dagegen sind weniger Unternehmer als Verwalter, Ausführer einer von oben kommenden Initiative" (Hamer 1984, S. 59). Der Leiter sei „in der Hierarchie letztlich nur ein untergeordneter und nach Weisungen handelnder Angestellter" (Hamer 1984, S. 59f.). Die andere Extremaussage kommt von R. W. Campbell, einem der führenden amerikanischen Ost-Experten: „There is a kind of bargaining relationship between the people at the top who think they have power and the people at the bottom who know they have the power. They are the ones who have to take the actions to make the improvements. And the people at center do not know how to make them take those actions" (Campbell 1984, S. 53).

Nimmt man den ersten Satz von Campbell, so kollidiert diese Aussage stark mit aktuellen Aussagen führender sowjetischer Politiker, Manager und Wissenschaftler über die immer noch praktizierte „kleinliche Bevormundung der Betriebe". Richtig ist, daß bargaining ein bedeutendes konstitutives Element der vertikalen Koordination in der UdSSR ist, richtig ist aber auch, daß die bargaining-Macht vieler Unternehmen schwach ist, weil z. B. ein Unternehmensleiter – er mag sogar erheblich managerial skill besitzen – sich weder auf persönliche noch auf politische Kontakte stützen kann. Campbells Aussage liegt insofern näher zur Realität, als sie zumindest die Möglichkeit von *entrepreneurship* beim sowjetischen Unternehmungsleiter sieht, während diese von Hamer gleichsam „herausdefiniert" wird.

Wie in westlichen Ländern mit einer starken staatswirtschaftlichen Tradition und Komponente ist *entrepreneurship* auch in der UdSSR anders verteilt als z. B. in westlichen, primär marktwirtschaftlich verfaßten Ländern. Entrepreneurs wird man weniger im Staatlichen Plankomitee antreffen, wie Hamer meint, sondern eher in der Partei, in bestimmten staatlichen Wirtschaftsorganen, im Militär und vor allem auch in den Unternehmungen selbst und – wie im Westen – bei schattenwirtschaftlichen Aktivitäten. Partei-entrepreneur kann z. B. der Parteisekretär einer administrativen Region sein. Der amerikanische Politikwissenschaftler J. Hough hat sich in verschiedenen Publikationen mit dem regionalen Parteisekretär – dem „Soviet Prefect" – und seinen wirtschaftlichen Möglichkeiten und Aktivitäten befaßt (vgl. insbesondere Hough 1969). Der „sowjetische Präfekt" ist nicht nur in hohem Maße in die Wirtschaft allgemein und in die „laufenden Geschäfte" seiner Region involviert, sondern in vielen Fällen auch „developmental prefect". Es gibt hier ebenso Ansätze „neomerkantilischer" Politik, wie wir sie aus westlichen Ländern kennen; man denke an die Bundesrepublik Deutschland und an Länderchefs als „Entwicklungsagenten" ihrer Länder.

Zweifellos engen die Entscheidungsdominanz der Partei, die Eigentumsverfassung und die zentrale Leitung und Planung der Wirtschaft die *Handlungsmöglich-*

keiten des Unternehmenssektors in der UdSSR nach wie vor beträchtlich ein. Die Forderung nach mehr *Selbständigkeit* der Unternehmung gibt es in der UdSSR und in Osteuropa jetzt seit ungefähr 30 Jahren. Im Prinzip ist diese Diskussion in der UdSSR jedoch so alt wie die UdSSR selbst. Die bisherige Diskussion in der UdSSR zeigt aber, daß es an einem adäquaten *Reform-Modell* noch fehlt. Man will die Kompetenzen der Unternehmung erhöhen und gleichzeitig die zentrale Leitung und Planung stärken. Das ist per se noch kein Widerspruch, wie im Westen immer wieder behauptet wird, denn es sollen vor allem ja bürokratische Mittelinstanzen zugunsten der Unternehmung und des „Zentrums" aufgelöst bzw. weitgehend entmachtet werden. Es ist aber überhaupt nicht klar, welcher „Mechanismus" und welches Instrumentarium dieser Reorganisation, diesem institutionellen Umbau entsprechen soll bzw. könnte. Letztlich war die aktuelle Wirtschaftsorganisation doch ein „Ausfluß" des Wirtschaftsmechanismus und nicht umgekehrt. Immer noch und gerade jetzt wieder – durch die Zusammenlegung von Ministerien zu Mammutgebilden – zeigt sich die Überschätzung des Faktors (Re)Organisation.

In diesem Beitrag soll nicht die Position vertreten werden, daß es in der UdSSR nur Betriebe und keine Unternehmungen gäbe. Ein Konzept der „SU Inc." ist m. E. analytisch unergiebig oder sogar „kontraproduktiv". In der UdSSR gibt es viele Wirtschaftseinheiten, welche Rechtspersönlichkeit besitzen und auch über beträchtliche faktische Kompetenzen, insbesondere Ressourcen, verfügen. Richtig ist, daß sowohl das kodifizierte Recht als auch „Gewohnheitsrecht" häufig von der Administration verletzt wird. Es wird aber auch von den Unternehmungen „überschritten". Und in zahlreichen Fällen ist „Rechtmäßigkeit" nicht klar definiert. Die faktische Macht der Unternehmung liegt darin, daß die jeweilige übergeordnete Behörde erstens auf sie als „Planerfüller" angewiesen ist, daß sie zweitens sowohl über sachliche als auch Macht-Ressourcen verfügt und daß sie drittens als Besitzer von Informationen entscheidender Mitplaner ist.

Der sowjetische Unternehmungsleiter ist – wie der westliche – Träger einer Mehrzahl von Rollen. Er hat es aber ungleich viel schwerer, diese Rollen bzw. Rollenerwartungen „auszubalancieren". Erwartungen bzw. Forderungen an ihn haben nicht nur seine übergeordnete Wirtschafts-Behörde, andere staatliche Organe, Parteiorgane, Kommune oder Region, sondern auch die Belegschaft. „... a manager gets no support from any theory of management prerogatives if he resists criticisms and suggestions from the rank and file. When a manager stands on his authority and fails to listen to his workers, he may and sometimes does get into trouble" (E. C. Brown, zit. nach Andrle 1976, S. 68f.). Auch gegenüber seiner Belegschaft, nicht nur „nach oben", muß der Unternehmensleiter Flexibilität und bargaining-Qualität beweisen, wenn auch generell die Systemkonstruktion so ist, daß im Zweifelsfall für „die oben" entschieden werden muß.

„Unternehmungsgeist" (predpriimčivost') wird in der UdSSR zunehmend als ein zentrales Element für die Modernisierung der Unternehmungs- und Volks-Wirtschaft genannt. Es ist ein in der Diskussion relativ neuer Begriff, der z. B. im sowjetischen Standard-Wörterbuch von Lochowic von 1962 noch nicht zu finden ist. Die Kritik in der UdSSR und Osteuropa an fehlendem „Unternehmungsgeist" gibt es in der UdSSR im wesentlichen seit dem Beginn der relativen ideologisch-politischen und ökonomischen Liberalisierung der Chruščev-Ära. Generell zeigt sich heute eine gewisse Verschiebung vom „Mechanismus" zur Person (zum „subjektiven Faktor") und vom Manager zum entrepreneur, wenn es um die Faktoren geht, welche als relevant für die Modernisierung der sowjetischen Wirtschaft angesehen werden.

Das bisherige System der Leitung und Planung engte nicht nur die Beteiligung der Unternehmung an strategischen Entscheidungen erheblich ein, sondern auch die Partizipationsmöglichkeiten für die Belegschaften. Es gibt zwar eine Reihe von Formen und Foren der Mitbestimmung, aber deren weitgehende Scheintätigkeit wird auch in der UdSSR selbst kritisiert. Raum ist bislang im wesentlichen nur für Mitbestimmung auf Arbeitsplatzebene. Aber selbst hier sind die Widerstände erheblich. Wie die gesetzlichen und faktischen Intentionen und Möglichkeiten für mehr Mitbestimmung aussehen, wird in den Teilen 4 und 5 dieses Beitrags dargestellt werden. Teil 3 stellt die heutige Situation kurz dar und ebenfalls sehr kursorisch werden in den Teilen 1 und 2 die Grundzüge des Systems der Leitung und Planung sowie die für die sowjetische Unternehmung relevanten Entscheidungsträger dargestellt.

1. Grundzüge des Systems der Leitung und Planung

Im Westen gibt es eine Reihe von Begriffen, mit denen die sowjetische Wirtschaft bzw. das System der Leitung und Planung gekennzeichnet werden: „Befehlswirtschaft", „Zentrale Verwaltungswirtschaft", „Zentral geplante Wirtschaft" u. a. Alle Begriffe enthalten wichtige Elemente, enthalten Richtiges, suggerieren aber auch „Vollkommenheiten", welche realiter nicht gegeben sind. So stehen neben Befehlen bzw. administrativen Anweisungen, d. h. neben *bürokratischer Koordination*, drei andere Koordinationsmechanismen (vgl. Kornai 1984, S. 306ff.): die *marktmäßige*, die *ethische* und die *aggressive*. Märkte gibt es bei Arbeitskräften, bei Konsumgütern, vor allem auch in der „zweiten Wirtschaft". Bei der „ethischen Koordination" geht es um Abstimmungen, die nicht bürokratisch durchzusetzen oder marktwirtschaftlich zu induzieren sind. Und „aggressive Koordination" meint "a wilful force – not acknowledged by law and morality . . . coercion is not institutionalized . . . it is mostly not lasting but of occasional nature" (Kornai 1984, S. 308). Zur aggressiven Koordination gehört in der UdSSR z. B. die Fülle rechtsverletzender bürokratischer Handlungen gegenüber den Unternehmen. Behördliche Rechtsverletzungen gibt es im Hinblick auf Reformgesetze, wo neue Unternehmensrechte faktisch nicht „gewährt" werden. Generell gibt es zu viele Rechtslücken. „Eines der am wenigsten ausgearbeiteten Gebiete des Wirtschaftsrechts ist die Leitung durch den Plan". Während die Regelung des zivilrechtlichen

Bereichs hinsichtlich wirtschaftlicher Aspekte in adäquater Form erfolgte, wurde die „Leitung durch den Plan lange Zeit von konkreten und einmaligen Verwaltungsakten, unzähligen Richtlinien, Verfügungen und Vorschriften beherrscht" und hat sich weitgehend „der tatsächlichen rechtlichen Regelung entzogen. Und darin liegt eine der Hauptursachen für die Verbreitung des Voluntarismus in der Planung" (W. P. Schkredow, zit. nach Wolkonski 1985, S. 472). Die beträchtlichen Abweichungen von rational bürokratischem Handeln (im Sinne M. Webers) in der sowjetischen Verwaltung haben dazu geführt – leider auch in der Wissenschaft –, daß die „aggressive Koordination", d. h. eine bürokratische Deformation als „bürokratisch" bezeichnet, die Abweichung also als Essenz ausgegeben wird. Gerade weil die „Verwaltungswirtschaft" nur bedingt bürokratisch-rational strukturiert ist, bedarf es eben – wobei nicht die Möglichkeit „perfekter bürokratischer Verwaltung" oder „perfekter Planung" unterstellt werden soll – der anderen Koordinationsmechanismen. Generell kann man sagen, daß die real existierende *Verwaltungs*-Wirtschaft die *Plan*-Wirtschaft stark deformiert, d. h. für Planungs- und Plan-Mängel zwar nicht ausschließlich, aber doch in hohem Maße verantwortlich ist.

Die Sowjetunion hat es permanent mit fundamentalen *Planungleichgewichten* zu tun, aus folgenden Gründen. Erstens ist die „Ex-ante-Koordination", die ja das Wesen von Planung ausmachen soll, realiter nur bedingt gegeben: vieles wird nicht geplant; geplante outputs sind nicht voll mit der input-Seite „bilanziert" u. a. m. Zweitens führen „Überplanungen" (taut planning, „angespannte Pläne", d. h. sehr hohe bzw. zu hohe Planansätze) zu Gegenstrategien auf Seiten der Unternehmungen. Diese versuchen leichte („weiche") Pläne zu erhalten und vor allem Ressourcen-Reserven zu bilden, um gegen Unsicherheiten der Planrealisierung und gegen Planänderungen durch ihre Behörde gewappnet zu sein. Diese „planlose" Reservebildung, das Horten aller denkbaren Ressourcen, schafft per se bzw. erhöht das gesamtwirtschaftliche Ungleichgewicht. Drittens wird Ungleichgewichtigkeit ex ante in Kauf genommen, ja bewußt anvisiert durch ein System der *Prioritätenplanung*. Da Prioritäten aber in der Regel immer (zu) zahlreich sind, sie durch die Interdependenz der Wirtschaft schnell „explodieren" und auch bei der Planrealisierung viele Wirtschaftsverwalter ihre eigenen Zielfunktionen bzw. Prioritäten durchsetzen wollen, wird die Ungleichgewichtigkeit tendenziell noch verstärkt. Viertens ist auch das realiter stark dominierende Planungs-Prinzip der Planung "from the achieved level" (vgl. Birman 1978) Ursache von Ungleichgewichtigkeit.

Die durch „angespannte Pläne", Prioritätenplanungen, betriebliche Hortungen u. a. m. auftretenden *Knappheitserscheinungen* – auch zu wenig durch Preiserhöhungen „kuriert" – schaffen einen *Verkäufermarkt*, welcher wiederum negative Folgen für die *Qualität* der Produkte hat. Schlechte Qualität bedeutet aber *Ressourcen-Verschwendung* und diese bewirkt wiederum *Knappheit*. „Diese oder jene Waren müssen wir nicht deshalb teuer bezahlen, weil wir zu wenig davon haben, sondern umgekehrt, es gibt davon zu wenig, weil sie uns zu teuer zu stehen kommen, weil für jede Einheit Endprodukt mehr gesellschaftliche Ressourcen eingesetzt werden, als notwendig ist" (Birman 1984, S. 242). Und auch die Preisbildung trägt zur Knappheit entschieden bei. „Wenn die Preise von den Kosten abgeleitet werden (und das ist ... bisher die Hauptmethode der Preisbildung) nimmt das Defizit spürbar zu. Die ‚Kostenpreise' lassen sich schließlich mit geringer Leistung, mit überzähligen Arbeitskräften und mit einem aufgeblähten Verwaltungsapparat in Einklang bringen. Vermittels solcher Preise findet der Betrieb mit Leichtigkeit die Quellen für Lohn- und Prämienzahlungen. Alle sind zufrieden, und die Kasse stimmt" (Bunitsch 1982, S. 208).

Das *Qualitätsproblem* ist im existierenden „Wirtschaftsmechanismus" m. E. nicht annähernd befriedigend lösbar. Die unmittelbaren Verluste, die Kosten für „Nachbesserungen" bei Käufern, die Vermeidung schlechter Qualität durch Eigenproduktion („Selbstversorgung" statt Arbeitsteilung), hohe Reparaturkosten, eine zu kurze Lebensdauer vieler Produkte u. a. m. wirken sich negativ auf die volkswirtschaftliche Produktivität aus. „Qualität und noch einmal Qualität – das ist unsere Losung heute. Nur wenn man das Qualitätsproblem entschieden hat, kann man auch das Quantitätsproblem lösen" (Aganbegjan 1985, S. 19). Das Qualitätsproblem löst man aber grundlegend weder durch bürokratische Koordination (Qualitätssiegel u. a. m.) noch durch ethische (moralische Appelle), sondern primär nur durch marktmäßige Koordination. Dies setzt aber einen *„Käufermarkt"* voraus. Dieser wiederum ist nur möglich bei einem grundlegend veränderten *„Wirtschaftsmechanismus"*.

Die große Frage ist natürlich, wie die sowjetische Wirtschaft trotz der oben geschilderten Ungleichgewichte und Probleme dennoch einigermaßen „ins Lot" kommt, wie eine relative *„static efficiency"* erreicht wird. Daß hier unterschiedliche Koordinationsmechanismen zusammenwirken, wurde schon gesagt. Um noch etwas zu detaillieren, sei darauf hingewiesen, daß die Gesamtkoordination durch eine Fülle von *„Interventionen"* gekennzeichnet ist. Vielen Unternehmungen helfen *Ad-hoc-Entscheidungen* von Partei- und Staats-Funktionären oder -Organen; sie belasten aber auch die Volkswirtschaft. Sie belasten vor allem gut wirtschaftende Unternehmungen. Ein klassisches Beispiel von Partei-Intervention stellen die Aktivitäten des in der Einleitung schon vorgestellten „sowjetischen Präfekten" dar (Materialbeschaffung für Unternehmen seiner Region; Nutzung der „wohlhabenden" Unternehmen für ökonomische und soziale Zwecke der Region etc.). Letztlich kann man auch die Aktivitäten der ethischen und aggressiven Koordination unter die Interventionen einreihen. Hier sei an freiwillige Zusatzleistungen in der regulären Produktion gedacht (z. B. bei Produktionsverzug) oder an mehr oder weniger offenen Zwang von seiten einer Betriebsleitung, auch an von Unternehmungen seitens einer Behörde erzwungene Leistungen, z. B. für außerbetriebliche Aktivitäten. Neben den verschiedenen Interventionsformen spielt der *Markt* bzw. spielen *Märkte* eine viel größere Rolle als offiziell zugegeben wird und nicht nur außerhalb des Staatssektors. Chronische Produktionsmittel-Knappheit in Verbindung mit dem Fehlen offizieller Märkte hat auch im staatlichen Bereich eine „zweite Wirtschaft" entstehen lassen. Es gibt erhebliche graue bis schwarze Beschaffung, gegen Geld und gegen Produktionsmittel.

Während das „laufende Geschäft" der sowjetischen Wirtschaft gemeinsam von den vier Koordinations-Mechanismen noch relativ gut bewältigt werden kann, sind sie im Hinblick auf die *„dynamische Effizienz"*, die *Innovations-Effizienz*, viel weniger wirksam. Die unzureichenden Innovations-Ergebnisse der „bürokratischen Koordination" können durch die anderen drei Mechanismen kaum verbessert werden, jedenfalls nicht im Kontext des gegebenen „Wirtschaftsmechanismus". Die Innovations-Effizienz hängt andererseits vom „laufenden Geschäft" in starkem Maße ab. Die Energien und Ressourcen, die hierauf verwendet werden müssen, die Spezifik der dadurch bestimmten Anreizsysteme schafft wenig gute Voraussetzungen für die Entwicklung von Risiko- und Innovations-Bereitschaft bei den Unternehmensleitern. Hier hilft nur mehr Markt und Wettbewerb. Ein stärker marktmäßig gesteuertes Subsystem der sowjetischen Wirtschaft könnte z. B. der Bereich der Projektierung von neuen Anlagen sein. Das bürokratische Herangehen an diese Frage ließ „Wettbewerbsausschreibungen für neue Technik" bislang kaum zu. Die Bürokratie befürchtet u. a. Vergeudung von Arbeitskraft. Die Fragen der „Einführung einer modernen Technologie ... werden nicht selten subjektiv entschieden, so daß keine optimalen Lösungen gefunden werden" (Palterowitsch 1985, S. 485). D. Palterowitsch weist auf die möglichen großen volkswirtschaftlichen Gewinne durch die Auswahl zwischen Varianten und eine echte betriebliche Wirtschaftlichkeitsrechnung (Investitionsrechnung) hin. Die Situation von heute sei folgende: „Eben weil der Wettbewerb fehlt, werden zuweilen hohe Prämien für die Entwicklung und Einführung einer formal neuen, aber wenig effektiven Technik gezahlt. Viele Ökonomen schlagen heute Alarm, weil sich die Anzahl der jährlich neu entwickelten Maschinen verringert" (Palterowitsch 1985, S. 486). Palterowitsch kritisiert auch die Unterbewertung der „ökonomischen Kriterien für die Bewertung technischer Neuerungen" und weist darauf hin, daß Entscheidungen über Projekte „häufig nicht auf einer allseitigen Analyse der Qualität, des Neuheitsgrades, der ökologischen, ökonomischen und anderer Kennziffern, sondern auf einem Vergleich rein technischer Parameter" beruhen. Gefordert sei eine „grundlegende Verbesserung der ökonomischen Analyse. Heute hat der Ökonom oft nur noch die Aufgabe, irgendwie ‚nachzuweisen', daß eine schon beschlossene Neuerung effektiv ist, bei der Ausschreibungsmethode jedoch würde der Ökonom tätsächlich die Entscheidung zu fällen haben" (Palterowitsch 1985, S. 486). Besonders wichtig sei „ein solcher Wettbewerb im gegenwärtigen Moment, da die Bedingungen für eine breitere Entfaltung von Initiative und sozialistischem Unternehmungsgeist geschaffen werden" (Palterowitsch 1985, S. 486).

Überleitend zum nächsten Abschnitt sei T. Zaslavskaja zitiert. „Wie ... ist die tatsächliche Wechselwirkung von strikter administrativer Reglementierung und wirtschaftlicher Effizienz?" Sie ist nach T. Zaslavskaja für die Effizienzwirkung eindeutig negativ, aus drei Gründen. Die Undifferenziertheit vieler zentraler Regulierungen (in Bezug auf Regionen, Wirtschaftszweige, Betriebsgrößen u. a. m.) mache deren Realisierung häufig schwierig und ergäbe negative Resultate. Zweitens verlange verschärfte Reglementierung erhöhte administrative Kontrolle, der hohe Kontrollaufwand sei aber nicht realisierbar. Dadurch fehle „es in der Praxis häufig an einer täglichen Kontrolle der Einhaltung der Vorschriften, und diese bleiben unbeachtet" und drittens käme es „nahezu unausweichlich zu einer Einengung der kreativen Elemente der Arbeit ..." (Zaslavskaja 1984, S. A 11f.).

2. Die Entscheidungssituation der sowjetischen Unternehmung

Die sowjetische Unternehmung ist gekennzeichnet durch rechtliche Selbständigkeit (Rechtspersönlichkeit); sie hat aber nur partielle ökonomische Kompetenzen, die mit „operative Selbständigkeit" umschrieben werden. Nach sowjetischem Selbstverständnis liegen die strategischen Entscheidungen im wesentlichen bei der jeweils übergeordneten staatlichen Wirtschaftsverwaltungs-Instanz. Die sowjetische Unternehmung ist weder autonomer Planer noch autonomer Investor und der Unternehmensleiter wird vom Ministerium eingesetzt. Er ist diesem auch allein verantwortlich. Die Unternehmung soll im Rahmen der vorgegebenen (geplanten) output-Größen, bestimmter input-Normen, fixierter Preise und verschiedener Kennziffern, welche zentral für die Erfolgsbestimmung sind, *wirtschaftlich, kostendeckend* und nach Möglichkeit auch *rentabel* arbeiten *(„wirtschaftliche Rechnungsführung")*. Bei weitgehend fehlender güterwirtschaftlicher und finanzwirtschaftlicher Selbständigkeit hat sich das Prinzip der wirtschaftlichen Rechnungsführung aber weitgehend entleert (siehe unten).

Faktisch ist die Unternehmung jedoch an der strategischen Planung beteiligt, wenn auch unzureichend, gemessen an der Meinung reformfreudiger Politiker, Wissenschaftler und Manager. Ganz allgemein engt die Kurzfristigkeit und „Adhocery" vieler staatlicher Maßnahmen die strategische Unternehmensplanung extrem ein. Die Stärke der Unternehmung liegt in ihrer *Ressourcen-Macht*. Die stärkste Stellung hat sie im Hinblick auf *Informations-Ressourcen*. Sie allein kann etwas über das konkrete *Produktions-Potential* sagen. Bei der sehr begrenzten Möglichkeit direkter Kontrollen durch die Ministerien (Personal- und Qualifikationsfrage) sind diese auf die Informations-inputs der Unternehmungen angewiesen. Durch die Möglichkeiten der Verheimlichung und Manipulation von Informationen sind die Unternehmungen somit mehr als nur formal an der Planung beteiligt. Da die jeweilige Behörde diese Verhaltensweise kennt, nicht aber die jeweilige konkrete Situation, kann sie sich nur undifferenziert „wehren", mit „Durchschnitts"- bzw. normierten Anordnungen. Diese treffen alle gleich, Leistungsfähige und weniger Leistungsfähige. Und soweit Differenzierungen gewählt werden, wird – in Relation zu Durchschnittsnormen – unter Effizienz-Aspekten häufig nur der Teufel durch Belzebub ausgetrieben. Auf der anderen Seite wird durch den *Primat der Planerfüllung* Leistung nicht entsprechend belohnt. Im gegenwärtigen sowjetischen System wirken „zwei Systeme der Leistungsbewertung der Betriebe", das „eine ist der Mechanismus der Preise und der Kennziffern der wirtschaftlichen Rechnungsführung, der die faktischen Ergebnisse und Aufwendungen mißt, ... der andere ist der Mechanismus der Planausarbeitung und des Vergleichs der faktischen mit den geplanten Arbeitsergebnissen", bei einer „Nichtübereinstimmung dieser beiden Systeme" (Wolkonski 1985, S. 474). Das Kriterium Planerfüllung sage nichts „über die Effektivität der Nutzung der dieser Einheit zugewiesenen Ressourcen aus", denn die Effektivität „müßte vom Plan selbst zum Ausdruck gebracht werden" (Wolkonski 1985, S. 474).

Neben Informations-Ressourcen verfügt die Unternehmung auch über *sachliche Ressourcen, Arbeitskräfte, Infrastruktur-Kapital, politische Macht* und in vielen Fällen auch über gute *Beziehungen* zur übergeordneten Administration. Zwar hat die sowjetische Unternehmung im Hinblick auf die *sachlichen* Ressourcen nicht so viele property-rights wie die westliche Unternehmung, aber viel stärker als in Marktwirtschaften – das Gegenteil müßte man eigentlich von einer „zentral verwalteten" Wirtschaft erwarten – befinden sich die sachlichen Ressourcen bei den Industrie-Unternehmungen, und hier vor allem bei den Verbraucherbetrieben (wo sie volkswirtschaftlich weitgehend immobil werden). Sowohl für die sachlichen Ressourcen (Anlagegüter und Umlaufvermögen) als auch für *Arbeitskräfte* zahlt der Unternehmungssektor nach Ansicht führender sowjetischer Ökonomen zu wenig an den Staat, was den optimalen Ressourcen-Einsatz (Allokations-Effizienz) verhindere und Ressourcen-Verschwendung mitbewirke. Die Ressourcen-Ausstattung im Hinblick auf Arbeitskräfte wird vor allem bestimmt durch die zum Teil sehr unterschiedliche Modernität betrieblichen Anlagevermögens (per se Arbeitskräfte zu den gut Ausgestatteten lenkend) und die Ausstattung mit *Infrastruktur-Kapital* (insbesondere Wohnungen in Unternehmungs-Besitz), wo die Reichtümer sehr unterschiedlich verteilt sind. Die *politische Macht* ist bestimmt durch Kontakte des Unternehmungsleiters zu Partei- und Staats-Organen und durch die eigene Stellung in der Partei. Hier gibt es eine primär von Betriebsgröße und Branche bestimmte Differenzierung von Macht. *Persönliche Beziehungen* sind für die einzelne Unternehmung von zentraler Bedeutung. Auch diese „Ressource" ist ungleich verteilt (vgl. Andrle 1976, S. 30f.). „... structural circumstances of directive planning based on imperfect knowledge make mutual trust a scarce and highly valued commodity which can be obtained through the exchange of personal favours extended at personal risks. Thus there emerge cliques whose members use the ressources to which they have access through office for preferential treatment of each other's interests. Woe to the director who does not manage to develop personal bonds across institutional boundaries" (Andrle 1976, S. 31).

Zum Teil schon Gesagtes zusammenfassend, seien die für die Entscheidungsstruktur der sowjetischen Unternehmung m. E. zentralen Determinanten genannt: 1.) rechtliche Selbständigkeit, 2.) weitgehende ökonomische „Fremdbestimmung" durch die übergeordnete Behörde, 3.) „wirtschaftliche Rechnungsführung", 4.) Einzelleitung und Einzelverantwortung des Unternehmungsleiters gegenüber seiner Behörde, 5.) umfassende, aber insgesamt zurückhaltende Kontrolle durch die

Partei, 6.) begrenzte „worker's control", 7.) vielfältige, sich zum Teil überschneidende und teils hoch „formalisierte" Kontrolle durch andere staatliche und gesellschaftliche Organe und 8.) das Fehlen einer organisierten Interessengruppe der Industrie- bzw. Wirtschafts-Manager.

Zunehmend wird in der UdSSR von Juristen wie Ökonomen die unbefriedigende *Rechtslage* kritisiert, in der sich die Unternehmung befindet. Vor allem wird gefordert, daß erstens die Unternehmung berechtigt sein müsse, to "carry out all operations ... which are not forbidden, and not only those which are specifically allowed" (V. Laptev, zit. nach Andrle 1976, S. 14) und zweitens "that the application of the laws should not be qualifiable by administrative directives" (Andrle 1976, S. 15). Die Kritik an Rechtsvakuen, offenen Rechtsverletzungen und einer nicht rationalen Hierarchie der Vorschriften (niederes Recht kann höheres „brechen") geht hin bis zum Vorwurf der Eigentumsverletzung durch staatliche Behörden. „Warum darf ein Minister Umlaufmittel eines gut arbeitenden Betriebes vereinnahmen und sie einem schlecht arbeitenden Betrieb zusprechen, so als wäre es sein Eigentum? ... Die Umverteilung zentraler Mittel von gut arbeitenden Betrieben an solche, die diese Mittel uneffektiv verausgaben, ist doch nichts anderes als eine Verletzung des gesamtstaatlichen Eigentumsrechts an diesen Mitteln zugunsten schlecht arbeitender Betriebe ... Da die Betriebskollektive auch bestimmte Rechte im Hinblick auf das gesamtstaatliche Eigentum haben, müßten die Rechte des Ministers durch das Gesetz klar abgegrenzt sein" (Wolkonski 1985, S. 471). Dieser Argumentation entspricht es, wenn von politischer oder wissenschaftlicher Seite bestritten wird, daß die jeweils übergeordnete Instanz das allgemeine bzw. allgemeinere Interesse verträte.

Hinsichtlich der behördlichen *„Fremdbestimmung"* sei A. G. Aganbegjan zitiert: „Ministries still exercise excessively close supervision over the activities of associations and enterprises, whose independence has not been expanded" (A. G. Aganbegjan, in: CDSP. Nr. 48/1983, S. 1). Und T. Zaslavskaja kritisiert „das beschränkte Ausmaß an ökonomischen Rechten und dementsprechend auch an wirtschaftlicher Verantwortlichkeit der Betriebe für die Ergebnisse ihrer Tätigkeit" (Zaslavskaja 1984, S. A 5). „Durch einen einzigen Telefonanruf aus der Industrievereinigung kann die betriebliche Ergebniskennziffer abgeändert werden, oder das Ministerium wartet mit einem geänderten Plan auf. Oder aber der Zulieferbetrieb schickt Metall und Einzelteile nicht termingerecht, die Eisenbahn kommt mit dem Transport nicht zurecht, die Bauschaffenden halten die Termine für die Übergabe neuer Produktionskapazitäten nicht ein usw. usf. Und keiner von ihnen muß voll für den verursachten Schaden aufkommen. Somit hängt das Produktionsergebnis weitgehend nicht von den Arbeitern des betreffenden Betriebes selbst, sondern von äußeren Faktoren ab" (A. G. Aganbegjan 1983, S. 383).

Das gegenwärtige Lenkungssystem der UdSSR führt dazu, „daß eine Realisierung des gesellschaftlichen Eigentums mit Methoden, die auf der Trennung von Nutzungs- und Verfügungsfunktion beruhen, objektiv und unausweichlich zu einer Beschränkung der Selbständigkeit und Verantwortlichkeit der Produktionseinheiten führt. Die ökonomische Verantwortung trägt nicht derjenige, der falsche Entscheidungen trifft oder unrationell wirtschaftet, sondern die Gesellschaft insgesamt, vor allem die besser arbeitenden Betriebskollektive. Natürlich hemmt das die Initiative und ist wirtschaftlichem Verhalten nicht förderlich" (Jassin 1985, S. 465). Das Prinzip der betrieblichen *„wirtschaftlichen Rechnungsführung"* ist also weitgehend ausgehöhlt. Seine Herstellung bzw. Wiederherstellung wird in Wissenschaft und Praxis immer wieder gefordert, häufig unter dem Begriff der *„vollen* wirtschaftlichen Rechnungsführung". Wenn nicht „weitgehende Selbständigkeit (einschließlich der Planung des größten Teils der Produktion und der Wirtschaftsbeziehungen) sowie volle Eigenerwirtschaftung" (d. h. Unabhängigkeit der betrieblichen Finanzwirtschaft vom staatlichen Haushalt – H.E.G.) realisiert werden, vermindert sich das Niveau der wirtschaftlichen Rechnungsführung und wird sie letztlich etwas Formales" (Jassin 1985, S. 467). „Ökonomische Verantwortlichkeit ist Verantwortlichkeit auf der Grundlage wirtschaftlicher Rechnungsführung" (Wolkonski 1985, S. 470). Ihr gegenüber bestehe aber „ein gewisses Mißtrauen, da befürchtet wird, sie könne die zentrale Planung schwächen . . . Ressortgeist sei eine Folge der wirtschaftlichen Rechnungsführung" (Jassin 1985, S. 467). Nach Jassin könne sich eine solche Position nicht auf Lenin berufen. „Lenin sprach von einer Situation, in der das Ressortinteresse durch die wirtschaftliche Rechnungsführung auf die Effektivitätssteigerung gelenkt wird und in der ein Zusammenstoß dieses Interesses mit den Interessen der Arbeiter vom gesellschaftlichen Standpunkt aus produktiv ist. Heute dagegen verleiht die Monopolstellung der Ministerien und zentralen Ämter den Ressortinteressen eine völlig andere Richtung" (Jassin 1985, S. 468).

Das Prinzip *Einzelleitung* ist sowohl unter Lenkungs- als auch unter Mitbestimmungs-Aspekten von Interesse. Für die Entstehung der Einzelleitung (jedinonačalie) gab es politische Gründe (Beherrschung der bürgerlichen Spezialisten durch die „roten" Direktoren), ökonomische (Stärkung der Manager gegenüber Partei- und Gewerkschaftseinmischung; Begrenztheit qualifizierter Manager) sowie überzogene Vorstellungen im Hinblick auf die Effizienz strikt hierarchischer Lenkung. Die Begründungen für die Aufrechterhaltung des Prinzips sind eher vage und theoretisch dürftig (vgl. Gramatzki, in: Gramatzki/Lemân 1977, S. 67ff.).

Am Ende dieses Kapitels sei noch einmal der starke *bargaining-Charakter* der vertikalen Koordination zwischen Behörde und Unternehmung unterstrichen. Bargaining flexibilisiert zwar einzel- wie volkswirtschaftlich, ist aber andererseits mit Effizienzverlusten zu bezahlen, konserviert administrative Macht und schiebt daher Reformen auf. Dieses bargaining wird letztlich so lange existieren, wie Güter knapp sind (UdSSR) oder um finanzielle Mittel „gefeilscht" wird (Ungarn), solange Mittel (sachliche wie monetäre) „von oben" zugeteilt werden.

3. Kontrolle des Managements – Partizipation von Gewerkschaft und Belegschaft

Management-Kontrolle wird in der UdSSR von einer Reihe innerbetrieblicher wie außerbetrieblicher, professioneller wie gesellschaftlicher Kontrollorgane durchgeführt. Die *Kontroll-Effizienz* ist aber schon generell aus zwei Gründen begrenzt. Erstens ist die Kontrolle im Maßstab des Gesamtsystems gegenüber der Planung unterentwickelt – weniger quantitativ als qualitativ – und zweitens gibt es Interessen-Koalitionen zwischen Kontrolleuren und Kontrollierten. Die *Parteiorganisation* in der Unternehmung z. B. hat vor allem mit für den Unternehmungserfolg zu sorgen. Sich gegen den Leiter zu stellen, ist für den Parteisekretär in der Regel weder materiell noch karrieremäßig lohnend. Und *das* Partei-Interesse gibt es ebenso wenig wie *das* Unternehmungs-Interesse. Was das *Unternehmungs*-Interesse anbetrifft, um an die Erörterungen von G. Dlugos über *das* Unternehmungs-Interesse anzuknüpfen[1], gibt es natürlich in der UdSSR keine auf die sowjetische Unternehmung bezogene Diskussion, allerdings ein extremes Erhaltungsziel (siehe unten). Man kann aber die Kritik von G. Dlugos analog anwenden auf *das* Partei-Interesse und *das* gesellschaftliche Interesse. Auch hier findet eine „Mystifizierung“ (Ideologisierung) statt; auch hier wird so getan, als sei *das* gesellschaftliche Interesse etwas sui generis, getrennt von Teilinteressen Vorstellbares bzw. Bestimmbares. Die „Abdrängung“ der Unternehmung in die Funktion einer Exekutive der jeweiligen behördlichen „Zentrale“ und die extreme Praktizierung der Erhaltung einer Unternehmung (Liquidationen sind zwar nicht de iure, aber bis heute de facto ausgeschlossen) passen prima facie schlecht zusammen. Der hohe Rang des Erhaltungsziels ist aber eben nicht aus *dem* Unternehmungsinteresse ableitbar, und auch nur partiell aus beschäftigungspolitischen bzw. arbeitsrechtlichen Gründen, sondern primär eben gerade aus der Tatsache, daß die Unternehmung im Selbstverständnis der zentralen Planer „Exekutive“ ist und eine Liquidation daher als Planungs- bzw. Plan-Versagen hingestellt werden könnte.

Auch die *Betriebsgewerkschafts-Organisation* steht zwischen zwei Fronten. Sofern es sich nicht um eklatante Arbeitsrechtsverletzungen handelt, gibt es auch bei ihr eine beträchtliche „Produktionsnähe“. Und für den *Haupt-Buchhalter*, gleichsam das Trojanische Pferd des Finanzministeriums in der Unternehmung, ist bei Loyalitäts-Konflikten auch das Hemd näher als der Rock. Der entsprechenden *Staatsbank-Filiale* („Kontrolle durch den Rubel“) fehlt es sowohl an Experten als auch an Sanktionsinstrumenten. Für die Unternehmung sind Güter das Problem und nicht Geld. Die finanzielle Seite wird allenfalls die Prämiengestaltung tangieren, aber nicht die Existenz der Unternehmung. Wenn die Unternehmung – selbst oder fremd verursacht – in einen Liquiditätsengpaß kommt, muß die Bank helfen („soft budget“).

Somit ist die „Kontrolle durch den Rubel“ funktional nur eng begrenzt möglich. Solange naturale und wertmäßige bzw. finanzielle Planung so unvollkommen aufeinander abgestimmt sind wie heute – womit nicht gesagt werden soll, daß diese Aufgabe auch nur annähernd vollkommen gelöst werden könnte im Kontext dieses zentralisierten Systems –, solange die Quellen eines Unternehmungs-Mißerfolgs nur zum Teil innerhalb der Unternehmung liegen, kann die Bank nicht harte finanzwirtschaftliche Sanktionen ergreifen.

Die Kontrollgrenzen der übergeordneten *Fachorgane* (Unternehmensvereinigung, Ministerium, regionale oder lokale Behörde) wurden schon angesprochen. Es fehlt an Kontrollmöglichkeiten und auch an Kontrollwillen. Eine Offenlegung betrieblicher Reserven z. B. kann auch für ein Ministerium von Nachteil sein, da sie planerisch berücksichtigt werden, d. h. die Planansätze des Ministeriums erhöhen müßte. Dieses möchte aber gegenüber dem Ministerrat und dem Staatlichen Plankomitee gut erfüllbare Pläne durchsetzen. Es hat also im Hinblick auf die Planfixierung mit der Unternehmung weitgehend identische Interessen. Man schont gleichsam die Unternehmung bei der Planung und bittet sie dann bei der Planrealisierung „zur Kasse" (Mehrleistungen, Materialreduzierungen, Änderungen des Produktionsprogramms u. a. m.).

Die sonstigen *gesellschaftlichen Kontroll-Instanzen* sind sowohl im Hinblick auf Effizienz als auch auf Mitbestimmung nicht von sehr großer Bedeutung, so daß auf die *workers' control* übergegangen werden kann. Versucht man die Partizipationssituation zunächst ganz allgemein zu charakterisieren, dann verbinden sich systemische Hemmnisse für mehr Mitbestimmung, d. h. begrenzte *Möglichkeiten*, mit dem begrenzten *Willen* verschiedener Entscheidungsträger (Partei-, Wirtschaftsverwaltungs-Organe, Gewerkschaften, Unternehmungs-Management) stärker von „Scheinpartizipation" zu echter Partizipation überzugehen. Lenin sah „die Beschneidung der Rechte der Arbeiter nur als vorübergehend an und versuchte zwischen Skylla und Charybdis, zwischen Bürokratismus und Anarchosyndikalismus hindurch zu steuern" (Teckenberg 1975, S. 129). Heute ist ein Anarchosyndikalismus-Trauma faktisch sicherlich nicht mehr von großer Bedeutung, und Widerstände gegen Macht-Umverteilung sind primäres Hindernis für mehr Demokratisierung dieser Leitungsprozesse. „Anarcho-Syndikalismus" war aber immer auch die politisch-ideologische Keule, mit der man weitergehende Demokratisierungen in anderen sozialistischen Ländern und Forderungen in der UdSSR selbst „prophylaktisch" behandeln wollte.

Die allmähliche Reduktion der Mitbestimmung in der Lenin-Ära durch Entmachtung der „Arbeiter-Opposition" (vgl. Gramatzki, in: Gramatzki/Lemân 1977, S. 45–53) und die Entwicklungen der Stalin-Ära, in der Ende der 30er Jahre „beinahe kriegsrechtsähnliche arbeitsdisziplinarische Maßnahmen eingeführt ... und die Menschen ... als ‚Schräubchen' im volkswirtschaftlichen Mechanismus betrachtet wurden und sich auch nahezu so willfährig (und passiv) wie Maschinen und Materialien verhielten" (Zaslavskaja 1984, S. A 7), kann hier aus Raumgründen nicht dargestellt werden. Es sei auf die Darstellungen bei M. Tatur, W. Tekkenberg und beim Verfasser hingewiesen, sowie auf die dort genannten Literaturquellen. Nachfolgend soll nur eine kurze Skizze der aktuellen Situation gegeben werden. M. Tatur hebt drei Elemente aller Partizipationsorgane hervor („Partizipation“ ist im übrigen ein in der UdSSR nicht verwendeter Begriff, vgl. Huber 1983, S. 180): 1.) den „Bezug auf die Interessenharmonie, der eine Interessenvertretung einzelner sozialer Gruppen“ verbiete, wodurch 2.) „in den verschiedenen Organisationen und Partizipationsorganen nicht nur Arbeiter, sondern auch ingenieurtechnisches und Leitungspersonal vertreten“ seien und 3.) die „verwirrende Vielzahl von Organisationsformen und Organen mit einander überschneidenden Aufgaben und Kompetenzen“ (Tatur 1983, S. 118f.). Demgegenüber betont W. Teckenberg – mit Verweis auf sowjetische Soziologen – die große „soziale Distanz“ zwischen Ingenieur/Techniker und Arbeiter, zwischen qualifiziertem und „einfachem“ Arbeiter. Soziale Kontakte werden „fast nur mit Personen gesucht ..., deren soziale Position nur gering von der eigenen abweicht“ (Teckenberg 1975, S. 134). Eine Zentralposition unter dem Aspekt der funktionalen bzw. faktischen Partizipation haben die „hochqualifizierten Arbeiter, die ihre Konflikte informell regeln, oft in direktem Zugang zum Management, und sich selten an die Kommission für Arbeitsstreitigkeiten wenden. Sie gelten auch oft als Organisatoren der gesellschaftlichen Arbeit und sind mit verschiedenen Auszeichnungen versehen. Von der Position aus haben sie einen gewissen Einfluß auf das Management“ (Teckenberg 1975, S. 134).

Die sowjetische *Gewerkschaft* ist nicht nur – sowohl nach sowjetischem Selbstverständnis als auch faktisch – Multi-Funktionär (quasistaatliche Organisation im Bereich Soziales, betrieblicher Mitgestalter oder alleinverantwortlich in den Bereichen Produktion, Arbeit, Soziales und Kultur), sie wird auch noch als *der* Mitbestimmungs-Repräsentant definiert, dessen Leitung die *Foren* der Partizipation bzw. deren *Instrumentarium* obliegen. Die allgemeinen Foren (Organe) sind die *Arbeiterversammlung* und die *Ständige Produktionsberatung* als Repräsentativorgan. In der Ständigen Produktionsberatung sind sowohl die Belegschaft als auch die Partei- und Gewerkschafts-Organe der Unternehmung, funktionale Partizipations-Organe und auch das Unternehmungs-Management vertreten. Die als „wichtigste Form der sozialistischen Demokratie, der gesellschaftlichen Kontrolle und der praktischen Heranziehung der Werktätigen an die Leitung“ bezeichnete Ständige Produktionsberatung ist aber realiter als Partizipationsorgan dadurch eingeschränkt, daß sie „ohne eigene Machtmittel ... auf die Kooperationsbereitschaft der Betriebsverwaltung angewiesen“ sei (Tatur 1983, S. 123), daß durch die starke Beteiligung des Managements sogar die Einzelleitung in das Organ hineinreiche (vgl. Teckenberg 1975, S. 133), daß „oft nur ein kleiner Kreis von Aktivisten alles entscheide“ und sogar „Repräsentanten der Betriebsleitungen den Vorsitz führten und die Beratungen so zum verlängerten Arm der Verwaltung verkümmerten“ (Tatur 1983, S. 123) und daß „Formalismus“ für ihre Arbeit kennzeichnend sei (vgl. Gramatzki, in: Gramatzki / Lemân 1977, S. 90).

Die neben den allgemeinen Organen bestehenden *Funktional-Organe* für Partizipation haben klare Effizienzzielrichtungen, z. B. Produktivitätsreserven offenzulegen, die Arbeitsnormierung zu verbessern und vor allem Rationalisierung und

Innovation zu unterstützen. Auch sie sind daher in hohem Maße verlängerter Arm der Verwaltung, haben auch legitimatorische Funktionen für das Gesamtsystem bzw. dessen Führung (und sind dann in konkreten Fällen dem Unternehmungs-Management eher lästig). Und letztlich soll der zweite Schritt vor dem ersten getan werden: „betriebliches Vorschlagswesen" sozialistischer Provenienz vor der Ausweitung betrieblicher Entscheidungs-Kompetenz. Zusammenfassend kann man sagen, daß die Systemlogik, aber auch Management-Interesse eine solche Umkehrung der Schritte nur bedingt zulassen. „Die Entscheidungen fallen im engen Kreis der Verwaltung. Die Heranziehung der Öffentlichkeit (d. h. der unternehmungsinternen – H.E.G.) hat demonstrativen Charakter und ist nur die mechanische Approbation bereits getroffener Entscheidungen" (Tatur 1983, S. 131).

4. Innersowjetische Kritik und Reformdiskussion

Wenn auch in der UdSSR seit längerer Zeit relativ offen der hohe gesamt- und einzelwirtschaftliche Reformbedarf diskutiert wird, so hat sich diese Diskussion dennoch in den letzten Jahren nach Quantität und Qualität/Radikalität erheblich ausgeweitet. Es geht A. Aganbegjan, T. Zaslavskaja und anderen nicht nur um „technokratische" Reformen, sondern auch um eine echte Partizipation der Belegschaften. So verlangt Aganbegjan, daß das jetzt laufende „Experiment" einer wesentlich erweiterten Kompetenz für die Unternehmungen verschiedener Branchen (siehe Abschnitt 5.) mit der Partizipations-Komponente zu verbinden sei. Die „kollektiven Formen der Organisation und Stimulierung der Arbeit" (siehe Abschnitt 5.) seien „Formen der Selbstverwaltung der Beschäftigten, Ausdruck von Wirtschaftsdemokratie". Er zitiert Lenins Forderung, die „Organe der Macht" seien aus Organen „für die Arbeiter" in Organe der Verwaltung „durch die werktätigen Massen" umzuwandeln (vgl. Aganbegjan 1985, S. 21–24).

Von der Kritik und den Reformvorschlägen in der UdSSR sollen im folgenden in extrem knapper und selektiver Form diejenigen behandelt werden, die sich auf den *„Wirtschafts-Mechanismus"*, dessen *Anreizsystem*, die *Unternehmung* selbst, auf *predpriimčivost' (entrepreneurship)* des Unternehmungsleiters, auf *Partizipation* in der Unternehmung und auf den *privaten entrepreneur* beziehen.

Bei der Diskussion um den *Mechanismus* sind die Forderungen nach einem *radikalen Umbau* und einem *„systemischen" Herangehen* an die Reform zentrale Punkte. Das fünf Jahrzehnte alte „System staatlicher Wirtschaftslenkung" wurde niemals „einer qualitativen Veränderung unterzogen, welche die grundsätzlichen Wandlungen im Zustand der Produktivkräfte widergespiegelt hätte" (Zaslavskaja 1984, S. A 5). „Die Struktur der Volkswirtschaft ist schon längst so kompliziert geworden, daß man sie nicht mehr von einem einzigen Zentrum aus effektiv lenken kann". Die Vertiefung verschiedener „Disproportionen", d. h. struktureller Ungleichgewichte, beweist, „daß die Möglichkeiten zentral-administrativer Wirtschaftsführung erschöpft sind, daß es notwendig ist, aktiver „automatische" Regulatoren in Verbindung mit dem Ausbau von Marktbeziehungen für die Sicherstellung einer gleichgewichtigen Produktion zu nutzen" (Zaslavskaja 1984, S. A 7). Der „Übergang zu intensiven Wirtschaftsmethoden" könne „nicht durch ‚kosmetische' Operationen im Leitungsbereich vollzogen werden" (Prigoshin 1985, S. 477). Die „Intensivierung" müsse „nicht nur die eigentliche Produktion, sondern auch deren Leitung umfassen ... Während bei den extensiven Leitungsmethoden das Schwergewicht auf der Bildung neuer Organe und der detaillierten Reglementierung der Wirtschaftstätigkeit liegt, orientieren die intensiven Leitungsmethoden auf die Entfaltung und Stimulierung von Initiative, auf Interessiertheit und Selbständigkeit. Intensivierung der Leitung bedeutet eine engere Verbindung der Leitungsziele mit den Interessen der Kollektive und jedes einzelnen Werktätigen, sie bedeutet flexibles und rasches Reagieren auf Veränderungen der äußeren und inneren Bedingungen, Vereinfachung und Reduzierung der Verwaltungsstrukturen bei gleichzeitiger Verbesserung der Qualität der Leitung" (Prigoshin 1985, S. 474).

Nur durch ein *systemisches, ganzheitliches* Herangehen an eine Reform sei die *„dynamische Effizienz"* des Systems zu verbessern. Die Ursachen für die nachlassende Wachstums-Effizienz besteht nach T. Zaslavskaja „im Zurückbleiben des Systems der Produktionsverhältnisse und des sie widerspiegelnden Mechanismus der staatlichen Wirtschaftslenkung hinter dem Entwicklungsstand der Produktivkräfte, konkreter, in der Unfähigkeit dieses Systems, eine vollständige und genügend effiziente Nutzung des materiellen und intellektuellen Potentials der Gesellschaft zu gewährleisten" (Zaslavskaja 1984, S. A 4). Die bisherigen Ansätze bzw. Maßnahmen zur Erhöhung der „Dynamik" der sowjetischen Volkswirtschaft haben nach N. P. Fedorenko einen grundlegenden Konstruktionsfehler. Es wurden bislang mehr oder weniger „Maßnahmen zur Verbesserung der Leitung und Planung der Volkswirtschaft und andererseits Maßnahmen zur Beschleunigung des wissenschaftlich-technischen Fortschritts" getrennt voneinander konzipiert. Nach Fedorenko müßte jedoch der „Wirtschaftsmechanismus des Landes zu einem Mechanismus der Leitung des wissenschaftlich-technischen Fortschritts werden". Durch die Trennung der Planung der „Hauptproduktion" und der Produktion und Einführung von neuer Technik „erscheint alles, was wir als das *Neue* bezeichnen als Anhängsel dessen, was als das *Hauptsächliche* gilt. Aber gerade *das Neue muß das Hauptsächliche*, Wichtigste, Entscheidende sein" (Fedorenko 1982, S. 486).

Eine umfassende Reform des *Anreizsystems („Stimulierungssystems")* wird gefordert. Es differenziere „nicht genügend deutlich zwischen der Erfüllung niedriger und der Erfüllung hoher Planziele. Betriebe mit einem angespannten Plan schneiden bei der Abrechnung nicht selten schlechter ab, als Betriebe, die sich mit weniger angespannten, um nicht zu sagen mit weichen Planaufgaben, begnügen" (Batschurin 1983, S. 32). „Selbst wenn im Plan Verluste oder eine geringe Rentabilität vorgesehen sind, werden bei Planerfüllung im vollen Umfang Prämien gezahlt. Ein Betrieb hingegen, der anspruchsvolle Aufgaben übernimmt, kommt ins Hintertreffen" (P. Bunitsch 1982b, S. 493f.). Die Absurditäten des heutigen Anreizsystems pointiert W. A. Wolkonski. Die „optimale Strategie" der Unternehmung gegenüber dem Ministerium könne man „als Paradoxon formulieren: Um zu den Besten aufrücken zu können, muß man mit dem Plan wenigstens einmal so richtig ‚einbrechen'". Dieses Paradoxon entstehe durch die Planungspraxis des überzentralisierten Systems, die neuen Pläne am „erreichten Niveau" zu orientieren. Der Erfolgreiche habe Reserven mobilisiert und werde nun für seine gesamtwirtschaftlich positive Haltung bestraft. Er könne zukünftige Erfolge dann nur durch einen „Einbruch" erreichen, der ihm für die nächsten Jahre wieder Luft verschaffe (vgl. Wolkonski 1985, S. 472f.).

Viel Reformdiskussion bezieht sich auf die Beziehungen zwischen Behörden und *Unternehmung*, auf die Verletzung von Unternehmungs-Rechten sowie von ökonomischer ratio. „Anstatt den Betrieben unbegrenzt staatliche Ressourcen zu ‚schenken'", müßte die UdSSR „zu einem solchen System der Planung übergehen, bei dem nur die größten Aufwendungen zentral geplant werden. Die übrigen Mittel für die Entwicklung der Produktion aber sollten die Arbeitskollektive selbst erwirtschaften" (Bunitsch 1982, S. 494). „Statt Anweisungen auf Anweisungen zu erlassen, kann der Staat ... auf Fernsteuerung umschalten, indem er für mehrere Jahre im voraus Wertkennziffern festlegt" (Birman 1984, S. 243). „Dort, wo Betriebsleiter das Recht haben, die Produktionstechnik in eigener Verantwortung zu erneuern, springt ökonomisch das meiste heraus" (Miljukow 1984, S. 237). „Mangelnde Disziplin im Leitungsapparat versperrt den Weg zum Erfolg ... Warum wird auf Schritt und Tritt gegen die Ordnung über den staatlichen Betrieb verstoßen? Warum werden die Pläne weiterhin zum Nachteil der guten Betriebe und zum Vorteil der schlechter arbeitenden Betriebe geändert?" (Birman 1984, S. 248). W. A. Wolkonski plädiert für die Zuweisung der Ressourcen an den besten Wirt. „Die Ressourcen zur Erweiterung der Produktion müssen ... in der Regel jene Betriebe erhalten, von denen die Gesellschaft den größten Nutzen erwarten kann." Die Realität sei jedoch anders: „Wenn zu entscheiden ist, ob zusätzliche Ressourcen (deren Umfang immer begrenzt ist) einem hocheffektiven oder einem schlecht wirtschaftenden Betrieb zur Verfügung zu stellen sind, neigt man bei uns häufig dazu, den Zurückgebliebenen zu ‚helfen'" (Wolkonski 1985, S. 476). Fedorenko fordert für die Unternehmungen „weitgehende Rechte beim Abschluß von Wirtschaftsverträgen, bei der Wahl dieser oder jener Formen der Entlohnung und Stimulierung sowie bei der Verwendung ihrer finanziellen Ressourcen für wirtschaftliche und soziale Zwecke ..., damit die ‚Zone der Gleichgültigkeit' der Beschäftigten gegenüber der Qualität ihrer Arbeit und der Verwendung der Ressourcen verschwindet" (Fedorenko 1982, S. 491).

Die Diskussion um den *„sozialistischen Unternehmungsgeist"* verläuft in der UdSSR zum Teil extrem kontrovers und in „der Wirtschaftsliteratur sind die Probleme sozialistischen Unternehmungsgeists ... noch unzureichend ausgearbeitet" (Predpriimčivost' 1981, S. 107). Wie unterschiedlich *spontane Aktivitäten* immer noch beurteilt werden, zeigt sich vor allem bei „unorthodoxem" Vorgehen sowjetischer Manager im Falle von wirtschaftlichen Schwierigkeiten und vor allem auch bei individueller „Entwicklungsplanung" für die eigene Unternehmung. „Höchst fähiger entrepreneur" und „Krimineller" sind die Extrembeurteilungen. Mit der theoretischen wie der praktischen Seite der Vermittlung zwischen Reguliertem und nicht Reguliertem, Planung und Spontaneität, formaler und informeller Organisation tut sich die UdSSR bislang extrem schwer. T. Zaslavskaja lehnt eine nur negative Bewertung von „Spontaneität" (ein in der sowjetischen Literatur bis heute weitgehend negativ besetzter Begriff) ab. Für sie ist die „Rolle des spontanen, d. h. nicht regulierten Verhaltens ... nicht monovalent". Spontaneität ziehe zwar „nicht selten Verletzungen der Planmäßigkeit, das Entstehen von Disproportionen, verlangsamte Produktionsentwicklung usw. nach sich", führe aber auch zur „Freisetzung schöpferischer Kräfte der Arbeiter", ermögliche „die aktive Nutzung der sozialen Reserven einer effizienten Produktion" (Zaslavskaja 1984, S. A 10).

Verständlicherweise wird auch der entrepreneur der *„zweiten Wirtschaft"* extrem unterschiedlich beurteilt (wie bei uns). „In der Praxis ist auf Schritt und Tritt zu beobachten, daß sich privat-unternehmerische Elemente ‚auf leisen Sohlen' in eben diese gesellschaftliche Wirtschaft einschleichen, daß sie die ehrlichen Werktätigen ausplündern und übervorteilen und sich sogar noch als Wohltäter der Bevölkerung aufspielen" (Kossopalow 1985, S. 455). Dieser rein negativen Bewertung steht eine positive von A. Aganbegjan gegenüber. Er spricht sich für die Stärkung des *privaten entrepreneurs* aus, z. B. des privaten Pkw-Besitzers, der den staatlichen Taxisektor – „weder die Fahrzeuge noch die Fahrer reichen aus" – ergänzen könne und der kleinen Verkaufstellen, welche an Private verpachtet werden könnten, wobei „das flexiblere Stimulierungssystem" dazu beitragen würde, „die Qualität der Bedienung zu erhöhen und diese Arbeit rentabel zu machen", was „alles recht gut in einigen sozialistischen Ländern" klappe (vgl. Aganbegjan 1985, S. 368). Aganbegjan meint offensichtlich Ungarn und auch dessen relativ erfolgreiche Versuche die „zweite Wirtschaft" bzw. die „zweite Arbeit" zu legalisieren.

Neben den allgemeinen, das Gesamtsystem betreffenden *Partizipationsforderungen* wie sie z. B. von A. Aganbegjan (siehe oben) und T. Zaslavska in der „Novosibirsker Studie" vorgebracht wurden, gibt es auch spezifische Forderungen bezogen auf die Situation in den Unternehmungen. Bezüglich der schon länger zurückliegenden Partizipations-Analysen sowjetischer Soziologen sei auf M. Tatur und M. Huber verwiesen. An dieser Stelle sollen nur die wichtigsten Forderungen bzw. Vorschläge der Diskussion über den Gesetzentwurf für das „Gesetz über Arbeitskollektive" von 1983 (vgl. Abschnitt V.) genannt werden. Gefordert wurden vor allem *klare Rechte* für die Arbeiter, eine *Eigenvertretung* der Interessen durch eine *eigene Institution* (statt Vertretung durch das Management und die Gewerkschaften), eine Aufwertung der *Belegschafts-Versammlung* zu einem echten Partizipationsorgan, die Beteiligung bei *personalpolitischen Entscheidungen*, verbesserte *Informationen* und häufigere *Rechenschaftslegungen* durch das Management, bessere *Kontrolle* der Verträge zwischen Management und Betriebsgewerkschaftsorganisation.

5. Reformexperimente, Reformgesetze, Reformchancen

Bei einer Bewertung der *Reformchancen* in sehr globaler Form, muß man zwei Dinge in Betracht ziehen. Erstens ist das sowjetische System seit langer Zeit in eine Überzentralisierung hineingewachsen, sind vested interests und Verhaltensweisen extrem stark geprägt worden und zweitens sollen diejenigen, welche reformiert werden sollen, die Reform mit in die Hand nehmen. Hinsichtlich des Makrosystems sollen die Ministerien Agenten der Reform sein, hinsichtlich der Unternehmung in Richtung auf mehr Partizipation die Gewerkschaften. Beide haben einiges zu verlieren.

Alle drei im folgenden kurz skizzierten Reformobjekte: das *Wirtschaftsexperiment* erhöhter betrieblicher Autonomie, das *Gesetz über Arbeitskollektive* und die neue *Brigadeorganisation* belegen die beiden oben genannten grundlegenden Reform-Restriktionen.

Beim ,,*Experiment*" hatten seit 1983 die Betriebe von fünf Ministerien mehr Rechte erhalten, insbesondere in der Lohnpolitik, der Gewinnverwendung, der Investitions- und Innovationspolitik (vgl. Conert 1985). 1985 wurde das Experiment auf 26 Ministerien ausgedehnt und umfaßte bereits etwa ein Viertel der Industrieproduktion (vgl. Bunitsch 1985, S. 479). Zentral für die Prämiierung der betrieblichen Arbeit ist die Erfüllung der *Lieferverpflichtungen* (traditionelle Schwachstelle der Planrealisierung). Der Reformbeginn war doppelt begünstigt: in einem kleinen Segment waren Erfolge denkbar und der Erfolg wurde – wie häufig bei sowjetischen „Experimenten" – durch präferentielle Behandlung (insbesondere bei der Materialversorgung) sichergestellt. Aber auch im „Experiment" haben Ministerien – wie schon immer bei Reformprojekten in der Vergangenheit – wieder die Spielregeln nicht eingehalten und alte Auflagen (Kennziffern) beibehalten (vgl. Bunitsch 1985, S. 481). Bunič fordert generell den „Wirrwar" bei den Kennziffern zu beseitigen und er schlägt als „synthetische Kennziffer" den „Nettogewinnzuwachs" vor. Die vielfältigen Probleme, die schon bei dem stark „segmentierten" Experiment aufgetreten sind (vgl. insbesondere Bunitsch 1985; Conert 1985) müssen sich bei seiner Erweiterung noch viel stärker bemerkbar machen; vor allem präferentielle Behandlungen sind nicht mehr möglich. Die Übertragbarkeit des anfänglichen „Experiments" auf weit mehr Unternehmungen wurde von einigen sowjetischen Wissenschaftlern schon von Beginn des Experiments an in Frage gestellt. Partielle Verbesserungen für die Handlungsmöglichkeiten der Unternehmungen können sich ergeben, aber ohne grundlegende Änderung des ,,*Mechanismus*" der Wirtschaft (siehe oben) kann sich nichts Grundlegendes ändern.

Die Rahmenbedingungen für mehr *Partizipation auf Unternehmensebene* haben sich damit von der *systemischen* Seite her kaum gebessert, sicherlich etwas von seiten der Intentionen der politischen Führung. Dies spiegelt sich allerdings in der neuen Gesetzgebung über die Arbeitskollektive noch nicht wider. „The rather paltry results of the reform indicate that the Brezhnev approach to reform continued to characterise the Andropow period" (Slider 1985, S. 181). Das „Gesetz über die Arbeitskollektive und die Erhöhung ihrer Rolle bei der Leitung der Betriebe, Einrichtungen und Organisationen" (übersetzt in: UdSSR. Staat, Demokratie, Leitung. Dokumente. Berlin(Ost) 1983, S. 464 ff.) vom 17. 6. 1983 hat zentrale Forderungen von führenden Juristen und Kritikern bei der Diskussion des Gesetzentwurfs („Volksaussprache") nicht eingelöst (vgl. Lohmann 1985; Slider 1985). Die *Belegschafts-Versammlung* wurde nicht aufgewertet (durch größere Tagungshäufigkeit und geheime Abstimmungen), zwischen den Versammlungen „vertreten" Management und Gewerkschaften die Interessen der Belegschaft. Ein eigenes repräsentatives *Partizipations-Organ* wurde mithin nicht zugelassen. Ein in der „Volkssprache" häufiger geforderter „Rat des Arbeitskollektivs" (Management, Belegschaft, Partei, Gewerkschaft und andere unternehmungsinterne Organe) wurde nicht geschaffen. Die viel kritisierte *Einzelleitung* blieb in ihrer bisherigen Form voll erhalten; es wurden mithin Rechte gegeben, ohne dem Management welche zu nehmen, eine „Reformpraxis", die in der UdSSR häufig praktiziert wird und welche die oben schon angesprochene *Rechtsunklarheit* noch erhöht. Die Hauptkritik von Lohmann und Slider richtet sich auch gegen die rechtsdogmatische Qualität des neuen Gesetzes, gegen die Inflation der Begriffe für „Vollmacht". Aber dies war letztlich Ausfluß *politischen* Wollens bzw. Nicht-Wollens. Die personalpolitische Kompetenz der Partei, die Leitungskompetenz des Unternehmungs-Managements und die Partizipations-Kompetenz der Betriebsgewerkschaftsorganisation wurden nicht wesentlich reduziert.

Das neue Gesetz über die Arbeitskollektive schuf eine „imposante Reihe" neuer „Vollmachten". Es sind „Vollmachten" in den folgenden Bereichen

- Produktion und Innovation
- Arbeitsbedingungen (technische wie soziale)
- Lebensbedingungen (betriebliche Sozialpolitik)
- „Bildung und Erziehung der Werktätigen".

„Produzenten"-„Vollmachten" beziehen sich auf Beteiligung an der Planung, Eigentumssicherung, rationelle Ressourcennutzung, Innovation und Vorschlagswesen, Gewinnverteilung. Zum Bereich Arbeitsbedingungen gehören der Abschluß von Betriebs-Kollektivverträgen (Aufgaben eigentlich aller vier Bereiche), Arbeitsnormen, Lohnfragen, „Sozialistischer Wettbewerb", Arbeitsbedingungen und Arbeitsschutz (vgl. Lohmann 1985). Der relativ breiten Palette von „Vollmachten" stehen einmal eine geringe rechtliche Klarheit („bei insgesamt 108 Kompetenzzuschreibungen 52 verschiedene Ausdruck-Variationen", Lohmann 1985) und zum anderen eine fehlende institutionelle Absicherung gegenüber.

Das Gesetz über die Arbeitskollektive wurde sicherlich mit bestimmt durch die

„polnischen Ereignisse" von 1980/81, durch die Ablehnung einer Arbeiterselbstverwaltung, welche sich zum „Schlichter" betrieblicher Fragen machen und die Partei entmachten wollte. „Thus, one lesson leaders have drawn from the events in Poland is that worker movements independent of the party must never be allowed to emerge" (Slider 1985, S. 174). Das Gesetz wurde zweitens mitbestimmt durch die Kampagne für *Arbeitsdisziplin* in der Zeit von Andropov, d. h. eine eher autoritäre Grundstimmung.

Im Gegensatz zu der teils euphorischen Behandlung des Gesetzes in der sowjetischen Tages- und Fachpresse wurde es von Gorbačev auf dem XXVII. Parteitag eher kritisch behandelt. Es könne „noch nicht gesagt werden, daß es die Ergebnisse zeitigt", mit denen man gerechnet habe. Einer der bedeutendsten Teile der Gorbačev-Rede ist m. E. der Teil über Partizipationsfragen. Er knüpft in mehrfacher Hinsicht an die Forderungen der Volksaussprache an. „Schritt für Schritt soll der Kreis von Problemen erweitert werden, bei denen die Entscheidungen des Arbeitskollektivs definitiv sind, sollen die Rolle der Belegschaftsversammlungen und die Verantwortung für die Erfüllung ihrer Beschlüsse verstärkt werden." Und Gorbačev greift auch die Idee eines „Rats des Arbeitskollektivs" wieder auf, „dem Vertreter der Betriebsleitung, der Partei-, der Gewerkschafts- und der Komsomolorganisation, der Brigaderäte sowie Arbeiter und Fachleute angehören würden." Gorbačev propagiert – analog zu den gewählten Brigadieren der Chozrastčet-Brigaden – für die Ausdehnung der „Wählbarkeit auf alle Brigadiere und dann schrittweise auch auf einige andere Kategorien von leitenden Mitarbeitern der Betriebe ...: auf Meister, Schicht-, Bereichs- und Abteilungsleiter ...". Man sollte nach Formen „für eine Verknüpfung des Zentralismus mit der Demokratie, des Einzelleiterprinzips mit der Wählbarkeit bei der Lenkung und Leitung der Volkswirtschaft" suchen.

Gorbačev kritisiert auch die Verletzungen von *Genossenschaftsrechten*. Es seien „zu viele, die sich in das Leben von Genossenschaften einmischen. Die Partei und die Staatsorgane müssen darauf achten, daß die Selbstverwaltung der Kolchose und der anderen Genossenschaften einwandfrei funktioniert, und jegliche Versuche unterbinden, Druck auszuüben und zu administrieren" (Gorbačev 1986).

Wenn auch häufiger in den sozialistischen Ländern massive Kritik an dem primären Träger von Partizipation, d. h. den *Gewerkschaften* geübt wird, geht die Gorbačevsche Radikalkritik m. E. über das „Normalmaß" hinaus. Er wirft ihnen „Passivität" gerade im Hinblick auf „die Wahrnehmung der legitimen Interessen der Werktätigen, den Arbeits- und Unfallschutz, den Bau und das Funktionieren von Gesundheitseinrichtungen ..." vor. „Es leuchtet ein, daß eine solche Passivität jene Wirtschaftsfunktionäre zufriedenstellt, für die die Produktion mitunter den Menschen überschattet." Doch für die Gewerkschaften hätten „die Interessen der Werktätigen stets im Vordergrund zu stehen". Man könne „nicht darauf warten, daß jemand die Aufgaben, mit denen die Gewerkschaften betraut worden sind, für sie lösen wird" (Gorbačev 1986). Eine Kritik an die Adresse der KPdSU als der Erzeuger und ständige Begleiter dieser Gewerkschaften fehlt allerdings bei Gorbačev.

Gorbačev kritisiert auch die für Partizipation unzureichende *eigentumstheoretische und eigentumspolitische Basis* des sowjetischen Systems; sein eigener Beitrag ist jedoch ohne analytischen Tiefgang. Es sind Standardformulierungen, ohne Ursachenanalyse. Das betrifft vor allem auch seine Ansicht, daß Theorie-Defizite für die fehlenden Lösungen entscheidend seien, „die eine Einstellung zum sozialistischen Eigentum formen sollen, wie sie sich für die wirklichen Herren im Lande gebührt." Und diejenigen, die in starkem Maße die unterschiedlichen property rights in der UdSSR in den Händen haben, die Ministerien und andere staatliche Organe (nach Gorbačev „keine Eigentümer der Produktionsmittel") schließen es nicht nur (macht)politisch sondern systemisch aus, daß die Unternehmungen „voll und ganz dafür verantwortlich sind, daß ihre Arbeit keine Verluste bringt und der Staat nicht für ihre Verbindlichkeiten verantwortlich zeichnet" (Gorbačev 1986).

Zusammenfassend kann man sagen, daß die allgemeinen Rahmenbedingungen für Reformen heute (1985) sicherlich besser sind als zu Beginn der 1980er Jahre. Es ist allerdings noch nicht sichtbar, wie die *systemischen Hemmnisse* für mehr Demokratisierung überwunden werden können. „Die Ausarbeitung der theoretischen Grundlagen der Leitungsneuerungen ... befindet sich noch im Anfangsstadium" (Prigoshin 1985, S. 474). Sicherlich gibt es eine Reihe bürokratischer Deformationen, deren Beseitigung selbst beim gegebenen „Wirtschaftsmechanismus" möglich ist und die auch einen gesamtwirtschaftlichen Produktivitätsschub ermöglichen könnte. Aber ohne eine weitergehende Systemreform wird ein Reformprozeß schnell wieder gebremst werden. Die ungarische Systemreform zeigt, wie schwierig es ist – selbst nach grundlegendem Umbau des Mechanismus – Strukturen und Verhaltensweisen zu ändern. Im Bereich der Partizipation wird sich in der UdSSR so schnell sicherlich nichts ändern. Aber wie bei allen Mitbestimmungsregelungen in der Welt sind informelle Beziehungen zwischen Management- und Belegschafts-Vertretern wichtig; diese dürften tendenziell eher noch wichtiger werden.

„Ohne aktive, schöpferische Mitwirkung der Arbeitskollektive an der Ausarbeitung und Erfüllung der Wirtschafts- und Sozialpläne ... kann nicht erwartet werden, daß der Wirtschaftsmechanismus effektiv funktioniert" (Ryshkow 1986, S. 5). Dies ist zwar richtig – und der „Faktor Mensch" – um Ryshkows Terminologie zu verwenden – hat in jedem „Mechanismus", in jedem Wirtschaftssystem zentrale Bedeutung, aber mindestens ebenso wichtig ist die Leistungsfähigkeit des „Mechanismus". Und hier sind bislang keine revolutionierenden Änderungen erkennbar. Das gilt auch für die Elemente des „Experiments", welches noch nicht einmal „Eigenfinanzierung" enthält, d. h. finanzwirtschaftlich eine „offene Flanke" hat. Die grundlegenden Reformrestriktionen systemischer Art bleiben weitgehend bestehen: der begrenzte Wille der „Zentrale", die Unternehmen über das Produktionssortiment und die Netto-Investitionen, Erweiterungs- und Rationalisierungs-Investitionen entscheiden zu lassen, auf der input-Seite eine weitgehend „deregulierte" Materialversorgung herzustellen und alles finanzwirtschaftlich abzusichern. Die Widerstände gegen Reformen in der UdSSR wurden von

M. Gorbačev wie folgt umschrieben: In der UdSSR habe „eine Haltung Verbreitung gefunden, bei der in jeder Veränderung des Wirtschaftsmechanismus geradezu eine Abweichung von Grundsätzen des Sozialismus gesehen" werde (Gorbačev 1986). Dem steht die Neigung der westlichen Forschung gegenüber, sowjetische piecemeal-policy als nicht reformrelevant zu deklarieren.

Während die Rahmenbedingungen für mehr Partizipation auf Unternehmungsebene nach wie vor nicht günstig sind, stellt sich die Situation für die *Mitbestimmung am Arbeitsplatz* anders dar. Sie tangiert weniger die gegebene Machtstruktur, Partizipation wird dort am stärksten erlebbar und sie wird aus Effizienzgründen dort am meisten benötigt. Zumindest erhofft man sich von der *Brigade (Brigadeorganisation der Arbeit)* bzw. dem *Brigadevertrag* eine wesentliche Effizienzsteigerung. Die Brigade stellt auch ein zentrales Element der Kollektivierung der Arbeit im Gesetz für Arbeitskollektive (Art. 18) dar.

Zwischen der „traditionellen Form der Arbeitsorganisation" und dem Brigadevertrag „besteht ein qualitativer Unterschied", „traditionell" ist die „Höhe der Planerfüllung" entscheidend, bei dem Brigadevertrag entscheidet das „Endprodukt" über Löhne und Prämien, d. h. die faktische Leistung. Bislang hat aber erst ein geringerer Teil der Brigaden eine „volle wirtschaftliche Rechnungsführung", d. h. eine eigene Erfolgsrechnung. Es gibt – in der sowjetischen Literatur stark kritisiert – noch viel „Formalismus"; die alte Organisation bekam in den meisten Fällen nur ein neues Etikett (vgl. Popow, Schtscherbakow 1984, S. 634 f.). Die Angaben über die Leistungsentwicklung der Brigade mit Brigadevertrag sind widersprüchlich (vgl. einerseits Teckenberg 1985 und andererseits Popow, Schtscherbakow 1984, S. 635).

Das Hauptziel der Brigadeorganisation ist die „Anhebung kollektiver Verantwortung für das gemeinsame Arbeitsergebnis" (Tatur 1983, S. 97). Allerdings wählt noch nicht die Brigade ihren Leiter, den *Brigadier*, wie es häufig in der UdSSR vorgeschlagen wird. Der Brigadier wird „von oben" ernannt, allerdings gibt es seit dem Gesetz über die Arbeitskollektive eine *modifizierte Einzelleitung*, weil die Leitung bei der Ernennung die „Zustimmung" der Brigade einholen muß. Und die Brigade „hat das Recht, von der Leitung zu verlangen, den Brigadier von seinen Pflichten zu entbinden, wenn er das Vertrauen des Kollektivs nicht gerechtfertigt hat" (Art. 18).

In der Literatur werden folgende vier Merkmale des Brigadevertrags genannt:

- die Abgrenzbarkeit des Ergebnisses (Erfolgs)
- gleicher Lohn für jede Einheit Ertrag
- Unabhängigkeit der Gesamtlohnsumme von der Anzahl der Mitglieder, ihrer Lohngruppen und Tarifsätze
- die Verteilung der Lohnsumme durch die Brigade selbst (Popow, Schtscherbakow 1984, S. 634)

Als *Verteilungsprinzip* kann weder das reine *Gewinnprinzip* (Lohntarifierung für die Brigademitglieder voll „von außen") noch das reine *Einkommensprinzip* (eigene Lohnfixierung) in Frage kommen (vgl. Popow, Schtscherbakow 1984,

S. 634 ff.). Es kann damit für die „neue“ Brigade drei generelle *Verteilungskonflikte* geben: erstens über den Gesamtertrag (der ist ja von außen veränderbar, auch vom „erreichten Niveau“ abhängig zu machen und generell bleiben den Brigaden die alte „Umwelt“ des Prinzips Planerfüllung erhalten, sowie Lieferfriktionen, welche ihre Ertragslage durch „Leerzeiten“ verschlechtern können), zweitens über die Frage, wie Gewinnprinzip und Einkommensprinzip „gemischt“, d. h. welche Lohntarife (Basiseinkommen) von außen vorgegeben werden und drittens nach welchen Kriterien „innen“ verteilt wird (Qualifikation, Berufsjahre etc.). „Die Hauptrolle bei der Verteilung des Lohns muß die Brigade selbst spielen. Anders kann den Arbeitern nicht voll bewußt werden, daß die Höhe des Verdienstes allein von ihnen selbst abhängt“ (Popow / Schtescherbakow 1984, S. 635).

Zum *partizipatorischen Aspekt* ist folgendes zu sagen. Die Brigadeorganisation bewirkt zweifellos einen Solidarisierungsprozeß gegen das Management (vgl. Teckenberg 1985). Es bestehe „nun die Neigung, die Administration stärker verantwortlich zu machen“ und Konfliktformen richten sich nun „verstärkt auf die Rationalität der Arbeitsorganisation“ (Teckenberg 1985). Es gibt schon negative Erfahrungen von früheren Aktivitäten zur Brigadebildung. „Erhielt die Brigade keine Arbeit, forderte sie eine materielle Entschädigung. Und da eine organisierte Gruppe, die um den kollektiven Lohnfonds besorgt ist, entschiedener protestieren kann als ein einzelner Arbeiter, enden solche Konflikte häufig mit ungerechtfertigter „Stundenschreiberei“, Reduzierung der Normen und Pläne usw. ... Unter diesen Bedingungen konnte sich die Brigadeform der Arbeitsorganisation nicht weiter ausbreiten (Naumow 1985, S. 375). Wenn auch durch das „Experiment“ die Lieferdisziplin zentrales Kriterium der Erfolgsbemessung werden soll und damit die Chancen für eine Brigadeorganisation gegenüber früher gewachsen sind, ist dennoch Skepsis angebracht, denn die erheblichen Friktionen, welche sowohl das „Experiment“ als auch die Brigadeorganisation gefährden, können nur durch einen radikalen Umbau des Mechanismus in stärkerem Maße reduziert werden, welcher der Unternehmung weit mehr Entscheiungen zuweist, vor allem über das *Was* der Prouktion, zumindest partielle Preisbildungskompetenzen, Lohnkompetenzen, weitgehende Investitionsentscheidungen und prinzipiell Eigenfinanzierung der laufenden und Investitions-Aufwendungen. Die Unternehmung wird – im Unterschied zu Ungarn und den Reformintentionen Polens – nicht autonomer Planer, mit dessen Plänen die jeweilige „Zentrale“ ihre eigenen „harmonisieren“ müßte. Das Instrumentarium wird zwar geändert in Richtung auf „indirekte“ bzw. Verhaltens-Steuerung (Abbau von *Befehls*-Wirtschaft im engeren Sinne), die UdSSR bleibt aber Befehls-Wirtschaft im weiteren Sinne, da das Prinzip des demokratischen Zentralismus weiterhin Gültigkeit für die Wirtschaft haben soll, ein Prinzip, welches eigentlich ja ein Prinzip der Parteiorganisation ist. Dieses Parteiprinzip wird aber solange in die Wirtschaft hineinwirken, wie sie ihre „führende Rolle“ auch für die Wirtschaft im Sinne von day-to-day-Interventionen beibehält. Diese Intervention wurde von B. Jelzin, dem neuen Moskauer Parteisekretär, auf dem XXVII. Parteitag wie folgt kritisiert: „Die Parteiorgane sind schon so tief in die wirtschaftlichen Belange verstrickt, daß sie nicht selten ihre Positionen als Organe der politischen Führung verlieren" (zit. nach Schmidt-Häuer 1986). Die „angespannte" Planung bis zum Jahre 2000 macht es aber unwahrscheinlich, daß die Partei ökonomisch stärker in den Hintergrund treten wird. Adhoc-Interventionen und Kampagnen werden bleiben und die partielle Entregulierung wirtschaftlicher Entscheidungen erschweren.

Anmerkung

[1] Der Verfasser bezieht sich hier auf einen Vortrag, den Prof. Dlugos zum Thema „Unternehmungsinteresse" am Fachbereich Wirtschaftswissenschaft der Freien Universität Berlin im Wintersemester 1983/84 gehalten hat.

Literatur

Anganbegjan, E. G. (1985): Na novom etape ekonomičeskogo stroitelstva. In: *Eko* 8, S. 3–24.

Alijew, G. A. (1983): Das Gesetz der UdSSR über die Arbeitskollektive. In: *Sowjetwissenschaft* 36 (Nov./Dez.), S. 718–727 (Übers. aus Pravda, 18. 6. 1983).

Andrle, V. (1976): *Managerial Power in the Soviet Union.* Westmead, Farnborough (Engl.).

Bahro, R. (1977): *Die Alternative – Zur Kritik des real existierenden Sozialismus.* Köln, Frankfurt a. M.

Berliner, J. S. (1983): Entrepreneurship in the Soviet Period: The Overview. In: Guroff, G. / Carstensen, F. (Ed.), *Entrepreneurship in Imperial Russia and the Soviet Union,* S. 191–200.

Birman, I. (1978): From the Achieved Level. In: *Soviet Studies* 30 (2), S. 153–172.

Blue-Collar Workers (1981): *Blue-Collar Workers in Eastern Europe.* London, Boston, Sydney.

Bornstein, M. (1985): Improving the Soviet Economic Mechanism. In: *Soviet Studies,* Vol. XXXVII, January, S. 1–30.

Brus, W. (1971): *Funktionsprobleme der sozialistischen Wirtschaft* (Übersetzung aus dem Polnischen). Frankfurt a. M.

Conert, H. (1985): Der schwierige Weg zu ökonomischer Effizienz. Probleme und Erfahrungen des sowjetischen „Wirtschafts-Experiments". In: *Sozialismus,* Mai.

Dlugos, G. (1986): Das Unternehmungsinteresse – kritische Analyse eines fragwürdigen Konstruktes. In: Zukunftsaspekte der anwendungsorientierten Betriebswirtschaftslehre. Erwin Grochla zum 65. Geburtstag gewidmet. Hrsg. von E. Gaugler, H. G. Meissner, N. Thom. Stuttgart. S. 23–35.

Ellman, M. (1979): *Socialist Planning.* Cambridge et al.

Gorlin, A. C. (1985): The Power of Soviet Industrial Ministries in the 1980s. In: *Soviet* Studies 37 (3), S. 353–370.

Gramatzki, H. E. / Lemân, G. (1977): *Arbeiterselbstverwaltung und Mitbestimmung in den Staaten Osteuropas.* Hannover.

Grossman, G. (1983): The Party as an Entrepreneur. In: Guroff, G. / Carstensen, F. (Hrsg.), *Entrepreneurship in Imperial Russia and the Soviet Union.*

Guroff, G. / Carstensen, F. (Hrsg.) (1983): *Entrepreneurship in Imperial Russia and the Soviet Union.* Princeton, New Jersey.

Hamer, E. (1984): *Die Unternehmerlücke.* Stuttgart.

Hardt, J.P. / Frankel, T. (1974): Die Industriemanager. In: Skilling, H.G. / Griffiths, F. (Hrsg.), *Pressure Groups in der Sowjetunion.*

Höhmann, H.H. / Seidenstecher, G. (1980): Partizipation im System der administrativen Planwirtschaft von UdSSR und DDR. In: Höhmann, H.H. (Hrsg.), *Partizipation und Wirtschaftsplanung in Osteuropa und der VR China.* Stuttgart et al., S. 9–52.

Hofmann, W. (1956): *Die Arbeitsverfassung in der Sowjetunion.* Berlin.

Hough, J.F. (1969): *The Soviet Prefects: The Local Party Organs in Industrial Decision-making.* Cambridge/Mass.

Hough, J.F. (1974): Die Parteiapparatschiki. In: Skilling, H.G. / Griffiths, G. (Hrsg.), *Pressure Groups in der Sowjetunion*, S. 53–94.

Hough, J.F. (1930): *Soviet Leadership in Transition.* Washington D.C.

Huber, M. (1983): *Betriebliche Sozialplanung und Partizipation in der UdSSR.* Frankfurt a.M./New York.

Jeffries, J. (Hrsg.) (1981): *The Industrial Enterprise in Eastern Europe.* Eastbourne (Engl.), New York.

Jeffries, J. (1981): Introduction and Summary. In: Jeffries, J., *The Industrial Enterprise in Eastern Europe*, S. 1–28.

Kornai, J. (1971): *Anti-Equilibrium.* Amsterdam.

Kornai, J. (1980): *Economics of Shortage.* Amsterdam.

Kornai, J. (1984): Bureaucratic and Market Coordination. In: *Osteuropa-Wirtschaft*, H. 4, S. 306–319.

Kuromiya, H. (1984): Edinonachalie and the Soviet Industrial Manager, 1928–1937. In: *Soviet Studies*, Vol. XXXVI, No 2, April, S. 185–204.

Lindblom, Ch.E. (1980): *Jenseits von Markt und Staat* (Übers. aus dem Amerikanischen). Stuttgart.

Loeser, F. (1984): *Die unglaubwürdige Gesellschaft. Quo vadis, DDR?* Köln.

Lohmann, U. (1986): Das sowjetische Gesetz über die Arbeitskollektive. In: Gramatzki, H.E. / Nutzinger, H.G. (Hrsg.), *Betrieb und Partizipation in Osteuropa.* Frankfurt/M., New York.

Maksimova, I. (1985): Brigady na pereput'e. Zametki ob ekonomiki i nravstvennosti. In: *Eko* 8, S. 152–199, S. 289–307.

Masuch, M. (1981): *Kritik der Planung: Naturwüchsigkeit und Planung im realen Sozialismus.* Darmstadt/Neuwied.

Nove, A. (1977): *The Soviet Economic System.* London.

Nove, A. (1981): The Soviet Industrial Enterprise. In: Jeffries, J. (Hrsg.) (1981). The Industrial Enterprise in Eastern Europe. Eastbourne (Engl.), New York. S. 29–38.

Nove, A. (1983): *The Economics of Feasible Socialism.* London.

Political Economy (1984): *The Political Economy of the Soviet Union. Joint Economic Committee – Committee on Foreign Affairs.* Joint Hearings July 26 and September 29, 1983. Washington.

Predpriimčivost' (1981): Predpriimčivost' i chozjajstvennyj mechanizm. In: *Eko* 3, S. 104–122.

Reynolds, L. G. (1976): *The Three Worlds of Economics*. Second Printing. New Haven, London.

Samostojatel'nost' (1984): Samostojatel'nost': idei i voploščenie (Selbständigkeit: Ideen und Verwirklichung). In: *Eko* 12, S. 35–72.

Schachnasarow, G. Ch. (1973): *Die sozialistische Demokratie* (Übers. aus dem Russischen). Berlin(Ost).

Skilling, H. G. / F. Griffiths (Hrsg.) (1974): *Pressure Groups in der Sowjetunion* (Übers. aus dem Amerikanischen). Wien.

Slider, D. (1985): Reforming the Workplace: The 1983 Soviet Law on Labour Collectives. In: *Soviet Studies*, Vol. XXXVII, April, S. 173–183.

Smith, H. (1976): *Die Russen* (Übers. aus dem Amerikanischen). Bern, München.

Sorevnovanie (1985): Sorevnovanie i effektivnost' proizvodstva. In: *Eko* 8, S. 31–64.

Sozialistische Ethik (1980): Sozialistische Ethik oder wirtschaftliche Effizienz. In: *Wissenschaftlicher Dienst Südosteuropa* 6/7, S. 148–153.

Süß, W. (1981): *Der Betrieb in der UdSSR. Stellung, Organisation und Management 1917–1932*. Frankfurt a. M., Bern.

Tatur, M. (1978): Ansätze zur Partizipation von Industriearbeitern an Verwaltungsfunktionen im sowjetischen Industriebetrieb. In: *Osteuropa* 4, S. 318–337.

Tatur, M. (1983): *Taylorismus in der Sowjetunion – Die Rationalisierungspolitik der UdSSR in den siebziger Jahren*. Frankfurt a. M.

Teckenberg, W. (1975): Beteiligung der Arbeiter am Entscheidungsprozeß auf den unteren Verwaltungsebenen und Arbeitskonflikte in der Sowjetunion. In: B. Meissner, G. Brunner (Hrsg.), *Gruppeninteressen und Entscheidungsprozeß in der Sowjetunion*. Köln, S. 128–164.

Wedel Parlow, W. von (1976): *Betriebliche Zielausrichtung und die Eignung der Preise als Instrument der Plandurchsetzung*. Zur Unhaltbarkeit des indirekt zentralen Ansatzes der sozialistischen Planung. Arbeitspapiere des Fachbereichs Wirtschaftswissenschaft der Gesamthochschule Wuppertal, No 17.

Wedel Parlow, W. von (1977): Vorstudien zur Analyse betrieblicher Zielbildungsprozesse im sowjetischen Sozialismus. Berichte des Osteuropa-Instituts an der Freien Universität Berlin. Heft 113. Berlin(West).

Wilhelm, J. (1979): Does the Soviet Union Have a Planned Economy? A Comment on "From the Achieved Level". In: *Soviet Studies* 31, (2), S. 268–274.

Zaslavskaja, T. I. (1984): Die Studie von Nowosibirsk. In: *Osteuropa* 34 1, S. A 1–A 25 (Übers. aus dem Russischen).

Autoren

Adams, Roy J., Professor of Personnel and Industrial Relations of the Faculty of Business, McMaster University, Hamilton, Ontario

Albert, Hans, Professor an der Universität Mannheim, Lehrstuhl für Soziologie und Wissenschaftslehre

Becker, Werner, Professor an der Johann-Wolfgang-Goethe-Universität Frankfurt, Fachbereich Philosophie, Institut für Allgemeine Philosophie

Crispo, John, Professor of Industrial Relations and Public Policy at the Faculty of Management Studies, University of Toronto, Ontario

Danesy, Frank C., M.S.B.A. Boston University, Wissenschaftlicher Mitarbeiter an der Fachrichtung Unternehmungspolitik, Fachbereich Wirtschaftswissenschaft der Freien Universität Berlin

Dorow, Wolfgang, Dr. rer. pol., Dozent an der European School of Management Studies (E.A.P.), Paris, Oxford, Berlin, Assistenzprofessor/Hochschulassistent an der Fachrichtung Unternehmungspolitik, Freie Universität Berlin, von 1977–1984

Gramatzki, Hans-Erich, Dr. rer. pol., Wissenschaftlicher Mitarbeiter am Osteuropa-Institut an der Freien Universität Berlin

Jaggi, Bikki, Professor and Chairman of the Department of Accounting at the School of Business, Rutgers University, New Brunswick, New Jersey

Lemân, Gudrun, Dr. rer. pol., Wissenschaftliche Mitarbeiterin am Osteuropa-Institut der Freien Universität Berlin 1963–1974, gegenwärtig freiberufliche wissenschaftliche Tätigkeit

Müller, Helmut, Dr. rer. pol., ehem. Wissenschaftlicher Mitarbeiter am Lehrstuhl für Allgemeine Betriebswirtschaftslehre und Unternehmensführung der Friedrich-Alexander-Universität Erlangen–Nürnberg

Napierala, Mieczyslaw, Professor am Instytut Organizacji i Zarzadzania Politechniki Wroclawskiej

Nikolopoulos, Andreas, Assistenzprofessor an der Fachrichtung Unternehmungsführung, Hochschule für Wirtschafts- und Handelswissenschaften zu Athen

Ondrack, Daniel, Professor of Organizational Behavior at the Faculty of Management Studies, University of Toronto, Ontario

Reber, Gerhard, Professor an der Universität Linz, Sozialwissenschaftliche Fakultät, Lehrstuhl für Organisation und Wirtschaftsinformatik

Schwan, Alexander, Professor an der Freien Universität Berlin, Fachbereich Politische Wissenschaft, Institut für Grundfragen der Politik

Schwan, Gesine, Professor an der Freien Universität Berlin, Fachbereich für Politische Wissenschaft, Institut für Grundlagen der Politik

Staehle, Wolfgang H., Professor an der Freien Universität Berlin, Fachbereich Wirtschaftswissenschaft, Fachrichtung Organisation und Personalwesen
Steden, Werner, Professor an der Freien Universität Berlin, Fachbereich Wirtschaftswissenschaft, Fachrichtung Finanzpolitische Forschung
Steinmann, Horst, Professor an der Friedrich-Alexander-Universität Erlangen-Nürnberg, Lehrstuhl für Allgemeine Betriebswirtschaftslehre und Unternehmensführung
Szyperski, Norbert, Professor an der Universität zu Köln, Direktor des Seminars für Allgemeine Betriebswirtschaftslehre und Betriebswirtschaftliche Planung

Takahashi, Yoshiaki, Professor at Chuo University, Institute of Business Research, Tokyo

Weiermair, Klaus, Professor of Economics at the Faculty of Administrative Studies, York University, Downsview, Ontario
Wheeler, Hoyt N., Professor of Industrial Relations at the College of Business Administration, University of South Carolina, Columbia
Wilpert, Bernhard, Professor an der Technischen Universität Berlin, Institut für Psychologie
Wilson, H. T., Professor at the Faculty of Administrative Studies, the Faculty of Law and the Graduate Programmes in Social and Political Thought at York University, Downsview, Ontario
Wondracek, Jochen, Dr. rer. pol., Assistent an der Fachrichtung Unternehmungspolitik der Freien Universität Berlin 1976–1981, Geschäftsführer der Conplan GmbH., Berlin–Münster

Zander, Ernst, Honorarprofessor an der Freien Universität Berlin, Mitglied des Vorstandes der Reemtsma Cigarettenfabrik GmbH., Hamburg

Veröffentlichungen von Günter Dlugos zum Generalthema der Festschrift

1974: Unternehmungspolitik als betriebwirtschaftlich-politologische Teildisziplin. In: Wild, J. (Hrsg.), *Unternehmungsführung. Festschrift für Erich Kosiol zum 75. Geburtstag*. Berlin, S. 40–73.

1976: Unternehmungspolitik. In: Grochla, E. / Wittmann, W. (Hrsg.), *Handwörterbuch der Betriebswirtschaft*. 4. Aufl., Stuttgart, Sp. 4093–4103.

1977: Gesellschaftspolitische Implikationen unternehmungsinterner Konflikthandhabung. In: Die Betriebswirtschaft 37, S. 465–474. Wiederabdruck in: Chmielewicz, K. u. a. (Hrsg.), *Unternehmungsverfassung*. Stuttgart, S. 25–34.

1979: (mit Wondracek, J.) Grundüberlegungen zur Konstituierung einer unternehmungsbezogenen Konfliktforschung. In: Dlugos, G. (Hrsg.), *Unternehmungsbezogene Konfliktforschung. Methodologische und forschungsprogrammatische Grundfragen*. Stuttgart, S. 3–30.

1980: Mibestimmung. In: Grochla, E. (Hrsg.), *Handwörterbuch der Organisation*. Stuttgart, Sp. 1343–1356.

1981: Von der Betriebswirtschaftspolitik zur betriebswirtschaftlich-politologischen Unternehmungspolitik. In: Geist, M. N. / Köhler, R. (Hrsg.), *Die Führung des Betriebes*. Curt Sandig, zu seinem 80. Geburtstag gewidmet. Stuttgart, S. 53–70.

Die Unternehmungseffizienz im Interessenkonflikt der Unternehmungsmitglieder. In: Säcker, F. J. / Zander, E. (Hrsg.), *Mitbestimmung und Effizienz. Humanität und Rationalität der Produktionsstruktur in mitbestimmten Unternehmen* – Kontroverse Beiträge im Rahmen eines Seminars an der Freien Universität Berlin. Stuttgart, S. 1–18.

The Relationship between Changing Value Systems, Conflict, and Conflict-Handling in the Enterprise Sector. In: Dlugos, G. / Weiermair, K. in collaboration with Dorow, W. (Hrsg.), *Management under Differing Value Systems*. Political, Social and Economical Perspectives in a Changing World. Berlin, New York, S. 651–676.

1982: Beziehungen zwischen Wertwandel, Konflikt und Konflikthandhabung im Unternehmungssektor. In: Stachowiak, H. / Herrmann, Th. / Stapf, K. (Hrsg.), *Bedürfnisse, Werte und Normen im Wandel*. Bd. 2: Methoden und Analysen. München, Paderborn, Wien, Zürich, S. 293–319.

Aktuelle Probleme der Mitbestimmung in der Bundesrepublik Deutschland. In: Committee of International Programms No. 79 (japanisch), Meiji University; Ronsan, Shogaku, *The Journal of Commerce No. 1* (Übersetzung: Takahashi, Y.).

1984: Die Lehre von der Unternehmungspolitik – eine vergleichende Analyse der Konzeptionen. In: *Die Betriebswirtschaft* 44, S. 187–305.

Unternehmungseffizienz und Interessenpluralität. In: Dlugos, G. / Napierala, M. unter Mitarbeit von Schlingmann, St. (Hrsg.), *Probleme der Unternehmungseffizienz im Systemvergleich*. Bad Honnef, S. 41–59.

1986: Unternehmungspolitik als Führungsaufgabe. In: Kieser, A. / Reber, G. / Wunderer, R. (Hrsg.), *Handwörterbuch der Führung*. Stuttgart. (Im Druck)

Führungsforschung, wissenschaftstheoretische Grundfragen ... Kritischer Rationalismus. Mit Kamitz, R. In: *Handwörterbuch der Führung*. Stuttgart. (Im Druck)

Das Unternehmungsinteresse – kritische Analyse eines fragwürdigen Konstruktes. In: Gaugler, E. / Meissner, H. G. / Thom, N. (Hrsg.), *Zukunftsaspekte der anwendungsorientierten Betriebswirtschaftslehre*. Erwin Grochla zum 65. Geburtstag gewidmet. Stuttgart, S. 23–35.

Bei Fragen zur Produktsicherheit wenden Sie sich bitte an:
If you have any questions regarding product safety,
please contact:

Walter de Gruyter GmbH
Genthiner Straße 13
10785 Berlin
productsafety@degruyterbrill.com